THE
1989
Baseball
Encyclopedia
Update

THE
1989
Baseball
Encyclopedia
Update

COLLIER BOOKS
Macmillan Publishing Company
New York
COLLIER MACMILLAN PUBLISHERS
London

Collier Books
Macmillan Publishing Company
866 Third Avenue, New York, NY 10022
Collier Macmillan Canada, Inc.

Library of Congress Cataloging-in-Publication Data
The 1989 Baseball encyclopedia update.
p.   cm.
ISBN 0-02-028391-1
1. Baseball—United States—Statistics. I. Macmillan Publishing
Company. II. Baseball encyclopedia.
GV877.A135   1989   88-38396   CIP
796.357'0973'021—dc19

Macmillan books are available at special discounts for bulk purchases
for sales promotions, premiums, fund-raising, or educational use.
For details, contact:

Special Sales Director
Macmillan Publishing Company
866 Third Avenue
New York, NY 10022

10 9 8 7 6 5 4 3 2 1

Printed in the United States of America

Contents

THE
1989
Baseball
Encyclopedia
Update

The Teams and Their Players

The Teams and Their Players lists, for the 1988 season, each team, along with its manager and record, the regulars at each position, as well as the pitchers and the leading substitutes. The teams are presented in the order of the standings of the division. Substitutes are listed if they had at least 162 at bats or 20 runs batted in; pitchers are listed if they pitched 162 innings or had 9 or more decisions (including saves).

Fielding statistics listed for regulars are for the indicated position only. The position listed for substitutes may vary. If a substitute played 70% of his games at one position, that is the only position listed for him. If he did not play 70% of his games at one position, but played 90% of his games at two positions, he is listed with a combination position, such as "S2" for shortstop and second base, or "CO" for catcher and outfield. In such cases, the fielding statistics listed are combined for both positions. All outfield positions are considered one position for these purposes. If a player failed to meet either the 70% or 90% requirement listed above, he is listed as a utility player ("UT").

Any statistic that appears in bold faced print is a league-leading total for that category. An asterisk (*) next to a particular statistic would indicate that the player led the league, but since he was traded during the season, the figure listed there is not necessarily his league-leading final total or average. For batting averages or percentages, a batter must have 502 plate appearances to qualify for the title. Pitchers must have pitched 162 innings to qualify in any pitching average. Fielders must have appeared in 100 games at the position to qualify.

East

Team	POS	Player	AB	BA	HR	RBI	PO	A	E	DP	TC/G	FA	Pitcher	G	IP	W	L	SV	ERA
N. Y. W-100 L-60 Davey Johnson	1B	K. Hernandez	348	.276	11	55	734	77	2	63	8.7	.998	D. Gooden	34	248	18	9	0	3.19
	2B	W. Backman	294	.303	0	17	128	219	4	36	3.8	.989	R. Darling	34	241	17	9	0	3.25
	SS	K. Elster	406	.214	9	37	196	345	13	61	3.7	.977	D. Cone	35	231	20	3	0	2.22
	3B	H. Johnson	495	.230	24	68	65	187	13	16	2.0	.951	B. Ojeda	29	190	10	13	0	2.88
	RF	Strawberry	543	.269	**39**	101	297	4	9	3	2.1	.971	S. Fernandez	31	187	12	10	0	3.03
	CF	L. Dykstra	429	.270	8	33	270	3	1	0	2.4	.996	T. Leach	52	92	7	2	3	2.54
	LF	McReynolds	552	.288	27	99	252	**18**	4	**5**	1.9	.985	R. McDowell	62	89	5	5	16	2.63
	C	G. Carter	455	.242	11	46	**797**	54	9	5	**7.2**	.990	R. Myers	55	68	7	3	26	1.72
	OF	M. Wilson	378	.296	8	41	200	4	5	1	2.0	.976							
	13	D. Magadan	314	.277	1	35	459	99	10	42		.982							
	2B	T. Teufel	273	.234	4	31	153	212	7	48	4.4	.981							
Pit. W-85 L-75 Jim Leyland	1B	S. Bream	462	.264	10	65	1118	**140**	6	88	9.2	.995	D. Drabek	33	219	15	7	0	3.08
	2B	J. Lind	611	.262	2	49	333	473	11	73	5.3	.987	B. Walk	32	213	12	10	0	2.71
	SS	R. Belliard	286	.213	0	11	131	258	9	50	3.4	**.977**	J. Smiley	34	205	13	11	0	3.25
	3B	B. Bonilla	584	.274	24	100	121	**336**	32	17	**3.1**	.935	M. Dunne	30	170	7	11	0	3.92
	RF	R. Reynolds	323	.248	6	51	142	7	4	2	1.6	.974	B. Fisher	33	146	8	10	1	4.61
	CF	A. Van Slyke	587	.288	25	100	**406**	12	4	2	**2.8**	.991	J. Robinson	75	125	11	5	9	3.03
	LF	B. Bonds	538	.283	24	58	292	5	6	0	2.2	.980	J. Gott	67	77	6	6	34	3.49
	C	LaValliere	352	.261	2	47	565	55	8	6	5.5	.987							
	OF	D. Coles	211	.232	5	36	98	0	1	0	1.8	.990							
Mon. W-81 L-81 Buck Rodgers	1B	A. Galarraga	609	.302	29	92	1464	103	15	124	10.1	.991	D. Martinez	34	235	15	13	0	2.72
	2B	T. Foley	377	.265	5	43	164	255	12	46	4.8	.972	B. Smith	32	198	12	10	0	3.00
	SS	L. Rivera	371	.224	4	30	160	301	18	69	4.1	.962	P. Perez	27	188	12	8	0	2.44
	3B	T. Wallach	592	.257	12	69	**123**	328	18	**31**	3.1	.962	J. Dopson	26	169	3	11	0	3.04
	RF	H. Brooks	588	.279	20	90	261	8	9	1	1.9	.968	B. Holman	18	100	4	8	0	3.23
	CF	M. Webster	259	.255	2	13	153	2	1	0	2.2	.994	N. Heaton	32	97	3	10	2	4.99
	LF	T. Raines	429	.270	12	48	235	5	3	1	2.3	.988	J. Parrett	61	92	12	4	6	2.65
	C	Santovenia	309	.236	8	41	457	63	9	7	6.2	.983	McGaffigan	63	91	6	0	4	2.76
	OF	O. Nixon	271	.244	0	15	176	2	1	1	2.2	.994	T. Burke	61	82	3	5	18	3.40
	2S	R. Hudler	216	.273	4	14	113	168	10	30		.966	J. Hesketh	60	73	4	3	9	2.85
	OF	D. Martinez	191	.257	2	12	119	2	1	1	2.0	.992							
	C	Fitzgerald	155	.271	5	23	258	21	6	2	6.1	.979							
Chi. W-77 L-85 Don Zimmer	1B	M. Grace	486	.296	7	57	1182	87	**17**	91	9.7	.987	G. Maddux	34	249	18	8	0	3.18
	2B	R. Sandberg	618	.264	19	69	291	**522**	11	79	5.4	.987	R. Sutcliffe	32	226	13	14	0	3.86
	SS	S. Dunston	575	.249	9	56	**257**	455	20	76	4.8	.973	J. Moyer	34	202	9	15	0	3.48
	3B	V. Law	556	.293	11	78	111	272	19	22	2.7	.953	C. Schiraldi	29	166	9	13	1	4.38
	RF	A. Dawson	591	.303	24	79	267	7	3	1	1.9	.989	J. Pico	29	113	6	7	1	4.15
	CF	D. Martinez	256	.254	4	34	162	2	5	0	2.3	.970	F. DiPino	63	90	2	3	6	4.98
	LF	R. Palmeiro	580	.307	8	53	30	5	0	1	7.0	1.000	L. Lancaster	44	86	4	6	5	3.78
	C	D. Berryhill	309	.259	7	38	448	54	9	5	5.7	.982	G. Gossage	46	44	4	4	13	4.33
	OF	M. Webster	264	.265	4	26	169	1	5	0	2.7	.971							
	C	J. Davis	249	.229	6	33	383	32	2	1	5.6	.995							
	OF	D. Jackson	188	.266	6	20	116	1	2	0	1.6	.983							
	UT	M. Trillo	164	.250	1	14	177	81	3	19		.989							
St. L. W-76 L-86 Whitey Herzog	1B	B. Horner	206	.257	3	33	463	40	5	39	8.9	.990	J. DeLeon	34	225	13	10	0	3.67
	2B	L. Alicea	297	.212	1	24	206	240	14	52	5.1	.970	J. Magrane	24	165	5	9	0	**2.18**
	SS	O. Smith	575	.270	3	51	234	**519**	22	79	**5.2**	.972	J. Tudor	21	145	6	5	0	2.29
	3B	T. Pendleton	391	.253	6	53	75	239	12	13	3.2	.963	McWilliams	42	136	6	9	1	3.90
	RF	T. Brunansky	523	.245	22	79	267	10	1	0	1.9	**.996**	S. Terry	51	129	9	6	3	2.92
	CF	W. McGee	562	.292	3	50	348	9	9	0	2.7	.975	B. Forsch	30	109	9	4	0	3.73
	LF	V. Coleman	616	.260	3	38	290	14	9	1	2.1	.971	T. Worrell	68	90	5	9	32	3.00
	C	T. Pena	505	.263	10	51	777	70	5	8	6.0	**.994**	D. Cox	13	86	3	8	0	3.98
	UT	J. Oquendo	451	.277	7	46	268	315	11	61		.981	G. Mathews	13	68	4	6	0	4.24
	C1	T. Pagnozzi	195	.282	0	15	340	28	4	11		.989	K. Dayley	54	55	2	7	5	2.77
	1B	P. Guerrero	149	.268	5	30	348	22	0	18	10.0	1.000							
Phi. W-65 L-96 Lee Elia W-60 L-92 John Vukovich W-5 L-4	1B	V. Hayes	367	.272	6	45	712	55	8	66	9.1	.990	K. Gross	33	232	12	14	0	3.69
	2B	J. Samuel	629	.243	12	67	343	385	16	**92**	4.9	.978	D. Carman	36	201	10	14	0	4.29
	SS	S. Jeltz	379	.187	0	27	195	368	14	73	3.9	.976	S. Rawley	32	198	8	16	0	4.18
	3B	M. Schmidt	390	.249	12	62	73	222	19	17	3.0	.939	B. Ruffin	55	144	6	10	3	4.43
	RF	C. James	566	.242	19	66	26	44	6	3	2.5	.921	D. Palmer	22	129	7	9	0	4.47
	CF	M. Thompson	378	.288	2	33	278	5	5	1	2.6	.983	G. Harris	66	107	4	6	1	2.36
	3B	P. Bradley	569	.264	11	56	298	14	3	2	2.1	.990	K. Tekulve	70	80	3	7	4	3.60
	C	L. Parrish	424	.215	15	60	639	73	9	**11**	6.2	.988	S. Bedrosian	57	74	6	6	28	3.75
	1B	R. Jordan	273	.308	11	43	579	35	5	41	9.0	.992							
	OF	B. Dernier	166	.289	1	10	98	2	2	0	1.9	.980							
	OF	R. Jones	124	.290	8	26	70	1	0	0	2.2	1.000							

West

POS	Player	AB	BA	HR	RBI	PO	A	E	DP	TC/G	FA	Pitcher	G	IP	W	L	SV	ERA
L. A. W-94 L-67 Tommy Lasorda																		
1B	F. Stubbs	242	.223	8	34	521	57	13	41	7.0	.978	O. Hershiser	35	**267**	**23**	8	1	2.26
2B	S. Sax	**632**	.277	5	57	276	429	14	69	4.6	.981	T. Leary	35	229	17	11	0	2.91
SS	A. Griffin	316	.199	1	27	145	264	15	44	4.6	.965	T. Belcher	36	180	12	6	4	2.91
3B	J. Hamilton	309	.236	6	33	67	157	14	8	2.3	.941	Valenzuela	23	142	5	8	1	4.24
RF	M. Marshall	542	.277	20	82	468	45	2	31	9.7	.996	A. Pena	60	94	6	7	12	1.91
CF	J. Shelby	494	.263	10	64	329	7	6	1	2.4	.982	B. Holton	45	85	7	3	1	1.70
LF	K. Gibson	542	.290	25	76	311	6	12	3	2.2	.964	J. Howell	50	65	5	3	21	2.08
C	M. Scioscia	408	.257	3	35	748	63	7	10	6.7	.991	J. Orosco	55	53	3	2	9	2.72
SS	D. Anderson	285	.249	2	20	128	225	5	49	4.4	.986							
OF	M. Davis	281	.196	2	17	121	3	5	2	1.7	.961							
3B	P. Guerrero	215	.298	5	35	21	64	10	2	2.1	.895							
O1	M. Hatcher	191	.293	1	25	188	17	3	7		.986							
31	T. Woodson	173	.249	3	15	160	60	6	13		.973							
C	R. Dempsey	167	.251	7	30	333	29	4	4	4.9	.989							
Cin. W-87 L-74 Pete Rose W-11 L-12 Tommy Helms W-12 L-15 Pete Rose W-64 L-47																		
1B	N. Esasky	391	.243	15	62	982	52	6	70	9.0	.994	D. Jackson	35	261	**23**	8	0	2.73
2B	J. Treadway	301	.252	2	23	188	252	7	49	4.6	.984	T. Browning	36	251	18	5	0	3.41
SS	B. Larkin	588	.296	12	56	231	470	29	67	4.9	.960	J. Rijo	49	162	13	8	0	2.39
3B	C. Sabo	538	.271	11	44	75	318	14	31	3.0	**.966**	M. Soto	14	87	3	7	0	4.66
RF	P. O'Neill	485	.252	16	73	173	8	2	14	8.7	.989	J. Franco	70	86	6	6	39	1.57
CF	E. Davis	472	.273	26	93	300	2	6	0	2.4	.981	R. Robinson	17	79	3	7	0	4.12
LF	K. Daniels	495	.291	18	64	256	10	5	2	2.0	.982	J. Armstrong	14	65	4	7	0	5.79
C	B. Diaz	315	.219	10	35	468	44	5	9	5.9	.990							
UT	Concepcion	197	.198	0	8	151	131	2	36		.993							
OF	D. Collins	174	.236	0	14	53	2	2	0	1.6	.965							
S. D. W-83 L-78 Larry Bowa W-16 L-30 Jack McKeon W-67 L-48																		
1B	K. Moreland	511	.256	5	64	637	52	4	55	9.5	.994	E. Show	32	235	16	11	0	3.26
2B	R. Alomar	545	.266	9	41	319	459	16	88	5.6	.980	A. Hawkins	33	218	14	11	0	3.35
SS	G. Templeton	362	.249	3	36	168	316	16	62	4.8	.968	E. Whitson	34	205	13	11	0	3.77
3B	C. Brown	247	.235	2	19	54	131	10	15	2.7	.949	J. Jones	29	179	9	14	0	4.12
RF	T. Gwynn	521	**.313**	7	70	264	8	5	1	2.1	.982	D. Rasmussen	20	148	14	4	0	2.55
CF	M. Wynne	333	.264	11	42	216	5	3	2	2.0	.987	M. Davis	62	98	5	10	28	2.01
LF	C. Martinez	365	.236	18	65	287	26	3	29	7.7	.991	McCullers	60	98	3	6	10	2.49
C	B. Santiago	492	.248	10	46	725	75	12	11	6.0	.985	M. Grant	33	98	2	8	0	3.69
1O	J. Kruk	378	.241	9	44	634	37	3	45		.996							
UT	R. Ready	331	.266	7	39	112	153	11	22		.960							
SS	D. Thon	258	.264	1	18	82	168	12	28	3.7	.954							
3B	T. Flannery	170	.265	0	19	27	76	3	8	2.1	.972							
S. F. W-83 L-79 Roger Craig																		
1B	W. Clark	575	.282	29	**109**	**1492**	104	12	**126**	**10.2**	.993	R. Reuschel	36	245	19	11	0	3.12
2B	R. Thompson	477	.264	7	48	255	365	14	88	4.7	.970	D. Robinson	51	177	10	5	6	2.45
SS	J. Uribe	493	.252	3	35	212	404	19	77	4.5	.970	K. Downs	27	168	13	9	0	3.32
3B	K. Mitchell	505	.251	19	80	61	203	16	18	2.7	.943	A. Hammaker	43	145	9	9	5	3.73
RF	C. Maldonado	499	.255	12	68	251	5	10	1	1.9	.962	M. Krukow	20	125	7	4	0	3.54
CF	B. Butler	568	.287	6	43	395	3	5	1	2.6	.988	M. LaCoss	19	114	7	7	0	3.62
LF	M. Aldrete	389	.267	3	50	61	3	0	2	6.4	1.000	S. Garrelts	65	98	5	9	13	3.58
C	B. Melvin	273	.234	8	27	403	31	7	4	5.0	.984	C. Lefferts	64	92	3	8	11	2.92
C	B. Brenly	206	.189	5	22	334	27	6	2	5.3	.984	J. Price	38	62	1	6	4	3.94
UT	E. Riles	187	.294	3	28	46	133	3	17		.984							
UT	C. Speier	171	.216	3	18	70	142	3	26		.986							
OF	J. Leonard	160	.256	2	20	74	0	1	0	1.7	.987							
Hou. W-82 L-80 Hal Lanier																		
1B	G. Davis	561	.271	30	99	1355	103	6	104	9.7	**.996**	N. Ryan	33	220	12	11	0	3.52
2B	B. Doran	480	.248	7	53	260	371	8	73	4.9	**.987**	M. Scott	32	219	14	8	0	2.92
SS	R. Ramirez	566	.276	6	59	232	408	23	68	4.3	.965	J. Deshaies	31	207	11	14	0	3.00
3B	B. Bell	269	.253	7	37	31	114	12	8	2.4	.924	D. Darwin	44	192	8	13	3	3.84
RF	K. Bass	541	.255	14	72	267	7	6	2	1.9	.979	B. Knepper	27	175	14	5	0	3.14
CF	G. Young	576	.257	0	37	357	10	3	1	2.6	.992	J. Agosto	75	92	10	2	4	2.26
LF	B. Hatcher	530	.268	7	52	280	7	5	2	2.1	.983	L. Andersen	53	83	2	4	5	2.94
C	A. Trevino	193	.249	2	13	360	24	9	5	5.3	.977	D. Smith	51	57	4	5	27	2.67
OF	T. Puhl	234	.303	3	19	116	2	2	0	1.5	.983							
C	A. Ashby	227	.238	7	33	414	23	4	4	6.7	.991							
3B	D. Walling	176	.244	1	20	33	99	7	14	2.7	.950							
Atl. W-54 L-106 Chuck Tanner W-12 L-27 Russ Nixon W-42 L-79																		
1B	G. Perry	547	.300	8	74	1282	106	**17**	102	10.0	.988	R. Mahler	39	249	9	16	0	3.69
2B	R. Gant	563	.259	19	60	295	378	**26**	82	**5.7**	.963	P. Smith	32	195	7	15	0	3.69
SS	A. Thomas	606	.252	13	68	230	456	**29**	**90**	4.8	.959	T. Glavine	34	195	7	**17**	0	4.56
3B	K. Oberkfell	422	.277	3	40	83	207	15	21	2.7	.951	Z. Smith	23	140	5	10	0	4.30
RF	D. Murphy	592	.226	24	77	340	15	3	4	2.3	.992	C. Puleo	53	106	5	5	1	3.47
CF	A. Hall	231	.247	1	15	137	7	4	1	2.3	.973	J. Alvarez	60	102	5	6	3	2.99
LF	D. James	386	.256	3	30	222	5	3	0	1.9	.987	Assenmacher	64	79	8	7	5	3.06
C	O. Virgil	320	.256	9	31	448	45	5	3	5.2	.990	B. Sutter	38	45	1	4	14	4.76
C	B. Benedict	236	.242	0	19	384	54	5	5	5.0	.989							
OF	T. Blocker	198	.212	2	10	164	1	1	0	2.7	.994							
OF	K. Griffey	193	.249	2	19	61	2	2	0	1.5	.969							

BATTING AND BASE RUNNING LEADERS

Batting Average

T. Gwynn, SD	.313
R. Palmeiro, CHI	.307
A. Dawson, CHI	.303
A. Galarraga, MON	.302
G. Perry, ATL	.300

Slugging Average

Strawberry, NY	.545
A. Galarraga, MON	.540
W. Clark, SF	.508
A. Van Slyke, PIT	.506
A. Dawson, CHI	.504

Home Runs

Strawberry, NY	39
G. Davis, HOU	30
W. Clark, SF	29
A. Galarraga, MON	29
McReynolds, NY	27

Total Bases

A. Galarraga, MON	329
A. Dawson, CHI	298
A. Van Slyke, PIT	297
Strawberry, NY	296
W. Clark, SF	292

Runs Batted In

W. Clark, SF	109
Strawberry, NY	101
B. Bonilla, PIT	100
A. Van Slyke, PIT	100
McReynolds, NY	99
G. Davis, HOU	99

Stolen Bases

V. Coleman, STL	81
G. Young, HOU	65
O. Smith, STL	57
O. Nixon, MON	46
C. Sabo, CIN	46

Hits

A. Galarraga, MON	184
A. Dawson, CHI	179
R. Palmeiro, CHI	178

Base on Balls

W. Clark, SF	100
B. Butler, SF	97
K. Daniels, CIN	87

Home Run Percentage

Strawberry, NY	7.2
E. Davis, CIN	5.5
G. Davis, HOU	5.3

Runs Scored

B. Butler, SF	109
K. Gibson, LA	106
W. Clark, SF	102

Doubles

A. Galarraga, MON	42
R. Palmeiro, CHI	41
C. Sabo, CIN	40

Triples

A. Van Slyke, PIT	15
V. Coleman, STL	10

PITCHING LEADERS

Winning Percentage

D. Cone, NY	.870
T. Browning, CIN	.783
O. Hershiser, LA	.742
D. Jackson, CIN	.742
B. Knepper, HOU	.737

Earned Run Average

J. Magrane, STL	2.18
D. Cone, NY	2.22
O. Hershiser, LA	2.26
J. Tudor, LA, STL	2.32
J. Rijo, CIN	2.39

Wins

O. Hershiser, LA	23
D. Jackson, CIN	23
D. Cone, NY	20
R. Reuschel, SF	19

Saves

J. Franco, CIN	39
J. Gott, PIT	34
T. Worrell, STL	32
S. Bedrosian, PHI	28
M. Davis, SD	28

Strikeouts

N. Ryan, HOU	228
D. Cone, NY	213
J. DeLeon, STL	208
M. Scott, HOU	190
S. Fernandez, NY	189

Complete Games

O. Hershiser, LA	15
D. Jackson, CIN	15
E. Show, SD	13
R. Sutcliffe, CHI	12
D. Gooden, NY	10

Fewest Hits per 9 Innings

S. Fernandez, NY	6.11
P. Perez, MON	6.37
J. Rijo, CIN	6.67

Shutouts

O. Hershiser, LA	8
T. Leary, LA	6
D. Jackson, CIN	6

Fewest Walks per 9 Innings

B. Smith, MON	1.45
R. Mahler, ATL	1.52
R. Reuschel, SF	1.54

Most Strikeouts per 9 Inn.

N. Ryan, HOU	9.33
S. Fernandez, NY	9.10
J. Rijo, CIN	8.89

Innings

O. Hershiser, LA	267
D. Jackson, CIN	261
T. Browning, CIN	251

Games Pitched

R. Murphy, CIN	76
J. Robinson, PIT	75
J. Agosto, HOU	75

	W	L	PCT	GB	R	OR	2B	3B	HR	BA	SA	SB	E	DP	FA	CG	BB	SO	ShO	SV	ERA
EAST																					
NY	100	60	.625		703	532	251	24	152	.256	.396	140	115	127	.981	31	404	1100	17	46	2.91
PIT	85	75	.531	15	651	616	240	45	110	.247	.369	119	125	128	.980	12	469	790	4	46	3.47
MON	81	81	.500	20	628	592	260	48	107	.251	.373	189	142	145	.978	18	476	923	6	43	3.08
CHI	77	85	.475	24	660	694	262	46	113	.261	.383	120	125	128	.980	30	490	897	9	24	3.84
STL	76	86	.469	25	578	633	207	33	71	.249	.337	234	121	131	.981	17	486	881	7	42	3.47
PHI	65	96	.404	35.5	597	734	246	31	106	.239	.355	112	145	139	.976	16	628	859	3	36	4.14
WEST																					
LA	94	67	.584		628	544	217	25	99	.248	.352	131	142	126	.977	32	473	1029	15	49	2.97
CIN	87	74	.540	7	641	596	246	25	122	.246	.368	207	125	131	.980	24	504	934	10	43	3.35
SD	83	78	.516	11	594	583	205	35	94	.247	.351	123	120	147	.981	30	439	885	4	39	3.28
SF	83	79	.512	11.5	670	626	227	44	113	.248	.368	121	129	145	.980	25	422	875	11	42	3.39
HOU	82	80	.506	12.5	617	631	239	31	96	.244	.351	198	138	124	.978	21	478	1049	10	40	3.40
ATL	54	106	.338	39.5	555	741	228	28	96	.242	.348	95	151	138	.976	14	524	810	3	25	4.09
					7522	7522	2828	415	1279	.248	.363	1789	1578	1609	.979	270	5793	11032	99	480	3.45

East

Bos.   W-89 L-73   John McNamara   W-43 L-42   Joe Morgan   W-46 L-31

POS	Player	AB	BA	HR	RBI	PO	A	E	DP	TC/G	FA	Pitcher	G	IP	W	L	SV	ERA
1B	T. Benzinger	405	.254	13	70	520	38	5	47	6.6	.991	R. Clemens	35	264	18	12	0	2.93
2B	M. Barrett	612	.283	1	65	312	402	7	97	4.8	.990	B. Hurst	33	217	18	6	0	3.66
SS	J. Reed	338	.293	1	28	123	242	11	49	4.0	.971	W. Gardner	36	149	8	6	2	3.50
3B	W. Boggs	584	**.366**	5	58	**122**	250	11	17	2.5	.971	O. Boyd	23	130	9	7	0	5.34
RF	D. Evans	559	.293	21	111	460	30	7	39	7.8	.986	M. Smithson	31	127	9	6	0	5.97
CF	E. Burks	540	.294	18	92	370	9	9	0	2.7	.977	B. Stanley	57	102	6	4	5	3.19
LF	M. Greenwell	590	.325	22	119	302	6	6	2	2.1	.981	M. Boddicker	15	89	7	3	0	2.63
C	R. Gedman	299	.231	9	39	570	40	5	4	6.6	.992	L. Smith	64	84	4	5	29	2.80
DH	J. Rice	485	.264	15	72							D. Lamp	46	83	7	6	0	3.48
C	R. Cerone	264	.269	3	27	471	28	0	4	6.0	**1.000**							
SS	S. Owen	257	.249	5	18	102	192	10	34	4.0	.967							
1B	L. Parrish	158	.259	7	26	221	25	3	18	6.9	.988							

Det.   W-88 L-74   Sparky Anderson

POS	Player	AB	BA	HR	RBI	PO	A	E	DP	TC/G	FA	Pitcher	G	IP	W	L	SV	ERA
1B	D. Evans	437	.208	22	64	509	58	4	43	8.8	.993	J. Morris	34	235	15	13	0	3.94
2B	L. Whitaker	403	.275	12	55	218	284	8	53	4.6	.984	D. Alexander	34	229	14	11	0	4.32
SS	A. Trammell	466	.311	15	69	195	355	11	67	4.5	.980	W. Terrell	29	206	7	16	0	3.97
3B	T. Brookens	441	.243	5	38	101	234	17	16	2.6	.952	F. Tanana	32	203	14	11	0	4.21
RF	C. Lemon	512	.264	17	64	296	8	8	3	2.2	.974	J. Robinson	24	172	13	6	0	2.98
CF	G. Pettis	458	.210	3	36	361	5	5	0	2.9	.987	M. Henneman	65	91	9	6	22	1.87
LF	P. Sheridan	347	.254	11	47	203	2	4	0	1.9	.981	G. Hernandez	63	68	6	5	10	3.06
C	M. Nokes	382	.251	16	53	574	45	7	8	5.7	.989							
UT	L. Salazar	452	.270	12	62	199	151	10	22		.972							
1B	R. Knight	299	.217	3	33	432	33	4	40	7.3	.991							
UT	D. Bergman	289	.294	5	35	386	37	4	31		.991							
C	M. Heath	219	.247	5	18	357	24	6	3	5.2	.984							
2B	Walewander	175	.211	0	6	114	144	6	36	4.3	.977							
DH	L. Herndon	174	.224	4	20													

Mil.   W-87 L-75   Tom Trebelhorn

POS	Player	AB	BA	HR	RBI	PO	A	E	DP	TC/G	FA	Pitcher	G	IP	W	L	SV	ERA
1B	G. Brock	364	.212	6	50	915	102	7	89	9.0	.993	T. Higuera	31	227	16	9	0	2.45
2B	J. Gantner	539	.276	0	47	**325**	428	11	92	5.0	.986	B. Wegman	32	199	13	13	0	4.12
SS	D. Sveum	467	.242	9	51	208	370	**27**	93	4.8	.955	C. Bosio	38	182	7	15	6	3.36
3B	P. Molitor	609	.312	13	60	86	187	17	15	2.8	.941	D. August	24	148	13	7	0	3.09
RF	R. Deer	492	.252	23	85	284	10	3	3	2.2	.990	M. Birkbeck	23	124	10	8	0	4.72
CF	R. Yount	621	.306	13	91	444	12	2	2	2.9	.996	J. Nieves	25	110	7	5	1	4.08
LF	J. Leonard	374	.235	8	44	191	4	3	1	2.2	.985	C. Crim	**70**	105	7	6	9	2.91
C	B. Surhoff	493	.245	5	38	525	42	6	2	5.4	.990	T. Filer	19	102	5	8	0	4.43
D1	J. Meyer	327	.263	11	45	190	18	3	19	6.4	.986	D. Plesac	50	52	1	2	30	2.41
OF	G. Braggs	272	.261	10	42	134	1	3	0	2.6	.978							

Tor.   W-87 L-75   Jimy Williams

POS	Player	AB	BA	HR	RBI	PO	A	E	DP	TC/G	FA	Pitcher	G	IP	W	L	SV	ERA
1B	F. McGriff	536	.282	34	82	1344	93	5	143	9.4	**.997**	M. Flanagan	34	211	13	13	0	4.18
2B	M. Lee	381	.291	2	38	221	261	6	64	5.0	.988	D. Stieb	32	207	16	8	0	3.04
SS	T. Fernandez	648	.287	5	70	247	470	14	106	4.7	.981	J. Clancy	36	196	11	13	1	4.49
3B	K. Gruber	569	.278	16	81	114	**349**	14	31	3.1	.971	J. Key	21	131	12	5	0	3.29
RF	J. Barfield	468	.244	18	56	325	12	4	4	2.5	.988	J. Cerutti	46	124	6	7	1	3.13
CF	L. Moseby	472	.239	10	42	304	2	5	1	2.5	.984	D. Ward	64	112	9	3	15	3.30
LF	G. Bell	614	.269	24	97	253	8	15	1	1.9	.946	Stottlemyre	28	98	4	8	0	5.69
C	E. Whitt	398	.251	16	70	643	43	4	10	5.6	.994	J. Musselman	15	85	8	5	0	3.18
DH	R. Mulliniks	337	.300	12	48							T. Henke	52	68	4	4	25	2.91
2B	N. Liriano	276	.264	3	23	121	177	12	48	3.9	.961	D. Wells	41	64	3	5	4	4.62
OD	R. Leach	199	.276	0	23	74	1	0	0	1.5	1.000							
1B	C. Fielder	174	.230	9	23	99	10	1	10	6.5	.991							
C	P. Borders	154	.273	5	21	205	14	6	0	5.2	.973							

N. Y.   W-85 L-76   Billy Martin   W-40 L-28   Lou Piniella   W-45 L-48

POS	Player	AB	BA	HR	RBI	PO	A	E	DP	TC/G	FA	Pitcher	G	IP	W	L	SV	ERA
1B	D. Mattingly	599	.311	18	88	1250	99	9	131	9.5	.993	R. Rhoden	30	197	12	12	0	4.29
2B	W. Randolph	404	.230	2	34	254	339	7	83	**5.5**	.988	T. John	35	176	9	8	0	4.49
SS	R. Santana	480	.240	4	38	202	421	22	96	4.4	.966	R. Dotson	32	171	12	9	0	5.00
3B	Pagliarulo	444	.216	15	67	82	232	19	16	2.7	.943	Candelaria	25	157	13	7	1	3.38
RF	D. Winfield	559	.322	25	107	276	3	3	1	2.0	.989	N. Allen	41	117	5	3	0	3.84
CF	Washington	455	.308	11	64	309	5	5	1	2.7	.984	C. Hudson	28	106	6	6	2	4.49
LF	R. Henderson	554	.305	6	50	320	7	12	5	2.5	.965	D. Righetti	60	87	5	4	25	3.52
C	D. Slaught	322	.283	9	43	496	24	11	4	5.6	.979	S. Shields	39	82	5	5	0	4.37
DH	J. Clark	496	.242	27	93							C. Guante	56	75	5	6	11	2.88
C	J. Skinner	251	.227	4	23	395	16	4	5	4.9	.990							
OF	G. Ward	231	.225	4	24	130	0	1	0	2.4	.992							
DH	K. Phelps	107	.224	10	22													

Cle.   W-78 L-84   Doc Edwards

POS	Player	AB	BA	HR	RBI	PO	A	E	DP	TC/G	FA	Pitcher	G	IP	W	L	SV	ERA
1B	W. Upshaw	493	.245	11	50	1162	102	12	93	8.9	.991	G. Swindell	33	242	18	14	0	3.20
2B	J. Franco	613	.303	10	54	310	434	14	87	5.0	.982	T. Candiotti	31	217	14	8	0	3.28
SS	J. Bell	211	.218	2	21	103	170	10	37	3.9	.965	J. Farrell	31	210	14	10	0	4.24
3B	B. Jacoby	552	.241	9	49	99	298	10	23	2.7	.975	S. Bailes	37	145	9	14	0	4.90
RF	C. Snyder	511	.272	26	75	314	16	5	3	2.4	.985	R. Yett	23	134	9	6	0	4.62
CF	J. Carter	621	.271	27	98	444	8	7	3	2.9	.985	D. Jones	51	83	3	4	37	2.27
LF	M. Hall	515	.280	6	71	288	3	10	1	2.1	.967							
C	A. Allanson	434	.263	5	50	**691**	60	11	11	5.7	.986							
DH	R. Kittle	225	.258	18	43													
SS	Washington	223	.256	2	21	83	141	16	26	4.4	.933							
DH	T. Francona	212	.311	1	12													
OF	C. Castillo	176	.273	4	14	69	1	5	0	1.7	.933							

POS	Player	AB	BA	HR	RBI	PO	A	E	DP	TC/G	FA	Pitcher	G	IP	W	L	SV	ERA
Bal.																		
1B	E. Murray	603	.284	28	84	867	106	11	101	9.6	.989	J. Bautista	33	172	6	15	0	4.30
2B	B. Ripken	512	.207	2	34	309	440	12	110	5.1	.984	J. Tibbs	30	159	4	15	0	5.39
SS	C. Ripken	575	.264	23	81	**284**	480	21	119	4.9	.973	J. Ballard	25	153	8	12	0	4.40
3B	R. Gonzales	237	.215	2	15	45	153	7	19	2.6	.966	M. Boddicker	21	147	6	12	0	3.86
RF	J. Orsulak	379	.288	8	27	228	6	5	2	2.0	.979	D. Schmidt	41	130	8	5	2	3.40
CF	F. Lynn	301	.252	18	37	216	1	2	0	2.6	.991	Williamson	37	118	5	8	4	4.90
LF	P. Stanicek	261	.230	4	17	21	20	2	5	2.7	.953	O. Peraza	19	86	5	7	0	5.55
C	M. Tettleton	283	.261	11	37	361	31	3	1	4.9	.992	M. Thurmond	43	75	1	8	3	4.58
OD	L. Sheets	452	.230	10	47	139	9	4	0	2.0	.974	Niedenfuer	52	59	3	4	18	3.51
UT	J. Traber	352	.222	10	45	481	59	6	51		.989							
3B	R. Schu	270	.256	4	20	56	108	11	7	2.4	.937							
C	T. Kennedy	265	.226	3	16	332	23	2	3	4.5	.994							
OF	K. Gerhart	262	.195	9	23	192	3	5	1	2.2	.975							
OF	B. Anderson	177	.198	1	9	156	1	3	0	3.3	.981							

W-54 L-107
Cal Ripken
W-0 L-6
Frank Robinson
W-54 L-101

West

POS	Player	AB	BA	HR	RBI	PO	A	E	DP	TC/G	FA	Pitcher	G	IP	W	L	SV	ERA
Oak.																		
1B	M. McGwire	550	.260	32	99	1228	88	9	118	8.6	.993	D. Stewart	37	**276**	21	12	0	3.23
2B	G. Hubbard	294	.255	3	33	195	267	6	60	4.5	.987	B. Welch	36	245	17	9	0	3.64
SS	W. Weiss	452	.250	3	39	254	431	15	83	4.8	.979	S. Davis	33	202	16	7	0	3.70
3B	C. Lansford	556	.279	7	57	113	220	7	16	2.4	**.979**	C. Young	26	156	11	8	0	4.14
RF	J. Canseco	610	.307	**42**	**124**	304	11	7	3	2.2	.978	G. Nelson	54	112	9	6	3	3.06
CF	D. Henderson	507	.304	24	94	382	5	7	2	2.8	.982	T. Burns	17	103	8	2	1	3.16
LF	L. Polonia	288	.292	2	27	155	3	2	1	2.1	.988	R. Honeycutt	55	80	3	2	7	3.50
C	R. Hassey	323	.257	7	45	465	31	3	7	5.5	.994	E. Plunk	49	78	7	2	5	3.00
OF	S. Javier	397	.257	2	35	240	6	5	2	2.2	.980	D. Eckersley	60	73	4	2	45	2.35
DO	D. Parker	377	.257	12	55	58	3	3	0	1.9	.953	G. Cadaret	58	72	5	2	3	2.89
C	T. Steinbach	351	.265	9	51	484	48	9	5	6.4	.983							
UT	M. Gallego	277	.209	2	20	155	254	8	49		.981							
DH	D. Baylor	264	.220	7	34													
UT	T. Phillips	212	.203	2	17	84	80	10	18		.943							

W-104 L-58
Tony LaRussa

POS	Player	AB	BA	HR	RBI	PO	A	E	DP	TC/G	FA	Pitcher	G	IP	W	L	SV	ERA
Min.																		
1B	K. Hrbek	510	.312	25	76	842	57	3	92	8.6	.997	F. Viola	35	255	**24**	7	0	2.64
2B	Lombardozzi	287	.209	3	27	140	211	5	47	4.0	.986	B. Blyleven	33	207	10	17	0	5.43
SS	G. Gagne	461	.236	14	48	200	373	18	79	4.0	.970	A. Anderson	30	202	16	9	0	**2.45**
3B	G. Gaetti	468	.301	28	88	105	189	7	24	2.6	.977	C. Lea	24	130	7	7	0	4.85
RF	R. Bush	394	.261	14	51	19	2	0	1	3.5	1.000	F. Toliver	21	115	7	6	0	4.24
CF	K. Puckett	**657**	.356	24	121	**450**	12	3	4	2.9	.994	J. Berenguer	57	100	8	4	2	3.96
LF	D. Gladden	576	.269	11	62	0	0	0	**0**	.000	.000	K. Atherton	49	74	7	5	3	3.41
C	T. Laudner	375	.251	13	54	621	35	5	8	6.1	.992	J. Reardon	63	73	2	4	42	2.47
D1	G. Larkin	505	.267	8	70	466	28	3	46	8.3	.994							
2B	T. Herr	304	.263	1	21	140	195	4	54	4.6	.988							
UT	A. Newman	260	.223	0	19	97	155	6	33		.977							
OF	J. Moses	206	.316	2	12	123	1	0	0	1.5	1.000							
C	B. Harper	166	.295	3	20	207	15	2	0	4.7	.991							

W-91 L-71
Tom Kelly

POS	Player	AB	BA	HR	RBI	PO	A	E	DP	TC/G	FA	Pitcher	G	IP	W	L	SV	ERA
K. C.																		
1B	G. Brett	589	.306	24	103	1126	70	10	105	9.7	.992	M. Gubicza	35	270	20	8	0	2.70
2B	F. White	537	.235	8	58	293	426	4	88	4.9	**.994**	Saberhagen	35	261	14	16	0	3.80
SS	K. Stillwell	459	.251	10	53	170	349	13	60	4.3	.976	C. Leibrandt	35	243	13	12	0	3.19
3B	K. Seitzer	559	.304	5	60	93	297	**26**	33	2.8	.938	F. Bannister	31	189	12	13	0	4.33
RF	D. Tartabull	507	.274	26	102	227	8	9	1	1.9	.963	S. Farr	62	83	5	4	20	2.50
CF	W. Wilson	591	.262	1	37	365	1	4	0	2.6	.989	T. Power	22	80	5	6	0	5.94
LF	B. Jackson	439	.246	25	68	246	11	7	2	2.2	.973	Montgomery	45	63	7	2	1	3.45
C	J. Quirk	196	.240	8	25	409	31	8	5	5.7	.982	G. Garber	26	33	0	4	6	3.58
OF	P. Tabler	301	.309	1	49	68	1	1	0	1.9	.986							
D1	B. Buckner	242	.256	3	34	160	12	1	11	8.2	.994							
C	Macfarlane	211	.265	4	26	309	18	2	3	4.8	.994							
OF	Eisenreich	202	.218	1	19	109	0	4	0	1.8	.965							
UT	B. Pecota	178	.208	1	15	98	145	6	25		.976							

W-84 L-77
John Wathan

POS	Player	AB	BA	HR	RBI	PO	A	E	DP	TC/G	FA	Pitcher	G	IP	W	L	SV	ERA
Cal.																		
1B	W. Joyner	597	.295	13	85	**1369**	143	8	**148**	**9.7**	.995	M. Witt	34	250	13	16	0	4.15
2B	J. Ray	602	.306	6	83	194	328	15	64	5.2	.972	W. Fraser	34	195	12	13	0	5.41
SS	D. Schofield	527	.239	6	34	278	492	13	**125**	5.1	**.983**	C. Finley	31	194	9	15	0	4.17
3B	J. Howell	500	.254	16	63	96	249	17	19	2.4	.953	McCaskill	23	146	8	6	0	4.31
RF	C. Davis	600	.268	21	93	299	10	19	1	2.1	.942	D. Petry	22	140	3	9	0	4.38
CF	D. White	455	.259	11	51	364	7	9	2	**3.3**	.976	T. Clark	15	94	6	6	0	5.07
LF	T. Armas	368	.272	13	49	212	5	3	1	1.9	.986	G. Minton	44	79	4	5	7	2.85
C	B. Boone	352	.295	5	39	506	**66**	8	9	4.8	.986	B. Harvey	50	76	7	5	17	2.13
DH	B. Downing	484	.242	25	64							D. Moore	27	33	5	2	4	4.91
2B	M. McLemore	233	.240	2	16	107	171	6	52	4.5	.979							

W-75 L-87
Cookie Rojas
W-75 L-79
Larry Stubing
W-0 L-8

POS	Player	AB	BA	HR	RBI	PO	A	E	DP	TC/G	FA	Pitcher	G	IP	W	L	SV	ERA
Chi.																		
1B	G. Walker	377	.247	8	42	935	41	7	93	10.0	.993	M. Perez	32	197	12	10	0	3.79
2B	F. Manrique	345	.235	5	37	228	308	8	77	4.2	.985	J. Reuss	32	183	13	9	0	3.44
SS	O. Guillen	566	.261	0	39	273	**570**	20	115	**5.5**	.977	B. Long	47	174	8	11	2	4.03
3B	S. Lyons	472	.269	5	45	81	238	25	**36**	2.7	.927	D. LaPoint	26	161	10	11	0	3.40
RF	I. Calderon	264	.212	14	35	141	5	7	1	2.3	.954	J. McDowell	26	159	5	10	0	3.97
CF	D. Gallagher	347	.303	5	31	228	5	0	2	2.5	1.000	R. Horton	52	109	6	10	2	4.86
LF	D. Pasqua	422	.227	20	50	58	8	1	11	9.6	**.985**	B. Thigpen	68	90	5	8	34	3.30
C	C. Fisk	253	.277	19	50	338	36	2	7	5.1	.995							
DH	H. Baines	599	.277	13	81													
OF	D. Boston	281	.217	15	31	190	4	10	2	2.4	.951							
OF	G. Redus	262	.263	6	34	140	7	2	1	2.2	.987							
2B	D. Hill	221	.217	2	20	106	132	6	36	4.1	.975							
O3	K. Williams	220	.159	8	28	87	69	17	4		.902							
C	M. Salas	196	.250	3	9	251	35	6	5	4.2	.979							

W-71 L-90
Jim Fregosi

POS	Player	AB	BA	HR	RBI	PO	A	E	DP	TC/G	FA	Pitcher	G	IP	W	L	SV	ERA
Tex.												C. Hough	34	252	15	16	0	3.32
1B	P. O'Brien	547	.272	16	71	1346	140	8	124	9.6	.995	J. Guzman	30	207	11	13	0	3.70
2B	C. Wilkerson	338	.293	0	28	153	240	12	52	4.7	.970	P. Kilgus	32	203	12	15	0	4.16
SS	S. Fletcher	515	.276	0	47	215	414	11	90	4.6	.983	J. Russell	34	189	10	9	0	3.82
3B	S. Buechele	503	.250	16	58	110	297	16	25	2.8	.962	B. Witt	22	174	8	10	0	3.92
RF	R. Sierra	615	.254	23	91	310	11	7	3	2.1	.979	M. Williams	67	68	2	7	18	4.63
CF	O. McDowell	437	.247	6	37	267	2	3	1	2.4	.989	R. Hayward	12	63	4	6	0	5.46
LF	Incaviglia	418	.249	22	54	172	12	2	1	2.0	.989	D. Mohorcic	43	52	2	6	5	4.85
C	G. Petralli	351	.282	7	36	409	45	9	7	5.4	.981							
OF	C. Espy	347	.248	2	39	196	10	6	0	2.2	.972							
C	M. Stanley	249	.229	3	27	310	14	3	3	5.1	.991							
DH	L. Parrish	248	.190	7	26													
2B	J. Browne	214	.229	1	17	112	139	11	27	3.7	.958							
OF	B. Brower	201	.224	1	11	104	2	3	1	1.8	.972							
Sea.												M. Langston	35	261	15	11	0	3.34
1B	A. Davis	478	.295	18	69	980	65	6	111	9.1	.994	M. Moore	37	229	9	15	1	3.78
2B	H. Reynolds	598	.283	4	41	303	471	18	111	5.0	.977	B. Swift	38	175	8	12	0	4.59
SS	R. Quinones	499	.248	12	52	202	396	23	103	4.6	.963	S. Bankhead	21	135	7	9	0	3.07
3B	J. Presley	544	.230	14	62	112	234	22	25	2.5	.940	M. Campbell	20	115	6	10	0	5.89
RF	G. Wilson	284	.250	3	17	140	4	3	1	2.0	.980	M. Jackson	62	99	6	5	4	2.63
CF	H. Cotto	386	.259	8	33	253	6	2	0	2.2	.992	S. Trout	15	56	4	7	0	7.83
LF	M. Brantley	577	.263	15	56	327	5	6	1	2.3	.982	M. Schooler	40	48	5	8	15	3.54
C	S. Bradley	335	.257	4	33	524	37	5	6	6.7	.991							
D1	S. Balboni	350	.251	21	61	334	25	2	34	9.0	.994							
C	D. Valle	290	.231	10	50	484	47	6	7	6.4	.989							
OF	D. Coles	195	.292	10	34	66	3	1	0	1.5	.986							
OF	J. Buhner	192	.224	10	25	134	7	1	3	2.4	.993							
DH	K. Phelps	190	.284	14	32													

W-70 L-91 · SS S. Fletcher · Bobby Valentine (Texas)
W-68 L-93 · Dick Williams · W-24 L-33 Jimmy Snyder · W-44 L-60 (Seattle)

BATTING AND BASE RUNNING LEADERS

Batting Average
W. Boggs, BOS	.366
K. Puckett, MIN	.356
M. Greenwell, BOS	.325
D. Winfield, NY	.322
P. Molitor, MIL	.312

Slugging Average
J. Canseco, OAK	.569
F. McGriff, TOR	.552
G. Gaetti, MIN	.551
K. Puckett, MIN	.545
M. Greenwell, BOS	.531

Home Runs
J. Canseco, OAK	42
F. McGriff, TOR	34
M. McGwire, OAK	32
G. Gaetti, MIN	28
E. Murray, BAL	28

Total Bases
K. Puckett, MIN	358
J. Canseco, OAK	347
M. Greenwell, BOS	313
G. Brett, KC	300
J. Carter, CLE	297

Runs Batted In
J. Canseco, OAK	124
K. Puckett, MIN	121
M. Greenwell, BOS	119
D. Evans, BOS	111
D. Winfield, NY	107

Stolen Bases
R. Henderson, NY	93
G. Pettis, DET	44
P. Molitor, MIL	41
J. Canseco, OAK	40
W. Wilson, KC	35
H. Reynolds, SEA	35

Hits
K. Puckett, MIN	234
W. Boggs, BOS	214
M. Greenwell, BOS	192

Base on Balls
W. Boggs, BOS	125
J. Clark, NY	113
C. Ripken, BAL	102

Home Run Percentage
J. Canseco, OAK	6.9
F. McGriff, TOR	6.3
G. Gaetti, MIN	6.0

Runs Scored
W. Boggs, BOS	128
J. Canseco, OAK	120
R. Henderson, NY	118

Doubles
W. Boggs, BOS	45
G. Brett, KC	42
J. Ray, CAL	42
K. Puckett, MIN	42

Triples
W. Wilson, KC	11
H. Reynolds, SEA	11
R. Yount, MIL	11
M. Greenwell, BOS	8

PITCHING LEADERS

Winning Percentage
F. Viola, MIN	.774
B. Hurst, BOS	.750
M. Gubicza, KC	.714
S. Davis, OAK	.696
J. Robinson, DET	.684

Earned Run Average
A. Anderson, MIN	2.45
T. Higuera, MIL	2.45
F. Viola, MIN	2.64
M. Gubicza, KC	2.70
R. Clemens, BOS	2.93

Wins
F. Viola, MIN	24
D. Stewart, OAK	21
M. Gubicza, KC	20
B. Hurst, BOS	18
R. Clemens, BOS	18
G. Swindell, CLE	18

Saves
D. Eckersley, OAK	45
J. Reardon, MIN	42
D. Jones, CLE	37
B. Thigpen, CHI	34
D. Plesac, MIL	30

Strikeouts
R. Clemens, BOS	291
M. Langston, SEA	235
F. Viola, MIN	193
T. Higuera, MIL	192
D. Stewart, OAK	192

Complete Games
R. Clemens, BOS	14
D. Stewart, OAK	14
B. Witt, TEX	13
G. Swindell, CLE	12
M. Witt, CAL	12

Fewest Hits per 9 Innings
J. Robinson, DET	6.33
T. Higuera, MIL	6.65
D. Stieb, TOR	6.82

Shutouts
R. Clemens, BOS	8
D. Stieb, TOR	4
G. Swindell, CLE	4
M. Gubicza, KC	4

Fewest Walks per 9 Innings
A. Anderson, MIN	1.65
G. Swindell, CLE	1.67
D. Alexander, DET	1.81

Most Strikeouts per 9 Inn.
R. Clemens, BOS	9.92
M. Langston, SEA	8.09
B. Witt, TEX	7.64

Innings
D. Stewart, OAK	276
M. Gubicza, KC	270
R. Clemens, BOS	264

Games Pitched
C. Crim, MIL	70
B. Thigpen, CHI	68
M. Williams, TEX	67

	W	L	PCT	GB	R	OR	2B	3B	Batting HR	BA	SA	SB	E	Fielding DP	FA	CG	BB	Pitching SO	ShO	SV	ERA
EAST																					
BOS	89	73	.549		**813**	689	**310**	39	124	**.283**	.420	65	93	123	.984	26	493	**1085**	10	37	3.97
DET	88	74	.543	1	703	658	213	28	143	.250	.378	87	109	129	.982	34	497	890	6	36	3.71
MIL	87	75	.537	2	682	**616**	258	26	113	.257	.375	**159**	120	146	.981	30	**437**	832	6	51	3.45
TOR	87	75	.537	2	763	680	271	**47**	**158**	.268	.419	107	110	170	.982	16	528	904	7	47	3.80
NY	85	76	.528	3.5	772	748	272	12	148	.263	.395	146	134	161	.978	16	487	861	3	43	4.26
CLE	78	84	.481	11	666	731	235	28	134	.261	.387	97	124	131	.980	35	442	812	7	46	4.16
BAL	54	107	.335	34.5	550	789	199	20	137	.238	.359	69	119	172	.980	20	523	709	2	26	4.54
WEST																					
OAK	104	58	.642		800	620	251	22	156	.263	.399	129	105	151	.983	22	553	983	4	**64**	**3.44**
MIN	91	71	.562	13	759	672	294	31	151	.274	**.421**	107	**84**	155	**.986**	18	453	897	4	52	3.93
KC	84	77	.522	19.5	704	648	275	40	121	.259	.391	137	124	147	.980	29	465	886	9	32	3.66
CAL	75	87	.463	29	714	771	258	31	124	.261	.385	86	135	175	.979	26	568	817	6	33	4.31
CHI	71	90	.441	32.5	631	757	224	35	132	.244	.370	98	154	**177**	.976	11	533	754	2	43	4.12
TEX	70	91	.435	33.5	637	735	227	39	112	.252	.368	130	131	145	.979	**41**	654	912	8	31	4.05
SEA	68	93	.422	35.5	664	744	271	27	148	.257	.398	95	123	168	.980	28	558	981	8	28	4.15
					9858	9858	3558	425	1901	.259	.391	1512	1665	2150	.981	352	7191	12323	82	569	3.97

Player Register

The Player Register is an alphabetical listing of the career records of every man who appeared in a game in the 1988 season, with the exception of players who are primarily pitchers. Pitchers who have appeared in a minimum of 25 non-pitching games (pinch-hitting, pinch-running, or playing other positions) are listed in this section; all others have abbreviated batting records listed in the Pitcher Register.

Any statistics that appear in bold faced type indicate that the player led his league in that category that year. Where there is a tie for the league lead, all tied leaders are listed with bold faced figures. If a superscript "1" appears next to a statistic, as with Rickey Henderson's stolen base total in 1982, it indicates that he is the all-time single season leader in the category. Figures appearing in bold beneath a player's career totals means that the player ranks in the top ten in baseball history in that category. (Pete Rose, naturally, has "1st" beneath his career hits total.) Career leaders are also highlighted underneath the World Series totals.

	G	AB	H	2B	3B	HR	HR %	R	RBI	BB	SO	SB	BA	SA	Pinch Hit AB	Pinch Hit H	G by POS

Shawn Abner

ABNER, SHAWN WESLEY
B. June 17, 1966, Hamilton, Ohio

BR TR 6'1" 190 lbs.

	G	AB	H	2B	3B	HR	HR%	R	RBI	BB	SO	SB	BA	SA	PH AB	PH H	G by POS
1987 SD N	16	47	13	3	1	2	4.3	5	7	2	8	1	.277	.511	3	1	OF-14
1988	37	83	15	3	0	2	2.4	6	5	4	19	0	.181	.289	0	0	OF-35
2 yrs.	53	130	28	6	1	4	3.1	11	12	6	27	1	.215	.369	3	1	OF-49

Jim Adduci

ADDUCI, JAMES DAVID
B. Aug. 9, 1959, Chicago, Ill.

BL TL 6'4" 200 lbs.

	G	AB	H	2B	3B	HR	HR%	R	RBI	BB	SO	SB	BA	SA	PH AB	PH H	G by POS
1983 STL N	10	20	1	0	0	0	0.0	0	0	1	6	0	.050	.050	3	0	1B-6, OF-1
1986 MIL A	3	11	1	1	0	0	0.0	2	0	1	2	0	.091	.182	0	0	1B-3
1988	44	94	25	6	1	1	1.1	8	15	0	15	0	.266	.383	3	0	OF-24, DH-12, 1B-3
3 yrs.	57	125	27	7	1	1	0.8	10	15	2	23	0	.216	.312	6	0	OF-25, DH-12, 1B-12

Luis Aguayo

AGUAYO, LUIS
Born Luis Aguayo y Muriel.
B. Mar. 13, 1959, Vega Baja, Puerto Rico

BR TR 5'9" 173 lbs.

	G	AB	H	2B	3B	HR	HR%	R	RBI	BB	SO	SB	BA	SA	PH AB	PH H	G by POS
1980 PHI N	20	47	13	1	2	1	2.1	7	8	2	3	1	.277	.447	1	0	2B-14, SS-5
1981	45	84	18	4	0	1	1.2	11	7	6	15	1	.214	.298	3	1	SS-21, 2B-21, 3B-3
1982	50	56	15	1	2	3	5.4	11	7	5	7	1	.268	.518	5	1	2B-21, SS-15, 3B-5
1983	2	4	1	0	0	0	0.0	1	0	1	2	0	.250	.250	0	0	SS-2
1984	58	72	20	4	0	3	4.2	15	11	8	16	0	.278	.458	16	3	3B-14, 2B-12, SS-10
1985	91	165	46	7	3	6	3.6	27	21	22	26	1	.279	.467	8	3	SS-60, 2B-17, 3B-7
1986	62	133	28	6	1	4	3.0	17	13	8	26	1	.211	.361	14	2	2B-31, SS-20, 3B-1
1987	94	209	43	9	1	12	5.7	25	21	15	56	0	.206	.431	18	2	SS-78, 2B-6, 3B-2
1988 2 teams	PHI	N (49G –	.247)	NY	A	(50G –	.250)										
" total	99	237	59	7	0	6	2.5	21	13	20	50	2	.249	.354	13	4	3B-46, SS-33, 2B-15
9 yrs.	521	1007	243	39	9	36	3.6	135	101	87	201	7	.241	.405	78	21	SS-244, 2B-137, 3B-78

DIVISIONAL PLAYOFF SERIES

	G	AB	H	2B	3B	HR	HR%	R	RBI	BB	SO	SB	BA	SA	PH AB	PH H	G by POS
1981 PHI N	2	0	0	0	0	0	–	1	0	0	0	0	–	–	0	0	

Mike Aldrete

ALDRETE, MICHAEL PETER
B. Jan. 29, 1961, Carmel, Calif.

BL TL 5'11" 180 lbs.

	G	AB	H	2B	3B	HR	HR%	R	RBI	BB	SO	SB	BA	SA	PH AB	PH H	G by POS
1986 SF N	84	216	54	18	3	2	0.9	27	25	33	34	1	.250	.389	16	4	1B-37, OF-31
1987	126	357	116	18	2	9	2.5	50	51	43	50	6	.325	.462	25	6	OF-79, 1B-33
1988	139	389	104	15	0	3	0.8	44	50	56	65	6	.267	.329	29	11	OF-115, 1B-10
3 yrs.	349	962	274	51	5	14	1.5	121	126	132	149	13	.285	.392	70	21	OF-225, 1B-80

LEAGUE CHAMPIONSHIP SERIES

	G	AB	H	2B	3B	HR	HR%	R	RBI	BB	SO	SB	BA	SA	PH AB	PH H	G by POS
1987 SF N	5	10	1	0	0	0	0.0	0	1	0	2	0	.100	.100	2	0	OF-3

Luis Alicea

ALICEA, LUIS RENE
Born Luis Rene Alicea y DeJesus.
B. July 29, 1965, Santurce, Puerto Rico

BB TR 5'9" 165 lbs.

	G	AB	H	2B	3B	HR	HR%	R	RBI	BB	SO	SB	BA	SA	PH AB	PH H	G by POS
1988 STL N	93	297	63	10	4	1	0.3	20	24	25	32	1	.212	.283	5	1	2B-91

Andy Allanson

ALLANSON, ANDREW NEAL
B. Dec. 22, 1961, Richmond, Va.

BR TR 6'5" 220 lbs.

	G	AB	H	2B	3B	HR	HR%	R	RBI	BB	SO	SB	BA	SA	PH AB	PH H	G by POS
1986 CLE A	101	293	66	7	3	1	0.3	30	29	14	36	10	.225	.280	0	0	C-99
1987	50	154	41	6	0	3	1.9	17	16	9	30	1	.266	.364	0	0	C-50
1988	133	434	114	11	0	5	1.2	44	50	25	63	5	.263	.323	0	0	C-133
3 yrs.	284	881	221	24	3	9	1.0	91	95	48	129	16	.251	.316	0	0	C-282

Rod Allen

ALLEN, RODERICK BERNET
B. Oct. 5, 1959, Los Angeles, Calif.

BR TR 6'1" 185 lbs.

	G	AB	H	2B	3B	HR	HR%	R	RBI	BB	SO	SB	BA	SA	PH AB	PH H	G by POS
1983 SEA A	11	12	2	0	0	0	0.0	1	0	0	1	0	.167	.167	4	1	DH-3, OF-2
1984 DET A	15	27	8	1	0	0	0.0	6	3	2	8	1	.296	.333	3	1	DH-11, OF-2
1988 CLE A	5	11	1	1	0	0	0.0	1	0	0	2	0	.091	.182	2	1	DH-4
3 yrs.	31	50	11	2	0	0	0.0	8	3	2	11	1	.220	.260	9	3	DH-18, OF-4

Bill Almon

ALMON, WILLIAM FRANCIS
B. Nov. 21, 1952, Providence, R. I.

BR TR 6'3" 180 lbs.

	G	AB	H	2B	3B	HR	HR%	R	RBI	BB	SO	SB	BA	SA	PH AB	PH H	G by POS
1974 SD N	16	38	12	1	0	0	0.0	4	3	2	9	1	.316	.342	0	0	SS-14
1975	6	10	4	0	0	0	0.0	0	0	0	1	0	.400	.400	1	0	SS-2
1976	14	57	14	3	0	1	1.8	6	6	2	9	3	.246	.351	0	0	SS-14
1977	155	613	160	18	11	2	0.3	75	43	37	114	20	.261	.336	0	0	SS-155
1978	138	405	102	19	2	0	0.0	39	21	33	74	17	.252	.309	4	1	3B-114, SS-15, 2B-7
1979	100	198	45	3	0	1	0.5	20	8	21	48	6	.227	.258	3	0	2B-61, SS-25, OF-1
1980 2 teams	MON	N (18G –	.263)	NY	N	(48G –	.170)										
" total	66	150	29	4	3	0	0.0	15	7	9	32	2	.193	.260	4	0	SS-34, 2B-19, 3B-9
1981 CHI A	103	349	105	10	2	4	1.1	46	41	21	60	16	.301	.375	0	0	SS-103
1982	111	308	79	10	4	4	1.3	40	26	25	49	10	.256	.354	1	0	SS-108, DH-1
1983 OAK A	143	451	120	29	1	4	0.9	45	63	26	67	26	.266	.361	14	3	SS-52, 3B-40, 1B-38, OF-23, 2B-5, DH-4
1984	106	212	46	11	0	7	3.3	24	16	10	42	5	.217	.368	15	3	OF-48, 1B-44, DH-12, 3B-4, SS-1, C-1
1985 PIT N	88	244	66	17	0	6	2.5	33	29	22	61	10	.270	.414	14	5	SS-43, OF-32, 3B-7, 1B-7
1986	102	196	43	7	2	7	3.6	29	27	30	38	11	.219	.383	28	5	OF-54, 3B-28, SS-19, 1B-4
1987 2 teams	PIT	N (19G –	.200)	NY	N	(49G –	.241)										
" total	68	74	17	4	0	0	0.0	13	5	9	21	1	.230	.284	22	4	SS-26, 2B-10, OF-3, 1B-2, 3B-1
1988 PHI N	20	26	3	2	0	0	0.0	1	1	3	11	0	.115	.192	6	0	3B-9, SS-5, 1B-1
15 yrs.	1236	3331	845	138	25	36	1.1	390	296	250	636	128	.254	.343	112	21	SS-616, 3B-212, OF-161, 2B-102, 1B-96, DH-17, C-1

	G	AB	H	2B	3B	HR	HR %	R	RBI	BB	SO	SB	BA	SA	Pinch Hit AB	Pinch Hit H	G by POS

Roberto Alomar

ALOMAR, ROBERTO   BB TR 6'   155 lbs.
Born Roberto Alomar y Velasquez.   Son of Sandy Alomar.
Brother of Sandy Alomar.
B. Feb. 5, 1968, Salinas, Puerto Rico

	G	AB	H	2B	3B	HR	HR %	R	RBI	BB	SO	SB	BA	SA	PH AB	PH H	G by POS
1988 **SD** N	143	545	145	24	6	9	1.7	84	41	47	83	24	.266	.382	0	0	2B-143

Sandy Alomar

ALOMAR, SANTOS, JR.   BR TR 6'5"   200 lbs.
Born Santos Alomar y Velasquez.   Son of Sandy Alomar.
Brother of Roberto Alomar.
B. June 18, 1966, Salinas, Puerto Rico

	G	AB	H	2B	3B	HR	HR %	R	RBI	BB	SO	SB	BA	SA	PH AB	PH H	G by POS
1988 **SD** N	1	1	0	0	0	0	0.0	0	0	0	1	0	.000	.000	1	0	

Brady Anderson

ANDERSON, BRADY KEVIN   BL TL 6'1"   170 lbs.
B. Jan. 18, 1964, Silver Spring, Md.

	G	AB	H	2B	3B	HR	HR %	R	RBI	BB	SO	SB	BA	SA	PH AB	PH H	G by POS
1988 **2 teams**	**BOS** A (41G – .230)				**BAL** A (53G – .198)												
" total	94	325	69	13	4	1	0.3	31	21	23	75	10	.212	.286	7	0	OF-90

Dave Anderson

ANDERSON, DAVID CARTER   BR TR 6'2"   185 lbs.
B. Aug. 1, 1960, Louisville, Ky.

	G	AB	H	2B	3B	HR	HR %	R	RBI	BB	SO	SB	BA	SA	PH AB	PH H	G by POS
1983 **LA** N	61	115	19	4	2	1	0.9	12	2	12	15	6	.165	.261	2	1	SS-53, 3B-1
1984	121	374	94	16	2	3	0.8	51	34	45	55	15	.251	.329	5	0	SS-111, 3B-11
1985	77	221	44	6	0	4	1.8	24	18	35	42	5	.199	.281	4	2	3B-51, SS-25, 2B-2
1986	92	216	53	9	0	1	0.5	31	15	22	39	5	.245	.301	4	1	3B-51, SS-34, 2B-5
1987	108	265	62	12	3	1	0.4	32	13	24	43	9	.234	.313	6	2	SS-65, 3B-34, 2B-5
1988	116	285	71	10	2	2	0.7	31	20	32	45	4	.249	.319	7	2	SS-82, 3B-12, 2B-11
6 yrs.	575	1476	343	57	9	12	0.8	181	102	170	239	44	.232	.308	28	8	SS-370, 3B-161, 2B-23

LEAGUE CHAMPIONSHIP SERIES

	G	AB	H	2B	3B	HR	HR %	R	RBI	BB	SO	SB	BA	SA	PH AB	PH H	G by POS
1985 **LA** N	4	5	0	0	0	0	0.0	1	0	3	1	0	.000	.000	0	0	SS-3

WORLD SERIES

	G	AB	H	2B	3B	HR	HR %	R	RBI	BB	SO	SB	BA	SA	PH AB	PH H	G by POS
1988 **LA** N	1	1	0	0	0	0	0.0	0	0	0	1	0	.000	.000	1	0	DH-1

Tony Armas

ARMAS, ANTONIO RAFAEL   BR TR 5'11"   182 lbs.
Born Antonio Rafael Armas y Machado.
B. July 2, 1953, Anzoategui, Venezuela

	G	AB	H	2B	3B	HR	HR %	R	RBI	BB	SO	SB	BA	SA	PH AB	PH H	G by POS
1976 **PIT** N	4	6	2	0	0	0	0.0	0	1	0	2	0	.333	.333	2	0	OF-2
1977 **OAK** A	118	363	87	8	2	13	3.6	26	53	20	99	1	.240	.380	7	0	OF-112, SS-1
1978	91	239	51	6	1	2	0.8	17	13	10	62	1	.213	.272	4	0	OF-85, DH-3
1979	80	278	69	9	3	11	4.0	29	34	16	67	1	.248	.421	0	0	OF-80
1980	158	628	175	18	8	35	5.6	87	109	29	128	5	.279	.500	0	0	OF-158
1981	109	440	115	24	3	22	5.0	51	76	19	115	5	.261	.480	0	0	OF-109
1982	138	536	125	19	2	28	5.2	58	89	33	128	2	.233	.433	2	0	OF-135, DH-1
1983 **BOS** A	145	574	125	23	2	36	6.3	77	107	29	131	0	.218	.453	2	0	OF-126, DH-27
1984	157	639	171	29	5	43	6.7	107	123	32	156	1	.268	.531	0	0	OF-126, DH-31
1985	103	385	102	17	5	23	6.0	50	64	18	90	0	.265	.514	5	1	OF-79, DH-19
1986	121	425	112	21	4	11	2.6	40	58	24	77	0	.264	.409	4	1	OF-117, DH-1
1987 **CAL** A	28	81	16	3	1	3	3.7	8	9	1	11	1	.198	.370	6	2	OF-27
1988	120	368	100	20	2	13	3.5	42	49	22	87	1	.272	.443	9	2	OF-113, DH-5
13 yrs.	1372	4962	1250	197	38	240	4.8	592	785	253	1153	18	.252	.452	41	6	OF-1259, DH-87, SS-1

DIVISIONAL PLAYOFF SERIES

	G	AB	H	2B	3B	HR	HR %	R	RBI	BB	SO	SB	BA	SA	PH AB	PH H	G by POS
1981 **OAK** A	3	11	6	2	0	0	0.0	1	3	1	1	0	.545	.727	0	0	OF-3

LEAGUE CHAMPIONSHIP SERIES

	G	AB	H	2B	3B	HR	HR %	R	RBI	BB	SO	SB	BA	SA	PH AB	PH H	G by POS
1981 **OAK** A	3	12	2	0	0	0	0.0	0	0	0	5	0	.167	.167	0	0	OF-3
1986 **BOS** A	5	16	2	1	0	0	0.0	1	0	0	2	0	.125	.188	0	0	OF-5
2 yrs.	8	28	4	1	0	0	0.0	1	0	0	7	0	.143	.179	0	0	OF-8

WORLD SERIES

	G	AB	H	2B	3B	HR	HR %	R	RBI	BB	SO	SB	BA	SA	PH AB	PH H	G by POS
1986 **BOS** A	1	1	0	0	0	0	0.0	0	0	0	1	0	.000	.000	1	0	

Alan Ashby

ASHBY, ALAN DEAN   BB TR 6'2"   185 lbs.
B. July 8, 1951, Long Beach, Calif.

	G	AB	H	2B	3B	HR	HR %	R	RBI	BB	SO	SB	BA	SA	PH AB	PH H	G by POS
1973 **CLE** A	11	29	5	1	0	1	3.4	4	3	2	11	0	.172	.310	1	0	C-11
1974	10	7	1	0	0	0	0.0	1	0	1	2	0	.143	.143	1	1	C-9
1975	90	254	57	10	1	5	2.0	32	32	30	42	3	.224	.331	1	0	C-87, 1B-2, DH-1, 3B-1
1976	89	247	59	5	1	4	1.6	26	32	27	49	0	.239	.316	5	0	C-86, 1B-2, 3B-1
1977 **TOR** A	124	396	83	16	3	2	0.5	25	29	50	50	0	.210	.280	0	0	C-124
1978	81	264	69	15	0	9	3.4	27	29	28	32	1	.261	.420	0	0	C-81
1979 **HOU** N	108	336	68	15	2	2	0.6	25	35	26	70	0	.202	.277	3	1	C-105
1980	116	352	90	19	2	3	0.9	30	48	35	40	0	.256	.347	5	1	C-114
1981	83	255	69	13	0	4	1.6	20	33	35	33	0	.271	.369	4	2	C-81
1982	100	339	87	14	2	12	3.5	40	49	27	53	2	.257	.416	6	3	C-95
1983	87	275	63	18	1	8	2.9	31	34	31	38	0	.229	.389	5	2	C-85
1984	66	191	50	7	0	4	2.1	16	27	20	22	0	.262	.361	4	2	C-63
1985	65	189	53	8	0	8	4.2	20	25	24	27	0	.280	.450	4	1	C-60
1986	120	315	81	15	0	7	2.2	24	38	39	56	1	.257	.371	20	3	C-103
1987	125	386	111	16	0	14	3.6	53	63	50	52	0	.288	.438	16	1	C-110
1988	73	227	54	10	0	7	3.1	19	33	29	36	0	.238	.374	10	2	C-66
16 yrs.	1348	4062	1000	182	12	90	2.2	393	510	454	613	7	.246	.363	85	19	C-1280, 1B-4, 3B-2, DH-1

DIVISIONAL PLAYOFF SERIES

	G	AB	H	2B	3B	HR	HR %	R	RBI	BB	SO	SB	BA	SA	PH AB	PH H	G by POS
1981 **HOU** N	3	9	1	0	0	1	11.1	1	2	2	0	0	.111	.444	0	0	C-3

LEAGUE CHAMPIONSHIP SERIES

	G	AB	H	2B	3B	HR	HR %	R	RBI	BB	SO	SB	BA	SA	PH AB	PH H	G by POS
1980 **HOU** N	2	8	1	0	0	0	0.0	0	1	0	0	0	.125	.125	1	1	C-2
1986	6	23	3	1	0	1	4.3	2	2	2	1	0	.130	.304	0	0	C-6
2 yrs.	8	31	4	1	0	1	3.2	2	3	2	1	0	.129	.258	1	1	C-8

	G	AB	H	2B	3B	HR	HR %	R	RBI	BB	SO	SB	BA	SA	Pinch Hit AB	Pinch Hit H	G by POS

Wally Backman

BACKMAN, WALTER WAYNE   BB TR 5'9"   160 lbs.
B. Sept. 22, 1959, Hillsboro, Ore.

	G	AB	H	2B	3B	HR	HR %	R	RBI	BB	SO	SB	BA	SA	AB	H	G by POS
1980 NY N	27	93	30	1	1	0	0.0	12	9	11	14	2	.323	.355	0	0	2B-20, SS-8
1981	26	36	10	2	0	0	0.0	5	0	4	7	1	.278	.333	15	3	2B-11, 3B-1
1982	96	261	71	13	2	3	1.1	37	22	49	47	8	.272	.372	5	0	2B-88, 3B-6, SS-1
1983	26	42	7	0	1	0	0.0	6	3	2	8	0	.167	.214	16	3	2B-14, 3B-2
1984	128	436	122	19	2	1	0.2	68	26	56	63	32	.280	.339	11	3	2B-115, SS-7
1985	145	520	142	24	5	1	0.2	77	38	36	72	30	.273	.344	15	6	2B-140, SS-1
1986	124	387	124	18	2	1	0.3	67	27	36	32	13	.320	.385	15	5	2B-113
1987	94	300	75	6	1	1	0.3	43	23	25	43	11	.250	.287	12	2	2B-87
1988	99	294	89	12	0	0	0.0	44	17	41	49	9	.303	.344	6	1	2B-92
9 yrs.	765	2369	670	95	14	7	0.3	359	165	260	335	106	.283	.344	95	23	2B-680, SS-17, 3B-9

LEAGUE CHAMPIONSHIP SERIES

	G	AB	H	2B	3B	HR	HR %	R	RBI	BB	SO	SB	BA	SA	AB	H	G by POS
1986 NY N	6	21	5	0	0	0	0.0	5	2	2	4	1	.238	.238	0	0	2B-6
1988	7	22	6	1	0	0	0.0	2	2	2	5	1	.273	.318	0	0	2B-7
2 yrs.	13	43	11	1	0	0	0.0	7	4	4	9	2	.256	.279	0	0	2B-13

WORLD SERIES

	G	AB	H	2B	3B	HR	HR %	R	RBI	BB	SO	SB	BA	SA	AB	H	G by POS
1986 NY N	6	18	6	0	0	0	0.0	4	1	4	2	1	.333	.333	0	0	2B-6

Mark Bailey

BAILEY, JOHN MARK   BB TR 6'5"   195 lbs.
B. Nov. 14, 1961, Springfield, Mo.

	G	AB	H	2B	3B	HR	HR %	R	RBI	BB	SO	SB	BA	SA	AB	H	G by POS
1984 HOU N	108	344	73	16	1	9	2.6	38	34	53	71	0	.212	.343	0	0	C-108
1985	114	332	88	14	0	10	3.0	47	45	67	70	0	.265	.398	2	1	C-110, 1B-2
1986	57	153	27	5	0	4	2.6	9	15	28	45	1	.176	.288	5	2	C-53, 1B-1
1987	35	64	13	1	0	0	0.0	5	3	10	21	1	.203	.219	8	3	C-27
1988	8	23	3	0	0	0	0.0	1	0	5	6	0	.130	.130	0	0	C-8
5 yrs.	322	916	204	36	1	23	2.5	100	97	163	213	2	.223	.340	15	6	C-306, 1B-3

Harold Baines

BAINES, HAROLD DOUGLAS   BL TL 6'2"   175 lbs.
B. Mar. 15, 1959, Easton, Md.

	G	AB	H	2B	3B	HR	HR %	R	RBI	BB	SO	SB	BA	SA	AB	H	G by POS
1980 CHI A	141	491	125	23	6	13	2.6	55	49	19	65	2	.255	.405	9	1	OF-137, DH-1
1981	82	280	80	11	7	10	3.6	42	41	12	41	6	.286	.482	5	1	OF-80, DH-1
1982	161	608	165	29	8	25	4.1	89	105	49	95	10	.271	.469	1	0	OF-161
1983	156	596	167	33	2	20	3.4	76	99	49	85	7	.280	.443	1	1	OF-155
1984	147	569	173	28	10	29	5.1	72	94	54	75	1	.304	.541	1	0	OF-147
1985	160	640	198	29	3	22	3.4	86	113	42	89	1	.309	.467	1	0	OF-159, DH-1
1986	145	570	169	29	2	21	3.7	72	88	38	89	2	.296	.465	1	0	OF-141, DH-3
1987	132	505	148	26	4	20	4.0	59	93	46	82	0	.293	.479	9	3	DH-117, OF-8
1988	158	599	166	39	1	13	2.2	55	81	67	109	0	.277	.411	4	2	DH-147, OF-9
9 yrs.	1282	4858	1391	247	43	173	3.6	606	763	376	730	29	.286	.462	32	8	OF-997, DH-270

LEAGUE CHAMPIONSHIP SERIES

	G	AB	H	2B	3B	HR	HR %	R	RBI	BB	SO	SB	BA	SA	AB	H	G by POS
1983 CHI A	4	16	2	0	0	0	0.0	0	0	1	3	0	.125	.125	0	0	OF-4

Doug Baker

BAKER, DOUGLAS LEE   BB TR 5'9"   160 lbs.
B. Apr. 3, 1961, Fullerton, Calif.

	G	AB	H	2B	3B	HR	HR %	R	RBI	BB	SO	SB	BA	SA	AB	H	G by POS
1984 DET A	43	108	20	4	1	0	0.0	15	11	7	22	3	.185	.241	1	1	SS-39, 2B-5
1985	15	27	5	1	0	0	0.0	4	1	0	9	0	.185	.222	3	0	SS-12, 2B-1
1986	13	24	3	1	0	0	0.0	1	0	2	7	0	.125	.167	1	0	SS-10, 2B-2, DH-1
1987	8	1	0	0	0	0	0.0	0	0	0	1	0	.000	.000	1	0	SS-6, 3B-1, 2B-1
1988 MIN A	11	7	0	0	0	0	0.0	1	0	0	5	0	.000	.000	0	0	SS-9, 3B-1, 2B-1
5 yrs.	90	167	28	6	1	0	0.0	21	12	9	44	3	.168	.216	6	1	SS-76, 2B-10, 3B-2, DH-1

LEAGUE CHAMPIONSHIP SERIES

	G	AB	H	2B	3B	HR	HR %	R	RBI	BB	SO	SB	BA	SA	AB	H	G by POS
1984 DET A	1	0	0	0	0	0	—	0	0	0	0	0	—	—	0	0	SS-1

Steve Balboni

BALBONI, STEPHEN CHARLES (Bye-Bye)   BR TR 6'3"   225 lbs.
B. Jan. 16, 1957, Brockton, Mass.

	G	AB	H	2B	3B	HR	HR %	R	RBI	BB	SO	SB	BA	SA	AB	H	G by POS
1981 NY A	4	7	2	1	1	0	0.0	2	2	1	4	0	.286	.714	1	0	1B-3, DH-1
1982	33	107	20	2	1	2	1.9	8	4	6	34	0	.187	.280	5	1	1B-26, DH-5
1983	32	86	20	2	0	5	5.8	8	17	8	23	0	.233	.430	3	1	1B-23, DH-4
1984 KC A	126	438	107	23	2	28	6.4	58	77	45	139	0	.244	.498	1	0	1B-125, DH-1
1985	160	600	146	28	2	36	6.0	74	88	52	166	1	.243	.477	1	0	1B-160
1986	138	512	117	25	2	29	5.7	54	88	43	146	0	.229	.451	2	0	1B-137
1987	121	386	80	11	1	24	6.2	44	60	34	97	0	.207	.427	15	4	1B-55, DH-52
1988 2 teams	KC	A (21G – .143)				SEA	A (97G – .251)										
" total	118	413	97	17	2	23	5.6	46	66	24	87	0	.235	.448	9	2	DH-62, 1B-53
8 yrs.	732	2549	589	109	9	147	5.8	294	402	213	696	1	.231	.454	37	8	1B-582, DH-125

LEAGUE CHAMPIONSHIP SERIES

	G	AB	H	2B	3B	HR	HR %	R	RBI	BB	SO	SB	BA	SA	AB	H	G by POS
1984 KC A	3	10	1	0	0	0	0.0	0	0	1	4	0	.100	.100	0	0	1B-3
1985	7	25	3	0	0	0	0.0	1	1	2	8	0	.120	.120	0	0	1B-7
2 yrs.	10	35	4	0	0	0	0.0	1	1	3	12	0	.114	.114	0	0	1B-10

WORLD SERIES

	G	AB	H	2B	3B	HR	HR %	R	RBI	BB	SO	SB	BA	SA	AB	H	G by POS
1985 KC A	7	25	8	0	0	0	0.0	2	3	5	4	0	.320	.320	0	0	1B-7

Chris Bando

BANDO, CHRISTOPHER MICHAEL   BB TR 6'   195 lbs.
Brother of Sal Bando.
B. Feb. 4, 1956, Cleveland, Ohio

	G	AB	H	2B	3B	HR	HR %	R	RBI	BB	SO	SB	BA	SA	AB	H	G by POS
1981 CLE A	21	47	10	3	0	0	0.0	3	6	2	2	0	.213	.277	9	0	C-15, DH-2
1982	66	184	39	6	1	3	1.6	13	16	24	30	0	.212	.304	12	4	C-63, 3B-2
1983	48	121	31	3	0	4	3.3	15	15	15	19	0	.256	.380	9	2	C-43
1984	75	220	64	11	0	12	5.5	38	41	33	35	1	.291	.505	11	2	C-53, DH-1, 3B-1, 1B-1
1985	73	173	24	4	1	0	0.0	11	13	22	21	0	.139	.173	8	2	C-67
1986	92	254	68	9	0	2	0.8	28	26	22	49	0	.268	.327	13	2	C-86
1987	89	211	46	9	0	5	2.4	20	16	12	28	0	.218	.332	5	0	C-86

	G	AB	H	2B	3B	HR	HR %	R	RBI	BB	SO	SB	BA	SA	Pinch Hit AB	Pinch Hit H	G by POS

Chris Bando   continued

1988 2 teams   CLE A (32G – .125)   **DET A** (1G – .000)

	G	AB	H	2B	3B	HR	HR %	R	RBI	BB	SO	SB	BA	SA	AB	H	G by POS
" total	33	72	9	1	0	1	1.4	6	8	8	12	0	.125	.181	2	0	C-33
8 yrs.	497	1282	291	46	2	27	2.1	134	141	138	196	1	.227	.329	69	12	C-456, DH-3, 3B-3, 1B-1

Jesse Barfield

BARFIELD, JESSE LEE
B. Oct. 29, 1959, Joliet, Ill.   BR TR 6'1"   200 lbs.

	G	AB	H	2B	3B	HR	HR %	R	RBI	BB	SO	SB	BA	SA	AB	H	G by POS
1981 TOR A	25	95	22	3	2	2	2.1	7	9	4	19	4	.232	.368	0	0	OF-25
1982	139	394	97	13	2	18	4.6	54	58	42	79	1	.246	.426	21	6	OF-137, DH-1
1983	128	388	98	13	3	27	7.0	58	68	22	110	2	.253	.510	16	6	OF-120, DH-5
1984	110	320	91	14	1	14	4.4	51	49	35	81	8	.284	.466	20	8	OF-88, DH-9
1985	155	539	156	34	9	27	5.0	94	84	66	143	22	.289	.536	1	0	OF-154
1986	158	589	170	35	2	**40**	6.8	107	108	69	146	8	.289	.559	1	0	OF-157
1987	159	590	155	25	3	28	4.7	89	84	58	141	3	.263	.458	4	1	OF-158
1988	137	468	114	21	5	18	3.8	62	56	41	108	7	.244	.425	4	1	OF-136, DH-1
8 yrs.	1011	3383	903	158	27	174	5.1	522	516	337	827	55	.267	.484	67	22	OF-975, DH-16

LEAGUE CHAMPIONSHIP SERIES

	G	AB	H	2B	3B	HR	HR %	R	RBI	BB	SO	SB	BA	SA	AB	H	G by POS
1985 TOR A	7	25	7	1	0	1	4.0	3	4	3	7	1	.280	.440	0	0	OF-7

Marty Barrett

BARRETT, MARTIN GLENN
Brother of Tom Barrett.
B. June 23, 1958, Arcadia, Calif.   BR TR 5'11"   175 lbs.

	G	AB	H	2B	3B	HR	HR %	R	RBI	BB	SO	SB	BA	SA	AB	H	G by POS
1982 BOS A	8	18	1	0	0	0	0.0	0	0	0	1	0	.056	.056	0	0	2B-7
1983	33	44	10	1	0	0	0.0	7	2	3	1	0	.227	.295	0	0	2B-23, DH-5
1984	139	475	144	23	3	3	0.6	56	45	42	25	4	.303	.383	1	0	2B-136
1985	156	534	142	26	0	5	0.9	59	56	56	50	7	.266	.343	0	0	2B-155
1986	158	625	179	39	4	4	0.6	94	60	65	31	15	.286	.381	0	0	2B-158
1987	137	559	164	23	0	3	0.5	72	43	51	38	15	.293	.351	0	0	2B-137
1988	150	612	173	28	1	1	0.2	83	65	40	35	7	.283	.337	1	0	2B-150
7 yrs.	781	2867	813	140	9	16	0.6	371	271	257	181	48	.284	.355	2	0	2B-766, DH-5

LEAGUE CHAMPIONSHIP SERIES

	G	AB	H	2B	3B	HR	HR %	R	RBI	BB	SO	SB	BA	SA	AB	H	G by POS
1986 BOS A	7	30	11	2	0	0	0.0	4	5	2	2	0	.367	.433	0	0	2B-7
1988	4	15	1	0	0	0	0.0	2	0	1	0	0	.067	.067	0	0	2B-4
2 yrs.	11	45	12	2	0	0	0.0	6	5	3	2	0	.267	.311	0	0	2B-11

WORLD SERIES

	G	AB	H	2B	3B	HR	HR %	R	RBI	BB	SO	SB	BA	SA	AB	H	G by POS
1986 BOS A	7	30	13	2	0	0	0.0	1	4	5	2	0	.433	.500	0	0	2B-7

Tom Barrett

BARRETT, THOMAS LOREN
Brother of Marty Barrett.
B. Apr. 2, 1960, San Fernando, Calif.   BB TR 5'9"   157 lbs.

	G	AB	H	2B	3B	HR	HR %	R	RBI	BB	SO	SB	BA	SA	AB	H	G by POS
1988 PHI N	36	54	11	1	0	0	0.0	5	3	7	8	0	.204	.222	21	8	2B-10

Kevin Bass

BASS, KEVIN CHARLES
B. May 12, 1959, Redwood City, Calif.   BB TR 6'   183 lbs.

1982 2 teams   MIL A (18G – .000)   **HOU N** (12G – .042)

	G	AB	H	2B	3B	HR	HR %	R	RBI	BB	SO	SB	BA	SA	AB	H	G by POS
" total	30	33	1	0	0	0	0.0	6	1	1	9	0	.030	.030	1	0	OF-21, DH-2
1983 HOU N	88	195	46	7	3	2	1.0	25	18	6	27	2	.236	.333	43	11	OF-52
1984	121	331	86	17	5	2	0.6	33	29	6	57	5	.260	.360	44	13	OF-81
1985	150	539	145	27	5	16	3.0	72	68	31	63	19	.269	.427	12	4	OF-141
1986	157	591	184	33	5	20	3.4	83	79	38	72	22	.311	.486	2	2	OF-155
1987	157	592	168	31	5	19	3.2	83	85	53	77	21	.284	.449	2	1	OF-155
1988	157	541	138	27	2	14	2.6	57	72	42	65	31	.255	.390	16	6	OF-147
7 yrs.	860	2822	768	142	25	73	2.6	359	352	177	370	100	.272	.418	120	37	OF-752, DH-2

LEAGUE CHAMPIONSHIP SERIES

	G	AB	H	2B	3B	HR	HR %	R	RBI	BB	SO	SB	BA	SA	AB	H	G by POS
1986 HOU N	6	24	7	2	0	0	0.0	0	0	4	4	2	.292	.375	0	0	OF-6

Don Baylor

BAYLOR, DON EDWARD
B. June 28, 1949, Austin, Tex.   BR TR 6'1"   190 lbs.

	G	AB	H	2B	3B	HR	HR %	R	RBI	BB	SO	SB	BA	SA	AB	H	G by POS
1970 BAL A	8	17	4	0	0	0	0.0	4	4	2	3	1	.235	.235	0	0	OF-6
1971	1	2	0	0	0	0	0.0	0	1	2	1	0	.000	.000	0	0	OF-1
1972	102	320	81	13	3	11	3.4	33	38	29	50	24	.253	.416	16	5	OF-84, 1B-9
1973	118	405	116	20	4	11	2.7	64	51	35	48	32	.286	.437	12	2	OF-110, 1B-6, DH-1
1974	137	489	133	22	1	10	2.0	66	59	43	56	29	.272	.382	5	3	OF-129, 1B-8, DH-1
1975	145	524	148	21	6	25	4.8	79	76	53	64	32	.282	.489	1	1	OF-135, DH-7, 1B-2
1976 OAK A	157	595	147	25	1	15	2.5	85	68	58	72	52	.247	.368	2	0	OF-76, 1B-69, DH-23
1977 CAL A	154	561	141	27	0	25	4.5	87	75	62	76	26	.251	.433	1	0	OF-77, DH-61, 1B-18
1978	158	591	151	26	0	34	5.8	103	99	56	71	22	.255	.472	0	0	DH-100, OF-39, 1B-17
1979	162	628	186	33	3	36	5.7	**120**	**139**	71	51	22	.296	.530	0	0	OF-97, DH-65, 1B-1
1980	90	340	85	12	2	5	1.5	39	51	24	32	6	.250	.341	0	0	OF-54, DH-36
1981	103	377	90	18	1	17	4.5	52	66	42	51	3	.239	.427	1	1	DH-97, 1B-4, OF-1
1982	157	608	160	24	1	24	3.9	80	93	57	69	10	.263	.424	0	0	DH-155
1983 NY A	144	534	162	33	3	21	3.9	82	85	40	53	17	.303	.494	9	2	DH-136, OF-5, 1B-1
1984	134	493	129	29	1	27	5.5	84	89	39	67	1	.262	.489	10	2	DH-127, 1B-5
1985	142	477	110	24	1	23	4.8	70	91	52	90	0	.231	.430	13	5	DH-140
1986 BOS A	160	585	139	23	1	31	5.3	93	94	62	111	3	.238	.439	0	0	DH-143, 1B-13, OF-3
1987 2 teams BOS A (108G – .239) MIN A (20G – .286)																	
" total	128	388	95	9	0	16	4.1	67	63	45	59	5	.245	.392	17	6	DH-117
1988 OAK A	92	264	58	7	0	7	2.7	28	34	34	44	0	.220	.326	12	1	DH-80
19 yrs.	2292	8198	2135	366	28	338	4.1	1236	1276	806	1068	285	.260	.436	99	28	DH-1289, OF-817, 1B-153

LEAGUE CHAMPIONSHIP SERIES

	G	AB	H	2B	3B	HR	HR %	R	RBI	BB	SO	SB	BA	SA	AB	H	G by POS
1973 BAL A	4	11	3	0	0	0	0.0	3	1	3	5	0	.273	.273	0	0	OF-3
1974	4	15	4	0	0	0	0.0	0	0	0	2	0	.267	.267	0	0	OF-4
1979 CAL A	4	16	3	0	1	1	6.3	2	2	1	2	0	.188	.375	0	0	OF-1
1982	5	17	5	1	1	1	5.9	2	10	2	0	0	.294	.647	0	0	DH-5

	G	AB	H	2B	3B	HR	HR %	R	RBI	BB	SO	SB	BA	SA	Pinch Hit AB	Pinch Hit H	G by POS

Don Baylor continued

	G	AB	H	2B	3B	HR	HR %	R	RBI	BB	SO	SB	BA	SA	PH AB	PH H	G by POS
1986 BOS A	7	26	9	3	0	1	3.8	6	2	4	5	0	.346	.577	0	0	DH-7
1987 MIN A	2	5	2	0	0	0	0.0	0	1	0	0	0	.400	.400	1	1	DH-2
1988 OAK A	2	6	0	0	0	0	0.0	0	1	1	2	0	.000	.000	0	0	DH-2
7 yrs.	28	96	26	4	1	3	3.1	13	17	11	16	0	.271	.427	1	1	DH-16, OF-8

WORLD SERIES
	G	AB	H	2B	3B	HR	HR %	R	RBI	BB	SO	SB	BA	SA	PH AB	PH H	G by POS
1986 BOS A	4	11	2	1	0	0	0.0	1	1	1	3	0	.182	.273	1	0	DH-3
1987 MIN A	5	13	5	0	0	1	7.7	3	3	1	1	0	.385	.615	2	1	DH-3
1988 OAK A	1	1	0	0	0	0	0.0	0	0	0	1	0	.000	.000	1	0	
3 yrs.	10	25	7	1	0	1	4.0	4	4	2	5	0	.280	.440	4	1	DH-6

Billy Bean

BEAN, WILLIAM DARO
B. May 11, 1964, Santa Ana, Calif.
BL TL 6' 185 lbs.

	G	AB	H	2B	3B	HR	HR %	R	RBI	BB	SO	SB	BA	SA	PH AB	PH H	G by POS
1987 DET A	26	66	17	2	0	0	0.0	6	4	5	11	1	.258	.288	5	0	OF-24
1988	10	11	2	0	1	0	0.0	2	0	0	2	0	.182	.364	4	2	OF-4, 1B-2, DH-1
2 yrs.	36	77	19	2	1	0	0.0	8	4	5	13	1	.247	.299	9	2	OF-28, 1B-2, DH-1

Billy Beane

BEANE, WILLIAM LAMAR
B. Mar. 29, 1962, Orlando, Fla.
BR TR 6'4" 195 lbs.

	G	AB	H	2B	3B	HR	HR %	R	RBI	BB	SO	SB	BA	SA	PH AB	PH H	G by POS
1984 NY N	5	10	1	0	0	0	0.0	0	0	0	2	0	.100	.100	2	0	OF-5
1985	8	8	2	1	0	0	0.0	0	1	0	3	0	.250	.375	4	2	OF-2
1986 MIN A	80	183	39	6	0	3	1.6	20	15	11	54	0	.213	.295	11	1	OF-67, DH-5
1987	12	15	4	2	0	0	0.0	1	1	0	6	0	.267	.400	3	0	OF-7
1988 DET A	6	6	1	0	0	0	0.0	1	1	0	2	0	.167	.167	0	0	OF-6
5 yrs.	111	222	47	9	0	3	1.4	22	18	11	67	2	.212	.293	20	3	OF-87, DH-5

Buddy Bell

BELL, DAVID GUS
Son of Gus Bell.
B. Aug. 27, 1951, Pittsburgh, Pa.
BR TR 6'1" 180 lbs.

	G	AB	H	2B	3B	HR	HR %	R	RBI	BB	SO	SB	BA	SA	PH AB	PH H	G by POS
1972 CLE A	132	466	119	21	1	9	1.9	49	36	34	29	5	.255	.363	3	1	OF-123, 3B-6
1973	156	631	169	23	7	14	2.2	86	59	49	47	7	.268	.393	1	0	3B-154, OF-2
1974	116	423	111	15	1	7	1.7	51	46	35	29	1	.262	.352	0	0	3B-115, DH-1
1975	153	553	150	20	4	10	1.8	66	59	51	72	6	.271	.376	0	0	3B-153
1976	159	604	170	26	2	7	1.2	75	60	44	49	3	.281	.366	1	1	3B-158, 1B-2
1977	129	479	140	23	4	11	2.3	64	64	45	63	1	.292	.426	3	1	3B-118, OF-11
1978	142	556	157	27	8	6	1.1	71	62	39	43	1	.282	.392	3	1	3B-139, DH-1
1979 TEX A	162	670	200	42	3	18	2.7	89	101	30	45	5	.299	.451	0	0	3B-147, SS-33
1980	129	490	161	24	4	17	3.5	76	83	40	39	3	.329	.498	9	2	3B-123, SS-3
1981	97	360	106	16	1	10	2.8	44	64	42	30	3	.294	.428	1	0	3B-96, SS-1
1982	148	537	159	27	2	13	2.4	62	67	70	50	5	.296	.426	1	0	3B-145, SS-4
1983	156	618	171	35	3	14	2.3	75	66	50	48	3	.277	.411	2	0	3B-154
1984	148	553	174	36	5	11	2.0	87	83	63	54	2	.315	.458	0	0	3B-147
1985 2 teams	TEX A (84G – .236)						CIN N (67G – .219)										
" total	151	560	128	28	5	10	1.8	61	68	67	48	3	.229	.350	2	1	3B-150
1986 CIN N	155	568	158	29	3	20	3.5	89	75	73	49	2	.278	.445	4	2	3B-151, 2B-1
1987	143	522	148	19	2	17	3.3	74	70	71	39	4	.284	.425	1	0	3B-142
1988 2 teams	CIN N (21G – .185)						HOU N (74G – .253)										
" total	95	323	78	10	1	7	2.2	27	40	26	32	1	.241	.344	9	0	3B-79, 1B-9
17 yrs.	2371	8913	2499	421	56	201	2.3	1146	1103	829	766	55	.280	.408	40	9	3B-2177, OF-136, SS-41, 1B-11, DH-2, 2B-1

George Bell

BELL, JORGE ANTONIO MATHY
B. Oct. 21, 1959, San Pedro de Macoris, Dominican Republic
BR TR 6'1" 190 lbs.

	G	AB	H	2B	3B	HR	HR %	R	RBI	BB	SO	SB	BA	SA	PH AB	PH H	G by POS
1981 TOR A	60	163	38	2	1	5	3.1	19	12	5	27	3	.233	.350	5	3	OF-44, DH-8
1983	39	112	30	5	4	2	1.8	5	17	4	17	1	.268	.438	3	1	OF-34, DH-2
1984	159	606	177	39	4	26	4.3	85	87	24	86	11	.292	.498	8	3	OF-147, DH-7, 3B-3
1985	157	607	167	28	6	28	4.6	87	95	43	90	21	.275	.479	0	0	OF-157, 3B-2
1986	159	641	198	38	6	31	4.8	101	108	41	62	7	.309	.532	1	1	OF-147, DH-11, 3B-1
1987	156	610	188	32	4	47	7.7	111	134	39	75	5	.308	.605	1	0	OF-149, 3B-1
1988	156	614	165	27	5	24	3.9	78	97	34	66	4	.269	.446	2	0	OF-149, DH-7
7 yrs.	886	3353	963	171	30	163	4.9	486	550	190	423	52	.287	.502	20	8	OF-827, DH-35, 3B-7

LEAGUE CHAMPIONSHIP SERIES
	G	AB	H	2B	3B	HR	HR %	R	RBI	BB	SO	SB	BA	SA	PH AB	PH H	G by POS
1985 TOR A	7	28	9	3	0	0	0.0	4	1	0	4	0	.321	.429	0	0	OF-7

Jay Bell

BELL, JAY STUART
B. Dec. 11, 1965, Pensacola, Fla.
BR TR 6'1" 180 lbs.

	G	AB	H	2B	3B	HR	HR %	R	RBI	BB	SO	SB	BA	SA	PH AB	PH H	G by POS
1986 CLE A	5	14	5	2	0	1	7.1	3	4	2	3	0	.357	.714	1	0	DH-2, 2B-2
1987	38	125	27	9	1	2	1.6	14	13	8	31	2	.216	.352	0	0	SS-38
1988	73	211	46	5	1	2	0.9	23	21	21	53	4	.218	.280	0	0	SS-72
3 yrs.	116	350	78	16	2	5	1.4	40	38	31	87	6	.223	.323	1	0	SS-110, DH-2, 2B-2

Rafael Belliard

BELLIARD, RAFAEL LEONIDAS
Born Rafael Leonidas Belliard y Matias.
B. Oct. 24, 1961, Puerto Nuevo Mao, Dominican Republic
BB TR 5'9" 139 lbs.

	G	AB	H	2B	3B	HR	HR %	R	RBI	BB	SO	SB	BA	SA	PH AB	PH H	G by POS
1982 PIT N	9	2	1	0	0	0	0.0	3	0	0	0	1	.500	.500	1	1	SS-4
1983	4	1	0	0	0	0	0.0	1	0	0	1	0	.000	.000	0	0	SS-3
1984	20	22	5	0	0	0	0.0	3	0	0	1	4	.227	.227	0	0	SS-12, 2B-1
1985	17	20	4	0	0	0	0.0	1	0	0	5	0	.200	.200	2	0	SS-12
1986	117	309	72	5	2	0	0.0	33	31	26	54	12	.233	.262	4	0	SS-96, 2B-23
1987	81	203	42	4	3	1	0.5	26	15	20	25	5	.207	.271	1	0	SS-71, 2B-7
1988	122	286	61	0	4	0	0.0	28	11	26	47	7	.213	.241	0	0	SS-117, 2B-3
7 yrs.	370	843	185	9	9	1	0.1	95	58	72	133	29	.219	.255	9	1	SS-315, 2B-34

	G	AB	H	2B	3B	HR	HR %	R	RBI	BB	SO	SB	BA	SA	Pinch Hit AB	Pinch Hit H	G by POS

Bruce Benedict

BENEDICT, BRUCE EDWIN
B. Aug. 18, 1955, Birmingham, Ala.   BR TR 6'1"   175 lbs.

	G	AB	H	2B	3B	HR	HR %	R	RBI	BB	SO	SB	BA	SA	PH AB	PH H	G by POS
1978 **ATL N**	22	52	13	2	0	0	0.0	3	1	6	6	0	.250	.288	0	0	C-22
1979	76	204	46	11	0	0	0.0	14	15	33	18	1	.225	.279	1	0	C-76
1980	120	359	91	14	1	2	0.6	18	34	28	36	3	.253	.315	0	0	C-120
1981	90	295	78	12	1	5	1.7	26	35	33	21	1	.264	.363	0	0	C-90
1982	118	386	95	11	1	3	0.8	34	44	37	41	4	.246	.303	1	0	C-118
1983	134	423	126	13	1	2	0.5	43	43	61	24	1	.298	.348	0	0	C-134
1984	95	300	67	8	1	4	1.3	26	25	34	25	1	.223	.297	0	0	C-95
1985	70	208	42	6	0	0	0.0	12	20	22	12	0	.202	.231	0	0	C-70
1986	64	160	36	10	1	0	0.0	11	13	15	10	1	.225	.300	7	4	C-57
1987	37	95	14	1	0	1	1.1	4	5	17	15	0	.147	.189	2	0	C-35
1988	90	236	57	7	0	0	0.0	11	19	19	26	0	.242	.271	3	1	C-89
11 yrs.	916	2718	665	95	6	17	0.6	202	254	305	234	12	.245	.303	14	5	C-906

LEAGUE CHAMPIONSHIP SERIES

	G	AB	H	2B	3B	HR	HR %	R	RBI	BB	SO	SB	BA	SA	PH AB	PH H	G by POS
1982 **ATL N**	3	8	2	1	0	0	0.0	1	0	2	1	0	.250	.375	0	0	C-3

Juan Beniquez

BENIQUEZ, JUAN JOSE
Born Juan Jose Beniquez y Torres.
B. May 13, 1950, San Sebastian, Puerto Rico   BR TR 5'11"   150 lbs.

	G	AB	H	2B	3B	HR	HR %	R	RBI	BB	SO	SB	BA	SA	PH AB	PH H	G by POS
1971 **BOS A**	16	57	17	2	0	0	0.0	8	4	3	4	3	.298	.333	0	0	SS-15
1972	33	99	24	4	1	1	1.0	10	8	7	11	2	.242	.333	3	1	SS-27
1974	106	389	104	14	3	5	1.3	60	33	25	61	19	.267	.357	8	0	OF-97, DH-4
1975	78	254	74	14	4	2	0.8	43	17	25	26	7	.291	.402	8	5	OF-44, DH-20, 3B-14
1976 **TEX A**	145	478	122	14	4	0	0.0	49	33	39	56	17	.255	.301	4	1	OF-141, 2B-1
1977	123	424	114	19	6	10	2.4	56	50	43	43	26	.269	.413	0	0	OF-123
1978	127	473	123	17	3	11	2.3	61	50	20	59	10	.260	.378	2	0	OF-126
1979 **NY A**	62	142	36	6	1	4	2.8	19	17	9	17	3	.254	.394	1	0	OF-60, 3B-3
1980 **SEA A**	70	237	54	10	0	6	2.5	26	21	17	25	2	.228	.346	5	0	OF-65, DH-1
1981 **CAL A**	58	166	30	5	0	3	1.8	18	13	15	16	2	.181	.265	2	0	OF-55, DH-1
1982	112	196	52	11	2	3	1.5	25	24	15	21	3	.265	.388	3	1	OF-107
1983	92	315	96	15	0	3	1.0	44	34	15	29	4	.305	.381	3	1	OF-84, DH-6
1984	110	354	119	17	0	8	2.3	60	39	18	43	0	.336	.452	10	3	OF-98
1985	132	411	125	13	5	8	1.9	54	42	34	47	4	.304	.418	24	5	OF-71, 1B-46, DH-14, SS-1, 3B-1
1986 **BAL A**	113	343	103	15	0	6	1.7	48	36	40	49	2	.300	.397	19	9	OF-54, 3B-25, DH-16, 1B-14
1987 **2 teams**			KC	A	(57G –	.236)		TOR	A	(39G –	.284)						
" total	96	255	64	12	1	8	3.1	20	47	16	39	0	.251	.400	23	6	OF-29, DH-15, 1B-8, 3B-6
1988 **TOR A**	27	58	17	2	0	1	1.7	9	8	8	6	0	.293	.379	8	2	DH-19, OF-1
17 yrs.	1500	4651	1274	190	30	79	1.7	610	476	349	552	104	.274	.379	123	34	OF-1155, DH-96, 1B-68, 3B-49, SS-43, 2B-1

LEAGUE CHAMPIONSHIP SERIES

	G	AB	H	2B	3B	HR	HR %	R	RBI	BB	SO	SB	BA	SA	PH AB	PH H	G by POS
1975 **BOS A**	3	12	3	0	0	0	0.0	2	1	0	1	2	.250	.250	0	0	DH-3
1982 **CAL A**	2	0	0	0	0	0	–	0	0	0	0	0	–	–	0	0	OF-2
2 yrs.	5	12	3	0	0	0	0.0	2	1	0	1	2	.250	.250	0	0	DH-3, OF-2

WORLD SERIES

	G	AB	H	2B	3B	HR	HR %	R	RBI	BB	SO	SB	BA	SA	PH AB	PH H	G by POS
1975 **BOS A**	3	8	1	0	0	0	0.0	0	1	1	1	0	.125	.125	1	0	OF-2

Todd Benzinger

BENZINGER, TODD ERIC
B. Feb. 11, 1963, Dayton, Ky.   BB TR 6'1"   185 lbs.

	G	AB	H	2B	3B	HR	HR %	R	RBI	BB	SO	SB	BA	SA	PH AB	PH H	G by POS
1987 **BOS A**	73	223	62	11	1	8	3.6	36	43	22	41	5	.278	.444	8	2	OF-61, 1B-2
1988	120	405	103	28	1	13	3.2	47	70	22	80	2	.254	.425	7	3	1B-85, OF-48, DH-1
2 yrs.	193	628	165	39	2	21	3.3	83	113	44	121	7	.263	.432	15	5	OF-109, 1B-87, DH-1

LEAGUE CHAMPIONSHIP SERIES

	G	AB	H	2B	3B	HR	HR %	R	RBI	BB	SO	SB	BA	SA	PH AB	PH H	G by POS
1988 **BOS A**	4	11	1	0	0	0	0.0	0	0	1	3	0	.091	.091	1	0	1B-3

Dave Bergman

BERGMAN, DAVID BRUCE
B. June 6, 1953, Evanston, Ill.   BL TL 6'1½"   185 lbs.

	G	AB	H	2B	3B	HR	HR %	R	RBI	BB	SO	SB	BA	SA	PH AB	PH H	G by POS
1975 **NY A**	7	17	0	0	0	0	0.0	0	0	2	4	0	.000	.000	0	0	OF-6
1977	5	4	1	0	0	0	0.0	1	1	0	0	0	.250	.250	0	0	OF-3, 1B-2
1978 **HOU N**	104	186	43	5	1	0	0.0	15	12	39	32	2	.231	.269	16	2	1B-66, OF-29
1979	13	15	6	0	0	1	6.7	4	2	0	3	0	.400	.600	10	5	1B-4
1980	90	78	20	6	1	0	0.0	12	3	10	10	1	.256	.359	24	4	1B-59, OF-5
1981 **2 teams**			HOU	N	(6G –	.167)		SF	N	(63G –	.255)						
" total	69	151	38	9	0	4	2.6	17	14	19	18	2	.252	.391	23	4	1B-34, OF-15
1982 **SF N**	100	121	33	3	1	4	3.3	22	14	18	11	3	.273	.413	21	5	1B-69, OF-6
1983	90	140	40	4	1	6	4.3	16	24	24	21	2	.286	.457	31	11	1B-50, OF-6
1984 **DET A**	120	271	74	8	5	7	2.6	42	44	33	40	3	.273	.417	21	6	1B-114, OF-2
1985	69	140	25	2	0	3	2.1	8	7	14	15	0	.179	.257	24	6	1B-44, DH-5, OF-1
1986	65	130	30	6	1	1	0.8	14	9	21	16	0	.231	.315	22	5	1B-41, DH-8, OF-2
1987	91	172	47	7	3	6	3.5	25	22	30	23	0	.273	.453	21	4	1B-65, DH-7, OF-7
1988	116	289	85	14	0	5	1.7	37	35	38	34	0	.294	.394	24	3	1B-64, DH-30, OF-13
13 yrs.	939	1714	442	64	13	37	2.2	213	187	248	227	13	.258	.375	237	55	1B-612, OF-95, DH-50

LEAGUE CHAMPIONSHIP SERIES

	G	AB	H	2B	3B	HR	HR %	R	RBI	BB	SO	SB	BA	SA	PH AB	PH H	G by POS
1980 **HOU N**	4	3	1	0	1	0	0.0	0	2	0	0	0	.333	1.000	0	0	1B-4
1984 **DET A**	2	1	1	0	0	0	0.0	1	0	0	1	1	1.000	1.000	0	0	1B-1
1987	4	4	1	0	0	0	0.0	0	2	0	1	0	.250	.250	2	1	1B-1
3 yrs.	10	8	3	0	1	0	0.0	1	4	0	1	1	.375	.625	2	1	1B-6

WORLD SERIES

	G	AB	H	2B	3B	HR	HR %	R	RBI	BB	SO	SB	BA	SA	PH AB	PH H	G by POS
1984 **DET A**	5	5	0	0	0	0	0.0	0	0	0	1	0	.000	.000	0	0	1B-5

	G	AB	H	2B	3B	HR	HR %	R	RBI	BB	SO	SB	BA	SA	Pinch Hit AB	Pinch Hit H	G by POS

Damon Berryhill

BERRYHILL, DAMON SCOTT
B. Dec. 3, 1963, South Laguna, Calif.   BR TR 6'   205 lbs.

	G	AB	H	2B	3B	HR	HR %	R	RBI	BB	SO	SB	BA	SA	AB	H	G by POS
1987 CHI N	12	28	5	1	0	0	0.0	2	1	3	5	0	.179	.214	1	0	C-11
1988	95	309	80	19	1	7	2.3	19	38	17	56	1	.259	.395	6	1	C-90
2 yrs.	107	337	85	20	1	7	2.1	21	39	20	61	1	.252	.380	7	1	C-101

Dante Bichette

BICHETTE, ALPHONSE DANTE
B. Nov. 18, 1963, West Palm Beach, Fla.   BR TR 6'3"   215 lbs.

	G	AB	H	2B	3B	HR	HR %	R	RBI	BB	SO	SB	BA	SA	AB	H	G by POS
1988 CAL A	21	46	12	2	0	0	0.0	1	8	0	7	0	.261	.304	0	0	OF-21

Craig Biggio

BIGGIO, CRAIG ALAN
B. Dec. 14, 1965, Smithtown, N. Y.   BR TR 5'11"   185 lbs.

	G	AB	H	2B	3B	HR	HR %	R	RBI	BB	SO	SB	BA	SA	AB	H	G by POS
1988 HOU N	50	123	26	6	1	3	2.4	14	5	7	29	6	.211	.350	0	0	C-50

Lance Blankenship

BLANKENSHIP, LANCE ROBERT
B. Dec. 6, 1963, Portland, Ore.   BR TR 6'   185 lbs.

	G	AB	H	2B	3B	HR	HR %	R	RBI	BB	SO	SB	BA	SA	AB	H	G by POS
1988 OAK A	10	3	0	0	0	0	0.0	0	0	0	1	0	.000	.000	2	0	2B-4

Jeff Blauser

BLAUSER, JEFFREY SCOTT
B. Nov. 8, 1965, Los Gatos, Calif.   BR TR 6'   170 lbs.

	G	AB	H	2B	3B	HR	HR %	R	RBI	BB	SO	SB	BA	SA	AB	H	G by POS
1987 ATL N	51	165	40	6	3	2	1.2	11	15	18	34	7	.242	.352	1	0	SS-50
1988	18	67	16	3	1	2	3.0	7	7	2	11	0	.239	.403	1	0	2B-9, SS-8
2 yrs.	69	232	56	9	4	4	1.7	18	22	20	45	7	.241	.366	2	0	SS-58, 2B-9

Terry Blocker

BLOCKER, TERRY FENNELL
B. Aug. 18, 1959, Columbia, S. C.   BL TL 6'2"   195 lbs.

	G	AB	H	2B	3B	HR	HR %	R	RBI	BB	SO	SB	BA	SA	AB	H	G by POS
1985 NY N	18	15	1	0	0	0	0.0	1	0	1	2	0	.067	.067	5	0	OF-5
1988 ATL N	66	198	42	4	2	2	1.0	13	10	10	20	1	.212	.283	4	0	OF-61
2 yrs.	84	213	43	4	2	2	0.9	14	10	11	22	1	.202	.268	9	0	OF-66

Wade Boggs

BOGGS, WADE ANTHONY
B. June 15, 1958, Omaha, Neb.   BL TR 6'2"   190 lbs.

	G	AB	H	2B	3B	HR	HR %	R	RBI	BB	SO	SB	BA	SA	AB	H	G by POS
1982 BOS A	104	338	118	14	1	5	1.5	51	44	35	21	1	.349	.441	13	4	1B-49, 3B-44, DH-3, OF-1
1983	153	582	210	44	7	5	0.9	100	74	92	36	3	**.361**	.486	0	0	3B-153
1984	158	625	203	31	4	6	1.0	109	55	89	44	3	.325	.416	1	0	3B-155, DH-2
1985	161	653	**240**	42	3	8	1.2	107	78	96	61	2	**.368**	.478	0	0	3B-161
1986	149	580	207	47	2	8	1.4	107	71	**105**	44	0	**.357**	.486	0	0	3B-149
1987	147	551	200	40	6	24	4.4	108	89	105	48	1	.363	.588	1	0	3B-145, DH-1, 1B-1
1988	155	584	214	**45**	6	5	0.9	**128**	58	**125**	34	2	.366	.490	1	1	3B-151, DH-3
7 yrs.	1027	3913	1392	263	29	61	1.6	710	469	647	288	12	.356	.485	16	5	3B-958, 1B-50, DH-9, OF-1

LEAGUE CHAMPIONSHIP SERIES

	G	AB	H	2B	3B	HR	HR %	R	RBI	BB	SO	SB	BA	SA	AB	H	G by POS
1986 BOS A	7	30	7	1	1	0	0.0	3	2	4	1	0	.233	.333	0	0	3B-7
1988	4	13	5	0	0	0	0.0	2	3	3	4	0	.385	.385	0	0	3B-4
2 yrs.	11	43	12	1	1	0	0.0	5	5	7	5	0	.279	.349	0	0	3B-11

WORLD SERIES

	G	AB	H	2B	3B	HR	HR %	R	RBI	BB	SO	SB	BA	SA	AB	H	G by POS
1986 BOS A	7	31	9	3	0	0	0.0	3	3	3	2	0	.290	.387	0	0	3B-7

Barry Bonds

BONDS, BARRY LAMAR
Son of Bobby Bonds.
B. July 24, 1964, Riverside, Calif.   BL TL 6'1"   185 lbs.

	G	AB	H	2B	3B	HR	HR %	R	RBI	BB	SO	SB	BA	SA	AB	H	G by POS
1986 PIT N	113	413	92	26	3	16	3.9	72	48	65	102	36	.223	.416	3	1	OF-110
1987	150	551	144	34	9	25	4.5	99	59	54	88	32	.261	.492	7	1	OF-145
1988	144	538	152	30	5	24	4.5	97	58	72	82	17	.283	.491	11	2	OF-136
3 yrs.	407	1502	388	90	17	65	4.3	268	165	191	272	85	.258	.471	21	4	OF-391

Bobby Bonilla

BONILLA, ROBERTO MARTIN ANTONIO
B. Feb. 23, 1963, New York, N. Y.   BB TR 6'3"   210 lbs.

	G	AB	H	2B	3B	HR	HR %	R	RBI	BB	SO	SB	BA	SA	AB	H	G by POS
1986 2 teams		CHI A (75G – .269)				PIT N (63G – .240)											
" total	138	426	109	16	4	3	0.7	55	43	62	88	8	.256	.333	19	2	OF-94, 1B-34, 3B-4
1987 PIT N	141	466	140	33	3	15	3.2	58	77	39	64	3	.300	.481	17	6	3B-89, OF-46, 1B-6
1988	159	584	160	32	7	24	4.1	87	100	85	82	3	.274	.476	0	0	3B-159
3 yrs.	438	1476	409	81	14	42	2.8	200	220	186	234	14	.277	.436	36	8	3B-252, OF-140, 1B-40

Rod Booker

BOOKER, RODERICK STEWART
B. Sept. 4, 1958, Los Angeles, Calif.   BL TR 6'   175 lbs.

	G	AB	H	2B	3B	HR	HR %	R	RBI	BB	SO	SB	BA	SA	AB	H	G by POS
1987 STL N	44	47	13	1	1	0	0.0	9	8	7	7	2	.277	.340	18	4	2B-18, 3B-4, SS-1
1988	18	35	12	3	0	0	0.0	6	3	4	3	2	.343	.429	6	2	3B-13, 2B-1
2 yrs.	62	82	25	4	1	0	0.0	15	11	11	10	4	.305	.378	24	6	2B-19, 3B-17, SS-1

Bob Boone

BOONE, ROBERT RAYMOND
Son of Ray Boone.
B. Nov. 19, 1947, San Diego, Calif.   BR TR 6'2½"   195 lbs.

	G	AB	H	2B	3B	HR	HR %	R	RBI	BB	SO	SB	BA	SA	AB	H	G by POS
1972 PHI N	16	51	14	1	0	1	2.0	4	4	5	7	1	.275	.353	3	0	C-14
1973	145	521	136	20	2	10	1.9	42	61	41	36	3	.261	.365	0	0	C-145
1974	146	488	118	24	3	3	0.6	41	52	35	29	3	.242	.322	1	0	C-146
1975	97	289	71	14	2	2	0.7	28	20	32	14	1	.246	.329	6	1	C-92, 3B-3
1976	121	361	98	18	2	4	1.1	40	54	45	44	2	.271	.366	12	4	C-108, 1B-4
1977	132	440	125	26	4	11	2.5	55	66	42	54	5	.284	.436	1	0	C-131, 3B-2
1978	132	435	123	18	4	12	2.8	48	62	46	37	2	.283	.425	5	1	C-129, 1B-3, OF-1
1979	119	398	114	21	3	9	2.3	38	58	49	33	1	.286	.422	1	0	C-117, 3B-2
1980	141	480	110	23	1	9	1.9	34	55	48	41	3	.229	.338	4	1	C-138
1981	76	227	48	7	0	4	1.8	19	24	22	16	2	.211	.295	4	0	C-75
1982 CAL A	143	472	121	17	0	7	1.5	42	58	39	34	0	.256	.337	0	0	C-143
1983	142	468	120	18	0	9	1.9	46	52	24	42	4	.256	.353	0	0	C-142

Bob Boone continued

	G	AB	H	2B	3B	HR	HR %	R	RBI	BB	SO	SB	BA	SA	Pinch Hit AB	Pinch Hit H	G by POS
1984	139	450	91	16	1	3	0.7	33	32	25	45	3	.202	.262	2	2	C-137
1985	150	460	114	17	0	5	1.1	37	55	37	35	1	.248	.317	2	2	C-147
1986	144	442	98	12	2	7	1.6	48	49	43	30	1	.222	.305	0	0	C-144
1987	128	389	94	18	0	3	0.8	42	33	35	36	0	.242	.311	1	1	C-127, DH-1
1988	122	352	104	17	0	5	1.4	38	39	29	26	2	.295	.386	1	1	C-121
17 yrs.	2093	6723	1699	287	24	104	1.5	635	774	597	559	34	.253	.349	43	14	C-2056, 3B-7, 1B-7, DH-1, OF-1

DIVISIONAL PLAYOFF SERIES

	G	AB	H	2B	3B	HR	HR %	R	RBI	BB	SO	SB	BA	SA	Pinch Hit AB	Pinch Hit H	G by POS
1981 PHI N	3	5	0	0	0	0	0.0	0	0	0	0	0	.000	.000	0	0	C-3

LEAGUE CHAMPIONSHIP SERIES

	G	AB	H	2B	3B	HR	HR %	R	RBI	BB	SO	SB	BA	SA	Pinch Hit AB	Pinch Hit H	G by POS
1976 PHI N	3	7	2	0	0	0	0.0	0	1	1	0	0	.286	.286	0	0	C-3
1977	4	10	4	0	0	0	0.0	1	0	0	0	0	.400	.400	0	0	C-4
1978	3	11	2	0	0	0	0.0	0	0	0	1	0	.182	.182	0	0	C-3
1980	5	18	4	0	0	0	0.0	1	2	1	2	0	.222	.222	0	0	C-5
1982 CAL A	5	16	4	0	0	1	6.3	3	4	0	2	0	.250	.438	0	0	C-5
1986	7	22	10	0	0	1	4.5	4	2	1	3	0	.455	.591	0	0	C-7
6 yrs.	27	84	26	0	0	2	2.4	9	9	3	8	0	.310	.381	0	0	C-27

WORLD SERIES

	G	AB	H	2B	3B	HR	HR %	R	RBI	BB	SO	SB	BA	SA	Pinch Hit AB	Pinch Hit H	G by POS
1980 PHI N	6	17	7	2	0	0	0.0	3	4	4	0	0	.412	.529	0	0	C-6

Pat Borders

BORDERS, PATRICK LANCE
B. May 14, 1963, Columbus, Ohio   BR TR 6'2" 190 lbs.

	G	AB	H	2B	3B	HR	HR %	R	RBI	BB	SO	SB	BA	SA	Pinch Hit AB	Pinch Hit H	G by POS
1988 TOR A	56	154	42	6	3	5	3.2	15	21	3	24	0	.273	.448	15	5	C-43, 3B-1, 2B-1

Thad Bosley

BOSLEY, THADDIS
B. Sept. 17, 1956, Oceanside, Calif.   BL TL 6'3" 175 lbs.

	G	AB	H	2B	3B	HR	HR %	R	RBI	BB	SO	SB	BA	SA	Pinch Hit AB	Pinch Hit H	G by POS
1977 CAL A	58	212	63	10	2	0	0.0	19	19	16	32	5	.297	.363	4	2	OF-55
1978 CHI A	66	219	59	5	1	2	0.9	25	13	13	32	12	.269	.329	1	0	OF-64
1979	36	77	24	1	1	1	1.3	13	8	9	14	4	.312	.390	7	1	OF-28, DH-1
1980	70	147	33	2	0	2	1.4	12	14	10	27	3	.224	.279	25	8	OF-52
1981 MIL A	42	105	24	1	0	0	0.0	11	3	6	13	2	.229	.248	4	0	OF-37, DH-1
1982 SEA A	22	46	8	1	0	0	0.0	3	2	4	8	3	.174	.196	3	0	OF-19
1983 CHI N	43	72	21	4	1	2	2.8	12	12	10	12	1	.292	.458	18	4	OF-20
1984	55	98	29	2	2	2	2.0	17	14	13	22	5	.296	.418	23	6	OF-33
1985	108	180	59	6	3	7	3.9	25	27	20	29	5	.328	.511	60	20	OF-55
1986	87	120	33	4	1	1	0.8	15	9	18	24	3	.275	.350	51	16	OF-41
1987 KC A	80	140	39	6	1	1	0.7	13	16	9	26	0	.279	.357	42	12	OF-28, DH-13
1988 2 teams								KC A (15G – .190)		CAL A (35G – .280)							
" total	50	96	25	5	0	0	0.0	10	9	8	18	1	.260	.313	10	3	OF-32, DH-6
12 yrs.	717	1512	417	48	12	18	1.2	175	146	136	257	44	.276	.359	248	72	OF-464, DH-21

DIVISIONAL PLAYOFF SERIES

	G	AB	H	2B	3B	HR	HR %	R	RBI	BB	SO	SB	BA	SA	Pinch Hit AB	Pinch Hit H	G by POS
1981 MIL A	1	0	0	0	0	0	–	0	0	0	0	0	–	–	0	0	DH-1

LEAGUE CHAMPIONSHIP SERIES

	G	AB	H	2B	3B	HR	HR %	R	RBI	BB	SO	SB	BA	SA	Pinch Hit AB	Pinch Hit H	G by POS
1984 CHI N	2	2	0	0	0	0	0.0	0	0	0	2	0	.000	.000	2	0	

Daryl Boston

BOSTON, DARYL LAMONT
B. Jan. 4, 1963, Cincinnati, Ohio   BL TL 6'3" 185 lbs.

	G	AB	H	2B	3B	HR	HR %	R	RBI	BB	SO	SB	BA	SA	Pinch Hit AB	Pinch Hit H	G by POS
1984 CHI A	35	83	14	3	1	0	0.0	8	3	4	20	6	.169	.229	2	1	OF-34, DH-1
1985	95	232	53	13	1	3	1.3	20	15	14	44	8	.228	.332	5	1	OF-93, DH-2
1986	56	199	53	11	3	5	2.5	29	22	21	33	9	.266	.427	1	0	OF-53, DH-1
1987	103	337	87	21	2	10	3.0	51	29	25	68	12	.258	.421	10	2	OF-92, DH-5
1988	105	281	61	12	2	15	5.3	37	31	21	44	9	.217	.434	13	3	OF-85, DH-5
5 yrs.	394	1132	268	60	9	33	2.9	145	100	85	209	44	.237	.393	31	7	OF-357, DH-14

Phil Bradley

BRADLEY, PHILIP POOLE
B. Mar. 11, 1959, Bloomington, Ind.   BR TR 6' 185 lbs.

	G	AB	H	2B	3B	HR	HR %	R	RBI	BB	SO	SB	BA	SA	Pinch Hit AB	Pinch Hit H	G by POS
1983 SEA A	23	67	18	2	0	0	0.0	8	5	8	5	3	.269	.299	3	0	OF-21, DH-1
1984	124	322	97	12	4	0	0.0	49	24	34	61	21	.301	.363	3	0	OF-117, DH-3
1985	159	641	192	33	8	26	4.1	100	88	55	129	22	.300	.498	0	0	OF-159
1986	143	526	163	27	4	12	2.3	88	50	77	134	21	.310	.445	2	0	OF-140
1987	158	603	179	38	10	14	2.3	101	67	84	119	40	.297	.463	0	0	OF-158
1988 PHI N	154	569	150	30	5	11	1.9	77	56	54	106	11	.264	.392	2	0	OF-153
6 yrs.	761	2728	799	142	31	63	2.3	423	290	312	554	118	.293	.437	10	0	OF-748, DH-4

Scott Bradley

BRADLEY, SCOTT WILLIAM
B. Mar. 22, 1960, Glen Ridge, N. J.   BL TR 5'11" 175 lbs.

	G	AB	H	2B	3B	HR	HR %	R	RBI	BB	SO	SB	BA	SA	Pinch Hit AB	Pinch Hit H	G by POS
1984 NY A	9	21	6	1	0	0	0.0	3	2	1	1	0	.286	.333	1	0	OF-5, C-3
1985	19	49	8	2	1	0	0.0	4	1	1	5	0	.163	.245	7	1	DH-9, C-3
1986 2 teams								CHI A (9G – .286)		SEA A (68G – .302)							
" total	77	220	66	8	3	5	2.3	20	28	13	7	1	.300	.432	17	5	C-59, DH-9, OF-1
1987 SEA A	102	342	95	15	1	5	1.5	34	43	15	18	0	.278	.371	12	4	C-82, 3B-8, OF-2
1988	103	335	86	17	1	4	1.2	45	33	17	16	1	.257	.349	12	2	C-85, DH-4, OF-4, 3B-3, 1B-2
5 yrs.	310	967	261	43	6	14	1.4	106	107	47	47	2	.270	.370	49	12	C-232, DH-22, OF-12, 3B-11, 1B-2

Glenn Braggs

BRAGGS, GLENN ERICK
B. Oct. 17, 1962, San Bernardino, Calif.   BR TR 6'3" 210 lbs.

	G	AB	H	2B	3B	HR	HR %	R	RBI	BB	SO	SB	BA	SA	Pinch Hit AB	Pinch Hit H	G by POS
1986 MIL A	58	215	51	8	2	4	1.9	19	18	11	47	1	.237	.349	0	0	OF-56, DH-2
1987	132	505	136	28	7	13	2.6	67	77	47	96	12	.269	.430	3	0	OF-123, DH-8
1988	72	272	71	14	0	10	3.7	30	42	14	60	6	.261	.423	0	0	OF-54, DH-18
3 yrs.	262	992	258	50	9	27	2.7	116	137	72	203	19	.260	.410	3	0	OF-233, DH-28

	G	AB	H	2B	3B	HR	HR%	R	RBI	BB	SO	SB	BA	SA	Pinch Hit AB	Pinch Hit H	G by POS

Mickey Brantley

BRANTLEY, MICHAEL CHARLES
B. June 17, 1961, Catskill, N. Y.
BR TR 5'10" 180 lbs.

	G	AB	H	2B	3B	HR	HR%	R	RBI	BB	SO	SB	BA	SA	AB	H	G by POS
1986 SEA A	27	102	20	3	2	3	2.9	12	7	10	21	1	.196	.353	2	0	OF-25
1987	92	351	106	23	2	14	4.0	52	54	24	44	13	.302	.499	4	1	OF-82, DH-8
1988	149	577	152	25	4	15	2.6	76	56	26	64	18	.263	.399	1	1	OF-147
3 yrs.	268	1030	278	51	8	32	3.1	140	117	60	129	32	.270	.428	7	2	OF-254, DH-8

Sid Bream

BREAM, SIDNEY EUGENE
B. Aug. 3, 1960, Carlisle, Pa.
BL TL 6'4" 215 lbs.

	G	AB	H	2B	3B	HR	HR%	R	RBI	BB	SO	SB	BA	SA	AB	H	G by POS
1983 LA N	15	11	2	0	0	0	0.0	0	2	2	2	0	.182	.182	10	2	1B-4
1984	27	49	9	3	0	0	0.0	2	6	6	9	1	.184	.245	11	1	1B-14
1985 2 teams	LA	N (24G – .132)		PIT	N	(26G – .284)											
" total	50	148	34	7	0	6	4.1	18	21	18	24	0	.230	.399	10	2	1B-41
1986 PIT N	154	522	140	37	5	16	3.1	73	77	60	73	13	.268	.450	5	1	1B-153, OF-2
1987	149	516	142	25	3	13	2.5	64	65	49	69	9	.275	.411	7	2	1B-144
1988	148	462	122	37	0	10	2.2	50	65	47	64	9	.264	.409	16	6	1B-138
6 yrs.	543	1708	449	109	8	45	2.6	207	236	182	241	32	.263	.415	59	14	1B-494, OF-2

Bob Brenly

BRENLY, ROBERT EARL
B. Feb. 25, 1954, Coshocton, Ohio
BR TR 6'2" 210 lbs.

	G	AB	H	2B	3B	HR	HR%	R	RBI	BB	SO	SB	BA	SA	AB	H	G by POS
1981 SF N	19	45	15	2	1	1	2.2	5	4	6	4	0	.333	.489	1	0	C-14, 3B-3, OF-1
1982	65	180	51	4	1	4	2.2	26	15	18	26	6	.283	.383	9	3	C-61, 3B-1
1983	104	281	63	12	2	7	2.5	36	34	37	48	10	.224	.356	13	2	C-90, 1B-10, OF-2
1984	145	506	147	28	0	20	4.0	74	80	48	52	6	.291	.464	6	1	C-127, 1B-22, OF-3
1985	133	440	97	16	1	19	4.3	41	56	57	62	1	.220	.391	7	1	C-110, 3B-17, 1B-10
1986	149	472	116	26	0	16	3.4	60	62	74	97	10	.246	.403	8	0	C-101, 3B-45, 1B-19
1987	123	375	100	19	1	18	4.8	55	51	47	85	10	.267	.467	8	2	C-108, 1B-6, 3B-2
1988	73	206	39	7	0	5	2.4	13	22	20	40	1	.189	.296	5	0	C-69
8 yrs.	811	2505	628	114	6	90	3.6	310	324	307	414	44	.251	.409	57	9	C-680, 3B-68, 1B-67, OF-6

LEAGUE CHAMPIONSHIP SERIES

	G	AB	H	2B	3B	HR	HR%	R	RBI	BB	SO	SB	BA	SA	AB	H	G by POS
1987 SF N	6	17	4	1	0	1	5.9	3	2	3	7	0	.235	.471	1	0	C-6

George Brett

BRETT, GEORGE HOWARD
Brother of Ken Brett.
B. May 15, 1953, Glen Dale, W. Va.
BL TR 6' 185 lbs.

	G	AB	H	2B	3B	HR	HR%	R	RBI	BB	SO	SB	BA	SA	AB	H	G by POS
1973 KC A	13	40	5	2	0	0	0.0	2	0	0	5	0	.125	.175	1	0	3B-13
1974	133	457	129	21	5	2	0.4	49	47	21	38	8	.282	.363	2	0	3B-132, SS-1
1975	159	634	195	35	13	11	1.7	84	89	46	49	13	.308	.456	0	0	3B-159, SS-1
1976	159	645	215	34	14	7	1.1	94	67	49	36	21	.333	.462	0	0	3B-157, SS-4
1977	139	564	176	32	13	22	3.9	105	88	55	24	14	.312	.532	3	1	3B-135, DH-3, SS-1
1978	128	510	150	45	8	9	1.8	79	62	39	35	23	.294	.467	0	0	3B-128, SS-1
1979	154	645	212	42	20	23	3.6	119	107	51	36	17	.329	.563	0	0	3B-149, 1B-8, DH-1
1980	117	449	175	33	9	24	5.3	87	118	58	22	15	.390	.664	3	1	3B-112, 1B-1
1981	89	347	109	27	7	6	1.7	42	43	27	23	14	.314	.484	0	0	3B-88
1982	144	552	166	32	9	21	3.8	101	82	71	51	6	.301	.505	0	0	3B-134, OF-12
1983	123	464	144	38	2	25	5.4	90	93	57	39	0	.310	.563	1	1	3B-102, 1B-14, OF-13, DH-1
1984	104	377	107	21	3	13	3.4	42	69	38	37	0	.284	.459	3	1	3B-101
1985	155	550	184	38	5	30	5.5	108	112	103	49	9	.335	.585	2	0	3B-152, DH-1
1986	124	441	128	28	4	16	3.6	70	73	80	45	1	.290	.481	1	0	3B-115, DH-7, SS-2
1987	115	427	124	18	2	22	5.2	71	78	72	47	6	.290	.496	0	0	1B-83, DH-21, 3B-11
1988	157	589	180	42	3	24	4.1	90	103	82	51	14	.306	.509	0	0	1B-124, DH-33, SS-1
16 yrs.	2013	7691	2399	488	117	255	3.3	1233	1231	849	587	161	.312	.505	16	4	3B-1688, 1B-230, DH-67, OF-25, SS-11

DIVISIONAL PLAYOFF SERIES

	G	AB	H	2B	3B	HR	HR%	R	RBI	BB	SO	SB	BA	SA	AB	H	G by POS
1981 KC A	3	12	2	0	0	0	0.0	0	0	0	0	0	.167	.167	0	0	3B-3

LEAGUE CHAMPIONSHIP SERIES

	G	AB	H	2B	3B	HR	HR%	R	RBI	BB	SO	SB	BA	SA	AB	H	G by POS
1976 KC A	5	18	8	1	1	1	5.6	4	5	2	1	0	.444	.778	0	0	3B-5
1977	5	20	6	0	2	0	0.0	2	2	1	0	0	.300	.500	0	0	3B-5
1978	4	18	7	1	1	3	16.7	7	3	0	1	0	.389	1.056	0	0	3B-4
1980	3	11	3	1	0	2	18.2	3	4	1	0	0	.273	.909	0	0	3B-3
1984	3	13	3	0	0	0	0.0	0	0	0	2	0	.231	.231	0	0	3B-3
1985	7	23	8	2	0	3	13.0	6	5	7	5	0	.348	.826	0	0	3B-7
6 yrs.	27	103	35	5	4	9	8.7	22	19	11	9	0	.340	.728	0	0	3B-27

WORLD SERIES

	G	AB	H	2B	3B	HR	HR%	R	RBI	BB	SO	SB	BA	SA	AB	H	G by POS
1980 KC A	6	24	9	2	1	1	4.2	3	3	2	4	1	.375	.667	0	0	3B-6
1985	7	27	10	1	0	0	0.0	5	1	4	7	1	.370	.407	0	0	3B-7
2 yrs.	13	51	19	3	1	1	2.0	8	4	6	11	2	.373	.529	0	0	3B-13
													4th				

Greg Briley

BRILEY, GREGORY
B. May 24, 1965, Bethel, N. C.
BL TR 5'9" 170 lbs.

	G	AB	H	2B	3B	HR	HR%	R	RBI	BB	SO	SB	BA	SA	AB	H	G by POS
1988 SEA A	13	36	9	2	0	1	2.8	4	5	6	6	0	.250	.389	3	0	OF-11

Greg Brock

BROCK, GREGORY ALLEN
B. June 14, 1957, McMinnville, Ore.
BL TR 6'3" 200 lbs.

	G	AB	H	2B	3B	HR	HR%	R	RBI	BB	SO	SB	BA	SA	AB	H	G by POS
1982 LA N	18	17	2	1	0	0	0.0	1	1	1	5	0	.118	.176	13	2	1B-3
1983	146	455	102	14	2	20	4.4	64	66	83	81	5	.224	.396	6	1	1B-140
1984	88	271	61	6	0	14	5.2	33	34	39	37	8	.225	.402	8	0	1B-83
1985	129	438	110	19	0	21	4.8	64	66	54	72	4	.251	.438	9	2	1B-122
1986	115	325	76	13	0	16	4.9	33	52	37	60	2	.234	.422	23	4	1B-99
1987 MIL A	141	532	159	29	3	13	2.4	81	85	57	63	5	.299	.438	0	0	1B-141
1988	115	364	77	16	1	6	1.6	53	50	63	48	6	.212	.310	1	0	1B-114, DH-1
7 yrs.	752	2402	587	98	6	90	3.7	329	354	334	366	30	.244	.403	60	9	1B-702, DH-1

	G	AB	H	2B	3B	HR	HR %	R	RBI	BB	SO	SB	BA	SA	Pinch Hit AB	Pinch Hit H	G by POS

Greg Brock continued

LEAGUE CHAMPIONSHIP SERIES

	G	AB	H	2B	3B	HR	HR %	R	RBI	BB	SO	SB	BA	SA	AB	H	G by POS
1983 LA N	3	9	0	0	0	0	0.0	1	0	0	3	0	.000	.000	0	0	1B-3
1985	5	12	1	0	0	1	8.3	2	2	2	2	0	.083	.333	1	0	1B-4
2 yrs.	8	21	1	0	0	1	4.8	3	2	2	5	0	.048	.190	1	0	1B-7

Tom Brookens

BROOKENS, THOMAS DALE
B. Aug. 10, 1953, Chambersburg, Pa.   BR TR 5'10" 165 lbs.

	G	AB	H	2B	3B	HR	HR %	R	RBI	BB	SO	SB	BA	SA	AB	H	G by POS
1979 DET A	60	190	50	5	2	4	2.1	23	21	11	40	10	.263	.374	0	0	3B-42, 2B-19, DH-1
1980	151	509	140	25	9	10	2.0	64	66	32	71	13	.275	.418	4	1	3B-138, 2B-9, DH-1, SS-1
1981	71	239	58	10	1	4	1.7	19	25	14	43	5	.243	.343	1	0	3B-71
1982	140	398	92	15	3	9	2.3	40	58	27	63	5	.231	.352	6	2	3B-113, 2B-26, SS-9, OF-1
1983	138	332	71	13	3	6	1.8	50	32	29	46	10	.214	.325	10	1	3B-103, SS-30, 2B-10, DH-1
1984	113	224	55	11	4	5	2.2	32	26	19	33	6	.246	.397	3	2	3B-68, SS-28, 2B-26, DH-1
1985	156	485	115	34	6	7	1.4	54	47	27	78	14	.237	.375	1	1	3B-151, SS-8, 2B-3, DH-1, C-1
1986	98	281	76	11	2	3	1.1	42	25	20	42	11	.270	.356	7	1	3B-35, 2B-31, DH-14, SS-14, OF-3
1987	143	444	107	15	3	13	2.9	59	59	33	63	7	.241	.376	2	0	3B-122, SS-16, 2B-11
1988	136	441	107	23	5	5	1.1	62	38	44	74	4	.243	.351	5	1	3B-136, SS-3, 2B-1
10 yrs.	1206	3543	871	162	38	66	1.9	445	397	256	553	85	.246	.369	39	9	3B-979, 2B-136, SS-109, DH-19, OF-4, C-1

LEAGUE CHAMPIONSHIP SERIES

	G	AB	H	2B	3B	HR	HR %	R	RBI	BB	SO	SB	BA	SA	AB	H	G by POS
1984 DET A	2	2	0	0	0	0	0.0	0	0	0	1	0	.000	.000	0	0	3B-2
1987	5	13	0	0	0	0	0.0	0	0	0	3	0	.000	.000	0	0	3B-5
2 yrs.	7	15	0	0	0	0	0.0	0	0	0	4	0	.000	.000	0	0	3B-7

WORLD SERIES

	G	AB	H	2B	3B	HR	HR %	R	RBI	BB	SO	SB	BA	SA	AB	H	G by POS
1984 DET A	3	3	0	0	0	0	0.0	0	0	0	1	0	.000	.000	2	0	3B-3

Hubie Brooks

BROOKS, HUBERT JR.
B. Sept. 24, 1956, Los Angeles, Calif.   BR TR 6' 178 lbs.

	G	AB	H	2B	3B	HR	HR %	R	RBI	BB	SO	SB	BA	SA	AB	H	G by POS
1980 NY N	24	81	25	2	1	1	1.2	8	10	5	9	1	.309	.395	1	0	3B-23
1981	98	358	110	21	2	4	1.1	34	38	23	65	9	.307	.411	2	0	3B-93, OF-3, SS-1
1982	126	457	114	21	2	2	0.4	40	40	28	76	6	.249	.317	1	0	3B-126
1983	150	586	147	18	4	5	0.9	53	58	24	96	6	.251	.321	2	1	3B-145, 2B-7
1984	153	561	159	23	2	16	2.9	61	73	48	79	6	.283	.417	0	0	3B-129, SS-26
1985 MON N	156	605	163	34	7	13	2.1	67	100	34	79	6	.269	.413	2	1	SS-155
1986	80	306	104	18	5	14	4.6	50	58	25	60	4	.340	.569	0	0	SS-80
1987	112	430	113	22	3	14	3.3	57	72	24	72	4	.263	.426	3	2	SS-109
1988	151	588	164	35	2	20	3.4	61	90	35	108	7	.279	.447	2	1	OF-149
9 yrs.	1050	3972	1099	194	28	89	2.2	431	539	246	644	49	.277	.407	13	5	3B-516, SS-371, OF-152, 2B-7

Bob Brower

BROWER, ROBERT RICHARD
B. Jan. 10, 1960, Jamaica, N. Y.   BR TR 5'11" 185 lbs.

	G	AB	H	2B	3B	HR	HR %	R	RBI	BB	SO	SB	BA	SA	AB	H	G by POS
1986 TEX A	21	9	1	1	0	0	0.0	3	0	0	3	1	.111	.222	1	0	OF-17, DH-1
1987	127	303	79	10	3	14	4.6	63	46	36	66	15	.261	.452	9	1	OF-106, DH-7
1988	82	201	45	7	0	1	0.5	29	11	27	38	10	.224	.274	6	1	OF-59, DH-13
3 yrs.	230	513	125	18	3	15	2.9	95	57	63	107	26	.244	.378	16	2	OF-182, DH-21

Chris Brown

BROWN, JOHN CHRISTOPHER
B. Aug. 15, 1961, Jackson, Miss.   BR TR 6' 185 lbs.

	G	AB	H	2B	3B	HR	HR %	R	RBI	BB	SO	SB	BA	SA	AB	H	G by POS
1984 SF N	23	84	24	7	0	1	1.2	6	11	9	19	2	.286	.405	0	0	3B-23
1985	131	432	117	20	3	16	3.7	50	61	38	78	2	.271	.442	9	3	3B-120
1986	116	416	132	16	3	7	1.7	57	49	33	43	13	.317	.421	1	0	3B-111, SS-2
1987 2 teams	SF	N (38G – .242)			SD	N	(44G – .232)										
" total	82	287	68	9	0	12	4.2	34	40	20	46	4	.237	.394	3	2	3B-80, SS-1
1988 SD N	80	247	58	6	0	2	0.8	14	19	19	49	0	.235	.283	5	0	3B-72
5 yrs.	432	1466	399	58	6	38	2.6	161	180	119	235	21	.272	.398	18	5	3B-406, SS-3

Marty Brown

BROWN, MARTY LEO
B. Jan. 23, 1963, Lawton, Okla.   BR TR 6'1" 190 lbs.

	G	AB	H	2B	3B	HR	HR %	R	RBI	BB	SO	SB	BA	SA	AB	H	G by POS
1988 CIN N	10	16	3	1	0	0	0.0	0	2	1	2	0	.188	.250	4	1	3B-8

Mike Brown

BROWN, MICHAEL CHARLES
B. Dec. 29, 1959, San Francisco, Calif.   BR TR 6'2" 190 lbs.

	G	AB	H	2B	3B	HR	HR %	R	RBI	BB	SO	SB	BA	SA	AB	H	G by POS
1983 CAL A	31	104	24	5	1	3	2.9	12	9	7	20	1	.231	.385	0	0	OF-31
1984	62	148	42	8	3	7	4.7	19	22	13	23	0	.284	.520	14	3	OF-44, DH-3
1985 2 teams	CAL	A (60G – .268)			PIT	N	(57G – .332)										
" total	117	358	109	27	3	9	2.5	52	53	29	48	2	.304	.472	11	3	OF-104, DH-7
1986 PIT N	87	243	53	7	0	4	1.6	18	26	27	32	2	.218	.296	20	4	OF-71
1988 CAL A	18	50	11	2	0	0	0.0	4	3	1	12	0	.220	.260	2	0	OF-18
5 yrs.	315	903	239	49	7	23	2.5	105	113	77	135	5	.265	.411	47	10	OF-268, DH-10

Jerry Browne

BROWNE, JEROME AUSTIN
B. Feb. 13, 1966, Christiansted, Virgin Islands   BB TR 5'10" 140 lbs.

	G	AB	H	2B	3B	HR	HR %	R	RBI	BB	SO	SB	BA	SA	AB	H	G by POS
1986 TEX A	11	24	10	2	0	0	0.0	6	3	1	4	0	.417	.500	1	0	2B-8
1987	132	454	123	16	6	1	0.2	63	38	61	50	27	.271	.339	5	0	2B-130, DH-1
1988	73	214	49	9	2	1	0.5	26	17	25	32	7	.229	.304	3	0	2B-70, DH-1
3 yrs.	216	692	182	27	8	2	0.3	95	58	87	86	34	.263	.334	9	0	2B-208, DH-2

	G	AB	H	2B	3B	HR	HR %	R	RBI	BB	SO	SB	BA	SA	Pinch Hit AB	Pinch Hit H	G by POS

Tom Brunansky

BRUNANSKY, THOMAS ANDREW (Bruno)   BR TR 6'4" 205 lbs.
B. Aug. 20, 1960, Covina, Calif.

	G	AB	H	2B	3B	HR	HR %	R	RBI	BB	SO	SB	BA	SA	PH AB	PH H	G by POS
1981 CAL A	11	33	5	0	0	3	9.1	7	6	8	10	1	.152	.424	0	0	OF-11
1982 MIN A	127	463	126	30	1	20	4.3	77	46	71	101	1	.272	.471	0	0	OF-127
1983	151	542	123	24	5	28	5.2	70	82	61	95	2	.227	.445	2	0	OF-146, DH-4
1984	155	567	143	21	0	32	5.6	75	85	57	94	4	.252	.459	2	0	OF-153, DH-1
1985	157	567	137	28	4	27	4.8	71	90	71	86	5	.242	.448	3	1	OF-155
1986	157	593	152	28	1	23	3.9	69	75	53	98	12	.256	.423	5	1	OF-152, DH-2
1987	155	532	138	22	2	32	6.0	83	85	74	104	11	.259	.489	1	1	OF-138, DH-17
1988 2 teams	MIN A	(14G –	.184)			STL N	(143G –	.245)									
" total	157	572	137	23	4	23	4.0	74	85	86	93	17	.240	.414	0	0	OF-156, DH-1
8 yrs.	1070	3869	961	176	17	188	4.9	526	554	481	681	53	.248	.448	13	3	OF-1038, DH-25

LEAGUE CHAMPIONSHIP SERIES

	G	AB	H	2B	3B	HR	HR %	R	RBI	BB	SO	SB	BA	SA	PH AB	PH H	G by POS
1987 MIN A	5	17	7	4	0	2	11.8	5	9	4	3	0	.412	1.000	0	0	OF-5

WORLD SERIES

	G	AB	H	2B	3B	HR	HR %	R	RBI	BB	SO	SB	BA	SA	PH AB	PH H	G by POS
1987 MIN A	7	25	5	0	0	0	0.0	5	2	4	4	1	.200	.200	0	0	OF-7

Bill Buckner

BUCKNER, WILLIAM JOSEPH (Billy Bucks)   BL TL 6' 185 lbs.
B. Dec. 14, 1949, Vallejo, Calif.

	G	AB	H	2B	3B	HR	HR %	R	RBI	BB	SO	SB	BA	SA	PH AB	PH H	G by POS
1969 LA N	1	1	0	0	0	0	0.0	0	0	0	0	0	.000	.000	1	0	
1970	28	68	13	3	1	0	0.0	6	4	3	7	0	.191	.265	8	2	OF-20, 1B-1
1971	108	358	99	15	1	5	1.4	37	41	11	18	4	.277	.366	17	3	OF-86, 1B-11
1972	105	383	122	14	3	5	1.3	47	37	17	13	10	.319	.410	11	3	OF-61, 1B-35
1973	140	575	158	20	0	8	1.4	68	46	17	34	12	.275	.351	9	2	1B-93, OF-48
1974	145	580	182	30	3	7	1.2	83	58	30	24	31	.314	.412	9	1	OF-137, 1B-6
1975	92	288	70	11	2	6	2.1	30	31	17	15	8	.243	.358	19	3	OF-72
1976	154	642	193	28	4	7	1.1	76	60	26	26	28	.301	.389	1	1	OF-153, 1B-1
1977 CHI N	122	426	121	27	0	11	2.6	40	60	21	23	7	.284	.425	22	7	1B-99
1978	117	446	144	26	1	5	1.1	47	74	18	17	7	.323	.419	12	2	1B-105
1979	149	591	168	34	7	14	2.4	72	66	30	28	9	.284	.437	8	3	1B-140
1980	145	578	187	41	3	10	1.7	69	68	30	18	1	.324	.457	6	0	1B-94, OF-50
1981	106	421	131	35	3	10	2.4	45	75	26	16	5	.311	.480	2	1	1B-105
1982	161	657	201	34	5	15	2.3	93	105	36	26	15	.306	.441	0	0	1B-161
1983	153	626	175	38	6	16	2.6	79	66	25	30	12	.280	.436	2	1	1B-144, OF-15
1984 2 teams	CHI N	(21G –	.209)			BOS A	(114G –	.278)									
" total	135	482	131	21	2	11	2.3	54	69	25	39	2	.272	.392	12	3	1B-120, OF-2
1985 BOS A	162	673	201	46	3	16	2.4	89	110	30	36	18	.299	.447	0	0	1B-162
1986	153	629	168	39	2	18	2.9	73	102	40	25	6	.267	.421	0	0	1B-138, DH-15
1987 2 teams	BOS A	(75G –	.273)			CAL A	(57G –	.306)									
" total	132	469	134	18	2	5	1.1	39	74	22	26	2	.286	.365	15	8	1B-79, DH-39
1988 2 teams	CAL A	(19G –	.209)			KC A	(89G –	.256)									
" total	108	285	71	14	0	3	1.1	19	43	17	19	5	.249	.330	28	8	DH-53, 1B-22
20 yrs.	2416	9178	2669	494	48	172	1.9	1066	1189	441	440	182	.291	.411	182	48	1B-1516, OF-644, DH-107

LEAGUE CHAMPIONSHIP SERIES

	G	AB	H	2B	3B	HR	HR %	R	RBI	BB	SO	SB	BA	SA	PH AB	PH H	G by POS
1974 LA N	4	18	3	1	0	0	0.0	0	0	0	2	0	.167	.222	0	0	OF-4
1986 BOS A	7	28	6	1	0	0	0.0	3	3	0	2	0	.214	.250	0	0	1B-7
2 yrs.	11	46	9	2	0	0	0.0	3	3	0	4	0	.196	.239	0	0	1B-7, OF-4

WORLD SERIES

	G	AB	H	2B	3B	HR	HR %	R	RBI	BB	SO	SB	BA	SA	PH AB	PH H	G by POS
1974 LA N	5	20	5	1	0	1	5.0	1	1	0	1	0	.250	.450	0	0	OF-5
1986 BOS A	7	32	6	0	0	0	0.0	2	1	1	3	0	.188	.188	0	0	1B-7
2 yrs.	12	52	11	1	0	1	1.9	3	2	1	4	0	.212	.288	0	0	1B-7, OF-5

Steve Buechele

BUECHELE, STEVEN BERNARD   BR TR 6'2" 190 lbs.
B. Sept. 26, 1961, Lancaster, Calif.

	G	AB	H	2B	3B	HR	HR %	R	RBI	BB	SO	SB	BA	SA	PH AB	PH H	G by POS
1985 TEX A	69	219	48	6	3	6	2.7	22	21	14	38	3	.219	.356	0	0	3B-69, 2B-1
1986	153	461	112	19	2	18	3.9	54	54	35	98	5	.243	.410	2	1	3B-133, OF-2
1987	136	363	86	20	0	13	3.6	45	50	28	66	2	.237	.399	2	1	3B-123, 2B-18, OF-2
1988	155	503	126	21	4	16	3.2	68	58	65	79	2	.250	.404	2	0	3B-153, 2B-2
4 yrs.	513	1546	372	66	9	53	3.4	189	183	142	281	12	.241	.398	6	2	3B-482, 2B-54, OF-4

Jay Buhner

BUHNER, JAY CAMPBELL   BR TR 6'3" 205 lbs.
B. Aug. 13, 1964, Louisville, Ky.

	G	AB	H	2B	3B	HR	HR %	R	RBI	BB	SO	SB	BA	SA	PH AB	PH H	G by POS
1987 NY A	7	22	5	2	0	0	0.0	0	1	1	6	0	.227	.318	0	0	OF-7
1988 2 teams	NY A	(25G –	.188)			SEA A	(60G –	.224)									
" total	85	261	56	13	1	13	5.0	36	38	28	93	1	.215	.421	4	1	OF-81
2 yrs.	92	283	61	15	1	13	4.6	36	39	29	99	1	.216	.413	4	1	OF-88

Eric Bullock

BULLOCK, ERIC GERALD   BL TL 5'11" 185 lbs.
B. Feb. 16, 1960, Los Angeles, Calif.

	G	AB	H	2B	3B	HR	HR %	R	RBI	BB	SO	SB	BA	SA	PH AB	PH H	G by POS
1985 HOU N	18	25	7	2	0	0	0.0	3	2	1	3	0	.280	.360	12	3	OF-7
1986	6	21	1	0	0	0	0.0	0	1	0	3	2	.048	.048	0	0	OF-6
1988 MIN A	16	17	5	0	0	0	0.0	3	3	3	1	1	.294	.294	10	3	OF-4, DH-2
3 yrs.	40	63	13	2	0	0	0.0	6	6	4	7	3	.206	.238	22	6	OF-17, DH-2

Ellis Burks

BURKS, ELLIS RENA   BR TR 6'2" 175 lbs.
B. Sept. 11, 1964, Vicksburg, Miss.

	G	AB	H	2B	3B	HR	HR %	R	RBI	BB	SO	SB	BA	SA	PH AB	PH H	G by POS
1987 BOS A	133	558	152	30	2	20	3.6	94	59	41	98	27	.272	.441	0	0	OF-132
1988	144	540	159	37	5	18	3.3	93	92	62	89	25	.294	.481	0	0	OF-142, DH-2
2 yrs.	277	1098	311	67	7	38	3.5	187	151	103	187	52	.283	.461	0	0	OF-274, DH-2

LEAGUE CHAMPIONSHIP SERIES

	G	AB	H	2B	3B	HR	HR %	R	RBI	BB	SO	SB	BA	SA	PH AB	PH H	G by POS
1988 BOS A	4	17	4	1	0	0	0.0	2	1	0	3	0	.235	.294	0	0	OF-4

	G	AB	H	2B	3B	HR	HR %	R	RBI	BB	SO	SB	BA	SA	Pinch Hit AB	Pinch Hit H	G by POS

Randy Bush

BUSH, ROBERT RANDALL
B. Oct. 5, 1958, Dover, Del.
BL TL 6'1"   190 lbs.

	G	AB	H	2B	3B	HR	HR %	R	RBI	BB	SO	SB	BA	SA	PH AB	PH H	G by POS
1982 MIN A	55	119	29	6	1	4	3.4	13	13	8	28	0	.244	.412	25	3	DH-26, OF-6
1983	124	373	93	24	3	11	2.9	43	56	34	51	0	.249	.418	19	4	DH-103, 1B-3
1984	113	311	70	17	1	11	3.5	46	43	31	60	1	.225	.392	20	8	DH-89, 1B-2
1985	97	234	56	13	3	10	4.3	26	35	24	30	3	.239	.449	32	4	OF-41, DH-28, 1B-1
1986	130	357	96	19	7	7	2.0	50	45	39	63	5	.269	.420	30	13	OF-102, DH-6, 1B-3
1987	122	293	74	10	2	11	3.8	46	46	43	49	10	.253	.413	30	7	OF-75, DH-9, 1B-9
1988	136	394	103	20	3	14	3.6	51	51	58	49	8	.261	.434	19	6	OF-109, DH-17, 1B-6
7 yrs.	777	2081	521	109	20	68	3.3	275	289	237	330	27	.250	.420	175	45	OF-333, DH-278, 1B-24

LEAGUE CHAMPIONSHIP SERIES

	G	AB	H	2B	3B	HR	HR %	R	RBI	BB	SO	SB	BA	SA	PH AB	PH H	G by POS
1987 MIN A	4	12	3	0	1	0	0.0	4	2	3	2	3	.250	.417	0	0	DH-4

WORLD SERIES

	G	AB	H	2B	3B	HR	HR %	R	RBI	BB	SO	SB	BA	SA	PH AB	PH H	G by POS
1987 MIN A	4	6	1	1	0	0	0.0	1	2	0	1	0	.167	.333	3	0	DH-2

Sal Butera

BUTERA, SALVATORE PHILIP
B. Sept. 25, 1952, Richmond Hill, N. Y.
BR TR 6'   190 lbs.

	G	AB	H	2B	3B	HR	HR %	R	RBI	BB	SO	SB	BA	SA	PH AB	PH H	G by POS
1980 MIN A	34	85	23	1	0	0	0.0	4	2	3	6	0	.271	.282	2	0	C-32, DH-2
1981	62	167	40	7	1	0	0.0	13	18	22	14	0	.240	.293	1	0	C-59, DH-1, 1B-1
1982	54	126	32	2	0	0	0.0	9	8	17	12	0	.254	.270	1	0	C-53
1983 DET A	4	5	1	0	0	0	0.0	1	0	0	0	0	.200	.200	0	0	C-4
1984 MON N	3	3	0	0	0	0	0.0	0	0	1	0	0	.000	.000	0	0	C-2
1985	67	120	24	1	0	3	2.5	11	12	13	12	0	.200	.283	0	0	C-66, P-1
1986 CIN N	56	113	27	6	1	2	1.8	14	16	21	10	0	.239	.363	2	0	C-53, P-1
1987 2 teams	CIN	N (5G – .182)			MIN	A	(51G – .171)										
" total	56	122	21	5	0	2	1.6	8	14	8	22	0	.172	.262	0	0	C-56
1988 TOR A	23	60	14	2	1	1	1.7	3	6	1	9	0	.233	.350	1	0	C-23
9 yrs.	359	801	182	24	3	8	1.0	63	76	86	85	0	.227	.295	7	0	C-348, DH-3, P-2, 1B-1

LEAGUE CHAMPIONSHIP SERIES

	G	AB	H	2B	3B	HR	HR %	R	RBI	BB	SO	SB	BA	SA	PH AB	PH H	G by POS
1987 MIN A	1	3	2	0	0	0	0.0	0	0	0	0	0	.667	.667	0	0	C-1

WORLD SERIES

	G	AB	H	2B	3B	HR	HR %	R	RBI	BB	SO	SB	BA	SA	PH AB	PH H	G by POS
1987 MIN A	1	0	0	0	0	0	–	0	0	0	0	0	–	–	0	0	

Brett Butler

BUTLER, BRETT MORGAN
B. June 15, 1957, Los Angeles, Calif.
BL TL 5'10"   160 lbs.

	G	AB	H	2B	3B	HR	HR %	R	RBI	BB	SO	SB	BA	SA	PH AB	PH H	G by POS
1981 ATL N	40	126	32	2	3	0	0.0	17	4	19	17	9	.254	.317	2	1	OF-37
1982	89	240	52	2	0	0	0.0	35	7	25	35	21	.217	.225	6	1	OF-77
1983	151	549	154	21	13	5	0.9	84	37	54	56	39	.281	.393	6	1	OF-143
1984 CLE A	159	602	162	25	9	3	0.5	108	49	86	62	52	.269	.355	3	0	OF-156
1985	152	591	184	28	14	5	0.8	106	50	63	42	47	.311	.431	1	0	OF-150, DH-1
1986	161	587	163	17	14	4	0.7	92	51	70	65	32	.278	.375	1	0	OF-159
1987	137	522	154	25	8	9	1.7	91	41	91	55	33	.295	.425	0	0	OF-136
1988 SF N	157	568	163	27	9	6	1.1	109	43	97	64	43	.287	.398	2	0	OF-155
8 yrs.	1046	3785	1064	147	70	32	0.8	642	282	505	396	276	.281	.382	21	3	OF-1013, DH-1

LEAGUE CHAMPIONSHIP SERIES

	G	AB	H	2B	3B	HR	HR %	R	RBI	BB	SO	SB	BA	SA	PH AB	PH H	G by POS
1982 ATL N	2	1	0	0	0	0	0.0	0	0	0	0	0	.000	.000	1	0	OF-1

Randell Byers

BYERS, RANDELL PARKER
B. Oct. 2, 1964, Bridgeton, N. J.
BL TR 6'2"   180 lbs.

	G	AB	H	2B	3B	HR	HR %	R	RBI	BB	SO	SB	BA	SA	PH AB	PH H	G by POS
1987 SD N	10	16	5	1	0	0	0.0	1	1	1	5	1	.313	.375	3	0	OF-5
1988	11	10	2	1	0	0	0.0	0	0	0	5	0	.200	.300	10	2	OF-2
2 yrs.	21	26	7	2	0	0	0.0	1	1	1	10	1	.269	.346	13	2	OF-7

Ivan Calderon

CALDERON, IVAN PEREZ
Born Ivan Calderon y Perez.
B. Mar. 19, 1962, Fajardo, Puerto Rico
BR TR 5'11"   160 lbs.

	G	AB	H	2B	3B	HR	HR %	R	RBI	BB	SO	SB	BA	SA	PH AB	PH H	G by POS
1984 SEA A	11	24	5	1	0	1	4.2	2	1	2	5	1	.208	.375	0	0	OF-11
1985	67	210	60	16	4	8	3.8	37	28	19	45	4	.286	.514	10	3	OF-53, DH-3, 1B-2
1986 2 teams	SEA	A (37G – .237)			CHI	A	(13G – .303)										
" total	50	164	41	7	1	2	1.2	16	15	9	39	3	.250	.341	7	2	OF-37, DH-6
1987 CHI A	144	542	159	38	2	28	5.2	93	83	60	109	10	.293	.526	1	0	OF-139, DH-3
1988	73	264	56	14	0	14	5.3	40	35	34	66	4	.212	.424	1	0	OF-67, DH-3
5 yrs.	345	1204	321	76	7	53	4.4	188	162	124	264	22	.267	.473	19	5	OF-307, DH-15, 1B-2

Ken Caminiti

CAMINITI, KENNETH GENE
B. Apr. 21, 1963, Hanford, Calif.
BB TR 6'3"   200 lbs.

	G	AB	H	2B	3B	HR	HR %	R	RBI	BB	SO	SB	BA	SA	PH AB	PH H	G by POS
1987 HOU N	63	203	50	7	1	3	1.5	10	23	12	44	0	.246	.335	9	2	3B-61
1988	30	83	15	2	0	1	1.2	5	7	5	18	0	.181	.241	5	0	3B-28
2 yrs.	93	286	65	9	1	4	1.4	15	30	17	62	0	.227	.308	14	2	3B-89

Sil Campusano

CAMPUSANO, SILVESTRE
Born Silvestre Campusano y Diaz.
B. Dec. 31, 1965, Santo Domingo, Dominican Republic
BR TR 6'   160 lbs.

	G	AB	H	2B	3B	HR	HR %	R	RBI	BB	SO	SB	BA	SA	PH AB	PH H	G by POS
1988 TOR A	73	142	31	10	2	2	1.4	14	12	9	33	0	.218	.359	2	0	OF-69, DH-2

Casey Candaele

CANDAELE, CASEY TODD
B. Jan. 12, 1961, Lompoc, Calif.
BB TR 5'9"   160 lbs.

	G	AB	H	2B	3B	HR	HR %	R	RBI	BB	SO	SB	BA	SA	PH AB	PH H	G by POS
1986 MON N	30	104	24	4	1	0	0.0	9	6	5	15	3	.231	.288	3	1	2B-24, 3B-4
1987	138	449	122	23	4	1	0.2	62	23	38	28	7	.272	.347	12	3	2B-68, OF-67, SS-25, 1B-1
1988 2 teams	MON	N (36G – .172)			HOU	N	(21G – .161)										
" total	57	147	25	8	1	0	0.0	11	5	11	17	1	.170	.238	7	1	2B-45, OF-5, 3B-1
3 yrs.	225	700	171	35	6	1	0.1	82	34	54	60	11	.244	.316	22	5	2B-137, OF-72, SS-25, 3B-5, 1B-1

	G	AB	H	2B	3B	HR	HR %	R	RBI	BB	SO	SB	BA	SA	Pinch Hit AB	Pinch Hit H	G by POS

John Cangelosi

CANGELOSI, JOHN ANTHONY
B. Mar. 10, 1963, Brooklyn, N. Y.
BB TL 5'8" 150 lbs.

	G	AB	H	2B	3B	HR	HR %	R	RBI	BB	SO	SB	BA	SA	PH AB	PH H	G by POS
1985 CHI A	5	2	0	0	0	0	0.0	2	0	0	1	0	.000	.000	0	0	OF-3, DH-2
1986	137	438	103	16	3	2	0.5	65	32	71	61	50	.235	.299	1	0	OF-129, DH-3
1987 PIT N	104	182	50	8	3	4	2.2	44	18	46	33	21	.275	.418	50	10	OF-47
1988	75	118	30	4	1	0	0.0	18	8	17	16	9	.254	.305	42	12	OF-24, P-1
4 yrs.	321	740	183	28	7	6	0.8	129	58	134	111	80	.247	.328	93	22	OF-203, DH-5, P-1

Jose Canseco

CANSECO, JOSE
Born Jose Canseco y Capas.
B. July 2, 1964, Havana, Cuba
BR TR 6'3" 185 lbs.

	G	AB	H	2B	3B	HR	HR %	R	RBI	BB	SO	SB	BA	SA	PH AB	PH H	G by POS
1985 OAK A	29	96	29	3	0	5	5.2	16	13	4	31	1	.302	.490	4	1	OF-26
1986	157	600	144	29	1	33	5.5	85	117	65	175	15	.240	.457	1	1	OF-155, DH-1
1987	159	630	162	35	3	31	4.9	81	113	50	157	15	.257	.470	1	0	OF-130, DH-30
1988	158	610	187	34	0	42	6.9	120	124	78	128	40	.307	.569	1	0	OF-144, DH-13
4 yrs.	503	1936	522	101	4	111	5.7	302	367	197	491	71	.270	.498	7	2	OF-455, DH-44

LEAGUE CHAMPIONSHIP SERIES

	G	AB	H	2B	3B	HR	HR %	R	RBI	BB	SO	SB	BA	SA	PH AB	PH H	G by POS
1988 OAK A	4	16	5	1	0	3	18.8	4	4	1	2	1	.313	.938	0	0	OF-4

WORLD SERIES

	G	AB	H	2B	3B	HR	HR %	R	RBI	BB	SO	SB	BA	SA	PH AB	PH H	G by POS
1988 OAK A	5	19	1	0	0	1	5.3	1	5	2	5	1	.053	.211	0	0	OF-5

Nick Capra

CAPRA, NICK LEE
B. Mar. 8, 1958, Denver, Colo.
BR TR 5'8" 164 lbs.

	G	AB	H	2B	3B	HR	HR %	R	RBI	BB	SO	SB	BA	SA	PH AB	PH H	G by POS
1982 TEX A	13	15	4	0	0	1	6.7	2	1	3	4	2	.267	.467	0	0	OF-9
1983	8	2	0	0	0	0	0.0	2	0	0	0	0	.000	.000	2	0	OF-4
1985	8	8	1	0	0	0	0.0	1	0	0	0	0	.125	.125	0	0	OF-8
1988 KC A	14	29	4	1	0	0	0.0	3	0	2	3	1	.138	.172	1	0	OF-11
4 yrs.	43	54	9	1	0	1	1.9	8	1	5	7	3	.167	.241	3	0	OF-32

Mark Carreon

CARREON, MARK STEVEN
Son of Cam Carreon.
B. July 19, 1963, Chicago, Ill.
BR TL 6' 170 lbs.

	G	AB	H	2B	3B	HR	HR %	R	RBI	BB	SO	SB	BA	SA	PH AB	PH H	G by POS
1987 NY N	9	12	3	0	0	0	0.0	0	1	1	1	0	.250	.250	5	1	OF-5
1988	7	9	5	2	0	1	11.1	5	1	2	1	0	.556	1.111	2	0	OF-4
2 yrs.	16	21	8	2	0	1	4.8	5	2	3	2	0	.381	.619	7	1	OF-9

Gary Carter

CARTER, GARY EDMUND (The Kid)
B. Apr. 8, 1954, Culver City, Calif.
BR TR 6'2" 205 lbs.

	G	AB	H	2B	3B	HR	HR %	R	RBI	BB	SO	SB	BA	SA	PH AB	PH H	G by POS
1974 MON N	9	27	11	0	1	1	3.7	5	6	1	2	2	.407	.593	1	1	C-6, OF-2
1975	144	503	136	20	1	17	3.4	58	68	72	83	5	.270	.416	5	1	OF-92, C-66, 3B-1
1976	91	311	68	8	1	6	1.9	31	38	30	43	0	.219	.309	2	0	C-60, OF-36
1977	154	522	148	29	2	31	5.9	86	84	58	103	5	.284	.525	6	3	C-146, OF-1
1978	157	533	136	27	1	20	3.8	76	72	62	70	10	.255	.422	6	0	C-152, 1B-1
1979	141	505	143	26	5	22	4.4	74	75	40	62	3	.283	.485	3	0	C-138
1980	154	549	145	25	5	29	5.3	76	101	58	78	3	.264	.486	4	0	C-149
1981	100	374	94	20	2	16	4.3	48	68	35	35	1	.251	.444	0	0	C-100, 1B-1
1982	154	557	163	32	1	29	5.2	91	97	78	64	2	.293	.510	3	0	C-153
1983	145	541	146	37	3	17	3.1	63	79	51	57	1	.270	.444	2	0	C-144, 1B-1
1984	159	596	175	32	1	27	4.5	75	106	64	57	2	.294	.487	2	0	C-143, 1B-25
1985 NY N	149	555	156	17	1	32	5.8	83	100	69	46	1	.281	.488	2	0	C-143, 1B-6, OF-1
1986	132	490	125	14	2	24	4.9	81	105	62	63	1	.255	.439	1	0	C-122, 1B-9, OF-4, 3B-1
1987	139	523	123	18	2	20	3.8	55	83	42	73	0	.235	.392	4	0	C-135, 1B-4, OF-1
1988	130	455	110	16	2	11	2.4	39	46	34	52	0	.242	.358	7	4	C-119, 1B-10, 3B-1
15 yrs.	1958	7041	1879	321	30	302	4.3	941	1128	756	888	36	.267	.450	48	9	C-1776, OF-137, 1B-57, 3B-3

DIVISIONAL PLAYOFF SERIES

	G	AB	H	2B	3B	HR	HR %	R	RBI	BB	SO	SB	BA	SA	PH AB	PH H	G by POS
1981 MON N	5	19	8	3	0	2	10.5	3	6	1	1	0	.421	.895	0	0	C-5

LEAGUE CHAMPIONSHIP SERIES

	G	AB	H	2B	3B	HR	HR %	R	RBI	BB	SO	SB	BA	SA	PH AB	PH H	G by POS
1981 MON N	5	16	7	1	0	0	0.0	3	0	4	2	0	.438	.500	0	0	C-5
1986 NY N	6	27	4	1	0	0	0.0	1	2	2	5	0	.148	.185	0	0	C-6
1988	7	27	6	1	1	0	0.0	0	4	1	3	0	.222	.333	0	0	C-7
3 yrs.	18	70	17	3	1	0	0.0	4	6	7	10	0	.243	.314	0	0	C-18

WORLD SERIES

	G	AB	H	2B	3B	HR	HR %	R	RBI	BB	SO	SB	BA	SA	PH AB	PH H	G by POS
1986 NY N	7	29	8	2	0	2	6.9	4	9	0	4	0	.276	.552	0	0	C-7

Joe Carter

CARTER, JOSEPH CHRIS
B. Mar. 7, 1960, Oklahoma City, Okla.
BR TR 6'3" 210 lbs.

	G	AB	H	2B	3B	HR	HR %	R	RBI	BB	SO	SB	BA	SA	PH AB	PH H	G by POS
1983 CHI N	23	51	9	1	1	0	0.0	6	1	0	21	1	.176	.235	5	1	OF-16
1984 CLE A	66	244	67	6	1	13	5.3	32	41	11	48	2	.275	.467	7	5	OF-59, 1B-7
1985	143	489	128	27	0	15	3.1	64	59	25	74	24	.262	.409	4	0	OF-135, 1B-11, DH-7, 3B-1, 2B-1
1986	162	663	200	36	9	29	4.4	108	121	32	95	29	.302	.514	1	1	OF-104, 1B-70
1987	149	588	155	27	2	32	5.4	83	106	27	105	31	.264	.480	2	0	1B-84, OF-62, DH-5
1988	157	621	168	36	6	27	4.3	85	98	35	82	27	.271	.478	1	0	OF-156
6 yrs.	700	2656	727	133	19	116	4.4	378	426	130	425	114	.274	.469	20	7	OF-532, 1B-172, DH-12, 3B-1, 2B-1

Carmen Castillo

CASTILLO, MONTE CARMELO
B. June 8, 1958, San Pedro de Macoris, Dominican Republic
BR TR 6'1" 180 lbs.

	G	AB	H	2B	3B	HR	HR %	R	RBI	BB	SO	SB	BA	SA	PH AB	PH H	G by POS
1982 CLE A	47	120	25	4	0	2	1.7	11	11	6	17	0	.208	.292	3	0	OF-43, DH-2
1983	23	36	10	2	1	1	2.8	9	3	4	6	1	.278	.472	2	0	OF-19, DH-1
1984	87	211	55	9	2	10	4.7	36	36	21	32	1	.261	.464	18	3	OF-70, DH-2
1985	67	184	45	5	1	11	6.0	27	25	11	40	3	.245	.462	9	1	OF-51, DH-9
1986	85	205	57	9	0	8	3.9	34	32	9	48	2	.278	.439	21	3	OF-37, DH-35
1987	89	220	55	17	0	11	5.0	27	31	16	52	1	.250	.477	29	5	DH-43, OF-23

	G	AB	H	2B	3B	HR	HR %	R	RBI	BB	SO	SB	BA	SA	Pinch Hit AB	H	G by POS

Carmen Castillo continued

	G	AB	H	2B	3B	HR	HR %	R	RBI	BB	SO	SB	BA	SA	AB	H	G by POS
1988	66	176	48	8	0	4	2.3	12	14	5	31	6	.273	.386	16	4	OF-45, DH-9
7 yrs.	464	1152	295	54	4	47	4.1	156	152	72	226	14	.256	.432	98	16	OF-288, DH-101

Juan Castillo

CASTILLO, JUAN
Born Juan Castillo y Brayas.
B. Jan. 25, 1962, San Pedro de Macoris, Dominican Republic

BB   TR   5'11"   162 lbs.

	G	AB	H	2B	3B	HR	HR %	R	RBI	BB	SO	SB	BA	SA	AB	H	G by POS
1986 **MIL A**	26	54	9	0	1	0	0.0	6	5	5	12	1	.167	.204	0	0	2B-17, SS-4, DH-2, 3B-2, OF-1
1987	116	321	72	11	4	3	0.9	44	28	33	76	15	.224	.312	7	2	2B-97, SS-13, 3B-7
1988	54	90	20	0	0	0	0.0	10	2	3	14	2	.222	.222	0	0	2B-18, 3B-17, SS-13, DH-3, OF-1
3 yrs.	196	465	101	11	5	3	0.6	60	35	41	102	18	.217	.282	7	2	2B-132, SS-30, 3B-26, DH-5, OF-2

Rick Cerone

CERONE, RICHARD ALDO
B. May 19, 1954, Newark, N. J.

BR   TR   5'11"   192 lbs.

	G	AB	H	2B	3B	HR	HR %	R	RBI	BB	SO	SB	BA	SA	AB	H	G by POS
1975 **CLE A**	7	12	3	1	0	0	0.0	1	0	1	0	0	.250	.333	0	0	C-7
1976	7	16	2	0	0	0	0.0	1	1	0	2	0	.125	.125	1	1	C-6, DH-1
1977 **TOR A**	31	100	20	4	0	1	1.0	7	10	6	12	0	.200	.270	0	0	C-31
1978	88	282	63	8	2	3	1.1	25	20	23	32	0	.223	.298	4	1	C-84, DH-2
1979	136	469	112	27	4	7	1.5	47	61	37	40	1	.239	.358	2	0	C-136
1980 **NY A**	147	519	144	30	4	14	2.7	70	85	32	56	1	.277	.432	0	0	C-147
1981	71	234	57	13	2	2	0.9	23	21	12	24	0	.244	.342	2	2	C-69
1982	89	300	68	10	0	5	1.7	29	28	19	27	0	.227	.310	0	0	C-89
1983	80	246	54	7	0	2	0.8	18	22	15	29	0	.220	.272	2	0	C-78, 3B-1
1984	38	120	25	3	0	2	1.7	8	13	9	15	1	.208	.283	0	0	C-38
1985 **ATL N**	96	282	61	9	0	3	1.1	15	25	29	25	0	.216	.280	7	1	C-91
1986 **MIL A**	68	216	56	14	0	4	1.9	22	18	15	28	1	.259	.380	0	0	C-68
1987 **NY A**	113	284	69	12	1	4	1.4	28	23	30	46	0	.243	.335	6	2	C-111, 1B-2, P-2
1988 **BOS A**	84	264	71	13	1	3	1.1	31	27	20	32	0	.269	.360	4	1	C-83, DH-1
14 yrs.	1055	3344	805	151	14	50	1.5	325	354	248	368	4	.241	.339	28	8	C-1038, DH-4, 1B-2, P-2, 3B-1

DIVISIONAL PLAYOFF SERIES

	G	AB	H	2B	3B	HR	HR %	R	RBI	BB	SO	SB	BA	SA	AB	H	G by POS
1981 **NY A**	5	18	6	2	0	1	5.6	1	5	0	2	0	.333	.611	0	0	C-5

LEAGUE CHAMPIONSHIP SERIES

	G	AB	H	2B	3B	HR	HR %	R	RBI	BB	SO	SB	BA	SA	AB	H	G by POS
1980 **NY A**	3	12	4	0	0	1	8.3	1	2	0	1	0	.333	.583	0	0	C-3
1981	3	10	1	0	0	0	0.0	1	0	0	0	0	.100	.100	0	0	C-3
2 yrs.	6	22	5	0	0	1	4.5	2	2	0	1	0	.227	.364	0	0	C-6

WORLD SERIES

	G	AB	H	2B	3B	HR	HR %	R	RBI	BB	SO	SB	BA	SA	AB	H	G by POS
1981 **NY A**	6	21	4	1	0	1	4.8	2	3	4	2	0	.190	.381	0	0	C-6

Chris Chambliss

CHAMBLISS, CARROLL CHRISTOPHER
B. Dec. 26, 1948, Dayton, Ohio

BL   TR   6'1"   195 lbs.

	G	AB	H	2B	3B	HR	HR %	R	RBI	BB	SO	SB	BA	SA	AB	H	G by POS
1971 **CLE A**	111	415	114	20	4	9	2.2	49	48	40	83	2	.275	.407	2	0	1B-108
1972	121	466	136	27	2	6	1.3	51	44	26	63	3	.292	.397	2	0	1B-119
1973	155	572	156	30	2	11	1.9	70	53	58	76	4	.273	.390	1	0	1B-154
1974 **2 teams**				CLE	A	(17G –	.328)	NY	A	(110G –	.243)						
" total	127	467	119	20	3	6	1.3	46	50	28	48	0	.255	.349	4	0	1B-123
1975 **NY A**	150	562	171	38	4	9	1.6	66	72	29	50	0	.304	.434	3	0	1B-147
1976	156	641	188	32	6	17	2.7	79	96	27	80	1	.293	.441	0	0	1B-155, DH-1
1977	157	600	172	32	6	17	2.8	90	90	45	73	4	.287	.445	4	2	1B-157
1978	162	625	171	26	3	12	1.9	81	90	41	60	2	.274	.382	1	0	1B-155, DH-7
1979	149	554	155	27	3	18	3.2	61	63	34	53	3	.280	.437	2	1	1B-134, DH-16
1980 **ATL N**	158	602	170	37	2	18	3.0	83	72	49	73	7	.282	.440	0	0	1B-158
1981	107	404	110	25	2	8	2.0	44	51	44	41	4	.272	.403	0	0	1B-107
1982	157	534	144	25	2	20	3.7	57	86	57	57	7	.270	.436	11	5	1B-151
1983	131	447	125	24	3	20	4.5	59	78	63	68	2	.280	.481	8	5	1B-126
1984	133	389	100	14	0	9	2.3	47	44	58	54	1	.257	.362	24	4	1B-109
1985	101	170	40	7	0	3	1.8	16	21	18	22	0	.235	.329	54	11	1B-39
1986	97	122	38	8	0	2	1.6	13	14	15	24	0	.311	.426	68	20	1B-20
1988 **NY A**	1	0	0	0	0	0	0.0	0	0	0	0	0	.000	.000	1	0	
17 yrs.	2173	7571	2109	392	42	185	2.4	912	972	632	926	40	.279	.415	185	48	1B-1962, DH-24

LEAGUE CHAMPIONSHIP SERIES

	G	AB	H	2B	3B	HR	HR %	R	RBI	BB	SO	SB	BA	SA	AB	H	G by POS
1976 **NY A**	5	21	11	1	1	2	9.5	5	8	0	1	2	.524	.952	0	0	1B-5
1977	5	17	1	0	0	0	0.0	0	0	3	4	0	.059	.059	0	0	1B-5
1978	4	15	6	0	0	0	0.0	1	2	0	4	0	.400	.400	0	0	1B-4
1982 **ATL N**	3	10	0	0	0	0	0.0	0	0	1	0	0	.000	.000	0	0	1B-3
4 yrs.	17	63	18	1	1	2	3.2	6	10	4	9	2	.286	.429	0	0	1B-17

WORLD SERIES

	G	AB	H	2B	3B	HR	HR %	R	RBI	BB	SO	SB	BA	SA	AB	H	G by POS
1976 **NY A**	4	16	5	1	0	0	0.0	1	1	0	2	0	.313	.375	0	0	1B-4
1977	6	24	7	2	0	1	4.2	4	4	0	2	0	.292	.500	0	0	1B-6
1978	3	11	2	0	0	0	0.0	1	0	1	1	0	.182	.182	0	0	1B-3
3 yrs.	13	51	14	3	0	1	2.0	6	5	1	5	0	.275	.392	0	0	1B-13

John Christensen

CHRISTENSEN, JOHN LAWRENCE
B. Sept. 15, 1960, Downey, Calif.

BR   TR   6'3"   205 lbs.

	G	AB	H	2B	3B	HR	HR %	R	RBI	BB	SO	SB	BA	SA	AB	H	G by POS
1984 **NY N**	5	11	3	2	0	0	0.0	2	3	1	2	0	.273	.455	1	1	OF-5
1985	51	113	21	4	1	3	2.7	10	13	19	23	1	.186	.319	15	1	OF-38
1987 **SEA A**	53	132	32	6	1	2	1.5	19	12	12	28	2	.242	.348	13	2	OF-43, DH-8
1988 **MIN A**	23	38	10	4	0	0	0.0	5	5	3	5	0	.263	.368	6	2	OF-17
4 yrs.	132	294	66	16	2	5	1.7	36	33	35	58	3	.224	.344	35	6	OF-103, DH-8

	G	AB	H	2B	3B	HR	HR %	R	RBI	BB	SO	SB	BA	SA	Pinch Hit AB	Pinch Hit H	G by POS

Dave Clark

CLARK, DAVID EARL
B. Sept. 3, 1962, Tupelo, Miss. BL TR 6'2" 200 lbs.

	G	AB	H	2B	3B	HR	HR %	R	RBI	BB	SO	SB	BA	SA	AB	H	G by POS
1986 CLE A	18	58	16	1	0	3	5.2	10	9	7	11	1	.276	.448	0	0	OF-10, DH-7
1987	29	87	18	5	0	3	3.4	11	12	2	24	1	.207	.368	6	0	OF-13, DH-12
1988	63	156	41	4	1	3	1.9	11	18	17	28	0	.263	.359	19	4	DH-27, OF-23
3 yrs.	110	301	75	10	1	9	3.0	32	39	26	63	2	.249	.379	25	4	DH-46, OF-46

Jack Clark

CLARK, JACK ANTHONY (The Ripper)
B. Nov. 10, 1955, New Brighton, Pa. BR TR 6'2" 205 lbs.

	G	AB	H	2B	3B	HR	HR %	R	RBI	BB	SO	SB	BA	SA	AB	H	G by POS
1975 SF N	8	17	4	0	0	0	0.0	3	2	1	2	1	.235	.235	3	0	OF-3, 3B-2
1976	26	102	23	6	2	2	2.0	14	10	8	18	6	.225	.382	0	0	OF-26
1977	136	413	104	17	4	13	3.1	64	51	49	73	12	.252	.407	29	11	OF-114
1978	156	592	181	46	8	25	4.2	90	98	50	72	15	.306	.537	6	2	OF-152
1979	143	527	144	25	2	26	4.9	84	86	63	95	11	.273	.476	2	0	OF-140, 3B-2
1980	127	437	124	20	8	22	5.0	77	82	74	52	2	.284	.517	5	0	OF-120
1981	99	385	103	19	2	17	4.4	60	53	45	45	1	.268	.460	2	0	OF-98
1982	157	563	154	30	3	27	4.8	90	103	90	91	6	.274	.481	4	1	OF-155
1983	135	492	132	25	0	20	4.1	82	66	74	79	5	.268	.441	1	0	OF-133, 1B-2
1984	57	203	65	9	1	11	5.4	33	44	43	29	1	.320	.537	1	0	OF-54, 1B-4
1985 STL N	126	442	124	26	3	22	5.0	71	87	83	88	1	.281	.502	1	0	1B-121, OF-12
1986	65	232	55	12	2	9	3.9	34	23	45	61	1	.237	.422	1	1	1B-64
1987	131	419	120	23	1	35	8.4	93	106	136	139	1	.286	.597	4	0	1B-126, OF-1
1988 NY A	150	496	120	14	0	27	5.4	81	93	113	141	3	.242	.433	12	3	DH-112, OF-19, 1B-10
14 yrs.	1516	5320	1453	272	36	256	4.8	876	904	874	985	66	.273	.482	71	18	OF-1027, 1B-327, DH-112, 3B-4

LEAGUE CHAMPIONSHIP SERIES

	G	AB	H	2B	3B	HR	HR %	R	RBI	BB	SO	SB	BA	SA	AB	H	G by POS
1985 STL N	6	21	8	0	0	1	4.8	4	4	5	5	0	.381	.524	0	0	1B-6
1987	1	1	0	0	0	0	0.0	0	0	0	1	0	.000	.000	1	0	
2 yrs.	7	22	8	0	0	1	4.5	4	4	5	6	0	.364	.500	1	0	1B-6

WORLD SERIES

	G	AB	H	2B	3B	HR	HR %	R	RBI	BB	SO	SB	BA	SA	AB	H	G by POS
1985 STL N	7	25	6	2	0	0	0.0	1	4	3	9	0	.240	.320	0	0	1B-7

Jerald Clark

CLARK, JERALD DWAYNE
B. Aug. 10, 1963, Crockett, Tex. BR TR 6'4" 189 lbs.

	G	AB	H	2B	3B	HR	HR %	R	RBI	BB	SO	SB	BA	SA	AB	H	G by POS
1988 SD N	6	15	3	1	0	0	0.0	0	3	0	4	0	.200	.267	3	1	OF-4

Will Clark

CLARK, WILLIAM NUSCHLER (The Natural, The Thrill)
B. Mar. 13, 1964, New Orleans, La. BL TL 6'2" 190 lbs.

	G	AB	H	2B	3B	HR	HR %	R	RBI	BB	SO	SB	BA	SA	AB	H	G by POS
1986 SF N	111	408	117	27	2	11	2.7	66	41	34	76	4	.287	.444	9	6	1B-102
1987	150	529	163	29	5	35	6.6	89	91	49	98	5	.308	.580	11	3	1B-139
1988	162	575	162	31	6	29	5.0	102	109	100	129	9	.282	.508	5	0	1B-158
3 yrs.	423	1512	442	87	13	75	5.0	257	241	183	303	18	.292	.516	25	9	1B-399

LEAGUE CHAMPIONSHIP SERIES

	G	AB	H	2B	3B	HR	HR %	R	RBI	BB	SO	SB	BA	SA	AB	H	G by POS
1987 SF N	7	25	9	2	0	1	4.0	3	3	3	6	1	.360	.560	0	0	1B-7

Vince Coleman

COLEMAN, VINCENT MAURICE
B. Sept. 22, 1960, Jacksonville, Fla. BB TR 6' 170 lbs.

	G	AB	H	2B	3B	HR	HR %	R	RBI	BB	SO	SB	BA	SA	AB	H	G by POS
1985 STL N	151	636	170	20	10	1	0.2	107	40	50	115	110	.267	.335	1	0	OF-150
1986	154	600	139	13	8	0	0.0	94	29	60	98	107	.232	.280	2	1	OF-149
1987	151	623	180	14	10	3	0.5	121	43	70	126	109	.289	.358	1	0	OF-150
1988	153	616	160	20	10	3	0.5	77	38	49	111	81	.260	.339	2	0	OF-150
4 yrs.	609	2475	649	67	38	7	0.3	399	150	229	450	407	.262	.328	6	1	OF-599

LEAGUE CHAMPIONSHIP SERIES

	G	AB	H	2B	3B	HR	HR %	R	RBI	BB	SO	SB	BA	SA	AB	H	G by POS
1985 STL N	3	14	4	0	0	0	0.0	2	1	0	2	1	.286	.286	0	0	OF-3
1987	7	26	7	1	0	0	0.0	3	4	4	6	1	.269	.308	0	0	OF-7
2 yrs.	10	40	11	1	0	0	0.0	5	5	4	8	2	.275	.300	0	0	OF-10

WORLD SERIES

	G	AB	H	2B	3B	HR	HR %	R	RBI	BB	SO	SB	BA	SA	AB	H	G by POS
1987 STL N	7	28	4	2	0	0	0.0	5	2	2	10	6	.143	.214	0	0	OF-7

Darnell Coles

COLES, DARNELL
B. June 2, 1962, San Bernardino, Calif. BR TR 6'2" 175 lbs.

	G	AB	H	2B	3B	HR	HR %	R	RBI	BB	SO	SB	BA	SA	AB	H	G by POS
1983 SEA A	27	92	26	7	0	1	1.1	9	6	7	12	0	.283	.391	1	0	3B-26
1984	48	143	23	3	1	0	0.0	15	6	17	26	2	.161	.196	0	0	3B-42, DH-3, OF-3
1985	27	59	14	4	0	1	1.7	8	5	9	17	0	.237	.356	3	0	SS-15, 3B-7, DH-2, OF-2
1986 DET A	142	521	142	30	2	20	3.8	67	86	45	84	6	.273	.453	1	0	3B-133, DH-7, OF-2, SS-2
1987 2 teams	93	DET A (53G – .181)				PIT N (40G – .227)											
" total	93	268	54	13	1	10	3.7	34	39	34	43	1	.201	.369	9	2	3B-46, OF-34, 1B-10, DH-3, SS-1
1988 2 teams	123	PIT N (68G – .232)				SEA A (55G – .292)											
" total	123	406	106	23	2	15	3.7	52	70	37	67	4	.261	.438	11	0	OF-102, DH-7, 1B-2, 3B-1
6 yrs.	460	1489	365	80	6	47	3.2	185	212	149	249	13	.245	.402	25	2	3B-255, OF-143, DH-22, SS-18, 1B-12

Dave Collins

COLLINS, DAVID SCOTT
B. Oct. 20, 1952, Rapid City, S. D. BB TL 5'10" 175 lbs.

	G	AB	H	2B	3B	HR	HR %	R	RBI	BB	SO	SB	BA	SA	AB	H	G by POS
1975 CAL A	93	319	85	13	4	3	0.9	41	29	36	55	24	.266	.361	5	4	OF-75, DH-12
1976	99	365	96	12	1	4	1.1	45	28	40	55	32	.263	.334	2	0	OF-71, DH-22
1977 SEA A	120	402	96	9	3	5	1.2	46	28	33	66	25	.239	.313	7	4	OF-73, DH-40
1978 CIN N	102	102	22	1	0	0	0.0	13	7	15	18	7	.216	.225	64	14	OF-24
1979	122	396	126	16	4	3	0.8	59	35	27	48	16	.318	.402	28	9	OF-91, 1B-10
1980	144	551	167	20	4	3	0.5	94	35	53	68	79	.303	.370	3	1	OF-141
1981	95	360	98	18	6	3	0.8	63	23	41	41	26	.272	.381	1	0	OF-94
1982 NY A	111	348	88	12	3	3	0.9	41	25	28	49	13	.253	.330	7	1	OF-60, 1B-52, DH-1
1983 TOR A	118	402	109	12	4	1	0.2	55	34	43	67	31	.271	.328	18	5	OF-112, 1B-5, DH-1
1984	128	441	136	24	15	2	0.5	59	44	33	41	60	.308	.444	14	6	OF-108, 1B-6, DH-4
1985 OAK A	112	379	95	16	4	4	1.1	52	29	29	37	29	.251	.346	17	4	OF-91

	G	AB	H	2B	3B	HR	HR %	R	RBI	BB	SO	SB	BA	SA	Pinch Hit AB	Pinch Hit H	G by POS

Dave Collins continued

	G	AB	H	2B	3B	HR	HR %	R	RBI	BB	SO	SB	BA	SA	P.H. AB	P.H. H	G by POS
1986 **DET A**	124	419	113	18	2	1	0.2	44	27	44	49	27	.270	.329	11	1	OF-94, DH-24
1987 **CIN N**	57	85	25	5	0	0	0.0	19	5	11	12	9	.294	.353	35	8	OF-21
1988	99	174	41	6	2	0	0.0	12	14	11	27	7	.236	.293	58	12	OF-35, 1B-3
14 yrs.	1524	4743	1297	182	52	32	0.7	643	363	444	633	385	.273	.354	270	69	OF-1090, DH-104, 1B-76
LEAGUE CHAMPIONSHIP SERIES																	
1979 **CIN N**	3	14	5	1	0	0	0.0	0	1	0	2	2	.357	.429	0	0	OF-3

Dave Concepcion

CONCEPCION, DAVID ISMAEL
Born David Ismael Concepcion Bonitez.
B. June 17, 1948, Aragua, Venezuela

BR TR 6'2" 155 lbs.

	G	AB	H	2B	3B	HR	HR %	R	RBI	BB	SO	SB	BA	SA	P.H. AB	P.H. H	G by POS
1970 **CIN N**	101	265	69	6	3	1	0.4	38	19	23	45	10	.260	.317	5	1	SS-93, 2B-3
1971	130	327	67	4	4	1	0.3	24	20	18	51	9	.205	.251	1	0	SS-112, 2B-10, 3B-7, OF-5
1972	119	378	79	13	2	2	0.5	40	29	32	65	13	.209	.270	0	0	SS-114, 3B-9, 2B-1
1973	89	328	94	18	3	8	2.4	39	46	21	55	22	.287	.433	2	0	SS-88, OF-2
1974	160	594	167	25	1	14	2.4	70	82	44	79	41	.281	.397	1	0	SS-160
1975	140	507	139	23	1	5	1.0	62	49	39	51	33	.274	.353	8	2	SS-130, 3B-6
1976	152	576	162	28	7	9	1.6	74	69	49	68	21	.281	.401	3	1	SS-150
1977	156	572	155	26	3	8	1.4	59	64	46	77	29	.271	.369	0	0	SS-156
1978	153	565	170	33	4	6	1.1	75	67	51	83	23	.301	.405	3	1	SS-152
1979	149	590	166	25	3	16	2.7	91	84	64	73	19	.281	.415	1	0	SS-148
1980	156	622	162	31	8	5	0.8	72	77	37	107	12	.260	.360	2	0	SS-155, 2B-1
1981	106	421	129	28	0	5	1.2	57	67	37	61	4	.306	.409	0	0	SS-106
1982	147	572	164	25	4	5	0.9	48	53	45	61	13	.287	.371	3	1	SS-145, 3B-1, 1B-1
1983	143	528	123	22	0	1	0.2	54	47	56	81	14	.233	.280	3	1	SS-139, 3B-6, 1B-1
1984	154	531	130	26	1	4	0.8	46	58	52	72	22	.245	.320	13	1	SS-104, 3B-54, 1B-6
1985	155	560	141	19	2	7	1.3	59	48	50	67	16	.252	.330	6	0	SS-151, 3B-5
1986	90	311	81	13	2	3	1.0	42	30	26	43	13	.260	.344	8	1	SS-60, 1B-12, 3B-10, 2B-10
1987	104	279	89	15	0	1	0.4	32	33	28	24	4	.319	.384	24	8	2B-59, 1B-26, 3B-13, SS-2
1988	84	197	39	9	0	0	0.0	11	8	18	23	3	.198	.244	17	4	2B-46, 1B-16, SS-13, 3B-9, P-1
19 yrs.	2488	8723	2326	389	48	101	1.2	993	950	736	1186	321	.267	.357	100	21	SS-2178, 2B-130, 3B-120, 1B-62, OF-7, P-1
LEAGUE CHAMPIONSHIP SERIES																	
1970 **CIN N**	3	0	0	0	0	0	—	0	0	0	0	0	—	—	0	0	SS-3
1972	3	2	0	0	0	0	0.0	0	0	0	0	0	.000	.000	1	0	SS-1
1975	3	11	5	0	0	1	9.1	2	1	1	2	2	.455	.727	0	0	SS-3
1976	3	10	2	1	0	0	0.0	4	0	2	1	0	.200	.300	0	0	SS-3
1979	3	14	6	1	0	0	0.0	1	0	0	3	0	.429	.500	0	0	SS-3
5 yrs.	15	37	13	2	0	1	2.7	7	1	3	6	2	.351	.486	1	0	SS-13
WORLD SERIES																	
1970 **CIN N**	3	9	3	0	1	0	0.0	0	3	0	0	0	.333	.556	0	0	SS-3
1972	6	13	4	0	1	0	0.0	2	2	2	2	1	.308	.462	1	0	SS-5
1975	7	28	5	1	0	1	3.6	3	4	0	1	3	.179	.321	0	0	SS-7
1976	4	14	5	1	1	0	0.0	1	3	1	3	1	.357	.571	0	0	SS-4
4 yrs.	20	64	17	2	3	1	1.6	6	12	3	6	5	.266	.438	1	0	SS-19
					4th												

Henry Cotto

COTTO, HENRY
B. Jan. 5, 1961, Bronx, N. Y.

BR TR 6'2" 180 lbs.

	G	AB	H	2B	3B	HR	HR %	R	RBI	BB	SO	SB	BA	SA	P.H. AB	P.H. H	G by POS
1984 **CHI N**	105	146	40	5	0	0	0.0	24	8	10	23	9	.274	.308	13	3	OF-88
1985 **NY A**	34	56	17	1	0	1	1.8	4	6	3	12	1	.304	.375	4	1	OF-30
1986	35	80	17	3	0	1	1.3	11	6	2	17	3	.213	.288	2	0	OF-29, DH-1
1987	68	149	35	10	0	5	3.4	21	20	6	35	4	.235	.403	11	0	OF-57
1988 **SEA A**	133	386	100	18	1	8	2.1	50	33	23	53	27	.259	.373	7	1	OF-120, DH-2
5 yrs.	375	817	209	37	1	15	1.8	110	73	44	140	44	.256	.359	37	5	OF-324, DH-3
LEAGUE CHAMPIONSHIP SERIES																	
1984 **CHI N**	3	1	1	0	0	0	0.0	1	0	0	0	0	1.000	1.000	0	0	OF-3

Jose Cruz

CRUZ, JOSE (Cheo)
Born Jose Cruz y Dilan. Brother of Tommy Cruz.
Brother of Hector Cruz.
B. Aug. 8, 1947, Arroyo, Puerto Rico

BL TL 6' 170 lbs.

	G	AB	H	2B	3B	HR	HR %	R	RBI	BB	SO	SB	BA	SA	P.H. AB	P.H. H	G by POS
1970 **STL N**	6	17	6	1	0	0	0.0	2	1	4	0	0	.353	.412	1	1	OF-4
1971	83	292	80	13	2	9	3.1	46	27	49	35	6	.274	.425	2	1	OF-83
1972	117	332	78	14	4	2	0.6	33	23	36	54	9	.235	.319	13	5	OF-102
1973	132	406	92	22	5	10	2.5	51	57	51	66	10	.227	.379	14	3	OF-118
1974	107	161	42	4	3	5	3.1	24	20	20	27	4	.261	.416	47	11	OF-53, 1B-1
1975 **HOU N**	120	315	81	15	2	9	2.9	44	49	52	44	6	.257	.403	28	6	OF-94
1976	133	439	133	21	5	4	0.9	49	61	53	46	28	.303	.401	10	3	OF-125
1977	157	579	173	31	10	17	2.9	87	87	69	67	44	.299	.475	4	1	OF-155
1978	153	565	178	34	9	10	1.8	79	83	57	57	37	.315	.460	1	0	OF-152, 1B-2
1979	157	558	161	33	7	9	1.6	73	72	72	66	36	.289	.421	1	0	OF-156
1980	160	612	185	29	7	11	1.8	79	91	60	66	36	.302	.426	2	0	OF-158
1981	107	409	109	16	5	13	3.2	53	55	35	49	5	.267	.425	2	1	OF-105
1982	155	570	157	27	2	9	1.6	62	68	60	67	21	.275	.377	2	1	OF-155
1983	160	594	189	28	8	14	2.4	85	92	65	86	30	.318	.463	2	1	OF-160
1984	160	600	187	28	13	12	2.0	96	95	73	68	22	.312	.462	1	0	OF-160
1985	141	544	163	34	4	9	1.7	69	79	43	74	16	.300	.426	3	0	OF-137
1986	141	479	133	22	4	10	2.1	48	72	55	86	3	.278	.403	8	1	OF-134
1987	126	365	88	17	4	11	3.0	47	38	36	65	4	.241	.406	29	5	OF-97
1988 **NY A**	38	80	16	2	0	1	1.3	9	7	8	8	0	.200	.263	19	3	DH-12, OF-8
19 yrs.	2353	7917	2251	391	94	165	2.1	1036	1077	898	1031	317	.284	.420	189	43	OF-2156, DH-12, 1B-3

	G	AB	H	2B	3B	HR	HR %	R	RBI	BB	SO	SB	BA	SA	Pinch Hit AB	Pinch Hit H	G by POS

Jose Cruz continued

DIVISIONAL PLAYOFF SERIES
| 1981 HOU N | 5 | 20 | 6 | 1 | 0 | 0 | 0.0 | 0 | 0 | 1 | 3 | 1 | .300 | .350 | 0 | 0 | OF-5 |

LEAGUE CHAMPIONSHIP SERIES
1980 HOU N	5	15	6	1	1	0	0.0	3	4	8	1	0	.400	.600	0	0	OF-5
1986	6	26	5	0	0	0	0.0	0	2	1	8	0	.192	.192	0	0	OF-6
2 yrs.	11	41	11	1	1	0	0.0	3	6	9	9	0	.268	.341	0	0	OF-11

Kal Daniels

DANIELS, KALVOSKI
B. Aug. 20, 1963, Vienna, Ga.　　BL TR 5'11" 185 lbs.

1986 CIN N	74	181	58	10	4	6	3.3	34	23	22	30	15	.320	.519	23	11	OF-47
1987	108	368	123	24	1	26	7.1	73	64	60	62	26	.334	.617	12	2	OF-94
1988	140	495	144	29	1	18	3.6	95	64	87	94	27	.291	.463	1	0	OF-137
3 yrs.	322	1044	325	63	6	50	4.8	202	151	169	186	68	.311	.527	36	13	OF-278

Doug Dascenzo

DASCENZO, DOUGLAS CRAIG
B. June 30, 1964, Cleveland, Ohio　　BB TL 5'7" 150 lbs.

| 1988 CHI N | 26 | 75 | 16 | 3 | 0 | 0 | 0.0 | 9 | 4 | 9 | 4 | 6 | .213 | .253 | 5 | 0 | OF-20 |

Darren Daulton

DAULTON, DARREN ARTHUR
B. Jan. 3, 1962, Arkansas City, Kans.　　BL TR 6' 185 lbs.

1983 PHI N	2	3	1	0	0	0	0.0	1	0	1	1	0	.333	.333	0	0	C-2
1985	36	103	21	3	1	4	3.9	14	11	16	37	3	.204	.369	5	0	C-28
1986	49	138	31	4	0	8	5.8	18	21	38	41	2	.225	.428	1	0	C-48
1987	53	129	25	6	0	3	2.3	10	13	16	37	0	.194	.310	12	3	C-40, 1B-1
1988	58	144	30	6	0	1	0.7	13	12	17	26	2	.208	.271	15	4	C-44, 1B-1
5 yrs.	198	517	108	19	1	16	3.1	56	57	88	142	7	.209	.342	33	7	C-162, 1B-2

Mark Davidson

DAVIDSON, JOHN MARK
B. Feb. 15, 1961, Knoxville, Tenn.　　BR TR 6'2" 180 lbs.

1986 MIN A	36	68	8	3	0	0	0.0	5	2	6	22	2	.118	.162	2	1	OF-31, DH-3
1987	102	150	40	4	1	1	0.7	32	14	13	26	9	.267	.327	6	3	OF-86, DH-9
1988	100	106	23	7	0	1	0.9	22	10	10	20	3	.217	.311	9	4	OF-91, 3B-1
3 yrs.	238	324	71	14	1	2	0.6	59	26	29	68	14	.219	.287	17	8	OF-208, DH-12, 3B-1

LEAGUE CHAMPIONSHIP SERIES
| 1987 MIN A | 1 | 0 | 0 | 0 | 0 | 0 | – | 0 | 0 | 0 | 0 | 0 | – | – | 0 | 0 | |

WORLD SERIES
| 1987 MIN A | 2 | 1 | 0 | 0 | 0 | 0 | 0.0 | 0 | 0 | 0 | 0 | 0 | .000 | .000 | 1 | 0 | OF-1 |

Alvin Davis

DAVIS, ALVIN GLENN
B. Sept. 9, 1960, Riverside, Calif.　　BL TR 6'1" 190 lbs.

1984 SEA A	152	567	161	34	3	27	4.8	80	116	97	78	5	.284	.497	0	0	1B-147, DH-7
1985	155	578	166	33	1	18	3.1	78	78	90	71	1	.287	.441	1	1	1B-154
1986	135	479	130	18	1	18	3.8	66	72	76	68	0	.271	.426	4	0	1B-101, DH-32
1987	157	580	171	37	2	29	5.0	86	100	72	84	0	.295	.516	0	0	1B-157
1988	140	478	141	24	1	18	3.8	67	69	95	53	1	.295	.462	1	1	1B-115, DH-25
5 yrs.	739	2682	769	146	8	110	4.1	377	435	430	354	7	.287	.470	6	2	1B-674, DH-64

Butch Davis

DAVIS, WALLACE McARTHUR
B. June 19, 1958, Williamston, N. C.　　BR TR 6' 185 lbs.

1983 KC A	33	122	42	2	6	2	1.6	13	18	4	19	4	.344	.508	0	0	OF-33
1984	41	116	17	3	0	2	1.7	11	12	10	19	4	.147	.224	4	0	OF-35, DH-2
1987 PIT N	7	7	1	1	0	0	0.0	3	0	1	3	0	.143	.286	5	0	
1988 BAL A	13	25	6	1	0	0	0.0	2	0	0	8	1	.240	.280	1	0	OF-10, DH-1
4 yrs.	94	270	66	7	6	4	1.5	29	30	15	49	9	.244	.359	10	0	OF-78, DH-3

Chili Davis

DAVIS, CHARLES THEODORE
B. Jan. 17, 1960, Kingston, Jamaica　　BB TR 6'3" 195 lbs.

1981 SF N	8	15	2	0	0	0	0.0	1	0	1	2	2	.133	.133	3	1	OF-6
1982	154	641	167	27	6	19	3.0	86	76	45	115	24	.261	.410	1	1	OF-153
1983	137	486	113	21	2	11	2.3	54	59	55	108	10	.233	.352	4	1	OF-133
1984	137	499	157	21	6	21	4.2	87	81	42	74	12	.315	.507	15	6	OF-123
1985	136	481	130	25	2	13	2.7	53	56	62	74	15	.270	.412	9	2	OF-126
1986	153	526	146	28	3	13	2.5	71	70	84	96	16	.278	.416	7	1	OF-148
1987	149	500	125	22	1	24	4.8	80	76	72	109	16	.250	.442	20	3	OF-135
1988 CAL A	158	600	161	29	3	21	3.5	81	93	56	118	9	.268	.432	1	0	OF-153, DH-3
8 yrs.	1032	3748	1001	173	23	122	3.3	513	511	417	696	104	.267	.423	60	15	OF-977, DH-3

LEAGUE CHAMPIONSHIP SERIES
| 1987 SF N | 6 | 20 | 3 | 1 | 0 | 0 | 0.0 | 2 | 0 | 1 | 4 | 0 | .150 | .200 | 0 | 0 | OF-6 |

Doug Davis

DAVIS, DOUGLAS RAYMOND
B. Sept. 24, 1962, Bloomsburg, Pa.　　BR TR 6' 180 lbs.

| 1988 CAL A | 6 | 12 | 0 | 0 | 0 | 0 | 0.0 | 1 | 0 | 0 | 3 | 0 | .000 | .000 | 0 | 0 | 3B-3, C-3 |

Eric Davis

DAVIS, ERIC KEITH
B. May 29, 1962, Los Angeles, Calif.　　BR TR 6'3" 175 lbs.

1984 CIN N	57	174	39	10	1	10	5.7	33	30	24	48	10	.224	.466	6	1	OF-51
1985	56	122	30	3	3	8	6.6	26	18	7	39	16	.246	.516	8	1	OF-47
1986	132	415	115	15	3	27	6.5	97	71	68	100	80	.277	.523	4	0	OF-121
1987	129	474	139	23	4	37	7.8	120	100	84	134	50	.293	.593	1	0	OF-128
1988	135	472	129	18	3	26	5.5	81	93	65	124	35	.273	.489	3	1	OF-130
5 yrs.	509	1657	452	69	14	108	6.5	357	312	248	445	191	.273	.527	22	3	OF-477

	G	AB	H	2B	3B	HR	HR %	R	RBI	BB	SO	SB	BA	SA	Pinch Hit AB	Pinch Hit H	G by POS

Glenn Davis

DAVIS, GLENN EARLE
B. Mar. 28, 1961, Jacksonville, Fla.   BR TR 6'3"   205 lbs.

	G	AB	H	2B	3B	HR	HR %	R	RBI	BB	SO	SB	BA	SA	PH AB	PH H	G by POS
1984 **HOU N**	18	61	13	5	0	2	3.3	6	8	4	12	0	.213	.393	2	0	1B-16
1985	100	350	95	11	0	20	5.7	51	64	27	68	0	.271	.474	4	1	1B-89, OF-9
1986	158	574	152	32	3	31	5.4	91	101	64	72	3	.265	.493	2	0	1B-156
1987	151	578	145	35	2	27	4.7	70	93	47	84	4	.251	.458	1	0	1B-151
1988	152	561	152	26	0	30	5.3	78	99	53	77	4	.271	.478	2	0	1B-151
5 yrs.	579	2124	557	109	5	110	5.2	296	365	195	313	11	.262	.474	11	1	1B-563, OF-9

LEAGUE CHAMPIONSHIP SERIES

	G	AB	H	2B	3B	HR	HR %	R	RBI	BB	SO	SB	BA	SA	PH AB	PH H	G by POS
1986 **HOU N**	6	26	7	1	0	1	3.8	3	3	1	3	0	.269	.423	0	0	1B-6

Jody Davis

DAVIS, JODY RICHARD
B. Nov. 12, 1956, Gainesville, Ga.   BR TR 6'4"   192 lbs.

	G	AB	H	2B	3B	HR	HR %	R	RBI	BB	SO	SB	BA	SA	PH AB	PH H	G by POS
1981 **CHI N**	56	180	46	5	1	4	2.2	14	21	21	28	0	.256	.361	0	0	C-56
1982	130	418	109	20	2	12	2.9	41	52	36	92	0	.261	.404	1	0	C-129
1983	151	510	138	31	2	24	4.7	56	84	33	93	0	.271	.480	2	0	C-150
1984	150	523	134	24	2	19	3.6	55	94	47	99	5	.256	.419	4	1	C-146
1985	142	482	112	30	0	17	3.5	47	58	48	83	1	.232	.400	11	2	C-138
1986	148	528	132	27	2	21	4.0	61	74	41	110	0	.250	.428	4	0	C-145, 1B-1
1987	125	428	106	12	2	19	4.4	57	51	52	91	1	.248	.418	3	0	C-123
1988 **2 teams**	CHI	N (88G –	.229)		ATL	N (2G –	.250)										
" total	90	257	59	9	0	7	2.7	21	36	29	52	0	.230	.346	13	1	C-76
8 yrs.	992	3326	836	158	11	123	3.7	352	470	307	648	7	.251	.416	38	4	C-963, 1B-1

LEAGUE CHAMPIONSHIP SERIES

	G	AB	H	2B	3B	HR	HR %	R	RBI	BB	SO	SB	BA	SA	PH AB	PH H	G by POS
1984 **CHI N**	5	18	7	2	0	2	11.1	3	6	0	3	0	.389	.833	0	0	C-5

Mike Davis

DAVIS, MICHAEL DWAYNE
B. June 11, 1959, San Diego, Calif.   BL TL 6'2"   175 lbs.

	G	AB	H	2B	3B	HR	HR %	R	RBI	BB	SO	SB	BA	SA	PH AB	PH H	G by POS
1980 **OAK A**	51	95	20	2	1	1	1.1	11	8	7	14	2	.211	.284	22	4	OF-18, 1B-7, DH-6
1981	17	20	1	1	0	0	0.0	0	0	2	4	0	.050	.100	10	0	DH-3, OF-2, 1B-1
1982	23	75	30	4	0	1	1.3	12	10	2	8	3	.400	.493	4	1	OF-13, 1B-7
1983	128	443	122	24	4	8	1.8	61	62	27	74	32	.275	.402	6	3	OF-121, DH-3
1984	134	382	88	18	3	9	2.4	47	46	31	66	14	.230	.364	6	2	OF-127, DH-4
1985	154	547	157	34	1	24	4.4	92	82	50	99	24	.287	.484	3	0	OF-151
1986	142	489	131	28	3	19	3.9	77	55	34	91	27	.268	.454	7	2	OF-139
1987	139	494	131	32	1	22	4.5	69	72	42	94	19	.265	.468	11	2	OF-124, DH-14
1988 **LA N**	108	281	55	11	2	2	0.7	29	17	25	59	7	.196	.270	30	5	OF-76
9 yrs.	896	2826	735	154	15	86	3.0	398	352	220	509	128	.260	.416	99	19	OF-771, DH-30, 1B-15

LEAGUE CHAMPIONSHIP SERIES

	G	AB	H	2B	3B	HR	HR %	R	RBI	BB	SO	SB	BA	SA	PH AB	PH H	G by POS
1981 **OAK A**	1	1	1	0	0	0	0.0	0	0	0	0	0	1.000	1.000	1	1	
1988 **LA N**	4	2	0	0	0	0	0.0	0	0	0	1	0	.000	.000	2	0	
2 yrs.	5	3	1	0	0	0	0.0	0	0	0	1	0	.333	.333	3	1	

WORLD SERIES

	G	AB	H	2B	3B	HR	HR %	R	RBI	BB	SO	SB	BA	SA	PH AB	PH H	G by POS
1988 **LA N**	4	7	1	0	0	1	14.3	3	2	4	0	2	.143	.571	0	0	OF-1

Andre Dawson

DAWSON, ANDRE FERNANDO (Hawk)
B. July 10, 1954, Miami, Fla.   BR TR 6'3"   180 lbs.

	G	AB	H	2B	3B	HR	HR %	R	RBI	BB	SO	SB	BA	SA	PH AB	PH H	G by POS
1976 **MON N**	24	85	20	4	1	0	0.0	9	7	5	13	1	.235	.306	0	0	OF-24
1977	139	525	148	26	9	19	3.6	64	65	34	93	21	.282	.474	5	0	OF-136
1978	157	609	154	24	8	25	4.1	84	72	30	128	28	.253	.442	5	2	OF-153
1979	155	639	176	24	12	25	3.9	90	92	27	115	35	.275	.468	0	0	OF-153
1980	151	577	178	41	7	17	2.9	96	87	44	69	34	.308	.492	3	1	OF-147
1981	103	394	119	21	3	24	6.1	71	64	35	50	26	.302	.553	0	0	OF-103
1982	148	608	183	37	7	23	3.8	107	83	34	96	39	.301	.498	0	0	OF-147
1983	159	633	189	36	10	32	5.1	104	113	38	81	25	.299	.539	1	1	OF-157
1984	138	533	132	23	6	17	3.2	73	86	41	80	13	.248	.409	4	0	OF-134
1985	139	529	135	27	2	23	4.3	65	91	29	92	13	.255	.444	9	3	OF-131
1986	130	496	141	32	2	20	4.0	65	78	37	79	18	.284	.478	3	1	OF-127
1987 **CHI N**	153	621	178	24	2	49	7.9	90	137	32	103	11	.287	.568	2	1	OF-152
1988	157	591	179	31	8	24	4.1	78	79	37	73	12	.303	.504	8	2	OF-147
13 yrs.	1753	6840	1932	350	77	298	4.4	996	1054	423	1072	276	.282	.487	40	11	OF-1711

DIVISIONAL PLAYOFF SERIES

	G	AB	H	2B	3B	HR	HR %	R	RBI	BB	SO	SB	BA	SA	PH AB	PH H	G by POS
1981 **MON N**	5	20	6	0	1	0	0.0	1	0	1	6	2	.300	.400	0	0	OF-5

LEAGUE CHAMPIONSHIP SERIES

	G	AB	H	2B	3B	HR	HR %	R	RBI	BB	SO	SB	BA	SA	PH AB	PH H	G by POS
1981 **MON N**	5	20	3	0	0	0	0.0	2	0	0	4	0	.150	.150	0	0	OF-5

Rob Deer

DEER, ROBERT GEORGE
B. Sept. 29, 1960, Orange, Calif.   BR TR 6'3"   215 lbs.

	G	AB	H	2B	3B	HR	HR %	R	RBI	BB	SO	SB	BA	SA	PH AB	PH H	G by POS
1984 **SF N**	13	24	4	0	0	3	12.5	5	3	7	10	1	.167	.542	3	0	OF-9
1985	78	162	30	5	1	8	4.9	22	20	23	71	0	.185	.377	30	5	OF-37, 1B-10
1986 **MIL A**	134	466	108	17	3	33	7.1	75	86	72	179	5	.232	.494	1	1	OF-131, 1B-4
1987	134	474	113	15	2	28	5.9	71	80	86	186	12	.238	.494	2	0	OF-135, DH-4
1988	135	492	124	24	0	23	4.7	71	85	51	153	9	.252	.441	1	0	OF-133, DH-1
5 yrs.	494	1618	379	61	6	95	5.9	244	274	239	599	27	.234	.456	37	6	OF-445, 1B-14, DH-5

Ivan DeJesus

DeJESUS, IVAN ALVAREZ
Born Ivan DeJesus y Alvarez.
B. Jan. 9, 1953, Santurce, Puerto Rico   BR TR 5'11"   175 lbs.

	G	AB	H	2B	3B	HR	HR %	R	RBI	BB	SO	SB	BA	SA	PH AB	PH H	G by POS
1974 **LA N**	3	3	1	0	0	0	0.0	1	0	0	2	0	.333	.333	1	0	SS-2
1975	63	87	16	2	1	0	0.0	10	2	11	15	1	.184	.230	2	0	SS-63
1976	22	41	7	2	1	0	0.0	4	2	4	9	0	.171	.268	1	0	SS-13, 3B-7
1977 **CHI N**	155	624	166	31	7	3	0.5	91	40	56	90	24	.266	.353	0	0	SS-154
1978	160	619	172	24	7	3	0.5	104	35	74	78	41	.278	.354	0	0	SS-160
1979	160	636	180	26	10	5	0.8	92	52	59	82	24	.283	.379	0	0	SS-160
1980	157	618	160	26	3	3	0.5	78	33	60	81	44	.259	.325	0	0	SS-156

	G	AB	H	2B	3B	HR	HR %	R	RBI	BB	SO	SB	BA	SA	Pinch Hit AB	Pinch Hit H	G by POS

Ivan DeJesus continued

	G	AB	H	2B	3B	HR	HR %	R	RBI	BB	SO	SB	BA	SA	AB	H	G by POS
1981	106	403	78	8	4	0	0.0	49	13	46	61	21	.194	.233	0	0	SS-106
1982 **PHI** **N**	161	536	128	21	5	3	0.6	53	59	54	70	14	.239	.313	0	0	SS-154, 3B-7
1983	158	497	126	15	7	4	0.8	60	45	53	77	11	.254	.336	0	0	SS-158
1984	144	435	112	15	3	0	0.0	40	35	43	76	12	.257	.306	2	0	SS-141
1985 **STL** **N**	59	72	16	5	0	0	0.0	11	7	4	16	2	.222	.292	24	6	3B-20, SS-13
1986 **NY** **A**	7	4	0	0	0	0	0.0	1	0	1	1	0	.000	.000	0	0	SS-7
1987 **SF** **N**	9	10	2	0	0	0	0.0	0	1	0	2	0	.200	.200	1	0	SS-9
1988 **DET** **A**	7	17	3	0	0	0	0.0	1	0	1	4	0	.176	.176	0	0	SS-7
15 yrs.	1371	4602	1167	175	48	21	0.5	595	324	466	664	194	.254	.326	31	6	SS-1303, 3B-34

LEAGUE CHAMPIONSHIP SERIES

	G	AB	H	2B	3B	HR	HR %	R	RBI	BB	SO	SB	BA	SA	AB	H	G by POS
1983 **PHI** **N**	4	12	3	0	0	0	0.0	0	1	3	3	0	.250	.250	0	0	SS-4

WORLD SERIES

	G	AB	H	2B	3B	HR	HR %	R	RBI	BB	SO	SB	BA	SA	AB	H	G by POS
1983 **PHI** **N**	5	16	2	0	0	0	0.0	0	0	1	2	0	.125	.125	0	0	SS-5
1985 **STL** **N**	1	1	0	0	0	0	0.0	0	0	0	0	0	.000	.000	1	0	
2 yrs.	6	17	2	0	0	0	0.0	0	0	1	2	0	.118	.118	1	0	SS-5

Luis De Los Santos

DE LOS SANTOS, LUIS MANUEL
B. Dec. 29, 1966, San Cristobal, Dominican Republic

BR TR 6'5" 190 lbs.

	G	AB	H	2B	3B	HR	HR %	R	RBI	BB	SO	SB	BA	SA	AB	H	G by POS
1988 **KC** **A**	11	22	2	1	1	0	0.0	1	4	4	0	.091	.227	2	0	1B-5, DH-3

Rick Dempsey

DEMPSEY, JOHN RIKARD
B. Sept. 13, 1949, Fayetteville, Tenn.

BR TR 6' 180 lbs.

	G	AB	H	2B	3B	HR	HR %	R	RBI	BB	SO	SB	BA	SA	AB	H	G by POS
1969 **MIN** **A**	5	6	3	1	0	0	0.0	1	0	1	1	0	.500	.667	1	0	C-3
1970	5	7	0	0	0	0	0.0	1	0	1	1	0	.000	.000	1	0	C-3
1971	6	13	4	1	0	0	0.0	2	0	1	1	0	.308	.385	0	0	C-6
1972	25	40	8	1	0	0	0.0	0	0	6	8	0	.200	.225	2	1	C-23
1973 **NY** **A**	6	11	2	0	0	0	0.0	0	0	1	3	0	.182	.182	0	0	C-5
1974	43	109	26	3	0	2	1.8	12	12	8	7	1	.239	.321	12	2	C-31, OF-2, DH-1
1975	71	145	38	8	0	1	0.7	18	11	21	15	0	.262	.338	23	5	C-19, DH-18, OF-8, 3B-1
1976 2 teams	**NY**	**A** (21G –	.119)		**BAL**	**A** (59G –	.213)										
" total	80	216	42	2	0	0	0.0	12	12	18	21	1	.194	.204	6	1	C-67, OF-7
1977 **BAL** **A**	91	270	61	7	4	3	1.1	27	34	34	34	2	.226	.315	1	1	C-91
1978	136	441	114	25	0	6	1.4	41	32	48	54	7	.259	.356	4	1	C-135
1979	124	368	88	23	0	6	1.6	48	41	38	37	0	.239	.351	39	11	C-112, OF-6, 1B-2, DH-1
1980	119	362	95	26	3	9	2.5	51	40	36	45	3	.262	.425	9	1	C-112, OF-6, 1B-2, DH-1
1981	92	251	54	10	1	6	2.4	24	15	32	36	0	.215	.335	7	0	C-90, DH-1
1982	125	344	88	15	1	5	1.5	35	36	46	37	0	.256	.349	8	3	C-124, DH-1
1983	128	347	80	16	2	4	1.2	33	32	40	54	1	.231	.323	7	0	C-128
1984	109	330	76	11	0	11	3.3	37	34	40	58	1	.230	.364	0	0	C-108
1985	132	362	92	19	0	12	3.3	54	52	50	87	0	.254	.406	6	1	C-131
1986	122	327	68	15	1	13	4.0	42	29	45	78	1	.208	.379	9	1	C-121
1987 **CLE** **A**	60	141	25	10	0	1	0.7	16	9	23	29	0	.177	.270	2	1	C-59
1988 **LA** **N**	77	167	42	13	0	7	4.2	25	30	25	44	1	.251	.455	8	1	C-74
20 yrs.	1556	4257	1006	206	12	86	2.0	479	419	514	649	18	.236	.351	145	30	C-1454, OF-23, DH-22, 1B-2, 3B-1

LEAGUE CHAMPIONSHIP SERIES

	G	AB	H	2B	3B	HR	HR %	R	RBI	BB	SO	SB	BA	SA	AB	H	G by POS
1979 **BAL** **A**	3	10	4	2	0	0	0.0	3	2	1	0	1	.400	.600	0	0	C-3
1983	4	12	2	0	0	0	0.0	1	0	1	1	0	.167	.167	0	0	C-4
1988 **LA** **N**	4	5	2	2	0	0	0.0	1	2	1	0	0	.400	.800	1	0	C-3
3 yrs.	11	27	8	4	0	0	0.0	5	4	3	1	1	.296	.444	1	0	C-10

WORLD SERIES

	G	AB	H	2B	3B	HR	HR %	R	RBI	BB	SO	SB	BA	SA	AB	H	G by POS
1979 **BAL** **A**	7	21	6	2	0	0	0.0	3	0	1	3	0	.286	.381	0	0	C-6
1983	5	13	5	4	0	1	7.7	3	2	2	2	0	.385	.923	0	0	C-5
1988 **LA** **N**	2	5	1	1	0	0	0.0	0	1	1	2	0	.200	.400	0	0	C-2
3 yrs.	14	39	12	7	0	1	2.6	6	3	4	7	0	.308	.564	0	0	C-13
				9th													

Bob Dernier

DERNIER, ROBERT EUGENE
B. Jan. 5, 1957, Kansas City, Mo.

BR TR 6' 160 lbs.

	G	AB	H	2B	3B	HR	HR %	R	RBI	BB	SO	SB	BA	SA	AB	H	G by POS
1980 **PHI** **N**	10	7	4	0	0	0	0.0	5	1	1	0	3	.571	.571	0	0	OF-3
1981	10	4	3	0	0	0	0.0	0	0	0	2	0	.750	.750	0	0	OF-5
1982	122	370	92	10	2	4	1.1	56	21	36	69	42	.249	.319	1	0	OF-119
1983	122	221	51	10	0	1	0.5	41	15	18	21	35	.231	.290	3	0	OF-107
1984 **CHI** **N**	143	536	149	26	5	3	0.6	94	32	63	60	45	.278	.362	2	0	OF-140
1985	121	469	119	20	3	1	0.2	63	21	40	44	31	.254	.316	4	0	OF-116
1986	108	324	73	14	1	4	1.2	32	18	22	41	27	.225	.312	2	2	OF-105
1987	93	199	63	4	4	8	4.0	38	21	19	19	16	.317	.497	31	7	OF-71
1988 **PHI** **N**	68	166	48	3	1	1	0.6	19	10	9	19	13	.289	.337	12	5	OF-54
9 yrs.	797	2296	602	87	16	22	1.0	348	139	208	273	214	.262	.343	55	14	OF-720

LEAGUE CHAMPIONSHIP SERIES

	G	AB	H	2B	3B	HR	HR %	R	RBI	BB	SO	SB	BA	SA	AB	H	G by POS
1983 **PHI** **N**	1	0	0	0	0	0	–	0	0	0	0	0	–	–	0	0	OF-1
1984 **CHI** **N**	5	17	4	2	0	1	5.9	5	1	5	4	2	.235	.529	0	0	OF-5
2 yrs.	6	17	4	2	0	1	5.9	5	1	5	4	2	.235	.529	0	0	OF-6

WORLD SERIES

	G	AB	H	2B	3B	HR	HR %	R	RBI	BB	SO	SB	BA	SA	AB	H	G by POS
1983 **PHI** **N**	1	0	0	0	0	0	–	1	0	0	0	0	–	–	0	0	

Orestes Destrade

DESTRADE, ORESTES
Born Orestes Destrade y Cucuas.
B. May 8, 1962, Santiago, Cuba

BB TR 6'4" 210 lbs.

	G	AB	H	2B	3B	HR	HR %	R	RBI	BB	SO	SB	BA	SA	AB	H	G by POS
1987 **NY** **A**	9	19	5	0	0	0	0.0	5	1	5	5	0	.263	.263	4	0	1B-3, DH-2
1988 **PIT** **N**	36	47	7	1	0	1	2.1	2	3	5	17	0	.149	.234	24	4	1B-8
2 yrs.	45	66	12	1	0	1	1.5	7	4	10	22	0	.182	.242	28	4	1B-11, DH-2

	G	AB	H	2B	3B	HR	HR %	R	RBI	BB	SO	SB	BA	SA	Pinch Hit AB	Pinch Hit H	G by POS

Mike Devereaux

DEVEREAUX, MICHAEL
B. Apr. 10, 1963, Casper, Wyo.
BR TR 6' 195 lbs.

	G	AB	H	2B	3B	HR	HR %	R	RBI	BB	SO	SB	BA	SA	PH AB	PH H	G by POS
1987 LA N	19	54	12	3	0	0	0.0	7	4	3	10	3	.222	.278	5	0	OF-18
1988	30	43	5	1	0	0	0.0	4	2	2	10	0	.116	.140	7	1	OF-26
2 yrs.	49	97	17	4	0	0	0.0	11	6	5	20	3	.175	.216	12	1	OF-44

Bo Diaz

DIAZ, BAUDILIO JOSE
Born Baudilio Jose Diaz y Seijas.
B. Mar. 23, 1953, Cua, Venezuela
BR TR 5'11" 185 lbs.

	G	AB	H	2B	3B	HR	HR %	R	RBI	BB	SO	SB	BA	SA	PH AB	PH H	G by POS
1977 BOS A	2	1	0	0	0	0	0.0	0	0	0	1	0	.000	.000	1	0	C-2
1978 CLE A	44	127	30	4	0	2	1.6	12	11	4	17	0	.236	.315	0	0	C-44
1979	15	32	5	2	0	0	0.0	0	1	2	6	0	.156	.219	0	0	C-15
1980	76	207	47	11	2	3	1.4	15	32	7	27	1	.227	.343	9	2	C-75
1981	63	182	57	19	0	7	3.8	25	38	13	23	2	.313	.533	12	3	C-51, DH-3
1982 PHI N	144	525	151	29	1	18	3.4	69	85	36	87	3	.288	.450	2	1	C-144
1983	136	471	111	17	0	15	3.2	49	64	38	57	1	.236	.367	4	2	C-134
1984	27	75	16	4	0	1	1.3	5	9	5	13	0	.213	.307	4	0	C-23
1985 2 teams		PHI	N (26G –	.211)		CIN	N (51G –	.261)									
" total	77	237	58	13	1	5	2.1	21	31	21	25	0	.245	.371	3	0	C-75
1986 CIN N	134	474	129	21	0	10	2.1	50	56	40	52	1	.272	.380	3	0	C-134
1987	140	496	134	28	1	15	3.0	49	82	19	73	1	.270	.421	2	0	C-137
1988	92	315	69	9	0	10	3.2	26	35	7	41	0	.219	.343	7	0	C-88
12 yrs.	950	3142	807	157	5	86	2.7	321	444	192	422	9	.257	.392	44	8	C-922, DH-3

LEAGUE CHAMPIONSHIP SERIES

	G	AB	H	2B	3B	HR	HR %	R	RBI	BB	SO	SB	BA	SA	PH AB	PH H	G by POS
1983 PHI N	4	13	2	1	0	0	0.0	0	0	2	1	0	.154	.231	0	0	C-4

WORLD SERIES

	G	AB	H	2B	3B	HR	HR %	R	RBI	BB	SO	SB	BA	SA	PH AB	PH H	G by POS
1983 PHI N	5	15	5	1	0	0	0.0	1	0	1	2	0	.333	.400	0	0	C-5

Mario Diaz

DIAZ, MARIO RAFAEL
Born Mario Rafael Diaz y Torres.
B. Jan. 10, 1962, Humacao, Puerto Rico
BR TR 5'10" 145 lbs.

	G	AB	H	2B	3B	HR	HR %	R	RBI	BB	SO	SB	BA	SA	PH AB	PH H	G by POS
1987 SEA A	11	23	7	0	1	0	0.0	4	3	0	4	0	.304	.391	1	0	SS-10
1988	28	72	22	5	0	0	0.0	6	9	3	5	0	.306	.375	3	1	SS-21, 2B-4, 3B-1, 1B-1
2 yrs.	39	95	29	5	1	0	0.0	10	12	3	9	0	.305	.379	4	1	SS-31, 2B-4, 3B-1, 1B-1

Mike Diaz

DIAZ, MICHAEL ANTHONY
B. Apr. 15, 1960, San Francisco, Calif.
BR TR 6'2" 205 lbs.

	G	AB	H	2B	3B	HR	HR %	R	RBI	BB	SO	SB	BA	SA	PH AB	PH H	G by POS
1983 CHI N	6	7	2	1	0	0	0.0	2	1	0	0	0	.286	.429	3	1	C-3
1986 PIT N	97	209	56	9	0	12	5.7	22	36	19	43	0	.268	.483	33	11	OF-38, 1B-20, 3B-5, C-1
1987	103	241	58	8	2	16	6.6	28	48	31	42	1	.241	.490	32	7	OF-37, 1B-32, C-8
1988 2 teams		PIT	N (47G –	.230)		CHI	A (40G –	.237)									
" total	87	226	53	9	0	3	1.3	18	17	21	43	0	.235	.314	18	2	1B-45, OF-19, DH-1, C-1
4 yrs.	293	683	169	27	2	31	4.5	70	102	71	128	1	.247	.429	86	21	1B-97, OF-94, C-13, 3B-5, DH-1

Benny Distefano

DISTEFANO, BENITO JAMES
B. Jan. 23, 1962, Brooklyn, N. Y.
BL TL 6'1" 195 lbs.

	G	AB	H	2B	3B	HR	HR %	R	RBI	BB	SO	SB	BA	SA	PH AB	PH H	G by POS
1984 PIT N	45	78	13	1	2	3	3.8	10	9	5	13	0	.167	.346	14	2	OF-20, 1B-17
1986	31	39	7	1	0	1	2.6	3	5	1	5	0	.179	.282	20	3	OF-9, 1B-1
1988	16	29	10	3	1	1	3.4	6	6	3	4	0	.345	.621	8	3	1B-5, OF-2
3 yrs.	92	146	30	5	3	5	3.4	19	20	9	22	0	.205	.384	42	8	OF-31, 1B-23

Pat Dodson

DODSON, PATRICK NEAL
B. Oct. 11, 1959, Santa Monica, Calif.
BL TL 6'4" 210 lbs.

	G	AB	H	2B	3B	HR	HR %	R	RBI	BB	SO	SB	BA	SA	PH AB	PH H	G by POS
1986 BOS A	9	12	5	2	0	1	8.3	3	3	3	3	0	.417	.833	2	1	1B-7
1987	26	42	7	3	0	2	4.8	4	6	8	13	0	.167	.381	3	1	1B-21, DH-1
1988	17	45	8	3	1	1	2.2	5	1	6	17	0	.178	.356	2	0	1B-17
3 yrs.	52	99	20	8	1	4	4.0	12	10	17	33	0	.202	.424	7	2	1B-45, DH-1

Bill Doran

DORAN, WILLIAM DONALD
B. May 28, 1958, Cincinnati, Ohio
BB TR 6' 175 lbs.

	G	AB	H	2B	3B	HR	HR %	R	RBI	BB	SO	SB	BA	SA	PH AB	PH H	G by POS
1982 HOU N	26	97	27	3	0	0	0.0	11	6	4	11	5	.278	.309	0	0	2B-26
1983	154	535	145	12	7	8	1.5	70	39	86	67	12	.271	.364	3	1	2B-153
1984	147	548	143	18	11	4	0.7	92	41	66	69	21	.261	.356	2	0	2B-139, SS-13
1985	148	578	166	31	6	14	2.4	84	59	71	69	23	.287	.434	2	1	2B-147
1986	145	550	152	29	3	6	1.1	92	37	81	57	42	.276	.373	1	0	2B-144
1987	162	625	177	23	3	16	2.6	82	79	82	64	31	.283	.406	0	0	2B-162, SS-3
1988	132	480	119	18	1	7	1.5	66	53	65	60	17	.248	.333	2	1	2B-130
7 yrs.	914	3413	929	134	31	55	1.6	497	314	455	397	151	.272	.378	10	3	2B-901, SS-16

LEAGUE CHAMPIONSHIP SERIES

	G	AB	H	2B	3B	HR	HR %	R	RBI	BB	SO	SB	BA	SA	PH AB	PH H	G by POS
1986 HOU N	6	27	6	0	0	1	3.7	3	3	2	2	2	.222	.333	0	0	2B-6

Brian Dorsett

DORSETT, BRIAN RICHARD
B. Apr. 9, 1961, Terre Haute, Ind.
BR TR 6'3" 215 lbs.

	G	AB	H	2B	3B	HR	HR %	R	RBI	BB	SO	SB	BA	SA	PH AB	PH H	G by POS
1987 CLE A	5	11	3	0	0	1	9.1	2	3	0	3	0	.273	.545	2	1	C-4
1988 CAL A	7	11	1	0	0	0	0.0	0	2	1	5	0	.091	.091	0	0	C-7
2 yrs.	12	22	4	0	0	1	4.5	2	5	1	8	0	.182	.318	2	1	C-11

Brian Downing

DOWNING, BRIAN JAY
B. Oct. 9, 1950, Los Angeles, Calif.
BR TR 5'10" 170 lbs.

	G	AB	H	2B	3B	HR	HR %	R	RBI	BB	SO	SB	BA	SA	PH AB	PH H	G by POS
1973 CHI A	34	73	13	1	0	2	2.7	4	4	10	17	0	.178	.274	8	2	OF-13, C-11, 3B-8
1974	108	293	66	12	1	10	3.4	41	39	51	72	0	.225	.375	5	0	C-63, OF-39, DH-9
1975	138	420	101	12	1	7	1.7	58	41	76	75	13	.240	.324	0	0	C-137, DH-1
1976	104	317	81	14	0	3	0.9	38	30	40	55	7	.256	.328	3	1	C-93, DH-11
1977	69	169	48	4	2	4	2.4	28	25	34	21	1	.284	.402	3	1	C-61, OF-3, DH-2
1978 CAL A	133	412	105	15	0	7	1.7	42	46	52	47	3	.255	.342	3	1	C-128, DH-2

	G	AB	H	2B	3B	HR	HR %	R	RBI	BB	SO	SB	BA	SA	Pinch Hit AB	Pinch Hit H	G by POS

Brian Downing continued

	G	AB	H	2B	3B	HR	HR%	R	RBI	BB	SO	SB	BA	SA	AB	H	G by POS
1979	148	509	166	27	3	12	2.4	87	75	77	57	3	.326	.462	3	1	C-129, DH-18
1980	30	93	27	6	0	2	2.2	5	25	12	12	0	.290	.419	2	0	C-16, DH-13
1981	93	317	79	14	0	9	2.8	47	41	46	35	1	.249	.379	2	0	OF-56, C-37, DH-5
1982	158	623	175	37	2	28	4.5	109	84	86	58	2	.281	.482	1	0	OF-158
1983	113	403	99	15	1	19	4.7	68	53	62	59	1	.246	.429	3	1	OF-84, DH-26
1984	156	539	148	28	2	23	4.3	66	91	70	66	0	.275	.462	3	1	OF-131, DH-21
1985	150	520	137	23	1	20	3.8	80	85	78	60	5	.263	.427	7	0	OF-121, DH-25
1986	152	513	137	27	4	20	3.9	90	95	90	84	4	.267	.452	8	0	OF-138, DH-10
1987	155	567	154	29	3	29	5.1	110	77	106	85	5	.272	.487	4	0	DH-118, OF-34
1988	135	484	117	18	2	25	5.2	80	64	81	63	3	.242	.442	3	1	DH-132
16 yrs.	1876	6252	1653	282	22	220	3.5	953	875	971	866	48	.264	.422	58	9	OF-777, C-675, DH-393, 3B-8

LEAGUE CHAMPIONSHIP SERIES

	G	AB	H	2B	3B	HR	HR%	R	RBI	BB	SO	SB	BA	SA	AB	H	G by POS
1979 CAL A	4	15	3	0	0	0	0.0	1	1	1	1	0	.200	.200	0	0	C-4
1982	5	19	3	1	0	0	0.0	4	0	3	2	0	.158	.211	0	0	OF-5
1986	7	27	6	0	0	1	3.7	2	7	4	5	0	.222	.333	0	0	OF-7
3 yrs.	16	61	12	1	0	1	1.6	7	8	8	8	0	.197	.262	0	0	OF-12, C-4

Cameron Drew

DREW, CAMERON STEWARD
B. Feb. 12, 1964, Boston, Mass.

BL TR 6'5"   215 lbs.

	G	AB	H	2B	3B	HR	HR%	R	RBI	BB	SO	SB	BA	SA	AB	H	G by POS
1988 HOU N	7	16	3	0	1	0	0.0	1	1	0	1	0	.188	.313	2	0	OF-5

Rob Ducey

DUCEY, ROBERT THOMAS
B. May 24, 1965, Toronto, Ontario, Canada

BL TR 6'2"   175 lbs.

	G	AB	H	2B	3B	HR	HR%	R	RBI	BB	SO	SB	BA	SA	AB	H	G by POS
1987 TOR A	34	48	9	1	0	1	2.1	12	6	8	10	2	.188	.271	3	1	OF-28
1988	27	54	17	4	1	0	0.0	15	6	5	7	1	.315	.426	0	0	OF-26
2 yrs.	61	102	26	5	1	1	1.0	27	12	13	17	3	.255	.353	3	1	OF-54

Shawon Dunston

DUNSTON, SHAWON DONNELL (Thunder Pup)
B. Mar. 21, 1963, Brooklyn, N. Y.

BR TR 6'1"   175 lbs.

	G	AB	H	2B	3B	HR	HR%	R	RBI	BB	SO	SB	BA	SA	AB	H	G by POS
1985 CHI N	74	250	65	12	4	4	1.6	40	18	19	42	11	.260	.388	0	0	SS-73
1986	150	581	145	36	3	17	2.9	66	68	21	114	13	.250	.410	2	1	SS-149
1987	95	346	85	18	3	5	1.4	40	22	10	68	12	.246	.358	1	0	SS-94
1988	155	575	143	23	6	9	1.6	69	56	16	108	30	.249	.357	3	0	SS-151
4 yrs.	474	1752	438	89	16	35	2.0	215	164	66	332	66	.250	.379	6	1	SS-467

Leon Durham

DURHAM, LEON (Bull)
B. July 31, 1957, Cincinnati, Ohio

BL TL 6'1"   185 lbs.

	G	AB	H	2B	3B	HR	HR%	R	RBI	BB	SO	SB	BA	SA	AB	H	G by POS
1980 STL N	96	303	82	15	4	8	2.6	42	42	18	55	8	.271	.426	16	5	OF-78, 1B-8
1981 CHI N	87	328	95	14	6	10	3.0	42	35	27	53	25	.290	.460	3	1	OF-83, 1B-3
1982	148	539	168	33	7	22	4.1	84	90	66	77	28	.312	.521	5	2	OF-143, 1B-1
1983	100	337	87	18	8	12	3.6	58	55	66	83	12	.258	.466	1	0	OF-95, 1B-6
1984	137	473	132	30	4	23	4.9	86	96	69	86	16	.279	.505	8	2	1B-130
1985	153	542	153	32	2	21	3.9	58	75	64	99	7	.282	.465	2	0	1B-151
1986	141	484	127	18	7	20	4.1	66	65	67	98	8	.262	.452	2	0	1B-141
1987	131	439	120	22	1	27	6.2	70	63	51	92	2	.273	.513	8	2	1B-123
1988 2 teams				CHI	N	(24G –	.219)		CIN	N	(21G –	.216)					
" total	45	124	27	9	1	4	3.2	14	8	14	32	0	.218	.403	8	0	1B-37
9 yrs.	1038	3569	991	191	40	147	4.1	520	529	442	675	106	.278	.477	53	12	1B-600, OF-399

LEAGUE CHAMPIONSHIP SERIES

	G	AB	H	2B	3B	HR	HR%	R	RBI	BB	SO	SB	BA	SA	AB	H	G by POS
1984 CHI N	5	20	3	0	0	2	10.0	2	4	1	4	0	.150	.450	0	0	1B-5

Jim Dwyer

DWYER, JAMES EDWARD
B. Jan. 3, 1950, Evergreen Park, Ill.

BL TL 5'10"   165 lbs.

	G	AB	H	2B	3B	HR	HR%	R	RBI	BB	SO	SB	BA	SA	AB	H	G by POS
1973 STL N	28	57	11	1	1	0	0.0	7	0	1	5	0	.193	.246	8	1	OF-20
1974	74	86	24	1	0	2	2.3	13	11	11	16	0	.279	.360	41	10	OF-25, 1B-3
1975 2 teams				STL	N	(21G –	.194)		MON	N	(60G –	.286)					
" total	81	206	56	8	1	3	1.5	26	21	27	36	4	.272	.364	21	6	OF-61
1976 2 teams				MON	N	(50G –	.185)		NY	N	(11G –	.154)					
" total	61	105	19	3	1	0	0.0	9	5	13	11	0	.181	.229	38	6	OF-21
1977 STL N	13	31	7	1	0	0	0.0	3	2	4	5	0	.226	.258	2	1	OF-12
1978 2 teams				STL	N	(34G –	.215)		SF	N	(73G –	.225)					
" total	107	238	53	12	2	6	2.5	30	26	37	32	7	.223	.366	24	5	OF-58, 1B-29
1979 BOS A	76	113	30	7	0	2	1.8	19	14	17	9	3	.265	.381	22	7	1B-25, OF-19, DH-4
1980	93	260	74	11	1	9	3.5	41	38	28	23	3	.285	.438	11	2	OF-65, DH-12, 1B-9
1981 BAL A	68	134	30	0	1	3	2.2	16	10	20	19	0	.224	.306	6	0	OF-59, 1B-3, DH-1
1982	71	148	45	4	3	6	4.1	28	15	27	24	2	.304	.493	23	6	OF-49, DH-1, 1B-1
1983	100	196	56	17	1	8	4.1	37	38	31	29	1	.286	.505	33	8	OF-56, 1B-4
1984	76	161	41	9	1	2	1.2	22	21	23	24	0	.255	.360	27	7	OF-52, DH-3
1985	101	233	58	8	3	7	3.0	35	36	37	31	0	.249	.399	26	5	OF-78, DH-3
1986	93	160	39	13	1	8	5.0	18	31	22	31	0	.244	.488	42	9	DH-24, OF-24, 1B-1
1987	92	241	66	7	1	15	6.2	54	33	37	57	4	.274	.498	24	7	DH-41, OF-30
1988 2 teams				BAL	A	(35G –	.226)		MIN	A	(20G –	.293)					
" total	55	94	24	1	0	2	2.1	9	18	25	19	0	.255	.330	24	6	DH-30, OF-2
16 yrs.	1189	2463	633	103	17	73	3.0	367	319	360	371	24	.257	.402	372	86	OF-631, DH-119, 1B-75

LEAGUE CHAMPIONSHIP SERIES

	G	AB	H	2B	3B	HR	HR%	R	RBI	BB	SO	SB	BA	SA	AB	H	G by POS
1983 BAL A	2	4	1	1	0	0	0.0	1	0	1	0	0	.250	.500	1	0	OF-1

WORLD SERIES

	G	AB	H	2B	3B	HR	HR%	R	RBI	BB	SO	SB	BA	SA	AB	H	G by POS
1983 BAL A	2	8	3	1	0	1	12.5	3	1	0	0	0	.375	.875	0	0	OF-2

	G	AB	H	2B	3B	HR	HR %	R	RBI	BB	SO	SB	BA	SA	Pinch Hit AB	Pinch Hit H	G by POS

Len Dykstra

DYKSTRA, LEONARD KYLE (Nails)
B. Feb. 10, 1963, Santa Ana, Calif.
BL TL 5'10" 160 lbs.

	G	AB	H	2B	3B	HR	HR%	R	RBI	BB	SO	SB	BA	SA	PH AB	PH H	G by POS
1985 NY N	83	236	60	9	3	1	0.4	40	19	30	24	15	.254	.331	9	3	OF-74
1986	147	431	127	27	7	8	1.9	77	45	58	55	31	.295	.445	14	4	OF-139
1987	132	431	123	37	3	10	2.3	86	43	40	67	27	.285	.455	18	5	OF-118
1988	126	429	116	19	3	8	1.9	57	33	30	43	30	.270	.385	12	5	OF-112
4 yrs.	488	1527	426	92	16	27	1.8	260	140	158	189	103	.279	.413	53	17	OF-443

LEAGUE CHAMPIONSHIP SERIES

	G	AB	H	2B	3B	HR	HR%	R	RBI	BB	SO	SB	BA	SA	PH AB	PH H	G by POS
1986 NY N	6	23	7	1	1	1	4.3	3	3	2	4	1	.304	.565	2	1	OF-6
1988	7	14	6	3	0	1	7.1	6	3	4	0	0	.429	.857	0	0	OF-7
2 yrs.	13	37	13	4	1	2	5.4	9	6	6	4	1	.351	.676	2	1	OF-13

WORLD SERIES

	G	AB	H	2B	3B	HR	HR%	R	RBI	BB	SO	SB	BA	SA	PH AB	PH H	G by POS
1986 NY N	7	27	8	0	0	2	7.4	4	3	2	7	0	.296	.519	1	1	OF-7

Jim Eisenreich

EISENREICH, JAMES MICHAEL
B. Apr. 18, 1959, St. Cloud, Minn.
BL TL 5'11" 175 lbs.

	G	AB	H	2B	3B	HR	HR%	R	RBI	BB	SO	SB	BA	SA	PH AB	PH H	G by POS
1982 MIN A	34	99	30	6	0	2	2.0	10	9	11	13	0	.303	.424	3	1	OF-30
1983	2	7	2	1	0	0	0.0	1	0	1	1	0	.286	.429	0	0	OF-2
1984	12	32	7	1	0	0	0.0	1	3	2	4	2	.219	.250	3	1	DH-6, OF-3
1987 KC A	44	105	25	8	2	4	3.8	10	21	7	13	1	.238	.467	15	5	DH-26
1988	82	202	44	8	1	1	0.5	26	19	6	31	9	.218	.282	9	1	OF-64, DH-13
5 yrs.	174	445	108	24	3	7	1.6	48	52	27	62	12	.243	.357	30	8	OF-99, DH-45

Kevin Elster

ELSTER, KEVIN DANIEL
B. Aug. 3, 1964, San Pedro, Calif.
BR TR 6'2" 180 lbs.

	G	AB	H	2B	3B	HR	HR%	R	RBI	BB	SO	SB	BA	SA	PH AB	PH H	G by POS
1986 NY N	19	30	5	1	0	0	0.0	3	0	3	8	0	.167	.200	0	0	SS-19
1987	5	10	4	2	0	0	0.0	1	1	0	1	0	.400	.600	2	2	SS-3
1988	149	406	87	11	1	9	2.2	41	37	35	47	2	.214	.313	1	0	SS-148
3 yrs.	173	446	96	14	1	9	2.0	45	38	38	56	2	.215	.312	3	2	SS-170

LEAGUE CHAMPIONSHIP SERIES

	G	AB	H	2B	3B	HR	HR%	R	RBI	BB	SO	SB	BA	SA	PH AB	PH H	G by POS
1986 NY N	4	3	0	0	0	0	0.0	0	0	0	1	0	.000	.000	0	0	SS-4
1988	5	8	2	1	0	0	0.0	1	1	3	0	0	.250	.375	0	0	SS-5
2 yrs.	9	11	2	1	0	0	0.0	1	1	3	1	0	.182	.273	0	0	SS-9

WORLD SERIES

	G	AB	H	2B	3B	HR	HR%	R	RBI	BB	SO	SB	BA	SA	PH AB	PH H	G by POS
1986 NY N	1	1	0	0	0	0	0.0	0	0	0	0	0	.000	.000	0	0	SS-1

Dave Engle

ENGLE, RALPH DAVID
B. Nov. 30, 1956, San Diego, Calif.
BR TR 6'3" 210 lbs.

	G	AB	H	2B	3B	HR	HR%	R	RBI	BB	SO	SB	BA	SA	PH AB	PH H	G by POS
1981 MIN A	82	248	64	14	4	5	2.0	29	32	13	37	0	.258	.407	1	0	OF-76, DH-1, 3B-1
1982	58	186	42	7	2	4	2.2	20	16	10	22	0	.226	.349	13	3	OF-34, DH-20
1983	120	374	114	22	4	8	2.1	46	43	28	39	2	.305	.449	20	6	C-73, OF-29, OF-4
1984	109	391	104	20	1	4	1.0	56	38	26	22	0	.266	.353	6	0	C-86, DH-22
1985	70	172	44	8	2	7	4.1	28	25	21	28	2	.256	.448	18	4	DH-38, C-17, OF-3
1986 DET A	35	86	22	7	0	0	0.0	6	4	7	13	0	.256	.337	5	1	1B-23, DH-5, OF-4, C-3
1987 MON N	59	84	19	4	0	1	1.2	7	14	6	11	1	.226	.310	41	11	OF-11, C-6, 1B-2, 3B-1
1988	34	37	8	3	0	0	0.0	4	1	5	5	0	.216	.297	23	2	C-9, OF-4, 3B-1
8 yrs.	567	1578	417	85	13	29	1.8	196	173	116	177	5	.264	.390	127	27	C-194, OF-136, DH-115, 1B-25, 3B-3

Jim Eppard

EPPARD, JAMES GERHARD
B. Apr. 27, 1960, South Bend, Ind.
BL TL 6'2" 180 lbs.

	G	AB	H	2B	3B	HR	HR%	R	RBI	BB	SO	SB	BA	SA	PH AB	PH H	G by POS
1987 CAL A	8	9	3	0	0	0	0.0	2	0	2	0	0	.333	.333	5	3	OF-1
1988	56	113	32	3	1	0	0.0	7	14	11	15	0	.283	.327	26	8	OF-17, DH-10, 1B-6
2 yrs.	64	122	35	3	1	0	0.0	9	14	13	15	0	.287	.328	31	11	OF-18, DH-10, 1B-6

Nick Esasky

ESASKY, NICHOLAS ANDREW
B. Feb. 24, 1960, Hialeah, Fla.
BR TR 6'3" 190 lbs.

	G	AB	H	2B	3B	HR	HR%	R	RBI	BB	SO	SB	BA	SA	PH AB	PH H	G by POS
1983 CIN N	85	302	80	10	5	12	4.0	41	46	27	99	6	.265	.450	1	0	3B-84
1984	113	322	62	10	5	10	3.1	30	45	52	103	1	.193	.348	12	0	3B-82, 1B-25
1985	125	413	108	21	0	21	5.1	61	66	41	102	3	.262	.465	10	4	3B-62, OF-54, 1B-12
1986	102	330	76	17	2	12	3.6	35	41	47	97	0	.230	.403	5	1	1B-70, OF-42, 3B-1
1987	100	346	94	19	2	22	6.4	48	59	29	76	0	.272	.529	6	1	1B-93, OF-1, 3B-1
1988	122	391	95	17	2	15	3.8	40	62	48	104	7	.243	.412	11	0	1B-116
6 yrs.	647	2104	515	94	16	92	4.4	255	319	244	581	17	.245	.436	45	6	1B-316, 3B-230, OF-97

Angel Escobar

ESCOBAR, ANGEL RUBENQUE
Born Angel Rubenque Escobar y Rivas.
B. May 12, 1965, LaSabana, Venezuela
BB TR 6' 160 lbs.

	G	AB	H	2B	3B	HR	HR%	R	RBI	BB	SO	SB	BA	SA	PH AB	PH H	G by POS
1988 SF N	3	3	1	0	0	0	0.0	1	0	0	0	0	.333	.333	1	0	SS-1, 3B-1

Alvaro Espinoza

ESPINOZA, ALVARO ALBERTO
Born Alvaro Alberto Espinoza y Ramirez.
B. Feb. 19, 1962, Valencia, Venezuela
BR TR 6' 160 lbs.

	G	AB	H	2B	3B	HR	HR%	R	RBI	BB	SO	SB	BA	SA	PH AB	PH H	G by POS
1984 MIN A	1	0	0	0	0	0	–	0	0	0	0	0	–	–	0	0	SS-1
1985	32	57	15	2	0	0	0.0	5	9	1	9	0	.263	.298	0	0	SS-31
1986	37	42	9	1	0	0	0.0	4	1	1	10	0	.214	.238	1	0	2B-19, SS-18
1988 NY A	3	3	0	0	0	0	0.0	0	0	0	0	0	.000	.000	0	0	2B-2, SS-1
4 yrs.	73	102	24	3	0	0	0.0	9	10	2	19	0	.235	.265	1	0	SS-51, 2B-21

Cecil Espy

ESPY, CECIL EDWARD
B. Jan. 20, 1963, San Diego, Calif.
BB TR 6'3" 190 lbs.

	G	AB	H	2B	3B	HR	HR%	R	RBI	BB	SO	SB	BA	SA	PH AB	PH H	G by POS
1983 LA N	20	11	3	1	0	0	0.0	4	1	1	2	0	.273	.364	2	1	OF-15
1987 TEX A	1	0	0	0	0	0	0.0	1	0	1	3	2	.000	.000	1	0	OF-8
1988	123	347	86	17	6	2	0.6	46	39	20	83	33	.248	.349	13	5	OF-98, DH-12, SS-3, C-2, 2B-1, 1B-1
3 yrs.	157	366	89	18	6	2	0.5	51	40	22	88	35	.243	.342	16	6	OF-121, DH-12, SS-3, C-2, 2B-1, 1B-1

	G	AB	H	2B	3B	HR	HR%	R	RBI	BB	SO	SB	BA	SA	Pinch Hit AB	Pinch Hit H	G by POS

Darrell Evans

EVANS, DARRELL WAYNE
B. May 26, 1947, Pasadena, Calif.   BL TR 6'2"   200 lbs.

	G	AB	H	2B	3B	HR	HR%	R	RBI	BB	SO	SB	BA	SA	AB	H	G by POS
1969 ATL N	12	26	6	0	0	0	0.0	3	1	1	8	0	.231	.231	4	0	3B-6
1970	12	44	14	1	1	0	0.0	4	9	7	5	0	.318	.386	0	0	3B-12
1971	89	260	63	11	1	12	4.6	42	38	39	54	2	.242	.431	10	1	3B-72, OF-3
1972	125	418	106	12	0	19	4.5	67	71	90	58	4	.254	.419	1	0	3B-123
1973	161	595	167	25	8	41	6.9	114	104	124	104	6	.281	.556	2	0	3B-146, 1B-20
1974	160	571	137	21	3	25	4.4	99	79	126	88	4	.240	.419	0	0	3B-160
1975	156	567	138	22	2	22	3.9	82	73	105	106	12	.243	.406	3	1	3B-156, 1B-3
1976 2 teams	ATL	N	(44G –	.173)		SF	N	(92G –	.222)								
" total	136	396	81	9	1	11	2.8	53	46	72	71	9	.205	.316	7	0	1B-119, 3B-12
1977 SF N	144	461	117	18	3	17	3.7	64	72	69	50	9	.254	.416	16	4	OF-81, 1B-41, 3B-35
1978	159	547	133	24	2	20	3.7	82	78	105	64	4	.243	.404	5	1	3B-155
1979	160	562	142	23	2	17	3.0	68	70	91	80	6	.253	.391	2	1	3B-159
1980	154	556	147	23	0	20	3.6	69	78	83	65	17	.264	.414	4	1	3B-140, 1B-14
1981	102	357	92	13	4	12	3.4	51	48	54	33	2	.258	.417	2	0	3B-87, 1B-12
1982	141	465	119	20	4	16	3.4	64	61	77	64	5	.256	.419	12	2	3B-84, 1B-49, SS-13
1983	142	523	145	29	3	30	5.7	94	82	84	81	6	.277	.516	2	1	1B-113, 3B-32, SS-9
1984 DET A	131	401	93	11	1	16	4.0	60	63	77	70	2	.232	.384	18	3	DH-62, 1B-47, 3B-19
1985	151	505	125	17	0	40	7.9	81	94	85	85	0	.248	.519	10	2	1B-113, DH-33, 3B-7
1986	151	507	122	15	0	29	5.7	78	85	91	105	3	.241	.442	8	3	1B-105, DH-42, 3B-2
1987	150	499	128	20	0	34	6.8	90	99	100	84	6	.257	.501	10	6	1B-105, DH-44, 3B-7
1988	144	437	91	9	0	22	5.0	48	64	84	89	1	.208	.380	23	3	DH-72, 1B-65
20 yrs.	2580	8697	2166	323	35	403	4.6	1313	1315	1564	1364	98	.249	.433	139	29	3B-1414, 1B-806, DH-253,
										10th							OF-84, SS-22

LEAGUE CHAMPIONSHIP SERIES

	G	AB	H	2B	3B	HR	HR%	R	RBI	BB	SO	SB	BA	SA	AB	H	G by POS
1984 DET A	3	10	3	1	0	0	0.0	1	1	1	0	1	.300	.400	0	0	1B-3
1987	5	17	5	0	0	0	0.0	0	0	4	2	0	.294	.294	0	0	1B-5
2 yrs.	8	27	8	1	0	0	0.0	1	1	5	2	1	.296	.333	0	0	1B-8

WORLD SERIES

	G	AB	H	2B	3B	HR	HR%	R	RBI	BB	SO	SB	BA	SA	AB	H	G by POS
1984 DET A	5	15	1	0	0	0	0.0	1	1	4	4	0	.067	.067	0	0	1B-4

Dwight Evans

EVANS, DWIGHT MICHAEL (Dewey)
B. Nov. 3, 1951, Santa Monica, Calif.   BR TR 6'2"   180 lbs.

	G	AB	H	2B	3B	HR	HR%	R	RBI	BB	SO	SB	BA	SA	AB	H	G by POS
1972 BOS A	18	57	15	3	1	1	1.8	2	6	7	13	0	.263	.404	1	1	OF-17
1973	119	282	63	13	1	10	3.5	46	32	40	52	5	.223	.383	3	0	OF-113
1974	133	463	130	19	8	10	2.2	60	70	38	77	4	.281	.421	12	2	OF-122, DH-7
1975	128	412	113	24	6	13	3.2	61	56	47	60	3	.274	.456	6	0	OF-115, DH-7
1976	146	501	121	34	5	17	3.4	61	62	57	92	6	.242	.431	2	1	OF-145, DH-1
1977	73	230	66	9	2	14	6.1	39	36	28	58	4	.287	.526	7	1	OF-63, DH-17
1978	147	497	123	24	2	24	4.8	75	63	65	119	8	.247	.449	4	1	OF-142, DH-4
1979	152	489	134	24	1	21	4.3	69	58	69	76	6	.274	.456	5	1	OF-149
1980	148	463	123	37	5	18	3.9	72	60	64	98	3	.266	.484	5	0	OF-144, DH-2
1981	108	412	122	19	4	22	5.3	84	71	85	85	3	.296	.522	0	0	OF-108
1982	162	609	178	37	7	32	5.3	122	98	112	125	3	.292	.534	0	0	OF-161, DH-1
1983	126	470	112	19	4	22	4.7	74	58	70	97	3	.238	.436	5	2	OF-99, DH-21
1984	162	630	186	37	8	32	5.1	121	104	96	115	3	.295	.532	0	0	OF-161, DH-1
1985	159	617	162	29	1	29	4.7	110	78	114	105	7	.263	.454	0	0	OF-152, DH-7
1986	152	529	137	33	2	26	4.9	86	97	97	117	3	.259	.476	1	0	OF-149, DH-1
1987	154	541	165	37	2	34	6.3	109	123	106	98	4	.305	.569	2	0	1B-79, OF-77, DH-4
1988	149	559	164	31	7	21	3.8	96	111	76	99	5	.293	.487	2	1	OF-85, 1B-64, DH-6
17 yrs.	2236	7761	2114	429	66	346	4.5	1287	1183	1171	1486	70	.272	.478	55	10	OF-2002, 1B-143, DH-79

LEAGUE CHAMPIONSHIP SERIES

	G	AB	H	2B	3B	HR	HR%	R	RBI	BB	SO	SB	BA	SA	AB	H	G by POS
1975 BOS A	3	10	1	1	0	0	0.0	1	1	1	2	0	.100	.200	0	0	OF-3
1986	7	28	6	1	0	1	3.6	2	4	3	3	0	.214	.357	0	0	OF-7
1988	4	12	2	1	0	0	0.0	1	1	3	5	0	.167	.250	0	0	OF-4
3 yrs.	14	50	9	3	0	1	2.0	4	6	7	10	0	.180	.300	0	0	OF-14

WORLD SERIES

	G	AB	H	2B	3B	HR	HR%	R	RBI	BB	SO	SB	BA	SA	AB	H	G by POS
1975 BOS A	7	24	7	1	1	1	4.2	3	5	3	4	0	.292	.542	0	0	OF-7
1986	7	26	8	2	0	2	7.7	4	9	4	3	0	.308	.615	0	0	OF-7
2 yrs.	14	50	15	3	1	3	6.0	7	14	7	7	0	.300	.580	0	0	OF-14

Mike Felder

FELDER, MICHAEL OTIS
B. Nov. 18, 1961, Vallejo, Calif.   BB TR 5'8"   160 lbs.

	G	AB	H	2B	3B	HR	HR%	R	RBI	BB	SO	SB	BA	SA	AB	H	G by POS
1985 MIL A	15	56	11	1	0	0	0.0	8	0	5	6	4	.196	.214	1	1	OF-14
1986	44	155	37	2	4	1	0.6	24	13	13	16	16	.239	.323	0	0	OF-42, DH-1
1987	108	289	77	5	7	2	0.7	48	31	28	23	34	.266	.353	7	1	OF-99, DH-3, 2B-1
1988	50	81	14	1	0	0	0.0	14	5	0	11	8	.173	.185	2	0	OF-28, DH-16, 2B-1
4 yrs.	217	581	139	9	11	3	0.5	94	49	46	56	62	.239	.308	10	2	OF-183, DH-20, 2B-2

Felix Fermin

FERMIN, FELIX JOSE
Born Felix Jose Fermin y Minaya.
B. Oct. 9, 1963, Mao Valverde, Dominican Republic   BR TR 5'11"   160 lbs.

	G	AB	H	2B	3B	HR	HR%	R	RBI	BB	SO	SB	BA	SA	AB	H	G by POS
1987 PIT N	23	68	17	0	0	0	0.0	6	4	4	9	0	.250	.250	0	0	SS-23
1988	43	87	24	0	2	0	0.0	9	2	8	10	3	.276	.322	1	0	SS-43
2 yrs.	66	155	41	0	2	0	0.0	15	6	12	19	3	.265	.290	1	0	SS-66

Tony Fernandez

FERNANDEZ, OCTAVIO ANTONIO CASTRO
Born Octavio Antonio Fernandez y Castro.
B. Aug. 6, 1962, San Pedro de Macoris, Dominican Republic   BB TR 6'1"   160 lbs.

	G	AB	H	2B	3B	HR	HR%	R	RBI	BB	SO	SB	BA	SA	AB	H	G by POS
1983 TOR A	15	34	9	1	1	0	0.0	5	2	2	2	0	.265	.353	2	1	SS-13, DH-1
1984	88	233	63	5	3	3	1.3	29	19	17	15	5	.270	.356	6	1	SS-73, 3B-10, DH-1
1985	161	564	163	31	10	2	0.4	71	51	43	41	13	.289	.390	3	1	SS-160
1986	163	687	213	33	9	10	1.5	91	65	27	52	25	.310	.428	1	1	SS-163
1987	146	578	186	29	8	5	0.9	90	67	51	48	32	.322	.426	1	0	SS-146

	G	AB	H	2B	3B	HR	HR %	R	RBI	BB	SO	SB	BA	SA	Pinch Hit AB	Pinch Hit H	G by POS

Tony Fernandez continued

	G	AB	H	2B	3B	HR	HR %	R	RBI	BB	SO	SB	BA	SA	AB	H	G by POS
1988	154	648	186	41	4	5	0.8	76	70	45	65	15	.287	.386	0	0	SS-154
6 yrs.	727	2744	820	140	35	25	0.9	362	274	185	223	90	.299	.403	13	4	SS-709, 3B-10, DH-2

LEAGUE CHAMPIONSHIP SERIES
	G	AB	H	2B	3B	HR	HR %	R	RBI	BB	SO	SB	BA	SA	AB	H	G by POS
1985 **TOR A**	7	24	8	2	0	0	0.0	2	2	1	2	0	.333	.417	0	0	SS-7

Cecil Fielder

FIELDER, CECIL GRANT   BR TR 6'3"   230 lbs.
B. Sept. 21, 1963, Los Angeles, Calif.

	G	AB	H	2B	3B	HR	HR %	R	RBI	BB	SO	SB	BA	SA	AB	H	G by POS
1985 **TOR A**	30	74	23	4	0	4	5.4	6	16	6	16	0	.311	.527	4	1	1B-25
1986	34	83	13	2	0	4	4.8	7	13	6	27	0	.157	.325	9	1	DH-22, 1B-7, 3B-2, OF-1
1987	82	175	47	7	1	14	8.0	30	32	20	48	0	.269	.560	19	4	DH-55, 1B-16, 3B-2
1988	74	174	40	6	1	9	5.2	24	23	14	53	0	.230	.431	21	5	1B-17, 3B-3, 2B-2
4 yrs.	220	506	123	19	2	31	6.1	67	84	46	144	0	.243	.472	53	11	DH-77, 1B-65, 3B-7, 2B-2, OF-1

LEAGUE CHAMPIONSHIP SERIES
	G	AB	H	2B	3B	HR	HR %	R	RBI	BB	SO	SB	BA	SA	AB	H	G by POS
1985 **TOR A**	3	3	1	1	0	0	0.0	0	0	0	1	0	.333	.667	3	1	

Bruce Fields

FIELDS, BRUCE ALAN   BL TR 6'   185 lbs.
B. Oct. 6, 1960, Cleveland, Ohio

	G	AB	H	2B	3B	HR	HR %	R	RBI	BB	SO	SB	BA	SA	AB	H	G by POS
1986 **DET A**	16	43	12	1	1	0	0.0	4	6	1	6	1	.279	.349	2	1	OF-14, DH-1
1988 **SEA A**	39	67	18	5	0	1	1.5	8	5	4	11	0	.269	.388	12	3	OF-23, DH-6
2 yrs.	55	110	30	6	1	1	0.9	12	11	5	17	1	.273	.373	14	4	OF-37, DH-7

Dan Firova

FIROVA, DANIEL MICHAEL   BR TR 6'   185 lbs.
B. Oct. 16, 1956, Refugio, Tex.

	G	AB	H	2B	3B	HR	HR %	R	RBI	BB	SO	SB	BA	SA	AB	H	G by POS
1981 **SEA A**	13	2	0	0	0	0	0.0	0	0	0	1	0	.000	.000	0	0	C-13
1982	3	5	0	0	0	0	0.0	0	0	0	0	0	.000	.000	0	0	C-3
1988 **CLE A**	1	0	0	0	0	0	–	0	0	0	0	0	–	–	0	0	C-1
3 yrs.	17	7	0	0	0	0	0.0	0	0	0	1	0	.000	.000	0	0	C-17

John Fishel

FISHEL, JOHN ALAN   BR TR 5'11"   185 lbs.
B. Nov. 8, 1962, Fullerton, Calif.

	G	AB	H	2B	3B	HR	HR %	R	RBI	BB	SO	SB	BA	SA	AB	H	G by POS
1988 **HOU N**	19	26	6	0	0	1	3.8	1	2	3	6	0	.231	.346	16	3	OF-6

Carlton Fisk

FISK, CARLTON ERNEST (Pudge)   BR TR 6'3"   200 lbs.
B. Dec. 26, 1947, Bellows Falls, Vt.

	G	AB	H	2B	3B	HR	HR %	R	RBI	BB	SO	SB	BA	SA	AB	H	G by POS
1969 **BOS A**	2	5	0	0	0	0	0.0	0	0	0	2	0	.000	.000	1	0	C-1
1971	14	48	15	2	1	2	4.2	7	6	1	10	0	.313	.521	0	0	C-14
1972	131	457	134	28	9	22	4.8	74	61	52	83	5	.293	.538	0	0	C-131
1973	135	508	125	21	0	26	5.1	65	71	37	99	7	.246	.441	1	1	C-131, DH-3
1974	52	187	56	12	1	11	5.9	36	26	24	23	5	.299	.551	0	0	C-50, DH-2
1975	79	263	87	14	4	10	3.8	47	52	27	32	4	.331	.529	2	0	C-71, DH-6
1976	134	487	124	17	5	17	3.5	76	58	56	71	12	.255	.415	1	0	C-133, DH-1
1977	152	536	169	26	3	26	4.9	106	102	75	85	7	.315	.521	2	0	C-151
1978	157	571	162	39	5	20	3.5	94	88	71	83	7	.284	.475	2	1	C-154, DH-1, OF-1
1979	91	320	87	23	2	10	3.1	49	42	10	38	3	.272	.450	13	3	DH-42, C-39, OF-1
1980	131	478	138	25	3	18	3.8	73	62	36	62	11	.289	.467	0	0	C-115, DH-5, OF-5, 3B-3, 1B-3
1981 **CHI A**	96	338	89	12	0	7	2.1	44	45	38	37	3	.263	.361	0	0	C-95, OF-1, 3B-1, 1B-1
1982	135	476	127	17	3	14	2.9	66	65	46	60	17	.267	.403	3	1	C-133, 1B-2
1983	138	488	141	26	4	26	5.3	85	86	46	88	9	.289	.518	6	1	C-133, DH-2
1984	102	359	83	20	1	21	5.8	54	43	26	60	6	.231	.468	11	1	C-90, DH-5
1985	153	543	129	23	1	37	6.8	85	107	52	81	17	.238	.488	1	0	C-130, DH-28
1986	125	457	101	11	0	14	3.1	42	63	22	92	2	.221	.337	8	1	C-71, OF-31, DH-22
1987	135	454	116	22	1	23	5.1	68	71	39	72	1	.256	.460	12	3	C-122, 1B-9, OF-2
1988	76	253	70	8	1	19	7.5	37	50	37	40	0	.277	.542	6	0	C-74
19 yrs.	2038	7228	1953	346	44	323	4.5	1108	1098	695	1118	116	.270	.464	69	12	C-1838, DH-117, OF-41, 1B-15, 3B-4

LEAGUE CHAMPIONSHIP SERIES
	G	AB	H	2B	3B	HR	HR %	R	RBI	BB	SO	SB	BA	SA	AB	H	G by POS
1975 **BOS A**	3	12	5	1	0	0	0.0	4	2	0	2	1	.417	.500	0	0	C-3
1983 **CHI A**	4	17	3	1	0	0	0.0	0	0	1	3	0	.176	.235	0	0	C-4
2 yrs.	7	29	8	2	0	0	0.0	4	2	1	5	1	.276	.345	0	0	C-7

WORLD SERIES
	G	AB	H	2B	3B	HR	HR %	R	RBI	BB	SO	SB	BA	SA	AB	H	G by POS
1975 **BOS A**	7	25	6	0	0	2	8.0	5	4	7	7	0	.240	.480	0	0	C-7

Mike Fitzgerald

FITZGERALD, MICHAEL PATRICK   BR TR 6'1"   200 lbs.
B. Mar. 28, 1964, Savannah, Ga.

	G	AB	H	2B	3B	HR	HR %	R	RBI	BB	SO	SB	BA	SA	AB	H	G by POS
1988 **STL N**	13	46	9	1	0	0	0.0	4	1	0	9	0	.196	.217	1	0	1B-12

Mike Fitzgerald

FITZGERALD, MICHAEL ROY (Fitz)   BR TR 6'   185 lbs.
B. July 13, 1960, Long Beach, Calif.

	G	AB	H	2B	3B	HR	HR %	R	RBI	BB	SO	SB	BA	SA	AB	H	G by POS
1983 **NY N**	8	20	2	0	0	1	5.0	1	2	3	6	0	.100	.250	0	0	C-8
1984	112	360	87	15	1	2	0.6	20	33	24	71	1	.242	.306	7	1	C-107
1985 **MON N**	108	295	61	7	1	5	1.7	25	34	38	55	5	.207	.288	3	1	C-108
1986	73	209	59	13	1	6	2.9	20	37	27	34	3	.282	.440	3	0	C-71
1987	107	287	69	11	0	3	1.0	32	36	42	54	5	.240	.310	5	2	C-104, 2B-1, 1B-1
1988	63	155	42	6	1	5	3.2	17	23	19	22	2	.271	.419	15	4	C-47, 1B-1
6 yrs.	471	1326	320	52	4	22	1.7	115	165	153	242	16	.241	.336	33	8	C-445, OF-4, 2B-1, 1B-1

Tim Flannery

FLANNERY, TIMOTHY EARL   BL TR 5'11"   175 lbs.
B. Sept. 29, 1957, Tulsa, Okla.

	G	AB	H	2B	3B	HR	HR %	R	RBI	BB	SO	SB	BA	SA	AB	H	G by POS
1979 **SD N**	22	65	10	0	1	0	0.0	2	4	4	5	0	.154	.185	0	0	2B-21
1980	95	292	70	12	0	0	0.0	15	25	18	30	2	.240	.281	12	5	2B-53, 3B-41
1981	37	67	17	4	1	0	0.0	4	6	2	4	1	.254	.343	16	6	3B-15, 2B-7

	G	AB	H	2B	3B	HR	HR %	R	RBI	BB	SO	SB	BA	SA	Pinch Hit AB	H	G by POS

Tim Flannery continued

	G	AB	H	2B	3B	HR	HR %	R	RBI	BB	SO	SB	BA	SA	AB	H	G by POS
1982	122	379	100	11	7	0	0.0	40	30	30	32	1	.264	.330	16	3	2B-104, 3B-5, SS-2
1983	92	214	50	7	3	3	1.4	24	19	20	23	2	.234	.336	19	4	3B-52, 2B-21, SS-7
1984	86	128	35	3	3	2	1.6	24	10	12	17	4	.273	.391	40	7	2B-22, SS-14, 3B-14
1985	126	384	108	14	3	1	0.3	50	40	58	39	2	.281	.341	13	3	2B-121, 3B-1
1986	134	368	103	11	2	3	0.8	48	28	54	61	3	.280	.345	16	3	2B-108, 3B-23, SS-8
1987	106	276	63	5	1	0	0.0	23	20	42	30	2	.228	.254	23	2	2B-84, 3B-8, SS-2
1988	79	170	45	5	4	0	0.0	16	19	24	32	3	.265	.341	26	8	3B-51, 2B-2, SS-1
10 yrs.	899	2343	601	72	25	9	0.4	246	201	264	273	20	.257	.320	181	41	2B-543, 3B-210, SS-34

LEAGUE CHAMPIONSHIP SERIES

	G	AB	H	2B	3B	HR	HR %	R	RBI	BB	SO	SB	BA	SA	AB	H	G by POS
1984 **SD N**	3	2	1	0	0	0	0.0	2	0	0	0	0	.500	.500	2	1	

WORLD SERIES

	G	AB	H	2B	3B	HR	HR %	R	RBI	BB	SO	SB	BA	SA	AB	H	G by POS
1984 **SD N**	1	1	1	0	0	0	0.0	0	0	0	0	0	1.000	1.000	1	1	2B-1

Scott Fletcher

FLETCHER, SCOTT BRIAN
B. July 30, 1958, Fort Walton Beach, Fla.

BR TR 5'11" 168 lbs.

	G	AB	H	2B	3B	HR	HR %	R	RBI	BB	SO	SB	BA	SA	AB	H	G by POS
1981 **CHI N**	19	46	10	4	0	0	0.0	6	1	2	4	0	.217	.304	0	0	2B-13, SS-4, 3B-1
1982	11	24	4	0	0	0	0.0	4	1	4	5	1	.167	.167	0	0	SS-11
1983 **CHI A**	114	262	62	16	5	3	1.1	42	31	29	22	5	.237	.370	0	0	SS-100, 2B-12, 3B-7, DH-1
1984	149	456	114	13	3	3	0.7	46	35	46	46	10	.250	.311	0	0	SS-134, 2B-28, 3B-3
1985	119	301	77	8	1	2	0.7	38	31	35	47	5	.256	.309	12	3	3B-55, SS-44, 2B-37, DH-2
1986 **TEX A**	147	530	159	34	5	3	0.6	82	50	47	59	12	.300	.400	0	0	SS-136, 3B-12, 2B-11, DH-1
1987	156	588	169	28	4	5	0.9	82	63	61	66	13	.287	.374	3	1	SS-155
1988	140	515	142	19	4	0	0.0	59	47	62	34	8	.276	.328	2	0	SS-139
8 yrs.	855	2722	737	122	22	16	0.6	359	259	286	283	54	.271	.349	17	4	SS-723, 2B-101, 3B-78, DH-4

LEAGUE CHAMPIONSHIP SERIES

	G	AB	H	2B	3B	HR	HR %	R	RBI	BB	SO	SB	BA	SA	AB	H	G by POS
1983 **CHI A**	3	7	0	0	0	0	0.0	0	0	1	0	0	.000	.000	0	0	SS-3

Tom Foley

FOLEY, THOMAS MICHAEL
B. Sept. 9, 1959, Fort Benning, Ga.

BL TR 6'1" 160 lbs.

	G	AB	H	2B	3B	HR	HR %	R	RBI	BB	SO	SB	BA	SA	AB	H	G by POS
1983 **CIN N**	68	98	20	4	1	0	0.0	7	9	13	17	1	.204	.265	20	4	SS-37, 2B-5
1984	106	277	70	8	3	5	1.8	26	27	24	36	3	.253	.357	13	5	SS-83, 2B-10, 3B-1
1985 2 teams		CIN N (43G – .196)			PHI N (46G – .266)												
" total	89	250	60	13	1	3	1.2	24	23	19	34	2	.240	.336	12	1	SS-60, 2B-18, 3B-1
1986 2 teams		PHI N (39G – .295)			MON N (64G – .257)												
" total	103	263	70	15	3	1	0.4	26	23	30	37	10	.266	.357	22	5	SS-53, 2B-26, 3B-16
1987 **MON N**	106	280	82	18	3	5	1.8	35	28	11	40	6	.293	.432	24	5	SS-49, 2B-39, 3B-9
1988	127	377	100	21	3	5	1.3	33	43	30	49	2	.265	.377	14	1	2B-89, SS-32, 3B-9
6 yrs.	599	1545	402	79	14	19	1.2	151	153	127	213	24	.260	.366	105	21	SS-314, 2B-187, 3B-36

Curt Ford

FORD, CURTIS GLENN
B. Oct. 11, 1960, Jackson, Miss.

BL TR 5'10" 150 lbs.

	G	AB	H	2B	3B	HR	HR %	R	RBI	BB	SO	SB	BA	SA	AB	H	G by POS
1985 **STL N**	11	12	6	2	0	0	0.0	2	3	4	1	1	.500	.667	4	2	OF-4
1986	85	214	53	15	2	2	0.9	30	29	23	29	13	.248	.364	25	5	OF-64
1987	89	228	65	9	5	3	1.3	32	26	14	32	11	.285	.408	18	7	OF-75
1988	91	128	25	6	0	1	0.8	11	18	8	26	6	.195	.266	40	9	OF-40, 1B-7
4 yrs.	276	582	149	32	7	6	1.0	75	76	49	88	31	.256	.366	87	23	OF-183, 1B-7

LEAGUE CHAMPIONSHIP SERIES

	G	AB	H	2B	3B	HR	HR %	R	RBI	BB	SO	SB	BA	SA	AB	H	G by POS
1987 **STL N**	4	9	3	0	0	0	0.0	2	0	1	1	0	.333	.333	1	1	OF-4

WORLD SERIES

	G	AB	H	2B	3B	HR	HR %	R	RBI	BB	SO	SB	BA	SA	AB	H	G by POS
1987 **STL N**	5	13	4	0	0	0	0.0	1	2	1	1	0	.308	.308	1	0	OF-4

Julio Franco

FRANCO, JULIO CESAR ROBLES
Born Julio Cesar Franco y Robles.
B. Aug. 23, 1958, Hato Mayor, Puerto Rico

BB TR 6' 160 lbs.

	G	AB	H	2B	3B	HR	HR %	R	RBI	BB	SO	SB	BA	SA	AB	H	G by POS
1982 **PHI N**	16	29	8	1	0	0	0.0	3	3	2	4	0	.276	.310	0	0	SS-11, 3B-2
1983 **CLE A**	149	560	153	24	8	8	1.4	68	80	27	50	32	.273	.388	0	0	SS-149
1984	160	658	188	22	5	3	0.5	82	79	43	68	19	.286	.348	0	0	SS-159, DH-1
1985	160	636	183	33	4	6	0.9	97	90	54	74	13	.288	.381	2	0	SS-151, 2B-8, DH-1
1986	149	599	183	30	5	10	1.7	80	74	32	66	10	.306	.422	1	0	SS-134, 2B-13, DH-3
1987	128	495	158	24	3	8	1.6	86	52	57	56	32	.319	.428	1	1	SS-111, 2B-9, DH-8
1988	152	613	186	23	6	10	1.6	88	54	56	72	25	.303	.409	0	0	2B-151, DH-1
7 yrs.	914	3590	1059	157	31	45	1.3	504	432	271	390	131	.295	.394	4	1	SS-715, 2B-181, DH-14, 3B-2

Terry Francona

FRANCONA, TERRY JON
Son of Tito Francona.
B. Apr. 22, 1959, Aberdeen, S. D.

BB TL 6'1" 190 lbs.

	G	AB	H	2B	3B	HR	HR %	R	RBI	BB	SO	SB	BA	SA	AB	H	G by POS
1981 **MON N**	34	95	26	0	1	1	1.1	11	8	5	6	1	.274	.326	10	5	OF-26, 1B-1
1982	46	131	42	3	0	0	0.0	14	9	8	11	2	.321	.344	7	2	OF-33, 1B-16
1983	120	230	59	11	1	3	1.3	21	22	6	20	0	.257	.352	38	8	OF-51, 1B-47
1984	58	214	74	19	2	1	0.5	18	18	5	12	0	.346	.467	3	0	1B-50, OF-6
1985	107	281	75	15	1	2	0.7	19	31	12	12	5	.267	.349	31	6	1B-57, OF-28, 3B-1
1986 **CHI N**	86	124	31	3	0	2	1.6	13	8	6	8	0	.250	.323	42	8	OF-30, 1B-23
1987 **CIN N**	102	207	47	5	0	3	1.4	16	12	10	12	2	.227	.295	43	11	1B-57, OF-8
1988 **CLE A**	62	212	66	8	0	1	0.5	24	12	5	18	0	.311	.363	15	5	DH-38, OF-5, 1B-5
8 yrs.	615	1494	420	64	5	13	0.9	136	120	57	99	10	.281	.357	189	45	1B-256, OF-187, DH-38, 3B-1

DIVISIONAL PLAYOFF SERIES

	G	AB	H	2B	3B	HR	HR %	R	RBI	BB	SO	SB	BA	SA	AB	H	G by POS
1981 **MON N**	5	12	4	0	0	0	0.0	0	0	2	2	2	.333	.333	0	0	OF-5

	G	AB	H	2B	3B	HR	HR %	R	RBI	BB	SO	SB	BA	SA	Pinch Hit AB	H	G by POS

Terry Francona continued

LEAGUE CHAMPIONSHIP SERIES

	G	AB	H	2B	3B	HR	HR %	R	RBI	BB	SO	SB	BA	SA	AB	H	G by POS
1981 **MON N**	2	1	0	0	0	0	0.0	0	0	0	1	0	.000	.000	1	0	OF-1

Gary Gaetti

GAETTI, GARY JOSEPH
B. Aug. 19, 1958, Centralia, Ill.

BR TR 6'   180 lbs.

	G	AB	H	2B	3B	HR	HR %	R	RBI	BB	SO	SB	BA	SA	AB	H	G by POS
1981 **MIN A**	9	26	5	0	0	2	7.7	4	3	0	6	0	.192	.423	0	0	3B-8, DH-1
1982	145	508	117	25	4	25	4.9	59	84	37	107	0	.230	.443	1	0	3B-142, SS-2
1983	157	584	143	30	3	21	3.6	81	78	54	121	7	.245	.414	2	1	3B-154, SS-3, DH-1
1984	162	588	154	29	4	5	0.9	55	65	44	81	11	.262	.350	0	0	3B-154, OF-8, SS-2
1985	160	560	138	31	0	20	3.6	71	63	37	89	13	.246	.409	1	0	3B-156, OF-4, DH-1, 1B-1
1986	157	596	171	34	1	34	5.7	91	108	52	108	14	.287	.518	1	0	3B-156, SS-2, OF-1, 2B-1
1987	154	584	150	36	2	31	5.3	95	109	37	92	10	.257	.485	3	2	3B-150, DH-2
1988	133	468	141	29	2	28	6.0	66	88	36	85	7	.301	.551	14	4	3B-115, DH-5, SS-2
8 yrs.	1077	3914	1019	214	16	166	4.2	522	598	297	689	62	.260	.450	22	7	3B-1035, OF-13, SS-11, DH-10, 2B-1, 1B-1

LEAGUE CHAMPIONSHIP SERIES

	G	AB	H	2B	3B	HR	HR %	R	RBI	BB	SO	SB	BA	SA	AB	H	G by POS
1987 **MIN A**	5	20	6	1	0	2	10.0	5	5	1	3	0	.300	.650	0	0	3B-5

WORLD SERIES

	G	AB	H	2B	3B	HR	HR %	R	RBI	BB	SO	SB	BA	SA	AB	H	G by POS
1987 **MIN A**	7	27	7	2	1	1	3.7	4	4	2	5	2	.259	.519	0	0	3B-7

Greg Gagne

GAGNE, GREGORY CHRISTOPHER
B. Nov. 12, 1961, Fall River, Mass.

BR TR 5'11"   175 lbs.

	G	AB	H	2B	3B	HR	HR %	R	RBI	BB	SO	SB	BA	SA	AB	H	G by POS
1983 **MIN A**	10	27	3	1	0	0	0.0	2	3	0	6	0	.111	.148	0	0	SS-10
1984	2	1	0	0	0	0	0.0	0	0	0	0	0	.000	.000	1	0	
1985	114	293	66	15	3	2	0.7	37	23	20	57	10	.225	.317	4	1	SS-106, DH-5
1986	156	472	118	22	6	12	2.5	63	54	30	108	12	.250	.398	0	0	SS-155, 2B-4
1987	137	437	116	28	7	10	2.3	68	40	25	84	6	.265	.430	0	0	SS-136, OF-4, 2B-1
1988	149	461	109	20	6	14	3.0	70	48	27	110	15	.236	.397	1	0	SS-146, OF-2, 3B-1, 2B-1
6 yrs.	568	1691	412	86	22	38	2.2	240	168	102	365	43	.244	.388	6	1	SS-553, OF-6, 2B-6, DH-5, 3B-1

LEAGUE CHAMPIONSHIP SERIES

	G	AB	H	2B	3B	HR	HR %	R	RBI	BB	SO	SB	BA	SA	AB	H	G by POS
1987 **MIN A**	5	18	5	3	0	2	11.1	5	3	3	4	0	.278	.778	0	0	SS-5

WORLD SERIES

	G	AB	H	2B	3B	HR	HR %	R	RBI	BB	SO	SB	BA	SA	AB	H	G by POS
1987 **MIN A**	7	30	6	1	0	1	3.3	5	3	1	6	0	.200	.333	0	0	SS-7

Andres Galarraga

GALARRAGA, ANDRES JOSE (Big Cat)
Born Andres Jose Padovani y Galarraga.
B. June 18, 1961, Caracas, Venezuela

BR TR 6'3"   235 lbs.

	G	AB	H	2B	3B	HR	HR %	R	RBI	BB	SO	SB	BA	SA	AB	H	G by POS
1985 **MON N**	24	75	14	1	0	2	2.7	9	4	3	18	1	.187	.280	2	1	1B-23
1986	105	321	87	13	0	10	3.1	39	42	30	79	6	.271	.405	7	1	1B-102
1987	147	551	168	40	3	13	2.4	72	90	41	127	7	.305	.459	1	0	1B-146
1988	157	609	184	42	8	29	4.8	99	92	39	153	13	.302	.540	2	1	1B-156
4 yrs.	433	1556	453	96	11	54	3.5	219	228	113	377	27	.291	.471	12	3	1B-427

Dave Gallagher

GALLAGHER, DAVID THOMAS
B. Sept. 20, 1960, Trenton, N. J.

BR TR 6'   180 lbs.

	G	AB	H	2B	3B	HR	HR %	R	RBI	BB	SO	SB	BA	SA	AB	H	G by POS
1987 **CLE A**	15	36	4	1	1	0	0.0	2	1	2	5	2	.111	.194	0	0	OF-14
1988 **CHI A**	101	347	105	15	3	5	1.4	59	31	29	40	5	.303	.406	11	2	OF-95, DH-2
2 yrs.	116	383	109	16	4	5	1.3	61	32	31	45	7	.285	.386	11	2	OF-109, DH-2

Mike Gallego

GALLEGO, MICHAEL ANTHONY
B. Oct. 31, 1960, Whittier, Calif.

BR TR 5'8"   160 lbs.

	G	AB	H	2B	3B	HR	HR %	R	RBI	BB	SO	SB	BA	SA	AB	H	G by POS
1985 **OAK A**	76	77	16	5	1	1	1.3	13	9	12	14	1	.208	.338	2	0	2B-42, SS-21, 3B-12
1986	20	37	10	2	0	0	0.0	2	4	1	6	0	.270	.324	0	0	2B-19, 3B-2, SS-1
1987	72	124	31	6	0	2	1.6	18	14	12	21	0	.250	.347	4	0	2B-31, 3B-24, SS-17
1988	129	277	58	8	0	2	0.7	38	20	34	53	2	.209	.260	3	0	2B-83, SS-42, 3B-16
4 yrs.	297	515	115	21	1	5	1.0	71	47	59	94	3	.223	.297	9	1	2B-175, SS-81, 3B-54

LEAGUE CHAMPIONSHIP SERIES

	G	AB	H	2B	3B	HR	HR %	R	RBI	BB	SO	SB	BA	SA	AB	H	G by POS
1988 **OAK A**	4	12	1	0	0	0	0.0	1	0	0	3	0	.083	.083	0	0	2B-4

WORLD SERIES

	G	AB	H	2B	3B	HR	HR %	R	RBI	BB	SO	SB	BA	SA	AB	H	G by POS
1988 **OAK A**	1	0	0	0	0	0	–	0	0	0	0	0	–	–	0	0	2B-1

Ron Gant

GANT, RONALD EDWIN
B. Mar. 2, 1965, Victoria, Tex.

BR TR 6'   172 lbs.

	G	AB	H	2B	3B	HR	HR %	R	RBI	BB	SO	SB	BA	SA	AB	H	G by POS
1987 **ATL N**	21	83	22	4	0	2	2.4	9	9	1	11	4	.265	.386	1	0	2B-20
1988	146	563	146	28	8	19	3.4	85	60	46	118	19	.259	.439	2	0	2B-122, 3B-22
2 yrs.	167	646	168	32	8	21	3.3	94	69	47	129	23	.260	.432	3	0	2B-142, 3B-22

Jim Gantner

GANTNER, JAMES ELMER
B. Jan. 5, 1953, Fond du Lac, Wis.

BL TR 6'   180 lbs.

	G	AB	H	2B	3B	HR	HR %	R	RBI	BB	SO	SB	BA	SA	AB	H	G by POS
1976 **MIL A**	26	69	17	1	0	0	0.0	6	7	6	11	1	.246	.261	1	0	3B-24, DH-2
1977	14	47	14	1	0	1	2.1	4	2	2	5	2	.298	.383	1	1	3B-14
1978	43	97	21	1	0	1	1.0	14	8	5	10	2	.216	.258	4	1	3B-21, 2B-15, SS-1, 1B-1
1979	70	208	59	10	3	2	1.0	29	22	16	17	3	.284	.389	0	0	3B-42, 2B-22, SS-3, P-1
1980	132	415	117	21	3	4	1.0	47	40	30	29	11	.282	.376	2	0	3B-69, 2B-66, SS-1
1981	107	352	94	14	1	2	0.6	35	33	29	29	3	.267	.330	3	0	2B-107
1982	132	447	132	17	2	4	0.9	48	43	26	36	6	.295	.369	4	1	2B-131
1983	161	603	170	23	8	11	1.8	85	74	38	46	5	.282	.401	3	0	2B-158
1984	153	613	173	27	1	3	0.5	61	56	30	51	6	.282	.344	2	1	2B-153
1985	143	523	133	15	4	5	1.0	63	44	33	42	11	.254	.327	1	1	2B-124, 3B-24, SS-1
1986	139	497	136	25	1	7	1.4	58	38	26	50	13	.274	.370	2	0	2B-135, 3B-3, DH-1, SS-1
1987	81	265	72	14	0	4	1.5	37	30	19	22	6	.272	.370	3	1	2B-57, 3B-38, DH-2

	G	AB	H	2B	3B	HR	HR %	R	RBI	BB	SO	SB	BA	SA	Pinch Hit AB	Pinch Hit H	G by POS

Jim Gantner continued

	G	AB	H	2B	3B	HR	HR%	R	RBI	BB	SO	SB	BA	SA	PH AB	PH H	G by POS
1988	155	539	149	28	2	0	0.0	67	47	34	50	20	.276	.336	2	1	2B-154, 3B-1
13 yrs.	1356	4675	1287	197	25	44	0.9	554	444	294	398	89	.275	.356	28	7	2B-1128, 3B-230, SS-7, DH-4, 1B-1, P-1

DIVISIONAL PLAYOFF SERIES
| 1981 MIL A | 4 | 14 | 2 | 1 | 0 | 0 | 0.0 | 1 | 0 | 0 | 2 | 0 | .143 | .214 | 0 | 0 | 2B-4 |

LEAGUE CHAMPIONSHIP SERIES
| 1982 MIL A | 5 | 16 | 3 | 0 | 0 | 0 | 0.0 | 1 | 2 | 1 | 1 | 0 | .188 | .188 | 0 | 0 | 2B-5 |

WORLD SERIES
| 1982 MIL A | 7 | 24 | 8 | 4 | 1 | 0 | 0.0 | 5 | 4 | 1 | 1 | 0 | .333 | .583 | 0 | 0 | 2B-7 |

Barbaro Garbey

GARBEY, BARBARO GARBEY
Born Barbaro Garbey y Garbey.
B. Dec. 4, 1956, Santiago, Cuba

BR TR 5'10" 170 lbs.

	G	AB	H	2B	3B	HR	HR%	R	RBI	BB	SO	SB	BA	SA	PH AB	PH H	G by POS
1984 DET A	110	327	94	17	1	5	1.5	45	52	17	35	6	.287	.391	25	8	1B-65, 3B-20, DH-18, OF-10, 2B-3
1985	86	237	61	9	1	6	2.5	27	29	15	37	3	.257	.380	20	3	1B-37, OF-24, DH-21, 3B-1
1988 TEX A	30	62	12	2	0	0	0.0	4	5	4	11	0	.194	.226	10	3	OF-8, 1B-7, 3B-3
3 yrs.	226	626	167	28	2	11	1.8	76	86	36	83	9	.267	.371	55	14	1B-109, OF-42, DH-39, 3B-24, 2B-3

LEAGUE CHAMPIONSHIP SERIES
| 1984 DET A | 3 | 9 | 3 | 0 | 0 | 0 | 0.0 | 1 | 0 | 0 | 1 | 0 | .333 | .333 | 1 | 0 | DH-2 |

WORLD SERIES
| 1984 DET A | 4 | 12 | 0 | 0 | 0 | 0 | 0.0 | 0 | 0 | 0 | 2 | 0 | .000 | .000 | 1 | 0 | DH-3 |

Damaso Garcia

GARCIA, DAMASO DOMINGO SANCHEZ
Born Damaso Domingo Garcia y Sanchez.
B. Feb. 7, 1957, Moca, Dominican Republic

BR TR 6'1" 165 lbs.

	G	AB	H	2B	3B	HR	HR%	R	RBI	BB	SO	SB	BA	SA	PH AB	PH H	G by POS
1978 NY A	18	41	8	0	0	0	0.0	5	1	2	6	1	.195	.195	0	0	2B-16, SS-3
1979	11	38	10	1	0	0	0.0	3	4	0	2	2	.263	.289	0	0	SS-10, 3B-1
1980 TOR A	140	543	151	30	7	4	0.7	50	46	12	55	13	.278	.381	2	0	2B-138, DH-1
1981	64	250	63	8	1	1	0.4	24	13	9	32	13	.252	.304	1	0	2B-62, DH-1
1982	147	597	185	32	3	5	0.8	89	42	21	44	54	.310	.399	0	0	2B-141, DH-4
1983	131	525	161	23	6	3	0.6	84	38	24	34	31	.307	.390	2	0	2B-130
1984	152	633	180	32	5	5	0.8	79	46	16	46	46	.284	.374	2	0	2B-149, DH-1
1985	146	600	169	25	4	8	1.3	70	65	15	41	28	.282	.377	4	1	2B-143
1986	122	424	119	22	0	6	1.4	57	46	13	32	9	.281	.375	5	3	2B-106, DH-11, 1B-1
1988 ATL N	21	60	7	1	0	1	1.7	3	4	3	10	1	.117	.183	8	1	2B-13
10 yrs.	952	3711	1053	174	26	33	0.9	464	305	115	302	198	.284	.371	24	7	2B-898, DH-18, SS-13, 3B-1, 1B-1

LEAGUE CHAMPIONSHIP SERIES
| 1985 TOR A | 7 | 30 | 7 | 4 | 0 | 0 | 0.0 | 4 | 1 | 3 | 3 | 0 | .233 | .367 | 0 | 0 | 2B-7 |

Leo Garcia

GARCIA, LEONARDO ANTONIO
Born Leonardo Antonio Garcia y Peralta.
B. Nov. 6, 1962, Santiago, Dominican Republic

BL TL 5'8" 160 lbs.

	G	AB	H	2B	3B	HR	HR%	R	RBI	BB	SO	SB	BA	SA	PH AB	PH H	G by POS
1987 CIN N	31	30	6	0	0	1	3.3	8	2	4	8	3	.200	.300	9	2	OF-14
1988	23	28	4	1	0	0	0.0	2	0	4	5	0	.143	.179	12	3	OF-9
2 yrs.	54	58	10	1	0	1	1.7	10	2	8	13	3	.172	.241	21	5	OF-23

Phil Garner

GARNER, PHILIP MASON (Scrap Iron)
B. Apr. 30, 1948, Jefferson City, Tenn.

BR TR 5'10" 175 lbs.

	G	AB	H	2B	3B	HR	HR%	R	RBI	BB	SO	SB	BA	SA	PH AB	PH H	G by POS
1973 OAK A	9	5	0	0	0	0	0.0	0	0	0	3	0	.000	.000	0	0	3B-9
1974	30	28	5	1	0	0	0.0	4	1	1	5	1	.179	.214	0	0	SS-8, 2B-3, DH-2
1975	160	488	120	21	5	6	1.2	46	54	30	65	4	.246	.346	0	0	2B-138, SS-1
1976	159	555	145	29	12	8	1.4	54	74	36	71	35	.261	.400	0	0	2B-159
1977 PIT N	153	585	152	35	10	17	2.9	99	77	55	65	32	.260	.441	2	0	3B-107, 2B-50, SS-12
1978	154	528	138	25	9	10	1.9	66	66	66	71	27	.261	.400	1	0	3B-81, 2B-81, SS-4
1979	150	549	161	32	8	11	2.0	76	59	55	74	17	.293	.441	0	0	2B-83, 3B-78, SS-14
1980	151	548	142	27	6	5	0.9	62	58	46	53	32	.259	.358	0	0	2B-151, SS-1
1981 2 teams			PIT	N (56G –		.254)		HOU	N	(31G –	.239)						
" total	87	294	73	9	3	1	0.3	35	26	36	32	10	.248	.310	3	2	2B-81
1982 HOU N	155	588	161	33	8	13	2.2	65	83	40	92	24	.274	.423	1	0	2B-136, 3B-18
1983	154	567	135	24	2	14	2.5	76	79	63	84	18	.238	.362	0	0	3B-154
1984	128	374	104	17	6	4	1.1	60	45	43	63	3	.278	.388	24	6	3B-82, 2B-35
1985	135	463	124	23	10	6	1.3	65	51	34	72	4	.268	.400	15	7	3B-123, 2B-15
1986	107	313	83	14	3	9	2.9	43	41	30	45	12	.265	.415	16	3	3B-84, 2B-7
1987 2 teams			HOU	N (43G –		.223)		LA	N	(70G –	.190)						
" total	113	238	49	9	0	5	2.1	29	23	28	44	6	.206	.307	24	4	3B-82, 2B-14, SS-2
1988 SF N	15	13	2	0	0	0	0.0	0	1	1	3	0	.154	.154	13	2	3B-2
16 yrs.	1860	6136	1594	299	82	109	1.8	780	738	564	842	225	.260	.389	99	24	2B-975, 3B-820, SS-42, DH-2

DIVISIONAL PLAYOFF SERIES
| 1981 HOU N | 5 | 18 | 2 | 0 | 0 | 0 | 0.0 | 1 | 0 | 3 | 3 | 0 | .111 | .111 | 0 | 0 | 2B-5 |

LEAGUE CHAMPIONSHIP SERIES
1975 OAK A	3	5	0	0	0	0	0.0	0	0	0	1	0	.000	.000	0	0	2B-3
1979 PIT N	3	12	5	0	1	1	8.3	4	1	1	0	0	.417	.833	0	0	2B-3
1986 HOU N	3	9	2	1	0	0	0.0	1	2	1	2	0	.222	.333	0	0	3B-3
3 yrs.	9	26	7	1	1	1	3.8	5	3	2	3	0	.269	.500	0	0	2B-6, 3B-3

WORLD SERIES
| 1979 PIT N | 7 | 24 | 12 | 4 | 0 | 0 | 0.0 | 4 | 5 | 3 | 1 | 0 | .500 | .667 | 0 | 0 | 2B-7 |

	G	AB	H	2B	3B	HR	HR %	R	RBI	BB	SO	SB	BA	SA	Pinch Hit AB	Pinch Hit H	G by POS

Rich Gedman

GEDMAN, RICHARD LEO
B. Sept. 26, 1959, Worcester, Mass.
BL TR 6'   210 lbs.

	G	AB	H	2B	3B	HR	HR %	R	RBI	BB	SO	SB	BA	SA	PH AB	PH H	G by POS
1980 **BOS A**	9	24	5	0	0	0	0.0	2	1	0	5	0	.208	.208	5	0	DH-4, C-2
1981	62	205	59	15	0	5	2.4	22	26	9	31	0	.288	.434	3	1	C-59
1982	92	289	72	17	2	4	1.4	30	26	10	37	0	.249	.363	9	2	C-86
1983	81	204	60	16	1	2	1.0	21	18	15	37	0	.294	.412	19	5	C-69
1984	133	449	121	26	4	24	5.3	54	72	29	72	0	.269	.506	15	5	C-125
1985	144	498	147	30	5	18	3.6	66	80	50	79	2	.295	.484	9	4	C-139
1986	135	462	119	29	0	16	3.5	49	65	37	61	1	.258	.424	9	4	C-134
1987	52	151	31	8	0	1	0.7	11	13	10	24	0	.205	.278	4	1	C-51
1988	95	299	69	14	0	9	3.0	33	39	18	49	0	.231	.368	2	0	C-93, DH-1
9 yrs.	803	2581	683	155	12	79	3.1	288	340	178	395	3	.265	.426	75	22	C-758, DH-5

LEAGUE CHAMPIONSHIP SERIES

	G	AB	H	2B	3B	HR	HR %	R	RBI	BB	SO	SB	BA	SA	PH AB	PH H	G by POS
1986 **BOS A**	7	28	10	1	0	1	3.6	4	6	0	4	0	.357	.500	0	0	C-7
1988	4	14	5	0	0	1	7.1	1	1	2	1	0	.357	.571	0	0	C-4
2 yrs.	11	42	15	1	0	2	4.8	5	7	2	5	0	.357	.524	0	0	C-11

WORLD SERIES

	G	AB	H	2B	3B	HR	HR %	R	RBI	BB	SO	SB	BA	SA	PH AB	PH H	G by POS
1986 **BOS A**	7	30	6	1	0	1	3.3	1	1	0	10	0	.200	.333	0	0	C-7

Bob Geren

GEREN, ROBERT PETER
B. Sept. 22, 1961, San Diego, Calif.
BR TR 6'3"   205 lbs.

	G	AB	H	2B	3B	HR	HR %	R	RBI	BB	SO	SB	BA	SA	PH AB	PH H	G by POS
1988 **NY A**	10	10	1	0	0	0	0.0	0	0	2	3	0	.100	.100	0	0	C-10

Ken Gerhart

GERHART, HAROLD KENNETH
B. May 19, 1961, Charleston, S. C.
BR TR 6'   190 lbs.

	G	AB	H	2B	3B	HR	HR %	R	RBI	BB	SO	SB	BA	SA	PH AB	PH H	G by POS
1986 **BAL A**	20	69	16	2	0	1	1.4	4	7	4	18	0	.232	.304	1	0	OF-20
1987	92	284	69	10	2	14	4.9	41	34	17	53	9	.243	.440	3	1	OF-91
1988	103	262	51	10	1	9	3.4	27	23	21	57	7	.195	.344	8	2	OF-93, DH-3
3 yrs.	215	615	136	22	3	24	3.9	72	64	42	128	16	.221	.384	12	3	OF-204, DH-3

Kirk Gibson

GIBSON, KIRK HAROLD
B. May 28, 1957, Pontiac, Mich.
BL TL 6'3"   215 lbs.

	G	AB	H	2B	3B	HR	HR %	R	RBI	BB	SO	SB	BA	SA	PH AB	PH H	G by POS
1979 **DET A**	12	38	9	3	0	1	2.6	3	4	1	3	3	.237	.395	2	0	OF-10
1980	51	175	46	2	1	9	5.1	23	16	10	45	4	.263	.440	5	1	OF-49, DH-1
1981	83	290	95	11	3	9	3.1	41	40	18	64	17	.328	.479	8	1	OF-67, DH-9
1982	69	266	74	16	2	8	3.0	34	35	25	41	9	.278	.444	1	0	OF-64, DH-4
1983	128	401	91	12	9	15	3.7	60	51	53	96	14	.227	.414	20	5	DH-66, OF-54
1984	149	531	150	23	10	27	5.1	92	91	63	103	29	.282	.516	11	1	OF-139, DH-6
1985	154	581	167	37	5	29	5.0	96	97	71	137	30	.287	.518	3	2	OF-144, DH-8
1986	119	441	118	11	2	28	6.3	84	86	68	107	34	.268	.492	2	1	OF-114, DH-4
1987	128	487	135	25	3	24	4.9	95	79	71	117	26	.277	.489	3	0	OF-121, DH-4
1988 **LA N**	150	542	157	28	1	25	4.6	106	76	73	120	31	.290	.483	3	0	OF-148
10 yrs.	1043	3752	1042	168	36	175	4.7	634	575	453	833	197	.278	.482	58	11	OF-910, DH-102

LEAGUE CHAMPIONSHIP SERIES

	G	AB	H	2B	3B	HR	HR %	R	RBI	BB	SO	SB	BA	SA	PH AB	PH H	G by POS
1984 **DET A**	3	12	5	1	0	1	8.3	2	2	2	1	1	.417	.750	0	0	OF-3
1987	5	21	6	1	0	1	4.8	4	4	3	8	3	.286	.476	0	0	OF-5
1988 **LA N**	7	26	4	0	0	2	7.7	2	6	3	6	2	.154	.385	0	0	OF-7
3 yrs.	15	59	15	2	0	4	6.8	8	12	8	15	6	.254	.492	0	0	OF-15

WORLD SERIES

	G	AB	H	2B	3B	HR	HR %	R	RBI	BB	SO	SB	BA	SA	PH AB	PH H	G by POS
1984 **DET A**	5	18	6	0	0	2	11.1	4	7	4	4	3	.333	.667	0	0	OF-5
1988 **LA N**	1	1	1	0	0	1	0.0	1	2	0	0	0	1.000	4.000	1	1	
2 yrs.	6	19	7	0	0	3	15.8	5	9	4	4	3	.368	.842	1	1	OF-5

Dan Gladden

GLADDEN, CLINTON DANIEL III
B. July 7, 1957, San Jose, Calif.
BR TR 5'11"   175 lbs.

	G	AB	H	2B	3B	HR	HR %	R	RBI	BB	SO	SB	BA	SA	PH AB	PH H	G by POS
1983 **SF N**	18	63	14	2	0	1	1.6	6	9	5	11	4	.222	.302	1	0	OF-18
1984	86	342	120	17	2	4	1.2	71	31	33	37	31	.351	.447	2	0	OF-85
1985	142	502	122	15	8	7	1.4	64	41	40	78	32	.243	.347	19	8	OF-124
1986	102	351	97	16	1	4	1.1	55	29	39	59	27	.276	.362	9	1	OF-89
1987 **MIN A**	121	438	109	21	2	8	1.8	69	38	38	72	25	.249	.361	9	2	OF-111, DH-4
1988	141	576	155	32	6	11	1.9	91	62	46	74	28	.269	.403	4	1	OF-140, 3B-1, 2B-1, P-1
6 yrs.	610	2272	617	103	19	35	1.5	356	210	201	331	147	.272	.380	44	12	OF-567, DH-4, 3B-1, 2B-1, P-1

LEAGUE CHAMPIONSHIP SERIES

	G	AB	H	2B	3B	HR	HR %	R	RBI	BB	SO	SB	BA	SA	PH AB	PH H	G by POS
1987 **MIN A**	5	20	7	2	0	0	0.0	5	5	2	1	0	.350	.450	0	0	OF-5

WORLD SERIES

	G	AB	H	2B	3B	HR	HR %	R	RBI	BB	SO	SB	BA	SA	PH AB	PH H	G by POS
1987 **MIN A**	7	31	9	2	1	1	3.2	3	7	3	4	2	.290	.516	0	0	OF-7

Rene Gonzales

GONZALES, RENE ADRIAN
B. Sept. 23, 1960, Austin, Tex.
BR TR 6'3"   180 lbs.

	G	AB	H	2B	3B	HR	HR %	R	RBI	BB	SO	SB	BA	SA	PH AB	PH H	G by POS
1984 **MON N**	29	30	7	1	0	0	0.0	5	2	2	5	0	.233	.267	0	0	SS-27
1986	11	26	3	0	0	0	0.0	1	0	2	7	0	.115	.115	0	0	SS-6, 3B-5
1987 **BAL A**	37	60	16	2	1	1	1.7	14	7	3	11	1	.267	.383	0	0	3B-29, 2B-6, SS-1
1988	92	237	51	6	0	2	0.8	13	15	13	32	2	.215	.266	0	0	3B-80, 2B-14, SS-2, OF-1, 1B-1
4 yrs.	169	353	77	9	1	3	0.8	33	24	20	55	3	.218	.275	0	0	3B-114, SS-36, 2B-20, OF-1, 1B-1

Denny Gonzalez

GONZALEZ, DENIO MARIANO MANZUETA
Born Denio Mariano Gonzalez y Manzueta.
B. July 22, 1963, Sabana Grande Boya, Dominican Republic
BR TR 5'11"   165 lbs.

	G	AB	H	2B	3B	HR	HR %	R	RBI	BB	SO	SB	BA	SA	PH AB	PH H	G by POS
1984 **PIT N**	26	82	15	3	0	0	0.0	9	4	7	21	1	.183	.244	0	0	3B-11, SS-10, OF-3
1985	35	124	28	4	0	4	3.2	11	12	13	27	2	.226	.355	1	0	3B-21, OF-13, 2B-6
1987	5	7	0	0	0	0	0.0	1	0	1	2	0	.000	.000	4	0	SS-1
1988	24	32	6	1	0	0	0.0	5	1	6	10	0	.188	.219	10	3	SS-14, 2B-4, 3B-2
4 yrs.	90	245	49	8	1	4	1.6	26	17	27	60	3	.200	.290	15	3	3B-34, SS-25, OF-16, 2B-10

	G	AB	H	2B	3B	HR	HR %	R	RBI	BB	SO	SB	BA	SA	Pinch Hit AB	Pinch Hit H	G by POS

Jose Gonzalez

Playing record listed under Jose Uribe

Jose Gonzalez

GONZALEZ, JOSE RAFAEL   BR   TR   6'3"   197 lbs.
Born Jose Rafael Gonzalez y Gutierrez.
B. Nov. 23, 1964, Puerta Plata, Dominican Republic

	G	AB	H	2B	3B	HR	HR %	R	RBI	BB	SO	SB	BA	SA	PH AB	PH H	G by POS
1985 LA N	23	11	3	2	0	0	0.0	6	0	1	3	1	.273	.455	1	0	OF-18
1986	57	93	20	5	1	2	2.2	15	6	7	29	4	.215	.355	5	1	OF-57
1987	19	16	3	2	0	0	0.0	2	1	1	2	5	.188	.313	2	0	OF-16
1988	37	24	2	1	0	0	0.0	7	0	2	10	3	.083	.125	9	2	OF-24
4 yrs.	136	144	28	10	1	2	1.4	30	7	11	44	13	.194	.319	17	3	OF-115
LEAGUE CHAMPIONSHIP SERIES																	
1988 LA N	5	0	0	0	0	0	–	2	0	0	0	0	–	–	0	0	OF-4
WORLD SERIES																	
1988 LA N	4	2	0	0	0	0	0.0	0	0	0	2	0	.000	.000	2	0	OF-3

Mark Grace

GRACE, MARK EUGENE   BL   TL   6'2"   190 lbs.
B. June 28, 1964, Winston-Salem, N. C.

	G	AB	H	2B	3B	HR	HR %	R	RBI	BB	SO	SB	BA	SA	PH AB	PH H	G by POS
1988 CHI N	134	486	144	23	4	7	1.4	65	57	60	43	3	.296	.403	7	3	1B-133

Mike Greenwell

GREENWELL, MICHAEL LEWIS   BL   TR   6'   170 lbs.
B. July 18, 1963, Louisville, Ky.

	G	AB	H	2B	3B	HR	HR %	R	RBI	BB	SO	SB	BA	SA	PH AB	PH H	G by POS
1985 BOS A	17	31	10	1	0	4	12.9	7	8	3	4	1	.323	.742	1	0	OF-17
1986	31	35	11	2	0	0	0.0	4	4	5	7	0	.314	.371	12	2	OF-15, DH-3
1987	125	412	135	31	6	19	4.6	71	89	35	40	5	.328	.570	17	5	OF-91, DH-15, C-1
1988	158	590	192	39	8	22	3.7	86	119	87	38	16	.325	.531	0	0	OF-147, DH-11
4 yrs.	331	1068	348	73	14	45	4.2	168	220	130	89	22	.326	.547	30	7	OF-270, DH-29, C-1
LEAGUE CHAMPIONSHIP SERIES																	
1986 BOS A	2	2	1	0	0	1	50.0	2	2	0	0	0	.500	.500	2	1	
1988	4	14	3	1	0	1	7.1	2	3	3	0	0	.214	.500	0	0	OF-4
2 yrs.	6	16	4	1	0	1	6.3	2	3	3	0	0	.250	.500	2	1	OF-4
WORLD SERIES																	
1986 BOS A	4	3	0	0	0	0	0.0	0	0	1	2	0	.000	.000	3	0	

Tommy Gregg

GREGG, WILLIAM THOMAS   BL   TL   6'1"   190 lbs.
B. July 29, 1963, Boone, N. C.

	G	AB	H	2B	3B	HR	HR %	R	RBI	BB	SO	SB	BA	SA	PH AB	PH H	G by POS
1987 PIT N	10	8	2	1	0	0	0.0	3	0	0	2	0	.250	.375	7	2	OF-4
1988 2 teams					PIT N (14G – .200)			ATL N (11G – .345)									
" total	25	44	13	4	0	1	2.3	5	7	3	6	0	.295	.455	12	2	OF-13
2 yrs.	35	52	15	5	0	1	1.9	8	7	3	8	0	.288	.442	19	4	OF-17

Ken Griffey

GRIFFEY, GEORGE KENNETH   BL   TL   5'11"   190 lbs.
B. Apr. 10, 1950, Donora, Pa.

	G	AB	H	2B	3B	HR	HR %	R	RBI	BB	SO	SB	BA	SA	PH AB	PH H	G by POS
1973 CIN N	25	86	33	5	1	3	3.5	19	14	6	10	4	.384	.570	3	2	OF-21
1974	88	227	57	9	5	2	0.9	24	19	27	43	9	.251	.361	15	4	OF-70
1975	132	463	141	15	9	4	0.9	95	46	67	67	16	.305	.402	10	2	OF-119
1976	148	562	189	28	9	6	1.1	111	74	62	65	34	.336	.450	10	3	OF-144
1977	154	585	186	35	8	12	2.1	117	57	69	84	17	.318	.467	4	1	OF-147
1978	158	614	177	33	8	10	1.6	90	63	54	70	23	.288	.417	6	3	OF-154
1979	95	380	120	27	4	8	2.1	62	32	36	39	12	.316	.471	4	1	OF-93
1980	146	544	160	28	10	13	2.4	89	85	62	77	23	.294	.454	7	4	OF-138
1981	101	396	123	21	6	2	0.5	65	34	39	42	12	.311	.409	1	0	OF-99
1982 NY A	127	484	134	23	2	12	2.5	70	54	39	58	10	.277	.407	7	1	OF-125
1983	118	458	140	21	3	11	2.4	60	46	34	45	6	.306	.437	5	1	1B-101, OF-14, DH-2
1984	120	399	109	20	1	7	1.8	44	56	29	32	2	.273	.381	18	5	OF-82, 1B-27, DH-2
1985	127	438	120	28	4	10	2.3	68	69	41	51	7	.274	.425	18	2	OF-110, DH-7, 1B-1
1986 2 teams					NY A (59G – .303)			ATL N (80G – .308)									
" total	139	490	150	22	3	21	4.3	69	58	35	67	14	.306	.492	19	8	OF-128, DH-2, 1B-1
1987 ATL N	122	399	114	24	1	14	3.5	65	64	46	54	4	.286	.456	18	11	OF-110
1988 2 teams					ATL N (69G – .249)			CIN N (25G – .280)									
" total	94	243	62	6	0	4	1.6	26	23	19	31	1	.255	.329	31	5	OF-42, 1B-21
16 yrs.	1894	6768	2015	345	74	139	2.1	1074	794	665	835	194	.298	.432	173	53	OF-1596, 1B-151, DH-13
LEAGUE CHAMPIONSHIP SERIES																	
1973 CIN N	3	7	1	1	0	0	0.0	0	0	0	1	0	.143	.286	1	0	OF-2
1975	3	12	4	1	0	0	0.0	4	4	0	3	3	.333	.417	0	0	OF-3
1976	3	13	5	0	1	0	0.0	2	2	2	1	2	.385	.538	0	0	OF-3
3 yrs.	9	32	10	2	1	0	0.0	6	6	2	5	5	.313	.438	1	0	OF-8
WORLD SERIES																	
1975 CIN N	7	26	7	3	1	0	0.0	4	4	4	2	2	.269	.462	0	0	OF-7
1976	4	17	1	0	0	0	0.0	2	1	0	1	1	.059	.059	0	0	OF-4
2 yrs.	11	43	8	3	1	0	0.0	6	5	4	3	3	.186	.302	0	0	OF-11

Alfredo Griffin

GRIFFIN, ALFREDO CLAUDINO   BB   TR   5'11"   160 lbs.
Born Alfredo Claudino Baptist y Griffin.
B. Oct. 6, 1957, Santo Domingo, Dominican Republic

	G	AB	H	2B	3B	HR	HR %	R	RBI	BB	SO	SB	BA	SA	PH AB	PH H	G by POS
1976 CLE A	12	4	1	0	0	0	0.0	0	0	0	2	0	.250	.250	0	0	SS-6, DH-4
1977	14	41	6	1	0	0	0.0	5	3	3	5	2	.146	.171	0	0	SS-13, DH-1
1978	5	4	2	1	0	0	0.0	1	0	2	1	0	.500	.750	0	0	SS-2
1979 TOR A	153	624	179	22	10	2	0.3	81	31	40	59	21	.287	.364	0	0	SS-153
1980	155	653	166	26	15	2	0.3	63	41	24	58	18	.254	.349	0	0	SS-155
1981	101	388	81	19	6	0	0.0	30	21	17	38	8	.209	.289	1	0	SS-97, 3B-4, 2B-1
1982	162	539	130	20	8	1	0.2	57	48	22	48	10	.241	.314	0	0	SS-162
1983	162	528	132	22	9	4	0.8	62	47	27	44	8	.250	.348	0	0	SS-157, 2B-5, DH-1
1984	140	419	101	8	2	4	1.0	53	30	4	33	11	.241	.298	0	0	SS-115, 2B-21, DH-5
1985 OAK A	162	614	166	18	7	2	0.3	75	64	20	50	24	.270	.332	0	0	SS-162

	G	AB	H	2B	3B	HR	HR %	R	RBI	BB	SO	SB	BA	SA	Pinch Hit AB	Pinch Hit H	G by POS

Alfredo Griffin continued

	G	AB	H	2B	3B	HR	HR %	R	RBI	BB	SO	SB	BA	SA	AB	H	G by POS
1986	162	594	169	23	6	4	0.7	74	51	35	52	33	.285	.364	0	0	SS-162
1987	144	494	130	23	5	3	0.6	69	60	28	41	26	.263	.348	0	0	SS-137, 2B-1
1988 LA N	95	316	63	8	3	1	0.3	39	27	24	30	7	.199	.253	0	0	SS-93
13 yrs.	1467	5218	1326	191	71	23	0.4	609	423	246	461	168	.254	.331	1	0	SS-1414, 2B-28, DH-11, 3B-4

LEAGUE CHAMPIONSHIP SERIES

	G	AB	H	2B	3B	HR	HR %	R	RBI	BB	SO	SB	BA	SA	AB	H	G by POS
1988 LA N	7	25	4	1	0	0	0.0	1	3	0	5	0	.160	.200	0	0	SS-7

WORLD SERIES

	G	AB	H	2B	3B	HR	HR %	R	RBI	BB	SO	SB	BA	SA	AB	H	G by POS
1988 LA N	5	16	3	0	0	0	0.0	2	0	2	4	0	.188	.188	0	0	SS-5

Greg Gross

GROSS, GREGORY EUGENE
B. Aug. 1, 1952, York, Pa.

BL TL 5'10"   160 lbs.

	G	AB	H	2B	3B	HR	HR %	R	RBI	BB	SO	SB	BA	SA	AB	H	G by POS
1973 HOU N	14	39	9	2	1	0	0.0	5	1	4	4	2	.231	.333	4	0	OF-9
1974	156	589	185	21	8	0	0.0	78	36	76	39	12	.314	.377	5	2	OF-151
1975	132	483	142	14	10	0	0.0	67	41	63	37	2	.294	.364	8	1	OF-121
1976	128	426	122	12	3	0	0.0	52	27	64	39	2	.286	.329	13	1	OF-115
1977 CHI N	115	239	77	10	4	5	2.1	43	32	33	19	0	.322	.460	39	10	OF-71
1978	124	347	92	12	7	1	0.3	34	39	33	19	3	.265	.349	20	5	OF-111
1979 PHI N	111	174	58	6	3	0	0.0	21	15	29	5	5	.333	.402	51	14	OF-73
1980	127	154	37	7	2	0	0.0	19	12	24	7	1	.240	.312	39	10	OF-91, 1B-1
1981	83	102	23	6	1	0	0.0	14	7	15	5	2	.225	.304	39	6	OF-55
1982	119	134	40	4	0	0	0.0	14	10	19	8	4	.299	.328	53	19	OF-71
1983	136	245	74	12	3	0	0.0	25	29	34	16	3	.302	.376	33	7	OF-110, 1B-1
1984	112	202	65	9	1	0	0.0	19	16	24	11	1	.322	.376	46	13	OF-48, 1B-28
1985	93	169	44	5	2	0	0.0	21	14	32	9	1	.260	.314	41	7	OF-52, 1B-8
1986	87	101	25	5	0	0	0.0	11	8	21	11	1	.248	.297	52	13	OF-27, 1B-5, P-1
1987	114	133	38	4	1	1	0.8	14	12	25	12	0	.286	.353	55	15	OF-50, 1B-11
1988	98	133	27	1	0	0	0.0	10	5	16	3	0	.203	.211	52	13	OF-37, 1B-14
16 yrs.	1749	3670	1058	130	46	7	0.2	447	304	512	244	39	.288	.354	550 **1st**	136 **3rd**	OF-1192, 1B-68, P-1

DIVISIONAL PLAYOFF SERIES

	G	AB	H	2B	3B	HR	HR %	R	RBI	BB	SO	SB	BA	SA	AB	H	G by POS
1981 PHI N	4	4	0	0	0	0	0.0	0	0	0	0	0	.000	.000	3	0	OF-2

LEAGUE CHAMPIONSHIP SERIES

	G	AB	H	2B	3B	HR	HR %	R	RBI	BB	SO	SB	BA	SA	AB	H	G by POS
1980 PHI N	4	4	3	0	0	0	0.0	2	1	0	0	0	.750	.750	2	2	OF-1
1983	4	5	0	0	0	0	0.0	1	0	2	2	0	.000	.000	0	0	OF-3
2 yrs.	8	9	3	0	0	0	0.0	3	1	2	2	0	.333	.333	2	2	OF-4

WORLD SERIES

	G	AB	H	2B	3B	HR	HR %	R	RBI	BB	SO	SB	BA	SA	AB	H	G by POS
1980 PHI N	4	2	0	0	0	0	0.0	0	0	0	0	0	.000	.000	1	0	OF-3
1983	2	6	0	0	0	0	0.0	0	0	0	0	0	.000	.000	0	0	OF-2
2 yrs.	6	8	0	0	0	0	0.0	0	0	0	0	0	.000	.000	1	0	OF-5

Kelly Gruber

GRUBER, KELLY WAYNE
B. Feb. 26, 1962, Houston, Tex.

BR TR 6'   175 lbs.

	G	AB	H	2B	3B	HR	HR %	R	RBI	BB	SO	SB	BA	SA	AB	H	G by POS
1984 TOR A	15	16	1	0	0	1	6.3	1	2	1	5	0	.063	.250	4	1	3B-12, OF-2, SS-1
1985	5	13	3	0	0	0	0.0	0	1	0	3	0	.231	.231	1	1	3B-5, 2B-1
1986	87	143	28	4	1	5	3.5	20	15	5	27	2	.196	.343	9	2	3B-42, DH-14, 2B-14, OF-9, SS-5
1987	138	341	80	14	3	12	3.5	50	36	17	70	12	.235	.399	16	2	3B-119, SS-21, 2B-7, OF-2
1988	158	569	158	33	5	16	2.8	75	81	38	92	23	.278	.438	3	0	3B-156, 2B-7, OF-2, SS-1
5 yrs.	403	1082	270	51	9	34	3.1	146	135	60	197	37	.250	.408	33	6	3B-334, 2B-29, SS-28, OF-15, DH-14

Pedro Guerrero

GUERRERO, PEDRO
B. June 29, 1956, San Pedro de Macoris, Dominican Republic

BR TR 5'11"   176 lbs.

	G	AB	H	2B	3B	HR	HR %	R	RBI	BB	SO	SB	BA	SA	AB	H	G by POS
1978 LA N	5	8	5	0	1	0	0.0	3	1	0	0	0	.625	.875	1	1	1B-4
1979	25	62	15	2	0	2	3.2	7	9	1	14	2	.242	.371	7	3	OF-12, 1B-8, 3B-3
1980	75	183	59	9	1	7	3.8	27	31	12	31	2	.322	.497	17	11	OF-40, 2B-12, 3B-3, 1B-2
1981	98	347	104	17	2	12	3.5	46	48	34	57	5	.300	.464	4	1	OF-75, 3B-21, 1B-1
1982	150	575	175	27	5	32	5.6	87	100	65	89	22	.304	.536	0	0	OF-137, 3B-24
1983	160	584	174	28	6	32	5.5	87	103	72	110	23	.298	.531	1	1	3B-157, 1B-2
1984	144	535	162	29	4	16	3.0	85	72	49	105	9	.303	.462	7	1	3B-76, OF-58, 1B-16
1985	137	487	156	22	2	33	6.8	99	87	83	68	12	.320	**.577**	3	0	OF-81, 3B-44, 1B-12
1986	31	61	15	3	0	5	8.2	7	10	2	19	0	.246	.541	17	3	OF-10, 1B-4
1987	152	545	184	25	2	27	5.0	89	89	74	85	9	.338	.539	4	0	OF-109, 1B-40
1988 2 teams	LA	N	(59G –	.298)				STL	N	(44G –	.268)						
" total	103	364	104	14	2	10	2.7	40	65	46	59	4	.286	.418	1	0	1B-52, 3B-45, OF-9
11 yrs.	1080	3751	1153	176	25	176	4.7	577	615	438	637	88	.307	.508	62	21	OF-531, 3B-373, 1B-141, 2B-12

DIVISIONAL PLAYOFF SERIES

	G	AB	H	2B	3B	HR	HR %	R	RBI	BB	SO	SB	BA	SA	AB	H	G by POS
1981 LA N	5	17	3	1	0	1	5.9	1	1	2	4	1	.176	.412	0	0	3B-5

LEAGUE CHAMPIONSHIP SERIES

	G	AB	H	2B	3B	HR	HR %	R	RBI	BB	SO	SB	BA	SA	AB	H	G by POS
1981 LA N	5	19	2	0	0	1	5.3	1	2	1	4	0	.105	.263	0	0	OF-5
1983	4	12	3	1	1	0	0.0	1	2	3	3	0	.250	.500	0	0	3B-4
1985	6	20	5	1	0	0	0.0	2	4	5	2	2	.250	.300	0	0	OF-6
3 yrs.	15	51	10	2	1	1	2.0	4	8	9	9	2	.196	.333	0	0	OF-11, 3B-4

WORLD SERIES

	G	AB	H	2B	3B	HR	HR %	R	RBI	BB	SO	SB	BA	SA	AB	H	G by POS
1981 LA N	6	21	7	1	1	2	9.5	2	7	2	6	0	.333	.762	0	0	OF-6

	G	AB	H	2B	3B	HR	HR%	R	RBI	BB	SO	SB	BA	SA	Pinch Hit AB	Pinch Hit H	G by POS

Ozzie Guillen

GUILLEN, OSWALDO JOSE
Born Oswaldo Jose Guillen y Barrios.
B. Jan. 20, 1964, Oculare del Tuy, Venezuela

BL TR 5'11" 160 lbs.

	G	AB	H	2B	3B	HR	HR%	R	RBI	BB	SO	SB	BA	SA	PH AB	PH H	G by POS
1985 CHI A	150	491	134	21	9	1	0.2	71	33	12	36	7	.273	.358	13	1	SS-150
1986	159	547	137	19	4	2	0.4	58	47	12	52	8	.250	.311	2	0	SS-157, DH-1
1987	149	560	156	22	7	2	0.4	64	51	22	52	25	.279	.354	2	1	SS-149
1988	156	566	148	16	7	0	0.0	58	39	25	40	25	.261	.314	0	0	SS-156
4 yrs.	614	2164	575	78	27	5	0.2	251	170	71	180	65	.266	.334	17	2	SS-612, DH-1

Jackie Gutierrez

GUTIERREZ, JOAQUIN FERNANDO HERNANDEZ
Born Joaquin Fernando Gutierrez y Hernandez.
B. June 27, 1960, Cartagena, Colombia

BR TR 5'11" 168 lbs.

	G	AB	H	2B	3B	HR	HR%	R	RBI	BB	SO	SB	BA	SA	PH AB	PH H	G by POS
1983 BOS A	5	10	3	0	0	0	0.0	2	0	1	1	0	.300	.300	0	0	SS-4
1984	151	449	118	12	3	2	0.4	55	29	15	49	12	.263	.316	0	0	SS-150
1985	103	275	60	5	2	2	0.7	33	21	12	37	10	.218	.273	1	0	SS-99
1986 BAL A	61	145	27	3	0	0	0.0	8	4	3	27	3	.186	.207	0	0	2B-53, 3B-6, DH-1
1987	3	1	0	0	0	0	0.0	0	0	0	0	0	.000	.000	0	0	3B-1, 2B-1
1988 PHI N	33	77	19	4	0	0	0.0	8	9	2	9	0	.247	.299	1	0	SS-22, 3B-13
6 yrs.	356	957	227	24	5	4	0.4	106	63	33	123	25	.237	.285	2	0	SS-275, 2B-54, 3B-20, DH-1

Chris Gwynn

GWYNN, CHRISTOPHER KARLTON
Brother of Tony Gwynn.
B. Oct. 13, 1964, Los Angeles, Calif.

BL TL 6' 200 lbs.

	G	AB	H	2B	3B	HR	HR%	R	RBI	BB	SO	SB	BA	SA	PH AB	PH H	G by POS
1987 LA N	17	32	7	1	0	0	0.0	2	1	1	7	0	.219	.250	6	0	OF-10
1988	12	11	2	0	0	0	0.0	1	0	1	2	0	.182	.182	9	2	OF-4
2 yrs.	29	43	9	1	0	0	0.0	3	2	2	9	0	.209	.233	15	2	OF-14

Tony Gwynn

GWYNN, ANTHONY KEITH
Brother of Chris Gwynn.
B. May 9, 1960, Los Angeles, Calif.

BL TL 5'11" 185 lbs.

	G	AB	H	2B	3B	HR	HR%	R	RBI	BB	SO	SB	BA	SA	PH AB	PH H	G by POS
1982 SD N	54	190	55	12	2	1	0.5	33	17	14	16	8	.289	.389	4	1	OF-52
1983	86	304	94	12	2	1	0.3	34	37	23	21	7	.309	.372	6	1	OF-81
1984	158	606	213	21	10	5	0.8	88	71	59	23	33	.351	.444	2	1	OF-156
1985	154	622	197	29	5	6	1.0	90	46	45	33	14	.317	.408	2	0	OF-152
1986	160	642	211	33	7	14	2.2	107	59	52	35	37	.329	.467	1	0	OF-160
1987	157	589	218	36	13	7	1.2	119	54	82	35	56	.370	.511	2	1	OF-156
1988	133	521	163	22	5	7	1.3	64	70	51	40	26	.313	.415	0	0	OF-133
7 yrs.	902	3474	1151	165	44	41	1.2	535	354	326	203	181	.331	.440	17	4	OF-890

LEAGUE CHAMPIONSHIP SERIES

	G	AB	H	2B	3B	HR	HR%	R	RBI	BB	SO	SB	BA	SA	PH AB	PH H	G by POS
1984 SD N	5	19	7	3	0	0	0.0	6	3	1	2	0	.368	.526	0	0	OF-5

WORLD SERIES

	G	AB	H	2B	3B	HR	HR%	R	RBI	BB	SO	SB	BA	SA	PH AB	PH H	G by POS
1984 SD N	5	19	5	0	0	0	0.0	1	0	3	2	1	.263	.263	0	0	OF-5

Jerry Hairston

HAIRSTON, JERRY WAYNE
Brother of John Hairston. Son of Sam Hairston.
B. Feb. 16, 1952, Birmingham, Ala.

BB TR 5'10" 170 lbs.

	G	AB	H	2B	3B	HR	HR%	R	RBI	BB	SO	SB	BA	SA	PH AB	PH H	G by POS
1973 CHI A	60	210	57	11	1	0	0.0	25	23	33	30	0	.271	.333	2	0	OF-33, 1B-19, DH-8
1974	45	109	25	7	0	0	0.0	8	8	13	18	0	.229	.294	12	2	OF-22, DH-10
1975	69	219	62	8	0	0	0.0	26	23	46	23	1	.283	.320	3	0	OF-59, DH-8
1976	44	119	27	2	2	0	0.0	20	10	24	19	1	.227	.277	4	1	OF-40
1977 2 teams				CHI	A (13G –	.308)		PIT	N	(51G –	.192)						
" total	64	78	18	4	0	2	2.6	8	10	11	17	0	.231	.359	34	7	OF-25, 2B-1
1981 CHI A	9	25	7	1	0	1	4.0	5	6	2	4	0	.280	.440	2	1	OF-7
1982	85	90	21	5	0	5	5.6	11	18	9	15	0	.233	.456	47	11	OF-36, DH-2
1983	101	126	37	9	1	5	4.0	17	22	23	16	0	.294	.500	62	17	OF-32, DH-4
1984	115	227	59	13	2	5	2.2	41	19	41	29	2	.260	.401	59	18	OF-37, DH-20
1985	95	140	34	8	0	2	1.4	9	20	29	18	0	.243	.343	53	14	DH-29, OF-5
1986	101	225	61	15	0	5	2.2	32	26	26	26	0	.271	.404	46	14	DH-19, 1B-19, OF-11
1987	66	126	29	8	0	5	4.0	14	20	25	25	0	.230	.413	32	8	DH-13, OF-13, 1B-7
1988	2	2	0	0	0	0	0.0	0	0	0	0	0	.000	.000	2	0	
13 yrs.	856	1696	437	91	6	30	1.8	216	205	282	240	4	.258	.371	358	93	OF-320, DH-123, 1B-45, 2B-1

LEAGUE CHAMPIONSHIP SERIES

	G	AB	H	2B	3B	HR	HR%	R	RBI	BB	SO	SB	BA	SA	PH AB	PH H	G by POS
1983 CHI A	2	3	0	0	0	0	0.0	0	0	1	1	0	.000	.000	2	0	OF-2

Albert Hall

HALL, ALBERT
B. Mar. 7, 1958, Birmingham, Ala.

BB TR 5'11" 155 lbs.

	G	AB	H	2B	3B	HR	HR%	R	RBI	BB	SO	SB	BA	SA	PH AB	PH H	G by POS
1981 ATL N	6	2	0	0	0	0	0.0	1	0	1	1	0	.000	.000	1	0	OF-2
1982	5	0	0	0	0	0	–	1	0	0	0	0	–	–	0	0	
1983	10	8	0	0	0	0	0.0	2	0	2	2	1	.000	.000	1	0	OF-4
1984	87	142	37	6	1	1	0.7	25	9	10	18	6	.261	.338	13	5	OF-66
1985	54	47	7	0	1	0	0.0	5	3	9	12	1	.149	.191	32	5	OF-13
1986	16	50	12	2	0	0	0.0	6	1	5	6	8	.240	.280	1	0	OF-14
1987	92	292	83	20	4	3	1.0	54	24	38	36	33	.284	.411	25	7	OF-69
1988	85	231	57	7	1	1	0.4	27	15	21	35	15	.247	.299	16	2	OF-63
8 yrs.	355	772	196	35	7	5	0.6	121	52	86	110	64	.254	.337	89	19	OF-231

Mel Hall

HALL, MELVIN, JR.
B. Sept. 16, 1960, Lyons, N. Y.

BL TL 6' 185 lbs.

	G	AB	H	2B	3B	HR	HR%	R	RBI	BB	SO	SB	BA	SA	PH AB	PH H	G by POS
1981 CHI N	10	11	1	0	0	1	9.1	1	2	1	4	0	.091	.364	7	1	OF-3
1982	24	80	21	3	2	0	0.0	6	4	5	17	0	.263	.350	1	0	OF-22
1983	112	410	116	23	5	17	4.1	60	56	42	101	6	.283	.488	2	1	OF-112
1984 2 teams				CHI	N (48G –	.280)		CLE	A	(83G –	.257)						
" total	131	407	108	24	4	11	2.7	68	52	47	78	3	.265	.425	14	3	OF-115, DH-9
1985 CLE A	23	66	21	6	0	0	0.0	7	12	8	12	0	.318	.409	6	2	OF-15, DH-5
1986	140	442	131	29	2	18	4.1	68	77	33	65	6	.296	.493	19	6	OF-126, DH-7

	G	AB	H	2B	3B	HR	HR %	R	RBI	BB	SO	SB	BA	SA	Pinch Hit AB	Pinch Hit H	G by POS

Mel Hall continued

	G	AB	H	2B	3B	HR	HR%	R	RBI	BB	SO	SB	BA	SA	AB	H	G by POS
1987	142	485	136	21	1	18	3.7	57	76	20	68	5	.280	.439	17	2	OF-122, DH-14
1988	150	515	144	32	4	6	1.2	69	71	28	50	7	.280	.392	11	4	OF-141, DH-6
8 yrs.	732	2416	678	138	18	71	2.9	336	350	184	395	27	.281	.441	77	19	OF-656, DH-14

Darryl Hamilton

HAMILTON, DARRYL QUINN
B. Dec. 3, 1963, Baton Rouge, La.

BL TR 6'1''   180 lbs.

	G	AB	H	2B	3B	HR	HR%	R	RBI	BB	SO	SB	BA	SA	AB	H	G by POS
1988 MIL A	44	103	19	4	0	1	1.0	14	11	12	9	7	.184	.252	3	1	OF-37, DH-3

Jeff Hamilton

HAMILTON, JEFFREY ROBERT
B. Mar. 19, 1964, Flint, Mich.

BR TR 6'3''   190 lbs.

	G	AB	H	2B	3B	HR	HR%	R	RBI	BB	SO	SB	BA	SA	AB	H	G by POS
1986 LA N	71	147	33	5	0	5	3.4	22	19	2	43	0	.224	.361	6	2	3B-66, SS-2
1987	35	83	18	3	0	0	0.0	5	1	7	22	0	.217	.253	6	0	3B-31, SS-1
1988	111	309	73	14	2	6	1.9	34	33	10	51	0	.236	.353	9	3	3B-105, SS-2, 1B-1
3 yrs.	217	539	124	22	2	11	2.0	61	53	19	116	0	.230	.340	21	5	3B-202, SS-5, 1B-1

LEAGUE CHAMPIONSHIP SERIES

	G	AB	H	2B	3B	HR	HR%	R	RBI	BB	SO	SB	BA	SA	AB	H	G by POS
1988 LA N	7	23	5	0	0	0	0.0	2	1	3	4	0	.217	.217	0	0	3B-7

WORLD SERIES

	G	AB	H	2B	3B	HR	HR%	R	RBI	BB	SO	SB	BA	SA	AB	H	G by POS
1988 LA N	5	19	2	0	0	0	0.0	1	0	1	4	0	.105	.105	0	0	3B-5

Brian Harper

HARPER, BRIAN DAVID
B. Oct. 16, 1959, Los Angeles, Calif.

BR TR 6'2''   195 lbs.

	G	AB	H	2B	3B	HR	HR%	R	RBI	BB	SO	SB	BA	SA	AB	H	G by POS
1979 CAL A	1	2	0	0	0	0	0.0	0	0	0	1	0	.000	.000	1	0	DH-1
1981	4	11	3	0	0	0	0.0	1	1	0	0	1	.273	.273	1	0	OF-2, DH-1
1982 PIT N	20	29	8	1	0	2	6.9	4	4	1	4	0	.276	.517	12	5	OF-8
1983	61	131	29	4	1	7	5.3	16	20	2	15	0	.221	.427	27	6	OF-35, 1B-1
1984	48	112	29	4	0	2	1.8	4	11	5	11	0	.259	.348	11	2	OF-37, C-2
1985 STL N	43	52	13	4	0	0	0.0	5	8	2	3	0	.250	.327	26	7	OF-13, 3B-6, C-2, 1B-1
1986 DET A	19	36	5	1	0	0	0.0	2	3	3	3	0	.139	.167	4	2	OF-11, DH-6, 1B-2, C-2
1987 OAK A	11	17	4	1	0	0	0.0	1	3	0	4	0	.235	.294	4	1	DH-7, OF-1
1988 MIN A	60	166	49	11	1	3	1.8	15	20	10	12	0	.295	.428	7	1	C-48, DH-5, 3B-2
9 yrs.	267	556	140	26	2	14	2.5	48	70	23	53	1	.252	.381	93	24	OF-107, C-54, DH-20, 3B-8, 1B-4

LEAGUE CHAMPIONSHIP SERIES

	G	AB	H	2B	3B	HR	HR%	R	RBI	BB	SO	SB	BA	SA	AB	H	G by POS
1985 STL N	1	1	0	0	0	0	0.0	0	0	0	0	0	.000	.000	1	0	

WORLD SERIES

	G	AB	H	2B	3B	HR	HR%	R	RBI	BB	SO	SB	BA	SA	AB	H	G by POS
1985 STL N	4	4	1	0	0	0	0.0	0	1	0	1	0	.250	.250	4	1	

Lenny Harris

HARRIS, LEONARD ANTHONY
B. Oct. 28, 1964, Miami, Fla.

BL TR 5'10''   195 lbs.

	G	AB	H	2B	3B	HR	HR%	R	RBI	BB	SO	SB	BA	SA	AB	H	G by POS
1988 CIN N	16	43	16	1	0	0	0.0	7	8	5	4	4	.372	.395	0	0	3B-10, 2B-6

Ron Hassey

HASSEY, RONALD WILLIAM
B. Feb. 27, 1953, Tucson, Ariz.

BL TR 6'2''   200 lbs.

	G	AB	H	2B	3B	HR	HR%	R	RBI	BB	SO	SB	BA	SA	AB	H	G by POS
1978 CLE A	25	74	15	0	0	2	2.7	5	9	5	7	2	.203	.284	1	0	C-24
1979	75	223	64	14	0	4	1.8	20	32	19	19	1	.287	.404	7	2	C-68, 1B-2, DH-1
1980	130	390	124	18	4	8	2.1	43	65	49	51	0	.318	.446	18	6	C-113, DH-7, 1B-3
1981	61	190	44	4	0	1	0.5	8	25	17	11	0	.232	.268	4	2	C-56, DH-5, 1B-1
1982	113	323	81	18	0	5	1.5	33	34	53	32	3	.251	.353	10	3	C-105, DH-2, 1B-2
1983	117	341	92	21	0	6	1.8	48	42	38	35	2	.270	.384	9	3	C-113, DH-1
1984 2 teams		CLE A	(48G –	.255)				CHI N	(19G –	.333)							
" total	67	182	49	5	1	2	1.1	16	24	19	32	1	.269	.341	9	2	C-50, 1B-5, DH-1
1985 NY A	92	267	79	16	1	13	4.9	31	42	28	21	0	.296	.509	20	5	C-69, DH-2, 1B-2
1986 2 teams		NY A	(64G –	.298)				CHI A	(49G –	.353)							
" total	113	341	110	25	1	9	2.6	45	49	46	27	1	.323	.481	18	10	C-62, DH-37
1987 CHI A	49	145	31	9	0	3	2.1	15	12	17	11	0	.214	.338	6	0	C-24, DH-18
1988 OAK A	107	323	83	15	0	7	2.2	32	45	30	42	2	.257	.368	14	2	C-91, DH-9
11 yrs.	949	2799	772	145	7	60	2.1	296	379	321	288	12	.276	.397	116	35	C-775, DH-79, 1B-19

LEAGUE CHAMPIONSHIP SERIES

	G	AB	H	2B	3B	HR	HR%	R	RBI	BB	SO	SB	BA	SA	AB	H	G by POS
1988 OAK A	4	8	4	1	0	1	12.5	2	3	1	1	0	.500	1.000	0	0	C-4

WORLD SERIES

	G	AB	H	2B	3B	HR	HR%	R	RBI	BB	SO	SB	BA	SA	AB	H	G by POS
1988 OAK A	5	8	2	0	0	0	0.0	0	1	3	3	0	.250	.250	1	1	C-4

Billy Hatcher

HATCHER, WILLIAM AUGUSTUS
B. Oct. 4, 1960, Williams, Ariz.

BR TR 5'9''   175 lbs.

	G	AB	H	2B	3B	HR	HR%	R	RBI	BB	SO	SB	BA	SA	AB	H	G by POS
1984 CHI N	8	9	1	0	0	0	0.0	1	0	1	0	2	.111	.111	3	0	OF-4
1985	53	163	40	12	1	2	1.2	24	10	8	12	2	.245	.368	9	1	OF-44
1986 HOU N	127	419	108	15	4	6	1.4	55	36	22	52	38	.258	.356	4	0	OF-121
1987	141	564	167	28	3	11	2.0	96	63	42	70	53	.296	.415	1	1	OF-140
1988	145	530	142	25	4	7	1.3	79	52	37	56	32	.268	.370	5	1	OF-142
5 yrs.	474	1685	458	80	12	26	1.5	255	161	110	190	127	.272	.380	22	3	OF-451

LEAGUE CHAMPIONSHIP SERIES

	G	AB	H	2B	3B	HR	HR%	R	RBI	BB	SO	SB	BA	SA	AB	H	G by POS
1986 HOU N	6	25	7	0	0	1	4.0	4	2	3	2	3	.280	.400	0	0	OF-6

Mickey Hatcher

HATCHER, MICHAEL VAUGHN, JR.
B. Mar. 15, 1955, Cleveland, Ohio

BR TR 6'2''   200 lbs.

	G	AB	H	2B	3B	HR	HR%	R	RBI	BB	SO	SB	BA	SA	AB	H	G by POS
1979 LA N	33	93	25	4	1	1	1.1	9	5	7	12	1	.269	.366	6	1	OF-19, 3B-17
1980	57	84	19	2	0	1	1.2	4	5	2	12	0	.226	.286	21	4	OF-25, 3B-18
1981 MIN A	99	377	96	23	2	3	0.8	36	37	15	29	3	.255	.350	2	1	OF-91, 1B-7, 3B-2, DH-1
1982	84	277	69	13	2	3	1.1	23	26	8	27	0	.249	.343	9	3	OF-47, DH-29, 3B-5
1983	105	375	119	15	3	9	2.4	50	47	14	19	2	.317	.445	15	6	OF-56, DH-39, 1B-7, 3B-1
1984	152	576	174	35	5	5	0.9	61	69	37	34	0	.302	.406	2	0	OF-100, DH-37, 1B-17, 3B-1

	G	AB	H	2B	3B	HR	HR %	R	RBI	BB	SO	SB	BA	SA	Pinch Hit AB	Pinch Hit H	G by POS

Mickey Hatcher continued

	G	AB	H	2B	3B	HR	HR%	R	RBI	BB	SO	SB	BA	SA	AB	H	G by POS
1985	116	444	125	28	0	3	0.7	46	49	16	23	0	.282	.365	6	2	OF-97, DH-11, 1B-4
1986	115	317	88	13	3	3	0.9	40	32	19	26	2	.278	.366	38	6	OF-46, DH-28, 1B-22, 3B-3
1987 LA N	101	287	81	19	1	7	2.4	27	42	20	19	2	.282	.429	16	1	3B-49, 1B-37, OF-7
1988	88	191	56	8	0	1	0.5	22	25	7	7	0	.293	.351	38	12	OF-29, 1B-25, 3B-3
10 yrs.	950	3021	852	160	17	36	1.2	318	337	145	208	10	.282	.382	153	36	OF-517, DH-145, 1B-119, 3B-99

LEAGUE CHAMPIONSHIP SERIES

	G	AB	H	2B	3B	HR	HR%	R	RBI	BB	SO	SB	BA	SA	AB	H	G by POS
1988 LA N	6	21	5	2	0	0	0.0	4	3	3	0	0	.238	.333	0	0	1B-6

WORLD SERIES

	G	AB	H	2B	3B	HR	HR%	R	RBI	BB	SO	SB	BA	SA	AB	H	G by POS
1988 LA N	5	19	7	1	0	2	10.5	5	5	1	3	0	.368	.737	0	0	OF-5

Charlie Hayes

HAYES, CHARLES DEWAYNE
B. May 29, 1965, Hattiesburg, Miss.

BR TR 6' 190 lbs.

	G	AB	H	2B	3B	HR	HR%	R	RBI	BB	SO	SB	BA	SA	AB	H	G by POS
1988 SF N	7	11	1	0	0	0	0.0	0	0	0	3	0	.091	.091	2	0	OF-4, 3B-3

Von Hayes

HAYES, VON FRANCIS
B. Aug. 31, 1958, Stockton, Calif.

BL TR 6'5" 185 lbs.

	G	AB	H	2B	3B	HR	HR%	R	RBI	BB	SO	SB	BA	SA	AB	H	G by POS
1981 CLE A	43	109	28	8	2	1	0.9	21	17	14	10	8	.257	.394	9	4	DH-21, OF-13, 3B-5
1982	150	527	132	25	3	14	2.7	65	82	42	63	32	.250	.389	11	2	OF-139, 3B-5, 1B-4
1983 PHI N	124	351	93	9	5	6	1.7	45	32	36	55	20	.265	.370	21	5	OF-103
1984	152	561	164	27	6	16	2.9	85	67	59	84	48	.292	.447	12	2	OF-148
1985	152	570	150	30	4	13	2.3	76	70	61	99	21	.263	.398	6	4	OF-146
1986	158	610	186	46	2	19	3.1	107	98	74	77	24	.305	.480	2	0	1B-134, OF-31
1987	158	556	154	36	5	21	3.8	84	84	121	77	16	.277	.473	4	0	1B-144, OF-32
1988	104	367	100	28	2	6	1.6	43	45	49	59	20	.272	.409	5	1	1B-85, OF-16, 3B-3
8 yrs.	1041	3651	1007	209	29	96	2.6	526	495	456	524	189	.276	.428	70	18	OF-628, 1B-367, DH-21, 3B-13

LEAGUE CHAMPIONSHIP SERIES

	G	AB	H	2B	3B	HR	HR%	R	RBI	BB	SO	SB	BA	SA	AB	H	G by POS
1983 PHI N	2	2	0	0	0	0	0.0	0	0	0	0	0	.000	.000	1	0	OF-1

WORLD SERIES

	G	AB	H	2B	3B	HR	HR%	R	RBI	BB	SO	SB	BA	SA	AB	H	G by POS
1983 PHI N	4	3	0	0	0	0	0.0	0	0	0	1	0	.000	.000	3	0	OF-1

Ed Hearn

HEARN, EDWARD JOHN
B. Aug. 23, 1960, Stuart, Fla.

BR TR 6'3" 215 lbs.

	G	AB	H	2B	3B	HR	HR%	R	RBI	BB	SO	SB	BA	SA	AB	H	G by POS
1986 NY N	49	136	36	5	0	4	2.9	16	10	12	19	0	.265	.390	6	2	C-45
1987 KC A	6	17	5	2	0	0	0.0	2	3	4	2	0	.294	.412	1	0	C-5
1988	7	18	4	2	0	0	0.0	1	1	0	1	0	.222	.333	2	1	C-4, DH-2
3 yrs.	62	171	45	9	0	4	2.3	19	14	16	22	0	.263	.386	9	3	C-54, DH-2

Mike Heath

HEATH, MICHAEL THOMAS
B. Feb. 5, 1955, Tampa, Fla.

BR TR 5'11" 180 lbs.

	G	AB	H	2B	3B	HR	HR%	R	RBI	BB	SO	SB	BA	SA	AB	H	G by POS
1978 NY A	33	92	21	3	1	0	0.0	6	8	4	9	0	.228	.283	0	0	C-33
1979 OAK A	74	258	66	8	0	3	1.2	19	27	17	18	1	.256	.322	5	3	OF-46, C-22, 3B-7, DH-3
1980	92	305	74	10	2	1	0.3	27	33	16	28	3	.243	.298	6	1	C-47, DH-31, OF-8
1981	84	301	71	7	1	8	2.7	26	30	13	36	3	.236	.346	4	2	C-78, OF-6
1982	101	318	77	18	4	3	0.9	43	39	27	36	8	.242	.352	2	1	C-90, OF-10, 3B-5
1983	96	345	97	17	0	6	1.7	45	33	18	59	3	.281	.383	3	1	C-80, OF-24, DH-2, 3B-2
1984	139	472	118	21	5	13	2.8	48	64	26	72	7	.250	.398	10	1	C-108, OF-45, 3B-2, SS-1
1985	138	436	109	18	6	13	3.0	71	55	41	63	7	.250	.408	6	3	C-112, OF-35, 3B-13
1986 2 teams	STL N (65G – .205)				DET A (30G – .265)												
" total	95	288	65	11	1	8	2.8	30	36	27	53	6	.226	.354	4	0	C-92, OF-2, 3B-1
1987 DET A	93	270	76	16	0	8	3.0	34	33	21	42	1	.281	.430	12	3	C-67, OF-24, 3B-4, 1B-4, SS-3, DH-1, 2B-1
1988	86	219	54	7	2	5	2.3	24	18	18	32	1	.247	.365	6	0	C-75, OF-9
11 yrs.	1031	3304	828	136	22	68	2.1	373	376	228	448	40	.251	.367	58	15	C-804, OF-209, DH-37, 3B-34, 1B-4, SS-3, 2B-1

DIVISIONAL PLAYOFF SERIES

	G	AB	H	2B	3B	HR	HR%	R	RBI	BB	SO	SB	BA	SA	AB	H	G by POS
1981 OAK A	2	8	0	0	0	0	0.0	0	0	0	1	0	.000	.000	0	0	C-2

LEAGUE CHAMPIONSHIP SERIES

	G	AB	H	2B	3B	HR	HR%	R	RBI	BB	SO	SB	BA	SA	AB	H	G by POS
1981 OAK A	3	6	2	0	0	0	0.0	1	0	0	1	0	.333	.333	0	0	C-2
1987 DET A	3	7	2	0	0	1	14.3	1	2	0	0	0	.286	.714	0	0	C-3
2 yrs.	6	13	4	0	0	1	7.7	2	2	0	1	0	.308	.538	0	0	C-5

WORLD SERIES

	G	AB	H	2B	3B	HR	HR%	R	RBI	BB	SO	SB	BA	SA	AB	H	G by POS
1978 NY A	1	0	0	0	0	0	–	0	0	0	0	0	–	–	0	0	C-1

Danny Heep

HEEP, DANIEL WILLIAM
B. July 3, 1957, San Antonio, Tex.

BL TL 5'11" 185 lbs.

	G	AB	H	2B	3B	HR	HR%	R	RBI	BB	SO	SB	BA	SA	AB	H	G by POS
1979 HOU N	14	14	2	0	0	0	0.0	0	2	1	4	0	.143	.143	10	1	OF-2
1980	33	87	24	8	0	0	0.0	6	6	8	9	0	.276	.368	8	2	1B-22
1981	33	96	24	3	0	0	0.0	6	11	10	11	0	.250	.281	9	4	1B-22, OF-1
1982	85	198	47	14	1	4	2.0	16	22	21	31	0	.237	.379	23	6	OF-39, 1B-16
1983 NY N	115	253	64	12	0	8	3.2	30	21	29	40	3	.253	.395	40	11	OF-61, 1B-14
1984	99	199	46	9	2	1	0.5	36	12	27	22	3	.231	.312	38	8	OF-48, 1B-10
1985	95	271	76	17	0	7	2.6	26	42	27	27	2	.280	.421	13	1	OF-78, 1B-4
1986	86	195	55	8	2	5	2.6	24	33	30	31	1	.282	.421	30	9	OF-56
1987 LA N	60	98	16	4	0	0	0.0	7	9	8	10	1	.163	.204	35	5	OF-22, 1B-6
1988	95	149	36	2	0	0	0.0	14	11	22	13	2	.242	.255	44	4	OF-32, 1B-12, P-1
10 yrs.	715	1560	390	77	5	25	1.6	165	169	183	198	12	.250	.354	250	51	OF-339, 1B-106, P-1

LEAGUE CHAMPIONSHIP SERIES

	G	AB	H	2B	3B	HR	HR%	R	RBI	BB	SO	SB	BA	SA	AB	H	G by POS
1980 HOU N	5	1	0	0	0	0	0.0	0	0	0	0	0	.000	.000	1	0	
1986 NY N	5	4	1	0	0	0	0.0	0	1	0	2	0	.250	.250	3	1	OF-1

	G	AB	H	2B	3B	HR	HR %	R	RBI	BB	SO	SB	BA	SA	Pinch Hit AB	Pinch Hit H	G by POS

Danny Heep continued

	G	AB	H	2B	3B	HR	HR %	R	RBI	BB	SO	SB	BA	SA	PH AB	PH H	G by POS
1988 LA N	3	1	0	0	0	0	0.0	0	0	1	1	0	.000	.000	1	0	
3 yrs.	13	6	1	0	0	0	0.0	0	1	1	3	0	.167	.167	5	1	OF-1

WORLD SERIES

	G	AB	H	2B	3B	HR	HR %	R	RBI	BB	SO	SB	BA	SA	PH AB	PH H	G by POS
1986 NY N	5	11	1	0	0	0	0.0	0	2	1	1	0	.091	.091	2	0	OF-1
1988 LA N	3	8	2	1	0	0	0.0	0	0	0	2	0	.250	.375	2	0	OF-1
2 yrs.	8	19	3	1	0	0	0.0	0	2	1	3	0	.158	.211	4	0	OF-2

Dave Henderson

HENDERSON, DAVID LEE   BR TR 6'2"   210 lbs.
B. July 21, 1958, Merced, Calif.

	G	AB	H	2B	3B	HR	HR %	R	RBI	BB	SO	SB	BA	SA	PH AB	PH H	G by POS
1981 SEA A	59	126	21	3	0	6	4.8	17	13	16	24	2	.167	.333	6	1	OF-58
1982	104	324	82	17	1	14	4.3	47	48	36	67	2	.253	.441	4	0	OF-101
1983	137	484	130	24	5	17	3.5	50	55	28	93	9	.269	.444	4	1	OF-133, DH-3
1984	112	350	98	23	0	14	4.0	42	43	19	56	5	.280	.466	5	1	OF-97, DH-10
1985	139	502	121	28	2	14	2.8	70	68	48	104	6	.241	.388	2	1	OF-138
1986 2 teams	SEA	A	(103G –	.276)		BOS	A	(36G –	.196)								
" total	139	388	103	22	4	15	3.9	59	47	39	110	2	.265	.459	8	2	OF-112, DH-22
1987 2 teams	BOS	A	(75G –	.234)		SF	N	(15G –	.238)								
" total	90	205	48	12	0	8	3.9	32	26	30	53	3	.234	.410	15	3	OF-73
1988 OAK A	146	507	154	38	1	24	4.7	100	94	47	92	2	.304	.525	6	3	OF-143
8 yrs.	926	2886	757	167	13	112	3.9	417	394	263	599	31	.262	.446	50	12	OF-855, DH-35

LEAGUE CHAMPIONSHIP SERIES

	G	AB	H	2B	3B	HR	HR %	R	RBI	BB	SO	SB	BA	SA	PH AB	PH H	G by POS
1986 BOS A	5	9	1	0	0	1	11.1	3	4	2	2	0	.111	.444	0	0	OF-5
1988 OAK A	4	16	6	1	0	1	6.3	2	4	1	7	0	.375	.625	0	0	OF-4
2 yrs.	9	25	7	1	0	2	8.0	5	8	3	9	0	.280	.560	0	0	OF-9

WORLD SERIES

	G	AB	H	2B	3B	HR	HR %	R	RBI	BB	SO	SB	BA	SA	PH AB	PH H	G by POS
1986 BOS A	7	25	10	1	1	2	8.0	6	5	2	6	0	.400	.760	0	0	OF-7
1988 OAK A	5	20	6	2	0	0	0.0	1	1	2	7	0	.300	.400	0	0	OF-5
2 yrs.	12	45	16	3	1	2	4.4	7	6	4	13	0	.356	.600	0	0	OF-12

Rickey Henderson

HENDERSON, RICKEY HENLEY   BR TL 5'10"   180 lbs.
B. Dec. 25, 1957, Chicago, Ill.

	G	AB	H	2B	3B	HR	HR %	R	RBI	BB	SO	SB	BA	SA	PH AB	PH H	G by POS
1979 OAK A	89	351	96	13	3	1	0.3	49	26	34	39	33	.274	.336	0	0	OF-88
1980	158	591	179	22	4	9	1.5	111	53	117	54	100	.303	.399	0	0	OF-157, DH-1
1981	108	423	135	18	7	6	1.4	89	35	64	68	56	.319	.437	1	0	OF-107
1982	149	536	143	24	4	10	1.9	119	51	116	94	130	.267	.382	0	0	OF-144, DH-4
1983	145	513	150	25	7	9	1.8	105	48	103	80	108	.292	.421	6	1	OF-142, DH-1
1984	142	502	147	27	4	16	3.2	113	58	86	81	66	.293	.458	2	0	OF-140
1985 NY A	143	547	172	28	5	24	4.4	146	72	99	65	80	.314	.516	1	0	OF-141, DH-1
1986	153	608	160	31	5	28	4.6	130	74	89	81	87	.263	.469	3	0	OF-146, DH-5
1987	95	358	104	17	3	17	4.7	78	37	80	52	41	.291	.497	2	0	OF-69, DH-24
1988	140	554	169	30	2	6	1.1	118	50	82	54	93	.305	.399	0	0	OF-136, DH-3
10 yrs.	1322	4983	1455	235	44	126	2.5	1058	504	870	668	794 / 3rd	.292	.433	15	1	OF-1270, DH-39

DIVISIONAL PLAYOFF SERIES

	G	AB	H	2B	3B	HR	HR %	R	RBI	BB	SO	SB	BA	SA	PH AB	PH H	G by POS
1981 OAK A	3	11	2	0	0	0	0.0	3	0	2	0	2	.182	.182	0	0	OF-3

LEAGUE CHAMPIONSHIP SERIES

	G	AB	H	2B	3B	HR	HR %	R	RBI	BB	SO	SB	BA	SA	PH AB	PH H	G by POS
1981 OAK A	3	11	4	2	1	0	0.0	0	1	1	2	2	.364	.727	0	0	OF-3

Steve Henderson

HENDERSON, STEPHEN CURTIS (Hendu)   BR TR 6'2"   190 lbs.
B. Nov. 18, 1952, Houston, Tex.

	G	AB	H	2B	3B	HR	HR %	R	RBI	BB	SO	SB	BA	SA	PH AB	PH H	G by POS
1977 NY N	99	350	104	16	6	12	3.4	67	65	43	79	6	.297	.480	2	0	OF-97
1978	157	587	156	30	9	10	1.7	83	65	60	109	13	.266	.399	4	4	OF-155
1979	98	350	107	16	8	5	1.4	42	39	38	58	13	.306	.440	3	2	OF-94
1980	143	513	149	17	8	8	1.6	75	58	62	90	23	.290	.402	8	1	OF-136
1981 CHI N	82	287	84	9	5	5	1.7	32	35	42	61	5	.293	.411	4	0	OF-77
1982	92	257	60	12	4	2	0.8	23	29	22	64	6	.233	.335	25	6	OF-70
1983 SEA A	121	436	128	32	3	10	2.3	50	54	44	82	10	.294	.450	6	1	OF-112, DH-6
1984	109	325	85	12	3	10	3.1	42	35	38	62	2	.262	.409	15	4	OF-53, DH-51
1985 OAK A	85	193	58	8	3	3	1.6	25	31	18	34	0	.301	.420	27	8	OF-58, DH-1
1986	11	26	2	1	0	0	0.0	2	3	0	5	0	.077	.115	2	0	OF-7, DH-1
1987	46	114	33	7	0	3	2.6	14	9	12	19	0	.289	.430	11	1	OF-31, DH-9
1988 HOU N	42	46	10	2	0	0	0.0	4	5	7	14	1	.217	.261	30	6	OF-8, 1B-1
12 yrs.	1085	3484	976	162	49	68	2.0	459	428	386	677	79	.280	.413	137	33	OF-898, DH-68, 1B-1

George Hendrick

HENDRICK, GEORGE ANDREW   BR TR 6'3"   195 lbs.
B. Oct. 18, 1949, Los Angeles, Calif.

	G	AB	H	2B	3B	HR	HR %	R	RBI	BB	SO	SB	BA	SA	PH AB	PH H	G by POS
1971 OAK A	42	114	27	4	1	0	0.0	8	8	3	20	0	.237	.289	5	2	OF-36
1972	58	121	22	1	1	4	3.3	10	15	3	22	3	.182	.306	19	5	OF-41
1973 CLE A	113	440	118	18	0	21	4.8	64	61	25	71	7	.268	.452	3	1	OF-110
1974	139	495	138	23	1	19	3.8	65	67	33	73	6	.279	.444	5	0	OF-133, DH-1
1975	145	561	145	21	2	24	4.3	82	86	40	78	6	.258	.431	2	1	OF-143
1976	149	551	146	20	2	25	4.5	72	81	51	82	4	.265	.448	1	1	OF-146
1977 SD N	152	541	168	25	2	23	4.3	75	81	61	74	11	.311	.492	9	2	OF-142
1978 2 teams	SD	N	(36G –	.243)		STL	N	(102G –	.288)								
" total	138	493	137	31	1	20	4.1	64	75	40	60	2	.278	.467	5	3	OF-134
1979 STL N	140	493	148	27	1	16	3.2	67	75	49	62	2	.300	.456	7	2	OF-138
1980	150	572	173	33	2	25	4.4	73	109	32	67	6	.302	.498	3	0	OF-149
1981	101	394	112	19	3	18	4.6	67	61	41	44	4	.284	.485	0	0	OF-101
1982	136	515	145	20	5	19	3.7	65	104	37	80	3	.282	.450	2	1	OF-134
1983	144	529	168	33	3	18	3.4	73	97	51	76	3	.318	.493	5	1	1B-92, OF-51
1984	120	441	122	28	1	9	2.0	57	69	32	75	0	.277	.406	4	0	OF-116, 1B-1
1985 2 teams	PIT	N	(69G –	.230)		CAL	A	(16G –	.122)								
" total	85	297	64	16	0	4	1.3	28	31	22	50	1	.215	.310	6	2	OF-77, DH-1
1986 CAL A	102	283	77	13	1	14	4.9	45	47	26	41	1	.272	.473	11	3	OF-93, 1B-7, DH-4

	G	AB	H	2B	3B	HR	HR %	R	RBI	BB	SO	SB	BA	SA	Pinch Hit AB	Pinch Hit H	G by POS

George Hendrick continued

	G	AB	H	2B	3B	HR	HR %	R	RBI	BB	SO	SB	BA	SA	PH AB	PH H	G by POS
1987	65	162	39	10	0	5	3.1	14	25	14	18	0	.241	.395	15	6	OF-45, 1B-9, DH-5
1988	69	127	31	1	0	3	2.4	12	19	7	20	0	.244	.323	29	8	OF-24, 1B-12, DH-3
18 yrs.	2048	7129	1980	343	27	267	3.7	941	1111	567	1013	59	.278	.446	131	38	OF-1813, 1B-121, DH-14

LEAGUE CHAMPIONSHIP SERIES
	G	AB	H	2B	3B	HR	HR %	R	RBI	BB	SO	SB	BA	SA	PH AB	PH H	G by POS
1972 OAK A	5	7	1	0	0	0	0.0	2	0	0	1	0	.143	.143	4	1	OF-1
1982 STL N	3	13	4	0	0	0	0.0	2	2	1	2	0	.308	.308	0	0	OF-3
1986 CAL A	3	12	1	0	0	0	0.0	0	0	0	2	0	.083	.083	0	0	1B-1
3 yrs.	11	32	6	0	0	0	0.0	4	2	1	5	0	.188	.188	4	1	OF-4, 1B-1

WORLD SERIES
	G	AB	H	2B	3B	HR	HR %	R	RBI	BB	SO	SB	BA	SA	PH AB	PH H	G by POS
1972 OAK A	5	15	2	0	0	0	0.0	3	0	1	2	0	.133	.133	0	0	OF-5
1982 STL N	7	28	9	0	0	0	0.0	5	5	2	1	0	.321	.321	0	0	OF-7
2 yrs.	12	43	11	0	0	0	0.0	8	5	3	3	0	.256	.256	0	0	OF-12

Dave Hengel

HENGEL, DAVID LEE
B. Dec. 18, 1961, Oakland, Calif.
BR TR 6' 185 lbs.

	G	AB	H	2B	3B	HR	HR %	R	RBI	BB	SO	SB	BA	SA	PH AB	PH H	G by POS
1986 SEA A	21	63	12	1	0	1	1.6	3	6	1	13	0	.190	.254	4	1	DH-11, OF-8
1987	10	19	6	0	0	1	5.3	2	4	0	4	0	.316	.474	4	2	OF-7, DH-1
1988	26	60	10	1	0	2	3.3	3	7	1	15	0	.167	.283	8	1	DH-12, OF-12
3 yrs.	57	142	28	2	0	4	2.8	8	17	2	32	0	.197	.296	16	4	OF-27, DH-24

Keith Hernandez

HERNANDEZ, KEITH (Mex)
B. Oct. 20, 1953, San Francisco, Calif.
BL TL 6' 180 lbs.

	G	AB	H	2B	3B	HR	HR %	R	RBI	BB	SO	SB	BA	SA	PH AB	PH H	G by POS
1974 STL N	14	34	10	1	2	0	0.0	3	2	7	8	0	.294	.441	3	1	1B-9
1975	64	188	47	8	2	3	1.6	20	20	17	26	0	.250	.362	9	3	1B-56
1976	129	374	108	21	5	7	1.9	54	46	49	53	4	.289	.428	17	4	1B-110
1977	161	560	163	41	4	15	2.7	90	91	79	88	7	.291	.459	6	1	1B-158
1978	159	542	138	32	4	11	2.0	90	64	82	68	13	.255	.389	5	1	1B-158
1979	161	610	210	48	11	11	1.8	116	105	80	78	11	.344	.513	2	2	1B-160
1980	159	595	191	39	8	16	2.7	111	99	86	73	14	.321	.494	2	0	1B-157
1981	103	376	115	27	4	8	2.1	65	48	61	45	12	.306	.463	2	0	1B-98, OF-3
1982	160	579	173	33	6	7	1.2	79	94	100	67	19	.299	.413	1	1	1B-158, OF-4
1983 2 teams			STL	N	(55G –	.284)		NY	N	(95G –	.306)						
" total	150	538	160	23	7	12	2.2	77	63	88	72	9	.297	.433	5	1	1B-144
1984 NY N	154	550	171	31	0	15	2.7	83	94	97	89	2	.311	.449	1	0	1B-153
1985	158	593	183	34	4	10	1.7	87	91	77	59	3	.309	.430	3	1	1B-157
1986	149	551	171	34	1	13	2.4	94	83	94	69	2	.310	.446	0	0	1B-149
1987	154	587	170	28	2	18	3.1	87	89	81	104	0	.290	.436	1	0	1B-154
1988	95	348	96	16	0	11	3.2	43	55	31	57	2	.276	.417	1	0	1B-93
15 yrs.	1970	7025	2106	416	60	157	2.2	1099	1044	1029	956	98	.300	.443	58	15	1B-1914, OF-7

LEAGUE CHAMPIONSHIP SERIES
	G	AB	H	2B	3B	HR	HR %	R	RBI	BB	SO	SB	BA	SA	PH AB	PH H	G by POS
1982 STL N	3	12	4	0	0	0	0.0	3	1	2	3	0	.333	.333	0	0	1B-3
1986 NY N	6	26	7	1	1	0	0.0	3	3	3	6	0	.269	.385	0	0	1B-6
1988	7	26	7	0	0	1	3.8	2	5	6	7	1	.269	.385	0	0	1B-7
3 yrs.	16	64	18	1	1	1	1.6	8	9	11	16	1	.281	.375	0	0	1B-16

WORLD SERIES
	G	AB	H	2B	3B	HR	HR %	R	RBI	BB	SO	SB	BA	SA	PH AB	PH H	G by POS
1982 STL N	7	27	7	2	0	1	3.7	4	8	4	2	0	.259	.444	0	0	1B-7
1986 NY N	7	26	6	0	0	0	0.0	1	4	5	1	0	.231	.231	0	0	1B-7
2 yrs.	14	53	13	2	0	1	1.9	5	12	9	3	0	.245	.340	0	0	1B-14

Larry Herndon

HERNDON, LARRY DARNELL
B. Nov. 3, 1953, Sunflower, Tex.
BR TR 6'3" 190 lbs.

	G	AB	H	2B	3B	HR	HR %	R	RBI	BB	SO	SB	BA	SA	PH AB	PH H	G by POS
1974 STL N	12	1	1	0	0	0	0.0	3	0	0	0	0	1.000	1.000	0	0	OF-1
1976 SF N	115	337	97	11	3	2	0.6	42	23	23	45	12	.288	.356	6	2	OF-110
1977	49	109	26	4	3	1	0.9	13	5	5	20	4	.239	.358	5	1	OF-44
1978	151	471	122	15	9	1	0.2	52	32	35	71	13	.259	.335	4	2	OF-149
1979	132	354	91	14	5	7	2.0	35	36	29	70	8	.257	.384	19	7	OF-122
1980	139	493	127	17	11	8	1.6	54	49	19	91	8	.258	.385	21	6	OF-122
1981	96	364	105	15	8	5	1.4	48	41	20	55	15	.288	.415	4	0	OF-93
1982 DET A	157	614	179	21	13	23	3.7	92	88	38	92	12	.292	.480	3	0	OF-155, DH-3
1983	153	603	182	28	9	20	3.3	88	92	46	95	9	.302	.478	5	1	OF-133, DH-19
1984	125	407	114	18	5	7	1.7	52	43	32	63	6	.280	.400	24	7	OF-117, DH-4
1985	137	443	108	12	7	12	2.7	45	37	33	79	2	.244	.384	5	3	OF-136
1986	106	283	70	13	1	8	2.8	33	37	27	40	2	.247	.385	26	6	OF-83, DH-18
1987	89	225	73	13	2	9	4.0	32	47	23	35	1	.324	.520	21	8	OF-57, DH-23
1988	76	174	39	5	0	4	2.3	16	20	23	37	0	.224	.322	17	4	OF-35, DH-15
14 yrs.	1537	4878	1334	186	76	107	2.2	605	550	353	793	92	.273	.409	160	47	OF-1337, DH-120

LEAGUE CHAMPIONSHIP SERIES
	G	AB	H	2B	3B	HR	HR %	R	RBI	BB	SO	SB	BA	SA	PH AB	PH H	G by POS
1984 DET A	2	5	1	0	0	1	20.0	1	1	1	2	0	.200	.800	0	0	OF-2
1987	3	9	3	1	0	0	0.0	1	2	1	1	0	.333	.444	1	1	OF-2
2 yrs.	5	14	4	1	0	1	7.1	2	3	2	3	0	.286	.571	1	1	OF-4

WORLD SERIES
	G	AB	H	2B	3B	HR	HR %	R	RBI	BB	SO	SB	BA	SA	PH AB	PH H	G by POS
1984 DET A	5	15	5	0	0	1	6.7	1	3	3	2	0	.333	.533	2	0	OF-5

Tommy Herr

HERR, THOMAS MITCHELL
B. Apr. 4, 1956, Lancaster, Pa.
BB TR 6' 175 lbs.

	G	AB	H	2B	3B	HR	HR %	R	RBI	BB	SO	SB	BA	SA	PH AB	PH H	G by POS
1979 STL N	14	10	2	0	0	0	0.0	4	1	2	2	1	.200	.200	1	0	2B-6
1980	76	222	55	12	5	0	0.0	29	15	16	21	9	.248	.347	9	2	2B-58, SS-14
1981	103	411	110	14	9	0	0.0	50	46	39	30	23	.268	.345	0	0	2B-103
1982	135	493	131	19	4	0	0.0	83	36	57	56	25	.266	.320	5	2	2B-128
1983	89	313	101	14	4	2	0.6	43	31	43	27	6	.323	.412	5	2	2B-86
1984	145	558	154	23	2	4	0.7	67	49	49	56	13	.276	.346	1	1	2B-144
1985	159	596	180	38	3	8	1.3	97	110	80	55	31	.302	.416	1	1	2B-158
1986	152	559	141	30	4	2	0.4	48	61	73	75	22	.252	.331	0	0	2B-152
1987	141	510	134	29	0	2	0.4	73	83	68	62	19	.263	.331	2	1	2B-137

	G	AB	H	2B	3B	HR	HR %	R	RBI	BB	SO	SB	BA	SA	Pinch Hit AB	Pinch Hit H	G by POS

Tommy Herr continued

		G	AB	H	2B	3B	HR	HR%	R	RBI	BB	SO	SB	BA	SA	AB	H	G by POS
1988 2 teams	STL N (15G – .260)							MIN A (86G – .263)										
" total		101	354	93	16	0	2	0.6	46	24	51	51	13	.263	.325	10	3	2B-88, DH-3, SS-2
10 yrs.		1115	4026	1101	195	31	20	0.5	540	456	478	435	162	.273	.352	34	12	2B-1060, SS-16, DH-3

LEAGUE CHAMPIONSHIP SERIES

		G	AB	H	2B	3B	HR	HR%	R	RBI	BB	SO	SB	BA	SA	AB	H	G by POS
1982 STL N		3	13	3	1	0	0	0.0	1	0	1	2	0	.231	.308	0	0	2B-3
1985		6	21	7	4	0	1	4.8	0	6	5	2	1	.333	.667	0	0	2B-6
1987		7	27	6	0	0	0	0.0	2	3	0	1	1	.222	.222	0	0	2B-7
3 yrs.		16	61	16	5	0	1	1.6	3	9	6	5	2	.262	.393	0	0	2B-16

WORLD SERIES

		G	AB	H	2B	3B	HR	HR%	R	RBI	BB	SO	SB	BA	SA	AB	H	G by POS
1982 STL N		7	25	4	2	0	0	0.0	2	5	3	3	0	.160	.240	0	0	2B-7
1985		7	26	4	2	0	0	0.0	2	0	2	2	0	.154	.231	0	0	2B-7
1987		7	28	7	0	0	1	3.6	2	1	2	2	0	.250	.357	0	0	2B-7
3 yrs.		21	79	15	4	0	1	1.3	6	6	7	7	0	.190	.278	0	0	2B-21

Donnie Hill

HILL, DONALD EARL
B. Nov. 12, 1960, Pomona, Calif.　　　BB TR 5'10"　165 lbs.

		G	AB	H	2B	3B	HR	HR%	R	RBI	BB	SO	SB	BA	SA	AB	H	G by POS
1983 OAK A		53	158	42	7	0	2	1.3	20	15	4	21	1	.266	.348	1	0	SS-53
1984		73	174	40	6	0	2	1.1	21	16	5	12	1	.230	.299	5	0	SS-66, 2B-4, DH-2, 3B-2
1985		123	393	112	13	2	3	0.8	45	48	23	33	8	.285	.351	2	0	2B-122
1986		108	339	96	16	2	4	1.2	37	29	23	38	5	.283	.378	15	4	2B-68, 3B-33, DH-3, SS-2
1987 CHI A		111	410	98	14	6	9	2.2	57	46	30	35	1	.239	.368	3	1	2B-84, 3B-32, DH-1
1988		83	221	48	6	1	2	0.9	17	20	26	32	3	.217	.281	12	3	2B-59, 3B-12, DH-5
6 yrs.		551	1695	436	62	11	22	1.3	197	174	111	171	19	.257	.346	38	8	2B-337, SS-121, 3B-79, DH-11

Sam Horn

HORN, SAMUEL LEE
B. Nov. 2, 1963, Dallas, Tex.　　　BL TL 6'5"　215 lbs.

		G	AB	H	2B	3B	HR	HR%	R	RBI	BB	SO	SB	BA	SA	AB	H	G by POS
1987 BOS A		46	158	44	7	0	14	8.9	31	34	17	55	0	.278	.589	6	1	DH-40
1988		24	61	9	0	0	2	3.3	4	8	11	20	0	.148	.246	4	0	DH-16
2 yrs.		70	219	53	7	0	16	7.3	35	42	28	75	0	.242	.493	10	1	DH-56

Bob Horner

HORNER, JAMES ROBERT
B. Aug. 6, 1957, Junction City, Kans.　　　BR TR 6'1"　195 lbs.

		G	AB	H	2B	3B	HR	HR%	R	RBI	BB	SO	SB	BA	SA	AB	H	G by POS
1978 ATL N		89	323	86	17	1	23	7.1	50	63	24	42	0	.266	.539	0	0	3B-89
1979		121	487	153	15	1	33	6.8	66	98	22	74	0	.314	.552	1	0	3B-82, 1B-45
1980		124	463	124	14	1	35	7.6	81	89	27	50	3	.268	.529	3	1	3B-121, 1B-1
1981		79	300	83	10	0	15	5.0	42	42	32	39	2	.277	.460	0	0	3B-79
1982		140	499	130	24	0	32	6.4	85	97	66	75	3	.261	.501	3	0	3B-137
1983		104	386	117	25	1	20	5.2	75	68	50	63	4	.303	.528	0	0	3B-104, 1B-1
1984		32	113	31	8	0	3	2.7	15	19	14	17	0	.274	.425	0	0	3B-32
1985		130	483	129	25	3	27	5.6	61	89	50	57	1	.267	.499	4	1	1B-87, 3B-40
1986		141	517	141	22	0	27	5.2	70	87	52	72	1	.273	.472	2	1	1B-139
1988 STL N		60	206	53	9	1	3	1.5	15	33	32	23	0	.257	.354	3	2	1B-57
10 yrs.		1020	3777	1047	169	8	218	5.8	560	685	369	512	14	.277	.499	16	6	3B-684, 1B-330

LEAGUE CHAMPIONSHIP SERIES

		G	AB	H	2B	3B	HR	HR%	R	RBI	BB	SO	SB	BA	SA	AB	H	G by POS
1982 ATL N		3	11	1	0	0	0	0.0	0	0	0	2	0	.091	.091	0	0	3B-3

Dave Hostetler

HOSTETLER, DAVID ALAN
B. Mar. 27, 1956, Pasadena, Calif.　　　BR TR 6'4"　215 lbs.

		G	AB	H	2B	3B	HR	HR%	R	RBI	BB	SO	SB	BA	SA	AB	H	G by POS
1981 MON N		5	6	3	0	0	1	16.7	1	1	0	2	0	.500	1.000	3	0	1B-2
1982 TEX A		113	418	97	12	3	22	5.3	53	67	42	113	2	.232	.433	1	0	1B-109, DH-3
1983		94	304	67	9	2	11	3.6	31	46	42	103	0	.220	.372	8	1	DH-88, 1B-2
1984		37	82	18	2	1	3	3.7	7	10	13	27	0	.220	.378	9	2	1B-14, DH-13
1988 PIT N		6	8	2	0	0	0	0.0	0	0	0	3	0	.250	.250	4	1	1B-4, C-1
5 yrs.		255	818	187	23	6	37	4.5	92	124	97	248	2	.229	.407	25	4	1B-131, DH-104, C-1

Jack Howell

HOWELL, JACK ROBERT
B. Aug. 18, 1961, Tucson, Ariz.　　　BL TR 6'　185 lbs.

		G	AB	H	2B	3B	HR	HR%	R	RBI	BB	SO	SB	BA	SA	AB	H	G by POS
1985 CAL A		43	137	27	4	0	5	3.6	19	18	16	33	1	.197	.336	2	1	3B-42
1986		63	151	41	14	2	4	2.6	26	21	19	28	2	.272	.470	16	4	3B-39, OF-8, DH-2
1987		138	449	110	18	5	23	5.1	64	64	57	118	4	.245	.461	18	6	OF-89, 3B-48, 2B-13
1988		154	500	127	32	2	16	3.2	59	63	46	130	2	.254	.422	4	1	3B-152, OF-2
4 yrs.		398	1237	305	68	9	48	3.9	168	166	138	309	9	.247	.432	40	12	3B-281, OF-99, 2B-13, DH-2

LEAGUE CHAMPIONSHIP SERIES

		G	AB	H	2B	3B	HR	HR%	R	RBI	BB	SO	SB	BA	SA	AB	H	G by POS
1986 CAL A		2	1	0	0	0	0	0.0	0	0	1	1	0	.000	.000	1	0	

Kent Hrbek

HRBEK, KENT ALLEN (Herbie)
B. May 21, 1960, Minneapolis, Minn.　　　BL TR 6'4"　200 lbs.

		G	AB	H	2B	3B	HR	HR%	R	RBI	BB	SO	SB	BA	SA	AB	H	G by POS
1981 MIN A		24	67	16	5	0	1	1.5	5	7	5	9	0	.239	.358	5	2	1B-13, DH-8
1982		140	532	160	21	4	23	4.3	82	92	54	80	3	.301	.485	1	0	1B-138, DH-2
1983		141	515	153	41	5	16	3.1	75	84	57	71	4	.297	.489	3	0	1B-137, DH-2
1984		149	559	174	31	3	27	4.8	80	107	65	87	1	.311	.522	1	1	1B-148, DH-1
1985		158	593	165	31	2	21	3.5	78	93	67	87	1	.278	.444	5	2	1B-156, DH-2
1986		149	550	147	27	1	29	5.3	85	91	71	81	2	.267	.478	3	0	1B-147, DH-1
1987		143	477	136	20	1	34	7.1	85	90	84	60	5	.285	.545	5	1	1B-137, DH-1
1988		143	510	159	31	0	25	4.9	75	76	67	54	0	.312	.520	2	1	1B-105, DH-37
8 yrs.		1047	3803	1110	207	16	176	4.6	565	640	470	529	16	.292	.494	25	7	1B-981, DH-54

LEAGUE CHAMPIONSHIP SERIES

		G	AB	H	2B	3B	HR	HR%	R	RBI	BB	SO	SB	BA	SA	AB	H	G by POS
1987 MIN A		5	20	3	0	0	1	5.0	4	1	3	0	0	.150	.300	0	0	1B-5

WORLD SERIES

		G	AB	H	2B	3B	HR	HR%	R	RBI	BB	SO	SB	BA	SA	AB	H	G by POS
1987 MIN A		7	24	5	0	0	1	4.2	4	6	5	3	0	.208	.333	0	0	1B-7

	G	AB	H	2B	3B	HR	HR %	R	RBI	BB	SO	SB	BA	SA	Pinch Hit AB	Pinch Hit H	G by POS

Glenn Hubbard

HUBBARD, GLENN DEE
B. Sept. 25, 1957, Hahn, West Germany
BR TR 5'9" 150 lbs.

	G	AB	H	2B	3B	HR	HR %	R	RBI	BB	SO	SB	BA	SA	AB	H	G by POS
1978 ATL N	44	163	42	4	0	2	1.2	15	13	10	20	2	.258	.319	0	0	2B-44
1979	97	325	75	12	0	3	0.9	34	29	27	43	0	.231	.295	6	1	2B-91
1980	117	431	107	21	3	9	2.1	55	43	49	69	7	.248	.374	0	0	2B-117
1981	99	361	85	13	5	6	1.7	39	33	33	59	4	.235	.349	0	0	2B-98
1982	145	532	132	25	1	9	1.7	75	59	59	62	4	.248	.350	0	0	2B-144
1983	148	517	136	24	6	12	2.3	65	70	55	71	3	.263	.402	1	0	2B-148
1984	120	397	93	27	2	9	2.3	53	43	55	61	4	.234	.380	4	2	2B-117
1985	142	439	102	21	0	5	1.1	51	39	56	54	4	.232	.314	4	1	2B-140
1986	143	408	94	16	1	4	1.0	42	36	66	74	3	.230	.304	0	0	2B-142
1987	141	443	117	33	2	5	1.1	69	38	77	57	1	.264	.381	2	0	2B-139
1988 OAK A	105	294	75	12	2	3	1.0	35	33	33	50	1	.255	.340	2	0	2B-104, DH-1
11 yrs.	1301	4310	1058	208	22	67	1.6	533	436	520	620	33	.245	.351	19	4	2B-1284, DH-1

LEAGUE CHAMPIONSHIP SERIES

1982 ATL N	3	9	2	0	0	0	0.0	1	1	0	3	0	.222	.222	0	0	2B-3

WORLD SERIES

1988 OAK A	4	12	3	0	0	0	0.0	2	0	1	2	1	.250	.250	0	0	2B-4

Rex Hudler

HUDLER, REX ALLEN
B. Sept. 2, 1960, Tempe, Ariz.
BR TR 6'1" 180 lbs.

1984 NY A	9	7	1	1	0	0	0.0	2	0	1	5	0	.143	.286	0	0	2B-9
1985	20	51	8	0	1	0	0.0	4	1	1	9	0	.157	.196	0	0	2B-16, SS-1, 1B-1
1986 BAL A	14	1	0	0	0	0	0.0	1	0	0	0	1	.000	.000	0	0	2B-13, 3B-1
1988 MON N	77	216	59	14	2	4	1.9	38	14	10	34	29	.273	.412	3	0	2B-41, SS-27, OF-4
4 yrs.	120	275	68	15	3	4	1.5	45	15	12	48	30	.247	.367	3	0	2B-79, SS-28, OF-4, 3B-1, 1B-1

Keith Hughes

HUGHES, KEITH WILLS
B. Sept. 12, 1963, Bryn Mawr, Pa.
BL TL 6'3" 210 lbs.

1987 2 teams		NY	A	(4G –	.000)		PHI	N	(37G –	.263)							
" total	41	80	20	2	0	0	0.0	8	10	7	13	0	.250	.275	23	8	OF-23
1988 BAL A	41	108	21	4	2	2	1.9	10	14	16	27	1	.194	.324	8	0	OF-31
2 yrs.	82	188	41	6	2	2	1.1	18	24	23	40	1	.218	.303	31	8	OF-54

Jeff Huson

HUSON, JEFFREY KENT
B. Aug. 15, 1964, Scottsdale, Ariz.
BL TR 6'3" 183 lbs.

1988 MON N	20	42	13	2	0	0	0.0	7	3	4	3	2	.310	.357	2	2	SS-15, 2B-2, OF-1, 3B-1

Pete Incaviglia

INCAVIGLIA, PETER JOSEPH (Inky)
B. Apr. 2, 1964, Pebble Beach, Calif.
BR TR 6'1" 225 lbs.

1986 TEX A	153	540	135	21	2	30	5.6	82	88	55	**185**	3	.250	.463	4	0	OF-114, DH-36
1987	139	509	138	26	4	27	5.3	85	80	48	168	9	.271	.497	3	0	OF-132, DH-6
1988	116	418	104	19	3	22	5.3	59	54	39	153	6	.249	.467	0	0	OF-93, DH-21
3 yrs.	408	1467	377	66	9	79	5.4	226	222	142	506	18	.257	.476	7	0	OF-339, DH-63

Alex Infante

INFANTE, FERMIN ALEXIS
Born Fermin Alexis Infante y Carpio.
B. Dec. 4, 1961, Barquisimeto, Venezuela
BR TR 5'10" 175 lbs.

1987 TOR A	1	0	0	0	0	0	–	0	0	0	0	0	–	–	0	0	SS-1
1988	19	15	3	0	0	0	0.0	7	0	2	4	0	.200	.200	0	0	3B-9, SS-2
2 yrs.	20	15	3	0	0	0	0.0	7	0	2	4	0	.200	.200	0	0	3B-9, SS-3

Bo Jackson

JACKSON, VINCENT EDWARD
B. Nov. 30, 1962, Bessemer, Ala.
BR TR 6'1" 222 lbs.

1986 KC A	25	82	17	2	1	2	2.4	9	9	7	34	3	.207	.329	0	0	OF-23, DH-1
1987	116	396	93	17	2	22	5.6	46	53	30	158	10	.235	.455	2	0	OF-113, DH-1
1988	124	439	108	16	4	25	5.7	63	68	25	146	27	.246	.472	1	0	OF-121, DH-2
3 yrs.	265	917	218	35	7	49	5.3	118	130	62	338	40	.238	.451	3	0	OF-257, DH-4

Chuck Jackson

JACKSON, CHARLES LEO
B. Mar. 19, 1963, Seattle, Wash.
BR TR 6' 185 lbs.

1987 HOU N	35	71	15	3	0	1	1.4	3	6	7	19	1	.211	.296	5	1	3B-16, OF-13, SS-1
1988	46	83	19	5	1	1	1.2	7	8	7	16	1	.229	.349	9	2	3B-32, OF-3, SS-3
2 yrs.	81	154	34	8	1	2	1.3	10	14	14	35	2	.221	.325	14	3	3B-48, OF-16, SS-4

Darrin Jackson

JACKSON, DARRIN JAY
B. Aug. 22, 1963, Los Angeles, Calif.
BR TR 6' 185 lbs.

1985 CHI N	5	11	1	0	0	0	0.0	0	0	0	3	0	.091	.091	1	0	OF-4
1987	7	5	4	1	0	0	0.0	2	0	0	0	0	.800	1.000	4	3	OF-5
1988	100	188	50	11	3	6	3.2	29	20	5	28	4	.266	.452	21	5	OF-74
3 yrs.	112	204	55	12	3	6	2.9	31	20	5	31	4	.270	.446	26	8	OF-83

Brook Jacoby

JACOBY, BROOK WALLACE
B. Nov. 23, 1959, Philadelphia, Pa.
BR TR 5'11" 175 lbs.

1981 ATL N	11	10	2	0	0	0	0.0	0	1	0	3	0	.200	.200	8	2	3B-3
1983	4	8	0	0	0	0	0.0	0	0	0	1	0	.000	.000	2	0	3B-2
1984 CLE A	126	439	116	19	3	7	1.6	64	40	32	73	3	.264	.369	0	0	3B-126, SS-1
1985	161	606	166	26	3	20	3.3	72	87	48	120	2	.274	.426	1	0	3B-161, 2B-1
1986	158	583	168	30	4	17	2.9	83	80	56	137	2	.288	.441	0	0	3B-158
1987	155	540	162	26	4	32	5.9	73	69	75	73	2	.300	.541	2	1	3B-144, 1B-7, DH-4
1988	152	552	133	25	0	9	1.6	59	49	48	101	2	.241	.335	1	0	3B-151
7 yrs.	767	2738	747	126	14	85	3.1	351	326	259	508	11	.273	.422	14	3	3B-745, 1B-7, DH-4, SS-1, 2B-1

	G	AB	H	2B	3B	HR	HR %	R	RBI	BB	SO	SB	BA	SA	Pinch Hit AB	Pinch Hit H	G by POS

Chris James

JAMES, DONALD CHRIS
B. Oct. 4, 1962, Rusk, Tex.
BR TR 6'1" 190 lbs.

	G	AB	H	2B	3B	HR	HR%	R	RBI	BB	SO	SB	BA	SA	PH AB	PH H	G by POS
1986 PHI N	16	46	13	3	0	1	2.2	5	5	1	13	0	.283	.413	6	2	OF-11
1987	115	358	105	20	6	17	4.7	48	54	27	67	3	.293	.525	9	5	OF-108
1988	150	566	137	24	1	19	3.4	57	66	31	73	7	.242	.389	4	1	OF-116, 3B-31
3 yrs.	281	970	255	47	7	37	3.8	110	125	59	153	10	.263	.440	19	8	OF-235, 3B-31

Dion James

JAMES, DION
B. Nov. 9, 1962, Philadelphia, Pa.
BL TL 6'1" 170 lbs.

	G	AB	H	2B	3B	HR	HR%	R	RBI	BB	SO	SB	BA	SA	PH AB	PH H	G by POS
1983 MIL A	11	20	2	0	0	0	0.0	1	1	2	2	1	.100	.100	0	0	OF-9, DH-2
1984	128	387	114	19	5	1	0.3	52	30	32	41	10	.295	.377	17	3	OF-118
1985	18	49	11	1	0	0	0.0	5	3	6	6	0	.224	.245	4	0	OF-11, DH-3
1987 ATL N	134	494	154	37	6	10	2.0	80	61	70	63	10	.312	.472	11	1	OF-126
1988	132	386	99	17	5	3	0.8	46	30	58	59	9	.256	.350	15	3	OF-120
5 yrs.	423	1336	380	74	16	14	1.0	184	125	168	171	30	.284	.3.5	47	7	OF-384, DH-5

Stan Javier

JAVIER, STANLEY JULIAN
Born Stanley Julian Javier y DeJavier. Son of Julian Javier.
B. Sept. 1, 1965, San Francisco De Macoris, Dominican Republic
BB TR 6' 180 lbs.

	G	AB	H	2B	3B	HR	HR%	R	RBI	BB	SO	SB	BA	SA	PH AB	PH H	G by POS
1984 NY A	7	7	1	0	0	0	0.0	1	0	0	1	0	.143	.143	0	0	OF-5
1986 OAK A	59	114	23	8	0	0	0.0	13	8	16	27	8	.202	.272	0	0	OF-51, DH-2
1987	81	151	28	3	1	2	1.3	22	9	19	33	3	.185	.258	7	0	OF-71, 1B-6, DH-1
1988	125	397	102	13	3	2	0.5	49	35	32	63	20	.257	.320	9	2	OF-115, 1B-4, DH-2
4 yrs.	272	669	154	24	4	4	0.6	85	52	67	124	31	.230	.296	16	2	OF-242, 1B-10, DH-5

LEAGUE CHAMPIONSHIP SERIES

	G	AB	H	2B	3B	HR	HR%	R	RBI	BB	SO	SB	BA	SA	PH AB	PH H	G by POS
1988 OAK A	2	4	2	0	0	0	0.0	0	1	1	0	0	.500	.500	0	0	OF-2

WORLD SERIES

	G	AB	H	2B	3B	HR	HR%	R	RBI	BB	SO	SB	BA	SA	PH AB	PH H	G by POS
1988 OAK A	3	4	2	0	0	0	0.0	0	2	0	1	0	.500	.500	0	0	OF-2

Gregg Jefferies

JEFFERIES, GREGORY SCOTT
B. Aug. 1, 1967, Burlingame, Calif.
BB TR 5'11" 175 lbs.

	G	AB	H	2B	3B	HR	HR%	R	RBI	BB	SO	SB	BA	SA	PH AB	PH H	G by POS
1987 NY N	6	6	3	1	0	0	0.0	0	2	0	0	0	.500	.667	6	3	
1988	29	109	35	8	2	6	5.5	19	17	8	10	5	.321	.596	1	0	3B-20, 2B-10
2 yrs.	35	115	38	9	2	6	5.2	19	19	8	10	5	.330	.600	7	3	3B-20, 2B-10

LEAGUE CHAMPIONSHIP SERIES

	G	AB	H	2B	3B	HR	HR%	R	RBI	BB	SO	SB	BA	SA	PH AB	PH H	G by POS
1988 NY N	7	27	9	2	0	0	0.0	2	1	4	0	0	.333	.407	0	0	3B-7

Stan Jefferson

JEFFERSON, STANLEY
B. Dec. 4, 1962, New York, N. Y.
BB TR 5'11" 175 lbs.

	G	AB	H	2B	3B	HR	HR%	R	RBI	BB	SO	SB	BA	SA	PH AB	PH H	G by POS
1986 NY N	14	24	5	1	0	1	4.2	6	3	2	8	0	.208	.375	5	0	OF-7
1987 SD N	116	422	97	8	7	8	1.9	59	29	39	92	34	.230	.339	9	0	OF-107
1988	49	111	16	1	2	1	0.9	16	4	9	22	5	.144	.216	3	0	OF-38
3 yrs.	179	557	118	10	9	10	1.8	81	36	50	122	39	.212	.316	17	0	OF-152

Steve Jeltz

JELTZ, LARRY STEVEN
B. May 28, 1959, Paris, France
BB TR 5'11" 180 lbs.

	G	AB	H	2B	3B	HR	HR%	R	RBI	BB	SO	SB	BA	SA	PH AB	PH H	G by POS
1983 PHI N	13	8	1	0	1	0	0.0	0	1	1	2	0	.125	.375	3	0	2B-4, SS-2, 3B-2
1984	28	68	14	0	1	1	1.5	7	7	7	11	2	.206	.279	0	0	SS-27, 3B-1
1985	89	196	37	4	1	0	0.0	17	12	26	55	1	.189	.219	0	0	SS-86
1986	145	439	96	11	4	0	0.0	44	36	65	97	6	.219	.262	5	2	SS-141
1987	114	293	68	9	6	0	0.0	37	12	39	54	1	.232	.304	1	1	SS-114, OF-1
1988	148	379	71	11	4	0	0.0	39	27	59	58	3	.187	.237	3	0	SS-148
6 yrs.	537	1383	287	35	17	1	0.1	144	95	197	277	13	.208	.260	12	3	SS-518, 2B-4, 3B-3, OF-1

Doug Jennings

JENNINGS, JAMES DOUGLAS
B. Sept. 30, 1964, Atlanta, Ga.
BL TL 5'10" 165 lbs.

	G	AB	H	2B	3B	HR	HR%	R	RBI	BB	SO	SB	BA	SA	PH AB	PH H	G by POS
1988 OAK A	71	101	21	6	0	1	1.0	9	15	21	28	0	.208	.297	27	5	OF-23, 1B-14, DH-2

Houston Jimenez

JIMENEZ, ALFONSO GONZALEZ
Born Alfonso Jimenez y Gonzalez.
B. Oct. 30, 1957, Navojoa, Mexico
BR TR 5'8" 144 lbs.

	G	AB	H	2B	3B	HR	HR%	R	RBI	BB	SO	SB	BA	SA	PH AB	PH H	G by POS
1983 MIN A	36	86	15	5	1	0	0.0	5	9	4	11	0	.174	.256	0	0	SS-36
1984	108	298	60	11	1	0	0.0	28	19	15	34	0	.201	.245	0	0	SS-107
1987 PIT N	5	6	0	0	0	0	0.0	0	0	1	2	0	.000	.000	1	0	SS-2, 2B-2
1988 CLE A	9	21	1	0	0	0	0.0	1	1	0	2	0	.048	.048	0	0	2B-7, SS-2
4 yrs.	158	411	76	16	2	0	0.0	34	29	20	49	0	.185	.234	1	0	SS-147, 2B-9

Howard Johnson

JOHNSON, HOWARD MICHAEL (Hojo)
B. Nov. 29, 1960, Clearwater, Fla.
BB TR 5'11" 175 lbs.

	G	AB	H	2B	3B	HR	HR%	R	RBI	BB	SO	SB	BA	SA	PH AB	PH H	G by POS
1982 DET A	54	155	49	5	0	4	2.6	23	14	16	30	7	.316	.426	7	1	3B-33, DH-10, OF-9
1983	27	66	14	0	0	3	4.5	11	5	7	10	0	.212	.348	6	2	3B-21, DH-2
1984	116	355	88	14	1	12	3.4	43	50	40	67	10	.248	.394	7	2	3B-108, SS-9, DH-4, OF-1, 1B-1
1985 NY N	126	389	94	18	4	11	2.8	38	46	34	78	6	.242	.393	12	4	3B-113, SS-7, OF-1
1986	88	220	54	14	0	10	4.5	30	39	31	64	8	.245	.445	17	2	3B-55, SS-34, OF-1
1987	157	554	147	22	1	36	6.5	93	99	83	113	32	.265	.504	2	1	3B-140, SS-38, OF-2
1988	148	495	114	21	1	24	4.8	85	68	86	104	23	.230	.422	3	1	3B-131, SS-52
7 yrs.	716	2234	560	94	7	100	4.5	323	321	297	466	86	.251	.433	54	13	3B-591, SS-140, DH-16, OF-14, 1B-1

LEAGUE CHAMPIONSHIP SERIES

	G	AB	H	2B	3B	HR	HR%	R	RBI	BB	SO	SB	BA	SA	PH AB	PH H	G by POS
1986 NY N	2	1	0	0	0	0	0.0	0	0	0	0	0	.000	.000	2	0	
1988	6	18	1	0	0	0	0.0	3	0	1	6	1	.056	.056	2	0	3B-1
2 yrs.	8	20	1	0	0	0	0.0	3	0	1	6	1	.050	.050	4	0	3B-1

WORLD SERIES

	G	AB	H	2B	3B	HR	HR%	R	RBI	BB	SO	SB	BA	SA	PH AB	PH H	G by POS
1984 DET A	1	1	0	0	0	0	0.0	0	0	0	0	0	.000	.000	1	0	

	G	AB	H	2B	3B	HR	HR %	R	RBI	BB	SO	SB	BA	SA	Pinch Hit AB	Pinch Hit H	G by POS

Howard Johnson continued

	G	AB	H	2B	3B	HR	HR %	R	RBI	BB	SO	SB	BA	SA	AB	H	G by POS
1986 **NY N**	2	5	0	0	0	0	0.0	0	0	0	2	0	.000	.000	1	0	3B-1
2 yrs.	3	6	0	0	0	0	0.0	0	0	0	2	0	.000	.000	2	0	3B-1

Lance Johnson

JOHNSON, KENNETH LANCE
B. July 6, 1963, Cincinnati, Ohio
BL TL 5'10" 160 lbs.

	G	AB	H	2B	3B	HR	HR %	R	RBI	BB	SO	SB	BA	SA	AB	H	G by POS
1987 **STL N**	33	59	13	2	1	0	0.0	4	7	4	6	6	.220	.288	8	2	OF-25
1988 **CHI A**	33	124	23	4	1	0	0.0	11	6	6	11	6	.185	.234	3	0	OF-31, DH-1
2 yrs.	66	183	36	6	2	0	0.0	15	13	10	17	12	.197	.251	11	2	OF-56, DH-1

LEAGUE CHAMPIONSHIP SERIES

	G	AB	H	2B	3B	HR	HR %	R	RBI	BB	SO	SB	BA	SA	AB	H	G by POS
1987 **STL N**	1	0	0	0	0	0	–	1	0	0	0	1	–	–	0	0	

WORLD SERIES

	G	AB	H	2B	3B	HR	HR %	R	RBI	BB	SO	SB	BA	SA	AB	H	G by POS
1987 **STL N**	1	0	0	0	0	0	–	0	0	0	0	1	–	–	0	0	

Wallace Johnson

JOHNSON, WALLACE DARNELL
B. Dec. 25, 1956, Gary, Ind.
BB TR 6' 173 lbs.

	G	AB	H	2B	3B	HR	HR %	R	RBI	BB	SO	SB	BA	SA	AB	H	G by POS
1981 **MON N**	11	9	2	0	1	0	0.0	1	3	1	1	1	.222	.444	7	2	2B-1
1982	36	57	11	0	2	0	0.0	5	2	5	5	4	.193	.263	21	4	2B-13
1983 **2 teams**			**MON**	**N**	(3G –	.500)		**SF**	**N**	(7G –	.125)						
" total	10	10	2	0	0	0	0.0	1	1	1	0	1	.200	.200	7	1	2B-1
1984 **MON N**	17	24	5	0	0	0	0.0	3	4	5	4	0	.208	.208	10	3	1B-4
1986	61	127	36	3	1	1	0.8	13	10	7	9	6	.283	.346	37	11	1B-27
1987	75	85	21	5	0	1	1.2	7	14	7	6	5	.247	.341	61	17	1B-9
1988	86	94	29	5	1	0	0.0	7	3	12	15	0	.309	.383	64	22	1B-13, 2B-1
7 yrs.	296	406	106	13	5	2	0.5	37	37	38	40	17	.261	.333	207	60	1B-53, 2B-16

DIVISIONAL PLAYOFF SERIES

	G	AB	H	2B	3B	HR	HR %	R	RBI	BB	SO	SB	BA	SA	AB	H	G by POS
1981 **MON N**	2	2	1	0	0	0	0.0	0	1	0	0	0	.500	.500	2	1	

Ron Jones

JONES, RONALD GLEN
B. June 11, 1964, Sequin, Tex.
BL TR 5'10" 200 lbs.

	G	AB	H	2B	3B	HR	HR %	R	RBI	BB	SO	SB	BA	SA	AB	H	G by POS
1988 **PHI N**	33	124	36	6	1	8	6.5	15	26	2	14	0	.290	.548	1	0	OF-32

Tim Jones

JONES, WILLIAM TIMOTHY
B. Dec. 1, 1962, Sumter, S. C.
BL TR 5'10" 172 lbs.

	G	AB	H	2B	3B	HR	HR %	R	RBI	BB	SO	SB	BA	SA	AB	H	G by POS
1988 **STL N**	31	52	14	0	0	0	0.0	2	3	4	10	4	.269	.269	9	1	SS-9, 2B-8, 3B-1

Tracy Jones

JONES, TRACY DONALD
B. Mar. 31, 1961, Hawthorne, Calif.
BR TR 6'3" 180 lbs.

	G	AB	H	2B	3B	HR	HR %	R	RBI	BB	SO	SB	BA	SA	AB	H	G by POS
1986 **CIN N**	46	86	30	3	0	2	2.3	16	10	9	5	7	.349	.453	12	2	OF-24, 1B-2
1987	117	359	104	17	3	10	2.8	53	44	23	40	31	.290	.437	25	6	OF-95
1988 **2 teams**			**CIN**	**N**	(37G –	.229)		**MON**	**N**	(53G –	.333)						
" total	90	224	66	6	1	3	1.3	29	24	20	18	18	.295	.371	23	6	OF-68
3 yrs.	253	669	200	26	4	15	2.2	98	78	52	63	56	.299	.417	60	14	OF-187, 1B-2

Ricky Jordan

JORDAN, PAUL SCOTT
B. May 26, 1965, Richmond, Calif.
BR TR 6'5" 210 lbs.

	G	AB	H	2B	3B	HR	HR %	R	RBI	BB	SO	SB	BA	SA	AB	H	G by POS
1988 **PHI N**	69	273	84	15	1	11	4.0	41	43	7	39	1	.308	.491	0	0	1B-69

Scott Jordan

JORDAN, SCOTT ALLAN
B. May 27, 1963, Waco, Tex.
BR TR 6' 178 lbs.

	G	AB	H	2B	3B	HR	HR %	R	RBI	BB	SO	SB	BA	SA	AB	H	G by POS
1988 **CLE A**	7	9	1	0	0	0	0.0	0	0	0	3	0	.111	.111	0	0	OF-6

Felix Jose

JOSE, DOMINGO FELIX
B. May 8, 1965, Santo Domingo, Dominican Republic
BB TR 6'1" 190 lbs.

	G	AB	H	2B	3B	HR	HR %	R	RBI	BB	SO	SB	BA	SA	AB	H	G by POS
1988 **OAK A**	8	6	2	1	0	0	0.0	2	1	0	1	1	.333	.500	2	0	OF-6

Wally Joyner

JOYNER, WALLACE KEITH (Wally World)
B. June 16, 1962, Atlanta, Ga.
BL TL 6'2" 185 lbs.

	G	AB	H	2B	3B	HR	HR %	R	RBI	BB	SO	SB	BA	SA	AB	H	G by POS
1986 **CAL A**	154	593	172	27	3	22	3.7	82	100	57	58	5	.290	.457	4	1	1B-152
1987	149	564	161	33	1	34	6.0	100	117	72	64	8	.285	.528	2	0	1B-149
1988	158	597	176	31	2	13	2.2	81	85	55	51	8	.295	.419	4	2	1B-156
3 yrs.	461	1754	509	91	6	69	3.9	263	302	184	173	21	.290	.467	10	3	1B-457

LEAGUE CHAMPIONSHIP SERIES

	G	AB	H	2B	3B	HR	HR %	R	RBI	BB	SO	SB	BA	SA	AB	H	G by POS
1986 **CAL A**	3	11	5	2	0	1	9.1	3	2	2	0	0	.455	.909	0	0	1B-3

Ed Jurak

JURAK, EDWARD JAMES (Lizard)
B. Oct. 24, 1957, Hollywood, Calif.
BR TR 6'2" 185 lbs.

	G	AB	H	2B	3B	HR	HR %	R	RBI	BB	SO	SB	BA	SA	AB	H	G by POS
1982 **BOS A**	12	21	7	0	0	0	0.0	3	7	2	4	0	.333	.333	0	0	3B-11, OF-1
1983	75	159	44	8	4	0	0.0	19	18	18	25	1	.277	.377	4	2	SS-38, 1B-19, 3B-12, DH-5, 2B-1
1984	47	66	16	3	1	1	1.5	6	7	12	12	0	.242	.364	3	1	1B-19, 2B-14, 3B-9, SS-2
1985	26	13	3	0	0	0	0.0	4	0	1	3	0	.231	.231	3	0	3B-7, SS-3, DH-2, OF-1, 1B-1
1988 **OAK A**	3	1	0	0	0	0	0.0	0	0	0	0	0	.000	.000	1	0	3B-1
5 yrs.	163	260	70	11	5	1	0.4	33	32	33	44	1	.269	.362	11	3	SS-43, 3B-40, 1B-39, 2B-15, DH-7, OF-2

Ron Karkovice

KARKOVICE, RONALD JOSEPH
B. Aug. 8, 1963, Union, N. J.
BR TR 6'1" 210 lbs.

	G	AB	H	2B	3B	HR	HR %	R	RBI	BB	SO	SB	BA	SA	AB	H	G by POS
1986 **CHI A**	37	97	24	7	0	4	4.1	13	13	9	37	1	.247	.443	0	0	C-37
1987	39	85	6	0	0	2	2.4	7	7	7	40	3	.071	.141	0	0	C-37
1988	46	115	20	4	0	3	2.6	10	9	7	30	4	.174	.287	0	0	C-46
3 yrs.	122	297	50	11	0	9	3.0	30	29	23	107	8	.168	.296	0	0	C-120

Roberto Kelly

KELLY, ROBERTO CONRADO
Born Roberto Conrado Kelly y Gray.
B. Oct. 1, 1964, Panama City, Panama

BR TR 6'2" 180 lbs.

	G	AB	H	2B	3B	HR	HR%	R	RBI	BB	SO	SB	BA	SA	Pinch Hit AB	Pinch Hit H	G by POS
1987 NY A	23	52	14	3	0	1	1.9	12	7	5	15	9	.269	.385	0	0	OF-17
1988	38	77	19	4	1	1	1.3	9	7	3	15	5	.247	.364	1	1	OF-30
2 yrs.	61	129	33	7	1	2	1.6	21	14	8	30	14	.256	.372	1	1	OF-47

Steve Kemp

KEMP, STEVEN F.
B. Aug. 7, 1954, San Angelo, Tex.

BL TL 6' 195 lbs.

	G	AB	H	2B	3B	HR	HR%	R	RBI	BB	SO	SB	BA	SA	Pinch Hit AB	Pinch Hit H	G by POS
1977 DET A	151	552	142	29	4	18	3.3	75	88	71	93	3	.257	.422	3	0	OF-148
1978	159	582	161	18	4	15	2.6	75	79	97	87	2	.277	.399	2	1	OF-157
1979	134	490	156	26	3	26	5.3	88	105	68	70	5	.318	.543	4	1	OF-120, DH-11
1980	135	508	149	23	3	21	4.1	88	101	69	64	5	.293	.474	6	2	OF-85, DH-46
1981	105	372	103	18	4	9	2.4	52	49	70	48	9	.277	.419	3	1	OF-92, DH-12
1982 CHI A	160	580	166	23	1	19	3.3	91	98	89	83	7	.286	.428	3	1	OF-154, DH-2
1983 NY A	109	373	90	17	3	12	3.2	53	49	41	37	1	.241	.399	9	2	OF-101, DH-2
1984	94	313	91	12	1	7	2.2	37	41	40	54	4	.291	.403	9	2	OF-75, DH-12
1985 PIT N	92	236	59	13	2	2	0.8	19	21	25	54	1	.250	.347	27	9	OF-63
1986	13	16	3	0	0	1	6.3	1	1	4	6	1	.188	.375	5	0	OF-4
1988 TEX A	16	36	8	0	0	0	0.0	2	2	2	9	1	.222	.222	5	1	DH-7, OF-5, 1B-1
11 yrs.	1168	4058	1128	179	25	130	3.2	581	634	576	605	39	.278	.431	76	20	OF-1004, DH-92, 1B-1

Terry Kennedy

KENNEDY, TERRENCE EDWARD
Son of Bob Kennedy.
B. June 4, 1956, Euclid, Ohio

BL TR 6'3" 220 lbs.

	G	AB	H	2B	3B	HR	HR%	R	RBI	BB	SO	SB	BA	SA	Pinch Hit AB	Pinch Hit H	G by POS
1978 STL N	10	29	5	0	0	0	0.0	0	2	4	3	0	.172	.172	1	0	C-10
1979	33	109	31	7	0	2	1.8	11	17	6	20	0	.284	.404	5	1	C-32
1980	84	248	63	12	3	4	1.6	28	34	28	34	0	.254	.375	12	2	C-41, OF-28
1981 SD N	101	382	115	24	1	2	0.5	32	41	22	53	0	.301	.385	3	0	C-100
1982	153	562	166	42	1	21	3.7	75	97	26	91	1	.295	.486	5	2	C-139, 1B-12
1983	149	549	156	27	2	17	3.1	47	98	51	89	1	.284	.434	4	2	C-143, 1B-4
1984	148	530	127	16	1	14	2.6	54	57	33	99	1	.240	.353	5	0	C-147
1985	143	532	139	27	1	10	1.9	54	74	31	102	0	.261	.372	5	2	C-140, 1B-5
1986	141	432	114	22	1	12	2.8	46	57	37	74	0	.264	.403	23	11	C-123
1987 BAL A	143	512	128	13	1	18	3.5	51	62	35	112	1	.250	.385	5	0	C-142
1988	85	265	60	10	0	3	1.1	20	16	15	53	0	.226	.298	8	1	C-79
11 yrs.	1190	4150	1104	200	11	103	2.5	418	555	288	730	4	.266	.394	76	21	C-1096, OF-28, 1B-21

LEAGUE CHAMPIONSHIP SERIES

	G	AB	H	2B	3B	HR	HR%	R	RBI	BB	SO	SB	BA	SA	Pinch Hit AB	Pinch Hit H	G by POS
1984 SD N	5	18	4	0	0	0	0.0	2	1	1	3	0	.222	.222	0	0	C-5

WORLD SERIES

	G	AB	H	2B	3B	HR	HR%	R	RBI	BB	SO	SB	BA	SA	Pinch Hit AB	Pinch Hit H	G by POS
1984 SD N	5	19	4	1	0	1	5.3	2	3	1	1	0	.211	.421	0	0	C-5

Steve Kiefer

KIEFER, STEVEN GEORGE
B. Oct. 18, 1960, Chicago, Ill.

BR TR 6'1" 175 lbs.

	G	AB	H	2B	3B	HR	HR%	R	RBI	BB	SO	SB	BA	SA	Pinch Hit AB	Pinch Hit H	G by POS
1984 OAK A	23	40	7	1	2	0	0.0	7	2	2	10	2	.175	.300	1	1	SS-17, DH-3, 3B-2
1985	40	66	13	1	1	1	1.5	8	10	1	18	0	.197	.288	1	0	3B-34, DH-2
1986 MIL A	2	6	0	0	0	0	0.0	0	0	0	4	0	.000	.000	0	0	SS-2
1987	28	99	20	4	0	5	5.1	17	17	7	28	0	.202	.394	2	1	3B-26, 2B-4
1988	7	10	3	1	0	1	10.0	2	1	2	3	0	.300	.700	1	0	3B-4, 2B-4
5 yrs.	100	221	43	7	3	7	3.2	34	30	12	63	2	.195	.348	5	2	3B-66, SS-19, 2B-8, DH-5

Mike Kingery

KINGERY, MICHAEL SCOTT
B. Mar. 29, 1961, St. James, Minn.

BL TL 6' 180 lbs.

	G	AB	H	2B	3B	HR	HR%	R	RBI	BB	SO	SB	BA	SA	Pinch Hit AB	Pinch Hit H	G by POS
1986 KC A	62	209	54	8	5	3	1.4	25	14	12	30	7	.258	.388	5	0	OF-59
1987 SEA A	120	354	99	25	4	9	2.5	38	52	27	43	7	.280	.449	9	3	OF-114, DH-4
1988	57	123	25	6	0	1	0.8	21	9	19	23	3	.203	.276	5	0	OF-44, 1B-10
3 yrs.	239	686	178	39	9	13	1.9	84	75	58	96	17	.259	.399	19	5	OF-217, 1B-10, DH-4

Ron Kittle

KITTLE, RONALD DALE (Kitty)
B. Jan. 5, 1958, Gary, Ind.

BR TR 6'4" 200 lbs.

	G	AB	H	2B	3B	HR	HR%	R	RBI	BB	SO	SB	BA	SA	Pinch Hit AB	Pinch Hit H	G by POS
1982 CHI A	20	29	7	2	0	1	3.4	3	7	3	12	0	.241	.414	13	2	OF-5, DH-3
1983	145	520	132	19	3	35	6.7	75	100	39	150	8	.254	.504	6	0	OF-139, DH-2
1984	139	466	100	15	0	32	6.9	67	74	49	137	3	.215	.453	13	4	OF-124, DH-7
1985	116	379	87	12	0	26	6.9	51	58	31	92	1	.230	.467	9	0	DH-57, OF-57
1986 2 teams		CHI A (86G – .213)				NY A (30G – .238)											
" total	116	376	82	13	0	21	5.6	42	60	35	110	4	.218	.420	12	2	DH-86, OF-21
1987 NY A	59	159	44	5	0	12	7.5	21	28	10	36	0	.277	.535	13	1	DH-49, OF-2
1988 CLE A	75	225	58	8	0	18	8.0	31	43	16	65	0	.258	.533	13	5	DH-63
7 yrs.	670	2154	510	74	3	145	6.7	290	370	183	602	16	.237	.476	79	14	OF-348, DH-267

LEAGUE CHAMPIONSHIP SERIES

	G	AB	H	2B	3B	HR	HR%	R	RBI	BB	SO	SB	BA	SA	Pinch Hit AB	Pinch Hit H	G by POS
1983 CHI A	3	7	2	1	0	0	0.0	1	0	1	2	0	.286	.429	0	0	OF-3

Ray Knight

KNIGHT, CHARLES RAY
B. Dec. 28, 1952, Albany, Ga.

BR TR 6'1" 185 lbs.

	G	AB	H	2B	3B	HR	HR%	R	RBI	BB	SO	SB	BA	SA	Pinch Hit AB	Pinch Hit H	G by POS
1974 CIN N	14	11	2	1	0	0	0.0	1	2	1	2	0	.182	.273	0	0	3B-14
1977	80	92	24	5	1	1	1.1	8	13	9	16	1	.261	.370	26	6	3B-37, 2B-17, OF-5, SS-3
1978	83	65	13	3	0	1	1.5	7	4	3	13	0	.200	.292	16	2	3B-60, 2B-4, OF-3, SS-1, 1B-1
1979	150	551	175	37	4	10	1.8	64	79	38	57	4	.318	.454	1	0	3B-150
1980	162	618	163	39	7	14	2.3	71	78	36	62	1	.264	.417	1	0	3B-162
1981	106	386	100	23	1	6	1.6	43	34	33	51	2	.259	.370	1	0	3B-105
1982 HOU N	158	609	179	36	6	6	1.0	72	70	48	58	2	.294	.402	0	0	1B-96, 3B-67
1983	145	507	154	36	4	9	1.8	43	70	42	62	0	.304	.444	4	0	1B-143
1984 2 teams		HOU N (88G – .223)				NY N (27G – .280)											
" total	115	371	88	14	0	3	0.8	28	35	21	43	0	.237	.299	10	4	3B-81, 1B-27
1985 NY N	90	271	59	12	0	6	2.2	22	36	13	32	1	.218	.328	16	1	3B-73, 2B-2, 1B-1
1986	137	486	145	24	2	11	2.3	51	76	40	63	0	.298	.424	6	2	3B-132, 1B-1

	G	AB	H	2B	3B	HR	HR %	R	RBI	BB	SO	SB	BA	SA	Pinch Hit AB	Pinch Hit H	G by POS

Ray Knight continued

	G	AB	H	2B	3B	HR	HR %	R	RBI	BB	SO	SB	BA	SA	AB	H	G by POS
1987 **BAL A**	150	563	144	24	0	14	2.5	46	65	39	90	0	.256	.373	1	1	3B-130, DH-14, 1B-6
1988 **DET A**	105	299	65	12	2	3	1.0	34	33	20	30	1	.217	.301	23	2	1B-64, 3B-11, OF-2
13 yrs.	1495	4829	1311	266	27	84	1.7	490	595	343	579	14	.271	.390	105	18	3B-1021, 1B-339, 2B-23, DH-14, OF-10, SS-4

LEAGUE CHAMPIONSHIP SERIES

	G	AB	H	2B	3B	HR	HR %	R	RBI	BB	SO	SB	BA	SA	AB	H	G by POS
1979 **CIN N**	3	14	4	1	0	0	0.0	0	0	0	2	1	.286	.357	0	0	3B-3
1986 **NY N**	6	24	4	0	0	0	0.0	1	2	1	5	0	.167	.167	0	0	3B-6
2 yrs.	9	38	8	1	0	0	0.0	1	2	1	7	1	.211	.237	0	0	3B-9

WORLD SERIES

	G	AB	H	2B	3B	HR	HR %	R	RBI	BB	SO	SB	BA	SA	AB	H	G by POS
1986 **NY N**	7	23	9	1	0	1	4.3	4	5	2	2	0	.391	.565	0	0	3B-6

Chad Kreuter

KREUTER, CHAD MICHAEL
B. Aug. 26, 1964, Greenbrae, Calif.

BB TR 6'2"   190 lbs.

	G	AB	H	2B	3B	HR	HR %	R	RBI	BB	SO	SB	BA	SA	AB	H	G by POS
1988 **TEX A**	16	51	14	2	1	1	2.0	3	5	7	13	0	.275	.412	0	0	C-16

John Kruk

KRUK, JOHN MARTIN
B. Feb. 9, 1961, Charleston, W. Va.

BL TL 5'10"   170 lbs.

	G	AB	H	2B	3B	HR	HR %	R	RBI	BB	SO	SB	BA	SA	AB	H	G by POS
1986 **SD N**	122	278	86	16	2	4	1.4	33	38	45	58	2	.309	.424	32	8	OF-74, 1B-9
1987	138	447	140	14	2	20	4.5	72	91	73	93	18	.313	.488	12	6	1B-101, OF-29
1988	120	378	91	17	1	9	2.4	54	44	80	68	5	.241	.362	7	2	1B-63, OF-55
3 yrs.	380	1103	317	47	5	33	3.0	159	173	198	219	25	.287	.429	51	16	1B-173, OF-158

Jeff Kunkel

KUNKEL, JEFFREY WILLIAM
Son of Bill Kunkel.
B. Mar. 25, 1962, West Palm Beach, Fla.

BR TR 6'2"   175 lbs.

	G	AB	H	2B	3B	HR	HR %	R	RBI	BB	SO	SB	BA	SA	AB	H	G by POS
1984 **TEX A**	50	142	29	2	3	3	2.1	13	7	2	35	4	.204	.324	0	0	SS-48, DH-1
1985	2	4	1	0	0	0	0.0	1	0	0	3	0	.250	.250	0	0	SS-2
1986	8	13	3	0	0	1	7.7	3	2	0	2	0	.231	.462	1	0	SS-5, DH-1
1987	15	32	7	0	0	1	3.1	1	2	0	10	0	.219	.313	1	0	2B-10, OF-3, 3B-3, DH-1, SS-1, 1B-1
1988	55	154	35	8	3	2	1.3	14	15	4	35	0	.227	.357	3	0	2B-28, SS-19, 3B-10, OF-6, DH-3, P-1
5 yrs.	130	345	75	10	6	7	2.0	32	26	6	85	4	.217	.342	5	0	SS-75, 2B-38, 3B-13, OF-9, DH-6, 1B-1, P-1

Randy Kutcher

KUTCHER, RANDY SCOTT
B. Apr. 30, 1960, Anchorage, Alaska

BR TR 5'11"   170 lbs.

	G	AB	H	2B	3B	HR	HR %	R	RBI	BB	SO	SB	BA	SA	AB	H	G by POS
1986 **SF N**	71	186	44	9	1	7	3.8	28	16	11	41	6	.237	.409	13	1	OF-51, SS-13, 3B-4, 2B-3
1987	14	16	3	1	1	0	0.0	7	1	1	5	1	.188	.375	2	0	OF-6, 3B-2, 2B-2, SS-1
1988 **BOS A**	19	12	2	1	0	0	0.0	2	0	0	2	0	.167	.250	0	0	OF-7, 3B-2
3 yrs.	104	214	49	11	2	7	3.3	37	17	12	48	7	.229	.397	15	1	OF-64, SS-14, 3B-8, 2B-5

Mike Laga

LAGA, MICHAEL RUSSELL
B. June 14, 1960, Ridgewood, N. J.

BL TL 6'2"   210 lbs.

	G	AB	H	2B	3B	HR	HR %	R	RBI	BB	SO	SB	BA	SA	AB	H	G by POS
1982 **DET A**	27	88	23	9	0	3	3.4	6	11	4	23	1	.261	.466	4	1	1B-19, DH-8
1983	12	21	4	0	0	0	0.0	2	2	1	9	0	.190	.190	3	1	DH-6, 1B-5
1984	9	11	6	0	0	0	0.0	1	1	1	2	0	.545	.545	3	3	DH-4, 1B-4
1985	9	36	6	1	0	2	5.6	3	6	0	9	0	.167	.361	0	0	DH-5, 1B-4
1986 **2 teams**			DET	A	(15G –	.200)		STL	N	(18G –	.217)						
" total	33	91	19	5	0	6	6.6	13	16	10	31	0	.209	.462	5	0	1B-28, DH-3
1987 **STL N**	17	29	4	1	0	1	3.4	4	4	2	7	0	.138	.276	5	1	1B-12
1988	41	100	13	0	0	1	1.0	5	4	2	21	0	.130	.160	5	0	1B-37
7 yrs.	148	376	75	16	0	13	3.5	34	44	20	102	1	.199	.346	25	6	1B-109, DH-26

Steve Lake

LAKE, STEVEN MICHAEL
B. Mar. 14, 1957, Inglewood, Calif.

BR TR 6'1"   180 lbs.

	G	AB	H	2B	3B	HR	HR %	R	RBI	BB	SO	SB	BA	SA	AB	H	G by POS
1983 **CHI N**	38	85	22	4	1	1	1.2	9	7	2	6	0	.259	.365	5	0	C-32
1984	25	54	12	4	0	2	3.7	4	7	0	7	0	.222	.407	1	0	C-24
1985	58	119	18	2	0	1	0.8	5	11	3	21	1	.151	.193	4	1	C-55
1986 **2 teams**			CHI	N	(10G –	.421)		STL	N	(26G –	.245)						
" total	36	68	20	2	0	2	2.9	8	14	3	7	0	.294	.412	0	0	C-36
1987 **STL N**	74	179	45	7	2	2	1.1	19	19	10	18	0	.251	.346	14	4	C-59
1988	36	54	15	3	0	1	1.9	5	4	3	15	0	.278	.389	17	5	C-19
6 yrs.	267	559	132	22	3	9	1.6	50	62	21	74	1	.236	.335	41	10	C-225

LEAGUE CHAMPIONSHIP SERIES

	G	AB	H	2B	3B	HR	HR %	R	RBI	BB	SO	SB	BA	SA	AB	H	G by POS
1984 **CHI N**	1	1	1	1	0	0	0.0	0	0	0	0	0	1.000	2.000	0	0	C-1

WORLD SERIES

	G	AB	H	2B	3B	HR	HR %	R	RBI	BB	SO	SB	BA	SA	AB	H	G by POS
1987 **STL N**	3	3	1	0	0	0	0.0	0	1	0	0	0	.333	.333	0	0	C-3

Tom Lampkin

LAMPKIN, THOMAS MICHAEL
B. Mar. 4, 1964, Cincinnati, Ohio

BL TR 5'11"   185 lbs.

	G	AB	H	2B	3B	HR	HR %	R	RBI	BB	SO	SB	BA	SA	AB	H	G by POS
1988 **CLE A**	4	4	0	0	0	0	0.0	0	0	1	0	0	.000	.000	1	0	C-3

Tito Landrum

LANDRUM, TERRY LEE
B. Oct. 25, 1954, Joplin, Mo.

BR TR 5'11"   175 lbs.

	G	AB	H	2B	3B	HR	HR %	R	RBI	BB	SO	SB	BA	SA	AB	H	G by POS
1980 **STL N**	35	77	19	2	2	0	0.0	6	7	6	17	3	.247	.325	5	1	OF-29
1981	81	119	31	5	4	0	0.0	13	10	6	14	4	.261	.370	11	3	OF-67
1982	99	72	20	3	0	2	2.8	12	14	8	18	0	.278	.403	18	4	OF-56
1983 **2 teams**			STL	N	(6G –	.200)		BAL	A	(26G –	.310)						
" total	32	47	14	2	1	1	2.1	8	4	2	13	1	.298	.447	9	2	OF-31
1984 **STL N**	105	173	47	9	1	3	1.7	21	26	10	27	3	.272	.387	23	9	OF-88
1985	85	161	45	8	2	4	2.5	21	21	19	30	1	.280	.429	24	8	OF-73
1986	96	205	43	7	1	2	1.0	24	17	20	41	3	.210	.283	28	5	OF-78

	G	AB	H	2B	3B	HR	HR %	R	RBI	BB	SO	SB	BA	SA	Pinch Hit AB	Pinch Hit H	G by POS

Tito Landrum continued

	G	AB	H	2B	3B	HR	HR %	R	RBI	BB	SO	SB	BA	SA	AB	H	G by POS
1987 2 teams	STL N (30G – .200)				LA N (51G – .239)												
" total	81	117	26	4	0	1	0.9	13	10	10	30	2	.222	.282	35	8	OF-54, 1B-1
1988 BAL A	13	24	3	0	1	0	0.0	2	2	4	6	0	.125	.208	1	0	OF-12, DH-1
9 yrs.	607	995	248	40	12	13	1.3	120	111	85	196	17	.249	.353	154	40	OF-488, DH-1, 1B-1

LEAGUE CHAMPIONSHIP SERIES

	G	AB	H	2B	3B	HR	HR %	R	RBI	BB	SO	SB	BA	SA	AB	H	G by POS
1983 BAL A	4	10	2	0	0	1	10.0	2	1	0	2	0	.200	.500	1	0	OF-3
1985 STL N	6	14	6	0	0	0	0.0	2	4	1	1	1	.429	.429	1	1	OF-5
2 yrs.	10	24	8	0	0	1	4.2	4	5	1	3	1	.333	.458	2	1	OF-8

WORLD SERIES

	G	AB	H	2B	3B	HR	HR %	R	RBI	BB	SO	SB	BA	SA	AB	H	G by POS
1983 BAL A	3	0	0	0	0	0	–	0	0	0	0	1	–	–	0	0	OF-3
1985 STL N	7	25	9	2	0	1	4.0	3	1	0	2	0	.360	.560	0	0	OF-7
2 yrs.	10	25	9	2	0	1	4.0	3	1	0	2	1	.360	.560	0	0	OF-10

Carney Lansford

LANSFORD, CARNEY RAY
Brother of Joe Lansford.
B. Feb. 7, 1957, San Jose, Calif.

BR TR 6'2"   195 lbs.

	G	AB	H	2B	3B	HR	HR %	R	RBI	BB	SO	SB	BA	SA	AB	H	G by POS
1978 CAL A	121	453	133	23	2	8	1.8	63	52	31	67	20	.294	.406	2	0	3B-117, SS-2, DH-1
1979	157	654	188	30	5	19	2.9	114	79	39	115	20	.287	.436	0	0	3B-157
1980	151	602	157	27	3	15	2.5	87	80	50	93	14	.261	.390	1	1	3B-150
1981 BOS A	102	399	134	23	3	4	1.0	61	52	34	28	15	.336	.439	1	0	3B-86, DH-16
1982	128	482	145	28	4	11	2.3	65	63	46	48	9	.301	.444	1	0	3B-114, DH-13
1983 OAK A	80	299	92	16	2	10	3.3	43	45	22	33	3	.308	.475	3	1	3B-78, SS-1
1984	151	597	179	31	5	14	2.3	70	74	40	62	9	.300	.439	0	0	3B-151
1985	98	401	111	18	2	13	3.2	51	46	18	27	2	.277	.429	1	0	3B-97
1986	151	591	168	16	4	19	3.2	80	72	39	51	16	.284	.421	1	0	3B-100, 1B-60, DH-2, 2B-1
1987	151	554	160	27	4	19	3.4	89	76	60	44	27	.289	.455	2	1	3B-142, 1B-17, DH-4
1988	150	556	155	20	2	7	1.3	80	57	35	35	29	.279	.360	4	0	3B-143, 1B-9, 2B-1
11 yrs.	1440	5588	1622	259	36	139	2.5	803	696	414	603	164	.290	.424	16	3	3B-1335, 1B-86, DH-36, SS-3, 2B-2

LEAGUE CHAMPIONSHIP SERIES

	G	AB	H	2B	3B	HR	HR %	R	RBI	BB	SO	SB	BA	SA	AB	H	G by POS
1979 CAL A	4	17	5	0	0	0	0.0	2	3	1	2	1	.294	.294	0	0	3B-4
1988 OAK A	4	17	5	1	0	1	5.9	4	2	0	2	0	.294	.529	0	0	3B-4
2 yrs.	8	34	10	1	0	1	2.9	6	5	1	4	1	.294	.412	0	0	3B-8

WORLD SERIES

	G	AB	H	2B	3B	HR	HR %	R	RBI	BB	SO	SB	BA	SA	AB	H	G by POS
1988 OAK A	5	18	3	0	0	0	0.0	0	2	1	2	0	.167	.167	0	0	3B-5

Barry Larkin

LARKIN, BARRY LOUIS
B. Apr. 28, 1964, Cincinnati, Ohio

BR TR 6'   180 lbs.

	G	AB	H	2B	3B	HR	HR %	R	RBI	BB	SO	SB	BA	SA	AB	H	G by POS
1986 CIN N	41	159	45	4	3	3	1.9	27	19	9	21	8	.283	.403	4	0	SS-36, 2B-3
1987	125	439	107	16	2	12	2.7	64	43	36	52	21	.244	.371	4	1	SS-119
1988	151	588	174	32	5	12	2.0	91	56	41	24	40	.296	.429	2	0	SS-148
3 yrs.	317	1186	326	52	10	27	2.3	182	118	86	97	69	.275	.404	10	1	SS-303, 2B-3

Gene Larkin

LARKIN, EUGENE THOMAS
B. Oct. 24, 1962, Flushing, N. Y.

BB TR 6'3"   195 lbs.

	G	AB	H	2B	3B	HR	HR %	R	RBI	BB	SO	SB	BA	SA	AB	H	G by POS
1987 MIN A	85	233	62	11	2	4	1.7	23	28	25	31	1	.266	.382	17	5	DH-40, 1B-26
1988	149	505	135	30	2	8	1.6	56	70	68	55	3	.267	.382	4	0	DH-86, 1B-60
2 yrs.	234	738	197	41	4	12	1.6	79	98	93	86	4	.267	.382	21	5	DH-126, 1B-86

LEAGUE CHAMPIONSHIP SERIES

	G	AB	H	2B	3B	HR	HR %	R	RBI	BB	SO	SB	BA	SA	AB	H	G by POS
1987 MIN A	1	1	1	1	0	0	0.0	0	1	0	0	0	1.000	2.000	1	1	

WORLD SERIES

	G	AB	H	2B	3B	HR	HR %	R	RBI	BB	SO	SB	BA	SA	AB	H	G by POS
1987 MIN A	5	3	0	0	0	0	0.0	1	0	1	0	0	.000	.000	3	0	1B-1

Tim Laudner

LAUDNER, TIMOTHY JON
B. June 7, 1958, Mason City, Iowa

BR TR 6'3"   212 lbs.

	G	AB	H	2B	3B	HR	HR %	R	RBI	BB	SO	SB	BA	SA	AB	H	G by POS
1981 MIN A	14	43	7	2	0	2	4.7	4	5	3	17	0	.163	.349	0	0	C-12, DH-2
1982	93	306	78	19	1	7	2.3	37	33	34	74	0	.255	.392	0	0	C-93
1983	62	168	31	9	0	6	3.6	20	18	15	49	0	.185	.345	4	2	C-57, DH-4
1984	87	262	54	16	1	10	3.8	31	35	18	78	0	.206	.389	8	2	C-81, DH-2
1985	72	164	39	5	0	7	4.3	16	19	12	45	0	.238	.396	6	0	C-68, 1B-1
1986	76	193	47	10	0	10	5.2	21	29	24	56	1	.244	.451	15	2	C-68
1987	113	288	55	7	1	16	5.6	30	43	23	80	1	.191	.389	7	1	C-101, 1B-7, DH-2
1988	117	375	94	18	1	13	3.5	38	54	36	89	0	.251	.408	4	0	C-109, DH-4, 1B-3
8 yrs.	634	1799	405	86	4	71	3.9	197	236	165	488	2	.225	.396	44	7	C-589, DH-14, 1B-11

LEAGUE CHAMPIONSHIP SERIES

	G	AB	H	2B	3B	HR	HR %	R	RBI	BB	SO	SB	BA	SA	AB	H	G by POS
1987 MIN A	5	14	1	1	0	0	0.0	1	2	2	5	0	.071	.143	0	0	C-5

WORLD SERIES

	G	AB	H	2B	3B	HR	HR %	R	RBI	BB	SO	SB	BA	SA	AB	H	G by POS
1987 MIN A	7	22	7	1	0	1	4.5	4	4	5	4	0	.318	.500	0	0	C-7

Mile LaValliere

LaVALLIERE, MICHAEL EUGENE (Spanky)
B. Aug. 18, 1960, Charlotte, N. C.

BL TR 5'10"   180 lbs.

	G	AB	H	2B	3B	HR	HR %	R	RBI	BB	SO	SB	BA	SA	AB	H	G by POS
1984 PHI N	6	7	0	0	0	0	0.0	0	0	2	2	0	.000	.000	0	0	C-6
1985 STL N	12	34	5	1	0	0	0.0	2	6	7	3	0	.147	.176	0	0	C-12
1986	110	303	71	10	2	3	1.0	18	30	36	37	0	.234	.310	4	0	C-108
1987 PIT N	121	340	102	19	0	1	0.3	33	36	43	32	0	.300	.365	14	5	C-112
1988	120	352	92	18	0	2	0.6	24	47	50	34	3	.261	.330	10	1	C-114
5 yrs.	369	1036	270	48	2	6	0.6	77	119	138	108	3	.261	.328	28	6	C-352

	G	AB	H	2B	3B	HR	HR%	R	RBI	BB	SO	SB	BA	SA	Pinch Hit AB	Pinch Hit H	G by POS

Vance Law

LAW, VANCE AARON
Son of Vern Law.
B. Oct. 1, 1956, Boise, Ida.   BR TR 6'2"   185 lbs.

	G	AB	H	2B	3B	HR	HR%	R	RBI	BB	SO	SB	BA	SA	PH AB	PH H	G by POS
1980 PIT N	25	74	17	2	2	0	0.0	11	3	3	7	2	.230	.311	3	1	2B-11, SS-8, 3B-1
1981	30	67	9	0	1	0	0.0	1	3	2	15	1	.134	.164	2	0	2B-19, SS-7, 3B-2
1982 CHI A	114	359	101	20	1	5	1.4	40	54	26	46	4	.281	.384	1	1	SS-85, 3B-39, 2B-10, OF-1
1983	145	408	99	21	5	4	1.0	55	42	51	56	3	.243	.348	0	0	3B-139, 2B-3, SS-2, DH-1, OF-1
1984	151	481	121	18	2	17	3.5	60	59	41	75	4	.252	.403	4	2	3B-137, 2B-22, OF-5, SS-4
1985 MON N	147	519	138	30	6	10	1.9	75	52	86	96	6	.266	.405	5	0	2B-126, 1B-20, 3B-11, OF-1
1986	112	360	81	17	2	5	1.4	37	44	37	66	3	.225	.325	6	1	2B-94, 1B-20, 3B-13, P-3, OF-1
1987	133	436	119	27	1	12	2.8	52	56	51	62	8	.273	.422	5	1	2B-106, 3B-22, 1B-17, P-3
1988 CHI N	151	556	163	29	2	11	2.0	73	78	55	79	1	.293	.412	1	0	3B-150, OF-1
9 yrs.	1008	3260	848	164	22	64	2.0	404	391	352	502	32	.260	.383	27	6	3B-514, 2B-391, SS-106, 1B-57, OF-10, P-6, DH-1

LEAGUE CHAMPIONSHIP SERIES

	G	AB	H	2B	3B	HR	HR%	R	RBI	BB	SO	SB	BA	SA	PH AB	PH H	G by POS
1983 CHI A	4	11	2	0	0	0	0.0	0	1	1	3	0	.182	.182	0	0	3B-4

Tom Lawless

LAWLESS, THOMAS JAMES
B. Dec. 19, 1956, Erie, Pa.   BR TR 5'11"   170 lbs.

	G	AB	H	2B	3B	HR	HR%	R	RBI	BB	SO	SB	BA	SA	PH AB	PH H	G by POS
1982 CIN N	49	165	35	6	0	0	0.0	19	4	9	30	16	.212	.248	1	0	2B-47
1984 2 teams	CIN N (43G – .250)				MON N (11G – .176)												
" total	54	97	23	3	0	1	1.0	11	2	8	16	7	.237	.299	5	1	2B-32, 3B-6
1985 STL N	47	58	12	3	1	0	0.0	8	8	5	4	2	.207	.293	9	2	3B-13, 2B-11
1986	46	39	11	1	0	0	0.0	5	3	2	8	8	.282	.308	12	2	3B-12, 2B-7, OF-1
1987	19	25	2	1	0	0	0.0	5	0	3	5	2	.080	.120	5	0	2B-7, 3B-3, OF-1
1988	54	65	10	2	1	1	1.5	9	3	7	9	6	.154	.262	10	1	3B-24, OF-6, 2B-5, 1B-1
6 yrs.	269	449	93	16	2	2	0.4	57	20	34	72	41	.207	.265	42	6	2B-109, 3B-58, OF-8, 1B-1

LEAGUE CHAMPIONSHIP SERIES

	G	AB	H	2B	3B	HR	HR%	R	RBI	BB	SO	SB	BA	SA	PH AB	PH H	G by POS
1987 STL N	3	6	2	0	0	0	0.0	0	0	1	1	0	.333	.333	2	1	3B-2

WORLD SERIES

	G	AB	H	2B	3B	HR	HR%	R	RBI	BB	SO	SB	BA	SA	PH AB	PH H	G by POS
1985 STL N	1	0	0	0	0	0	–	0	0	0	0	0	–	–	0	0	
1987	3	10	1	0	0	1	10.0	1	3	0	4	0	.100	.400	0	0	3B-3
2 yrs.	4	10	1	0	0	1	10.0	1	3	0	4	0	.100	.400	0	0	3B-3

Rick Leach

LEACH, RICHARD MAX
B. May 4, 1957, Ann Arbor, Mich.   BL TL 6'1"   180 lbs.

	G	AB	H	2B	3B	HR	HR%	R	RBI	BB	SO	SB	BA	SA	PH AB	PH H	G by POS
1981 DET A	54	83	16	3	1	1	1.2	9	11	16	15	0	.193	.289	10	2	1B-32, OF-15, DH-2
1982	82	218	52	7	2	3	1.4	23	12	21	29	4	.239	.330	14	2	1B-56, OF-14, DH-4
1983	99	242	60	17	0	3	1.2	22	26	19	21	2	.248	.355	18	4	1B-73, OF-13, DH-3
1984 TOR A	65	88	23	6	2	0	0.0	11	7	8	14	0	.261	.375	22	8	OF-23, 1B-15, DH-6, P-1
1985	16	35	7	0	1	0	0.0	2	1	3	9	0	.200	.257	4	1	1B-10, OF-4
1986	110	246	76	14	1	5	2.0	35	39	13	24	0	.309	.435	31	10	DH-42, OF-39, 1B-7
1987	98	195	55	13	1	3	1.5	26	25	25	25	0	.282	.405	28	7	
1988	87	199	55	13	1	0	0.0	21	23	18	27	0	.276	.352	19	1	OF-49, DH-25, 1B-4
8 yrs.	611	1306	344	73	9	15	1.1	149	144	123	164	6	.263	.368	146	35	1B-197, OF-157, DH-82, P-1

Manny Lee

LEE, MANUEL LORA
Born Manuel Lora y Lee.
B. June 17, 1965, San Pedro de Macoris, Dominican Republic.   BB TR 5'9"   150 lbs.

	G	AB	H	2B	3B	HR	HR%	R	RBI	BB	SO	SB	BA	SA	PH AB	PH H	G by POS
1985 TOR A	64	40	8	0	0	0	0.0	9	0	2	9	1	.200	.200	3	1	2B-38, DH-8, SS-8, 3B-5
1986	35	78	16	0	1	1	1.3	8	7	4	10	0	.205	.269	0	0	2B-29, SS-5, 3B-2
1987	56	121	31	2	3	1	0.8	14	11	6	13	2	.256	.347	3	2	2B-27, SS-26
1988	116	381	111	16	3	2	0.5	38	38	26	64	3	.291	.365	2	0	2B-98, SS-23, 3B-8
4 yrs.	271	620	166	18	7	4	0.6	69	56	38	96	6	.268	.339	8	3	2B-192, SS-62, 3B-15, DH-8

LEAGUE CHAMPIONSHIP SERIES

	G	AB	H	2B	3B	HR	HR%	R	RBI	BB	SO	SB	BA	SA	PH AB	PH H	G by POS
1985 TOR A	1	0	0	0	0	0	–	0	0	0	0	0	–	–	0	0	2B-1

Mark Lemke

LEMKE, MARK ALAN
B. Aug. 13, 1965, Utica, N.Y.   BB TR 5'9"   165 lbs.

	G	AB	H	2B	3B	HR	HR%	R	RBI	BB	SO	SB	BA	SA	PH AB	PH H	G by POS
1988 ATL N	16	58	13	4	0	0	0.0	8	2	4	5	0	.224	.293	0	0	2B-16

Chet Lemon

LEMON, CHESTER EARL
B. Feb. 12, 1955, Jackson, Miss.   BR TR 6'   185 lbs.

	G	AB	H	2B	3B	HR	HR%	R	RBI	BB	SO	SB	BA	SA	PH AB	PH H	G by POS
1975 CHI A	9	35	9	2	0	0	0.0	2	1	2	6	1	.257	.314	1	0	3B-6, DH-2, OF-1
1976	132	451	111	15	5	4	0.9	46	38	28	65	13	.246	.328	1	0	OF-131
1977	150	553	151	38	4	19	3.4	99	67	52	88	8	.273	.459	0	0	OF-149
1978	105	357	107	24	6	13	3.6	51	55	39	46	5	.300	.510	1	0	OF-95, DH-10
1979	148	556	177	44	2	17	3.1	79	86	56	68	7	.318	.496	0	0	OF-147, DH-1
1980	147	514	150	32	6	11	2.1	76	51	71	56	6	.292	.442	1	0	OF-139, DH-6, 2B-1
1981	94	328	99	23	6	9	2.7	50	50	33	48	5	.302	.491	0	0	OF-93
1982 DET A	125	436	116	20	1	19	4.4	75	52	56	69	1	.266	.447	2	1	OF-121, DH-1
1983	145	491	125	21	5	24	4.9	78	69	54	70	0	.255	.464	2	1	OF-145
1984	141	509	146	34	6	20	3.9	77	76	51	83	5	.287	.495	3	1	OF-140, DH-1
1985	145	517	137	28	4	18	3.5	69	68	45	93	0	.265	.439	1	0	OF-144
1986	126	403	101	21	3	12	3.0	45	53	39	53	2	.251	.407	8	2	OF-124
1987	146	470	130	30	3	20	4.3	75	75	70	82	0	.277	.481	11	5	OF-145
1988	144	512	135	29	4	17	3.3	67	64	59	65	1	.264	.436	2	0	OF-144
14 yrs.	1757	6132	1694	361	55	203	3.3	889	805	655	892	54	.276	.452	33	10	OF-1718, DH-21, 3B-6, 2B-1

	G	AB	H	2B	3B	HR	HR %	R	RBI	BB	SO	SB	BA	SA	Pinch Hit AB	Pinch Hit H	G by POS

Chet Lemon continued

LEAGUE CHAMPIONSHIP SERIES

	G	AB	H	2B	3B	HR	HR %	R	RBI	BB	SO	SB	BA	SA	Pinch Hit AB	Pinch Hit H	G by POS
1984 **DET** **A**	3	13	0	0	0	0	0.0	1	0	0	1	0	.000	.000	0	0	OF-3
1987	5	18	5	0	0	2	11.1	4	4	1	4	0	.278	.611	0	0	OF-5
2 yrs.	8	31	5	0	0	2	6.5	5	4	1	5	0	.161	.355	0	0	OF-8

WORLD SERIES

	G	AB	H	2B	3B	HR	HR %	R	RBI	BB	SO	SB	BA	SA	Pinch Hit AB	Pinch Hit H	G by POS
1984 **DET** **A**	5	17	5	0	0	0	0.0	1	1	2	2	2	.294	.294	0	0	OF-5

Jeffrey Leonard

LEONARD, JEFFERY (Hack-Man)
B. Sept. 22, 1955, Philadelphia, Pa.

BR TR 6'2" 200 lbs.

	G	AB	H	2B	3B	HR	HR %	R	RBI	BB	SO	SB	BA	SA	Pinch Hit AB	Pinch Hit H	G by POS
1977 **LA** **N**	11	10	3	0	1	0	0.0	1	2	1	4	0	.300	.500	3	0	OF-10
1978 **HOU** **N**	8	26	10	2	0	0	0.0	2	4	1	2	0	.385	.462	1	0	OF-8
1979	134	411	119	15	5	0	0.0	47	47	46	68	23	.290	.350	11	2	OF-123
1980	88	216	46	7	5	3	1.4	29	20	19	46	4	.213	.333	24	6	OF-56, 1B-11
1981 **2 teams**	**HOU** **N** (7G – .167)			**SF**	**N**	(37G – .307)											
" total	44	145	42	12	4	4	2.8	21	29	12	25	5	.290	.510	6	1	1B-30, OF-7
1982 **SF** **N**	80	278	72	16	1	9	3.2	32	49	19	65	18	.259	.421	2	1	OF-74, 1B-1
1983	139	516	144	17	7	21	4.1	74	87	35	116	26	.279	.461	4	2	OF-136
1984	136	514	155	27	2	21	4.1	76	86	47	123	17	.302	.484	4	0	OF-131
1985	133	507	122	20	3	17	3.4	49	62	21	107	11	.241	.393	7	1	OF-126
1986	89	341	95	11	3	6	1.8	48	42	20	62	16	.279	.381	4	2	OF-87
1987	131	503	141	29	4	19	3.8	70	63	21	68	16	.280	.467	11	6	OF-127
1988 **2 teams**	**SF**	**N**	(44G – .256)			**MIL**	**A**	(94G – .235)									
" total	138	534	129	27	1	10	1.9	57	64	25	92	17	.242	.352	3	0	OF-134, DH-2
12 yrs.	1131	4001	1078	183	36	110	2.7	506	555	267	778	153	.269	.416	80	21	OF-1019, 1B-42, DH-2

LEAGUE CHAMPIONSHIP SERIES

	G	AB	H	2B	3B	HR	HR %	R	RBI	BB	SO	SB	BA	SA	Pinch Hit AB	Pinch Hit H	G by POS
1980 **HOU** **N**	3	3	0	0	0	0	0.0	0	0	0	2	0	.000	.000	2	0	OF-1
1987 **SF** **N**	7	24	10	0	0	4	16.7	5	5	3	4	0	.417	.917	0	0	OF-7
2 yrs.	10	27	10	0	0	4	14.8	5	5	3	6	0	.370	.815	2	0	OF-8

Jose Lind

LIND, JOSE
Born Jose Lind y Salgado.
B. May 1, 1964, Toabaja, Puerto Rico

BR TR 5'11" 155 lbs.

	G	AB	H	2B	3B	HR	HR %	R	RBI	BB	SO	SB	BA	SA	Pinch Hit AB	Pinch Hit H	G by POS
1987 **PIT** **N**	35	143	46	8	4	0	0.0	21	11	8	12	2	.322	.434	0	0	2B-35
1988	154	611	160	24	4	2	0.3	82	49	42	75	15	.262	.324	4	2	2B-153
2 yrs.	189	754	206	32	8	2	0.3	103	60	50	87	17	.273	.345	4	2	2B-188

Jim Lindeman

LINDEMAN, JAMES WILLIAM
B. Jan. 10, 1962, Evanston, Ill.

BR TR 6'1" 200 lbs.

	G	AB	H	2B	3B	HR	HR %	R	RBI	BB	SO	SB	BA	SA	Pinch Hit AB	Pinch Hit H	G by POS
1986 **STL** **N**	19	55	14	1	0	1	1.8	7	6	2	10	1	.255	.327	2	1	1B-17, OF-1, 3B-1
1987	75	207	43	13	0	8	3.9	20	28	11	56	3	.208	.386	13	2	OF-49, 1B-20
1988	17	43	9	1	0	2	4.7	3	7	2	9	0	.209	.372	4	2	OF-24, 1B-6
3 yrs.	111	305	66	15	0	11	3.6	30	41	15	75	4	.216	.374	19	5	OF-74, 1B-43, 3B-1

LEAGUE CHAMPIONSHIP SERIES

	G	AB	H	2B	3B	HR	HR %	R	RBI	BB	SO	SB	BA	SA	Pinch Hit AB	Pinch Hit H	G by POS
1987 **STL** **N**	5	13	4	0	0	1	7.7	1	3	0	3	0	.308	.538	1	0	1B-5

WORLD SERIES

	G	AB	H	2B	3B	HR	HR %	R	RBI	BB	SO	SB	BA	SA	Pinch Hit AB	Pinch Hit H	G by POS
1987 **STL** **N**	6	15	5	1	0	0	0.0	3	2	0	3	0	.333	.400	1	0	1B-6

Nelson Liriano

LIRIANO, NELSON ARTURO
Born Nelson Arturo Liriano y Bonilla.
B. June 3, 1964, Santo Domingo, Dominican Republic

BB TR 5'10" 165 lbs.

	G	AB	H	2B	3B	HR	HR %	R	RBI	BB	SO	SB	BA	SA	Pinch Hit AB	Pinch Hit H	G by POS
1987 **TOR** **A**	37	158	38	6	2	2	1.3	29	10	16	22	13	.241	.342	1	1	2B-37
1988	99	276	73	6	2	3	1.1	36	23	11	40	12	.264	.333	16	4	2B-80, DH-11, 3B-1
2 yrs.	136	434	111	12	4	5	1.2	65	33	27	62	25	.256	.336	17	5	2B-117, DH-11, 3B-1

Steve Lombardozzi

LOMBARDOZZI, STEPHEN PAUL (Lombo)
B. Apr. 26, 1960, Malden, Mass.

BR TR 6' 175 lbs.

	G	AB	H	2B	3B	HR	HR %	R	RBI	BB	SO	SB	BA	SA	Pinch Hit AB	Pinch Hit H	G by POS
1985 **MIN** **A**	28	54	20	4	1	0	0.0	10	6	6	6	3	.370	.481	1	0	2B-26
1986	156	453	103	20	5	8	1.8	53	33	52	76	3	.227	.347	0	0	2B-155
1987	136	432	103	19	3	8	1.9	51	38	33	66	5	.238	.352	0	0	2B-133
1988	103	287	60	15	2	3	1.0	34	27	35	48	2	.209	.307	1	1	2B-90, SS-12, 3B-5
4 yrs.	423	1226	286	58	11	19	1.5	148	104	126	196	13	.233	.345	2	1	2B-404, SS-12, 3B-5

LEAGUE CHAMPIONSHIP SERIES

	G	AB	H	2B	3B	HR	HR %	R	RBI	BB	SO	SB	BA	SA	Pinch Hit AB	Pinch Hit H	G by POS
1987 **MIN** **A**	5	15	4	0	0	0	0.0	2	1	2	2	0	.267	.267	0	0	2B-5

WORLD SERIES

	G	AB	H	2B	3B	HR	HR %	R	RBI	BB	SO	SB	BA	SA	Pinch Hit AB	Pinch Hit H	G by POS
1987 **MIN** **A**	7	17	7	1	0	1	5.9	3	4	2	2	0	.412	.647	0	0	2B-6

Torey Lovullo

LOVULLO, SALVATORE ANTHONY
B. July 25, 1965, Santa Monica, Calif.

BB TR 6' 185 lbs.

	G	AB	H	2B	3B	HR	HR %	R	RBI	BB	SO	SB	BA	SA	Pinch Hit AB	Pinch Hit H	G by POS
1988 **DET** **A**	12	21	8	1	1	1	4.8	2	2	1	2	0	.381	.667	0	0	2B-9, 3B-3

Dwight Lowry

LOWRY, DWIGHT
Born Dwight Lowery.
B. Oct. 23, 1957, Lumberton, N. C.

BL TR 6'3" 210 lbs.

	G	AB	H	2B	3B	HR	HR %	R	RBI	BB	SO	SB	BA	SA	Pinch Hit AB	Pinch Hit H	G by POS
1984 **DET** **A**	32	45	11	2	0	2	4.4	8	7	3	11	0	.244	.422	4	1	C-31
1986	56	150	46	4	0	3	2.0	21	18	17	19	0	.307	.393	0	0	C-55, OF-1, 1B-1
1987	13	25	5	2	0	0	0.0	0	1	0	6	0	.200	.280	1	0	C-12, 1B-1
1988 **MIN** **A**	7	7	0	0	0	0	0.0	0	0	0	2	0	.000	.000	2	0	C-5
4 yrs.	108	227	62	8	0	5	2.2	29	26	20	38	0	.273	.374	7	1	C-103, 1B-2, OF-1

	G	AB	H	2B	3B	HR	HR %	R	RBI	BB	SO	SB	BA	SA	Pinch Hit AB	Pinch Hit H	G by POS

Scott Lusader

LUSADER, SCOTT EDWARD
B. Sept. 30, 1964, Chicago, Ill.
BL TL 5'10" 165 lbs.

	G	AB	H	2B	3B	HR	HR %	R	RBI	BB	SO	SB	BA	SA	PH AB	PH H	G by POS
1987 DET A	23	47	15	3	1	1	2.1	8	8	5	7	1	.319	.489	0	0	OF-22, DH-1
1988	16	16	1	0	0	1	6.3	3	3	1	4	0	.063	.250	5	0	DH-6, OF-4
2 yrs.	39	63	16	3	1	2	3.2	11	11	6	11	1	.254	.429	5	0	OF-26, DH-7

Fred Lynn

LYNN, FREDRIC MICHAEL
B. Feb. 3, 1952, Chicago, Ill.
BL TL 6'1" 185 lbs.

	G	AB	H	2B	3B	HR	HR %	R	RBI	BB	SO	SB	BA	SA	PH AB	PH H	G by POS
1974 BOS A	15	43	18	2	2	2	4.7	5	10	6	6	0	.419	.698	2	0	OF-15, DH-1
1975	145	528	175	47	7	21	4.0	103	105	62	90	10	.331	.566	2	1	OF-144
1976	132	507	159	32	8	10	2.0	76	65	48	67	14	.314	.467	1	0	OF-128, DH-5
1977	129	497	129	29	5	18	3.6	81	76	51	63	2	.260	.447	3	0	OF-125, DH-1
1978	150	541	161	33	3	22	4.1	75	82	75	50	3	.298	.492	0	0	OF-149
1979	147	531	177	42	1	39	7.3	116	122	82	79	2	.333	.637	4	1	OF-143, DH-1
1980	110	415	125	32	3	12	2.9	67	61	58	39	12	.301	.480	0	0	OF-110
1981 CAL A	76	256	56	8	1	5	2.0	28	31	38	42	1	.219	.316	9	1	OF-69
1982	138	472	141	38	1	21	4.4	89	86	58	72	7	.299	.517	10	5	OF-133
1983	117	437	119	20	3	22	5.0	56	74	55	83	2	.272	.483	3	0	OF-113, DH-2
1984	142	517	140	28	4	23	4.4	84	79	77	98	2	.271	.474	5	2	OF-140
1985 BAL A	124	448	118	12	1	23	5.1	59	68	53	100	7	.263	.449	1	0	OF-123
1986	112	397	114	13	1	23	5.8	67	67	53	59	2	.287	.499	7	3	OF-107, DH-1
1987	111	396	100	24	0	23	5.8	49	60	39	72	3	.253	.487	4	1	OF-101, DH-8
1988 2 teams		BAL	A (87G –	.252)		DET	A (27G –	.222)									
" total	114	391	96	14	1	25	6.4	46	56	33	82	2	.246	.478	7	2	OF-105, DH-5
15 yrs.	1762	6376	1828	374	41	289	4.5	1001	1042	788	1002	69	.287	.494	58	16	OF-1705, DH-24

LEAGUE CHAMPIONSHIP SERIES

	G	AB	H	2B	3B	HR	HR %	R	RBI	BB	SO	SB	BA	SA	PH AB	PH H	G by POS
1975 BOS A	3	11	4	1	0	0	0.0	1	3	0	0	0	.364	.455	0	0	OF-3
1982 CAL A	5	18	11	2	0	1	5.6	4	5	2	3	0	.611	.889	0	0	OF-5
2 yrs.	8	29	15	3	0	1	3.4	5	8	2	3	0	.517	.724	0	0	OF-8

WORLD SERIES

	G	AB	H	2B	3B	HR	HR %	R	RBI	BB	SO	SB	BA	SA	PH AB	PH H	G by POS
1975 BOS A	7	25	7	1	0	1	4.0	3	5	3	5	0	.280	.440	0	0	OF-7

Barry Lyons

LYONS, BARRY STEPHEN
B. June 3, 1960, Biloxi, Miss.
BR TR 6'1" 205 lbs.

	G	AB	H	2B	3B	HR	HR %	R	RBI	BB	SO	SB	BA	SA	PH AB	PH H	G by POS
1986 NY N	6	9	0	0	0	0	0.0	1	2	1	2	0	.000	.000	2	0	C-3
1987	53	130	33	4	1	4	3.1	15	24	8	24	0	.254	.392	4	1	C-49
1988	50	91	21	7	1	0	0.0	5	11	3	12	0	.231	.330	18	3	C-32, 1B-1
3 yrs.	109	230	54	11	2	4	1.7	21	37	12	38	0	.235	.352	24	4	C-84, 1B-1

Steve Lyons

LYONS, STEPHEN JOHN (Psycho)
B. June 3, 1960, Tacoma, Wash.
BL TR 6'3" 190 lbs.

	G	AB	H	2B	3B	HR	HR %	R	RBI	BB	SO	SB	BA	SA	PH AB	PH H	G by POS
1985 BOS A	133	371	98	14	3	5	1.3	52	30	32	64	12	.264	.358	13	2	OF-114, DH-5, SS-1, 3B-1
1986 2 teams		BOS	A (59G –	.250)		CHI	A (42G –	.203)									
" total	101	247	56	9	3	1	0.4	30	20	19	47	4	.227	.300	7	1	OF-90, 3B-3, DH-1, 1B-1
1987 CHI A	76	193	54	11	1	1	0.5	26	19	12	37	3	.280	.363	4	0	3B-51, OF-15, 2B-1
1988	146	472	127	28	3	5	1.1	59	45	32	59	1	.269	.373	3	1	3B-128, OF-14, 2B-4, C-2, 1B-1
4 yrs.	456	1283	335	62	10	12	0.9	167	114	95	207	20	.261	.353	27	4	OF-233, 3B-183, DH-6, 2B-5, 1B-2, C-2, SS-1

Mike Macfarlane

MACFARLANE, MICHAEL ANDREW
B. Apr. 12, 1964, Stockton, Calif.
BR TR 6'1" 200 lbs.

	G	AB	H	2B	3B	HR	HR %	R	RBI	BB	SO	SB	BA	SA	PH AB	PH H	G by POS
1987 KC A	8	19	4	1	0	0	0.0	0	3	2	2	0	.211	.263	0	0	C-8
1988	70	211	56	15	0	4	1.9	25	26	21	37	0	.265	.393	4	0	C-68
2 yrs.	78	230	60	16	0	4	1.7	25	29	23	39	0	.261	.383	4	0	C-76

Shane Mack

MACK, SHANE LEE
B. Dec. 7, 1963, Los Angeles, Calif.
BR TR 6' 185 lbs.

	G	AB	H	2B	3B	HR	HR %	R	RBI	BB	SO	SB	BA	SA	PH AB	PH H	G by POS
1987 SD N	105	238	57	11	3	4	1.7	28	25	18	47	4	.239	.361	20	3	OF-91
1988	56	119	29	3	0	0	0.0	13	12	14	21	5	.244	.269	0	0	OF-55
2 yrs.	161	357	86	14	3	4	1.1	41	37	32	68	9	.241	.331	20	3	OF-146

Scotti Madison

MADISON, CHARLES SCOTT
B. Sept. 12, 1959, Pensacola, Fla.
BB TR 5'11" 185 lbs.

	G	AB	H	2B	3B	HR	HR %	R	RBI	BB	SO	SB	BA	SA	PH AB	PH H	G by POS
1985 DET A	6	11	0	0	0	0	0.0	0	1	2	0	0	.000	.000	2	0	DH-3, C-1
1986	2	7	0	0	0	0	0.0	0	0	1	3	0	.000	.000	0	0	DH-1, 3B-1
1987 KC A	7	15	4	3	0	0	0.0	4	0	1	5	0	.267	.467	1	0	1B-4, C-3
1988	16	35	6	2	0	0	0.0	4	2	4	5	1	.171	.229	6	0	C-4, OF-3, 1B-2
4 yrs.	31	68	10	5	0	0	0.0	8	4	7	13	1	.147	.221	9	0	C-8, 1B-6, DH-4, OF-3, 3B-1

Dave Magadan

MAGADAN, DAVID JOSEPH
B. Sept. 30, 1962, Tampa, Fla.
BL TR 6'3" 190 lbs.

	G	AB	H	2B	3B	HR	HR %	R	RBI	BB	SO	SB	BA	SA	PH AB	PH H	G by POS
1986 NY N	10	18	8	0	0	0	0.0	3	3	3	1	0	.444	.444	1	1	1B-9
1987	85	192	61	13	1	3	1.6	21	24	22	22	0	.318	.443	30	6	3B-50, 1B-13
1988	112	314	87	15	0	1	0.3	39	35	60	39	0	.277	.334	12	1	1B-71, 3B-48
3 yrs.	207	524	156	28	1	4	0.8	63	62	85	62	0	.298	.378	43	8	3B-98, 1B-93

LEAGUE CHAMPIONSHIP SERIES

	G	AB	H	2B	3B	HR	HR %	R	RBI	BB	SO	SB	BA	SA	PH AB	PH H	G by POS
1988 NY N	3	3	0	0	0	0	0.0	0	0	0	2	0	.000	.000	3	0	

Candy Maldonado

MALDONADO, CANDIDO GUADARRAMA
Born Candido Maldonado y Guadarrama.
B. Sept. 5, 1960, Humacao, Puerto Rico
BR TR 6' 185 lbs.

	G	AB	H	2B	3B	HR	HR %	R	RBI	BB	SO	SB	BA	SA	PH AB	PH H	G by POS
1981 LA N	11	12	1	0	0	0	0.0	0	0	0	5	0	.083	.083	4	0	OF-9
1982	6	4	0	0	0	0	0.0	0	0	1	2	0	.000	.000	2	0	OF-3
1983	42	62	12	1	1	1	1.6	5	6	5	14	0	.194	.290	9	2	OF-33

	G	AB	H	2B	3B	HR	HR %	R	RBI	BB	SO	SB	BA	SA	Pinch Hit AB	Pinch Hit H	G by POS

Candy Maldonado continued

	G	AB	H	2B	3B	HR	HR%	R	RBI	BB	SO	SB	BA	SA	AB	H	G by POS
1984	116	254	68	14	0	5	2.0	25	28	19	29	0	.268	.382	31	9	OF-102, 3B-4
1985	121	213	48	7	1	5	2.3	20	19	19	40	1	.225	.338	31	7	OF-113
1986 SF N	133	405	102	31	3	18	4.4	49	85	20	77	4	.252	.477	40	17	OF-101, 3B-1
1987	118	442	129	28	4	20	4.5	69	85	34	78	8	.292	.509	4	1	OF-116
1988	142	499	127	23	1	12	2.4	53	68	37	89	6	.255	.377	5	0	OF-139
8 yrs.	689	1891	487	104	10	61	3.2	221	291	135	334	19	.258	.420	126	36	OF-616, 3B-5

LEAGUE CHAMPIONSHIP SERIES

	G	AB	H	2B	3B	HR	HR%	R	RBI	BB	SO	SB	BA	SA	AB	H	G by POS
1983 LA N	2	2	0	0	0	0	0.0	0	0	0	1	0	.000	.000	2	0	
1985	4	7	1	0	0	0	0.0	0	1	0	3	0	.143	.143	1	0	OF-3
1987 SF N	5	19	4	1	0	0	0.0	2	2	0	3	0	.211	.263	0	0	OF-5
3 yrs.	11	28	5	1	0	0	0.0	2	3	0	7	0	.179	.214	3	0	OF-8

Fred Manrique

MANRIQUE, FRED ELOI REYES
Born Fred Eloy Manrique y Reyes.
B. May 11, 1961, Edo Bolivar, Venezuela

BR TR 6'1"   175 lbs.

	G	AB	H	2B	3B	HR	HR%	R	RBI	BB	SO	SB	BA	SA	AB	H	G by POS
1981 TOR A	14	28	4	0	0	0	0.0	1	1	0	12	0	.143	.143	2	1	SS-11, 3B-2, DH-1
1984	10	9	3	0	0	0	0.0	0	1	0	1	0	.333	.333	1	0	2B-9, DH-1
1985 MON N	9	13	4	1	1	1	7.7	5	1	1	3	0	.308	.769	4	2	SS-2, 2B-2, 3B-1
1986 STL N	13	17	3	0	0	1	5.9	2	1	1	1	1	.176	.353	7	1	3B-4, 2B-1
1987 CHI N	115	298	77	13	3	4	1.3	30	29	19	69	5	.258	.362	1	0	2B-92, SS-23
1988	140	345	81	10	6	5	1.4	43	37	21	54	6	.235	.342	5	1	2B-129, SS-12
6 yrs.	301	710	172	24	10	11	1.5	81	70	42	140	12	.242	.351	20	5	2B-233, SS-48, 3B-7, DH-2

Kirt Manwaring

MANWARING, KIRT DEAN
B. July 15, 1965, Elmira, N. Y.

BR TR 6'1"   195 lbs.

	G	AB	H	2B	3B	HR	HR%	R	RBI	BB	SO	SB	BA	SA	AB	H	G by POS
1987 SF N	6	7	1	0	0	0	0.0	0	0	0	1	0	.143	.143	0	0	C-6
1988	40	116	29	7	0	1	0.9	12	15	2	21	0	.250	.336	0	0	C-40
2 yrs.	46	123	30	7	0	1	0.8	12	15	2	22	0	.244	.325	0	0	C-46

Mike Marshall

MARSHALL, MICHAEL ALLEN (Bigfoot)
B. Jan. 12, 1960, Libertyville, Ill.

BR TR 6'5"   215 lbs.

	G	AB	H	2B	3B	HR	HR%	R	RBI	BB	SO	SB	BA	SA	AB	H	G by POS
1981 LA N	14	25	5	3	0	0	0.0	2	1	1	4	0	.200	.320	7	3	3B-3, 1B-3, OF-2
1982	49	95	23	3	0	5	5.3	10	9	13	23	2	.242	.432	20	3	OF-19, 1B-13
1983	140	465	132	17	1	17	3.7	47	65	43	127	7	.284	.434	6	1	OF-109, 1B-33
1984	134	495	127	27	0	21	4.2	69	65	40	93	4	.257	.438	7	2	OF-118, 1B-15
1985	135	518	152	27	2	28	5.4	72	95	37	137	3	.293	.515	3	0	OF-125, 1B-7
1986	103	330	77	11	0	19	5.8	47	53	27	90	4	.233	.439	1	0	OF-97
1987	104	402	118	19	0	16	4.0	45	72	18	79	0	.294	.460	2	1	OF-102
1988	144	542	150	27	2	20	3.7	63	82	24	93	4	.277	.445	4	0	OF-90, 1B-53
8 yrs.	823	2872	784	134	5	126	4.4	355	442	203	646	24	.273	.455	50	10	OF-662, 1B-124, 3B-3

DIVISIONAL PLAYOFF SERIES

	G	AB	H	2B	3B	HR	HR%	R	RBI	BB	SO	SB	BA	SA	AB	H	G by POS
1981 LA N	1	1	0	0	0	0	0.0	0	0	0	1	0	.000	.000	1	0	

LEAGUE CHAMPIONSHIP SERIES

	G	AB	H	2B	3B	HR	HR%	R	RBI	BB	SO	SB	BA	SA	AB	H	G by POS
1983 LA N	4	15	2	1	0	1	6.7	1	2	1	6	0	.133	.400	0	0	1B-3
1985	6	23	5	2	0	1	4.3	1	3	1	3	0	.217	.435	0	0	OF-6
1988	7	30	7	1	0	0	0.0	3	5	2	9	0	.233	.333	0	0	OF-7
3 yrs.	17	68	14	4	0	2	2.9	5	10	4	18	0	.206	.382	0	0	OF-13, 1B-3

WORLD SERIES

	G	AB	H	2B	3B	HR	HR%	R	RBI	BB	SO	SB	BA	SA	AB	H	G by POS
1988 LA N	5	13	3	0	1	1	7.7	2	3	0	5	0	.231	.615	0	0	OF-5

Carlos Martinez

MARTINEZ, CARLOS ALBERTO
B. Aug. 11, 1964, LaGuaira, Venezuela

BR TR 6'5"   175 lbs.

	G	AB	H	2B	3B	HR	HR%	R	RBI	BB	SO	SB	BA	SA	AB	H	G by POS
1988 CHI A	17	55	9	1	0	0	0.0	5	0	0	12	1	.164	.182	0	0	3B-15

Carmelo Martinez

MARTINEZ, CARMELO SALGADO
Born Carmelo Martinez y Salgado.
B. July 28, 1960, Dorado, Puerto Rico

BR TR 6'2"   185 lbs.

	G	AB	H	2B	3B	HR	HR%	R	RBI	BB	SO	SB	BA	SA	AB	H	G by POS
1983 CHI N	29	89	23	3	0	6	6.7	8	16	4	19	0	.258	.494	4	1	1B-26, OF-1, 3B-1
1984 SD N	149	488	122	28	2	13	2.7	64	66	68	82	1	.250	.395	4	0	OF-142, 1B-2
1985	150	514	130	28	1	21	4.1	64	72	87	82	0	.253	.434	0	0	OF-150, 1B-3
1986	113	244	58	10	0	9	3.7	28	25	35	46	1	.238	.389	36	8	OF-60, 1B-26, 3B-1
1987	139	447	122	21	2	15	3.4	59	70	70	82	5	.273	.430	7	1	OF-78, 1B-65
1988	121	365	86	12	0	18	4.9	48	65	35	57	1	.236	.416	28	8	OF-64, 1B-41
6 yrs.	701	2147	541	102	5	82	3.8	271	314	299	368	8	.252	.419	79	18	OF-495, 1B-163, 3B-2

LEAGUE CHAMPIONSHIP SERIES

	G	AB	H	2B	3B	HR	HR%	R	RBI	BB	SO	SB	BA	SA	AB	H	G by POS
1984 SD N	5	17	3	0	0	0	0.0	1	0	2	4	0	.176	.176	0	0	OF-5

WORLD SERIES

	G	AB	H	2B	3B	HR	HR%	R	RBI	BB	SO	SB	BA	SA	AB	H	G by POS
1984 SD N	5	17	3	0	0	0	0.0	0	0	1	9	0	.176	.176	0	0	OF-5

Dave Martinez

MARTINEZ, DAVID
B. Sept. 26, 1964, New York, N. Y.

BL TL 5'10"   150 lbs.

	G	AB	H	2B	3B	HR	HR%	R	RBI	BB	SO	SB	BA	SA	AB	H	G by POS
1986 CHI N	53	108	15	1	1	1	0.9	13	7	6	22	4	.139	.194	5	1	OF-46
1987	142	459	134	18	8	8	1.7	70	36	57	96	16	.292	.418	11	3	OF-139
1988 2 teams		CHI	N (75G –	.254)		MON	N (63G –	.257)									
" total	138	447	114	13	6	6	1.3	51	46	38	94	23	.255	.351	11	1	OF-132
3 yrs.	333	1014	263	32	15	15	1.5	134	89	101	212	43	.259	.365	27	5	OF-317

Edgar Martinez

MARTINEZ, EDGAR
B. Jan. 2, 1963, New York, N. Y.

BR TR 6'   175 lbs.

	G	AB	H	2B	3B	HR	HR%	R	RBI	BB	SO	SB	BA	SA	AB	H	G by POS
1987 SEA A	13	43	16	5	2	0	0.0	6	5	2	5	0	.372	.581	1	0	3B-12, DH-1
1988	14	32	9	4	0	0	0.0	0	5	4	7	0	.281	.406	1	1	3B-13
2 yrs.	27	75	25	9	2	0	0.0	6	10	6	12	0	.333	.507	2	1	3B-25, DH-1

	G	AB	H	2B	3B	HR	HR %	R	RBI	BB	SO	SB	BA	SA	Pinch Hit AB	Pinch Hit H	G by POS

John Marzano

MARZANO, JOHN ROBERT
B. Feb. 14, 1963, Philadelphia, Pa.

BR TR 5'11" 185 lbs.

	G	AB	H	2B	3B	HR	HR %	R	RBI	BB	SO	SB	BA	SA	PH AB	PH H	G by POS
1987 BOS A	52	168	41	11	0	5	3.0	20	24	7	41	0	.244	.399	1	0	C-52
1988	10	29	4	1	0	0	0.0	3	1	1	3	0	.138	.172	0	0	C-10
2 yrs.	62	197	45	12	0	5	2.5	23	25	8	44	0	.228	.365	1	0	C-62

Don Mattingly

MATTINGLY, DONALD ARTHUR
B. Apr. 20, 1961, Evansville, Ind.

BL TL 6' 185 lbs.

	G	AB	H	2B	3B	HR	HR %	R	RBI	BB	SO	SB	BA	SA	PH AB	PH H	G by POS
1982 NY A	7	12	2	0	0	0	0.0	0	1	0	1	0	.167	.167	1	0	OF-6, 1B-1
1983	91	279	79	15	4	4	1.4	34	32	21	31	0	.283	.409	8	1	OF-48, 1B-42, 2B-1
1984	153	603	207	44	2	23	3.8	91	110	41	33	1	.343	.537	3	1	1B-133, OF-19
1985	159	652	211	48	3	35	5.4	107	145	56	41	2	.324	.567	0	0	1B-159
1986	162	677	238	53	2	31	4.6	117	113	53	35	0	.352	.573	0	0	1B-160, 3B-3, DH-1
1987	141	569	186	38	2	30	5.3	93	115	51	38	1	.327	.559	1	0	1B-140, DH-1
1988	144	599	186	37	0	18	3.0	94	88	41	29	1	.311	.462	1	0	1B-143, DH-1, OF-1
7 yrs.	857	3391	1109	235	13	141	4.2	536	604	263	208	5	.327	.529	14	2	1B-778, OF-74, DH-3, 3B-3, 2B-1

Lee Mazzilli

MAZZILLI, LEE LOUIS (Maz)
B. Mar. 25, 1955, New York, N.Y.

BB TR 6'1" 180 lbs.

	G	AB	H	2B	3B	HR	HR %	R	RBI	BB	SO	SB	BA	SA	PH AB	PH H	G by POS
1976 NY N	24	77	15	2	0	2	2.6	9	7	14	10	5	.195	.299	2	1	OF-23
1977	159	537	134	24	3	6	1.1	66	46	72	72	22	.250	.339	5	2	OF-156
1978	148	542	148	28	5	16	3.0	78	61	69	82	20	.273	.432	5	1	OF-144
1979	158	597	181	34	4	15	2.5	78	79	93	74	34	.303	.449	1	0	OF-143, 1B-15
1980	152	578	162	31	4	16	2.8	82	76	82	92	41	.280	.431	2	0	1B-92, OF-66
1981	95	324	74	14	5	6	1.9	36	34	46	53	17	.228	.358	6	2	OF-89
1982 2 teams		TEX A (58G – .241)				NY N (37G – .266)											
" total	95	323	81	10	0	10	3.1	43	34	43	41	13	.251	.375	11	1	DH-33, OF-28, 1B-23
1983 PIT N	109	246	59	9	0	5	2.0	37	24	49	43	15	.240	.337	41	6	OF-57, 1B-7
1984	111	266	63	11	1	4	1.5	37	21	40	42	8	.237	.331	32	6	OF-74, 1B-5
1985	92	117	33	8	0	1	0.9	20	9	29	17	4	.282	.376	56	16	1B-19, OF-5
1986 2 teams		PIT N (61G – .226)				NY N (39G – .276)											
" total	100	151	37	5	1	3	2.0	28	15	38	36	4	.245	.351	54	8	OF-28, 1B-15
1987 NY N	88	124	38	8	1	3	2.4	26	24	21	14	5	.306	.460	55	17	OF-25, 1B-13
1988	68	116	17	2	0	0	0.0	9	12	12	16	4	.147	.164	30	7	OF-18, 1B-16
13 yrs.	1399	3998	1042	186	24	87	2.2	549	442	608	592	192	.261	.384	300	67	OF-856, 1B-205, DH-33

LEAGUE CHAMPIONSHIP SERIES

	G	AB	H	2B	3B	HR	HR %	R	RBI	BB	SO	SB	BA	SA	PH AB	PH H	G by POS
1986 NY N	5	5	1	0	0	0	0.0	0	0	0	3	0	.200	.200	5	1	
1988	3	2	1	0	0	0	0.0	0	0	0	0	1	.500	.500	2	1	
2 yrs.	8	7	2	0	0	0	0.0	0	0	0	3	1	.286	.286	7	2	

WORLD SERIES

	G	AB	H	2B	3B	HR	HR %	R	RBI	BB	SO	SB	BA	SA	PH AB	PH H	G by POS
1986 NY N	4	5	2	0	0	0	0.0	2	0	0	0	0	.400	.400	4	2	OF-1

Lloyd McClendon

McCLENDON, LLOYD GLENN
B. Jan. 11, 1959, Gary, Ind.

BR TR 5'10" 195 lbs.

	G	AB	H	2B	3B	HR	HR %	R	RBI	BB	SO	SB	BA	SA	PH AB	PH H	G by POS
1987 CIN N	45	72	15	5	0	2	2.8	8	13	4	15	1	.208	.361	24	6	C-12, 1B-5, OF-1, 3B-1
1988	72	137	30	4	0	3	2.2	9	14	15	22	4	.219	.314	24	6	C-23, OF-17, 1B-12, 3B-2
2 yrs.	117	209	45	9	0	5	2.4	17	27	19	37	5	.215	.330	48	12	C-35, OF-18, 1B-17, 3B-3

Oddibe McDowell

McDOWELL, ODDIBE JR.
B. Aug. 25, 1962, Hollywood, Fla.

BL TL 5'9" 165 lbs.

	G	AB	H	2B	3B	HR	HR %	R	RBI	BB	SO	SB	BA	SA	PH AB	PH H	G by POS
1985 TEX A	111	406	97	14	5	18	4.4	63	42	36	85	25	.239	.431	8	2	OF-103, DH-4
1986	154	572	152	24	7	18	3.1	105	49	65	112	33	.266	.427	8	2	OF-148, DH-1
1987	128	407	98	26	4	14	3.4	65	52	51	99	24	.241	.428	11	1	OF-125
1988	120	437	108	19	5	6	1.4	55	37	41	89	33	.247	.355	9	2	OF-113, DH-3
4 yrs.	513	1822	455	83	21	56	3.1	288	180	193	385	115	.250	.411	36	7	OF-489, DH-8

Willie McGee

McGEE, WILLIE DEAN
B. Nov. 2, 1958, San Francisco, Calif.

BB TR 6'1" 176 lbs.

	G	AB	H	2B	3B	HR	HR %	R	RBI	BB	SO	SB	BA	SA	PH AB	PH H	G by POS
1982 STL N	123	422	125	12	8	4	0.9	43	56	12	58	24	.296	.391	15	6	OF-117
1983	147	601	172	22	8	5	0.8	75	75	26	98	39	.286	.374	3	2	OF-145
1984	145	571	166	19	11	6	1.1	82	50	29	80	43	.291	.394	5	0	OF-141
1985	152	612	216	26	18	10	1.6	114	82	34	86	56	.353	.503	4	2	OF-149
1986	124	497	127	22	7	7	1.4	65	48	37	82	19	.256	.370	2	1	OF-121
1987	153	620	177	37	11	11	1.8	76	105	24	90	16	.285	.434	2	1	OF-152, SS-1
1988	137	562	164	24	6	3	0.5	73	50	32	84	41	.292	.372	2	1	OF-135
7 yrs.	981	3885	1147	162	69	46	1.2	528	466	194	578	238	.295	.408	33	12	OF-960, SS-1

LEAGUE CHAMPIONSHIP SERIES

	G	AB	H	2B	3B	HR	HR %	R	RBI	BB	SO	SB	BA	SA	PH AB	PH H	G by POS
1982 STL N	3	13	4	0	2	1	7.7	4	5	0	5	0	.308	.846	0	0	OF-3
1985	6	26	7	1	0	0	0.0	6	3	3	6	2	.269	.308	0	0	OF-6
1987	7	26	8	1	1	0	0.0	2	2	0	5	0	.308	.423	0	0	OF-7
3 yrs.	16	65	19	2	3	1	1.5	12	10	3	16	2	.292	.462	0	0	OF-16

WORLD SERIES

	G	AB	H	2B	3B	HR	HR %	R	RBI	BB	SO	SB	BA	SA	PH AB	PH H	G by POS
1982 STL N	6	25	6	0	0	2	8.0	6	5	1	3	2	.240	.480	0	0	OF-6
1985	7	27	7	2	0	1	3.7	2	2	1	3	1	.259	.444	0	0	OF-7
1987	7	27	10	2	0	0	0.0	2	4	0	9	0	.370	.444	0	0	OF-7
3 yrs.	20	79	23	4	0	3	3.8	10	11	2	15	3	.291	.456	0	0	OF-20

Fred McGriff

McGRIFF, FREDERICK STANLEY
B. Oct. 31, 1963, Tampa, Fla.

BL TL 6'3" 200 lbs.

	G	AB	H	2B	3B	HR	HR %	R	RBI	BB	SO	SB	BA	SA	PH AB	PH H	G by POS
1986 TOR A	3	5	1	0	0	0	0.0	1	0	0	2	0	.200	.200	0	0	DH-2, 1B-1
1987	107	295	73	16	0	20	6.8	58	43	60	104	3	.247	.505	14	1	DH-90, 1B-14
1988	154	536	151	35	4	34	6.3	100	82	79	149	6	.282	.552	5	2	1B-153
3 yrs.	264	836	225	51	4	54	6.5	159	125	139	255	9	.269	.533	19	3	1B-168, DH-92

	G	AB	H	2B	3B	HR	HR %	R	RBI	BB	SO	SB	BA	SA	Pinch Hit AB	Pinch Hit H	G by POS

Terry McGriff

McGRIFF, TERENCE ROY
B. Sept. 23, 1963, Fort Pierce, Fla.

BR TR 6'2" 190 lbs.

Year Team Lg	G	AB	H	2B	3B	HR	HR%	R	RBI	BB	SO	SB	BA	SA	PH AB	PH H	G by POS
1987 CIN N	34	89	20	3	0	2	2.2	6	11	8	17	0	.225	.326	0	0	C-33
1988	35	96	19	3	0	1	1.0	9	4	12	31	1	.198	.260	1	0	C-32
2 yrs.	69	185	39	6	0	3	1.6	15	15	20	48	1	.211	.292	1	0	C-65

Bill McGuire

McGUIRE, WILLIAM PATRICK
B. Feb. 14, 1964, Omaha, Neb.

BR TR 6'3" 195 lbs.

Year Team Lg	G	AB	H	2B	3B	HR	HR%	R	RBI	BB	SO	SB	BA	SA	PH AB	PH H	G by POS
1988 SEA A	9	16	3	0	0	0	0.0	1	2	3	2	0	.188	.188	0	0	C-9

Mark McGwire

McGWIRE, MARK DAVID
B. Oct. 1, 1963, Pomona, Calif.

BR TR 6'5" 215 lbs.

Year Team Lg	G	AB	H	2B	3B	HR	HR%	R	RBI	BB	SO	SB	BA	SA	PH AB	PH H	G by POS
1986 OAK A	18	53	10	1	0	3	5.7	10	9	4	18	0	.189	.377	3	1	3B-16
1987	151	557	161	28	4	49	8.8	97	118	71	131	1	.289	.618	2	1	1B-145, 3B-8, OF-3
1988	155	550	143	22	1	32	5.8	87	99	76	117	0	.260	.478	4	2	1B-154, OF-1
3 yrs.	324	1160	314	51	5	84	7.2	194	226	151	266	1	.271	.541	9	4	1B-299, 3B-24, OF-4

LEAGUE CHAMPIONSHIP SERIES

Year Team Lg	G	AB	H	2B	3B	HR	HR%	R	RBI	BB	SO	SB	BA	SA	PH AB	PH H	G by POS
1988 OAK A	4	15	5	0	0	1	6.7	4	3	1	5	0	.333	.533	0	0	1B-4

WORLD SERIES

Year Team Lg	G	AB	H	2B	3B	HR	HR%	R	RBI	BB	SO	SB	BA	SA	PH AB	PH H	G by POS
1988 OAK A	5	17	1	0	0	1	5.9	1	1	3	4	0	.059	.235	0	0	1B-5

Mark McLemore

McLEMORE, MARK TREMELL
B. Oct. 4, 1964, San Diego, Calif.

BB TR 5'11" 175 lbs.

Year Team Lg	G	AB	H	2B	3B	HR	HR%	R	RBI	BB	SO	SB	BA	SA	PH AB	PH H	G by POS
1986 CAL A	5	4	0	0	0	0	0.0	0	0	1	2	0	.000	.000	0	0	2B-2
1987	138	433	102	13	3	3	0.7	61	41	48	72	25	.236	.300	1	0	2B-132, SS-6, DH-3
1988	77	233	56	11	2	2	0.9	38	16	25	28	13	.240	.330	9	3	2B-63, 3B-5, DH-1
3 yrs.	220	670	158	24	5	5	0.7	99	57	74	102	38	.236	.309	10	3	2B-197, SS-6, 3B-5, DH-4

Kevin McReynolds

McREYNOLDS, WALTER KEVIN (Big Mac)
B. Oct. 16, 1959, Little Rock, Ark.

BR TR 6'1" 205 lbs.

Year Team Lg	G	AB	H	2B	3B	HR	HR%	R	RBI	BB	SO	SB	BA	SA	PH AB	PH H	G by POS
1983 SD N	39	140	31	3	1	4	2.9	15	14	12	29	2	.221	.343	2	1	OF-38
1984	147	525	146	26	6	20	3.8	68	75	34	69	3	.278	.465	5	1	OF-143
1985	152	564	132	24	4	15	2.7	61	75	43	81	4	.234	.371	2	0	OF-150
1986	158	560	161	31	6	26	4.6	89	96	66	83	8	.288	.504	4	1	OF-154
1987 NY N	151	590	163	32	5	29	4.9	86	95	39	70	14	.276	.495	3	2	OF-150
1988	147	552	159	30	2	27	4.9	82	99	38	56	21	.288	.496	3	1	OF-147
6 yrs.	794	2931	792	146	24	121	4.1	401	454	232	388	52	.270	.460	19	6	OF-782

LEAGUE CHAMPIONSHIP SERIES

Year Team Lg	G	AB	H	2B	3B	HR	HR%	R	RBI	BB	SO	SB	BA	SA	PH AB	PH H	G by POS
1984 SD N	4	10	3	0	0	1	10.0	2	4	3	1	0	.300	.600	0	0	OF-4
1988 NY N	7	28	7	2	0	2	7.1	4	4	3	5	2	.250	.536	0	0	OF-7
2 yrs.	11	38	10	2	0	3	7.9	6	8	6	6	2	.263	.553	0	0	OF-11

Bobby Meacham

MEACHAM, ROBERT ANDREW
B. Aug. 25, 1960, Los Angeles, Calif.

BB TR 6'1" 180 lbs.

Year Team Lg	G	AB	H	2B	3B	HR	HR%	R	RBI	BB	SO	SB	BA	SA	PH AB	PH H	G by POS
1983 NY A	22	51	12	2	0	0	0.0	5	4	4	10	8	.235	.275	0	0	SS-18, 3B-4
1984	99	360	91	13	4	2	0.6	62	25	32	70	9	.253	.328	0	0	SS-96, 2B-2
1985	156	481	105	16	2	1	0.2	70	47	54	102	25	.218	.266	0	0	SS-155
1986	56	161	36	7	1	0	0.0	19	10	17	39	3	.224	.280	0	0	SS-56
1987	77	203	55	11	1	5	2.5	28	21	19	33	6	.271	.409	1	1	SS-56, 2B-25
1988	47	115	25	9	0	0	0.0	18	7	14	22	7	.217	.296	1	1	SS-24, 2B-21, 3B-5
6 yrs.	457	1371	324	58	8	8	0.6	202	114	140	276	58	.236	.308	2	1	SS-405, 2B-48, 3B-9

Louie Meadows

MEADOWS, MICHAEL RAY
B. Apr. 29, 1961, Maysville, N. C.

BL TL 5'11" 190 lbs.

Year Team Lg	G	AB	H	2B	3B	HR	HR%	R	RBI	BB	SO	SB	BA	SA	PH AB	PH H	G by POS
1986 HOU N	6	6	2	0	0	0	0.0	1	0	0	0	1	.333	.333	6	2	OF-1
1988	35	42	8	0	1	2	4.8	5	3	6	8	4	.190	.381	18	3	OF-10
2 yrs.	41	48	10	0	1	2	4.2	6	3	6	8	5	.208	.375	24	5	OF-11

Luis Medina

MEDINA, LUIS MAIN
B. Mar. 26, 1963, Santa Monica, Calif.

BR TL 6'3" 190 lbs.

Year Team Lg	G	AB	H	2B	3B	HR	HR%	R	RBI	BB	SO	SB	BA	SA	PH AB	PH H	G by POS
1988 CLE A	16	51	13	0	0	6	11.8	10	8	2	18	0	.255	.608	1	0	1B-16

Dave Meier

MEIER, DAVID KEITH
B. Aug. 8, 1959, Helena, Mont.

BR TR 6' 195 lbs.

Year Team Lg	G	AB	H	2B	3B	HR	HR%	R	RBI	BB	SO	SB	BA	SA	PH AB	PH H	G by POS
1984 MIN A	59	147	35	8	1	0	0.0	18	13	6	9	0	.238	.306	9	1	OF-50, DH-4, 3B-1
1985	71	104	27	6	0	1	1.0	15	8	18	12	0	.260	.346	11	0	OF-63, DH-3
1987 TEX A	13	21	6	1	0	0	0.0	4	0	0	4	0	.286	.333	3	0	OF-8
1988 CHI N	2	5	2	0	0	0	0.0	0	1	0	1	0	.400	.400	1	1	3B-1
4 yrs.	145	277	70	15	1	1	0.4	37	22	24	26	0	.253	.325	24	2	OF-121, DH-7, 3B-2

Francisco Melendez

MELENDEZ, FRANCISCO JAVIER VILLEGAS
Born Francisco Javier Melendez y Villegas.
B. Jan. 25, 1964, Rio Piedras, Puerto Rico

BL TL 6' 170 lbs.

Year Team Lg	G	AB	H	2B	3B	HR	HR%	R	RBI	BB	SO	SB	BA	SA	PH AB	PH H	G by POS
1984 PHI N	21	23	3	0	0	0	0.0	0	2	1	5	0	.130	.130	13	1	1B-10
1986	9	8	2	0	0	0	0.0	0	0	0	2	0	.250	.250	7	1	1B-2
1987 SF N	12	16	5	0	0	1	6.3	2	1	0	3	0	.313	.500	10	1	1B-5
1988	23	26	5	0	0	0	0.0	1	3	3	2	0	.192	.192	16	4	1B-6, OF-1
4 yrs.	65	73	15	0	0	1	1.4	3	6	4	12	0	.205	.247	46	7	1B-23, OF-1

Bob Melvin

MELVIN, ROBERT PAUL
B. Oct. 28, 1961, Palo Alto, Calif.

BR TR 6'4" 205 lbs.

Year Team Lg	G	AB	H	2B	3B	HR	HR%	R	RBI	BB	SO	SB	BA	SA	PH AB	PH H	G by POS
1985 DET A	41	82	18	4	1	0	0.0	10	4	3	21	0	.220	.293	0	0	C-41
1986 SF N	89	268	60	14	2	5	1.9	24	25	15	69	3	.224	.347	6	1	C-84, 3B-1
1987	84	246	49	8	0	11	4.5	31	31	17	44	0	.199	.366	8	1	C-78, 1B-1
1988	92	273	64	13	1	8	2.9	23	27	13	46	0	.234	.377	4	1	C-89, 1B-1
4 yrs.	306	869	191	39	4	24	2.8	88	87	48	180	3	.220	.357	18	3	C-292, 1B-2, 3B-1

	G	AB	H	2B	3B	HR	HR %	R	RBI	BB	SO	SB	BA	SA	Pinch Hit AB	H	G by POS

Bob Melvin continued

LEAGUE CHAMPIONSHIP SERIES

	G	AB	H	2B	3B	HR	HR %	R	RBI	BB	SO	SB	BA	SA	AB	H	G by POS
1987 SF N	3	7	3	0	0	0	0.0	0	0	1	1	0	.429	.429	1	0	C-2

Orlando Mercado

MERCADO, ORLANDO RODRIGUEZ BR TR 6' 180 lbs.
Born Orlando Mercado y Rodriguez.
B. Nov. 7, 1961, Arecibo, Puerto Rico

	G	AB	H	2B	3B	HR	HR %	R	RBI	BB	SO	SB	BA	SA	AB	H	G by POS
1982 SEA A	9	17	2	0	0	1	5.9	1	6	0	5	0	.118	.294	0	0	C-8, DH-1
1983	66	178	35	11	2	1	0.6	10	16	14	27	2	.197	.298	2	0	C-65
1984	30	78	17	3	1	0	0.0	5	5	4	12	1	.218	.282	3	1	C-29
1986 TEX A	46	102	24	1	1	1	1.0	7	7	6	13	0	.235	.294	1	0	C-45
1987 LA N	7	5	3	1	0	0	0.0	1	1	1	1	0	.600	.800	0	0	C-7
1988 OAK A	16	24	3	0	0	1	4.2	3	1	3	8	0	.125	.250	0	0	C-16
6 yrs.	174	404	84	16	4	4	1.0	27	36	28	66	3	.208	.297	6	1	C-170, DH-1

Joey Meyer

MEYER, TANNER JOE BR TR 6'3" 250 lbs.
B. May 10, 1962, Honolulu, Hawaii

	G	AB	H	2B	3B	HR	HR %	R	RBI	BB	SO	SB	BA	SA	AB	H	G by POS
1988 MIL A	103	327	86	18	0	11	3.4	22	45	23	88	0	.263	.419	4	1	DH-66, 1B-33

Darrell Miller

MILLER, DARRELL KEITH BR TR 6'2" 200 lbs.
B. Feb. 26, 1958, Washington, D. C.

	G	AB	H	2B	3B	HR	HR %	R	RBI	BB	SO	SB	BA	SA	AB	H	G by POS
1984 CAL A	17	41	7	0	0	0	0.0	5	1	4	9	0	.171	.171	1	0	1B-16, OF-1
1985	51	48	18	2	1	2	4.2	8	7	1	10	0	.375	.583	6	3	OF-45, DH-4, 3B-1, C-1
1986	33	57	13	2	1	0	0.0	6	4	4	8	0	.228	.298	5	2	OF-23, C-10, DH-2
1987	53	108	26	5	0	4	3.7	14	16	9	13	1	.241	.398	9	4	C-33, OF-18, 3B-1
1988	70	140	31	4	1	2	1.4	21	7	9	29	2	.221	.307	9	2	C-53, OF-8, DH-1
5 yrs.	224	394	95	13	3	8	2.0	54	35	27	69	3	.241	.350	30	11	C-97, OF-95, 1B-16, DH-7, 3B-2

Keith Miller

MILLER, KEITH ALAN BR TR 5'11" 175 lbs.
B. June 12, 1963, Midland, Mich.

	G	AB	H	2B	3B	HR	HR %	R	RBI	BB	SO	SB	BA	SA	AB	H	G by POS
1987 NY N	25	51	19	2	0	0	0.0	14	1	2	6	8	.373	.490	0	0	2B-16
1988	40	70	15	1	1	1	1.4	9	5	6	10	0	.214	.300	9	2	2B-16, SS-8, 3B-6, OF-1
2 yrs.	65	121	34	3	3	1	0.8	23	6	8	16	8	.281	.380	9	2	2B-32, SS-8, 3B-6, OF-1

Keith Miller

MILLER, NEAL KEITH BB TR 5'11" 175 lbs.
B. Mar. 7, 1963, Dallas, Tex.

	G	AB	H	2B	3B	HR	HR %	R	RBI	BB	SO	SB	BA	SA	AB	H	G by POS
1988 PHI N	47	48	8	3	0	0	0.0	4	6	5	13	0	.167	.229	37	6	OF-4, 3B-3, SS-1

Randy Milligan

MILLIGAN, RANDY ANDRE BR TR 6'2" 200 lbs.
B. Nov. 27, 1961, San Diego, Calif.

	G	AB	H	2B	3B	HR	HR %	R	RBI	BB	SO	SB	BA	SA	AB	H	G by POS
1987 NY N	3	1	0	0	0	0	0.0	0	0	1	1	0	.000	.000	1	0	
1988 PIT N	40	82	18	5	0	3	3.7	10	8	20	24	1	.220	.390	13	3	1B-25, OF-1
2 yrs.	43	83	18	5	0	3	3.6	10	8	21	25	1	.217	.386	14	3	1B-25, OF-1

Eddie Milner

MILNER, EDWARD JAMES (Greyhound) BL TL 5'11" 173 lbs.
B. May 21, 1955, Columbus, Ohio

	G	AB	H	2B	3B	HR	HR %	R	RBI	BB	SO	SB	BA	SA	AB	H	G by POS
1980 CIN N	6	3	0	0	0	0	0.0	1	0	0	0	0	.000	.000	3	0	
1981	8	5	1	1	0	0	0.0	0	1	0	1	0	.200	.400	3	0	OF-4
1982	113	407	109	23	5	4	1.0	61	31	41	40	18	.268	.378	6	2	OF-107
1983	146	502	131	23	6	9	1.8	77	33	68	60	41	.261	.384	8	2	OF-139
1984	117	336	78	8	4	7	2.1	44	29	51	50	21	.232	.342	14	2	OF-108
1985	145	453	115	19	7	3	0.7	82	33	61	31	35	.254	.347	12	5	OF-135
1986	145	424	110	22	6	15	3.5	70	47	36	56	18	.259	.446	15	3	OF-127
1987 SF N	101	214	54	14	0	4	1.9	38	19	24	33	10	.252	.374	19	4	OF-84
1988 CIN N	23	51	9	1	0	0	0.0	3	2	4	9	2	.176	.196	7	0	OF-15
9 yrs.	804	2395	607	111	28	42	1.8	376	195	286	280	145	.253	.376	87	18	OF-719

LEAGUE CHAMPIONSHIP SERIES

	G	AB	H	2B	3B	HR	HR %	R	RBI	BB	SO	SB	BA	SA	AB	H	G by POS
1987 SF N	6	7	1	0	0	0	0.0	0	0	0	3	0	.143	.143	1	1	OF-4

Kevin Mitchell

MITCHELL, KEVIN DARNELL (Mitch, World) BR TR 5'10" 185 lbs.
B. Jan. 13, 1962, San Diego, Calif.

	G	AB	H	2B	3B	HR	HR %	R	RBI	BB	SO	SB	BA	SA	AB	H	G by POS
1984 NY N	7	14	3	0	0	0	0.0	0	1	0	3	0	.214	.214	4	1	3B-5
1986	108	328	91	22	2	12	3.7	51	43	33	61	3	.277	.466	20	3	OF-68, SS-24, 3B-7, 1B-2
1987 2 teams		SD	N (62G –		.245)		SF	N (69G –		.306)							
" total	131	464	130	20	2	22	4.7	68	70	48	84	9	.280	.474	9	2	3B-119, OF-6, SS-1
1988 SF N	148	505	127	25	7	19	3.8	60	80	48	85	5	.251	.442	10	2	3B-102, OF-40
4 yrs.	394	1311	351	67	11	53	4.0	179	194	129	237	17	.268	.457	43	8	3B-233, OF-114, SS-25, 1B-2

LEAGUE CHAMPIONSHIP SERIES

	G	AB	H	2B	3B	HR	HR %	R	RBI	BB	SO	SB	BA	SA	AB	H	G by POS
1986 NY N	2	8	2	0	0	0	0.0	1	0	0	1	0	.250	.250	0	0	OF-2
1987 SF N	7	30	8	1	0	1	3.3	2	2	0	3	1	.267	.400	0	0	3B-7
2 yrs.	9	38	10	1	0	1	2.6	3	2	0	4	1	.263	.368	0	0	3B-7, OF-2

WORLD SERIES

	G	AB	H	2B	3B	HR	HR %	R	RBI	BB	SO	SB	BA	SA	AB	H	G by POS
1986 NY N	5	8	2	0	0	0	0.0	1	0	0	3	0	.250	.250	2	1	OF-2

Paul Molitor

MOLITOR, PAUL LEO BR TR 6' 185 lbs.
B. Aug. 22, 1956, St. Paul, Minn.

	G	AB	H	2B	3B	HR	HR %	R	RBI	BB	SO	SB	BA	SA	AB	H	G by POS
1978 MIL A	125	521	142	26	4	6	1.2	73	45	19	54	30	.273	.372	3	0	2B-91, SS-31, DH-2, 3B-1
1979	140	584	188	27	16	9	1.5	88	62	48	48	33	.322	.469	2	0	2B-122, SS-10, DH-5
1980	111	450	137	29	2	9	2.0	81	37	48	48	34	.304	.438	2	1	2B-91, SS-12, DH-7, 3B-1
1981	64	251	67	11	0	2	0.8	45	19	25	29	10	.267	.335	1	0	OF-46, DH-16
1982	160	666	201	26	8	19	2.9	136	71	69	93	41	.302	.450	0	0	3B-150, DH-6, SS-4
1983	152	608	164	28	6	15	2.5	95	47	59	74	41	.270	.410	2	0	3B-146, DH-2
1984	13	46	10	1	0	0	0.0	3	6	2	8	1	.217	.239	2	0	3B-7, DH-4

	G	AB	H	2B	3B	HR	HR %	R	RBI	BB	SO	SB	BA	SA	Pinch Hit AB	H	G by POS

Paul Molitor continued

	G	AB	H	2B	3B	HR	HR %	R	RBI	BB	SO	SB	BA	SA	AB	H	G by POS
1985	140	576	171	28	3	10	1.7	93	48	54	80	21	.297	.408	1	0	3B-135, DH-4
1986	105	437	123	24	6	9	2.1	62	55	40	81	20	.281	.426	0	0	3B-91, DH-10, OF-4
1987	118	465	164	41	6	16	3.4	114	75	69	67	45	.353	.566	1	0	DH-58, 3B-41, 2B-19
1988	154	609	190	34	6	13	2.1	115	60	71	54	41	.312	.452	0	0	3B-105, DH-49, 2B-1
11 yrs.	1282	5213	1557	275	56	108	2.1	905	525	504	636	317	.299	.435	14	1	3B-677, 2B-324, DH-166, SS-57, OF-50

DIVISIONAL PLAYOFF SERIES

	G	AB	H	2B	3B	HR	HR %	R	RBI	BB	SO	SB	BA	SA	AB	H	G by POS
1981 **MIL A**	5	20	5	0	0	1	5.0	2	1	2	5	0	.250	.400	0	0	OF-5

LEAGUE CHAMPIONSHIP SERIES

	G	AB	H	2B	3B	HR	HR %	R	RBI	BB	SO	SB	BA	SA	AB	H	G by POS
1982 **MIL A**	5	19	6	1	0	2	10.5	4	5	2	3	1	.316	.684	0	0	3B-5

WORLD SERIES

	G	AB	H	2B	3B	HR	HR %	R	RBI	BB	SO	SB	BA	SA	AB	H	G by POS
1982 **MIL A**	7	31	11	0	0	0	0.0	5	2	2	4	1	.355	.355	0	0	3B-7

Keith Moreland

MORELAND, BOBBY KEITH
B. May 2, 1954, Dallas, Tex.

BR TR 6'   190 lbs.

	G	AB	H	2B	3B	HR	HR %	R	RBI	BB	SO	SB	BA	SA	AB	H	G by POS
1978 **PHI N**	1	2	0	0	0	0	0.0	0	0	0	0	0	.000	.000	0	0	C-1
1979	14	48	18	3	2	0	0.0	3	8	3	5	0	.375	.521	1	0	C-13
1980	62	159	50	8	0	4	2.5	13	29	8	14	3	.314	.440	17	7	C-39, 3B-4, OF-2
1981	61	196	50	7	0	6	3.1	16	37	15	13	1	.255	.383	5	1	C-50, 3B-7, OF-2, 1B-2
1982 **CHI N**	138	476	124	17	2	15	3.2	50	68	46	71	0	.261	.399	6	1	OF-86, C-44, 3B-2
1983	154	533	161	30	3	16	3.0	76	70	68	73	0	.302	.460	2	0	OF-151, C-3
1984	140	495	138	17	3	16	3.2	59	80	34	71	1	.279	.422	15	2	OF-103, 1B-29, 3B-8, C-3
1985	161	587	180	30	3	14	2.4	74	106	68	58	12	.307	.440	2	1	OF-148, 1B-12, 3B-11, C-2
1986	156	586	159	30	0	12	2.0	72	79	53	48	3	.271	.384	4	1	OF-121, 3B-24, C-13, 1B-12
1987	153	563	150	29	1	27	4.8	63	88	39	66	3	.266	.465	1	0	3B-150, 1B-1
1988 **SD N**	143	511	131	23	0	5	1.0	40	64	40	51	2	.256	.331	3	1	1B-73, OF-64, 3B-2
11 yrs.	1183	4156	1161	194	14	115	2.8	466	629	374	470	25	.279	.416	56	14	OF-677, 3B-208, C-168, 1B-129

DIVISIONAL PLAYOFF SERIES

	G	AB	H	2B	3B	HR	HR %	R	RBI	BB	SO	SB	BA	SA	AB	H	G by POS
1981 **PHI N**	4	13	6	0	0	1	7.7	2	3	1	1	0	.462	.692	0	0	C-4

LEAGUE CHAMPIONSHIP SERIES

	G	AB	H	2B	3B	HR	HR %	R	RBI	BB	SO	SB	BA	SA	AB	H	G by POS
1980 **PHI N**	2	1	0	0	0	0	0.0	0	1	0	0	0	.000	.000	1	0	C-1
1984 **CHI N**	5	18	6	2	0	0	0.0	3	2	1	1	0	.333	.444	0	0	OF-5
2 yrs.	7	19	6	2	0	0	0.0	3	3	1	1	0	.316	.421	1	0	OF-5, C-1

WORLD SERIES

	G	AB	H	2B	3B	HR	HR %	R	RBI	BB	SO	SB	BA	SA	AB	H	G by POS
1980 **PHI N**	3	12	4	0	0	0	0.0	1	1	0	1	0	.333	.333	0	0	DH-3

Russ Morman

MORMAN, RUSSELL LEE
B. Apr. 28, 1962, Independence, Mo.

BR TR 6'4"   215 lbs.

	G	AB	H	2B	3B	HR	HR %	R	RBI	BB	SO	SB	BA	SA	AB	H	G by POS
1986 **CHI A**	49	159	40	5	0	4	2.5	18	17	16	36	1	.252	.358	1	0	1B-47
1988	40	75	18	2	0	0	0.0	8	3	3	17	0	.240	.267	5	2	1B-22, OF-10, DH-3
2 yrs.	89	234	58	7	0	4	1.7	26	20	19	53	1	.248	.329	6	2	1B-69, OF-10, DH-3

Hal Morris

MORRIS, WILLIAM HAROLD
B. Apr. 9, 1965, Fort Rucker, Ala.

BL TL 6'3"   200 lbs.

	G	AB	H	2B	3B	HR	HR %	R	RBI	BB	SO	SB	BA	SA	AB	H	G by POS
1988 **NY A**	15	20	2	0	0	0	0.0	1	0	1	9	0	.100	.100	10	2	OF-4, DH-1

John Morris

MORRIS, JOHN DANIEL
B. Feb. 23, 1961, Freeport, N. Y.

BL TL 6'1"   185 lbs.

	G	AB	H	2B	3B	HR	HR %	R	RBI	BB	SO	SB	BA	SA	AB	H	G by POS
1986 **STL N**	39	100	24	0	1	1	1.0	8	14	7	15	6	.240	.290	11	3	OF-31
1987	101	157	41	6	4	3	1.9	22	23	11	22	5	.261	.408	30	10	OF-74
1988	20	38	11	2	1	0	0.0	3	3	1	7	0	.289	.395	6	2	OF-16
3 yrs.	160	295	76	8	6	4	1.4	33	40	19	44	11	.258	.366	47	15	OF-121

LEAGUE CHAMPIONSHIP SERIES

	G	AB	H	2B	3B	HR	HR %	R	RBI	BB	SO	SB	BA	SA	AB	H	G by POS
1987 **STL N**	2	3	0	0	0	0	0.0	0	0	0	0	0	.000	.000	0	0	OF-2

WORLD SERIES

	G	AB	H	2B	3B	HR	HR %	R	RBI	BB	SO	SB	BA	SA	AB	H	G by POS
1987 **STL N**	1	2	0	0	0	0	0.0	0	0	0	0	0	.000	.000	0	0	OF-1

Jim Morrison

MORRISON, JAMES FORREST
B. Sept. 23, 1952, Pensacola, Fla.

BR TR 5'11"   175 lbs.

	G	AB	H	2B	3B	HR	HR %	R	RBI	BB	SO	SB	BA	SA	AB	H	G by POS
1977 **PHI N**	5	7	3	0	0	0	0.0	3	1	1	1	0	.429	.429	0	0	3B-5
1978	53	108	17	1	0	3	2.8	12	10	10	21	1	.157	.269	12	0	2B-31, 3B-3, OF-1
1979 **CHI N**	67	240	66	14	0	14	5.8	38	35	15	48	11	.275	.508	4	0	2B-48, 3B-29
1980	162	604	171	40	0	15	2.5	66	57	36	74	9	.283	.424	0	0	2B-161, DH-1, SS-1
1981	90	290	68	8	1	10	3.4	27	34	10	29	3	.234	.372	2	0	3B-87, DH-1, 2B-1
1982 2 teams		CHI	**A** (51G – .223)			PIT	**N** (44G – .279)										
" total	95	252	61	11	4	11	4.4	27	34	18	29	2	.242	.448	16	3	3B-76, OF-2, DH-1, SS-1, 2B-1
1983 **PIT N**	66	158	48	7	2	6	3.8	16	25	9	25	2	.304	.487	15	4	2B-28, 3B-25, SS-7
1984	100	304	87	14	2	11	3.6	38	45	20	52	0	.286	.454	13	1	3B-61, 2B-26, SS-2, 1B-1
1985	92	244	62	11	0	4	1.6	17	22	8	44	3	.254	.348	19	4	3B-59, 2B-15, OF-1
1986	154	537	147	35	4	23	4.3	58	88	47	88	9	.274	.482	4	1	3B-151, SS-1, 2B-1
1987 2 teams		PIT	**N** (96G – .264)			DET	**A** (34G – .205)										
" total	130	465	116	23	2	13	2.8	56	65	29	83	10	.249	.391	11	2	3B-98, SS-20, 2B-12, DH-8, OF-3, 1B-1
1988 2 teams		DET	**A** (24G – .216)			ATL	**N** (51G – .152)										
" total	75	166	30	7	0	2	1.2	13	19	10	27	0	.181	.259	31	6	3B-24, DH-14, OF-6, 1B-4, P-3, SS-1
12 yrs.	1089	3375	876	171	16	112	3.3	371	435	213	521	50	.260	.419	127	21	3B-618, 2B-324, SS-33, DH-25, OF-13, 1B-6, P-3

	G	AB	H	2B	3B	HR	HR %	R	RBI	BB	SO	SB	BA	SA	Pinch Hit AB	H	G by POS

Jim Morrison continued

LEAGUE CHAMPIONSHIP SERIES

	G	AB	H	2B	3B	HR	HR %	R	RBI	BB	SO	SB	BA	SA	AB	H	G by POS
1978 **PHI N**	1	1	0	0	0	0	0.0	0	0	0	1	0	.000	.000	1	0	
1987 **DET A**	2	5	2	0	0	0	0.0	1	0	0	1	0	.400	.400	0	0	3B-1
2 yrs.	3	6	2	0	0	0	0.0	1	0	0	2	0	.333	.333	1	0	3B-1

Lloyd Moseby

MOSEBY, LLOYD ANTHONY
B. Nov. 5, 1959, Portland, Ark.

BL TR 6'3"   200 lbs.

	G	AB	H	2B	3B	HR	HR %	R	RBI	BB	SO	SB	BA	SA	AB	H	G by POS
1980 **TOR A**	114	389	89	24	1	9	2.3	44	46	25	85	4	.229	.365	2	0	OF-104, DH-6
1981	100	378	88	16	2	9	2.4	36	43	24	86	11	.233	.357	2	0	OF-100
1982	147	487	115	20	9	9	1.8	51	52	33	106	11	.236	.370	7	3	OF-145
1983	151	539	170	31	7	18	3.3	104	81	51	85	27	.315	.499	9	4	OF-147
1984	158	592	166	28	15	18	3.0	97	92	78	122	39	.280	.470	3	1	OF-156
1985	152	584	151	30	7	18	3.1	92	71	76	91	37	.259	.426	1	0	OF-152
1986	152	589	149	24	5	21	3.6	89	86	64	122	32	.253	.418	4	0	OF-147, DH-3
1987	155	592	167	27	4	26	4.4	106	96	70	124	39	.282	.473	0	0	OF-153, DH-2
1988	128	472	113	17	7	10	2.1	77	42	70	93	11	.239	.369	3	0	OF-125, DH-1
9 yrs.	1257	4622	1208	217	57	138	3.0	696	609	491	914	231	.261	.423	31	8	OF-1229, DH-12

LEAGUE CHAMPIONSHIP SERIES

	G	AB	H	2B	3B	HR	HR %	R	RBI	BB	SO	SB	BA	SA	AB	H	G by POS
1985 **TOR A**	7	31	7	1	0	0	0.0	5	4	2	3	1	.226	.258	0	0	OF-7

John Moses

MOSES, JOHN WILLIAM
B. Aug. 9, 1957, Los Angeles, Calif.

BB TL 5'10"   165 lbs.

	G	AB	H	2B	3B	HR	HR %	R	RBI	BB	SO	SB	BA	SA	AB	H	G by POS
1982 **SEA A**	22	44	14	5	1	1	2.3	7	3	4	5	5	.318	.545	2	1	OF-19
1983	93	130	27	4	1	0	0.0	19	6	12	20	11	.208	.254	4	1	OF-71, DH-10
1984	19	35	12	1	1	0	0.0	3	2	2	5	1	.343	.429	0	0	OF-19, DH-1
1985	33	62	12	0	0	0	0.0	4	3	2	8	5	.194	.194	0	0	OF-29
1986	103	399	102	16	3	3	0.8	56	34	34	65	25	.256	.333	2	0	OF-93, 1B-7, DH-4
1987	116	390	96	16	4	3	0.8	58	38	29	49	23	.246	.331	3	1	OF-116, DH-5
1988 **MIN A**	105	206	65	10	3	2	1.0	33	12	15	21	11	.316	.422	21	6	OF-82, DH-2
7 yrs.	491	1266	328	52	13	9	0.7	180	98	98	173	81	.259	.342	32	9	OF-429, DH-22, 1B-7

Rance Mulliniks

MULLINIKS, STEVEN RANCE
B. Jan. 15, 1956, Tulare, Calif.

BL TR 5'11"   162 lbs.

	G	AB	H	2B	3B	HR	HR %	R	RBI	BB	SO	SB	BA	SA	AB	H	G by POS
1977 **CAL A**	78	271	73	13	2	3	1.1	36	21	23	36	1	.269	.365	1	0	SS-77
1978	50	119	22	3	1	1	0.8	6	6	8	23	2	.185	.252	1	0	SS-47, DH-2
1979	22	68	10	0	0	1	1.5	7	8	4	14	0	.147	.191	0	0	SS-22
1980 **KC A**	36	54	14	3	0	0	0.0	8	6	7	10	0	.259	.315	0	0	SS-18, 2B-14
1981	24	44	10	3	0	0	0.0	6	5	2	7	0	.227	.295	0	0	2B-10, SS-7, 3B-5
1982 **TOR A**	112	311	76	25	0	4	1.3	32	35	37	49	3	.244	.363	22	3	3B-102, SS-16
1983	129	364	100	34	3	10	2.7	54	49	57	43	0	.275	.467	23	10	3B-116, SS-15, 2B-2
1984	125	343	111	21	5	3	0.9	41	42	33	44	2	.324	.440	18	6	3B-119, SS-3, 2B-1
1985	129	366	108	26	1	10	2.7	55	56	55	54	2	.295	.454	19	9	3B-119
1986	117	348	90	22	0	11	3.2	50	45	43	60	1	.259	.417	16	2	3B-110, DH-5, 2B-1
1987	124	332	103	28	1	11	3.3	37	44	34	55	1	.310	.500	24	8	3B-96, DH-22, SS-1
1988	119	337	101	21	1	12	3.6	49	48	56	57	1	.300	.475	17	6	DH-108, 3B-7
12 yrs.	1065	2957	818	199	14	66	2.2	381	365	359	452	13	.277	.420	141	44	3B-674, SS-206, DH-137, 2B-28

LEAGUE CHAMPIONSHIP SERIES

	G	AB	H	2B	3B	HR	HR %	R	RBI	BB	SO	SB	BA	SA	AB	H	G by POS
1985 **TOR A**	5	11	4	1	0	1	9.1	1	3	2	2	0	.364	.727	2	2	3B-5

Jerry Mumphrey

MUMPHREY, JERRY WAYNE
B. Sept. 9, 1952, Tyler, Tex.

BB TR 6'2"   185 lbs.

	G	AB	H	2B	3B	HR	HR %	R	RBI	BB	SO	SB	BA	SA	AB	H	G by POS
1974 **STL N**	5	2	0	0	0	0	0.0	2	0	0	0	0	.000	.000	0	0	OF-1
1975	11	16	6	2	0	0	0.0	2	1	4	3	0	.375	.500	4	2	OF-3
1976	112	384	99	15	5	1	0.3	51	26	37	53	22	.258	.331	10	3	OF-94
1977	145	463	133	20	10	2	0.4	73	38	47	70	22	.287	.387	16	3	OF-133
1978	125	367	96	13	4	2	0.5	41	37	30	40	14	.262	.335	16	5	OF-116
1979	124	339	100	10	3	3	0.9	53	32	26	39	16	.295	.369	16	5	OF-114
1980 **SD N**	160	564	168	24	3	4	0.7	61	59	49	90	52	.298	.372	6	1	OF-153
1981 **NY A**	80	319	98	11	5	6	1.9	44	32	24	27	14	.307	.429	0	0	OF-79
1982	123	477	143	24	10	9	1.9	76	68	50	66	11	.300	.449	0	0	OF-123
1983 2 teams	NY		A	(83G —	.262)			HOU	N	(44G —	.336)						
" total	127	410	118	21	6	8	2.0	58	53	50	56	7	.288	.427	2	0	OF-126
1984 **HOU N**	151	524	152	20	3	9	1.7	66	83	56	79	15	.290	.391	13	5	OF-137
1985	130	444	123	25	2	8	1.8	52	61	37	57	6	.277	.396	10	4	OF-126
1986 **CHI N**	111	309	94	11	2	5	1.6	37	32	26	45	2	.304	.401	29	10	OF-92
1987	118	309	103	19	2	13	4.2	41	44	35	47	1	.333	.534	35	12	OF-85
1988	63	66	9	2	0	0	0.0	3	9	7	16	0	.136	.167	50	5	OF-4
15 yrs.	1585	4993	1442	217	55	70	1.4	660	575	478	688	174	.289	.396	207	55	OF-1386

DIVISIONAL PLAYOFF SERIES

	G	AB	H	2B	3B	HR	HR %	R	RBI	BB	SO	SB	BA	SA	AB	H	G by POS
1981 **NY A**	5	21	2	0	0	0	0.0	2	0	0	1	1	.095	.095	0	0	OF-5

LEAGUE CHAMPIONSHIP SERIES

	G	AB	H	2B	3B	HR	HR %	R	RBI	BB	SO	SB	BA	SA	AB	H	G by POS
1981 **NY A**	3	12	6	1	0	0	0.0	2	0	3	2	0	.500	.583	0	0	OF-3

WORLD SERIES

	G	AB	H	2B	3B	HR	HR %	R	RBI	BB	SO	SB	BA	SA	AB	H	G by POS
1981 **NY A**	5	15	3	0	0	0	0.0	2	0	3	4	1	.200	.200	0	0	OF-5

Dale Murphy

MURPHY, DALE BRYAN
B. Mar. 12, 1956, Portland, Ore.

BR TR 6'4"   210 lbs.

	G	AB	H	2B	3B	HR	HR %	R	RBI	BB	SO	SB	BA	SA	AB	H	G by POS
1976 **ATL N**	19	65	17	6	0	0	0.0	3	9	7	9	0	.262	.354	0	0	C-19
1977	18	76	24	8	1	2	2.6	5	14	0	8	0	.316	.526	0	0	C-18
1978	151	530	120	14	3	23	4.3	66	79	42	145	11	.226	.394	7	3	1B-129, C-21
1979	104	384	106	7	2	21	5.5	53	57	38	67	6	.276	.469	2	0	1B-76, C-27
1980	156	569	160	27	2	33	5.8	98	89	59	133	9	.281	.510	1	0	OF-154, 1B-1

	G	AB	H	2B	3B	HR	HR %	R	RBI	BB	SO	SB	BA	SA	Pinch Hit AB	Pinch Hit H	G by POS

Dale Murphy continued

	G	AB	H	2B	3B	HR	HR %	R	RBI	BB	SO	SB	BA	SA	PH AB	PH H	G by POS
1981	104	369	91	12	1	13	3.5	43	50	44	72	14	.247	.390	2	0	OF-103, 1B-3
1982	162	598	168	23	2	36	6.0	113	109	93	134	23	.281	.507	1	1	OF-162
1983	162	589	178	24	4	36	6.1	131	121	90	110	30	.302	.540	2	0	OF-160
1984	162	607	176	32	8	36	5.9	94	100	79	134	19	.290	.547	2	0	OF-160
1985	162	616	185	32	2	37	6.0	118	111	90	141	10	.300	.539	0	0	OF-161
1986	160	614	163	29	7	29	4.7	89	83	75	141	7	.265	.477	1	1	OF-159
1987	159	566	167	27	1	44	7.8	115	105	115	136	16	.295	.580	0	0	OF-159
1988	156	592	134	35	4	24	4.1	77	77	74	125	3	.226	.421	1	0	OF-156
13 yrs.	1675	6175	1689	276	37	334	5.4	1005	1004	806	1355	148	.274	.492	19	5	OF-1374, 1B-209, C-85

LEAGUE CHAMPIONSHIP SERIES

	G	AB	H	2B	3B	HR	HR %	R	RBI	BB	SO	SB	BA	SA	PH AB	PH H	G by POS
1982 ATL N	3	11	3	0	0	0	0.0	1	0	0	2	1	.273	.273	0	0	OF-3

Dwayne Murphy

MURPHY, DWAYNE KEITH
B. Mar. 18, 1955, Merced, Calif.

BL TR 6'1" 180 lbs.

	G	AB	H	2B	3B	HR	HR %	R	RBI	BB	SO	SB	BA	SA	PH AB	PH H	G by POS
1978 OAK A	60	52	10	2	0	0	0.0	15	5	7	14	0	.192	.231	4	1	OF-45, DH-5
1979	121	388	99	10	4	11	2.8	57	40	84	80	15	.255	.387	2	1	OF-118
1980	159	573	157	18	2	13	2.3	86	68	102	96	26	.274	.380	0	0	OF-158
1981	107	390	98	10	3	15	3.8	58	60	73	91	10	.251	.408	0	0	OF-106, DH-1
1982	151	543	129	15	1	27	5.0	84	94	93	122	26	.238	.418	3	0	OF-147, DH-1, SS-1
1983	130	471	107	17	2	17	3.6	55	75	62	105	7	.227	.380	1	0	OF-124, DH-7
1984	153	559	143	18	2	33	5.9	93	88	74	111	4	.256	.472	0	0	OF-153
1985	152	523	122	21	3	20	3.8	77	59	84	123	4	.233	.400	0	0	OF-150
1986	98	329	83	11	3	9	2.7	50	39	56	80	3	.252	.386	2	2	OF-97, DH-1
1987	82	219	51	7	0	8	3.7	39	35	58	61	4	.233	.374	5	0	OF-80, 2B-1
1988 DET A	49	144	36	5	0	4	2.8	14	19	24	26	1	.250	.368	4	1	OF-43, DH-3
11 yrs.	1262	4191	1035	134	20	157	3.7	628	582	717	909	100	.247	.401	21	5	OF-1221, DH-18, SS-1, 2B-1

DIVISIONAL PLAYOFF SERIES

	G	AB	H	2B	3B	HR	HR %	R	RBI	BB	SO	SB	BA	SA	PH AB	PH H	G by POS
1981 OAK A	3	11	6	1	0	1	9.1	4	2	1	1	0	.545	.909	0	0	OF-3

LEAGUE CHAMPIONSHIP SERIES

	G	AB	H	2B	3B	HR	HR %	R	RBI	BB	SO	SB	BA	SA	PH AB	PH H	G by POS
1981 OAK A	3	8	2	1	0	0	0.0	0	1	2	3	0	.250	.375	0	0	OF-3

Eddie Murray

MURRAY, EDDIE CLARENCE
Brother of Rich Murray.
B. Feb. 24, 1956, Los Angeles, Calif.

BB TR 6'2" 190 lbs.

	G	AB	H	2B	3B	HR	HR %	R	RBI	BB	SO	SB	BA	SA	PH AB	PH H	G by POS
1977 BAL A	160	611	173	29	2	27	4.4	81	88	48	104	0	.283	.470	4	0	DH-111, 1B-42, OF-3
1978	161	610	174	32	3	27	4.4	85	95	70	97	6	.285	.480	0	0	1B-157, 3B-3, DH-1
1979	159	606	179	30	2	25	4.1	90	99	72	78	10	.295	.475	0	0	1B-157, DH-1
1980	158	621	186	36	2	32	5.2	100	116	54	71	7	.300	.519	3	1	1B-154, DH-1
1981	99	378	111	21	2	22	5.8	57	78	40	43	2	.294	.534	0	0	1B-99
1982	151	550	174	30	1	32	5.8	87	110	70	82	7	.316	.549	0	0	1B-149, DH-2
1983	156	582	178	30	3	33	5.7	115	111	86	90	5	.306	.538	2	0	1B-153, DH-2
1984	162	588	180	26	3	29	4.9	97	110	107	87	10	.306	.509	0	0	1B-159, DH-3
1985	156	583	173	37	1	31	5.3	111	124	84	68	5	.297	.523	0	0	1B-154, DH-2
1986	137	495	151	25	1	17	3.4	61	84	78	49	3	.305	.463	2	0	1B-119, DH-16
1987	160	618	171	28	3	30	4.9	89	91	73	80	1	.277	.477	0	0	1B-156, DH-4
1988	161	603	171	27	2	28	4.6	75	84	75	78	5	.284	.474	0	0	1B-160, DH-58
12 yrs.	1820	6845	2021	351	25	333	4.9	1048	1190	857	927	61	.295	.500	11	1	1B-1602, DH-202, OF-3, 3B-3

LEAGUE CHAMPIONSHIP SERIES

	G	AB	H	2B	3B	HR	HR %	R	RBI	BB	SO	SB	BA	SA	PH AB	PH H	G by POS
1979 BAL A	4	12	5	0	0	1	8.3	3	5	5	2	0	.417	.667	0	0	1B-4
1983	4	15	4	0	0	1	6.7	5	3	3	3	1	.267	.467	0	0	1B-4
2 yrs.	8	27	9	0	0	2	7.4	8	8	8	5	1	.333	.556	0	0	1B-8

WORLD SERIES

	G	AB	H	2B	3B	HR	HR %	R	RBI	BB	SO	SB	BA	SA	PH AB	PH H	G by POS
1979 BAL A	7	26	4	1	0	1	3.8	3	2	4	4	1	.154	.308	0	0	1B-7
1983	5	20	5	0	0	2	10.0	2	3	1	4	0	.250	.550	0	0	1B-5
2 yrs.	12	46	9	1	0	3	6.5	5	5	5	8	1	.196	.413	0	0	1B-12

Rob Nelson

NELSON, ROBERT AUGUSTUS
B. May 17, 1964, Pasadena, Calif.

BL TL 6'4" 215 lbs.

	G	AB	H	2B	3B	HR	HR %	R	RBI	BB	SO	SB	BA	SA	PH AB	PH H	G by POS
1986 OAK A	5	9	2	1	0	0	0.0	1	0	1	4	0	.222	.333	2	1	1B-2, DH-1
1987 2 teams	OAK A (7G – .167)					SD	N (10G – .091)										
" total	17	35	5	1	0	0	0.0	1	1	1	20	0	.143	.171	7	1	1B-9
1988 SD N	7	21	4	0	0	1	4.8	4	3	2	9	0	.190	.333	2	0	1B-5
3 yrs.	29	65	11	2	0	1	1.5	6	4	4	33	0	.169	.246	11	2	1B-16, DH-1

Graig Nettles

NETTLES, GRAIG
Brother of Jim Nettles.
B. Aug. 20, 1944, San Diego, Calif.

BL TR 6' 180 lbs.

	G	AB	H	2B	3B	HR	HR %	R	RBI	BB	SO	SB	BA	SA	PH AB	PH H	G by POS
1967 MIN A	3	3	1	1	0	0	0.0	0	0	0	0	0	.333	.667	3	1	
1968	22	76	17	2	1	5	6.6	13	8	7	20	0	.224	.474	0	0	OF-16, 3B-5, 1B-3
1969	96	225	50	9	2	7	3.1	27	26	32	47	1	.222	.373	28	4	OF-54, 3B-21
1970 CLE A	157	549	129	13	1	26	4.7	81	62	81	77	3	.235	.404	5	1	3B-154, OF-3
1971	158	598	156	18	1	28	4.7	78	86	82	56	7	.261	.435	0	0	3B-158
1972	150	557	141	28	0	17	3.1	65	70	57	50	2	.253	.395	0	0	3B-150
1973 NY A	160	552	129	18	0	22	4.0	65	81	78	76	0	.234	.386	1	0	3B-157, DH-2
1974	155	566	139	21	1	22	3.9	74	75	59	75	1	.246	.403	1	0	3B-154, SS-1
1975	157	581	155	24	4	21	3.6	71	91	51	88	1	.267	.430	0	0	3B-157
1976	158	583	148	29	2	32	5.5	88	93	62	94	11	.254	.475	1	0	3B-158, SS-1
1977	158	589	150	23	4	37	6.3	99	107	68	79	2	.255	.496	0	0	3B-156, DH-1
1978	159	587	162	23	2	27	4.6	81	93	59	69	1	.276	.460	0	0	3B-159, SS-2
1979	145	521	132	15	1	20	3.8	71	73	59	53	1	.253	.401	2	0	3B-144
1980	89	324	79	14	0	16	4.9	52	45	42	42	0	.244	.435	3	1	3B-88, SS-1

	G	AB	H	2B	3B	HR	HR %	R	RBI	BB	SO	SB	BA	SA	Pinch Hit AB	Pinch Hit H	G by POS

Graig Nettles continued

	G	AB	H	2B	3B	HR	HR%	R	RBI	BB	SO	SB	BA	SA	PH AB	PH H	G by POS
1981	103	349	85	7	1	15	4.3	46	46	47	49	0	.244	.398	3	1	3B-97, DH-4
1982	122	405	94	11	2	18	4.4	47	55	51	49	1	.232	.402	10	1	3B-113, DH-3
1983	129	462	123	17	3	20	4.3	56	75	51	65	0	.266	.446	6	3	3B-126, DH-1
1984 SD N	124	395	90	11	1	20	5.1	56	65	58	55	0	.228	.413	13	3	3B-119
1985	137	440	115	23	1	15	3.4	66	61	72	59	0	.261	.420	9	2	3B-130
1986	126	354	77	9	0	16	4.5	36	55	41	62	0	.218	.379	19	5	3B-114
1987 ATL N	112	177	37	8	1	5	2.8	16	33	22	25	1	.209	.350	72	13	3B-40, 1B-6
1988 MON N	80	93	16	4	0	1	1.1	5	14	9	19	0	.172	.247	54	13	3B-12, 1B-5
22 yrs.	2700	8986	2225	328	28	390	4.3	1193	1314	1088	1209	32	.248	.421	230	48	3B-2412, OF-73, 1B-14, DH-11, SS-5

DIVISIONAL PLAYOFF SERIES

	G	AB	H	2B	3B	HR	HR%	R	RBI	BB	SO	SB	BA	SA	PH AB	PH H	G by POS
1981 NY A	5	17	1	0	0	0	0.0	1	1	3	1	0	.059	.059	0	0	3B-5

LEAGUE CHAMPIONSHIP SERIES

	G	AB	H	2B	3B	HR	HR%	R	RBI	BB	SO	SB	BA	SA	PH AB	PH H	G by POS
1969 MIN A	1	1	1	0	0	0	0.0	0	0	0	0	0	1.000	1.000	1	1	
1976 NY A	5	17	4	1	0	2	11.8	2	4	3	3	0	.235	.647	0	0	3B-5
1977	5	20	3	0	0	0	0.0	1	1	0	3	0	.150	.150	0	0	3B-5
1978	4	15	5	0	1	1	6.7	3	2	0	1	0	.333	.667	0	0	3B-4
1980	2	6	1	0	0	1	16.7	1	1	0	1	0	.167	.667	1	0	3B-2
1981	3	12	6	2	0	1	8.3	2	9	1	0	0	.500	.917	0	0	3B-3
1984 SD N	4	14	2	0	0	0	0.0	1	2	1	1	0	.143	.143	0	0	3B-4
7 yrs.	24	85	22	3	1	5	5.9	10	19	5	9	0	.259	.494	2	1	3B-23

WORLD SERIES

	G	AB	H	2B	3B	HR	HR%	R	RBI	BB	SO	SB	BA	SA	PH AB	PH H	G by POS
1976 NY A	4	12	3	0	0	0	0.0	0	2	3	1	0	.250	.250	0	0	3B-4
1977	6	21	4	1	0	0	0.0	1	2	2	3	0	.190	.238	0	0	3B-6
1978	6	25	4	0	0	0	0.0	2	1	0	6	0	.160	.160	0	0	3B-6
1981	3	10	4	1	0	0	0.0	1	0	1	1	0	.400	.500	0	0	3B-3
1984 SD N	5	12	3	0	0	0	0.0	2	2	5	0	0	.250	.250	0	0	3B-5
5 yrs.	24	80	18	2	0	0	0.0	6	7	11	11	0	.225	.250	0	0	3B-24

Al Newman

NEWMAN, ALBERT DWAYNE
B. June 30, 1960, Kansas City, Mo.
BB TR 5'9" 175 lbs.

	G	AB	H	2B	3B	HR	HR%	R	RBI	BB	SO	SB	BA	SA	PH AB	PH H	G by POS
1985 MON N	25	29	5	1	0	0	0.0	7	1	3	4	2	.172	.207	2	0	2B-15, SS-2
1986	95	185	37	3	0	1	0.5	23	8	21	20	11	.200	.232	14	2	2B-59, SS-22
1987 MIN A	110	307	68	15	5	0	0.0	44	29	34	27	15	.221	.303	6	0	SS-55, 2B-47, 3B-12, DH-5, OF-2
1988	105	260	58	7	0	0	0.0	35	19	29	34	12	.223	.250	3	0	3B-60, SS-28, 2B-23
4 yrs.	335	781	168	26	5	1	0.1	109	57	87	85	40	.215	.265	25	2	2B-144, SS-107, 3B-72, DH-5, OF-2

LEAGUE CHAMPIONSHIP SERIES

	G	AB	H	2B	3B	HR	HR%	R	RBI	BB	SO	SB	BA	SA	PH AB	PH H	G by POS
1987 MIN A	1	2	0	0	0	0	0.0	0	0	0	0	0	.000	.000	0	0	2B-1

WORLD SERIES

	G	AB	H	2B	3B	HR	HR%	R	RBI	BB	SO	SB	BA	SA	PH AB	PH H	G by POS
1987 MIN A	4	5	1	0	0	0	0.0	0	0	1	1	0	.200	.200	1	0	2B-3

Carl Nichols

NICHOLS, CARL EDWARD
B. Oct. 14, 1962, Los Angeles, Calif.
BR TR 6' 184 lbs.

	G	AB	H	2B	3B	HR	HR%	R	RBI	BB	SO	SB	BA	SA	PH AB	PH H	G by POS
1986 BAL A	5	5	0	0	0	0	0.0	0	0	1	4	0	.000	.000	0	0	C-5
1987	13	21	8	1	0	0	0.0	4	3	1	4	0	.381	.429	0	0	C-13
1988	18	47	9	1	0	0	0.0	2	1	3	10	0	.191	.213	1	0	C-13, OF-3
3 yrs.	36	73	17	2	0	0	0.0	6	4	5	18	0	.233	.260	1	0	C-31, OF-3

Tom Nieto

NIETO, THOMAS ANDREW
B. Oct. 27, 1960, Downey, Calif.
BR TR 6'1" 205 lbs.

	G	AB	H	2B	3B	HR	HR%	R	RBI	BB	SO	SB	BA	SA	PH AB	PH H	G by POS
1984 STL N	33	86	24	4	0	3	3.5	7	12	5	18	0	.279	.430	2	0	C-32
1985	95	253	57	10	2	0	0.0	15	34	26	37	0	.225	.281	1	0	C-95
1986 MON N	30	65	13	3	1	1	1.5	5	7	6	21	0	.200	.323	1	1	C-30
1987 MIN A	41	105	21	7	1	1	1.0	7	12	8	24	0	.200	.314	1	1	C-40, DH-1
1988	24	60	4	0	0	0	0.0	1	0	1	17	0	.067	.067	0	0	C-24
5 yrs.	223	569	119	24	4	5	0.9	35	65	46	117	0	.209	.292	5	2	C-221, DH-1

LEAGUE CHAMPIONSHIP SERIES

	G	AB	H	2B	3B	HR	HR%	R	RBI	BB	SO	SB	BA	SA	PH AB	PH H	G by POS
1985 STL N	1	3	0	0	0	0	0.0	1	0	1	2	0	.000	.000	0	0	C-1

WORLD SERIES

	G	AB	H	2B	3B	HR	HR%	R	RBI	BB	SO	SB	BA	SA	PH AB	PH H	G by POS
1985 STL N	2	5	0	0	0	0	0.0	0	1	1	2	0	.000	.000	0	0	C-2

Donnell Nixon

NIXON, ROBERT DONNELL
Brother of Otis Nixon.
B. Dec. 31, 1961, Evergreen, N. C.
BR TR 6'1" 185 lbs.

	G	AB	H	2B	3B	HR	HR%	R	RBI	BB	SO	SB	BA	SA	PH AB	PH H	G by POS
1987 SEA A	46	132	33	4	0	3	2.3	17	12	13	28	21	.250	.348	0	0	OF-32, DH-6
1988 SF N	59	78	27	3	0	0	0.0	15	6	10	12	11	.346	.385	5	1	OF-46
2 yrs.	105	210	60	7	0	3	1.4	32	18	23	40	32	.286	.362	5	1	OF-78, DH-6

Otis Nixon

NIXON, OTIS JUNIOR
Brother of Donnell Nixon.
B. Jan. 9, 1959, Evergreen, N. C.
BB TR 6'2" 175 lbs.

	G	AB	H	2B	3B	HR	HR%	R	RBI	BB	SO	SB	BA	SA	PH AB	PH H	G by POS
1983 NY A	13	14	2	0	0	0	0.0	2	0	1	5	2	.143	.143	0	0	OF-9
1984 CLE A	49	91	14	0	0	0	0.0	16	1	8	11	12	.154	.154	0	0	OF-46
1985	104	162	38	4	0	3	1.9	34	9	8	27	20	.235	.315	2	0	OF-80, DH-11
1986	105	95	25	4	1	0	0.0	33	8	13	12	23	.263	.326	3	1	OF-95, DH-5
1987	19	17	1	0	0	0	0.0	2	1	3	4	2	.059	.059	0	0	OF-17
1988 MON N	90	271	66	8	2	0	0.0	47	15	28	42	46	.244	.288	11	6	OF-82
6 yrs.	380	650	146	16	3	3	0.5	134	34	61	101	105	.225	.272	16	7	OF-329, DH-16

	G	AB	H	2B	3B	HR	HR%	R	RBI	BB	SO	SB	BA	SA	Pinch Hit AB	Pinch Hit H	G by POS

Junior Noboa

NOBOA, MILCIADES ARTURO DIAZ
Born Milciades Arturo Noboa y Diaz.
B. Nov. 10, 1964, Azua, Dominican Republic — BR TR 5'10" 155 lbs.

	G	AB	H	2B	3B	HR	HR%	R	RBI	BB	SO	SB	BA	SA	PH AB	PH H	G by POS
1984 CLE A	23	11	4	0	0	0	0.0	3	0	0	2	1	.364	.364	0	0	2B-19, DH-1
1987	39	80	18	2	1	0	0.0	7	7	3	6	1	.225	.275	2	0	2B-21, SS-8, 3B-5
1988 CAL A	21	16	1	0	0	0	0.0	4	0	0	1	0	.063	.063	0	0	2B-9, SS-3, 3B-2
3 yrs.	83	107	23	2	1	0	0.0	14	7	3	9	2	.215	.252	2	0	2B-49, SS-11, 3B-7, DH-1

Matt Nokes

NOKES, MATTHEW DODGE
B. Oct. 31, 1963, San Diego, Calif. — BL TR 6'1" 180 lbs.

	G	AB	H	2B	3B	HR	HR%	R	RBI	BB	SO	SB	BA	SA	PH AB	PH H	G by POS
1985 SF N	19	53	11	2	0	2	3.8	3	5	1	9	0	.208	.358	5	0	C-14
1986 DET A	7	24	8	1	0	1	4.2	2	2	1	1	0	.333	.500	0	0	C-7
1987	135	461	133	14	2	32	6.9	69	87	35	70	2	.289	.536	19	4	C-109, OF-3, 3B-2
1988	122	382	96	18	0	16	4.2	53	53	34	58	0	.251	.424	16	3	C-110, DH-4
4 yrs.	283	920	248	35	2	51	5.5	127	147	71	138	2	.270	.478	40	7	C-240, DH-4, OF-3, 3B-2

LEAGUE CHAMPIONSHIP SERIES

	G	AB	H	2B	3B	HR	HR%	R	RBI	BB	SO	SB	BA	SA	PH AB	PH H	G by POS
1987 DET A	5	14	2	0	0	1	7.1	2	2	1	4	0	.143	.357	2	0	C-3

Ken Oberkfell

OBERKFELL, KENNETH RAY (Obie)
B. May 4, 1956, Highland, Ill. — BL TR 6' 175 lbs.

	G	AB	H	2B	3B	HR	HR%	R	RBI	BB	SO	SB	BA	SA	PH AB	PH H	G by POS
1977 STL N	9	9	1	0	0	0	0.0	0	1	0	3	0	.111	.111	3	0	2B-6
1978	24	50	6	1	0	0	0.0	7	0	3	1	0	.120	.140	3	0	2B-17, 3B-4
1979	135	369	111	19	5	1	0.3	53	35	57	35	4	.301	.388	13	3	2B-117, 3B-17, SS-2
1980	116	422	128	27	6	3	0.7	58	46	51	23	4	.303	.417	1	0	2B-101, 3B-16
1981	102	376	110	12	6	2	0.5	43	45	37	28	13	.293	.372	1	0	3B-102, SS-1
1982	137	470	136	22	5	2	0.4	55	34	40	31	11	.289	.370	3	1	3B-135, 2B-1
1983	151	488	143	26	5	3	0.6	62	38	61	27	12	.293	.385	8	3	3B-127, 2B-32, SS-1
1984 2 teams		STL N (50G – .309)			ATL N (50G – .233)												
" total	100	324	87	19	2	1	0.3	38	21	31	27	2	.269	.349	6	1	3B-91, 2B-6, SS-1
1985 ATL N	134	412	112	19	4	3	0.7	30	35	51	38	1	.272	.359	10	2	3B-117, 2B-16
1986	151	503	136	24	3	5	1.0	62	48	83	40	7	.270	.360	4	1	3B-130, 2B-41
1987	135	508	142	29	2	3	0.6	59	48	48	29	3	.280	.362	5	0	3B-126, 2B-11
1988 2 teams		ATL N (120G – .277)			PIT N (20G – .222)												
" total	140	476	129	22	4	3	0.6	49	42	37	34	4	.271	.353	15	2	3B-115, 2B-12, SS-3, 1B-1
12 yrs.	1334	4407	1241	220	42	26	0.6	516	393	499	316	61	.282	.368	72	13	3B-980, 2B-360, SS-8, 1B-1

LEAGUE CHAMPIONSHIP SERIES

	G	AB	H	2B	3B	HR	HR%	R	RBI	BB	SO	SB	BA	SA	PH AB	PH H	G by POS
1982 STL N	3	15	3	0	0	0	0.0	1	2	0	0	0	.200	.200	0	0	3B-3

WORLD SERIES

	G	AB	H	2B	3B	HR	HR%	R	RBI	BB	SO	SB	BA	SA	PH AB	PH H	G by POS
1982 STL N	7	24	7	1	0	0	0.0	4	1	2	1	2	.292	.333	0	0	3B-7

Charlie O'Brien

O'BRIEN, CHARLES HUGH
B. May 1, 1960, Tulsa, Okla. — BR TR 6'2" 195 lbs.

	G	AB	H	2B	3B	HR	HR%	R	RBI	BB	SO	SB	BA	SA	PH AB	PH H	G by POS
1985 OAK A	16	11	3	1	0	0	0.0	3	1	3	3	0	.273	.364	0	0	C-16
1987 MIL A	10	35	7	3	1	0	0.0	2	0	4	4	0	.200	.343	0	0	C-10
1988	40	118	26	6	0	2	1.7	12	9	5	16	0	.220	.322	0	0	C-40
3 yrs.	66	164	36	10	1	2	1.2	17	10	12	23	0	.220	.329	0	0	C-66 .

Pete O'Brien

O'BRIEN, PETER MICHAEL
B. Feb. 9, 1958, Santa Monica, Calif. — BL TL 6' 180 lbs.

	G	AB	H	2B	3B	HR	HR%	R	RBI	BB	SO	SB	BA	SA	PH AB	PH H	G by POS
1982 TEX A	20	67	16	4	1	4	6.0	13	13	6	8	1	.239	.507	0	0	OF-11, DH-4, 1B-3
1983	154	524	124	24	5	8	1.5	53	53	58	62	5	.237	.347	6	2	1B-133, OF-27, DH-1
1984	142	520	149	26	2	18	3.5	57	80	53	50	3	.287	.448	2	1	1B-141, OF-1
1985	159	573	153	34	3	22	3.8	69	92	69	53	5	.267	.452	3	0	1B-159
1986	156	551	160	23	3	23	4.2	86	90	87	66	4	.290	.468	3	1	1B-155
1987	159	569	163	26	1	23	4.0	84	88	59	61	0	.286	.457	3	0	1B-158, OF-2
1988	156	547	149	24	1	16	2.9	57	71	72	73	1	.272	.408	5	1	1B-155, DH-1
7 yrs.	946	3351	914	161	16	114	3.4	419	487	404	373	19	.273	.432	22	5	1B-904, OF-41, DH-6

Ron Oester

OESTER, RONALD JOHN
B. May 5, 1956, Cincinnati, Ohio — BB TR 6'2" 185 lbs.

	G	AB	H	2B	3B	HR	HR%	R	RBI	BB	SO	SB	BA	SA	PH AB	PH H	G by POS
1978 CIN N	6	8	3	0	0	0	0.0	1	1	0	2	0	.375	.375	0	0	SS-6
1979	6	3	0	0	0	0	0.0	0	0	0	1	0	.000	.000	1	0	SS-2
1980	100	303	84	16	2	2	0.7	40	20	26	44	6	.277	.363	10	3	2B-79, SS-17, 3B-3
1981	105	354	96	16	7	5	1.4	45	42	42	49	2	.271	.398	0	0	2B-103, SS-9
1982	151	549	143	19	4	9	1.6	63	47	35	82	5	.260	.359	6	1	2B-118, SS-29, 3B-13
1983	157	549	145	23	5	11	2.0	63	58	49	106	2	.264	.384	5	2	2B-154
1984	150	553	134	26	3	3	0.5	54	38	41	97	7	.242	.316	6	2	2B-147, SS-1
1985	152	526	155	26	3	1	0.2	59	34	51	65	5	.295	.361	2	0	2B-149
1986	153	523	135	23	2	8	1.5	52	44	52	84	9	.258	.356	4	0	2B-151
1987	69	237	60	9	6	2	0.8	28	23	22	51	2	.253	.367	0	0	2B-69
1988	54	150	42	7	0	0	0.0	20	10	9	24	0	.280	.327	3	1	2B-49, SS-5
11 yrs.	1103	3755	997	165	32	41	1.1	425	317	327	605	38	.266	.359	37	9	2B-1019, SS-69, 3B-16

Tom O'Malley

O'MALLEY, THOMAS PATRICK
B. Dec. 25, 1960, Orange, N. J. — BL TR 6' 170 lbs.

	G	AB	H	2B	3B	HR	HR%	R	RBI	BB	SO	SB	BA	SA	PH AB	PH H	G by POS
1982 SF N	92	291	80	12	4	2	0.7	26	27	33	39	0	.275	.364	9	3	3B-83, SS-1, 2B-1
1983	135	410	106	16	1	5	1.2	40	45	52	47	2	.259	.339	17	5	3B-117
1984 2 teams		SF N (13G – .120)			CHI A (12G – .125)												
" total	25	41	5	0	0	0	0.0	2	3	2	7	0	.122	.122	13	2	3B-13
1985 BAL A	8	14	1	0	0	1	7.1	1	2	0	2	0	.071	.286	5	0	3B-3
1986	56	181	46	9	0	1	0.6	19	18	17	21	0	.254	.320	4	0	3B-55
1987 TEX A	45	117	32	8	0	1	0.9	10	12	15	9	0	.274	.368	8	2	3B-40, 2B-1
1988 MON N	14	27	7	0	0	0	0.0	3	2	3	4	0	.259	.259	5	1	3B-7
7 yrs.	375	1081	277	45	5	10	0.9	101	109	122	129	2	.256	.335	61	13	3B-318, 2B-2, SS-1

	G	AB	H	2B	3B	HR	HR %	R	RBI	BB	SO	SB	BA	SA	Pinch Hit AB	Pinch Hit H	G by POS

Paul O'Neill

O'NEILL, PAUL ANDREW
B. Feb. 25, 1963, Columbus, Ohio

BL TL 6'4" 200 lbs.

	G	AB	H	2B	3B	HR	HR %	R	RBI	BB	SO	SB	BA	SA	PH AB	PH H	G by POS
1985 CIN N	5	12	4	1	0	0	0.0	1	1	0	2	0	.333	.417	3	1	OF-2
1986	3	2	0	0	0	0	0.0	0	0	1	1	0	.000	.000	2	0	
1987	84	160	41	14	1	7	4.4	24	28	18	29	2	.256	.488	37	11	OF-42, 1B-2, P-1
1988	145	485	122	25	3	16	3.3	58	73	38	65	8	.252	.414	11	0	OF-118, 1B-21
4 yrs.	237	659	167	40	4	23	3.5	83	102	57	97	10	.253	.431	53	12	OF-162, 1B-23, P-1

Jose Oquendo

OQUENDO, JOSE MANUEL CONTRERAS
Born Jose Manuel Oquendo y Contreras.
B. July 4, 1963, Rio Peidras, Puerto Rico

BB TR 5'10" 160 lbs.

	G	AB	H	2B	3B	HR	HR %	R	RBI	BB	SO	SB	BA	SA	PH AB	PH H	G by POS
1983 NY N	120	328	70	7	0	1	0.3	29	17	19	60	8	.213	.244	1	0	SS-116
1984	81	189	42	5	0	0	0.0	23	10	15	26	10	.222	.249	3	2	SS-67
1986 STL N	76	138	41	4	1	0	0.0	20	13	15	20	2	.297	.341	27	6	SS-29, 2B-21, OF-1, 3B-1
1987	116	248	71	9	0	1	0.4	43	24	54	29	4	.286	.335	26	10	OF-46, 2B-32, SS-23, 3B-8, 1B-3, P-1
1988	148	451	125	10	1	7	1.6	36	46	52	40	4	.277	.350	10	2	2B-69, 3B-47, SS-17, 1B-16, OF-15, C-1, P-1
5 yrs.	541	1354	349	35	2	9	0.7	151	110	155	175	28	.258	.306	67	20	SS-252, 2B-122, OF-62, 3B-56, 1B-19, P-2, C-1

LEAGUE CHAMPIONSHIP SERIES

	G	AB	H	2B	3B	HR	HR %	R	RBI	BB	SO	SB	BA	SA	PH AB	PH H	G by POS
1987 STL N	5	12	2	0	0	1	8.3	3	4	3	2	0	.167	.417	1	0	3B-1

WORLD SERIES

	G	AB	H	2B	3B	HR	HR %	R	RBI	BB	SO	SB	BA	SA	PH AB	PH H	G by POS
1987 STL N	7	24	6	0	0	0	0.0	2	2	1	4	0	.250	.250	0	0	3B-4

Joe Orsulak

ORSULAK, JOSEPH MICHAEL
B. May 31, 1962, Glen Ridge, N. J.

BL TL 6'1" 185 lbs.

	G	AB	H	2B	3B	HR	HR %	R	RBI	BB	SO	SB	BA	SA	PH AB	PH H	G by POS
1983 PIT N	7	11	2	0	0	0	0.0	0	1	0	2	0	.182	.182	3	0	OF-4
1984	32	67	17	1	2	0	0.0	12	3	1	7	3	.254	.328	6	1	OF-25
1985	121	397	119	14	6	0	0.0	54	21	26	27	24	.300	.365	8	4	OF-115
1986	138	401	100	19	6	2	0.5	60	19	28	38	24	.249	.342	22	4	OF-120
1988 BAL A	125	379	109	21	3	8	2.1	48	27	23	30	9	.288	.422	17	4	OF-117
5 yrs.	423	1255	347	55	17	10	0.8	174	71	78	104	60	.276	.371	56	13	OF-381

Junior Ortiz

ORTIZ, ADALBERTO COLON
Born Adalberto Ortiz y Colon.
B. Oct. 24, 1959, Humacao, Puerto Rico

BR TR 5'11" 174 lbs.

	G	AB	H	2B	3B	HR	HR %	R	RBI	BB	SO	SB	BA	SA	PH AB	PH H	G by POS
1982 PIT N	7	15	3	1	0	0	0.0	1	0	1	3	0	.200	.267	0	0	C-7
1983 2 teams		PIT	N (5G – .125)			NY	N (68G – .254)										
" total	73	193	48	5	0	0	0.0	11	12	4	34	1	.249	.275	5	2	C-71
1984 NY N	40	91	18	3	0	0	0.0	6	11	5	15	1	.198	.231	10	1	C-32
1985 PIT N	23	72	21	2	0	1	1.4	4	5	3	17	1	.292	.361	1	0	C-23
1986	49	110	37	6	0	0	0.0	11	14	9	13	0	.336	.391	11	3	C-36
1987	75	192	52	8	1	1	0.5	16	22	15	23	0	.271	.339	8	2	C-72
1988	49	118	33	6	0	2	1.7	8	18	9	9	1	.280	.381	12	3	C-40
7 yrs.	316	791	212	31	1	4	0.5	57	82	46	114	4	.268	.325	47	11	C-281

Dave Owen

OWEN, DAVID
Brother of Spike Owen.
B. Apr. 25, 1958, Cleburne, Tex.

BB TR 6'1" 175 lbs.

	G	AB	H	2B	3B	HR	HR %	R	RBI	BB	SO	SB	BA	SA	PH AB	PH H	G by POS
1983 CHI N	16	22	2	0	1	0	0.0	1	2	2	7	1	.091	.182	0	0	SS-14, 3B-3
1984	47	93	18	2	2	1	1.1	8	10	8	15	1	.194	.290	3	2	SS-35, 3B-6, 2B-4
1985	22	19	7	0	0	0	0.0	6	4	1	5	1	.368	.368	3	0	SS-7, 3B-7, 2B-4
1988 KC A	7	5	0	0	0	0	0.0	0	0	0	3	0	.000	.000	0	0	SS-7
4 yrs.	92	139	27	2	3	1	0.7	15	16	11	30	3	.194	.273	6	2	SS-63, 3B-16, 2B-8

Larry Owen

OWEN, LAWRENCE THOMAS
B. May 31, 1955, Cleveland, Ohio

BR TR 5'11" 185 lbs.

	G	AB	H	2B	3B	HR	HR %	R	RBI	BB	SO	SB	BA	SA	PH AB	PH H	G by POS
1981 ATL N	13	16	0	0	0	0	0.0	0	0	1	4	0	.000	.000	4	0	C-10
1982	2	3	1	1	0	0	0.0	1	0	0	1	0	.333	.667	0	0	C-2
1983	17	17	2	0	0	0	0.0	0	1	0	2	0	.118	.118	1	0	C-16
1985	26	71	17	3	0	2	2.8	7	12	8	17	0	.239	.366	2	0	C-25
1987 KC A	76	164	31	6	0	5	3.0	17	14	16	51	0	.189	.317	0	0	C-76
1988	37	81	17	1	0	1	1.2	5	3	9	23	0	.210	.259	0	0	C-37
6 yrs.	171	352	68	11	0	8	2.3	30	30	34	98	0	.193	.293	7	0	C-166

Spike Owen

OWEN, SPIKE DEE
Brother of Dave Owen.
B. Apr. 19, 1961, Cleburne, Tex.

BB TR 5'9" 160 lbs.

	G	AB	H	2B	3B	HR	HR %	R	RBI	BB	SO	SB	BA	SA	PH AB	PH H	G by POS
1983 SEA A	80	306	60	11	3	2	0.7	36	21	24	44	10	.196	.271	1	0	SS-80
1984	152	530	130	18	8	3	0.6	67	43	46	63	16	.245	.326	1	1	SS-151
1985	118	352	91	10	6	6	1.7	41	37	34	27	11	.259	.372	0	0	SS-117
1986 2 teams		SEA	A (112G – .246)			BOS	A (42G – .183)										
" total	154	528	122	24	7	1	0.2	67	45	51	51	4	.231	.309	0	0	SS-154
1987 BOS A	132	437	113	17	7	2	0.5	50	48	53	43	11	.259	.343	0	0	SS-130
1988	89	257	64	14	1	5	1.9	40	18	27	27	0	.249	.370	6	1	SS-76, DH-7
6 yrs.	725	2410	580	94	32	19	0.8	301	212	235	255	52	.241	.330	9	2	SS-708, DH-7

LEAGUE CHAMPIONSHIP SERIES

	G	AB	H	2B	3B	HR	HR %	R	RBI	BB	SO	SB	BA	SA	PH AB	PH H	G by POS
1986 BOS A	7	21	9	0	1	0	0.0	5	3	2	2	1	.429	.524	0	0	SS-7
1988	1	0	0	0	0	0	–	0	0	1	0	0	–	–	0	0	
2 yrs.	8	21	9	0	1	0	0.0	5	3	3	2	1	.429	.524	0	0	SS-7

WORLD SERIES

	G	AB	H	2B	3B	HR	HR %	R	RBI	BB	SO	SB	BA	SA	PH AB	PH H	G by POS
1986 BOS A	7	20	6	0	0	0	0.0	2	2	5	6	0	.300	.300	0	0	SS-7

	G	AB	H	2B	3B	HR	HR %	R	RBI	BB	SO	SB	BA	SA	Pinch Hit AB	Pinch Hit H	G by POS

Mike Pagliarulo

PAGLIARULO, MICHAEL TIMOTHY (Pags)
B. Mar. 15, 1960, Medford, Mass.   BL TR 6'2"   195 lbs.

	G	AB	H	2B	3B	HR	HR %	R	RBI	BB	SO	SB	BA	SA	AB	H	G by POS
1984 NY A	67	201	48	15	3	7	3.5	24	34	15	46	0	.239	.448	0	0	3B-67
1985	138	380	91	16	2	19	5.0	55	62	45	86	0	.239	.442	19	6	3B-134
1986	149	504	120	24	3	28	5.6	71	71	54	120	4	.238	.464	9	1	3B-143, SS-2
1987	150	522	122	26	3	32	6.1	76	87	53	111	1	.234	.479	8	0	3B-147, 1B-1
1988	125	444	96	20	1	15	3.4	46	67	37	104	1	.216	.367	9	0	3B-124
5 yrs.	629	2051	477	101	12	101	4.9	272	321	204	467	6	.233	.441	45	7	3B-615, SS-2, 1B-1

Tom Pagnozzi

PAGNOZZI, THOMAS ALAN
B. July 30, 1962, Tucson, Ariz.   BR TR 6'1"   190 lbs.

	G	AB	H	2B	3B	HR	HR %	R	RBI	BB	SO	SB	BA	SA	AB	H	G by POS
1987 STL N	27	48	9	1	0	2	4.2	8	9	4	13	1	.188	.333	7	2	C-25, 1B-1
1988	81	195	55	9	0	0	0.0	17	15	11	32	0	.282	.328	26	4	1B-28, C-28, 3B-5
2 yrs.	108	243	64	10	0	2	0.8	25	24	15	45	1	.263	.329	33	6	C-53, 1B-29, 3B-5

LEAGUE CHAMPIONSHIP SERIES

	G	AB	H	2B	3B	HR	HR %	R	RBI	BB	SO	SB	BA	SA	AB	H	G by POS
1987 STL N	1	1	0	0	0	0	0.0	0	0	0	0	0	.000	.000	1	0	

WORLD SERIES

	G	AB	H	2B	3B	HR	HR %	R	RBI	BB	SO	SB	BA	SA	AB	H	G by POS
1987 STL N	2	4	1	0	0	0	0.0	0	0	0	0	0	.250	.250	1	0	DH-1

Rey Palacios

PALACIOS, ROBERT REY
B. Nov. 8, 1962, Brooklyn, N. Y.   BR TR 5'10"   190 lbs.

	G	AB	H	2B	3B	HR	HR %	R	RBI	BB	SO	SB	BA	SA	AB	H	G by POS
1988 KC A	5	11	1	0	0	0	0.0	2	0	0	4	0	.091	.091	1	0	C-3, 3B-1

Rafael Palmeiro

PALMEIRO, RAFAEL
Born Rafael Palmeiro y Corrales.
B. Sept. 24, 1964, Havana, Cuba   BL TL 6'   180 lbs.

	G	AB	H	2B	3B	HR	HR %	R	RBI	BB	SO	SB	BA	SA	AB	H	G by POS
1986 CHI N	22	73	18	4	0	3	4.1	9	12	4	6	1	.247	.425	2	0	OF-20
1987	84	221	61	15	1	14	6.3	32	30	20	26	2	.276	.543	27	5	OF-45, 1B-18
1988	152	580	178	41	5	8	1.4	75	53	38	34	12	.307	.436	5	0	OF-147, 1B-5
3 yrs.	258	874	257	60	6	25	2.9	116	95	62	66	15	.294	.462	34	5	OF-212, 1B-23

Jim Pankovits

PANKOVITS, JAMES FRANKLIN
B. Aug. 6, 1955, Pennington Gap, Va.   BR TR 5'10"   170 lbs.

	G	AB	H	2B	3B	HR	HR %	R	RBI	BB	SO	SB	BA	SA	AB	H	G by POS
1984 HOU N	53	81	23	7	0	1	1.2	6	14	2	20	2	.284	.407	40	9	2B-15, SS-4, OF-3
1985	75	172	42	3	0	4	2.3	24	14	17	29	1	.244	.331	23	5	OF-33, 2B-21, SS-1, 3B-1
1986	70	113	32	6	1	1	0.9	12	7	11	25	1	.283	.381	38	11	2B-26, OF-5, C-1
1987	50	61	14	2	0	1	1.6	7	8	6	13	2	.230	.311	32	7	2B-9, OF-6, 3B-4
1988	68	140	31	7	1	2	1.4	13	12	8	28	2	.221	.329	27	2	2B-31, 3B-11, 1B-2
5 yrs.	316	567	142	25	2	9	1.6	62	55	44	115	8	.250	.349	160	34	2B-102, OF-47, 3B-16, SS-5, 1B-2, C-1

LEAGUE CHAMPIONSHIP SERIES

	G	AB	H	2B	3B	HR	HR %	R	RBI	BB	SO	SB	BA	SA	AB	H	G by POS
1986 HOU N	2	2	0	0	0	0	0.0	0	0	0	1	0	.000	.000	2	0	

Al Pardo

PARDO, ALBERTO JUDAS
B. Sept. 8, 1962, Oviedo, Spain   BB TR 6'2"   187 lbs.

	G	AB	H	2B	3B	HR	HR %	R	RBI	BB	SO	SB	BA	SA	AB	H	G by POS
1985 BAL A	34	75	10	1	0	0	0.0	3	1	3	15	0	.133	.147	7	0	C-29
1986	16	51	7	1	0	1	2.0	3	3	0	14	0	.137	.216	1	0	C-14, DH-1
1988 PHI N	2	2	0	0	0	0	0.0	0	0	0	2	0	.000	.000	0	0	C-2
3 yrs.	52	128	17	2	0	1	0.8	6	4	3	31	0	.133	.172	8	0	C-45, DH-1

Johnny Paredes

PAREDES, JHONNY ALFONSO
Born Jhonny Alfonso Paredes y Isambert.
B. Sept. 2, 1962, Maracaibo, Venezuela   BR TR 5'11"   165 lbs.

	G	AB	H	2B	3B	HR	HR %	R	RBI	BB	SO	SB	BA	SA	AB	H	G by POS
1988 MON N	35	91	17	2	0	1	1.1	6	10	9	17	5	.187	.242	2	2	2B-28, OF-1

Mark Parent

PARENT, MARK ALAN
B. Sept. 16, 1961, Ashland, Ore.   BR TR 6'5"   215 lbs.

	G	AB	H	2B	3B	HR	HR %	R	RBI	BB	SO	SB	BA	SA	AB	H	G by POS
1986 SD N	8	14	2	0	0	0	0.0	1	0	1	3	0	.143	.143	4	0	C-3
1987	12	25	2	0	0	0	0.0	0	2	0	9	0	.080	.080	2	0	C-10
1988	41	118	23	3	0	6	5.1	9	15	6	23	0	.195	.373	3	1	C-36
3 yrs.	61	157	27	3	0	6	3.8	10	17	7	35	0	.172	.306	9	1	C-49

Kelly Paris

PARIS, KELLY JAY
B. Oct. 17, 1957, Encino, Calif.   BB TR 6'   175 lbs.

	G	AB	H	2B	3B	HR	HR %	R	RBI	BB	SO	SB	BA	SA	AB	H	G by POS
1982 STL N	12	29	3	0	0	0	0.0	1	1	0	7	0	.103	.103	3	1	3B-5, SS-4
1983 CIN N	56	120	30	6	0	0	0.0	13	7	15	22	8	.250	.300	11	1	3B-16, 2B-10, SS-7, 1B-3
1985 BAL A	4	8	0	0	0	0	0.0	0	0	0	1	0	.000	.000	1	0	DH-2, 3B-2
1986	5	10	2	0	0	0	0.0	0	0	0	3	0	.200	.200	1	0	3B-3, DH-2
1988 CHI A	14	44	11	0	0	3	6.8	6	6	0	6	0	.250	.455	2	0	1B-9, 3B-4
5 yrs.	91	211	46	6	0	3	1.4	20	14	15	39	8	.218	.289	18	2	3B-28, 2B-12, 1B-12, SS-11, DH-4

Dave Parker

PARKER, DAVID GENE (The Cobra)
B. June 9, 1951, Calhoun, Miss.   BL TR 6'5"   230 lbs.

	G	AB	H	2B	3B	HR	HR %	R	RBI	BB	SO	SB	BA	SA	AB	H	G by POS
1973 PIT N	54	139	40	9	1	4	2.9	17	14	2	27	1	.288	.453	15	4	OF-39
1974	73	220	62	10	3	4	1.8	27	29	10	53	3	.282	.409	21	4	OF-49, 1B-6
1975	148	558	172	35	10	25	4.5	75	101	38	89	8	.308	.541	7	4	OF-141
1976	138	537	168	28	10	13	2.4	82	90	30	80	19	.313	.475	4	2	OF-134
1977	159	637	215	44	8	21	3.3	107	88	58	107	17	.338	.531	0	0	OF-158, 2B-1
1978	148	581	194	32	12	30	5.2	102	117	57	92	20	.334	.585	0	0	OF-147
1979	158	622	193	45	7	25	4.0	109	94	67	101	20	.310	.526	0	0	OF-158
1980	139	518	153	31	1	17	3.3	71	79	25	69	10	.295	.462	7	2	OF-130
1981	67	240	62	14	3	9	3.8	29	48	9	25	6	.258	.454	6	3	OF-60
1982	73	244	66	19	3	6	2.5	41	29	22	45	7	.270	.447	7	2	OF-63
1983	144	552	154	29	4	12	2.2	68	69	28	89	12	.279	.411	2	0	OF-142
1984 CIN N	156	607	173	28	0	16	2.6	73	94	41	89	11	.285	.410	2	0	OF-151

	G	AB	H	2B	3B	HR	HR %	R	RBI	BB	SO	SB	BA	SA	Pinch Hit AB	Pinch Hit H	G by POS

Dave Parker continued

	G	AB	H	2B	3B	HR	HR%	R	RBI	BB	SO	SB	BA	SA	AB	H	G by POS
1985	160	635	198	42	4	34	5.4	88	125	52	80	5	.312	.551	2	1	OF-159
1986	162	637	174	31	3	31	4.9	89	116	56	126	1	.273	.477	3	1	OF-159
1987	153	589	149	28	0	26	4.4	77	97	44	104	7	.253	.433	3	0	OF-151
1988 OAK A	101	377	97	18	1	12	3.2	43	55	32	70	0	.257	.406	9	4	DH-61, OF-34, 1B-1
16 yrs.	2033	7693	2270	443	70	285	3.7	1098	1245	571	1246	147	.295	.482	92	27	OF-1875, DH-61, 1B-7, 2B-1

LEAGUE CHAMPIONSHIP SERIES

	G	AB	H	2B	3B	HR	HR%	R	RBI	BB	SO	SB	BA	SA	AB	H	G by POS
1974 PIT N	3	8	1	0	0	0	0.0	0	0	0	1	0	.125	.125	1	0	OF-2
1975	3	10	0	0	0	0	0.0	2	0	1	3	0	.000	.000	0	0	OF-3
1979	3	12	4	0	0	0	0.0	2	2	2	3	1	.333	.333	0	0	OF-3
1988 OAK A	3	12	3	1	0	0	0.0	1	0	0	4	0	.250	.333	0	0	OF-1
4 yrs.	12	42	8	1	0	0	0.0	5	2	3	11	1	.190	.214	1	0	OF-9

WORLD SERIES

	G	AB	H	2B	3B	HR	HR%	R	RBI	BB	SO	SB	BA	SA	AB	H	G by POS
1979 PIT N	7	29	10	3	0	0	0.0	2	4	2	7	0	.345	.448	0	0	OF-7
1988 OAK A	4	15	3	0	0	0	0.0	0	0	2	4	0	.200	.200	0	0	OF-2
2 yrs.	11	44	13	3	0	0	0.0	2	4	4	11	0	.295	.364	0	0	OF-9

Lance Parrish

PARRISH, LANCE MICHAEL
B. June 15, 1956, Clairton, Pa.

BR TR 6'3" 210 lbs.

	G	AB	H	2B	3B	HR	HR%	R	RBI	BB	SO	SB	BA	SA	AB	H	G by POS
1977 DET A	12	46	9	2	0	3	6.5	10	7	5	12	0	.196	.435	0	0	C-12
1978	85	288	63	11	3	14	4.9	37	41	11	71	0	.219	.424	6	1	C-79
1979	143	493	136	26	3	19	3.9	65	65	49	105	6	.276	.456	3	1	C-142
1980	144	553	158	34	6	24	4.3	79	82	31	109	6	.286	.499	4	1	C-121, DH-16, OF-5, 1B-5
1981	96	348	85	18	2	10	2.9	39	46	34	52	2	.244	.394	0	0	C-90, DH-5
1982	133	486	138	19	2	32	6.6	75	87	40	99	3	.284	.529	2	1	C-132, OF-1
1983	155	605	163	42	3	27	4.5	80	114	44	106	1	.269	.483	2	0	C-131, DH-27
1984	147	578	137	16	2	33	5.7	75	98	41	120	2	.237	.443	3	1	C-127, DH-22
1985	140	549	150	27	1	28	5.1	64	98	41	90	2	.273	.479	1	1	C-120, DH-22
1986	91	327	84	6	1	22	6.7	53	62	38	83	0	.257	.483	4	0	C-85, DH-6
1987 PHI N	130	466	114	21	0	17	3.6	42	67	47	104	0	.245	.399	4	0	C-127
1988	123	424	91	17	2	15	3.5	44	60	47	93	0	.215	.370	3	2	C-117, 1B-1
12 yrs.	1399	5163	1328	239	25	244	4.7	663	827	428	1044	22	.257	.455	32	8	C-1283, DH-98, OF-6, 1B-6

LEAGUE CHAMPIONSHIP SERIES

	G	AB	H	2B	3B	HR	HR%	R	RBI	BB	SO	SB	BA	SA	AB	H	G by POS
1984 DET A	3	12	3	1	0	1	8.3	1	3	0	3	0	.250	.583	0	0	C-3

WORLD SERIES

	G	AB	H	2B	3B	HR	HR%	R	RBI	BB	SO	SB	BA	SA	AB	H	G by POS
1984 DET A	5	18	5	1	0	1	5.6	3	2	3	2	1	.278	.500	0	0	C-5

Larry Parrish

PARRISH, LARRY ALTON
B. Nov. 10, 1953, Winter Haven, Fla.

BR TR 6'3" 190 lbs.

	G	AB	H	2B	3B	HR	HR%	R	RBI	BB	SO	SB	BA	SA	AB	H	G by POS
1974 MON N	25	69	14	5	0	0	0.0	9	4	6	19	0	.203	.275	1	0	3B-24
1975	145	532	146	32	5	10	1.9	50	65	28	74	4	.274	.410	5	1	3B-143, SS-1, 2B-1
1976	154	543	126	28	5	11	2.0	65	61	41	91	2	.232	.363	1	0	3B-153
1977	123	402	99	19	2	11	2.7	50	46	37	71	2	.246	.386	14	4	3B-115
1978	144	520	144	39	4	15	2.9	68	70	32	103	2	.277	.454	5	3	3B-139
1979	153	544	167	39	2	30	5.5	83	82	41	101	5	.307	.551	0	0	3B-153
1980	126	452	115	27	3	15	3.3	55	72	36	80	2	.254	.427	1	0	3B-124
1981	97	349	85	19	3	8	2.3	41	44	28	73	0	.244	.384	1	0	3B-95
1982 TEX A	128	440	116	15	0	17	3.9	59	62	30	84	5	.264	.414	5	2	OF-124, 3B-3, DH-2
1983	145	555	151	26	4	26	4.7	76	88	46	91	0	.272	.474	0	0	OF-132, DH-13
1984	156	613	175	42	1	22	3.6	73	101	42	116	2	.285	.465	1	0	OF-81, DH-63, 3B-12
1985	94	346	86	11	1	17	4.9	44	51	33	77	0	.249	.434	1	0	OF-69, DH-22, 3B-2
1986	129	464	128	22	1	28	6.0	67	94	52	114	3	.276	.509	4	0	DH-99, 3B-30
1987	152	557	149	22	1	32	5.7	79	100	49	154	3	.268	.483	5	1	DH-122, 3B-28, OF-1
1988 2 teams		TEX A	(68G –	.190)		BOS A	(52G –	.259)									
" total	120	406	88	14	1	14	3.4	32	52	28	111	0	.217	.360	5	2	DH-81, 1B-36
15 yrs.	1891	6792	1789	360	33	256	3.8	851	992	529	1359	30	.263	.439	49	13	3B-1021, OF-407, DH-424, 1B-36, SS-1, 2B-1

DIVISIONAL PLAYOFF SERIES

	G	AB	H	2B	3B	HR	HR%	R	RBI	BB	SO	SB	BA	SA	AB	H	G by POS
1981 MON N	5	20	3	1	0	0	0.0	3	1	1	3	0	.150	.200	0	0	3B-5

LEAGUE CHAMPIONSHIP SERIES

	G	AB	H	2B	3B	HR	HR%	R	RBI	BB	SO	SB	BA	SA	AB	H	G by POS
1981 MON N	5	19	5	2	0	0	0.0	2	2	1	1	0	.263	.368	0	0	3B-5
1988 BOS A	4	6	0	0	0	0	0.0	0	0	0	2	0	.000	.000	3	0	1B-2
2 yrs.	9	25	5	2	0	0	0.0	2	2	1	3	0	.200	.280	3	0	3B-5, 1B-2

Dan Pasqua

PASQUA, DANIEL ANTHONY
B. Oct. 17, 1961, Yonkers, N. Y.

BL TL 6' 205 lbs.

	G	AB	H	2B	3B	HR	HR%	R	RBI	BB	SO	SB	BA	SA	AB	H	G by POS
1985 NY A	60	148	31	3	1	9	6.1	17	25	16	38	0	.209	.426	15	2	OF-37, DH-14
1986	102	280	82	17	0	16	5.7	44	45	47	78	2	.293	.525	22	7	OF-81, 1B-5, DH-3
1987	113	318	74	7	1	17	5.3	42	42	40	99	0	.233	.421	22	3	OF-86, DH-20
1988 CHI A	129	422	96	16	2	20	4.7	48	50	46	100	1	.227	.417	15	1	OF-112, 1B-7, DH-2
4 yrs.	404	1168	283	43	4	62	5.3	151	162	149	315	3	.242	.445	74	13	OF-316, DH-39, 1B-12

Bill Pecota

PECOTA, WILLIAM JOSEPH
B. Feb. 16, 1960, Redwood City, Calif.

BR TR 6'2" 195 lbs.

	G	AB	H	2B	3B	HR	HR%	R	RBI	BB	SO	SB	BA	SA	AB	H	G by POS
1986 KC A	12	29	6	2	0	0	0.0	3	2	3	3	0	.207	.276	0	0	3B-12, SS-2
1987	66	156	43	5	1	3	1.9	22	14	15	25	5	.276	.378	7	0	SS-36, 3B-17, 2B-15
1988	90	178	37	3	3	1	0.6	25	15	18	34	7	.208	.275	1	1	SS-41, 3B-21, 1B-11, OF-9, DH-4, 2B-3, C-1
3 yrs.	168	363	86	10	4	4	1.1	50	31	36	62	12	.237	.320	8	1	SS-79, 3B-50, 2B-18, 1B-11, OF-9, DH-4, C-1

	G	AB	H	2B	3B	HR	HR %	R	RBI	BB	SO	SB	BA	SA	Pinch Hit AB	Pinch Hit H	G by POS

Al Pedrique

PEDRIQUE, ALFREDO JOSE
Born Alfredo Jose Pedrique y Garcia.
B. Aug. 11, 1960, Aragua, Venezuela
BR TR 6'   155 lbs.

	G	AB	H	2B	3B	HR	HR%	R	RBI	BB	SO	SB	BA	SA	PH AB	PH H	G by POS
1987 2 teams							NY N (5G – .000)		PIT N (88G – .301)								
" total	93	252	74	10	1	1	0.4	24	27	19	29	5	.294	.353	7	0	SS-80, 3B-3, 2B-3
1988 PIT N	50	128	23	5	0	0	0.0	7	4	8	17	0	.180	.219	1	0	SS-46, 3B-5
2 yrs.	143	380	97	15	1	1	0.3	31	31	27	46	5	.255	.308	8	0	SS-126, 3B-8, 2B-3

Tony Pena

PENA, ANTONIO FRANCESCO PADILLA
Born Antonio Francesco Pena y Padilla.
B. June 4, 1957, Monte Cristi, Dominican Republic
BR TR 6'   175 lbs.

	G	AB	H	2B	3B	HR	HR%	R	RBI	BB	SO	SB	BA	SA	PH AB	PH H	G by POS
1980 PIT N	8	21	9	1	1	0	0.0	1	1	0	4	0	.429	.571	2	1	C-6
1981	66	210	63	9	1	2	1.0	16	17	8	23	1	.300	.381	2	1	C-64
1982	138	497	147	28	4	11	2.2	53	63	17	57	2	.296	.435	0	0	C-137
1983	151	542	163	22	3	15	2.8	51	70	31	73	6	.301	.435	1	0	C-149
1984	147	546	156	27	2	15	2.7	77	78	36	79	12	.286	.425	1	1	C-146
1985	147	546	136	27	2	10	1.8	53	59	29	67	12	.249	.361	0	0	C-146, 1B-1
1986	144	510	147	26	2	10	2.0	56	52	53	69	9	.288	.406	7	1	C-139, 1B-4
1987 STL N	116	384	82	13	4	5	1.3	40	44	36	54	6	.214	.307	4	1	C-112, 1B-4, OF-2
1988	149	505	133	23	1	10	2.0	55	51	33	60	6	.263	.372	8	1	C-142, 1B-3
9 yrs.	1066	3761	1036	176	20	78	2.1	402	435	243	486	54	.275	.395	26	7	C-1041, 1B-12, OF-2

LEAGUE CHAMPIONSHIP SERIES

	G	AB	H	2B	3B	HR	HR%	R	RBI	BB	SO	SB	BA	SA	PH AB	PH H	G by POS
1987 STL N	7	21	8	0	1	0	0.0	5	0	3	4	1	.381	.476	0	0	C-7

WORLD SERIES

	G	AB	H	2B	3B	HR	HR%	R	RBI	BB	SO	SB	BA	SA	PH AB	PH H	G by POS
1987 STL N	7	22	9	1	0	0	0.0	2	4	3	2	1	.409	.455	0	0	C-6

Terry Pendleton

PENDLETON, TERRY LEE
B. July 16, 1960, Los Angeles, Calif.
BB TR 5'9"   180 lbs.

	G	AB	H	2B	3B	HR	HR%	R	RBI	BB	SO	SB	BA	SA	PH AB	PH H	G by POS
1984 STL N	67	262	85	16	3	1	0.4	37	33	16	32	20	.324	.420	1	0	3B-66
1985	149	559	134	16	3	5	0.9	56	69	37	75	17	.240	.306	2	1	3B-149
1986	159	578	138	26	5	1	0.2	56	59	34	59	24	.239	.306	3	0	3B-156, OF-1
1987	159	583	167	29	4	12	2.1	82	96	70	74	19	.286	.412	1	1	3B-158
1988	110	391	99	20	2	6	1.5	44	53	21	51	3	.253	.361	11	4	3B-101
5 yrs.	644	2373	623	107	17	25	1.1	275	310	178	291	83	.263	.354	18	6	3B-630, OF-1

LEAGUE CHAMPIONSHIP SERIES

	G	AB	H	2B	3B	HR	HR%	R	RBI	BB	SO	SB	BA	SA	PH AB	PH H	G by POS
1985 STL N	6	24	5	1	0	0	0.0	2	4	1	2	0	.208	.250	0	0	3B-6
1987	6	19	4	0	1	0	0.0	3	1	0	6	0	.211	.316	0	0	3B-6
2 yrs.	12	43	9	1	1	0	0.0	5	5	1	8	0	.209	.279	0	0	3B-12

WORLD SERIES

	G	AB	H	2B	3B	HR	HR%	R	RBI	BB	SO	SB	BA	SA	PH AB	PH H	G by POS
1985 STL N	7	23	6	1	1	0	0.0	3	3	3	2	0	.261	.391	0	0	3B-7
1987	3	7	3	0	0	0	0.0	2	1	1	1	2	.429	.429	0	0	DH-2
2 yrs.	10	30	9	1	1	0	0.0	5	4	4	3	2	.300	.400	0	0	3B-7, DH-2

Tony Perezchica

PEREZCHICA, ANTONIO LLAMAS
B. Apr. 20, 1966, Mexicali, Mexico
BR TR 5'11"   165 lbs.

	G	AB	H	2B	3B	HR	HR%	R	RBI	BB	SO	SB	BA	SA	PH AB	PH H	G by POS
1988 SF N	7	8	1	0	0	0	0.0	1	1	2	1	0	.125	.125	0	0	2B-6

Gerald Perry

PERRY, GERALD JUNE
B. Oct. 30, 1960, Savannah, Ga.
BL TR 5'11"   172 lbs.

	G	AB	H	2B	3B	HR	HR%	R	RBI	BB	SO	SB	BA	SA	PH AB	PH H	G by POS
1983 ATL N	27	39	14	2	0	1	2.6	5	6	5	4	0	.359	.487	16	7	1B-7, OF-1
1984	122	347	92	12	2	7	2.0	52	47	61	38	15	.265	.372	16	8	1B-64, OF-53
1985	110	238	51	5	0	3	1.3	22	13	23	28	9	.214	.273	44	6	1B-55, OF-1
1986	29	70	19	2	0	2	2.9	6	11	8	4	0	.271	.386	11	3	OF-21, 1B-1
1987	142	533	144	35	2	12	2.3	77	74	48	63	42	.270	.411	5	1	1B-136, OF-7
1988	141	547	164	29	1	8	1.5	61	74	36	49	29	.300	.400	0	0	1B-141
6 yrs.	571	1774	484	85	5	33	1.9	223	225	181	186	95	.273	.382	92	25	1B-404, OF-83

Geno Petralli

PETRALLI, EUGENE JAMES
B. Sept. 25, 1959, Sacramento, Calif.
BB TR 6'1"   180 lbs.

	G	AB	H	2B	3B	HR	HR%	R	RBI	BB	SO	SB	BA	SA	PH AB	PH H	G by POS
1982 TOR A	16	44	16	2	0	0	0.0	3	1	4	6	0	.364	.409	3	1	C-12, 3B-3
1983	6	4	0	0	0	0	0.0	0	0	1	1	0	.000	.000	1	0	C-5, DH-1
1984	3	3	0	0	0	0	0.0	0	0	0	0	0	.000	.000	2	0	DH-1, C-1
1985 TEX A	42	100	27	2	0	0	0.0	7	11	8	12	1	.270	.290	3	0	C-41
1986	69	137	35	9	3	2	1.5	17	18	5	14	3	.255	.409	22	4	C-41, 3B-15, DH-2, 2B-2
1987	101	202	61	11	2	7	3.5	28	31	27	29	0	.302	.480	26	5	C-63, 3B-17, 1B-5, 2B-4, OF-3, DH-2
1988	129	351	99	14	2	7	2.0	35	36	41	52	0	.282	.393	23	6	C-85, 3B-23, 3B-9, 2B-2, 1B-2
7 yrs.	366	841	238	38	7	16	1.9	90	97	86	114	5	.283	.402	80	16	C-248, 3B-44, DH-29, 2B-8, 1B-7, OF-3

Gary Pettis

PETTIS, GARY GEORGE
B. Apr. 3, 1958, Oakland, Calif.
BB TR 6'1"   165 lbs.

	G	AB	H	2B	3B	HR	HR%	R	RBI	BB	SO	SB	BA	SA	PH AB	PH H	G by POS
1982 CAL A	10	5	1	0	0	1	20.0	5	1	0	2	0	.200	.800	0	0	OF-8
1983	22	85	25	2	3	3	3.5	19	6	7	15	8	.294	.494	0	0	OF-21
1984	140	397	90	11	6	2	0.5	63	29	60	115	48	.227	.300	2	0	OF-134
1985	125	443	114	10	8	1	0.2	67	32	62	125	56	.257	.323	0	0	OF-122
1986	154	539	139	23	4	5	0.9	93	58	69	132	50	.258	.343	0	0	OF-153, DH-1
1987	133	394	82	13	2	1	0.3	49	17	52	124	24	.208	.259	0	0	OF-131
1988 DET A	129	458	96	14	4	3	0.7	65	36	47	85	44	.210	.277	2	0	OF-126, DH-2
7 yrs.	713	2321	547	73	27	16	0.7	361	179	297	598	230	.236	.311	4	0	OF-695, DH-3

LEAGUE CHAMPIONSHIP SERIES

	G	AB	H	2B	3B	HR	HR%	R	RBI	BB	SO	SB	BA	SA	PH AB	PH H	G by POS
1986 CAL A	7	26	9	1	0	1	3.8	4	4	3	5	0	.346	.500	0	0	OF-7

	G	AB	H	2B	3B	HR	HR%	R	RBI	BB	SO	SB	BA	SA	Pinch Hit AB	Pinch Hit H	G by POS

Ken Phelps

PHELPS, KENNETH ALLEN
B. Aug. 6, 1954, Seattle, Wash. BL TL 6'1" 209 lbs.

	G	AB	H	2B	3B	HR	HR%	R	RBI	BB	SO	SB	BA	SA	Pinch Hit AB	Pinch Hit H	G by POS
1980 KC A	3	4	0	0	0	0	0.0	0	0	0	2	0	.000	.000	1	0	1B-2
1981	21	22	3	0	1	0	0.0	1	1	1	13	0	.136	.227	15	2	DH-4, 1B-2
1982 MON N	10	8	2	0	0	0	0.0	0	0	0	3	0	.250	.250	8	2	
1983 SEA A	50	127	30	4	1	7	5.5	10	16	13	25	0	.236	.449	11	3	1B-22, DH-19
1984	101	290	70	9	0	24	8.3	52	51	61	73	3	.241	.521	15	2	DH-84, 1B-9
1985	61	116	24	3	0	9	7.8	18	24	24	33	2	.207	.466	25	5	DH-25, 1B-8
1986	125	344	85	16	4	24	7.0	69	64	88	96	2	.247	.526	16	3	1B-55, DH-52
1987	120	332	86	13	1	27	8.1	68	68	80	75	1	.259	.548	12	2	DH-114, 1B-1
1988 2 teams		SEA A (72G – .284)						NY A (45G – .224)									
" total	117	297	78	13	0	24	8.1	54	54	70	61	1	.263	.549	17	2	DH-92, 1B-4
9 yrs.	608	1540	378	58	7	115	7.5	272	278	337	381	9	.245	.516	120	21	DH-390, 1B-103

Tony Phillips

PHILLIPS, KEITH ANTHONY
B. Apr. 25, 1959, Atlanta, Ga. BB TR 5'10" 160 lbs.

	G	AB	H	2B	3B	HR	HR%	R	RBI	BB	SO	SB	BA	SA	Pinch Hit AB	Pinch Hit H	G by POS
1982 OAK A	40	81	17	2	2	0	0.0	11	8	12	26	2	.210	.284	0	0	SS-39
1983	148	412	102	12	3	4	1.0	54	35	48	70	16	.248	.320	1	1	SS-101, 2B-63, 3B-4, DH-1
1984	154	451	120	24	3	4	0.9	62	37	42	86	10	.266	.359	2	0	SS-91, 2B-90, OF-1
1985	42	161	45	12	2	4	2.5	23	17	13	34	3	.280	.453	1	0	3B-31, 2B-24
1986	118	441	113	14	5	5	1.1	76	52	76	82	15	.256	.345	0	0	2B-88, 3B-30, OF-4, DH-2, SS-1
1987	111	379	91	20	0	10	2.6	48	46	57	76	7	.240	.372	6	1	2B-87, 3B-11, SS-9, OF-2
1988	79	212	43	8	4	2	0.9	32	17	36	50	0	.203	.307	5	1	3B-32, OF-31, 2B-27, SS-10, 1B-3
7 yrs.	692	2137	531	92	19	29	1.4	306	212	284	424	53	.248	.350	15	3	2B-379, SS-251, 3B-108, OF-38, DH-3, 1B-3

LEAGUE CHAMPIONSHIP SERIES

	G	AB	H	2B	3B	HR	HR%	R	RBI	BB	SO	SB	BA	SA	Pinch Hit AB	Pinch Hit H	G by POS
1988 OAK A	2	7	2	1	0	0	0.0	0	0	1	3	0	.286	.429	0	0	2B-1

WORLD SERIES

	G	AB	H	2B	3B	HR	HR%	R	RBI	BB	SO	SB	BA	SA	Pinch Hit AB	Pinch Hit H	G by POS
1988 OAK A	2	4	1	0	0	0	0.0	1	0	1	2	0	.250	.250	0	0	2B-1

Gus Polidor

POLIDOR, GUSTAVO ADOLFO
Born Gustavo Adolfo Polidor y Gonzalez.
B. Oct. 26, 1961, Caracas, Venezuela BR TR 6' 170 lbs.

	G	AB	H	2B	3B	HR	HR%	R	RBI	BB	SO	SB	BA	SA	Pinch Hit AB	Pinch Hit H	G by POS
1985 CAL A	2	1	1	0	0	0	0.0	1	0	0	0	0	1.000	1.000	0	0	OF-1, SS-1
1986	6	19	5	1	0	0	0.0	1	1	1	0	0	.263	.316	0	0	2B-4, SS-1, 3B-1
1987	63	137	36	3	0	2	1.5	12	15	2	15	0	.263	.328	3	1	SS-46, 3B-11, 2B-3
1988	54	81	12	3	0	0	0.0	4	4	3	11	0	.148	.185	8	2	SS-25, 3B-22, 2B-3
4 yrs.	125	238	54	7	0	2	0.8	18	20	6	26	0	.227	.282	11	3	SS-73, 3B-34, 2B-10, OF-1

Luis Polonia

POLONIA, LUIS ANDREW
Born Luis Andrew Polonia y Almonte.
B. Dec. 10, 1964, Santiago, Dominican Republic BB TL 5'8" 155 lbs.

	G	AB	H	2B	3B	HR	HR%	R	RBI	BB	SO	SB	BA	SA	Pinch Hit AB	Pinch Hit H	G by POS
1987 OAK A	125	435	125	16	10	4	0.9	78	49	32	64	29	.287	.398	8	3	OF-104, DH-18
1988	84	288	84	11	4	2	0.7	51	27	21	40	24	.292	.378	9	2	OF-76, DH-2
2 yrs.	209	723	209	27	14	6	0.8	129	76	53	104	53	.289	.390	17	5	OF-180, DH-20

LEAGUE CHAMPIONSHIP SERIES

	G	AB	H	2B	3B	HR	HR%	R	RBI	BB	SO	SB	BA	SA	Pinch Hit AB	Pinch Hit H	G by POS
1988 OAK A	3	5	2	0	0	0	0.0	0	0	1	2	0	.400	.400	0	0	OF-1

WORLD SERIES

	G	AB	H	2B	3B	HR	HR%	R	RBI	BB	SO	SB	BA	SA	Pinch Hit AB	Pinch Hit H	G by POS
1988 OAK A	3	9	1	0	0	0	0.0	0	0	0	2	0	.111	.111	2	0	OF-2

Jim Presley

PRESLEY, JAMES ARTHUR
B. Oct. 23, 1961, Pensacola, Fla. BR TR 6'1" 176 lbs.

	G	AB	H	2B	3B	HR	HR%	R	RBI	BB	SO	SB	BA	SA	Pinch Hit AB	Pinch Hit H	G by POS
1984 SEA A	70	251	57	12	1	10	4.0	27	36	6	63	1	.227	.402	1	0	3B-69, DH-1
1985	155	570	157	33	1	28	4.9	71	84	44	100	2	.275	.484	1	0	3B-154
1986	155	616	163	33	4	27	4.4	83	107	32	172	0	.265	.463	0	0	3B-155
1987	152	575	142	23	6	24	4.2	78	88	38	157	2	.247	.433	1	1	3B-148, SS-4, DH-1
1988	150	544	125	26	0	14	2.6	50	62	36	114	3	.230	.355	0	0	3B-146, DH-4
5 yrs.	682	2556	644	127	12	103	4.0	309	377	156	606	8	.252	.432	3	1	3B-672, DH-6, SS-4

Tom Prince

PRINCE, THOMAS ALBERT
B. Aug. 13, 1964, Kankakee, Ill. BR TR 5'11" 185 lbs.

	G	AB	H	2B	3B	HR	HR%	R	RBI	BB	SO	SB	BA	SA	Pinch Hit AB	Pinch Hit H	G by POS
1987 PIT N	4	9	2	1	0	1	11.1	1	2	0	2	0	.222	.667	0	0	C-4
1988	29	74	13	2	0	0	0.0	3	6	4	15	0	.176	.203	2	0	C-28
2 yrs.	33	83	15	3	0	1	1.2	4	8	4	17	0	.181	.253	2	0	C-32

Kirby Puckett

PUCKETT, KIRBY
B. Mar. 14, 1961, Chicago, Ill. BR TR 5'8" 178 lbs.

	G	AB	H	2B	3B	HR	HR%	R	RBI	BB	SO	SB	BA	SA	Pinch Hit AB	Pinch Hit H	G by POS
1984 MIN A	128	557	165	12	5	0	0.0	63	31	16	69	14	.296	.336	0	0	OF-128
1985	161	691	199	29	13	4	0.6	80	74	41	87	21	.288	.385	1	0	OF-161
1986	161	680	223	37	6	31	4.6	119	96	34	99	20	.328	.537	4	1	OF-160
1987	157	624	207	32	5	28	4.5	96	99	32	91	12	.332	.534	2	0	OF-147, DH-8
1988	158	657	234	42	5	24	3.7	109	121	23	83	6	.356	.545	1	0	OF-158
5 yrs.	765	3209	1028	152	34	87	2.7	467	421	146	429	73	.320	.470	8	1	OF-754, DH-8

LEAGUE CHAMPIONSHIP SERIES

	G	AB	H	2B	3B	HR	HR%	R	RBI	BB	SO	SB	BA	SA	Pinch Hit AB	Pinch Hit H	G by POS
1987 MIN A	5	24	5	1	0	1	4.2	3	3	0	5	1	.208	.375	0	0	OF-5

WORLD SERIES

	G	AB	H	2B	3B	HR	HR%	R	RBI	BB	SO	SB	BA	SA	Pinch Hit AB	Pinch Hit H	G by POS
1987 MIN A	7	28	10	1	1	0	0.0	5	3	2	1	1	.357	.464	0	0	OF-7

Terry Puhl

PUHL, TERRY STEPHEN   BL TR 6'2"   195 lbs.
B. July 8, 1956, Melville, Sask., Canada

	G	AB	H	2B	3B	HR	HR%	R	RBI	BB	SO	SB	BA	SA	Pinch Hit AB	Pinch Hit H	G by POS
1977 HOU N	60	229	69	13	5	0	0.0	40	10	30	31	10	.301	.402	0	0	OF-59
1978	149	585	169	25	6	3	0.5	87	35	48	46	32	.289	.368	1	1	OF-148
1979	157	600	172	22	4	8	1.3	87	49	58	46	30	.287	.377	5	1	OF-152
1980	141	535	151	24	5	13	2.4	75	55	60	52	27	.282	.419	6	0	OF-135
1981	96	350	88	19	4	3	0.9	43	28	31	49	22	.251	.354	8	1	OF-88
1982	145	507	133	17	9	8	1.6	64	50	51	49	17	.262	.379	7	3	OF-138
1983	137	465	136	25	7	8	1.7	66	44	36	48	24	.292	.428	15	4	OF-124
1984	132	449	135	19	7	9	2.0	66	55	59	45	13	.301	.434	5	2	OF-126
1985	57	194	55	14	3	2	1.0	34	23	18	23	6	.284	.418	3	1	OF-53
1986	81	172	42	10	0	3	1.7	17	14	15	24	3	.244	.355	28	8	OF-47
1987	90	122	28	5	0	2	1.6	9	15	11	16	1	.230	.320	52	15	OF-40
1988	113	234	71	7	2	3	1.3	42	19	35	30	22	.303	.389	36	11	OF-78
12 yrs.	1358	4442	1249	200	52	62	1.4	630	397	452	459	207	.281	.391	166	47	OF-1188

DIVISIONAL PLAYOFF SERIES

	G	AB	H	2B	3B	HR	HR%	R	RBI	BB	SO	SB	BA	SA	Pinch Hit AB	Pinch Hit H	G by POS
1981 HOU N	5	21	4	1	0	0	0.0	2	0	0	1	1	.190	.238	0	0	OF-5

LEAGUE CHAMPIONSHIP SERIES

	G	AB	H	2B	3B	HR	HR%	R	RBI	BB	SO	SB	BA	SA	Pinch Hit AB	Pinch Hit H	G by POS
1980 HOU N	5	19	10	2	0	0	0.0	4	3	3	2	2	.526	.632	1	0	OF-4
1986	3	3	2	0	0	0	0.0	0	0	0	0	1	.667	.667	3	2	
2 yrs.	8	22	12	2	0	0	0.0	4	3	3	2	3	.545	.636	4	2	OF-4

Luis Quinones

QUINONES, LUIS RAUL TORRUELLAS   BB TR 5'11"   165 lbs.
Born Luis Raul Quinones y Torruellas.
B. Apr. 28, 1962, Ponce, Puerto Rico

	G	AB	H	2B	3B	HR	HR%	R	RBI	BB	SO	SB	BA	SA	Pinch Hit AB	Pinch Hit H	G by POS
1983 OAK A	19	42	8	2	1	0	0.0	5	4	1	4	1	.190	.286	1	1	2B-6, DH-4, OF-4, 3B-4, SS-3
1986 SF N	71	106	19	1	3	0	0.0	13	11	3	17	3	.179	.245	7	0	SS-33, 3B-31, 2B-8
1987 CHI N	49	101	22	6	0	0	0.0	12	8	10	16	0	.218	.277	23	4	SS-28, 2B-4, 3B-1
1988 CIN N	23	52	12	3	0	1	1.9	4	11	2	11	1	.231	.346	6	1	SS-10, 3B-4, 2B-1
4 yrs.	162	301	61	12	4	1	0.3	34	34	16	48	5	.203	.279	37	6	SS-74, 3B-40, 2B-22, DH-4, OF-4

Rey Quinones

QUINONES, REY FRANCISCO   BR TR 5'11"   160 lbs.
Born Rey Francisco Quinones y Santiago.
B. Nov. 11, 1963, Rio Piedras, Puerto Rico

	G	AB	H	2B	3B	HR	HR%	R	RBI	BB	SO	SB	BA	SA	Pinch Hit AB	Pinch Hit H	G by POS
1986 2 teams		BOS	A	(62G –	.237)		SEA	A	(36G –	.189)							
" total	98	312	68	16	1	2	0.6	32	22	24	57	4	.218	.295	0	0	SS-98
1987 SEA A	135	478	132	18	2	12	2.5	55	56	26	71	1	.276	.397	0	0	SS-135
1988	140	499	124	30	3	12	2.4	63	52	23	71	0	.248	.393	2	0	SS-135, DH-4
3 yrs.	373	1289	324	64	6	26	2.0	150	130	73	199	5	.251	.371	2	0	SS-368, DH-4

Carlos Quintana

QUINTANA, CARLOS NARCIS   BR TR 6'   175 lbs.
B. Aug. 26, 1965, Estado, Mirana, Venezuela

	G	AB	H	2B	3B	HR	HR%	R	RBI	BB	SO	SB	BA	SA	Pinch Hit AB	Pinch Hit H	G by POS
1988 BOS A	5	6	2	0	0	0	0.0	1	2	2	3	0	.333	.333	0	0	OF-3, DH-1

Jamie Quirk

QUIRK, JAMES PATRICK   BL TR 6'4"   190 lbs.
B. Oct. 22, 1954, Whittier, Calif.

	G	AB	H	2B	3B	HR	HR%	R	RBI	BB	SO	SB	BA	SA	Pinch Hit AB	Pinch Hit H	G by POS
1975 KC A	14	39	10	0	0	1	2.6	2	5	2	7	0	.256	.333	1	1	OF-10, 3B-2, DH-1
1976	64	114	28	6	0	1	0.9	11	15	2	22	0	.246	.325	32	7	DH-19, SS-12, 3B-11, 1B-2
1977 MIL A	93	221	48	14	1	3	1.4	16	13	8	47	0	.217	.330	29	5	DH-53, OF-10, 3B-8
1978 KC A	17	29	6	2	0	0	0.0	3	2	5	4	0	.207	.276	4	2	3B-10, SS-2, DH-1
1979	51	79	24	6	1	1	1.3	8	11	5	13	0	.304	.443	30	3	DH-9, C-9, SS-5, 3B-3
1980	62	163	45	5	0	5	3.1	13	21	7	24	3	.276	.399	12	1	3B-28, C-15, OF-7, 1B-1
1981	46	100	25	7	0	0	0.0	8	10	6	17	0	.250	.320	18	4	C-22, 3B-8, DH-1, 2B-1
1982	36	78	18	3	0	1	1.3	8	5	3	15	0	.231	.308	7	1	C-29, 1B-6, OF-1, 3B-1
1983 STL N	48	86	18	2	1	2	2.3	3	11	6	27	0	.209	.326	17	1	C-22, 3B-7, SS-1
1984 2 teams		CHI	A	(3G –	.000)		CLE	A	(1G –	1.000)							
" total	4	3	1	0	0	0	33.3	1	2	0	2	0	.333	1.333	2	0	3B-1, C-1
1985 KC A	19	57	16	3	1	0	0.0	3	4	2	9	0	.281	.368	4	0	C-17, 1B-1
1986	80	219	47	10	0	8	3.7	24	26	17	41	0	.215	.370	20	4	C-41, SS-24, 1B-6, OF-1
1987	109	296	70	17	0	5	1.7	24	33	28	56	1	.236	.345	5	2	C-108, SS-1
1988	84	196	47	7	1	8	4.1	22	25	28	41	1	.240	.408	7	0	C-79, 3B-1, 1B-1
14 yrs.	727	1680	403	82	5	36	2.1	146	183	119	325	5	.240	.359	188	36	C-343, DH-84, 3B-80, SS-45, OF-29, 1B-17, 2B-1

LEAGUE CHAMPIONSHIP SERIES

	G	AB	H	2B	3B	HR	HR%	R	RBI	BB	SO	SB	BA	SA	Pinch Hit AB	Pinch Hit H	G by POS
1976 KC A	4	7	1	0	1	0	0.0	1	2	0	2	0	.143	.429	1	0	DH-2
1985	1	1	0	0	0	0	0.0	0	0	0	0	0	.000	.000	1	0	
2 yrs.	5	8	1	0	1	0	0.0	1	2	0	2	0	.125	.375	2	0	DH-2

Johnny Rabb

RABB, JOHN ANDREW   BR TR 6'1"   179 lbs.
B. June 23, 1960, Los Angeles, Calif.

	G	AB	H	2B	3B	HR	HR%	R	RBI	BB	SO	SB	BA	SA	Pinch Hit AB	Pinch Hit H	G by POS
1982 SF N	2	2	1	0	1	0	0.0	0	0	0	1	0	.500	1.500	1	0	OF-1
1983	40	104	24	9	0	1	1.0	10	14	9	17	1	.231	.346	6	2	C-31, OF-2
1984	54	82	16	1	0	3	3.7	10	9	10	33	1	.195	.317	28	2	1B-13, OF-8, C-6
1985 ATL N	3	2	0	0	0	0	0.0	0	0	0	1	0	.000	.000	2	0	OF-1
1988 SEA A	9	14	5	2	0	0	0.0	2	4	0	1	0	.357	.500	3	0	DH-5, OF-2, 1B-1
5 yrs.	108	204	46	12	1	4	2.0	22	27	19	53	2	.225	.353	40	4	C-37, OF-14, 1B-14, DH-5

Tim Raines

RAINES, TIMOTHY (Rock)   BB TR 5'8"   160 lbs.
B. Sept. 16, 1959, Sanford, Fla.

	G	AB	H	2B	3B	HR	HR%	R	RBI	BB	SO	SB	BA	SA	Pinch Hit AB	Pinch Hit H	G by POS
1979 MON N	6	0	0	0	0	0		3	0	0	0	2	–	–	0	0	2B-7, OF-1
1980	15	20	1	0	0	0	0.0	5	0	6	3	5	.050	.050	0	0	OF-81, 2B-1
1981	88	313	95	13	7	5	1.6	61	37	45	31	71	.304	.438	0	0	OF-81, 2B-1
1982	156	647	179	32	8	4	0.6	90	43	75	83	78	.277	.369	0	0	OF-120, 2B-36

	G	AB	H	2B	3B	HR	HR%	R	RBI	BB	SO	SB	BA	SA	Pinch Hit AB	Pinch Hit H	G by POS

Tim Raines continued

	G	AB	H	2B	3B	HR	HR%	R	RBI	BB	SO	SB	BA	SA	AB	H	G by POS
1983	156	615	183	32	8	11	1.8	**133**	71	97	70	**90**	.298	.429	1	1	OF-154, 2B-7
1984	160	622	192	**38**	9	8	1.3	106	60	87	69	**75**	.309	.437	0	0	OF-160, 2B-2
1985	150	575	184	30	13	11	1.9	115	41	81	60	70	.320	.475	7	0	OF-145
1986	151	580	194	35	10	9	1.6	91	62	78	60	70	**.334**	.476	4	1	OF-147
1987	139	530	175	34	8	18	3.4	**123**	68	90	52	50	.330	.526	0	0	OF-139
1988	109	429	116	19	7	12	2.8	66	48	53	44	33	.270	.431	1	0	OF-108
10 yrs.	1130	4331	1319	233	70	78	1.8	793	430	612	472	544	.305	.445	13	2	OF-1055, 2B-53

LEAGUE CHAMPIONSHIP SERIES

	G	AB	H	2B	3B	HR	HR%	R	RBI	BB	SO	SB	BA	SA	AB	H	G by POS
1981 **MON N**	5	21	5	2	0	0	0.0	1	1	0	3	0	.238	.333	0	0	OF-5

Rafael Ramirez

RAMIREZ, RAFAEL EMILIO PEGUERO (Raffy)
Born Rafael Emilio Ramirez y Peguero.
B. Feb. 18, 1958, San Pedro de Macoris, Dominican Republic

BR TR 6'   170 lbs.

	G	AB	H	2B	3B	HR	HR%	R	RBI	BB	SO	SB	BA	SA	AB	H	G by POS
1980 **ATL N**	50	165	44	6	1	2	1.2	17	11	2	33	2	.267	.352	0	0	SS-46
1981	95	307	67	16	2	2	0.7	30	20	24	47	7	.218	.303	0	0	SS-95
1982	157	609	169	24	4	10	1.6	74	52	36	49	27	.278	.379	0	0	SS-157
1983	152	622	185	13	5	7	1.1	82	58	36	48	16	.297	.368	1	0	SS-152
1984	145	591	157	22	4	2	0.3	51	48	26	70	14	.266	.327	0	0	SS-145
1985	138	568	141	25	4	5	0.9	54	58	20	63	2	.248	.333	3	2	SS-133
1986	134	496	119	21	1	8	1.6	57	33	21	60	19	.240	.335	5	1	SS-86, 3B-57, OF-3
1987	56	179	47	12	0	1	0.6	22	21	8	16	6	.263	.346	8	2	SS-38, 3B-12
1988 **HOU N**	155	566	156	30	5	6	1.1	51	59	18	61	3	.276	.378	4	3	SS-154
9 yrs.	1082	4103	1085	169	26	43	1.0	438	360	191	447	96	.264	.350	21	8	SS-1006, 3B-69, OF-3

LEAGUE CHAMPIONSHIP SERIES

	G	AB	H	2B	3B	HR	HR%	R	RBI	BB	SO	SB	BA	SA	AB	H	G by POS
1982 **ATL N**	3	11	2	0	0	0	0.0	1	1	1	1	0	.182	.182	0	0	SS-3

Domingo Ramos

RAMOS, DOMINGO ANTONIO de RAMOS
B. Mar. 29, 1958, Santiago, Dominican Republic

BR TR 5'10"   154 lbs.

	G	AB	H	2B	3B	HR	HR%	R	RBI	BB	SO	SB	BA	SA	AB	H	G by POS
1978 **NY A**	1	0	0	0	0	0	–	0	0	0	0	0	–	–	0	0	SS-1
1980 **TOR A**	5	16	2	0	0	0	0.0	0	0	2	5	0	.125	.125	0	0	SS-2, 2B-2
1982 **SEA A**	8	26	4	2	0	0	0.0	3	1	3	2	0	.154	.231	0	0	SS-8
1983	53	127	36	4	0	2	1.6	14	10	7	12	3	.283	.362	9	1	SS-28, 3B-8, 2B-8, DH-2
1984	59	81	15	2	0	0	0.0	6	2	5	12	2	.185	.210	2	0	3B-38, SS-13, 1B-5, 2B-3
1985	75	168	33	6	0	1	0.6	19	15	17	23	0	.196	.250	4	1	SS-36, 2B-20, 1B-14, 3B-7
1986	49	99	18	2	0	0	0.0	8	5	8	13	0	.182	.202	0	0	SS-21, 2B-16, 3B-8, DH-2
1987	42	103	32	6	0	2	1.9	9	11	3	12	0	.311	.427	1	0	SS-25, 3B-7, 2B-6
1988 2 teams	CLE	A	(22G –	.261)		CAL	A	(10G –	.133)								
" total	32	61	14	1	0	0	0.0	10	5	3	7	0	.230	.246	4	1	SS-11, 3B-10, 1B-5, SS-4, OF-1
9 yrs.	324	681	154	23	0	5	0.7	69	49	48	86	5	.226	.282	18	2	SS-138, 3B-78, 2B-66, 1B-24, DH-4, OF-1

Jim Randall

RANDALL, JAMES ODELL
B. Aug. 19, 1960, Mobile, Ala.

BB TR 5'11"   195 lbs.

	G	AB	H	2B	3B	HR	HR%	R	RBI	BB	SO	SB	BA	SA	AB	H	G by POS
1988 **CHI A**	4	12	0	0	0	0	0.0	1	1	2	3	0	.000	.000	0	0	1B-2, DH-1, OF-1

Willie Randolph

RANDOLPH, WILLIE LARRY
B. July 6, 1954, Holly Hill, S. C.

BR TR 5'11"   165 lbs.

	G	AB	H	2B	3B	HR	HR%	R	RBI	BB	SO	SB	BA	SA	AB	H	G by POS
1975 **PIT N**	30	61	10	1	0	0	0.0	9	3	7	6	1	.164	.180	8	2	2B-14, 3B-1
1976 **NY A**	125	430	115	15	4	1	0.2	59	40	58	39	37	.267	.328	1	0	2B-124
1977	147	551	151	28	11	4	0.7	91	40	64	53	13	.274	.387	0	0	2B-147
1978	134	499	139	18	6	3	0.6	87	42	82	51	36	.279	.357	0	0	2B-134
1979	153	574	155	15	13	5	0.9	98	61	95	39	33	.270	.368	0	0	2B-153
1980	138	513	151	23	7	7	1.4	99	46	**119**	45	30	.294	.407	0	0	2B-138
1981	93	357	83	14	3	2	0.6	59	24	57	24	14	.232	.305	0	0	2B-93
1982	144	553	155	21	4	3	0.5	85	36	75	35	16	.280	.349	0	0	2B-142, DH-1
1983	104	420	117	21	1	2	0.5	73	38	53	32	12	.279	.348	0	0	2B-104
1984	142	564	162	24	2	2	0.4	86	31	86	42	10	.287	.348	0	0	2B-142
1985	143	497	137	21	2	5	1.0	75	40	85	39	16	.276	.356	0	0	2B-143
1986	141	492	136	15	2	5	1.0	76	50	94	49	15	.276	.346	2	1	2B-139, DH-1
1987	120	449	137	24	2	7	1.6	96	67	82	25	11	.305	.414	0	0	2B-119, DH-1
1988	110	404	93	20	1	2	0.5	43	34	55	39	8	.230	.300	0	0	2B-110
14 yrs.	1724	6364	1741	260	58	48	0.8	1036	552	1012	518	252	.274	.355	11	3	2B-1702, DH-3, 3B-1

DIVISIONAL PLAYOFF SERIES

	G	AB	H	2B	3B	HR	HR%	R	RBI	BB	SO	SB	BA	SA	AB	H	G by POS
1981 **NY A**	5	20	4	0	0	0	0.0	0	1	1	4	0	.200	.200	0	0	2B-5

LEAGUE CHAMPIONSHIP SERIES

	G	AB	H	2B	3B	HR	HR%	R	RBI	BB	SO	SB	BA	SA	AB	H	G by POS
1975 **PIT N**	2	2	0	0	0	0	0.0	1	0	0	1	0	.000	.000	1	0	2B-1
1976 **NY A**	5	17	2	0	0	0	0.0	0	1	3	1	1	.118	.118	0	0	2B-5
1977	5	18	5	1	0	0	0.0	4	2	1	0	0	.278	.333	0	0	2B-5
1980	3	13	5	2	0	0	0.0	0	1	1	3	0	.385	.538	0	0	2B-3
1981	3	12	4	0	0	1	8.3	2	2	0	1	0	.333	.583	0	0	2B-3
5 yrs.	18	62	16	3	0	1	1.6	7	6	5	6	1	.258	.355	1	0	2B-17

WORLD SERIES

	G	AB	H	2B	3B	HR	HR%	R	RBI	BB	SO	SB	BA	SA	AB	H	G by POS
1976 **NY A**	4	14	1	0	0	0	0.0	1	0	1	3	0	.071	.071	0	0	2B-4
1977	6	25	4	2	0	1	4.0	5	1	2	2	0	.160	.360	0	0	2B-6
1981	6	18	4	1	1	2	11.1	5	3	9	0	1	.222	.722	0	0	2B-6
3 yrs.	16	57	9	3	1	3	5.3	11	4	12	5	1	.158	.404	0	0	2B-16

Johnny Ray

RAY, JOHNNY CORNELIUS
B. Mar. 1, 1957, Chouteau, Okla.

BB TR 5'11"   170 lbs.

	G	AB	H	2B	3B	HR	HR%	R	RBI	BB	SO	SB	BA	SA	AB	H	G by POS
1981 **PIT N**	31	102	25	11	0	0	0.0	10	6	6	9	0	.245	.353	2	1	2B-31
1982	162	647	182	30	7	7	1.1	79	63	36	34	16	.281	.382	0	0	2B-162
1983	151	576	163	**38**	7	5	0.9	68	53	35	26	18	.283	.399	5	1	2B-151, 3B-1
1984	155	555	173	**38**	6	6	1.1	75	67	37	31	11	.312	.434	9	3	2B-149

	G	AB	H	2B	3B	HR	HR %	R	RBI	BB	SO	SB	BA	SA	Pinch Hit AB	Pinch Hit H	G by POS

Johnny Ray continued

	G	AB	H	2B	3B	HR	HR %	R	RBI	BB	SO	SB	BA	SA	PH AB	PH H	G by POS
1985	154	594	163	33	3	7	1.2	67	70	46	24	13	.274	.375	4	1	2B-151
1986	155	579	174	33	0	7	1.2	67	78	58	47	6	.301	.394	8	2	2B-151
1987 2 teams		PIT	N	(123G –	.273)		CAL	A	(30G –	.346)							
" total	153	599	173	30	3	5	0.8	64	69	44	46	4	.289	.374	6	1	2B-148, DH-1
1988 CAL A	153	602	184	42	7	6	1.0	75	83	36	38	4	.306	.429	4	2	2B-104, OF-40, DH-6
8 yrs.	1114	4254	1237	255	33	43	1.0	505	489	298	255	72	.291	.397	38	11	2B-1047, OF-40, DH-7, 3B-1

Randy Ready

READY, RANDY MAX   BR TR 5'11"   175 lbs.
B. Jan. 8, 1960, San Mateo, Calif.

	G	AB	H	2B	3B	HR	HR %	R	RBI	BB	SO	SB	BA	SA	PH AB	PH H	G by POS
1983 MIL A	12	37	15	3	2	1	2.7	8	6	6	3	0	.405	.676	1	0	DH-6, 3B-3
1984	37	123	23	6	1	3	2.4	13	13	14	18	0	.187	.325	1	0	3B-36
1985	48	181	48	9	5	1	0.6	29	21	14	23	0	.265	.387	2	0	OF-37, 3B-7, 2B-3, DH-2
1986 2 teams		MIL	A	(23G –	.190)		SD	N	(1G –	.000)							
" total	24	82	15	4	0	1	1.2	8	4	9	10	2	.183	.268	2	0	OF-11, 2B-7, 3B-4, DH-1
1987 SD N	124	350	108	26	6	12	3.4	69	54	67	44	7	.309	.520	25	6	3B-52, 2B-51, OF-16
1988	114	331	88	16	2	7	2.1	43	39	39	38	6	.266	.390	24	5	3B-57, 2B-26, OF-16
6 yrs.	359	1104	297	64	16	25	2.3	170	137	149	136	15	.269	.424	55	11	3B-160, 2B-87, OF-80, DH-9

Joe Redfield

REDFIELD, JOSEPH RANDALL   BR TR 6'2"   185 lbs.
B. Jan. 14, 1961, Doylestown, Pa.

	G	AB	H	2B	3B	HR	HR %	R	RBI	BB	SO	SB	BA	SA	PH AB	PH H	G by POS
1988 CAL A	1	2	0	0	0	0	0.0	0	0	0	0	0	.000	.000	0	0	3B-1

Gary Redus

REDUS, GARY EUGENE   BR TR 6'1"   180 lbs.
B. Nov. 1, 1956, Tanner, Ala.

	G	AB	H	2B	3B	HR	HR %	R	RBI	BB	SO	SB	BA	SA	PH AB	PH H	G by POS
1982 CIN N	20	83	18	3	2	1	1.2	12	7	5	21	11	.217	.337	0	0	OF-20
1983	125	453	112	20	9	17	3.8	90	51	71	111	39	.247	.444	4	2	OF-120
1984	123	394	100	21	3	7	1.8	69	22	52	71	48	.254	.376	10	3	OF-114
1985	101	246	62	14	4	6	2.4	51	28	44	52	48	.252	.415	17	6	OF-85
1986 PHI N	90	340	84	22	4	11	3.2	62	33	47	78	25	.247	.432	2	0	OF-89
1987 CHI A	130	475	112	26	6	12	2.5	78	48	69	90	52	.236	.392	0	0	OF-123, DH-4
1988 2 teams		CHI	A	(77G –	.263)		PIT	N	(30G –	.197)							
" total	107	333	83	12	4	8	2.4	54	38	48	71	31	.249	.381	16	4	OF-87, DH-2
7 yrs.	696	2324	571	118	32	62	2.7	416	227	336	494	254	.246	.404	49	15	OF-638, DH-6

Jeff Reed

REED, JEFFREY SCOTT   BL TR 6'2"   185 lbs.
B. Nov. 12, 1962, Joliet, Ill.

	G	AB	H	2B	3B	HR	HR %	R	RBI	BB	SO	SB	BA	SA	PH AB	PH H	G by POS
1984 MIN A	18	21	3	3	0	0	0.0	3	1	2	6	0	.143	.286	0	0	C-18
1985	7	10	2	0	0	0	0.0	2	0	0	3	0	.200	.200	1	0	C-7
1986	68	165	39	6	1	2	1.2	13	9	16	19	1	.236	.321	7	3	C-64
1987 MON N	75	207	44	11	0	1	0.5	15	21	12	20	0	.213	.280	5	1	C-74
1988 2 teams		MON	N	(43G –	.220)		CIN	N	(49G –	.232)							
" total	92	265	60	9	2	1	0.4	20	16	28	41	1	.226	.287	6	1	C-88
5 yrs.	260	668	148	29	3	4	0.6	53	47	58	89	2	.222	.292	19	5	C-251

Jody Reed

REED, JODY ERIC   BR TR 5'9"   170 lbs.
B. July 26, 1962, Tampa, Fla.

	G	AB	H	2B	3B	HR	HR %	R	RBI	BB	SO	SB	BA	SA	PH AB	PH H	G by POS
1987 BOS A	9	30	9	1	1	0	0.0	4	8	4	0	1	.300	.400	0	0	SS-6, 2B-2, 3B-1
1988	109	338	99	23	1	1	0.3	60	28	45	21	1	.293	.376	0	0	SS-94, 2B-11, 3B-4
2 yrs.	118	368	108	24	2	1	0.3	64	36	49	21	2	.293	.378	0	0	SS-100, 2B-13, 3B-5

LEAGUE CHAMPIONSHIP SERIES

	G	AB	H	2B	3B	HR	HR %	R	RBI	BB	SO	SB	BA	SA	PH AB	PH H	G by POS
1988 BOS A	4	11	3	1	1	0	0.0	0	0	2	1	0	.273	.364	0	0	SS-4

Jessie Reid

REID, JESSIE THOMAS   BL TL 6'1"   200 lbs.
B. June 1, 1962, Honolulu, Hawaii

	G	AB	H	2B	3B	HR	HR %	R	RBI	BB	SO	SB	BA	SA	PH AB	PH H	G by POS
1987 SF N	6	8	1	0	0	1	12.5	1	1	1	5	0	.125	.500	5	0	OF-3
1988	2	2	0	0	0	0	0.0	0	0	0	1	0	.000	.000	2	0	
2 yrs.	8	10	1	0	0	1	10.0	1	1	1	6	0	.100	.400	7	0	OF-3

Kevin Reimer

REIMER, KEVIN MICHAEL   BL TR 6'2"   215 lbs.
B. June 28, 1964, Macon, Ga.

	G	AB	H	2B	3B	HR	HR %	R	RBI	BB	SO	SB	BA	SA	PH AB	PH H	G by POS
1988 TEX A	12	25	3	0	0	1	4.0	2	2	0	6	0	.120	.240	5	0	DH-7, OF-1

Rich Renteria

RENTERIA, RICHARD AVINA   BR TR 5'9"   172 lbs.
B. Dec. 25, 1961, Harbor City, Calif.

	G	AB	H	2B	3B	HR	HR %	R	RBI	BB	SO	SB	BA	SA	PH AB	PH H	G by POS
1986 PIT N	10	12	3	1	0	0	0.0	2	1	0	4	0	.250	.333	9	2	3B-1
1987 SEA A	12	10	1	1	0	0	0.0	2	0	1	2	1	.100	.200	3	0	DH-4, 2B-4, SS-1
1988	31	88	18	9	0	0	0.0	6	6	2	8	1	.205	.307	7	1	SS-11, 3B-5, 2B-4
3 yrs.	53	110	22	11	0	0	0.0	10	7	3	14	2	.200	.300	19	3	SS-12, 2B-8, 3B-6, DH-4

Gilberto Reyes

REYES, GILBERTO ROLANDO POLANCO   BR TR 6'3"   195 lbs.
Born Gilberto Rolando Reyes y Polanco.
B. Dec. 10, 1963, Santo Domingo, Dominican Republic

	G	AB	H	2B	3B	HR	HR %	R	RBI	BB	SO	SB	BA	SA	PH AB	PH H	G by POS
1983 LA N	19	31	5	2	0	0	0.0	1	0	0	5	0	.161	.226	0	0	C-19
1984	4	5	0	0	0	0	0.0	0	0	0	3	0	.000	.000	2	0	C-2
1985	6	1	0	0	0	0	0.0	0	0	0	1	0	.000	.000	1	0	C-6
1987	1	0	0	0	0	0	–	0	0	0	0	0	–	–	0	0	C-1
1988	5	9	1	0	0	0	0.0	1	0	0	3	0	.111	.111	1	0	C-5
5 yrs.	35	46	6	2	0	0	0.0	2	0	0	12	0	.130	.174	4	0	C-33

	G	AB	H	2B	3B	HR	HR %	R	RBI	BB	SO	SB	BA	SA	Pinch Hit AB	Pinch Hit H	G by POS

Craig Reynolds

REYNOLDS, GORDON CRAIG
B. Dec. 27, 1952, Houston, Tex.

BL TR 6'1" 175 lbs.

	G	AB	H	2B	3B	HR	HR %	R	RBI	BB	SO	SB	BA	SA	PH AB	PH H	G by POS
1975 PIT N	31	76	17	3	0	0	0.0	8	4	3	5	0	.224	.263	1	1	SS-30
1976	7	4	1	0	0	1	25.0	1	1	0	0	0	.250	1.000	0	0	SS-4, 2B-1
1977 SEA A	135	420	104	12	3	4	1.0	41	28	15	23	6	.248	.319	2	1	SS-134
1978	148	548	160	16	7	5	0.9	57	44	36	41	9	.292	.374	1	0	SS-146
1979 HOU N	146	555	147	20	9	0	0.0	63	39	21	49	12	.265	.333	5	1	SS-143
1980	137	381	86	9	6	3	0.8	34	28	20	39	2	.226	.304	2	0	SS-135
1981	87	323	84	10	12	4	1.2	43	31	12	31	3	.260	.402	2	1	SS-85
1982	54	118	30	2	3	1	0.8	16	7	11	9	3	.254	.347	5	0	SS-35, 3B-7
1983	65	98	21	3	0	1	1.0	10	6	6	10	0	.214	.276	12	2	2B-26, 3B-15, SS-8, OF-1
1984	146	527	137	15	11	6	1.1	61	60	22	53	7	.260	.364	4	2	SS-143, 3B-1
1985	107	379	103	18	8	4	1.1	43	32	12	30	4	.272	.393	10	3	SS-102, 2B-1
1986	114	313	78	7	3	6	1.9	32	41	12	31	3	.249	.348	22	9	SS-98, 1B-5, 3B-4, OF-2, P-1
1987	135	374	95	17	3	4	1.1	35	28	30	44	5	.254	.348	12	3	SS-129, 3B-2
1988	78	161	41	7	0	1	0.6	20	14	8	23	3	.255	.317	22	4	SS-22, 3B-19, 2B-11, 1B-10
14 yrs.	1390	4277	1104	139	65	40	0.9	464	363	208	388	57	.258	.349	100	27	SS-1214, 3B-48, 2B-39, 1B-15, OF-3, P-1

DIVISIONAL PLAYOFF SERIES

	G	AB	H	2B	3B	HR	HR %	R	RBI	BB	SO	SB	BA	SA	PH AB	PH H	G by POS
1981 HOU N	2	3	1	0	0	0	0.0	1	0	0	1	0	.333	.333	1	1	SS-1

LEAGUE CHAMPIONSHIP SERIES

	G	AB	H	2B	3B	HR	HR %	R	RBI	BB	SO	SB	BA	SA	PH AB	PH H	G by POS
1975 PIT N	2	1	0	0	0	0	0.0	0	0	0	0	0	.000	.000	0	0	SS-1
1980 HOU N	4	13	2	1	0	0	0.0	2	0	3	1	0	.154	.231	0	0	SS-4
1986	4	12	4	0	0	0	0.0	1	0	1	3	0	.333	.333	1	0	SS-4
3 yrs.	10	26	6	1	0	0	0.0	0	4	4	0	.231	.269	1	0	SS-9

Harold Reynolds

REYNOLDS, HAROLD CRAIG
Brother of Don Reynolds.
B. Nov. 26, 1960, Eugene, Ore.

BB TR 5'11" 165 lbs.

	G	AB	H	2B	3B	HR	HR %	R	RBI	BB	SO	SB	BA	SA	PH AB	PH H	G by POS
1983 SEA A	20	59	12	4	1	0	0.0	8	1	2	9	0	.203	.305	0	0	2B-18
1984	10	10	3	0	0	0	0.0	3	0	0	1	1	.300	.300	0	0	2B-6
1985	66	104	15	3	1	0	0.0	15	6	17	14	3	.144	.192	2	0	2B-61
1986	126	445	99	19	4	1	0.2	46	24	29	42	30	.222	.290	0	0	2B-126
1987	160	530	146	31	8	1	0.2	73	35	39	34	60	.275	.370	0	0	2B-160
1988	158	598	169	26	11	4	0.7	61	41	51	51	35	.283	.383	0	0	2B-158
6 yrs.	540	1746	444	83	25	6	0.3	206	107	138	151	129	.254	.341	2	0	2B-529

R. J. Reynolds

REYNOLDS, ROBERT JAMES
B. Apr. 19, 1959, Sacramento, Calif.

BB TR 6' 180 lbs.

	G	AB	H	2B	3B	HR	HR %	R	RBI	BB	SO	SB	BA	SA	PH AB	PH H	G by POS
1983 LA N	24	55	13	0	0	2	3.6	5	11	3	11	5	.236	.345	7	2	OF-18
1984	73	240	62	12	2	2	0.8	23	24	14	38	7	.258	.350	13	5	OF-63
1985 2 teams	LA	N (73G – .266)			PIT	N	(31G – .308)										
" total	104	337	95	15	7	3	0.9	44	42	22	49	18	.282	.395	19	3	OF-85
1986 PIT N	118	402	108	30	2	9	2.2	63	48	40	78	16	.269	.420	11	2	OF-112
1987	117	335	87	24	1	7	2.1	47	51	34	80	14	.260	.400	23	6	OF-99
1988	130	323	80	14	2	6	1.9	35	51	20	62	15	.248	.359	42	9	OF-95
6 yrs.	566	1692	445	95	14	29	1.7	217	227	133	318	75	.263	.387	115	27	OF-472

Jim Rice

RICE, JAMES EDWARD
B. Mar. 8, 1953, Anderson, S. C.

BR TR 6'2" 200 lbs.

	G	AB	H	2B	3B	HR	HR %	R	RBI	BB	SO	SB	BA	SA	PH AB	PH H	G by POS
1974 BOS A	24	67	18	2	1	1	1.5	6	13	4	12	0	.269	.373	6	0	DH-16, OF-3
1975	144	564	174	29	4	22	3.9	92	102	36	122	10	.309	.491	0	0	OF-90, DH-54
1976	153	581	164	25	8	25	4.3	75	85	28	123	8	.282	.482	3	1	OF-98, DH-54
1977	160	644	206	29	15	39	6.1	104	114	53	120	5	.320	.593	0	0	DH-116, OF-44
1978	163	677	213	25	15	46	6.8	121	139	58	126	7	.315	.600	0	0	OF-114, DH-49
1979	158	619	201	39	6	39	6.3	117	130	57	97	9	.325	.596	1	0	OF-125, DH-33
1980	124	504	148	22	6	24	4.8	81	86	30	87	8	.294	.504	0	0	OF-109, DH-15
1981	108	451	128	18	1	17	3.8	51	62	34	76	2	.284	.441	0	0	OF-108
1982	145	573	177	24	5	24	4.2	86	97	55	98	0	.309	.494	0	0	OF-145
1983	155	626	191	34	1	39	6.2	90	126	52	102	0	.305	.550	0	0	OF-151, DH-4
1984	159	657	184	25	7	28	4.3	98	122	44	102	4	.280	.467	0	0	OF-157, DH-2
1985	140	546	159	20	3	27	4.9	85	103	51	75	2	.291	.487	2	0	OF-130, DH-7
1986	157	618	200	39	2	20	3.2	98	110	62	78	0	.324	.490	0	0	OF-156, DH-1
1987	108	404	112	14	0	13	3.2	66	62	45	77	1	.277	.408	2	1	OF-94, DH-12
1988	135	485	128	18	3	15	3.1	57	72	48	89	1	.264	.406	5	2	DH-112, OF-19
15 yrs.	2033	8016	2403	363	77	379	4.7	1227	1423	657	1384	57	.300	.506	19	4	OF-1543, DH-475

LEAGUE CHAMPIONSHIP SERIES

	G	AB	H	2B	3B	HR	HR %	R	RBI	BB	SO	SB	BA	SA	PH AB	PH H	G by POS
1986 BOS A	7	31	5	1	0	2	6.5	8	6	1	8	0	.161	.387	0	0	OF-7
1988	4	13	2	0	0	0	0.0	0	1	2	4	0	.154	.154	0	0	DH-4
2 yrs.	11	44	7	1	0	2	4.5	8	7	3	12	0	.159	.318	0	0	OF-7, DH-4

WORLD SERIES

	G	AB	H	2B	3B	HR	HR %	R	RBI	BB	SO	SB	BA	SA	PH AB	PH H	G by POS
1986 BOS A	7	27	9	1	1	0	0.0	6	0	6	9	0	.333	.444	0	0	OF-7

Ernest Riles

RILES, ERNEST
B. Oct. 2, 1960, Cairo, Ga.

BL TR 6'1" 180 lbs.

	G	AB	H	2B	3B	HR	HR %	R	RBI	BB	SO	SB	BA	SA	PH AB	PH H	G by POS
1985 MIL A	116	448	128	12	7	5	1.1	54	45	36	54	2	.286	.377	1	0	SS-115, DH-1
1986	145	524	132	24	2	9	1.7	69	47	54	80	7	.252	.357	4	0	SS-142
1987	83	276	72	11	1	4	1.4	38	38	30	47	3	.261	.351	4	0	3B-65, SS-21
1988 2 teams	MIL	A (41G – .252)			SF	N	(79G – .294)										
" total	120	314	87	13	3	4	1.3	33	37	17	59	3	.277	.376	26	6	3B-58, SS-25, 2B-17, DH-5
4 yrs.	464	1562	419	60	13	22	1.4	194	167	137	240	15	.268	.366	35	6	SS-303, 3B-123, 2B-17, DH-6

	G	AB	H	2B	3B	HR	HR %	R	RBI	BB	SO	SB	BA	SA	Pinch Hit AB	Pinch Hit H	G by POS

Billy Ripken

RIPKEN, WILLIAM OLIVER
Son of Cal Ripken.   Brother of Cal Ripken.
B. Dec. 16, 1964, Havre de Grace, Md.

BR   TR   6'1"   180 lbs.

	G	AB	H	2B	3B	HR	HR %	R	RBI	BB	SO	SB	BA	SA	AB	H	G by POS
1987 **BAL A**	58	234	72	9	0	2	0.9	27	20	21	23	4	.308	.372	0	0	2B-58
1988	150	512	106	18	1	2	0.4	52	34	33	63	8	.207	.258	0	0	2B-149, 3B-2
2 yrs.	208	746	178	27	1	4	0.5	79	54	54	86	12	.239	.294	0	0	2B-207, 3B-2

Cal Ripken

RIPKEN, CALVIN EDWIN JR.
Son of Cal Ripken.   Brother of Billy Ripken.
B. Aug. 24, 1960, Havre de Grace, Md.

BR   TR   6'4"   200 lbs.

	G	AB	H	2B	3B	HR	HR %	R	RBI	BB	SO	SB	BA	SA	AB	H	G by POS
1981 **BAL A**	23	39	5	0	0	0	0.0	1	0	1	8	0	.128	.128	4	0	SS-12, 3B-6
1982	160	598	158	32	5	28	4.7	90	93	46	95	3	.264	.475	0	0	SS-94, 3B-71
1983	162	663	211	47	2	27	4.1	121	102	58	97	0	.318	.517	0	0	SS-162
1984	162	641	195	37	7	27	4.2	103	86	71	89	2	.304	.510	0	0	SS-162
1985	161	642	181	32	5	26	4.0	116	110	67	68	2	.282	.469	0	0	SS-161
1986	162	627	177	35	1	25	4.0	98	81	70	60	4	.282	.461	0	0	SS-162
1987	162	624	157	28	3	27	4.3	97	98	81	77	3	.252	.436	0	0	SS-162
1988	161	575	152	25	1	23	4.0	87	81	102	69	2	.264	.431	0	0	SS-161
8 yrs.	1153	4409	1236	236	24	183	4.2	713	651	496	563	16	.280	.469	4	0	SS-1076, 3B-77

LEAGUE CHAMPIONSHIP SERIES

	G	AB	H	2B	3B	HR	HR %	R	RBI	BB	SO	SB	BA	SA	AB	H	G by POS
1983 **BAL A**	4	15	6	2	0	0	0.0	5	1	2	3	0	.400	.533	0	0	SS-4

WORLD SERIES

	G	AB	H	2B	3B	HR	HR %	R	RBI	BB	SO	SB	BA	SA	AB	H	G by POS
1983 **BAL A**	5	18	3	0	0	0	0.0	2	1	3	4	0	.167	.167	0	0	SS-5

Luis Rivera

RIVERA, LUIS ANTONIO
Born Luis Antonio Rivera y Pedraza.
B. Jan. 3, 1964, Cidra, Puerto Rico

BR   TR   5'11"   165 lbs.

	G	AB	H	2B	3B	HR	HR %	R	RBI	BB	SO	SB	BA	SA	AB	H	G by POS
1986 **MON N**	55	166	34	11	1	0	0.0	20	13	17	33	1	.205	.283	2	0	SS-55
1987	18	32	5	2	0	0	0.0	0	1	1	8	0	.156	.219	3	1	SS-15
1988	123	371	83	17	3	4	1.1	35	30	24	69	3	.224	.318	8	2	SS-116
3 yrs.	196	569	122	30	4	4	0.7	55	44	42	110	4	.214	.302	13	3	SS-186

Bip Roberts

ROBERTS, LEON JOSEPH
B. Oct. 27, 1963, Berkeley, Calif.

BB   TR   5'7"   150 lbs.

	G	AB	H	2B	3B	HR	HR %	R	RBI	BB	SO	SB	BA	SA	AB	H	G by POS
1986 **SD N**	101	241	61	5	2	1	0.4	34	12	14	29	14	.253	.303	3	1	2B-87
1988	5	9	3	0	0	0	0.0	1	0	1	2	0	.333	.333	2	0	3B-2, 2B-1
2 yrs.	106	250	64	5	2	1	0.4	35	12	15	31	14	.256	.304	5	1	2B-88, 3B-2

Billy Jo Robidoux

ROBIDOUX, WILLIAM JOSEPH
B. Jan. 13, 1964, Ware, Mass.

BL   TR   6'1"   200 lbs.

	G	AB	H	2B	3B	HR	HR %	R	RBI	BB	SO	SB	BA	SA	AB	H	G by POS
1985 **MIL A**	18	51	9	2	0	3	5.9	5	8	12	16	0	.176	.392	4	0	OF-11, 1B-6, DH-1
1986	56	181	41	8	0	1	0.6	15	21	33	36	0	.227	.287	2	0	1B-43, DH-10
1987	23	62	12	0	0	0	0.0	9	4	8	17	0	.194	.194	4	0	DH-10, 1B-10
1988	33	91	23	5	0	0	0.0	9	5	8	14	1	.253	.308	3	1	1B-30, DH-1
4 yrs.	130	385	85	15	0	4	1.0	38	38	61	83	1	.221	.291	13	1	1B-89, DH-22, OF-11

Ruben Rodriguez

RODRIGUEZ, RUBEN DARIO
Born Ruben Dario Rodriguez y Martinez.
B. Aug. 4, 1964, Cabrera, Dominican Republic

BR   TR   6'   170 lbs.

	G	AB	H	2B	3B	HR	HR %	R	RBI	BB	SO	SB	BA	SA	AB	H	G by POS
1986 **PIT N**	2	3	0	0	0	0	0.0	0	0	0	1	0	.000	.000	0	0	C-2
1988	2	5	1	0	1	0	0.0	1	1	0	2	0	.200	.600	0	0	C-2
2 yrs.	4	8	1	0	1	0	0.0	1	1	0	3	0	.125	.375	0	0	C-4

Gary Roenicke

ROENICKE, GARY STEVEN
Brother of Ron Roenicke.
B. Dec. 5, 1954, Covina, Calif.

BR   TR   6'3"   205 lbs.

	G	AB	H	2B	3B	HR	HR %	R	RBI	BB	SO	SB	BA	SA	AB	H	G by POS
1976 **MON N**	29	90	20	3	1	2	2.2	9	5	4	18	0	.222	.344	4	1	OF-25
1978 **BAL A**	27	58	15	3	0	3	5.2	5	15	8	3	0	.259	.466	6	1	OF-20
1979	133	376	98	16	1	25	6.6	60	64	61	74	1	.261	.508	2	0	OF-130, DH-2
1980	118	297	71	13	0	10	3.4	40	28	41	49	2	.239	.384	12	6	OF-113
1981	85	219	59	16	0	3	1.4	31	20	23	29	1	.269	.384	16	3	OF-83
1982	137	393	106	25	1	21	5.3	58	74	70	73	6	.270	.499	18	5	OF-125, 1B-10
1983	115	323	84	13	0	19	5.9	45	64	30	35	2	.260	.477	38	8	OF-100, 1B-7, DH-2, 3B-2
1984	121	326	73	19	1	10	3.1	36	44	58	43	1	.224	.380	21	5	OF-117
1985	113	225	49	9	0	15	6.7	36	43	44	36	2	.218	.458	29	3	OF-88, DH-17
1986 **NY A**	69	136	36	5	0	3	2.2	11	18	27	30	1	.265	.368	18	6	OF-37, DH-15, 3B-3, 1B-2
1987 **ATL N**	67	151	33	8	0	9	6.0	25	28	32	23	0	.219	.450	15	3	OF-44, 1B-9
1988	49	114	26	5	0	1	0.9	11	7	8	15	0	.228	.298	16	1	OF-35, 1B-1
12 yrs.	1063	2708	670	135	4	121	4.5	367	410	406	428	16	.247	.434	195	42	OF-917, DH-36, 1B-29, 3B-5

LEAGUE CHAMPIONSHIP SERIES

	G	AB	H	2B	3B	HR	HR %	R	RBI	BB	SO	SB	BA	SA	AB	H	G by POS
1979 **BAL A**	2	5	1	0	0	0	0.0	1	1	0	0	0	.200	.200	1	0	OF-2
1983	3	4	3	1	0	1	25.0	4	4	5	0	0	.750	1.750	0	0	OF-3
2 yrs.	5	9	4	1	0	1	11.1	5	5	5	0	0	.444	.889	1	0	OF-5

WORLD SERIES

	G	AB	H	2B	3B	HR	HR %	R	RBI	BB	SO	SB	BA	SA	AB	H	G by POS
1979 **BAL A**	6	16	2	1	0	0	0.0	1	0	0	6	0	.125	.188	1	0	OF-5
1983	3	7	0	0	0	0	0.0	0	0	0	2	0	.000	.000	2	0	OF-2
2 yrs.	9	23	2	1	0	0	0.0	1	0	0	8	0	.087	.130	3	0	OF-7

Ron Roenicke

ROENICKE, RONALD JON
Brother of Gary Roenicke.
B. Aug. 19, 1956, Covina, Calif.

BB   TL   6'   180 lbs.

	G	AB	H	2B	3B	HR	HR %	R	RBI	BB	SO	SB	BA	SA	AB	H	G by POS
1981 **LA N**	22	47	11	0	0	0	0.0	6	0	6	8	1	.234	.234	4	0	OF-20
1982	109	143	37	8	0	1	0.7	18	12	21	32	5	.259	.336	44	13	OF-72

	G	AB	H	2B	3B	HR	HR %	R	RBI	BB	SO	SB	BA	SA	Pinch Hit AB	H	G by POS

Ron Roenicke continued

	G	AB	H	2B	3B	HR	HR %	R	RBI	BB	SO	SB	BA	SA	PH AB	PH H	G by POS
1983 2 teams LA N (81G – .221)					SEA A (59G – .253)												
" total	140	343	82	16	0	6	1.7	35	35	47	48	9	.239	.338	24	5	OF-116, 1B-6, DH-1
1984 SD N	12	20	6	1	0	1	5.0	4	2	2	5	0	.300	.500	2	0	OF-10
1985 SF N	65	133	34	9	1	3	2.3	23	13	35	27	6	.256	.406	23	4	OF-35
1986 PHI N	102	275	68	13	1	5	1.8	42	42	61	52	2	.247	.356	21	4	OF-83
1987	63	78	13	3	1	1	1.3	9	4	14	15	1	.167	.269	38	5	OF-26
1988 CIN N	14	37	5	1	0	0	0.0	4	5	4	8	0	.135	.162	2	1	OF-14
8 yrs.	527	1076	256	51	3	17	1.6	141	113	190	195	24	.238	.338	158	32	OF-376, 1B-6, DH-1
WORLD SERIES																	
1984 SD N	2	0	0	0	0	0	–	0	0	0	0	0	–	–	0	0	OF-1

Ed Romero

ROMERO, EDGARDO RALPH RIVERA
B. Dec. 9, 1957, Santurce, Puerto Rico

BR TR 5'11" 160 lbs.

	G	AB	H	2B	3B	HR	HR %	R	RBI	BB	SO	SB	BA	SA	PH AB	PH H	G by POS
1977 MIL A	10	25	7	1	0	0	0.0	4	2	4	3	0	.280	.320	0	0	SS-10
1980	42	104	27	7	0	1	1.0	20	10	9	11	2	.260	.356	1	0	SS-22, 2B-15, 3B-3
1981	44	91	18	3	0	1	1.1	6	10	4	9	0	.198	.264	0	0	SS-22, 2B-18, 3B-3
1982	52	144	36	8	0	1	0.7	18	7	8	16	0	.250	.326	2	1	2B-39, SS-10, 3B-2, OF-1
1983	59	145	46	7	0	1	0.7	17	18	8	8	1	.317	.386	14	6	SS-22, OF-15, DH-5, 3B-5, 2B-3
1984	116	357	90	12	0	1	0.3	36	31	29	25	3	.252	.294	1	0	3B-59, SS-39, 2B-11, 1B-4, DH-2, OF-1
1985	88	251	63	11	1	0	0.0	24	21	26	20	1	.251	.303	0	0	SS-43, 2B-31, OF-14, 3B-1
1986 BOS A	100	233	49	11	0	2	0.9	41	23	18	16	2	.210	.283	0	0	SS-75, 3B-18, 2B-4, OF-1
1987	88	235	64	5	0	0	0.0	23	14	18	22	0	.272	.294	6	1	2B-29, SS-24, 3B-24, 1B-8
1988	31	75	18	3	0	0	0.0	3	5	3	8	0	.240	.280	2	0	3B-15, SS-8, 2B-5, DH-1, 1B-1
10 yrs.	630	1660	418	68	1	7	0.4	192	141	127	138	9	.252	.307	26	8	SS-275, 2B-155, 3B-130, OF-32, 1B-13, DH-8
DIVISIONAL PLAYOFF SERIES																	
1981 MIL A	1	2	1	0	0	0	0.0	1	0	0	1	0	.500	.500	0	0	2B-1
LEAGUE CHAMPIONSHIP SERIES																	
1986 BOS A	1	2	0	0	0	0	0.0	0	0	0	0	0	.000	.000	0	0	SS-1
1988	1	0	0	0	0	0	–	0	0	0	0	0	–	–	0	0	
2 yrs.	2	2	0	0	0	0	0.0	0	0	0	0	0	.000	.000	0	0	SS-1
WORLD SERIES																	
1986 BOS A	3	1	0	0	0	0	0.0	0	0	0	0	0	.000	.000	0	0	SS-3

Kevin Romine

ROMINE, KEVIN ANDREW
B. May 23, 1961, Exeter, N. H.

BR TR 5'11" 185 lbs.

	G	AB	H	2B	3B	HR	HR %	R	RBI	BB	SO	SB	BA	SA	PH AB	PH H	G by POS
1985 BOS A	24	28	6	2	0	0	0.0	3	1	1	4	1	.214	.286	1	1	OF-23, DH-1
1986	35	35	9	2	0	0	0.0	6	2	3	9	2	.257	.314	1	0	OF-33
1987	9	24	7	2	0	0	0.0	5	2	2	6	0	.292	.375	1	0	OF-7, DH-2
1988	57	78	15	2	1	1	1.3	17	6	7	15	2	.192	.282	3	0	OF-45, DH-5
4 yrs.	125	165	37	8	1	1	0.6	31	11	13	34	5	.224	.303	6	1	OF-108, DH-8
LEAGUE CHAMPIONSHIP SERIES																	
1988 BOS A	2	0	0	0	0	0	–	1	0	0	0	0	–	–	0	0	

Rolando Roomes

ROOMES, ROLANDO AUDLEY
B. Feb. 15, 1962, Kingston, Jamaica

BR TR 6'3" 180 lbs.

	G	AB	H	2B	3B	HR	HR %	R	RBI	BB	SO	SB	BA	SA	PH AB	PH H	G by POS
1988 CHI N	17	16	3	0	0	0	0.0	3	0	0	4	0	.188	.188	4	0	OF-5

Wade Rowdon

ROWDON, WADE LEE
B. Sept. 7, 1960, Riverhead, N. Y.

BR TR 6'2" 170 lbs.

	G	AB	H	2B	3B	HR	HR %	R	RBI	BB	SO	SB	BA	SA	PH AB	PH H	G by POS
1984 CIN N	4	7	2	0	0	0	0.0	0	0	0	1	0	.286	.286	0	0	SS-1, 3B-1
1985	5	9	2	0	0	0	0.0	2	2	2	1	0	.222	.222	0	0	3B-4
1986	38	80	20	5	1	0	0.0	9	10	9	17	2	.250	.338	15	2	3B-7, SS-6, OF-5, 2B-3
1987 CHI N	11	31	7	1	1	1	3.2	2	4	3	10	0	.226	.419	2	0	3B-9
1988 BAL A	20	30	3	0	0	0	0.0	1	0	0	6	1	.100	.100	4	2	1B-8, DH-5, OF-5
5 yrs.	78	157	34	6	2	1	0.6	14	16	14	35	3	.217	.299	21	4	3B-29, OF-10, SS-7, DH-5, 2B-3

Jerry Royster

ROYSTER, JERON KENNIS
B. Oct. 18, 1952, Sacramento, Calif.

BR TR 6' 165 lbs.

	G	AB	H	2B	3B	HR	HR %	R	RBI	BB	SO	SB	BA	SA	PH AB	PH H	G by POS
1973 LA N	10	19	4	0	0	0	0.0	1	2	0	5	1	.211	.211	0	0	3B-6, 2B-1
1974	6	0	0	0	0	0	–	2	0	0	0	0	–	–	0	0	OF-1, 3B-1, 2B-1
1975	13	36	9	2	1	0	0.0	2	1	1	3	1	.250	.361	2	0	OF-7, 2B-4, 3B-3, SS-1
1976 ATL N	149	533	132	13	1	5	0.9	65	45	52	53	24	.248	.304	1	0	3B-148, SS-2
1977	140	445	96	10	2	6	1.3	64	28	38	67	28	.216	.288	4	0	3B-56, SS-51, 2B-38
1978	140	529	137	17	8	2	0.4	67	35	56	49	27	.259	.333	4	2	2B-75, SS-60, 3B-1
1979	154	601	164	25	6	3	0.5	103	51	62	59	35	.273	.349	3	0	3B-80, 2B-77
1980	123	392	95	17	5	1	0.3	42	20	37	48	22	.242	.319	4	1	2B-49, 3B-48, OF-41
1981	64	93	19	4	1	0	0.0	13	9	7	14	7	.204	.269	17	4	3B-24, 2B-13
1982	108	261	77	13	2	2	0.8	43	25	22	36	14	.295	.383	6	1	3B-62, OF-25, 2B-16, SS-10
1983	91	268	63	10	3	3	1.1	32	30	28	35	11	.235	.328	4	1	3B-47, 2B-26, OF-18, SS-13
1984	81	227	47	13	2	1	0.4	22	21	15	41	6	.207	.295	15	1	2B-29, 3B-17, SS-16, OF-11
1985 SD N	90	249	70	13	2	5	2.0	31	31	32	31	6	.281	.410	10	1	2B-58, 3B-29, SS-7, OF-2
1986	118	257	66	12	0	5	1.9	31	26	32	45	3	.257	.362	32	8	3B-59, SS-24, 2B-21, OF-7
1987 2 teams CHI A (55G – .240)					NY A (18G – .357)												
" total	73	196	52	13	0	7	3.6	26	27	23	32	4	.265	.439	9	2	3B-43, OF-14, 2B-6, SS-1

	G	AB	H	2B	3B	HR	HR %	R	RBI	BB	SO	SB	BA	SA	Pinch Hit AB	Pinch Hit H	G by POS

Jerry Royster *continued*

	G	AB	H	2B	3B	HR	HR %	R	RBI	BB	SO	SB	BA	SA	AB	H	G by POS
1988 **ATL N**	68	102	18	3	0	0	0.0	8	1	6	16	0	.176	.206	31	7	OF-26, 3B-10, SS-2, 2B-2
16 yrs.	1428	4208	1049	165	33	40	1.0	552	352	411	534	189	.249	.333	142	28	3B-634, 2B-416, SS-187, OF-152

LEAGUE CHAMPIONSHIP SERIES

	G	AB	H	2B	3B	HR	HR %	R	RBI	BB	SO	SB	BA	SA	AB	H	G by POS
1982 **ATL N**	3	11	2	0	0	0	0.0	0	0	0	2	0	.182	.182	0	0	OF-3

Paul Runge

RUNGE, PAUL WILLIAM
B. May 21, 1958, Kingston, N. Y.

BR TR 6'   165 lbs.

	G	AB	H	2B	3B	HR	HR %	R	RBI	BB	SO	SB	BA	SA	AB	H	G by POS
1981 **ATL N**	10	27	7	1	0	0	0.0	2	2	4	4	0	.259	.296	0	0	SS-10
1982	4	2	0	0	0	0	0.0	0	0	0	0	0	.000	.000	2	0	
1983	5	8	2	0	0	0	0.0	0	1	1	4	0	.250	.250	1	0	2B-2
1984	28	90	24	3	1	0	0.0	5	3	10	14	5	.267	.322	0	0	2B-22, SS-7, 3B-3
1985	50	87	19	3	0	1	1.1	15	5	18	18	0	.218	.287	12	2	3B-28, SS-5, 2B-2
1986	7	8	2	0	0	0	0.0	1	0	2	4	0	.250	.250	0	0	2B-5
1987	27	47	10	1	0	3	6.4	9	8	5	10	0	.213	.426	3	0	3B-10, SS-9, 2B-2
1988	52	76	16	5	0	0	0.0	11	7	14	21	0	.211	.276	21	4	3B-19, 2B-7, SS-6
8 yrs.	183	345	80	13	1	4	1.2	43	26	54	75	5	.232	.310	39	6	3B-60, 2B-40, SS-37

John Russell

RUSSELL, JOHN WILLIAM
B. Jan. 5, 1961, Oklahoma City, Okla.

BR TR 6'   195 lbs.

	G	AB	H	2B	3B	HR	HR %	R	RBI	BB	SO	SB	BA	SA	AB	H	G by POS
1984 **PHI N**	39	99	28	8	1	2	2.0	11	11	12	33	0	.283	.444	9	4	OF-29, C-2
1985	81	216	47	12	0	9	4.2	22	23	18	72	2	.218	.398	15	4	OF-49, 1B-18
1986	93	315	76	21	2	13	4.1	35	60	25	103	0	.241	.444	4	1	C-89
1987	24	62	9	1	0	3	4.8	5	8	3	17	0	.145	.306	6	2	OF-10, C-7
1988	22	49	12	1	0	2	4.1	5	4	3	15	0	.245	.388	7	0	C-15
5 yrs.	259	741	172	43	3	29	3.9	78	106	61	240	2	.232	.416	41	11	C-113, OF-88, 1B-18

Chris Sabo

SABO, CHRISTOPHER ANDREW (Spuds)
B. Jan. 19, 1962, Detroit, Mich.

BR TR 6'   185 lbs.

	G	AB	H	2B	3B	HR	HR %	R	RBI	BB	SO	SB	BA	SA	AB	H	G by POS
1988 **CIN N**	137	538	146	40	2	11	2.0	74	44	29	52	46	.271	.414	2	0	3B-135, SS-2

Mark Salas

SALAS, MARK BRUCE
B. Mar. 8, 1961, Montebello, Calif.

BL TR 6'   180 lbs.

	G	AB	H	2B	3B	HR	HR %	R	RBI	BB	SO	SB	BA	SA	AB	H	G by POS
1984 **STL N**	14	20	2	1	0	0	0.0	1	1	0	3	0	.100	.150	8	1	C-4, OF-3
1985 **MIN A**	120	360	108	20	5	9	2.5	51	41	18	37	0	.300	.458	12	1	C-115, DH-3
1986	91	258	60	7	4	8	3.1	28	33	18	32	3	.233	.384	25	5	C-69, DH-8
1987 **2 teams**		**MIN**	A (22G –	.378)		**NY**	A (50G –	.200)									
" total	72	160	40	6	0	6	3.8	21	21	15	23	0	.250	.400	19	4	C-55, DH-4, OF-1
1988 **CHI A**	75	196	49	7	0	3	1.5	17	9	12	17	0	.250	.332	7	1	C-69, DH-1
5 yrs.	372	994	259	41	9	26	2.6	118	105	63	112	3	.261	.398	71	12	C-312, DH-16, OF-4

Angel Salazar

SALAZAR, ARGENIS ANTONIO JUANA
Born Argenis Antonio Salazar y Yepez.
B. Nov. 4, 1961, Anaco-Anzoategui, Venezue,

BR TR 5'11"   180 lbs.

	G	AB	H	2B	3B	HR	HR %	R	RBI	BB	SO	SB	BA	SA	AB	H	G by POS
1983 **MON N**	36	37	8	1	0	0	0.0	5	1	1	8	0	.216	.297	2	0	SS-34
1984	80	174	27	4	2	0	0.0	12	12	4	38	1	.155	.201	0	0	SS-80
1986 **KC A**	117	298	73	20	2	0	0.0	24	24	7	47	1	.245	.326	1	0	SS-115, 2B-1
1987	116	317	65	7	0	2	0.6	24	21	6	46	4	.205	.246	0	0	SS-116
1988 **CHI N**	34	60	15	1	1	0	0.0	4	1	1	11	0	.250	.300	3	0	SS-29, 2B-2, 3B-1
5 yrs.	383	886	188	33	6	2	0.2	69	59	19	150	6	.212	.270	6	0	SS-374, 2B-3, 3B-1

Luis Salazar

SALAZAR, LLUIS ERNESTO GARCIA
Born Luis Ernesto Salazar y Garacia.
B. May 19, 1956, Barcelona, Venezuela

BR TR 6'   185 lbs.

	G	AB	H	2B	3B	HR	HR %	R	RBI	BB	SO	SB	BA	SA	AB	H	G by POS
1980 **SD N**	44	169	57	4	7	1	0.6	28	25	9	25	11	.337	.462	0	0	3B-42, OF-4
1981	109	400	121	19	6	3	0.8	37	38	16	72	11	.303	.403	2	0	3B-94, OF-23
1982	145	524	127	15	5	8	1.5	55	62	23	80	32	.242	.336	2	0	3B-129, SS-7, OF-1
1983	134	481	124	16	2	14	2.9	52	45	17	80	24	.258	.387	6	2	3B-118, SS-19
1984	93	228	55	7	4	3	1.3	20	17	6	38	11	.241	.329	14	4	3B-58, OF-24, SS-4
1985 **CHI A**	122	327	80	18	2	10	3.1	39	45	12	60	14	.245	.404	15	6	OF-84, 3B-39, DH-8, 1B-6
1986	4	7	1	0	0	0	0.0	0	1	0	1	0	.143	.143	2	0	DH-2
1987 **SD N**	84	189	48	5	0	3	1.6	13	17	14	30	3	.254	.328	18	3	3B-38, SS-22, OF-10, P-2, 1B-1
1988 **DET A**	130	452	122	14	1	12	2.7	61	62	21	70	6	.270	.385	9	5	OF-68, SS-37, 3B-31, 2B-5, 1B-1
9 yrs.	865	2777	735	98	25	54	1.9	306	311	119	458	112	.265	.376	68	20	3B-549, OF-214, SS-100, 1B-11, DH-10, 2B-5, P-2

LEAGUE CHAMPIONSHIP SERIES

	G	AB	H	2B	3B	HR	HR %	R	RBI	BB	SO	SB	BA	SA	AB	H	G by POS
1984 **SD N**	3	5	1	0	1	0	0.0	0	0	0	1	0	.200	.600	1	0	3B-1

WORLD SERIES

	G	AB	H	2B	3B	HR	HR %	R	RBI	BB	SO	SB	BA	SA	AB	H	G by POS
1984 **SD N**	4	3	1	0	0	0	0.0	0	0	0	0	0	.333	.333	1	1	3B-1

Juan Samuel

SAMUEL, JUAN MILTON ROMERO (Sammy)
Born Juan Milton Romero y Samuel.
B. Dec. 9, 1960, San Pedro de Macoris, Dominican Republic

BR TR 5'11"   170 lbs.

	G	AB	H	2B	3B	HR	HR %	R	RBI	BB	SO	SB	BA	SA	AB	H	G by POS
1983 **PHI N**	18	65	18	1	2	2	3.1	14	5	4	16	3	.277	.446	0	0	2B-18
1984	160	701	191	36	19	15	2.1	105	69	28	168	72	.272	.442	2	1	2B-160
1985	161	663	175	31	13	19	2.9	101	74	33	141	53	.264	.436	1	0	2B-159
1986	145	591	157	36	12	16	2.7	90	78	26	142	42	.266	.448	2	2	2B-143
1987	160	655	178	37	15	28	4.3	113	100	60	162	35	.272	.502	0	0	2B-160
1988	157	629	153	32	9	12	1.9	68	67	39	151	33	.243	.380	1	1	2B-152, OF-3, 3B-1
6 yrs.	801	3304	872	173	70	92	2.8	491	393	190	780	238	.264	.442	6	4	2B-792, OF-3, 3B-1

LEAGUE CHAMPIONSHIP SERIES

	G	AB	H	2B	3B	HR	HR %	R	RBI	BB	SO	SB	BA	SA	AB	H	G by POS
1983 **PHI N**	1	0	0	0	0	0	–	0	0	0	0	0	–	–	0	0	

Juan Samuel continued

WORLD SERIES

	G	AB	H	2B	3B	HR	HR%	R	RBI	BB	SO	SB	BA	SA	Pinch Hit AB	H	G by POS
1983 PHI N	3	1	0	0	0	0	0.0	0	0	0	0	0	.000	.000	1	0	

Ryne Sandberg

SANDBERG, RYNE DEE (Ryno)
B. Sept. 18, 1959, Spokane, Wash.
BR TR 6'1" 175 lbs.

	G	AB	H	2B	3B	HR	HR%	R	RBI	BB	SO	SB	BA	SA	Pinch Hit AB	H	G by POS
1981 PHI N	13	6	1	0	0	0	0.0	2	0	0	1	0	.167	.167	0	0	SS-5, 2B-1
1982 CHI N	156	635	172	33	5	7	1.1	103	54	36	90	32	.271	.372	1	0	3B-133, 2B-24
1983	158	633	165	25	4	8	1.3	94	48	51	79	37	.261	.351	4	2	2B-157, SS-1
1984	156	636	200	36	19	19	3.0	114	84	52	101	32	.314	.520	0	0	2B-156
1985	153	609	186	31	6	26	4.3	113	83	57	97	54	.305	.504	1	0	2B-153, SS-1
1986	154	627	178	28	5	14	2.2	68	76	46	79	34	.284	.411	1	1	2B-153
1987	132	523	154	25	2	16	3.1	81	59	59	79	21	.294	.442	2	1	2B-131
1988	155	618	163	23	8	19	3.1	77	69	54	91	25	.264	.419	2	0	2B-153
8 yrs.	1077	4287	1219	201	49	109	2.5	652	473	355	617	235	.284	.430	11	4	2B-928, 3B-133, SS-7

LEAGUE CHAMPIONSHIP SERIES

	G	AB	H	2B	3B	HR	HR%	R	RBI	BB	SO	SB	BA	SA	Pinch Hit AB	H	G by POS
1984 CHI N	5	19	7	2	0	0	0.0	3	2	3	2	3	.368	.474	0	0	2B-5

Rafael Santana

SANTANA, RAFAEL FRANCISCO de la CRUZ
Born Rafael Francisco Santana y de la Cruz.
B. Jan. 31, 1958, La Romana, Dominican Republic
BR TR 6'1" 156 lbs.

	G	AB	H	2B	3B	HR	HR%	R	RBI	BB	SO	SB	BA	SA	Pinch Hit AB	H	G by POS
1983 STL N	30	14	3	0	0	0	0.0	1	2	2	2	0	.214	.214	4	0	2B-9, SS-6, 3B-4
1984 NY N	51	152	42	11	1	1	0.7	14	12	9	17	0	.276	.382	1	0	SS-50
1985	154	529	136	19	1	1	0.2	41	29	29	54	1	.257	.302	1	0	SS-153
1986	139	394	86	11	0	1	0.3	38	28	36	43	0	.218	.254	2	0	SS-137, 2B-1
1987	139	439	112	21	2	5	1.1	41	44	29	57	1	.255	.346	1	0	SS-138
1988 NY A	148	480	115	12	1	4	0.8	50	38	33	61	1	.240	.294	0	0	SS-148
6 yrs.	661	2008	494	74	5	12	0.6	185	153	138	234	3	.246	.306	9	0	SS-632, 2B-10, 3B-4

LEAGUE CHAMPIONSHIP SERIES

	G	AB	H	2B	3B	HR	HR%	R	RBI	BB	SO	SB	BA	SA	Pinch Hit AB	H	G by POS
1986 NY N	6	17	3	0	0	0	0.0	0	0	0	3	0	.176	.176	0	0	SS-6

WORLD SERIES

	G	AB	H	2B	3B	HR	HR%	R	RBI	BB	SO	SB	BA	SA	Pinch Hit AB	H	G by POS
1986 NY N	7	20	5	0	0	0	0.0	3	2	2	5	0	.250	.250	0	0	SS-7

Benito Santiago

SANTIAGO, BENITO
Born Benito Santiago y Rivera.
B. Mar. 9, 1965, Ponce, Puerto Rico
BR TR 6'1" 180 lbs.

	G	AB	H	2B	3B	HR	HR%	R	RBI	BB	SO	SB	BA	SA	Pinch Hit AB	H	G by POS
1986 SD N	17	62	18	2	0	3	4.8	10	6	2	12	0	.290	.468	0	0	C-17
1987	146	546	164	33	2	18	3.3	64	79	16	112	21	.300	.467	0	0	C-146
1988	139	492	122	22	2	10	2.0	49	46	24	82	15	.248	.362	7	2	C-136
3 yrs.	302	1100	304	57	4	31	2.8	123	131	42	206	36	.276	.420	7	2	C-299

Nelson Santovenia

SANTOVENIA, NELSON GIL
Born Nelson Gil Santovenia y Mayol.
B. July 27, 1961, Pinar del Rio, Cuba
BR TR 6'3" 195 lbs.

	G	AB	H	2B	3B	HR	HR%	R	RBI	BB	SO	SB	BA	SA	Pinch Hit AB	H	G by POS
1987 MON N	2	1	0	0	0	0	0.0	0	0	0	0	0	.000	.000	1	0	C-1
1988	92	309	73	20	2	8	2.6	26	41	24	77	2	.236	.392	1	1	C-86, 1B-1
2 yrs.	94	310	73	20	2	8	2.6	26	41	24	77	2	.235	.390	2	1	C-87, 1B-1

Mackey Sasser

SASSER, MACK DANIEL
B. Aug. 3, 1962, Fort Gaines, Ga.
BL TR 6'1" 190 lbs.

	G	AB	H	2B	3B	HR	HR%	R	RBI	BB	SO	SB	BA	SA	Pinch Hit AB	H	G by POS
1987 2 teams	SF N (2G – .000)			PIT N (12G – .217)													
" total	14	27	5	0	0	0	0.0	2	2	0	2	0	.185	.185	9	4	C-6
1988 NY N	60	123	35	10	1	1	0.8	9	17	6	9	0	.285	.407	19	3	C-42, OF-1, 3B-1
2 yrs.	74	150	40	10	1	1	0.7	11	19	6	11	0	.267	.367	28	7	C-48, OF-1, 3B-1

LEAGUE CHAMPIONSHIP SERIES

	G	AB	H	2B	3B	HR	HR%	R	RBI	BB	SO	SB	BA	SA	Pinch Hit AB	H	G by POS
1988 NY N	4	5	1	0	0	0	0.0	0	0	0	1	0	.200	.200	2	0	C-2

Steve Sax

SAX, STEPHEN LOUIS
Brother of Dave Sax.
B. Jan. 29, 1960, Sacramento, Calif.
BR TR 5'11" 185 lbs.

	G	AB	H	2B	3B	HR	HR%	R	RBI	BB	SO	SB	BA	SA	Pinch Hit AB	H	G by POS
1981 LA N	31	119	33	2	0	2	1.7	15	9	7	14	5	.277	.345	2	1	2B-29
1982	150	638	180	23	7	4	0.6	88	47	49	53	49	.282	.359	1	1	2B-149
1983	155	623	175	18	5	5	0.8	94	41	58	73	56	.281	.350	4	1	2B-152
1984	145	569	138	24	4	1	0.2	70	35	47	53	34	.243	.304	3	0	2B-141
1985	136	488	136	8	4	1	0.2	62	42	54	43	27	.279	.318	1	0	2B-135, 3B-1
1986	157	633	210	43	4	6	0.9	91	56	59	58	40	.332	.441	3	1	2B-154
1987	157	610	171	22	7	6	1.0	84	46	44	61	37	.280	.369	5	0	2B-152, OF-1, 3B-1
1988	160	632	175	19	4	5	0.8	70	57	45	51	42	.277	.343	2	2	2B-158
8 yrs.	1091	4312	1218	159	35	30	0.7	574	333	363	406	290	.282	.356	21	6	2B-1070, 3B-2, OF-1

DIVISIONAL PLAYOFF SERIES

	G	AB	H	2B	3B	HR	HR%	R	RBI	BB	SO	SB	BA	SA	Pinch Hit AB	H	G by POS
1981 LA N	1	0	0	0	0	0	-	0	0	0	0	0	-	-	0	0	2B-1

LEAGUE CHAMPIONSHIP SERIES

	G	AB	H	2B	3B	HR	HR%	R	RBI	BB	SO	SB	BA	SA	Pinch Hit AB	H	G by POS
1981 LA N	1	0	0	0	0	0	-	0	0	0	0	0	-	-	0	0	2B-1
1983	4	16	4	0	0	0	0.0	0	0	1	0	1	.250	.250	0	0	2B-4
1985	6	20	6	3	0	0	0.0	1	1	1	5	0	.300	.450	0	0	2B-6
1988	7	30	8	0	0	0	0.0	7	3	3	3	5	.267	.267	0	0	2B-7
4 yrs.	18	66	18	3	0	0	0.0	8	4	5	8	6	.273	.318	0	0	2B-18

WORLD SERIES

	G	AB	H	2B	3B	HR	HR%	R	RBI	BB	SO	SB	BA	SA	Pinch Hit AB	H	G by POS
1981 LA N	2	1	0	0	0	0	0.0	0	0	0	0	0	.000	.000	1	0	2B-1
1988	5	20	6	0	0	0	0.0	3	0	1	1	1	.300	.300	0	0	2B-5
2 yrs.	7	21	6	0	0	0	0.0	3	0	1	1	1	.286	.286	0	0	2B-6

	G	AB	H	2B	3B	HR	HR%	R	RBI	BB	SO	SB	BA	SA	Pinch Hit AB	Pinch Hit H	G by POS

Mike Schmidt

SCHMIDT, MICHAEL JACK
B. Sept. 27, 1949, Dayton, Ohio — BR TR 6'2" 195 lbs.

	G	AB	H	2B	3B	HR	HR%	R	RBI	BB	SO	SB	BA	SA	PH AB	PH H	G by POS
1972 PHI N	13	34	7	0	0	1	2.9	2	3	5	15	0	.206	.294	1	0	3B-11, 2B-1
1973	132	367	72	11	0	18	4.9	43	52	62	136	8	.196	.373	9	2	3B-125, 2B-4, SS-2, 1B-2
1974	162	568	160	28	7	36	6.3	108	116	106	138	23	.282	.546	0	0	3B-162
1975	158	562	140	34	3	38	6.8	93	95	101	180	29	.249	.523	1	0	3B-151, SS-10
1976	160	584	153	31	4	38	6.5	112	107	100	149	14	.262	.524	0	0	3B-160
1977	154	544	149	27	11	38	7.0	114	101	104	122	15	.274	.574	2	0	3B-149, SS-2, 2B-1
1978	145	513	129	27	2	21	4.1	93	78	91	103	19	.251	.435	4	1	3B-140, SS-1
1979	160	541	137	25	4	45	8.3	109	114	120	115	9	.253	.564	2	0	3B-157, SS-2
1980	150	548	157	25	8	48	8.8	104	121	89	119	12	.286	.624	1	0	3B-149
1981	102	354	112	19	2	31	8.8	78	91	73	71	12	.316	.644	1	1	3B-101
1982	148	514	144	26	3	35	6.8	108	87	107	131	14	.280	.547	0	0	3B-148
1983	154	534	136	16	4	40	7.5	104	109	128	148	7	.255	.524	0	0	3B-153, SS-2
1984	151	528	146	23	3	36	6.8	93	106	92	116	5	.277	.536	4	3	3B-145, 1B-2, SS-1
1985	158	549	152	31	5	33	6.0	89	93	87	117	1	.277	.532	4	1	1B-106, 3B-54, SS-1
1986	160	552	160	29	1	37	6.7	97	119	89	84	1	.290	.547	8	2	3B-124, 1B-35
1987	147	522	153	28	0	35	6.7	88	113	83	80	2	.293	.548	6	1	3B-138, 1B-9, SS-3
1988	108	390	97	21	2	12	3.1	52	62	49	42	3	.249	.405	5	0	3B-104, 1B-3
17 yrs.	2362	8204	2204	401	59	542 7th	6.6 7th	1487	1567	1486	1866 4th	174	.269	.530	48	11	3B-2171, 1B-157, SS-24, 2B-6

DIVISIONAL PLAYOFF SERIES
| 1981 PHI N | 5 | 16 | 4 | 1 | 0 | 1 | 6.3 | 3 | 2 | 4 | 2 | 0 | .250 | .500 | 0 | 0 | 3B-5 |

LEAGUE CHAMPIONSHIP SERIES
1976 PHI N	3	13	4	2	0	0	0.0	1	2	0	1	0	.308	.462	0	0	3B-3
1977	4	16	1	0	0	0	0.0	2	1	2	3	0	.063	.063	0	0	3B-4
1978	4	15	3	2	0	0	0.0	1	1	2	2	0	.200	.333	0	0	3B-4
1980	5	24	5	1	0	0	0.0	1	1	1	6	1	.208	.250	0	0	3B-5
1983	4	15	7	2	0	1	6.7	5	2	2	3	0	.467	.800	0	0	3B-4
5 yrs.	20	83	20	7	0	1	1.2	10	7	7	15	1	.241	.361	0	0	3B-20

WORLD SERIES
1980 PHI N	6	21	8	1	0	2	9.5	6	7	4	3	0	.381	.714	0	0	3B-6
1983	5	20	1	0	0	0	0.0	0	0	0	6	0	.050	.050	0	0	3B-5
2 yrs.	11	41	9	1	0	2	4.9	6	7	4	9	0	.220	.390	0	0	3B-11

Dick Schofield

SCHOFIELD, RICHARD CRAIG
Son of Dick Schofield.
B. Nov. 21, 1962, Springfield, Ill. — BR TR 5'10" 175 lbs.

	G	AB	H	2B	3B	HR	HR%	R	RBI	BB	SO	SB	BA	SA	PH AB	PH H	G by POS
1983 CAL A	21	54	11	2	0	3	5.6	4	4	6	8	0	.204	.407	0	0	SS-21
1984	140	400	77	10	3	4	1.0	39	21	33	79	4	.193	.263	0	0	SS-140
1985	147	438	96	19	3	8	1.8	50	41	35	70	11	.219	.331	1	0	SS-147
1986	139	458	114	17	6	13	2.8	67	57	48	55	23	.249	.397	0	0	SS-137
1987	134	479	120	17	3	9	1.9	52	46	37	63	19	.251	.355	0	0	SS-131, 2B-2, DH-1
1988	155	527	126	11	6	6	1.1	61	34	40	57	20	.239	.317	0	0	SS-155
6 yrs.	736	2356	544	76	21	43	1.8	273	203	199	332	77	.231	.336	1	0	SS-731, 2B-2, DH-1

LEAGUE CHAMPIONSHIP SERIES
| 1986 CAL A | 7 | 30 | 9 | 1 | 0 | 1 | 3.3 | 4 | 2 | 1 | 5 | 1 | .300 | .433 | 0 | 0 | SS-7 |

Bill Schroeder

SCHROEDER, ALFRED WILLIAM III
B. Sept. 7, 1958, Baltimore, Md. — BR TR 6'2" 210 lbs.

	G	AB	H	2B	3B	HR	HR%	R	RBI	BB	SO	SB	BA	SA	PH AB	PH H	G by POS
1983 MIL A	23	73	13	2	1	3	4.1	7	7	3	23	0	.178	.356	0	0	C-23
1984	61	210	54	6	0	14	6.7	29	25	8	54	0	.257	.486	1	0	C-58, DH-3, 1B-1
1985	53	194	47	8	0	8	4.1	18	25	12	61	0	.242	.407	0	0	C-48, DH-4, 1B-1
1986	64	217	46	14	0	7	3.2	32	19	9	59	1	.212	.373	0	0	C-35, 1B-19, DH-10
1987	75	250	83	12	0	14	5.6	35	42	16	56	5	.332	.548	4	0	C-67, 1B-4, DH-2
1988	41	122	19	2	0	5	4.1	9	10	6	36	0	.156	.295	0	0	C-30, 1B-10, DH-1
6 yrs.	317	1066	262	44	1	51	4.8	130	128	54	289	6	.246	.432	5	0	C-261, 1B-35, DH-20

Rick Schu

SCHU, RICHARD SPENCER
B. Jan. 26, 1962, Philadelphia, Pa. — BR TR 6' 170 lbs.

	G	AB	H	2B	3B	HR	HR%	R	RBI	BB	SO	SB	BA	SA	PH AB	PH H	G by POS
1984 PHI N	17	29	8	2	1	2	6.9	12	5	6	6	0	.276	.621	2	0	3B-15
1985	112	416	105	21	4	7	1.7	54	24	38	78	8	.252	.373	1	0	3B-111
1986	92	208	57	10	1	8	3.8	32	25	18	44	2	.274	.447	29	7	3B-58
1987	92	196	46	6	3	7	3.6	24	23	20	36	0	.235	.403	24	4	3B-45, 1B-28
1988 BAL A	89	270	69	9	4	4	1.5	22	20	21	49	6	.256	.363	5	1	3B-72, DH-9, 1B-4
5 yrs.	402	1119	285	48	13	28	2.5	144	97	103	213	16	.255	.396	61	10	3B-301, 1B-32, DH-9

Mike Scioscia

SCIOSCIA, MICHAEL LORRI
B. Nov. 27, 1958, Upper Darby, Pa. — BL TR 6'2" 200 lbs.

	G	AB	H	2B	3B	HR	HR%	R	RBI	BB	SO	SB	BA	SA	PH AB	PH H	G by POS
1980 LA N	54	134	34	5	1	1	0.7	8	8	12	9	1	.254	.328	1	0	C-54
1981	93	290	80	10	0	2	0.7	27	29	36	18	0	.276	.331	2	1	C-91
1982	129	365	80	11	1	5	1.4	31	38	44	31	2	.219	.296	8	0	C-123
1983	12	35	11	3	0	1	2.9	3	7	5	2	0	.314	.486	1	0	C-11
1984	114	341	93	18	0	5	1.5	29	38	52	26	2	.273	.370	7	0	C-112
1985	141	429	127	26	3	7	1.6	47	53	77	21	3	.296	.420	7	1	C-139
1986	122	374	94	18	1	5	1.3	36	26	62	23	3	.251	.345	10	1	C-119
1987	142	461	122	26	1	6	1.3	44	38	55	29	7	.265	.364	11	4	C-138
1988	130	408	105	18	0	3	0.7	29	35	38	31	0	.257	.324	7	1	C-123
9 yrs.	937	2837	746	135	7	35	1.2	254	272	381	184	18	.263	.352	54	8	C-910

DIVISIONAL PLAYOFF SERIES
| 1981 LA N | 4 | 13 | 2 | 0 | 0 | 0 | 0.0 | 0 | 1 | 1 | 2 | 0 | .154 | .154 | 0 | 0 | C-4 |

LEAGUE CHAMPIONSHIP SERIES
1981 LA N	5	15	2	0	0	1	6.7	1	1	2	1	0	.133	.333	0	0	C-5
1985	6	16	4	0	0	0	0.0	2	1	4	0	0	.250	.250	0	0	C-6
1988	7	22	8	1	0	1	4.5	3	2	1	2	0	.364	.545	0	0	C-7
3 yrs.	18	53	14	1	0	2	3.8	6	4	7	3	0	.264	.396	0	0	C-18

	G	AB	H	2B	3B	HR	HR %	R	RBI	BB	SO	SB	BA	SA	Pinch Hit AB	Pinch Hit H	G by POS

Mike Scioscia continued

WORLD SERIES

	G	AB	H	2B	3B	HR	HR%	R	RBI	BB	SO	SB	BA	SA	PH AB	PH H	G by POS
1981 LA N	3	4	1	0	0	0	0.0	1	0	1	0	0	.250	.250	1	0	C-3
1988	4	14	3	0	0	0	0.0	0	1	0	2	0	.214	.214	0	0	C-4
2 yrs.	7	18	4	0	0	0	0.0	1	1	1	2	0	.222	.222	1	0	C-7

Larry See

SEE, RALPH LAURENCE
B. June 20, 1960, Norwalk, Calif.
BR TR 6'1" 195 lbs.

	G	AB	H	2B	3B	HR	HR%	R	RBI	BB	SO	SB	BA	SA	PH AB	PH H	G by POS
1986 LA N	13	20	5	2	0	0	0.0	1	2	2	7	0	.250	.350	4	1	1B-9
1988 TEX A	13	23	3	0	0	0	0.0	0	0	1	8	0	.130	.130	0	0	1B-2, C-2, 3B-1
2 yrs.	26	43	8	2	0	0	0.0	1	2	3	15	0	.186	.233	4	1	1B-11, C-2, 3B-1

Kevin Seitzer

SEITZER, KEVIN LEE
B. Mar. 26, 1962, Springfield, Ill.
BR TR 5'11" 180 lbs.

	G	AB	H	2B	3B	HR	HR%	R	RBI	BB	SO	SB	BA	SA	PH AB	PH H	G by POS
1986 KC A	28	96	31	4	1	2	2.1	16	11	19	14	0	.323	.448	1	1	1B-22, OF-5, 3B-3
1987	161	641	207	33	8	15	2.3	105	83	80	85	12	.323	.470	0	0	3B-141, 1B-25, OF-3
1988	149	559	170	32	5	5	0.9	90	60	72	64	10	.304	.406	1	0	3B-147, DH-1, OF-1
3 yrs.	338	1296	408	69	14	22	1.7	211	154	171	163	22	.315	.441	2	1	3B-291, 1B-47, OF-9, DH-1

Mike Sharperson

SHARPERSON, MICHAEL TYRONE
B. Oct. 4, 1961, Orangeburg, S. C.
BR TR 6'1" 175 lbs.

	G	AB	H	2B	3B	HR	HR%	R	RBI	BB	SO	SB	BA	SA	PH AB	PH H	G by POS
1987 2 teams	TOR A (32G – .208)		LA N (10G – .273)														
" total	42	129	29	6	1	0	0.0	11	10	11	20	2	.225	.287	0	0	2B-38, 3B-7
1988 LA N	46	59	16	1	0	0	0.0	8	4	1	12	0	.271	.288	22	3	2B-20, 3B-6, SS-4
2 yrs.	88	188	45	7	1	0	0.0	19	14	12	32	2	.239	.287	22	3	2B-58, 3B-13, SS-4

LEAGUE CHAMPIONSHIP SERIES

	G	AB	H	2B	3B	HR	HR%	R	RBI	BB	SO	SB	BA	SA	PH AB	PH H	G by POS
1988 LA N	2	1	0	0	0	0	0.0	0	1	1	0	0	.000	.000	1	0	3B-1

Larry Sheets

SHEETS, LARRY KENT
B. Dec. 6, 1959, Staunton, Va.
BL TR 6'4" 210 lbs.

	G	AB	H	2B	3B	HR	HR%	R	RBI	BB	SO	SB	BA	SA	PH AB	PH H	G by POS
1984 BAL A	8	16	7	1	0	1	6.3	3	2	1	3	0	.438	.688	1	0	OF-7
1985	113	328	86	8	0	17	5.2	43	50	28	52	0	.262	.442	16	4	DH-93, OF-9, 1B-1
1986	112	338	92	17	1	18	5.3	42	60	21	56	2	.272	.488	13	2	DH-58, OF-32, C-6, 1B-4, 3B-2
1987	135	469	148	23	0	31	6.6	74	94	31	67	1	.316	.563	6	3	OF-127, DH-7
1988	136	452	104	19	1	10	2.2	38	47	42	72	1	.230	.343	12	5	OF-76, DH-50, 1B-3
5 yrs.	504	1603	437	68	2	77	4.8	200	253	123	250	4	.273	.462	48	14	OF-251, DH-208, 1B-8, C-6, 3B-2

Gary Sheffield

SHEFFIELD, GARY ANTONIAN
B. Nov. 18, 1968, Tampa, Fla.
BR TR 5'11" 190 lbs.

	G	AB	H	2B	3B	HR	HR%	R	RBI	BB	SO	SB	BA	SA	PH AB	PH H	G by POS
1988 MIL A	24	80	19	1	0	4	5.0	12	12	7	7	3	.238	.400	0	0	SS-24

John Shelby

SHELBY, JOHN T. (T-Bone)
B. Feb. 23, 1958, Lexington, Ky.
BB TR 6'1" 175 lbs.

	G	AB	H	2B	3B	HR	HR%	R	RBI	BB	SO	SB	BA	SA	PH AB	PH H	G by POS
1981 BAL A	7	2	0	0	0	0	0.0	2	0	0	1	2	.000	.000	0	0	OF-4
1982	26	35	11	3	0	1	2.9	8	2	0	5	0	.314	.486	3	1	OF-24
1983	126	325	84	15	2	5	1.5	52	27	18	64	15	.258	.363	27	7	OF-115, DH-1
1984	128	383	80	12	5	6	1.6	44	30	20	71	12	.209	.313	12	4	OF-124
1985	69	205	58	6	2	7	3.4	28	27	7	44	5	.283	.434	12	3	OF-59, DH-3, 2B-1
1986	135	404	92	14	4	11	2.7	54	49	18	75	18	.228	.364	19	6	OF-121, DH-2
1987 2 teams	BAL A (21G – .188)		LA N (120G – .277)														
" total	141	508	138	26	0	22	4.3	65	72	32	110	16	.272	.453	3	1	OF-136, DH-1
1988 LA N	140	494	130	23	6	10	2.0	65	64	44	128	16	.263	.395	0	0	OF-140
8 yrs.	772	2356	593	99	19	62	2.6	318	271	139	498	84	.252	.389	76	22	OF-723, DH-7, 2B-1

LEAGUE CHAMPIONSHIP SERIES

	G	AB	H	2B	3B	HR	HR%	R	RBI	BB	SO	SB	BA	SA	PH AB	PH H	G by POS
1983 BAL A	3	9	2	0	0	0	0.0	1	0	1	3	1	.222	.222	0	0	OF-2
1988 LA N	7	24	4	0	0	0	0.0	3	3	5	12	2	.167	.167	0	0	OF-7
2 yrs.	10	33	6	0	0	0	0.0	4	3	6	15	3	.182	.182	0	0	OF-9

WORLD SERIES

	G	AB	H	2B	3B	HR	HR%	R	RBI	BB	SO	SB	BA	SA	PH AB	PH H	G by POS
1983 BAL A	5	9	4	0	0	0	0.0	1	1	0	4	0	.444	.444	3	0	OF-5
1988 LA N	5	18	4	1	0	0	0.0	0	1	2	7	1	.222	.278	0	0	OF-5
2 yrs.	10	27	8	1	0	0	0.0	1	2	2	11	1	.296	.333	3	0	OF-10

Pat Sheridan

SHERIDAN, PATRICK ARTHUR
B. Dec. 4, 1957, Ann Arbor, Mich.
BL TR 6'3" 175 lbs.

	G	AB	H	2B	3B	HR	HR%	R	RBI	BB	SO	SB	BA	SA	PH AB	PH H	G by POS
1981 KC A	3	1	0	0	0	0	0.0	0	0	0	1	0	.000	.000	0	0	OF-3
1983	109	333	90	12	2	7	2.1	43	36	20	64	12	.270	.381	19	5	OF-100
1984	138	481	136	24	4	8	1.7	64	53	41	91	19	.283	.399	8	4	OF-134
1985	78	206	47	9	2	3	1.5	18	17	23	38	11	.228	.335	10	1	OF-69, DH-1
1986 DET A	98	236	56	9	1	6	2.5	41	19	21	57	9	.237	.360	5	0	OF-90, DH-5
1987	141	421	109	19	3	6	1.4	57	49	44	90	18	.259	.361	16	2	OF-137
1988	127	347	88	9	5	11	3.2	47	47	44	64	8	.254	.403	16	2	OF-111, DH-3
7 yrs.	694	2025	526	82	17	41	2.0	270	221	193	405	77	.260	.378	74	14	OF-644, DH-9

LEAGUE CHAMPIONSHIP SERIES

	G	AB	H	2B	3B	HR	HR%	R	RBI	BB	SO	SB	BA	SA	PH AB	PH H	G by POS
1984 KC A	3	6	0	0	0	0	0.0	1	0	3	3	0	.000	.000	0	0	OF-3
1985	7	20	3	0	0	2	10.0	4	3	2	3	0	.150	.450	2	1	OF-6
1987 DET A	5	10	3	1	0	1	10.0	2	2	0	2	1	.300	.700	0	0	OF-4
3 yrs.	15	36	6	1	0	3	8.3	7	5	5	8	1	.167	.444	2	1	OF-13

WORLD SERIES

	G	AB	H	2B	3B	HR	HR%	R	RBI	BB	SO	SB	BA	SA	PH AB	PH H	G by POS
1985 KC A	5	18	4	2	0	0	0.0	0	1	0	7	0	.222	.333	1	1	OF-5

	G	AB	H	2B	3B	HR	HR %	R	RBI	BB	SO	SB	BA	SA	Pinch Hit AB	Pinch Hit H	G by POS

Ruben Sierra

SIERRA, RUBEN ANGEL
Born Ruben Angel Sierra y Garcia.
B. Oct. 6, 1965, Rio Piedras, Puerto Rico
BB   TR   6'1"   175 lbs.

	G	AB	H	2B	3B	HR	HR %	R	RBI	BB	SO	SB	BA	SA	AB	H	G by POS
1986 **TEX A**	113	382	101	13	10	16	4.2	50	55	22	65	7	.264	.476	6	1	OF-107, DH-3
1987	158	**643**	169	35	4	30	4.7	97	109	39	114	16	.263	.470	2	0	OF-157
1988	156	615	156	32	2	23	3.7	77	91	44	91	18	.254	.424	3	1	OF-153, DH-1
3 yrs.	427	1640	426	80	16	69	4.2	224	255	105	270	41	.260	.454	11	2	OF-417, DH-4

Ted Simmons

SIMMONS, TED LYLE
B. Aug. 9, 1949, Highland Park, Mich.
BB   TR   5'11"   193 lbs.

	G	AB	H	2B	3B	HR	HR %	R	RBI	BB	SO	SB	BA	SA	AB	H	G by POS
1968 **STL N**	2	3	1	0	0	0	0.0	0	0	1	1	0	.333	.333	0	0	C-2
1969	5	14	3	0	1	0	0.0	0	3	1	1	0	.214	.357	1	0	C-4
1970	82	284	69	8	2	3	1.1	29	24	37	37	2	.243	.317	4	1	C-79
1971	133	510	155	32	4	7	1.4	64	77	36	50	1	.304	.424	6	1	C-130
1972	152	594	180	36	6	16	2.7	70	96	29	57	1	.303	.465	2	0	C-135, 1B-15
1973	161	619	192	36	2	13	2.1	62	91	61	47	2	.310	.438	1	0	C-153, 1B-6, OF-2
1974	152	599	163	33	6	20	3.3	66	103	47	35	0	.272	.447	2	1	C-141, 1B-12
1975	157	581	193	32	3	18	3.1	80	100	63	35	1	.332	.491	5	1	C-154, OF-2, 1B-2
1976	150	546	159	35	3	5	0.9	60	75	73	35	0	.291	.394	7	4	C-113, 1B-30, OF-7, 3B-2
1977	150	516	164	25	3	21	4.1	82	95	79	37	2	.318	.500	17	2	C-144, OF-1
1978	152	516	148	40	5	22	4.3	71	80	77	39	1	.287	.512	10	3	C-134, OF-23
1979	123	448	127	22	0	26	5.8	68	87	61	34	0	.283	.507	4	0	C-122
1980	145	495	150	33	2	21	4.2	84	98	59	45	1	.303	.505	15	3	C-129, OF-5
1981 **MIL A**	100	380	82	13	3	14	3.7	45	61	23	32	0	.216	.376	3	1	C-75, DH-22, 1B-4
1982	137	539	145	29	0	23	4.3	73	97	32	40	0	.269	.451	2	1	C-121, DH-15
1983	153	600	185	39	3	13	2.2	76	108	41	51	4	.308	.448	4	0	C-86, DH-66
1984	132	497	110	23	2	4	0.8	44	52	30	40	3	.221	.300	6	1	DH-77, 1B-37, 3B-14
1985	143	528	144	28	2	12	2.3	60	76	57	32	1	.273	.402	3	1	DH-99, 1B-28, C-15, 3B-2
1986 **ATL N**	76	127	32	5	0	4	3.1	14	25	12	14	1	.252	.386	47	11	1B-14, C-10, 3B-9
1987	73	177	49	8	0	4	2.3	20	30	21	23	1	.277	.390	29	9	1B-26, C-15, 3B-2
1988	78	107	21	6	0	2	1.9	6	11	15	9	0	.196	.308	47	5	1B-19, C-10
21 yrs.	2456	8680	2472	483	47	248	2.9	1074	1389	855	694	21	.285	.437	215	45	C-1772, DH-279, 1B-195, OF-40, 3B-29

DIVISIONAL PLAYOFF SERIES

	G	AB	H	2B	3B	HR	HR %	R	RBI	BB	SO	SB	BA	SA	AB	H	G by POS
1981 **MIL A**	5	19	4	1	0	1	5.3	1	4	2	2	0	.211	.421	0	0	C-5

LEAGUE CHAMPIONSHIP SERIES

	G	AB	H	2B	3B	HR	HR %	R	RBI	BB	SO	SB	BA	SA	AB	H	G by POS
1982 **MIL A**	5	18	3	0	0	0	0.0	3	1	1	4	0	.167	.167	0	0	C-5

WORLD SERIES

	G	AB	H	2B	3B	HR	HR %	R	RBI	BB	SO	SB	BA	SA	AB	H	G by POS
1982 **MIL A**	7	23	4	0	0	2	8.7	2	3	5	3	0	.174	.435	0	0	C-7

Matt Sinatro

SINATRO, MATTHEW STEPHEN
B. Mar. 22, 1960, Hartford, Conn.
BR   TR   5'9"   174 lbs.

	G	AB	H	2B	3B	HR	HR %	R	RBI	BB	SO	SB	BA	SA	AB	H	G by POS
1981 **ATL N**	12	32	9	1	1	0	0.0	4	4	5	4	1	.281	.375	0	0	C-12
1982	37	81	11	2	0	1	1.2	10	4	4	9	0	.136	.198	0	0	C-35
1983	7	12	2	0	0	0	0.0	0	2	2	1	0	.167	.167	0	0	C-7
1984	2	4	0	0	0	0	0.0	0	0	0	0	0	.000	.000	0	0	C-2
1987 **OAK A**	6	3	0	0	0	0	0.0	0	0	0	1	0	.000	.000	2	0	C-6
1988	10	9	3	2	0	0	0.0	1	5	0	1	0	.333	.556	0	0	C-9
6 yrs.	74	141	25	5	1	1	0.7	15	15	11	16	1	.177	.248	2	0	C-71

Joel Skinner

SKINNER, JOEL PATRICK
Son of Bob Skinner.
B. Feb. 21, 1961, La Jolla, Calif.
BR   TR   6'4"   195 lbs.

	G	AB	H	2B	3B	HR	HR %	R	RBI	BB	SO	SB	BA	SA	AB	H	G by POS
1983 **CHI A**	6	11	3	0	0	0	0.0	2	1	0	1	0	.273	.273	0	0	C-6
1984	43	80	17	2	0	0	0.0	4	3	7	19	1	.213	.238	0	0	C-43
1985	22	44	15	4	1	1	2.3	9	5	5	13	0	.341	.545	2	0	C-21
1986 **2 teams**		CHI A (60G – .201)				NY A (54G – .259)											
" total	114	315	73	9	1	5	1.6	23	37	16	83	1	.232	.314	0	0	C-114
1987 **NY A**	64	139	19	4	0	3	2.2	9	14	8	46	0	.137	.230	1	0	C-64
1988	88	251	57	15	0	4	1.6	23	23	14	72	0	.227	.335	0	0	C-85, OF-2, 1B-1
6 yrs.	337	840	184	34	2	13	1.5	70	83	50	234	2	.219	.311	3	0	C-333, OF-2, 1B-1

Don Slaught

SLAUGHT, DONALD MARTIN
B. Sept. 11, 1958, Long Beach, Calif.
BR   TR   6'   185 lbs.

	G	AB	H	2B	3B	HR	HR %	R	RBI	BB	SO	SB	BA	SA	AB	H	G by POS
1982 **KC A**	43	115	32	6	0	3	2.6	14	8	9	12	0	.278	.409	0	0	C-43
1983	83	276	86	13	4	0	0.0	21	28	11	27	3	.312	.388	5	2	C-79, DH-1
1984	124	409	108	27	4	4	1.0	48	42	20	55	0	.264	.379	5	2	C-123, DH-1
1985 **TEX A**	102	343	96	17	4	8	2.3	34	35	20	41	5	.280	.423	1	0	C-102
1986	95	314	83	17	1	13	4.1	39	46	16	59	3	.264	.449	3	3	C-91, DH-2
1987	95	237	53	15	2	8	3.4	25	16	24	51	0	.224	.405	22	5	C-85, DH-5
1988 **NY A**	97	322	91	25	1	9	2.8	33	43	24	54	1	.283	.450	6	2	C-94, DH-1
7 yrs.	639	2016	549	120	16	45	2.2	214	218	124	299	12	.272	.415	42	14	C-617, DH-10

LEAGUE CHAMPIONSHIP SERIES

	G	AB	H	2B	3B	HR	HR %	R	RBI	BB	SO	SB	BA	SA	AB	H	G by POS
1984 **KC A**	3	11	4	0	0	0	0.0	0	0	0	0	0	.364	.364	0	0	C-3

Craig Smajstrla

SMAJSTRLA, CRAIG LEE
B. June 19, 1962, Houston, Tex.
BB   TR   5'8"   160 lbs.

	G	AB	H	2B	3B	HR	HR %	R	RBI	BB	SO	SB	BA	SA	AB	H	G by POS
1988 **HOU N**	8	3	0	0	0	0	0.0	0	0	0	1	0	.000	.000	2	0	2B-2

Brick Smith

SMITH, BRICK DUDLEY
B. May 2, 1959, Charlotte, N. C.
BR   TR   6'4"   225 lbs.

	G	AB	H	2B	3B	HR	HR %	R	RBI	BB	SO	SB	BA	SA	AB	H	G by POS
1987 **SEA A**	5	8	1	0	0	0	0.0	1	0	2	4	0	.125	.125	1	1	1B-3, DH-1
1988	4	10	1	0	0	0	0.0	1	1	0	1	0	.100	.100	0	0	1B-4
2 yrs.	9	18	2	0	0	0	0.0	2	1	2	5	0	.111	.111	1	1	1B-7, DH-1

	G	AB	H	2B	3B	HR	HR %	R	RBI	BB	SO	SB	BA	SA	Pinch Hit AB	Pinch Hit H	G by POS

Lonnie Smith

SMITH, LONNIE
B. Dec. 22, 1955, Chicago, Ill.   BR TR 5'9"   170 lbs.

Year/Team	G	AB	H	2B	3B	HR	HR%	R	RBI	BB	SO	SB	BA	SA	PH AB	PH H	G by POS
1978 PHI N	17	4	0	0	0	0	0.0	6	0	4	3	4	.000	.000	1	0	OF-11
1979	17	30	5	2	0	0	0.0	4	3	1	7	2	.167	.233	4	0	OF-11
1980	100	298	101	14	4	3	1.0	69	20	26	48	33	.339	.443	8	2	OF-82
1981	62	176	57	14	3	2	1.1	40	11	18	14	21	.324	.472	5	3	OF-51
1982 STL N	156	592	182	35	8	8	1.4	120	69	64	74	68	.307	.434	9	1	OF-149
1983	130	492	158	31	5	8	1.6	83	45	41	55	43	.321	.453	5	1	OF-126
1984	145	504	126	20	4	6	1.2	77	49	70	90	50	.250	.341	3	1	OF-140
1985 2 teams		STL	N	(28G –	.260)	KC	A	(120G –	.257)								
" total	148	544	140	25	6	6	1.1	92	48	56	89	52	.257	.358	2	0	OF-147
1986 KC A	134	508	146	25	7	8	1.6	80	44	46	78	26	.287	.411	4	2	OF-118, DH-10
1987	48	167	42	7	1	3	1.8	26	8	24	31	9	.251	.359	1	0	OF-32, DH-15
1988 ATL N	43	114	27	3	0	3	2.6	14	9	10	25	4	.237	.342	14	3	OF-35
11 yrs.	1000	3429	984	176	38	47	1.4	611	306	360	514	312	.287	.402	56	13	OF-902, DH-25

DIVISIONAL PLAYOFF SERIES

	G	AB	H	2B	3B	HR	HR%	R	RBI	BB	SO	SB	BA	SA	PH AB	PH H	G by POS
1981 PHI N	5	19	5	1	0	0	0.0	1	0	1	4	0	.263	.316	0	0	OF-5

LEAGUE CHAMPIONSHIP SERIES

	G	AB	H	2B	3B	HR	HR%	R	RBI	BB	SO	SB	BA	SA	PH AB	PH H	G by POS
1980 PHI N	3	5	3	0	0	0	0.0	2	0	0	0	1	.600	.600	0	0	OF-2
1982 STL N	3	11	3	0	0	0	0.0	1	1	0	1	0	.273	.273	0	0	OF-3
1985 KC A	7	28	7	2	0	0	0.0	2	1	3	6	1	.250	.321	0	0	OF-7
3 yrs.	13	44	13	2	0	0	0.0	5	2	3	7	2	.295	.341	0	0	OF-12

WORLD SERIES

	G	AB	H	2B	3B	HR	HR%	R	RBI	BB	SO	SB	BA	SA	PH AB	PH H	G by POS
1980 PHI N	6	19	5	1	0	0	0.0	2	1	1	1	0	.263	.316	0	0	OF-4
1982 STL N	7	28	9	4	1	0	0.0	6	1	1	5	2	.321	.536	0	0	OF-6
1985 KC A	7	27	9	3	0	0	0.0	5	4	3	8	2	.333	.444	0	0	OF-7
3 yrs.	20	74	23	8 (6th)	1	0	0.0	13	6	5	14	4	.311	.446	0	0	OF-17

Ozzie Smith

SMITH, OSBORNE EARL (The Wizard Of Oz)
B. Dec. 26, 1954, Mobile, Ala.   BB TR 5'11"   150 lbs.

Year/Team	G	AB	H	2B	3B	HR	HR%	R	RBI	BB	SO	SB	BA	SA	PH AB	PH H	G by POS
1978 SD N	159	590	152	17	6	1	0.2	69	46	47	43	40	.258	.312	1	0	SS-159
1979	156	587	124	18	6	0	0.0	77	27	37	37	28	.211	.262	0	0	SS-155
1980	158	609	140	18	5	0	0.0	67	35	71	49	57	.230	.276	0	0	SS-158
1981	110	450	100	11	2	0	0.0	53	21	41	37	22	.222	.256	0	0	SS-110
1982 STL N	140	488	121	24	1	2	0.4	58	43	68	32	25	.248	.314	1	0	SS-139
1983	159	552	134	30	6	3	0.5	69	50	64	36	34	.243	.335	2	0	SS-158
1984	124	412	106	20	5	1	0.2	53	44	56	17	35	.257	.337	0	0	SS-124
1985	158	537	148	22	3	6	1.1	70	54	65	27	31	.276	.361	0	0	SS-158
1986	153	514	144	19	4	0	0.0	67	54	79	27	31	.280	.333	8	2	SS-144
1987	158	600	182	40	4	0	0.0	104	75	89	36	43	.303	.383	2	1	SS-158
1988	153	575	155	27	1	3	0.5	80	51	74	43	57	.270	.336	2	0	SS-150
11 yrs.	1628	5914	1506	246	43	16	0.3	767	500	691	384	403	.255	.319	16	3	SS-1613

LEAGUE CHAMPIONSHIP SERIES

	G	AB	H	2B	3B	HR	HR%	R	RBI	BB	SO	SB	BA	SA	PH AB	PH H	G by POS
1982 STL N	3	9	5	0	0	0	0.0	0	3	3	0	1	.556	.556	0	0	SS-3
1985	6	23	10	1	1	1	4.3	4	3	3	1	1	.435	.696	0	0	SS-6
1987	7	25	5	0	1	0	0.0	2	1	3	4	0	.200	.280	0	0	SS-7
3 yrs.	16	57	20	1	2	1	1.8	6	7	9	5	2	.351	.491	0	0	SS-16

WORLD SERIES

	G	AB	H	2B	3B	HR	HR%	R	RBI	BB	SO	SB	BA	SA	PH AB	PH H	G by POS
1982 STL N	7	24	5	0	0	0	0.0	3	1	3	0	1	.208	.208	0	0	SS-7
1985	7	23	2	0	0	0	0.0	1	0	4	0	1	.087	.087	0	0	SS-7
1987	7	28	6	0	0	0	0.0	3	2	2	3	2	.214	.214	0	0	SS-7
3 yrs.	21	75	13	0	0	0	0.0	7	3	9	3	4	.173	.173	0	0	SS-21

Van Snider

SNIDER, VAN VOORHEES
B. Aug. 11, 1963, Birmingham, Ala.   BL TR 6'3"   185 lbs.

	G	AB	H	2B	3B	HR	HR%	R	RBI	BB	SO	SB	BA	SA	PH AB	PH H	G by POS
1988 CIN N	11	28	6	1	0	1	3.6	4	6	0	13	0	.214	.357	4	0	OF-8

Cory Snyder

SNYDER, JAMES CORY
B. Nov. 11, 1962, Inglewood, Calif.   BR TR 6'4"   175 lbs.

	G	AB	H	2B	3B	HR	HR%	R	RBI	BB	SO	SB	BA	SA	PH AB	PH H	G by POS
1986 CLE A	103	416	113	21	1	24	5.8	58	69	16	123	2	.272	.500	0	0	OF-74, SS-34, 3B-11, DH-1
1987	157	577	136	24	2	33	5.7	74	82	31	166	5	.236	.456	7	2	OF-139, SS-18
1988	142	511	139	24	3	26	5.1	71	75	42	101	5	.272	.483	1	0	OF-141
3 yrs.	402	1504	388	69	6	83	5.5	203	226	89	390	12	.258	.477	8	2	OF-354, SS-52, 3B-11, DH-1

Chris Speier

SPEIER, CHRIS EDWARD
B. June 28, 1950, Alameda, Calif.   BR TR 6'1"   175 lbs.

Year/Team	G	AB	H	2B	3B	HR	HR%	R	RBI	BB	SO	SB	BA	SA	PH AB	PH H	G by POS
1971 SF N	157	601	141	17	6	8	1.3	74	46	56	90	4	.235	.323	2	1	SS-156
1972	150	562	151	25	2	15	2.7	74	71	82	92	9	.269	.400	0	0	SS-150
1973	153	542	135	17	4	11	2.0	58	71	66	69	4	.249	.356	3	2	SS-150, 2B-1
1974	141	501	125	19	5	9	1.8	55	53	62	64	3	.250	.361	4	0	SS-135, 2B-4
1975	141	487	132	30	5	10	2.1	60	69	70	50	4	.271	.415	4	0	SS-136, 3B-1
1976	145	495	112	18	4	3	0.6	51	40	60	52	2	.226	.297	5	1	SS-135, 2B-7, 3B-5, 1B-1
1977 2 teams		SF	N	(6G –	.176)	MON	N	(139G –	.235)								
" total	145	548	128	31	6	5	0.9	59	38	67	81	1	.234	.339	2	0	SS-143
1978 MON N	150	501	126	18	3	5	1.0	47	51	60	75	1	.251	.329	2	0	SS-148
1979	113	344	78	13	1	7	2.0	31	26	43	45	0	.227	.331	0	0	SS-112
1980	128	388	103	14	4	1	0.3	35	32	52	38	0	.265	.330	4	0	SS-127, 2B-1
1981	96	307	69	10	2	2	0.7	33	25	38	29	1	.225	.290	0	0	SS-96
1982	156	530	136	26	4	7	1.3	41	60	47	67	1	.257	.360	1	0	SS-155
1983	88	261	67	12	2	2	0.8	31	22	29	37	2	.257	.341	5	1	SS-74, 3B-12, 2B-2
1984 3 teams		MON	N	(25G –	.150)	STL	N	(38G –	.178)	MIN	A	(12G –	.212)				
" total	75	191	34	7	1	3	1.6	12	10	13	34	0	.178	.272	16	3	SS-59, 3B-6
1985 CHI N	106	218	53	11	0	4	1.8	16	24	17	34	1	.243	.349	12	5	SS-58, 3B-31, 2B-13

	G	AB	H	2B	3B	HR	HR%	R	RBI	BB	SO	SB	BA	SA	Pinch Hit AB	Pinch Hit H	G by POS

Chris Speier continued

	G	AB	H	2B	3B	HR	HR%	R	RBI	BB	SO	SB	BA	SA	PH AB	PH H	G by POS
1986	95	155	44	8	0	6	3.9	21	23	15	32	2	.284	.452	17	7	3B-53, SS-23, 2B-7
1987 SF N	111	317	79	13	0	11	3.5	39	39	42	51	4	.249	.394	14	5	2B-55, 3B-44, SS-22
1988	82	171	37	9	1	3	1.8	26	18	23	39	3	.216	.333	10	1	2B-45, 3B-22, SS-12
18 yrs.	2232	7119	1750	298	50	112	1.6	763	718	842	979	42	.246	.349	97	28	SS-1891, 3B-174, 2B-135, 1B-1

DIVISIONAL PLAYOFF SERIES

	G	AB	H	2B	3B	HR	HR%	R	RBI	BB	SO	SB	BA	SA	PH AB	PH H	G by POS
1981 MON N	5	15	6	2	0	0	0.0	4	3	4	2	0	.400	.533	0	0	SS-5

LEAGUE CHAMPIONSHIP SERIES

	G	AB	H	2B	3B	HR	HR%	R	RBI	BB	SO	SB	BA	SA	PH AB	PH H	G by POS
1971 SF N	4	14	5	1	0	1	7.1	4	1	1	0	0	.357	.643	0	0	SS-4
1981 MON N	5	16	3	0	0	0	0.0	0	0	2	0	0	.188	.188	0	0	SS-5
1987 SF N	3	5	0	0	0	0	0.0	0	0	0	2	0	.000	.000	2	0	2B-1
3 yrs.	12	35	8	1	0	1	2.9	4	1	3	2	0	.229	.343	2	0	SS-9, 2B-1

Harry Spilman

SPILMAN, WILLIAM HARRY
B. July 18, 1954, Albany, Ga.

BL TR 6'1" 180 lbs.

	G	AB	H	2B	3B	HR	HR%	R	RBI	BB	SO	SB	BA	SA	PH AB	PH H	G by POS
1978 CIN N	4	4	1	0	0	0	0.0	1	0	0	1	0	.250	.250	4	1	
1979	43	56	12	3	0	0	0.0	7	5	7	5	0	.214	.268	22	5	1B-12, 3B-4
1980	65	101	27	4	0	4	4.0	14	19	9	19	0	.267	.426	41	12	1B-18, OF-2, 3B-1, C-1
1981 2 teams		CIN	N	(23G –	.167)		HOU	N	(28G –	.294)							
" total	51	58	14	1	0	0	0.0	9	4	5	10	0	.241	.259	29	9	1B-15, 3B-3
1982 HOU N	38	61	17	2	0	3	4.9	7	11	5	10	0	.279	.459	26	6	1B-11
1983	42	78	13	3	0	1	1.3	7	9	5	12	0	.167	.244	20	1	1B-19, C-6
1984	32	72	19	2	0	2	2.8	14	15	12	10	0	.264	.375	10	1	1B-18, C-8
1985	44	66	9	1	0	1	1.5	3	4	3	7	0	.136	.197	20	4	1B-19, C-2
1986 2 teams		DET	A	(24G –	.245)		SF	N	(58G –	.287)							
" total	82	143	39	9	0	5	3.5	18	30	15	21	0	.273	.441	42	16	1B-20, DH-11, 3B-7, C-2, OF-1, 2B-1
1987 SF N	83	90	24	5	0	1	1.1	5	14	9	20	1	.267	.356	61	13	3B-10, 1B-9, C-1
1988 2 teams		SF	N	(40G –	.175)		HOU	N	(7G –	.000)							
" total	47	45	7	1	1	2	2.2	4	3	4	9	0	.156	.289	34	4	1B-7, C-2, OF-1
11 yrs.	531	774	182	31	1	18	2.3	89	114	74	124	1	.235	.348	309	72	1B-148, 3B-25, C-22, DH-11, OF-4, 2B-1

DIVISIONAL PLAYOFF SERIES

	G	AB	H	2B	3B	HR	HR%	R	RBI	BB	SO	SB	BA	SA	PH AB	PH H	G by POS
1981 HOU N	1	1	0	0	0	0	0.0	0	0	0	0	0	.000	.000	1	0	

LEAGUE CHAMPIONSHIP SERIES

	G	AB	H	2B	3B	HR	HR%	R	RBI	BB	SO	SB	BA	SA	PH AB	PH H	G by POS
1979 CIN N	2	2	0	0	0	0	0.0	0	0	0	0	0	.000	.000	2	0	
1987 SF N	3	2	1	0	0	1	50.0	1	1	0	0	0	.500	2.000	2	1	
2 yrs.	5	4	1	0	0	1	25.0	1	1	0	0	0	.250	1.000	4	1	

Pete Stanicek

STANICEK, PETER LOUIS
Brother of Steve Stanicek.
B. Apr. 16, 1963, Harvey, Ill.

BB TR 5'11" 175 lbs.

	G	AB	H	2B	3B	HR	HR%	R	RBI	BB	SO	SB	BA	SA	PH AB	PH H	G by POS
1987 BAL A	30	113	31	3	0	0	0.0	9	9	8	19	8	.274	.301	0	0	2B-19, DH-10, 3B-2
1988	83	261	60	7	1	4	1.5	29	17	28	45	12	.230	.310	10	2	OF-65, 2B-16, DH-1
2 yrs.	113	374	91	10	1	4	1.1	38	26	36	64	20	.243	.307	10	2	OF-65, 2B-35, DH-11, 3B-2

Mike Stanley

STANLEY, ROBERT MICHAEL
B. June 25, 1963, Fort Lauderdale, Fla.

BR TR 6'1" 185 lbs.

	G	AB	H	2B	3B	HR	HR%	R	RBI	BB	SO	SB	BA	SA	PH AB	PH H	G by POS
1986 TEX A	15	30	10	3	0	1	3.3	4	1	3	7	1	.333	.533	5	2	3B-7, C-4, DH-3, OF-1
1987	78	216	59	8	1	6	2.8	34	37	31	48	3	.273	.403	6	4	C-61, 1B-12, OF-1
1988	94	249	57	8	0	3	1.2	21	27	37	62	0	.229	.297	15	3	C-64, 1B-7, 3B-2
3 yrs.	187	495	126	19	1	10	2.0	59	65	71	117	4	.255	.358	26	9	C-129, 1B-19, 3B-9, DH-3, OF-2

James Steels

STEELS, JAMES EARL
B. May 30, 1961, Bentonia, Miss.

BL TL 5'10" 185 lbs.

	G	AB	H	2B	3B	HR	HR%	R	RBI	BB	SO	SB	BA	SA	PH AB	PH H	G by POS
1987 SD N	62	68	13	1	1	0	0.0	9	6	11	14	3	.191	.235	31	8	OF-28
1988 TEX A	36	53	10	1	0	0	0.0	4	5	0	15	2	.189	.208	9	2	OF-17, DH-7, 1B-6
2 yrs.	98	121	23	2	1	0	0.0	13	11	11	29	5	.190	.223	40	10	OF-45, DH-7, 1B-6

Terry Steinbach

STEINBACH, TERRY LEE
B. Mar. 2, 1962, New Ulm, Minn.

BR TR 6'1" 195 lbs.

	G	AB	H	2B	3B	HR	HR%	R	RBI	BB	SO	SB	BA	SA	PH AB	PH H	G by POS
1986 OAK A	6	15	5	0	0	2	13.3	3	4	1	0	0	.333	.733	2	1	C-5
1987	122	391	111	16	3	16	4.1	66	56	32	66	1	.284	.463	7	4	C-107, 3B-10, 1B-1
1988	104	351	93	19	1	9	2.6	42	51	33	47	3	.265	.402	4	2	C-84, 3B-9, 1B-8, DH-7, OF-1
3 yrs.	232	757	209	35	4	27	3.6	111	111	66	113	4	.276	.440	13	7	C-196, 3B-19, 1B-9, DH-7, OF-1

LEAGUE CHAMPIONSHIP SERIES

	G	AB	H	2B	3B	HR	HR%	R	RBI	BB	SO	SB	BA	SA	PH AB	PH H	G by POS
1988 OAK A	2	4	1	0	0	0	0.0	0	0	2	0	0	.250	.250	0	0	C-2

WORLD SERIES

	G	AB	H	2B	3B	HR	HR%	R	RBI	BB	SO	SB	BA	SA	PH AB	PH H	G by POS
1988 OAK A	3	11	4	1	0	0	0.0	0	0	0	2	0	.364	.455	0	0	C-2

Kurt Stillwell

STILLWELL, KURT ANDREW
Son of Ron Stillwell.
B. June 4, 1965, Glendale, Calif.

BB TR 5'11" 165 lbs.

	G	AB	H	2B	3B	HR	HR%	R	RBI	BB	SO	SB	BA	SA	PH AB	PH H	G by POS
1986 CIN N	104	279	64	6	1	0	0.0	31	26	30	47	6	.229	.258	20	6	SS-80
1987	131	395	102	20	7	4	1.0	54	33	32	50	4	.258	.375	29	8	SS-51, 2B-37, 3B-20
1988 KC A	128	459	115	28	5	10	2.2	63	53	47	76	6	.251	.399	4	0	SS-124
3 yrs.	363	1133	281	54	13	14	1.2	148	112	109	173	16	.248	.356	53	14	SS-255, 2B-37, 3B-20

	G	AB	H	2B	3B	HR	HR %	R	RBI	BB	SO	SB	BA	SA	Pinch Hit AB	Pinch Hit H	G by POS

Jeff Stone

STONE, JEFFREY GLEN
B. Dec. 26, 1960, Kennett, Mo.   BL TR 6'   175 lbs.

	G	AB	H	2B	3B	HR	HR %	R	RBI	BB	SO	SB	BA	SA	AB	H	G by POS
1983 PHI N	9	4	3	0	2	0	0.0	2	3	0	1	4	.750	1.750	1	1	OF-1
1984	51	185	67	4	6	1	0.5	27	15	9	26	27	.362	.465	5	0	OF-46
1985	88	264	70	4	3	3	1.1	36	11	15	50	15	.265	.337	18	5	OF-69
1986	82	249	69	6	4	6	2.4	32	19	20	52	19	.277	.406	7	7	OF-58
1987	66	125	32	7	1	1	0.8	19	16	8	38	3	.256	.352	37	9	OF-25
1988 BAL A	26	61	10	1	0	0	0.0	4	1	4	11	4	.164	.180	7	2	OF-21, DH-1
6 yrs.	322	888	251	22	16	11	1.2	120	65	56	178	72	.283	.381	75	24	OF-220, DH-1

Darryl Strawberry

STRAWBERRY, DARRYL EUGENE (The Straw Man)
B. Mar. 12, 1962, Los Angeles, Calif.   BL TL 6'6"   190 lbs.

	G	AB	H	2B	3B	HR	HR %	R	RBI	BB	SO	SB	BA	SA	AB	H	G by POS
1983 NY N	122	420	108	15	7	26	6.2	63	74	47	128	19	.257	.512	4	0	OF-117
1984	147	522	131	27	4	26	5.0	75	97	75	131	27	.251	.467	4	2	OF-146
1985	111	393	109	15	4	29	7.4	78	79	73	96	26	.277	.557	2	0	OF-110
1986	136	475	123	27	5	27	5.7	76	93	72	141	28	.259	.507	8	0	OF-131
1987	154	532	151	32	5	39	7.3	108	104	97	122	36	.284	.583	3	1	OF-151
1988	153	543	146	27	3	**39**	**7.2**	101	101	85	127	29	.269	**.545**	2	0	OF-150
6 yrs.	823	2885	768	143	28	186	6.4	501	548	449	745	165	.266	.529	23	3	OF-805

LEAGUE CHAMPIONSHIP SERIES

	G	AB	H	2B	3B	HR	HR %	R	RBI	BB	SO	SB	BA	SA	AB	H	G by POS
1986 NY N	6	22	5	1	0	2	9.1	4	5	3	12	1	.227	.545	0	0	OF-6
1988	7	30	9	2	0	1	3.3	5	6	2	5	0	.300	.467	0	0	OF-7
2 yrs.	13	52	14	3	0	3	5.8	9	11	5	17	1	.269	.500	0	0	OF-13

WORLD SERIES

	G	AB	H	2B	3B	HR	HR %	R	RBI	BB	SO	SB	BA	SA	AB	H	G by POS
1986 NY N	7	24	5	1	0	1	4.2	4	1	4	6	3	.208	.375	0	0	OF-7

Franklin Stubbs

STUBBS, FRANKLIN LEE
B. Oct. 21, 1960, Richland, N. C.   BL TL 6'2"   205 lbs.

	G	AB	H	2B	3B	HR	HR %	R	RBI	BB	SO	SB	BA	SA	AB	H	G by POS
1984 LA N	87	217	42	2	3	8	3.7	22	17	24	63	2	.194	.341	22	4	1B-51, OF-20
1985	10	9	2	0	0	0	0.0	0	2	0	3	0	.222	.222	7	2	1B-4
1986	132	420	95	11	1	23	5.5	55	58	37	107	7	.226	.421	12	0	OF-124, 1B-13
1987	129	386	90	16	3	16	4.1	48	52	31	85	8	.233	.415	11	3	1B-111, OF-18
1988	115	242	54	13	0	8	3.3	30	34	23	61	11	.223	.376	26	8	1B-84, OF-13
5 yrs.	473	1274	283	42	7	55	4.3	155	163	115	319	28	.222	.396	78	17	1B-263, OF-175

LEAGUE CHAMPIONSHIP SERIES

	G	AB	H	2B	3B	HR	HR %	R	RBI	BB	SO	SB	BA	SA	AB	H	G by POS
1988 LA N	4	8	2	0	0	0	0.0	0	0	0	4	0	.250	.250	2	0	1B-3

WORLD SERIES

	G	AB	H	2B	3B	HR	HR %	R	RBI	BB	SO	SB	BA	SA	AB	H	G by POS
1988 LA N	5	17	5	2	0	0	0.0	3	2	1	3	0	.294	.412	0	0	1B-5

Jim Sundberg

SUNDBERG, JAMES HOWARD
B. May 18, 1951, Galesburg, Ill.   BR TR 6'   190 lbs.

	G	AB	H	2B	3B	HR	HR %	R	RBI	BB	SO	SB	BA	SA	AB	H	G by POS
1974 TEX A	132	368	91	13	3	3	0.8	45	36	62	61	2	.247	.323	1	0	C-132
1975	155	472	94	9	0	6	1.3	45	36	51	77	3	.199	.256	0	0	C-155
1976	140	448	102	24	2	3	0.7	33	34	37	61	0	.228	.310	1	1	C-140
1977	149	453	132	20	3	6	1.3	61	65	53	77	2	.291	.389	1	1	C-149
1978	149	518	144	23	6	6	1.2	54	58	64	70	2	.278	.380	1	0	C-148, DH-1
1979	150	495	136	23	4	5	1.0	50	64	51	51	3	.275	.368	1	0	C-150
1980	151	505	138	24	1	10	2.0	59	63	64	67	2	.273	.384	3	2	C-151
1981	102	339	94	17	2	3	0.9	42	28	50	48	2	.277	.366	2	1	C-98, OF-2
1982	139	470	118	22	5	10	2.1	37	47	49	57	2	.251	.383	7	1	C-132, OF-1
1983	131	378	76	14	0	2	0.5	30	28	35	64	0	.201	.254	1	0	C-131
1984 MIL A	110	348	91	19	4	7	2.0	43	43	38	63	1	.261	.399	3	0	C-109
1985 KC A	115	367	90	12	4	10	2.7	38	35	33	67	0	.245	.381	5	3	C-112
1986	140	429	91	9	1	12	2.8	41	42	57	91	1	.212	.322	8	2	C-134
1987 CHI N	61	139	28	2	0	4	2.9	9	15	19	40	0	.201	.302	8	3	C-57
1988 2 teams		CHI N	(24G –	.241)				TEX A	(38G –	.286)							
" total	62	145	39	5	0	6	4.1	21	22	13	32	0	.269	.428	9	1	C-56
15 yrs.	1886	5874	1464	236	35	93	1.6	608	616	676	926	20	.249	.349	51	15	C-1854, OF-3, DH-1

LEAGUE CHAMPIONSHIP SERIES

	G	AB	H	2B	3B	HR	HR %	R	RBI	BB	SO	SB	BA	SA	AB	H	G by POS
1985 KC A	7	24	4	1	1	1	4.2	3	6	1	7	0	.167	.417	0	0	C-7

WORLD SERIES

	G	AB	H	2B	3B	HR	HR %	R	RBI	BB	SO	SB	BA	SA	AB	H	G by POS
1985 KC A	7	24	6	2	0	0	0.0	6	1	6	4	0	.250	.333	0	0	C-7

B. J. Surhoff

SURHOFF, WILLIAM JAMES
Brother of Rick Surhoff.
B. Aug. 4, 1964, Bronx, N. Y.   BL TR 6'1"   185 lbs.

	G	AB	H	2B	3B	HR	HR %	R	RBI	BB	SO	SB	BA	SA	AB	H	G by POS
1987 MIL A	115	395	118	22	3	7	1.8	50	68	36	30	11	.299	.423	10	3	C-98, 3B-10, 1B-1
1988	139	493	121	21	0	5	1.0	47	38	31	49	21	.245	.318	9	2	C-106, 3B-31, 1B-2, OF-1, SS-1
2 yrs.	254	888	239	43	3	12	1.4	97	106	67	79	32	.269	.365	19	5	C-204, 3B-41, 1B-3, OF-1, SS-1

Dale Sveum

SVEUM, DALE CURTIS
B. Nov. 23, 1963, Richmond, Calif.   BB TR 6'2"   185 lbs.

	G	AB	H	2B	3B	HR	HR %	R	RBI	BB	SO	SB	BA	SA	AB	H	G by POS
1986 MIL A	91	317	78	13	2	7	2.2	35	35	32	63	4	.246	.366	2	0	3B-65, SS-13, 2B-2
1987	153	535	135	27	3	25	4.7	86	95	40	133	2	.252	.454	1	1	SS-142, 2B-13
1988	129	467	113	14	4	9	1.9	41	51	21	122	1	.242	.347	0	0	SS-127, DH-1, 2B-1
3 yrs.	373	1319	326	54	9	41	3.1	162	181	93	318	7	.247	.395	3	1	SS-282, 3B-65, 2B-27, DH-1

Pat Tabler

TABLER, PATRICK SEAN
B. Feb. 2, 1958, Hamilton, Ohio   BR TR 6'3"   175 lbs.

	G	AB	H	2B	3B	HR	HR %	R	RBI	BB	SO	SB	BA	SA	AB	H	G by POS
1981 CHI N	35	101	19	3	1	1	1.0	11	5	13	26	0	.188	.267	0	0	2B-35
1982	25	85	20	4	2	1	1.2	9	7	6	20	0	.235	.365	0	0	3B-25
1983 CLE A	124	430	125	23	5	6	1.4	56	65	56	63	2	.291	.409	5	2	OF-80, 3B-25, DH-6, 2B-2
1984	144	473	137	21	3	10	2.1	66	68	47	62	3	.290	.410	6	1	1B-67, OF-43, 3B-36, DH-1, 2B-1

	G	AB	H	2B	3B	HR	HR %	R	RBI	BB	SO	SB	BA	SA	Pinch Hit AB	Pinch Hit H	G by POS

Pat Tabler continued

	G	AB	H	2B	3B	HR	HR %	R	RBI	BB	SO	SB	BA	SA	AB	H	G by POS
1985	117	404	111	18	3	5	1.2	47	59	27	55	0	.275	.371	8	4	1B-92, DH-18, 3B-4, 2B-1
1986	130	473	154	29	2	6	1.3	61	48	29	75	3	.326	.433	9	1	1B-107, DH-18
1987	151	553	170	34	3	11	2.0	66	86	51	84	5	.307	.439	7	2	1B-82, DH-66
1988 2 teams		CLE	A	(41G –	.224)		KC	A	(89G –	.309)							
" total	130	444	125	22	3	2	0.5	53	66	46	68	3	.282	.358	8	2	OF-37, DH-29, 1B-17, 3B-1
8 yrs.	856	2963	861	154	22	42	1.4	369	404	275	453	16	.291	.400	43	12	1B-365, OF-160, DH-138, 3B-91, 2B-39

Danny Tartabull

TARTABULL, DANILO MORA   BR TR 6'1"   185 lbs.
Born Danilo Tartabull y Mora.   Son of Jose Tartabull.
B. Oct. 30, 1962, San Juan, Puerto Rico

	G	AB	H	2B	3B	HR	HR %	R	RBI	BB	SO	SB	BA	SA	AB	H	G by POS
1984 SEA A	10	20	6	1	0	2	10.0	3	7	2	3	0	.300	.650	1	0	SS-8, 2B-1
1985	19	61	20	7	1	1	1.6	8	7	8	14	1	.328	.525	3	1	SS-16, 3B-4
1986	137	511	138	25	6	25	4.9	76	96	61	157	4	.270	.489	2	1	OF-101, 2B-31, DH-3, 3B-1
1987 KC A	158	582	180	27	3	34	5.8	95	101	79	136	9	.309	.541	3	0	OF-149, DH-6
1988	146	507	139	38	3	26	5.1	80	102	76	119	8	.274	.515	4	1	OF-130, DH-13
5 yrs.	470	1681	483	98	13	88	5.2	262	313	226	429	22	.287	.518	13	3	OF-380, 2B-32, SS-24, DH-22, 3B-5

Wil Tejada

TEJADA, WILFREDO ARISTIDES   BR TR 6'   175 lbs.
Born Wilfredo Aristides Tejada y Andujar.
B. Nov. 12, 1962, Santo Domingo, Dominican Republic

	G	AB	H	2B	3B	HR	HR %	R	RBI	BB	SO	SB	BA	SA	AB	H	G by POS
1986 MON N	10	25	6	1	0	0	0.0	1	2	2	8	0	.240	.280	0	0	C-10
1988	8	15	4	2	0	0	0.0	1	2	0	4	0	.267	.400	1	0	C-7
2 yrs.	18	40	10	3	0	0	0.0	2	4	2	12	0	.250	.325	1	0	C-17

Garry Templeton

TEMPLETON, GARRY LEWIS (Jump Steady)   BB TR 5'11"   175 lbs.
B. Mar. 24, 1956, Lockney, Tex.

	G	AB	H	2B	3B	HR	HR %	R	RBI	BB	SO	SB	BA	SA	AB	H	G by POS
1976 STL N	53	213	62	8	2	1	0.5	32	17	7	33	11	.291	.362	1	0	SS-53
1977	153	621	200	19	18	8	1.3	94	79	15	70	28	.322	.449	2	0	SS-151
1978	155	647	181	31	13	2	0.3	82	47	22	87	34	.280	.377	2	0	SS-155
1979	154	672	211	32	19	9	1.3	105	62	18	91	26	.314	.458	1	0	SS-150
1980	118	504	161	19	9	4	0.8	83	43	18	43	31	.319	.417	2	0	SS-115
1981	80	333	96	16	8	1	0.3	47	33	14	55	8	.288	.393	4	0	SS-76
1982 SD N	141	563	139	25	8	6	1.1	76	64	26	82	27	.247	.352	6	1	SS-136
1983	126	460	121	20	2	3	0.7	39	40	21	57	16	.263	.335	3	0	SS-123
1984	148	493	127	19	3	2	0.4	40	35	39	81	8	.258	.320	2	0	SS-146
1985	148	546	154	30	2	6	1.1	63	55	41	88	16	.282	.377	0	0	SS-148
1986	147	510	126	21	2	2	0.4	42	44	35	86	10	.247	.308	9	4	SS-144
1987	148	510	113	13	5	5	1.0	42	48	42	92	14	.222	.296	1	0	SS-146
1988	110	362	90	15	7	3	0.8	35	36	20	50	8	.249	.354	5	0	SS-105, 3B-2
13 yrs.	1681	6434	1781	268	98	52	0.8	780	603	318	915	237	.277	.373	38	5	SS-1648, 3B-2

LEAGUE CHAMPIONSHIP SERIES

	G	AB	H	2B	3B	HR	HR %	R	RBI	BB	SO	SB	BA	SA	AB	H	G by POS
1984 SD N	5	15	5	1	0	0	0.0	2	2	2	0	1	.333	.400	0	0	SS-5

WORLD SERIES

	G	AB	H	2B	3B	HR	HR %	R	RBI	BB	SO	SB	BA	SA	AB	H	G by POS
1984 SD N	5	19	6	1	0	0	0.0	1	0	0	3	0	.316	.368	0	0	SS-5

Mickey Tettleton

TETTLETON, MICKEY LEE   BB TR 6'2"   190 lbs.
B. Sept. 16, 1960, Oklahoma City, Okla.

	G	AB	H	2B	3B	HR	HR %	R	RBI	BB	SO	SB	BA	SA	AB	H	G by POS
1984 OAK A	33	76	20	2	1	1	1.3	10	5	11	21	0	.263	.355	3	0	C-32
1985	78	211	53	12	0	3	1.4	23	15	28	59	2	.251	.351	3	1	C-76, DH-1
1986	90	211	43	9	0	10	4.7	26	35	39	51	7	.204	.389	2	0	C-89
1987	82	211	41	3	0	8	3.8	19	26	30	65	1	.194	.322	2	0	C-80, DH-1, 1B-1
1988 BAL A	86	283	74	11	1	11	3.9	31	37	28	70	0	.261	.424	9	0	C-80
5 yrs.	369	992	231	37	2	33	3.3	109	118	136	266	10	.233	.374	19	1	C-357, DH-2, 1B-1

Tim Teufel

TEUFEL, TIMOTHY SHAWN (Tuff)   BR TR 6'   175 lbs.
B. July 7, 1958, Greenwich, Conn.

	G	AB	H	2B	3B	HR	HR %	R	RBI	BB	SO	SB	BA	SA	AB	H	G by POS
1983 MIN A	21	78	24	7	1	3	3.8	11	6	2	8	0	.308	.538	2	0	2B-18, DH-1, SS-1
1984	157	568	149	30	3	14	2.5	76	61	76	73	1	.262	.400	0	0	2B-157
1985	138	434	113	24	3	10	2.3	58	50	48	70	4	.260	.399	6	1	2B-137, DH-1
1986 NY N	93	279	69	20	1	4	1.4	35	31	32	42	1	.247	.369	16	3	2B-84, 1B-3, 3B-1
1987	97	299	92	29	0	14	4.7	55	61	44	53	3	.308	.545	18	8	2B-92, 1B-1
1988	90	273	64	20	0	4	1.5	35	31	29	41	0	.234	.352	14	4	2B-84, 1B-3
6 yrs.	596	1931	511	130	8	49	2.5	270	240	231	287	9	.265	.416	56	16	2B-572, 1B-7, DH-2, SS-1, 3B-1

LEAGUE CHAMPIONSHIP SERIES

	G	AB	H	2B	3B	HR	HR %	R	RBI	BB	SO	SB	BA	SA	AB	H	G by POS
1986 NY N	2	6	1	0	0	0	0.0	0	0	0	0	0	.167	.167	0	0	2B-2
1988	1	3	0	0	0	0	0.0	0	0	0	1	0	.000	.000	0	0	2B-1
2 yrs.	3	9	1	0	0	0	0.0	0	0	0	1	0	.111	.111	0	0	2B-3

WORLD SERIES

	G	AB	H	2B	3B	HR	HR %	R	RBI	BB	SO	SB	BA	SA	AB	H	G by POS
1986 NY N	3	9	4	1	0	1	11.1	1	1	0	2	0	.444	.889	0	0	2B-3

Andres Thomas

THOMAS, ANDRES PERES   BR TR 6'1"   170 lbs.
Born Andres Peres Thomas.
B. Nov. 10, 1963, Boca Chica, Dominican Republic

	G	AB	H	2B	3B	HR	HR %	R	RBI	BB	SO	SB	BA	SA	AB	H	G by POS
1985 ATL N	15	18	5	0	0	0	0.0	6	2	0	2	0	.278	.278	1	1	SS-10
1986	102	323	81	17	2	6	1.9	26	32	8	49	4	.251	.372	6	3	SS-97
1987	82	324	75	11	0	5	1.5	29	39	14	50	6	.231	.312	1	0	SS-81
1988	153	606	153	22	2	13	2.1	54	68	14	95	7	.252	.360	3	1	SS-150
4 yrs.	352	1271	314	50	4	24	1.9	115	141	36	196	17	.247	.349	11	5	SS-338

Milt Thompson

THOMPSON, MILTON BERNARD
B. Jan. 5, 1959, Washington, D. C.   BL TR 5'11"   170 lbs.

	G	AB	H	2B	3B	HR	HR %	R	RBI	BB	SO	SB	BA	SA	Pinch Hit AB	Pinch Hit H	G by POS
1984 ATL N	25	99	30	1	0	2	2.0	16	4	11	11	14	.303	.374	2	2	OF-25
1985	73	182	55	7	2	0	0.0	17	6	7	36	9	.302	.363	30	13	OF-49
1986 PHI N	96	299	75	7	1	6	2.0	38	23	26	62	19	.251	.341	10	1	OF-89
1987	150	527	159	26	9	7	1.3	86	43	42	87	46	.302	.425	15	5	OF-146
1988	122	378	109	16	2	2	0.5	53	33	39	59	17	.288	.357	16	4	OF-112
5 yrs.	466	1485	428	57	14	17	1.1	210	109	125	255	105	.288	.380	73	25	OF-421

Robby Thompson

THOMPSON, ROBERT RANDALL
B. May 10, 1962, West Palm Beach, Fla.   BR TR 5'11"   165 lbs.

	G	AB	H	2B	3B	HR	HR %	R	RBI	BB	SO	SB	BA	SA	Pinch Hit AB	Pinch Hit H	G by POS
1986 SF N	149	549	149	27	3	7	1.3	73	47	42	112	12	.271	.370	1	0	2B-149, SS-1
1987	132	420	110	26	5	10	2.4	62	44	40	91	16	.262	.419	4	2	2B-126
1988	138	477	126	24	6	7	1.5	66	48	40	111	14	.264	.384	5	1	2B-134
3 yrs.	419	1446	385	77	14	24	1.7	201	139	122	314	42	.266	.389	10	3	2B-409, SS-1

LEAGUE CHAMPIONSHIP SERIES

	G	AB	H	2B	3B	HR	HR %	R	RBI	BB	SO	SB	BA	SA	Pinch Hit AB	Pinch Hit H	G by POS
1987 SF N	7	20	2	0	1	1	5.0	4	2	5	7	2	.100	.350	1	0	2B-6

Dickie Thon

THON, RICHARD WILLIAM
B. June 20, 1958, South Bend, Ind.   BR TR 5'11"   160 lbs.

	G	AB	H	2B	3B	HR	HR %	R	RBI	BB	SO	SB	BA	SA	Pinch Hit AB	Pinch Hit H	G by POS
1979 CAL A	35	56	19	3	0	0	0.0	6	8	5	10	0	.339	.393	0	0	2B-24, SS-8, DH-1, 3B-1
1980	80	267	68	12	2	0	0.0	32	15	10	28	7	.255	.315	13	2	SS-22, 2B-21, DH-15, 3B-10, 1B-1
1981 HOU N	49	95	26	6	0	0	0.0	13	3	9	13	6	.274	.337	2	0	2B-28, SS-13, 3B-5
1982	136	496	137	31	10	3	0.6	73	36	37	48	37	.276	.397	9	4	SS-119, 3B-8, 2B-1
1983	154	619	177	28	9	20	3.2	81	79	54	73	34	.286	.457	0	0	SS-154
1984	5	17	6	0	1	0	0.0	3	1	0	4	0	.353	.471	0	0	SS-5
1985	84	251	63	6	1	6	2.4	26	29	18	50	8	.251	.355	6	1	SS-79
1986	106	278	69	13	1	3	1.1	24	21	29	49	6	.248	.335	20	5	SS-104
1987	32	66	14	1	0	1	1.5	6	3	16	13	3	.212	.273	9	3	SS-31
1988 SD N	95	258	68	12	2	1	0.4	36	18	33	49	19	.264	.337	19	3	SS-70, 2B-2, 3B-1
10 yrs.	776	2403	647	112	26	34	1.4	300	213	211	337	120	.269	.380	78	18	SS-605, 2B-76, 3B-25, DH-16, 1B-1

DIVISIONAL PLAYOFF SERIES

	G	AB	H	2B	3B	HR	HR %	R	RBI	BB	SO	SB	BA	SA	Pinch Hit AB	Pinch Hit H	G by POS
1981 HOU N	4	11	2	0	0	0	0.0	0	0	1	0	0	.182	.182	1	0	SS-4

LEAGUE CHAMPIONSHIP SERIES

	G	AB	H	2B	3B	HR	HR %	R	RBI	BB	SO	SB	BA	SA	Pinch Hit AB	Pinch Hit H	G by POS
1979 CAL A	1	0	0	0	0	0	—	1	0	0	0	0	—	—	0	0	SS-1
1986 HOU N	6	12	3	0	0	1	8.3	1	1	0	1	0	.250	.500	1	0	SS-6
2 yrs.	7	12	3	0	0	1	8.3	2	1	0	1	0	.250	.500	1	0	SS-7

Lou Thornton

THORNTON, LOUIS JR.
B. Apr. 26, 1963, Montgomery, Ala.   BL TR 6'   170 lbs.

	G	AB	H	2B	3B	HR	HR %	R	RBI	BB	SO	SB	BA	SA	Pinch Hit AB	Pinch Hit H	G by POS
1985 TOR A	56	72	17	1	1	1	1.4	18	8	2	24	1	.236	.319	3	1	OF-35, DH-16
1987	12	2	1	0	0	0	0.0	5	0	1	0	0	.500	.500	0	0	OF-4
1988	11	2	0	0	0	0	0.0	1	0	0	0	0	.000	.000	0	0	OF-10
3 yrs.	79	76	18	1	1	1	1.3	24	8	3	24	1	.237	.316	3	1	OF-49, DH-16

LEAGUE CHAMPIONSHIP SERIES

	G	AB	H	2B	3B	HR	HR %	R	RBI	BB	SO	SB	BA	SA	Pinch Hit AB	Pinch Hit H	G by POS
1985 TOR A	2	0	0	0	0	0	—	1	0	0	0	0	—	—	0	0	

Gary Thurman

THURMAN, GARY MONTEZ
B. Nov. 12, 1964, Indianapolis, Ind.   BR TR 5'10"   170 lbs.

	G	AB	H	2B	3B	HR	HR %	R	RBI	BB	SO	SB	BA	SA	Pinch Hit AB	Pinch Hit H	G by POS
1987 KC A	27	81	24	2	0	0	0.0	12	5	8	20	7	.296	.321	0	0	OF-27
1988	35	66	11	1	0	0	0.0	6	2	4	20	5	.167	.182	1	0	OF-32, DH-1
2 yrs.	62	147	35	3	0	0	0.0	18	7	12	40	12	.238	.259	1	0	OF-59, DH-1

Rusty Tillman

TILLMAN, KERRY JEROME
B. Aug. 29, 1960, Jacksonville, Fla.   BR TR 6'   175 lbs.

	G	AB	H	2B	3B	HR	HR %	R	RBI	BB	SO	SB	BA	SA	Pinch Hit AB	Pinch Hit H	G by POS
1982 NY N	12	13	2	1	0	0	0.0	4	0	0	4	1	.154	.231	5	2	OF-3
1986 OAK A	22	39	10	1	0	1	2.6	6	6	3	11	2	.256	.359	5	0	OF-17
1988 SF N	4	4	1	0	0	1	25.0	1	3	2	1	0	.250	1.000	3	0	OF-1
3 yrs.	38	56	13	2	0	2	3.6	11	9	5	16	3	.232	.375	13	2	OF-21

Ron Tingley

TINGLEY, RONALD IRVIN
B. May 27, 1959, Presque Isle, Me.   BR TR 6'2"   160 lbs.

	G	AB	H	2B	3B	HR	HR %	R	RBI	BB	SO	SB	BA	SA	Pinch Hit AB	Pinch Hit H	G by POS
1982 SD N	8	20	2	0	0	0	0.0	0	0	0	7	0	.100	.100	0	0	C-8
1988 CLE A	9	24	4	0	0	1	4.2	1	2	2	8	0	.167	.292	1	1	C-9
2 yrs.	17	44	6	0	0	1	2.3	1	2	2	15	0	.136	.205	1	1	C-17

Wayne Tolleson

TOLLESON, JIMMY WAYNE
B. Nov. 22, 1955, Spartanburg, S. C.   BB TR 5'9"   160 lbs.

	G	AB	H	2B	3B	HR	HR %	R	RBI	BB	SO	SB	BA	SA	Pinch Hit AB	Pinch Hit H	G by POS
1981 TEX A	14	24	4	0	0	0	0.0	6	1	1	5	2	.167	.167	1	0	3B-6, SS-2
1982	38	70	8	1	0	0	0.0	6	2	5	14	1	.114	.129	0	0	SS-26, 3B-4, 2B-1
1983	134	470	122	13	2	3	0.6	64	20	40	68	33	.260	.315	0	0	2B-112, SS-26, DH-1
1984	118	338	72	9	2	0	0.0	35	9	27	47	22	.213	.251	0	0	2B-109, SS-7, 3B-5, DH-1, OF-1
1985	123	323	101	9	5	1	0.3	45	18	21	46	21	.313	.381	5	1	SS-81, 2B-29, 3B-12, DH-6
1986 2 teams	CHI A (81G — .250)							NY A (60G — .284)									
" total	141	475	126	16	5	3	0.6	61	43	52	76	17	.265	.339	3	0	SS-74, 3B-72, 2B-3, DH-2, OF-2
1987 NY A	121	349	77	4	0	1	0.3	48	24	43	72	5	.221	.241	0	0	SS-119, 3B-3
1988	21	59	15	2	0	0	0.0	8	5	8	12	1	.254	.288	1	0	2B-12, 3B-10, SS-1
8 yrs.	710	2108	525	54	14	8	0.4	273	120	197	340	102	.249	.299	10	1	SS-336, 2B-266, 3B-112, DH-10, OF-3

	G	AB	H	2B	3B	HR	HR %	R	RBI	BB	SO	SB	BA	SA	Pinch Hit AB	Pinch Hit H	G by POS

Kelvin Torve

TORVE, KELVIN CURTIS
B. Jan. 10, 1960, Rapid City, S. D.
BL TR 6'3"   185 lbs.

	G	AB	H	2B	3B	HR	HR %	R	RBI	BB	SO	SB	BA	SA	PH AB	PH H	G by POS
1988 MIN A	12	16	3	0	0	1	6.3	1	2	1	2	0	.188	.375	6	1	1B-4

Jim Traber

TRABER, JAMES JOSEPH
B. Dec. 26, 1961, Columbus, Ohio
BL TL 6'   194 lbs.

	G	AB	H	2B	3B	HR	HR %	R	RBI	BB	SO	SB	BA	SA	PH AB	PH H	G by POS
1984 BAL A	10	21	5	0	0	0	0.0	3	2	2	4	0	.238	.238	3	1	DH-9
1986	65	212	54	7	0	13	6.1	28	44	18	31	0	.255	.472	7	2	1B-29, DH-21, OF-8
1988	103	352	78	6	0	10	2.8	25	45	19	42	1	.222	.324	9	2	1B-57, DH-30, OF-11
3 yrs.	178	585	137	13	0	23	3.9	56	91	39	77	1	.234	.374	19	5	1B-86, DH-60, OF-19

Alan Trammell

TRAMMELL, ALAN STUART
B. Feb. 21, 1958, Garden Grove, Calif.
BR TR 6'   165 lbs.

	G	AB	H	2B	3B	HR	HR %	R	RBI	BB	SO	SB	BA	SA	PH AB	PH H	G by POS
1977 DET A	19	43	8	0	0	0	0.0	6	0	4	12	0	.186	.186	0	0	SS-19
1978	139	448	120	14	6	2	0.4	49	34	45	56	3	.268	.339	0	0	SS-139
1979	142	460	127	11	4	6	1.3	68	50	43	55	17	.276	.357	0	0	SS-142
1980	146	560	168	21	5	9	1.6	107	65	69	63	12	.300	.404	2	0	SS-144
1981	105	392	101	15	3	2	0.5	52	31	49	31	10	.258	.327	1	1	SS-105
1982	157	489	126	34	3	9	1.8	66	57	52	47	19	.258	.395	0	0	SS-157
1983	142	505	161	31	2	14	2.8	83	66	57	64	30	.319	.471	0	0	SS-140
1984	139	555	174	34	5	14	2.5	85	69	60	63	19	.314	.468	3	1	SS-114, DH-22
1985	149	605	156	21	7	13	2.1	79	57	50	71	14	.258	.380	0	0	SS-149
1986	151	574	159	33	7	21	3.7	107	75	59	57	25	.277	.469	1	0	SS-149, DH-2
1987	151	597	205	34	3	28	4.7	109	105	60	47	21	.343	.551	3	0	SS-149
1988	128	466	145	24	1	15	3.2	73	69	46	46	7	.311	.464	2	0	SS-125
12 yrs.	1568	5694	1650	272	46	133	2.3	884	678	594	612	177	.290	.424	12	4	SS-1532, DH-24

LEAGUE CHAMPIONSHIP SERIES

	G	AB	H	2B	3B	HR	HR %	R	RBI	BB	SO	SB	BA	SA	PH AB	PH H	G by POS
1984 DET A	3	11	4	0	1	1	9.1	2	3	3	1	0	.364	.818	0	0	SS-3
1987	5	20	4	1	0	0	0.0	3	2	1	2	0	.200	.250	0	0	SS-5
2 yrs.	8	31	8	1	1	1	3.2	5	5	4	3	0	.258	.452	0	0	SS-8

WORLD SERIES

	G	AB	H	2B	3B	HR	HR %	R	RBI	BB	SO	SB	BA	SA	PH AB	PH H	G by POS
1984 DET A	5	20	9	1	0	2	10.0	5	6	2	2	1	.450	.800	0	0	SS-5

Jeff Treadway

TREADWAY, HUGH JEFFREY
B. Jan. 22, 1963, Columbus, Ga.
BL TR 6'   175 lbs.

	G	AB	H	2B	3B	HR	HR %	R	RBI	BB	SO	SB	BA	SA	PH AB	PH H	G by POS
1987 CIN N	23	84	28	4	0	2	2.4	9	4	2	6	1	.333	.452	2	1	2B-21
1988	103	301	76	19	4	2	0.7	30	23	27	30	2	.252	.362	7	4	2B-97, 3B-2
2 yrs.	126	385	104	23	4	4	1.0	39	27	29	36	3	.270	.382	9	5	2B-118, 3B-2

Alex Trevino

TREVINO, ALEJANDRO CASTRO
Born Alejandro Trevino y Castro.   Brother of Bobby Trevino.
B. Aug. 26, 1957, Monterrey, Mexico
BR TR 5'10"   165 lbs.

	G	AB	H	2B	3B	HR	HR %	R	RBI	BB	SO	SB	BA	SA	PH AB	PH H	G by POS
1978 NY N	6	12	3	0	0	0	0.0	3	0	1	2	0	.250	.250	1	0	C-5, 3B-1
1979	79	207	56	11	1	0	0.0	24	20	20	27	2	.271	.333	16	5	C-36, 3B-27, 2B-8
1980	106	355	91	11	2	0	0.0	26	37	13	41	0	.256	.299	12	3	C-86, 3B-14, 2B-1
1981	56	149	39	2	0	0	0.0	17	10	13	19	3	.262	.275	10	3	C-45, 2B-4, OF-2, 3B-1
1982 CIN N	120	355	89	10	3	1	0.3	24	33	34	34	3	.251	.304	7	1	C-116, 3B-2
1983	74	167	36	8	1	0	0.0	14	13	17	20	0	.216	.293	7	2	C-63, 3B-4, 2B-1
1984 2 teams		CIN	N (6G – .167)			ATL	N	(79G – .244)									
" total	85	272	66	16	0	3	1.1	36	28	16	29	5	.243	.335	7	1	C-83
1985 SF N	57	157	34	10	1	6	3.8	17	19	20	24	0	.217	.408	2	0	C-55, 3B-1
1986 LA N	89	202	53	13	0	4	2.0	31	26	27	35	0	.262	.386	31	7	C-63, 1B-1
1987	72	144	32	7	1	3	2.1	16	16	6	28	1	.222	.347	33	7	C-45, OF-2, 3B-1
1988 HOU N	78	193	48	17	0	2	1.0	19	13	24	29	5	.249	.368	5	1	C-74, OF-1
11 yrs.	822	2213	547	105	9	20	0.9	227	215	191	288	19	.247	.330	131	30	C-671, 3B-51, 2B-14, OF-5, 1B-1

Manny Trillo

TRILLO, JESUS MANUEL MARCADO (Indio)
Born Jesus Manuel Marcano y Trillo.
B. Dec. 25, 1950, Carapito, Venezuela
BR TR 6'1"   150 lbs.

	G	AB	H	2B	3B	HR	HR %	R	RBI	BB	SO	SB	BA	SA	PH AB	PH H	G by POS
1973 OAK A	17	12	3	2	0	0	0.0	0	3	0	4	0	.250	.417	0	0	2B-16
1974	21	33	5	0	0	0	0.0	3	2	2	8	0	.152	.152	0	0	2B-21
1975 CHI N	154	545	135	12	2	7	1.3	55	70	45	78	1	.248	.316	1	0	2B-153, SS-1
1976	158	582	139	24	3	4	0.7	42	59	53	70	17	.239	.311	1	0	2B-156, SS-1
1977	152	504	141	18	5	7	1.4	51	57	44	58	3	.280	.377	5	0	2B-149
1978	152	552	144	17	5	4	0.7	55	55	50	67	0	.261	.332	2	2	2B-149
1979 PHI N	118	431	112	22	1	6	1.4	40	42	20	59	4	.260	.357	0	0	2B-118
1980	141	531	155	25	9	7	1.3	68	43	32	46	8	.292	.412	0	0	2B-140
1981	94	349	100	14	3	6	1.7	37	36	26	37	10	.287	.395	0	0	2B-94
1982	149	549	149	24	1	0	0.0	52	39	33	53	8	.271	.319	0	0	2B-149
1983 2 teams		CLE	A	(88G – .272)			MON	N	(31G – .264)								
" total	119	441	119	21	1	3	0.7	49	45	31	64	1	.270	.342	0	0	2B-118
1984 SF N	98	401	102	21	1	4	1.0	45	36	25	55	0	.254	.342	1	0	2B-96, 3B-4
1985	125	451	101	16	2	3	0.7	36	25	40	44	2	.224	.288	5	0	2B-120, 3B-1
1986 CHI N	81	152	45	10	0	1	0.7	22	19	16	21	0	.296	.382	14	3	3B-53, 1B-11, 2B-6
1987	108	214	63	8	0	8	3.7	27	26	25	37	0	.294	.444	23	7	1B-47, 3B-35, 2B-13, SS-6
1988	76	164	41	5	0	1	0.6	15	14	8	32	2	.250	.299	20	2	1B-24, 3B-17, 2B-13, SS-7
16 yrs.	1763	5911	1554	239	33	61	1.0	595	571	450	733	56	.263	.345	72	14	2B-1508, 3B-110, 1B-82, SS-15

DIVISIONAL PLAYOFF SERIES

	G	AB	H	2B	3B	HR	HR %	R	RBI	BB	SO	SB	BA	SA	PH AB	PH H	G by POS
1981 PHI N	5	16	3	0	0	0	0.0	1	1	4	0	0	.188	.188	0	0	2B-5

LEAGUE CHAMPIONSHIP SERIES

	G	AB	H	2B	3B	HR	HR %	R	RBI	BB	SO	SB	BA	SA	PH AB	PH H	G by POS
1974 OAK A	1	0	0	0	0	0	–	1	0	0	0	0	–	–	0	0	
1980 PHI N	5	21	8	2	1	0	0.0	1	4	0	2	0	.381	.571	0	0	2B-5
2 yrs.	6	21	8	2	1	0	0.0	2	4	0	2	0	.381	.571	0	0	2B-5

	G	AB	H	2B	3B	HR	HR %	R	RBI	BB	SO	SB	BA	SA	Pinch Hit AB	Pinch Hit H	G by POS

Manny Trillo continued

WORLD SERIES

	G	AB	H	2B	3B	HR	HR%	R	RBI	BB	SO	SB	BA	SA	AB	H	G by POS
1980 PHI N	6	23	5	2	0	0	0.0	4	2	0	0	0	.217	.304	0	0	2B-6

Shane Turner

TURNER, SHANE LEE
B. Jan. 8, 1963, Los Angeles, Calif.
BL TR 5'10" 180 lbs.

	G	AB	H	2B	3B	HR	HR%	R	RBI	BB	SO	SB	BA	SA	AB	H	G by POS
1988 PHI N	18	35	6	0	0	0	0.0	1	1	5	9	0	.171	.171	5	1	3B-8, SS-5

Willie Upshaw

UPSHAW, WILLIE CLAY
B. Apr. 27, 1957, Blanco, Tex.
BL TL 6' 185 lbs.

	G	AB	H	2B	3B	HR	HR%	R	RBI	BB	SO	SB	BA	SA	AB	H	G by POS
1978 TOR A	95	224	53	8	2	1	0.4	26	17	21	35	4	.237	.304	12	1	OF-52, DH-18, 1B-10
1980	34	61	13	3	1	1	1.6	10	5	6	14	1	.213	.344	9	2	1B-14, DH-12, OF-1
1981	61	111	19	3	1	4	3.6	15	10	11	16	2	.171	.324	17	4	DH-15, OF-14, 1B-14
1982	160	580	155	25	7	21	3.6	77	75	52	91	8	.267	.443	2	0	1B-155, DH-5
1983	160	579	177	26	7	27	4.7	99	104	61	98	10	.306	.515	4	1	1B-159, DH-1
1984	152	569	158	31	9	19	3.3	79	84	55	86	10	.278	.464	0	0	1B-151, DH-1
1985	148	501	138	31	5	15	3.0	79	65	48	71	8	.275	.447	2	0	1B-147, DH-1
1986	155	573	144	28	6	9	1.6	85	60	78	87	23	.251	.368	2	0	1B-154, DH-1
1987	150	512	125	22	4	15	2.9	68	58	58	78	10	.244	.391	7	2	1B-146
1988 CLE A	149	493	121	22	3	11	2.2	58	50	62	66	12	.245	.369	7	2	1B-144
10 yrs.	1264	4203	1103	199	45	123	2.9	596	528	452	642	88	.262	.419	62	12	1B-1094, OF-67, DH-54

LEAGUE CHAMPIONSHIP SERIES

	G	AB	H	2B	3B	HR	HR%	R	RBI	BB	SO	SB	BA	SA	AB	H	G by POS
1985 TOR A	7	26	6	2	0	0	0.0	2	1	1	4	0	.231	.308	0	0	1B-7

Jose Uribe

URIBE, JOSE ALTAGARCIA
Born Jose Altagarcia Gonzalez y Uribe.
B. Jan. 21, 1952, San Cristobal, Dominican Republic
BB TR 5'10" 156 lbs.

	G	AB	H	2B	3B	HR	HR%	R	RBI	BB	SO	SB	BA	SA	AB	H	G by POS
1984 STL N	8	19	4	0	0	0	0.0	4	3	0	2	1	.211	.211	0	0	SS-5, 2B-1
1985 SF N	147	476	113	20	4	3	0.6	46	26	30	57	8	.237	.315	2	0	SS-145, 2B-1
1986	157	453	101	15	1	3	0.7	46	43	61	76	22	.223	.280	2	1	SS-156
1987	95	309	90	16	5	5	1.6	44	30	24	35	12	.291	.424	3	1	SS-95
1988	141	493	124	10	7	3	0.6	47	35	36	69	14	.252	.318	0	0	SS-140
5 yrs.	548	1750	432	61	17	14	0.8	187	137	151	239	57	.247	.325	7	2	SS-541, 2B-2

LEAGUE CHAMPIONSHIP SERIES

	G	AB	H	2B	3B	HR	HR%	R	RBI	BB	SO	SB	BA	SA	AB	H	G by POS
1987 SF N	7	26	7	1	0	0	0.0	1	2	0	4	1	.269	.308	0	0	SS-7

Dave Valle

VALLE, DAVID
B. Oct. 30, 1960, Bayside, N. Y.
BR TR 6'2" 200 lbs.

	G	AB	H	2B	3B	HR	HR%	R	RBI	BB	SO	SB	BA	SA	AB	H	G by POS
1984 SEA A	13	27	8	1	0	1	3.7	4	4	1	5	0	.296	.444	0	0	C-13
1985	31	70	11	1	0	0	0.0	2	4	1	17	0	.157	.171	0	0	C-31
1986	22	53	18	3	0	5	9.4	10	15	7	7	0	.340	.679	8	2	C-12, 1B-4
1987	95	324	83	16	3	12	3.7	40	53	15	46	2	.256	.435	10	1	C-75, 1B-2, OF-1
1988	93	290	67	15	2	10	3.4	29	50	18	38	0	.231	.400	10	5	C-84, DH-3, 1B-1
5 yrs.	254	764	187	36	5	28	3.7	85	126	42	113	2	.245	.415	28	8	C-215, 1B-7, DH-3, OF-1

Andy Van Slyke

VAN SLYKE, ANDREW JAMES (Slick)
B. Dec. 21, 1960, Utica, N. Y.
BL TR 6'1" 190 lbs.

	G	AB	H	2B	3B	HR	HR%	R	RBI	BB	SO	SB	BA	SA	AB	H	G by POS
1983 STL N	101	309	81	15	5	8	2.6	51	38	46	64	21	.262	.421	5	1	OF-69, 3B-30, 1B-9
1984	137	361	88	16	4	7	1.9	45	50	63	71	28	.244	.368	11	4	OF-81, 3B-30, 1B-30
1985	146	424	110	25	6	13	3.1	61	55	47	54	34	.259	.439	19	4	OF-142, 1B-2
1986	137	418	113	23	7	13	3.1	48	61	47	85	21	.270	.452	10	2	OF-110, 1B-38
1987 PIT N	157	564	165	36	11	21	3.7	93	82	56	122	34	.293	.507	7	1	OF-151
1988	154	587	169	23	15	25	4.3	101	100	57	126	30	.288	.506	5	0	OF-152
6 yrs.	832	2663	726	138	48	87	3.3	399	386	316	522	168	.273	.459	57	12	OF-705, 1B-79, 3B-62

LEAGUE CHAMPIONSHIP SERIES

	G	AB	H	2B	3B	HR	HR%	R	RBI	BB	SO	SB	BA	SA	AB	H	G by POS
1985 STL N	5	11	1	0	0	0	0.0	1	1	2	1	0	.091	.091	0	0	OF-5

WORLD SERIES

	G	AB	H	2B	3B	HR	HR%	R	RBI	BB	SO	SB	BA	SA	AB	H	G by POS
1985 STL N	6	11	1	0	0	0	0.0	0	0	0	5	0	.091	.091	0	0	OF-5

Gary Varsho

VARSHO, GARY ANDREW
B. June 20, 1961, Marshfield, Wis.
BL TR 5'11" 190 lbs.

	G	AB	H	2B	3B	HR	HR%	R	RBI	BB	SO	SB	BA	SA	AB	H	G by POS
1988 CHI N	46	73	20	3	0	0	0.0	6	5	1	6	5	.274	.315	28	11	OF-18

Randy Velarde

VELARDE, RANDY LEE
B. Nov. 24, 1962, Midland, Tex.
BR TR 6' 185 lbs.

	G	AB	H	2B	3B	HR	HR%	R	RBI	BB	SO	SB	BA	SA	AB	H	G by POS
1987 NY A	8	22	4	0	0	0	0.0	1	1	0	6	0	.182	.182	0	0	SS-8
1988	48	115	20	6	0	5	4.3	18	12	8	24	1	.174	.357	0	0	2B-24, SS-14, 3B-11
2 yrs.	56	137	24	6	0	5	3.6	19	13	8	30	1	.175	.328	0	0	2B-24, SS-22, 3B-11

Ozzie Virgil

VIRGIL, OSVALDO JOSE LOPEZ
Born Osvaldo Jose Virgil y Lopez. Son of Ozzie Virgil.
B. Dec. 7, 1956, Mayaguez, Puerto Rico
BR TR 6'1" 205 lbs.

	G	AB	H	2B	3B	HR	HR%	R	RBI	BB	SO	SB	BA	SA	AB	H	G by POS
1980 PHI N	1	5	1	1	0	0	0.0	1	0	0	1	0	.200	.400	0	0	C-1
1981	6	6	0	0	0	0	0.0	0	0	0	2	0	.000	.000	5	0	C-1
1982	49	101	24	6	0	3	3.0	11	8	10	26	0	.238	.386	14	3	C-35
1983	55	140	30	7	0	6	4.3	11	23	8	34	0	.214	.393	8	2	C-51
1984	141	456	119	21	2	18	3.9	61	68	45	91	1	.261	.434	8	2	C-137
1985	131	426	105	16	3	19	4.5	47	55	49	85	0	.246	.432	12	4	C-120
1986 ATL N	114	359	80	9	0	15	4.2	45	48	63	73	1	.223	.373	5	0	C-111
1987	123	429	106	13	1	27	6.3	57	72	47	81	0	.247	.471	3	0	C-122
1988	107	320	82	10	0	9	2.8	23	31	22	54	2	.256	.372	15	7	C-96
9 yrs.	727	2242	547	83	6	97	4.3	256	305	244	447	4	.244	.416	70	18	C-674

LEAGUE CHAMPIONSHIP SERIES

	G	AB	H	2B	3B	HR	HR%	R	RBI	BB	SO	SB	BA	SA	AB	H	G by POS
1983 PHI N	1	1	0	0	0	0	0.0	0	0	0	1	0	.000	.000	1	0	

	G	AB	H	2B	3B	HR	HR%	R	RBI	BB	SO	SB	BA	SA	Pinch Hit AB	Pinch Hit H	G by POS

Ozzie Virgil continued

WORLD SERIES

	G	AB	H	2B	3B	HR	HR%	R	RBI	BB	SO	SB	BA	SA	PH AB	PH H	G by POS
1983 PHI N	3	2	1	0	0	0	0.0	0	1	0	0	0	.500	.500	2	1	C-1

Jim Walewander

WALEWANDER, JAMES   B. May 2, 1962, Chicago, Ill.   BB TR 5'10" 160 lbs.

	G	AB	H	2B	3B	HR	HR%	R	RBI	BB	SO	SB	BA	SA	PH AB	PH H	G by POS
1987 DET A	53	54	13	3	1	1	1.9	24	4	7	6	2	.241	.389	2	0	2B-24, 3B-17, SS-3
1988	88	175	37	5	0	0	0.0	23	6	12	26	11	.211	.240	2	0	2B-61, SS-8, 3B-3
2 yrs.	141	229	50	8	1	1	0.4	47	10	19	32	13	.218	.275	4	0	2B-85, 3B-20, SS-11

Chico Walker

WALKER, CLEOTHA   B. Nov. 25, 1957, Jackson, Miss.   BB TR 5'9" 170 lbs.

	G	AB	H	2B	3B	HR	HR%	R	RBI	BB	SO	SB	BA	SA	PH AB	PH H	G by POS
1980 BOS A	19	57	12	0	0	1	1.8	3	5	6	10	3	.211	.263	1	1	2B-11, DH-7
1981	6	17	6	0	0	0	0.0	3	2	1	2	0	.353	.353	1	0	2B-5
1983	4	5	2	0	2	0	0.0	2	1	0	0	0	.400	1.200	1	0	OF-3
1984	3	2	0	0	0	0	0.0	0	1	0	1	0	.000	.000	2	0	2B-1
1985 CHI N	21	12	1	0	0	0	0.0	3	0	0	5	1	.083	.083	8	1	OF-6, 2B-2
1986	28	101	28	3	2	1	1.0	21	7	10	20	15	.277	.376	2	0	OF-26
1987	47	105	21	4	0	0	0.0	15	7	12	23	11	.200	.238	6	0	OF-33, 3B-2
1988 CAL A	33	78	12	1	0	0	0.0	8	2	6	15	2	.154	.167	10	0	OF-17, 2B-7, 3B-2
8 yrs.	161	377	82	8	4	2	0.5	55	25	35	76	32	.218	.276	31	2	OF-85, 2B-26, DH-7, 3B-4

Duane Walker

WALKER, DUANE ALLEN   B. Mar. 13, 1957, Pasadena, Tex.   BL TL 6' 180 lbs.

	G	AB	H	2B	3B	HR	HR%	R	RBI	BB	SO	SB	BA	SA	PH AB	PH H	G by POS
1982 CIN N	86	239	52	10	0	5	2.1	26	22	27	58	9	.218	.322	14	2	OF-69
1983	109	225	53	12	1	2	0.9	14	29	20	43	6	.236	.324	48	16	OF-60
1984	83	195	57	10	3	10	5.1	35	28	33	35	7	.292	.528	14	4	OF-68
1985 2 teams			CIN N (37G – .167)			TEX A (53G – .174)											
" total	90	180	31	4	1	7	3.9	19	17	21	47	3	.172	.322	40	7	OF-42, DH-10
1988 STL N	24	22	4	1	0	0	0.0	1	3	2	7	0	.182	.227	19	4	OF-4, 1B-1
5 yrs.	392	861	197	37	5	24	2.8	95	99	103	190	25	.229	.367	135	33	OF-243, DH-10, 1B-1

Greg Walker

WALKER, GREGORY LEE   B. Oct. 6, 1959, Douglas, Ga.   BL TR 6'3" 205 lbs.

	G	AB	H	2B	3B	HR	HR%	R	RBI	BB	SO	SB	BA	SA	PH AB	PH H	G by POS
1982 CHI A	11	17	7	2	1	2	11.8	3	7	2	3	0	.412	1.000	4	2	DH-4
1983	118	307	83	16	3	10	3.3	32	55	28	57	2	.270	.440	35	13	1B-59, DH-21
1984	136	442	130	29	2	24	5.4	62	75	35	66	8	.294	.532	16	3	1B-101, DH-21
1985	163	601	155	38	4	24	4.0	77	92	44	100	5	.258	.454	9	3	1B-151, DH-7
1986	78	282	78	10	6	13	4.6	37	51	29	44	1	.277	.493	3	1	1B-77, DH-1
1987	157	566	145	33	2	27	4.8	85	94	75	112	2	.256	.465	4	0	1B-154, DH-3
1988	99	377	93	22	1	8	2.1	45	42	29	77	0	.247	.374	1	0	1B-98
7 yrs.	762	2592	691	150	19	108	4.2	341	416	242	459	18	.267	.464	72	22	1B-640, DH-57

LEAGUE CHAMPIONSHIP SERIES

	G	AB	H	2B	3B	HR	HR%	R	RBI	BB	SO	SB	BA	SA	PH AB	PH H	G by POS
1983 CHI A	2	3	1	0	0	0	0.0	0	0	1	2	0	.333	.333	1	0	1B-1

Tim Wallach

WALLACH, TIMOTHY CHARLES   B. Sept. 14, 1957, Huntington Park, Calif.   BR TR 6'3" 220 lbs.

	G	AB	H	2B	3B	HR	HR%	R	RBI	BB	SO	SB	BA	SA	PH AB	PH H	G by POS
1980 MON N	5	11	2	0	0	1	9.1	1	2	1	5	0	.182	.455	2	0	OF-3, 1B-1
1981	71	212	50	9	1	4	1.9	19	13	15	37	0	.236	.344	6	1	OF-35, 1B-16, 3B-15
1982	158	596	160	31	3	28	4.7	89	97	36	81	6	.268	.471	3	1	3B-156, OF-2, 1B-1
1983	156	581	156	33	3	19	3.3	54	70	55	97	0	.269	.434	0	0	3B-156
1984	160	582	143	25	4	18	3.1	55	72	50	101	3	.246	.395	0	0	3B-160, SS-1
1985	155	569	148	36	3	22	3.9	70	81	38	79	9	.260	.450	2	0	3B-154
1986	134	480	112	22	1	18	3.8	50	71	44	72	8	.233	.396	1	0	3B-132
1987	153	593	177	42	4	26	4.4	89	123	37	98	9	.298	.514	3	0	3B-150, P-1
1988	159	592	152	32	5	12	2.0	52	69	38	88	2	.257	.389	8	2	3B-153, 2B-1
9 yrs.	1151	4216	1100	230	24	148	3.5	479	598	314	658	37	.261	.432	25	4	3B-1076, OF-40, 1B-18, SS-1, 2B-1, P-1

DIVISIONAL PLAYOFF SERIES

	G	AB	H	2B	3B	HR	HR%	R	RBI	BB	SO	SB	BA	SA	PH AB	PH H	G by POS
1981 MON N	4	4	1	1	0	0	0.0	1	0	4	0	0	.250	.500	0	0	OF-3

LEAGUE CHAMPIONSHIP SERIES

	G	AB	H	2B	3B	HR	HR%	R	RBI	BB	SO	SB	BA	SA	PH AB	PH H	G by POS
1981 MON N	1	1	0	0	0	0	0.0	0	0	0	0	0	.000	.000	1	0	

Denny Walling

WALLING, DENNIS MARTIN   B. Apr. 17, 1954, Neptune, N. J.   BL TR 6' 180 lbs.

	G	AB	H	2B	3B	HR	HR%	R	RBI	BB	SO	SB	BA	SA	PH AB	PH H	G by POS
1975 OAK A	6	8	1	1	0	0	0.0	0	2	0	4	0	.125	.250	4	1	OF-3
1976	3	11	3	0	0	0	0.0	1	0	0	3	0	.273	.273	0	0	OF-3
1977 HOU N	6	21	6	0	1	0	0.0	1	6	2	4	0	.286	.381	1	1	OF-5
1978	120	247	62	11	3	3	1.2	30	36	30	24	9	.251	.356	39	10	OF-78
1979	82	147	48	8	4	3	2.0	21	31	17	21	3	.327	.497	37	14	OF-42
1980	100	284	85	6	5	3	1.1	30	29	35	26	4	.299	.387	21	4	1B-63, OF-19
1981	65	158	37	6	0	5	3.2	23	23	28	17	2	.234	.367	18	6	OF-27, 1B-27
1982	85	146	30	4	1	1	0.7	22	14	23	19	4	.205	.267	30	6	OF-32, 1B-20
1983	100	135	40	5	3	3	2.2	24	19	15	16	2	.296	.444	37	8	1B-42, OF-13, 3B-13
1984	87	249	70	11	5	3	1.2	37	31	16	24	7	.281	.402	26	7	3B-52, 1B-16, OF-6
1985	119	345	93	20	1	7	2.0	44	45	25	26	5	.270	.394	23	2	3B-51, 1B-46, OF-13
1986	130	382	119	23	1	13	3.4	54	58	36	31	1	.312	.479	31	12	3B-102, OF-11, 1B-4
1987	110	325	92	21	4	5	1.5	45	33	39	37	5	.283	.418	15	8	3B-79, 1B-16, OF-7
1988 2 teams			HOU N (65G – .244)			STL N (19G – .224)											
" total	84	234	56	13	2	1	0.4	22	21	17	25	2	.239	.325	20	3	3B-56, OF-12, 1B-4
14 yrs.	1097	2692	742	129	30	47	1.7	354	348	283	281	44	.276	.398	302	82	3B-353, OF-271, 1B-238

DIVISIONAL PLAYOFF SERIES

	G	AB	H	2B	3B	HR	HR%	R	RBI	BB	SO	SB	BA	SA	PH AB	PH H	G by POS
1981 HOU N	3	6	2	0	0	0	0.0	0	1	0	1	0	.333	.333	1	1	OF-1, 1B-1

	G	AB	H	2B	3B	HR	HR %	R	RBI	BB	SO	SB	BA	SA	Pinch Hit AB	Pinch Hit H	G by POS

Denny Walling continued

LEAGUE CHAMPIONSHIP SERIES

	G	AB	H	2B	3B	HR	HR %	R	RBI	BB	SO	SB	BA	SA	PH AB	PH H	G by POS
1980 HOU N	3	9	1	0	0	0	0.0	2	2	1	0	0	.111	.111	1	0	OF-2
1986	5	19	3	1	0	0	0.0	1	2	0	4	0	.158	.211	2	1	3B-5
2 yrs.	8	28	4	1	0	0	0.0	3	4	1	4	0	.143	.179	3	1	3B-5, OF-2

Gary Ward

WARD, GARY LAMELL
B. Dec. 6, 1953, Los Angeles, Calif.

BR TR 6'2" 195 lbs.

	G	AB	H	2B	3B	HR	HR %	R	RBI	BB	SO	SB	BA	SA	PH AB	PH H	G by POS
1979 MIN A	10	14	4	0	0	0	0.0	2	1	3	3	0	.286	.286	1	0	OF-5, DH-3
1980	13	41	19	6	2	1	2.4	11	10	3	6	0	.463	.780	2	0	OF-12
1981	85	295	78	7	6	3	1.0	42	29	28	48	5	.264	.359	5	1	OF-80, DH-2
1982	152	570	165	33	7	28	4.9	85	91	37	105	13	.289	.519	5	2	OF-150, DH-2
1983	157	623	173	34	5	19	3.0	76	88	44	98	8	.278	.440	4	0	OF-152, DH-2
1984 TEX A	153	602	171	21	7	21	3.5	97	79	55	95	7	.284	.447	4	0	OF-148, DH-5
1985	154	593	170	28	7	15	2.5	77	70	39	97	26	.287	.433	1	1	OF-153, DH-1
1986	105	380	120	15	2	5	1.3	54	51	31	72	12	.316	.405	0	0	OF-104, DH-1
1987 NY A	146	529	131	22	1	16	3.0	65	78	33	101	9	.248	.384	12	8	OF-94, DH-36, 1B-15
1988	91	231	52	8	0	4	1.7	26	24	24	41	0	.225	.312	17	5	OF-54, 1B-11, 3B-2
10 yrs.	1066	3878	1083	174	37	112	2.9	535	521	297	666	80	.279	.430	51	17	OF-952, DH-52, 1B-26, 3B-2

Claudell Washington

WASHINGTON, CLAUDELL
B. Aug. 31, 1954, Los Angeles, Calif.

BL TL 6' 190 lbs.

	G	AB	H	2B	3B	HR	HR %	R	RBI	BB	SO	SB	BA	SA	PH AB	PH H	G by POS
1974 OAK A	73	221	63	10	5	0	0.0	16	19	13	44	7	.285	.376	8	3	DH-38, OF-32
1975	148	590	182	24	7	10	1.7	86	77	32	80	40	.308	.424	2	1	OF-148
1976	134	490	126	20	6	5	1.0	65	53	30	90	37	.257	.353	3	2	OF-126, DH-6
1977 TEX A	129	521	148	31	2	12	2.3	63	68	25	112	21	.284	.420	2	0	OF-127
1978 2 teams			TEX	A	(12G –	.167)		CHI	A	(86G –	.264)						
" total	98	356	90	16	5	6	1.7	34	33	13	69	5	.253	.376	6	2	OF-89, DH-5
1979 CHI A	131	471	132	33	5	13	2.8	79	66	28	93	19	.280	.454	13	4	OF-122, DH-3
1980 2 teams			CHI	A	(32G –	.289)		NY	N	(79G –	.275)						
" total	111	374	104	20	6	11	2.9	53	54	25	82	21	.278	.452	17	1	OF-93, DH-2
1981 ATL N	85	320	93	22	3	5	1.6	37	37	15	47	12	.291	.425	5	3	OF-79
1982	150	563	150	24	6	16	2.8	94	80	50	107	33	.266	.416	7	0	OF-139
1983	134	496	138	24	8	9	1.8	75	44	35	103	31	.278	.413	7	2	OF-128
1984	120	416	119	21	2	17	4.1	62	61	59	77	21	.286	.469	12	2	OF-107
1985	122	398	110	14	6	15	3.8	62	43	40	66	14	.276	.455	26	6	OF-99
1986 2 teams			ATL	N	(40G –	.270)		NY	A	(54G –	.237)						
" total	94	272	69	16	0	11	4.0	36	30	21	59	10	.254	.434	28	5	OF-76
1987 NY A	102	312	87	17	0	9	2.9	42	44	27	54	10	.279	.420	21	4	OF-72, DH-13
1988	126	455	140	22	3	11	2.4	62	64	24	74	15	.308	.442	19	4	OF-117
15 yrs.	1757	6255	1751	314	64	150	2.4	866	773	437	1157	296	.280	.423	176	39	OF-1554, DH-67

LEAGUE CHAMPIONSHIP SERIES

	G	AB	H	2B	3B	HR	HR %	R	RBI	BB	SO	SB	BA	SA	PH AB	PH H	G by POS
1974 OAK A	4	11	3	1	0	0	0.0	1	0	0	0	0	.273	.364	1	1	OF-3
1975	3	12	3	1	0	0	0.0	1	1	0	2	0	.250	.333	0	0	OF-2
1982 ATL N	3	9	3	0	0	0	0.0	0	0	2	2	0	.333	.333	0	0	OF-3
3 yrs.	10	32	9	2	0	0	0.0	2	1	2	4	0	.281	.344	1	1	OF-8

WORLD SERIES

	G	AB	H	2B	3B	HR	HR %	R	RBI	BB	SO	SB	BA	SA	PH AB	PH H	G by POS
1974 OAK A	5	7	4	0	0	0	0.0	1	0	1	1	0	.571	.571	1	1	OF-5

Ron Washington

WASHINGTON, RONALD
B. Apr. 29, 1952, New Orleans, La.

BR TR 5'11" 156 lbs.

	G	AB	H	2B	3B	HR	HR %	R	RBI	BB	SO	SB	BA	SA	PH AB	PH H	G by POS
1977 LA N	10	19	7	0	0	0	0.0	4	1	0	2	1	.368	.368	0	0	SS-10
1981 MIN A	28	84	19	3	1	0	0.0	8	5	4	14	4	.226	.286	0	0	SS-26, OF-2
1982	119	451	122	17	6	5	1.1	48	39	14	79	3	.271	.368	2	0	SS-91, 2B-37, 3B-1
1983	99	317	78	7	3	4	1.3	28	26	22	50	10	.246	.325	4	1	SS-81, 2B-14, DH-1, 3B-1
1984	88	197	58	11	5	3	1.5	25	23	4	31	1	.294	.447	12	2	SS-71, 2B-9, DH-4, 3B-2
1985	69	135	37	6	4	1	0.7	24	14	8	15	5	.274	.400	12	2	SS-31, 2B-24, DH-7, 3B-7, 1B-1
1986	48	74	19	3	0	4	5.4	15	11	3	21	1	.257	.459	10	2	2B-16, DH-15, SS-7, 3B-3
1987 BAL A	26	79	16	3	1	1	1.3	7	6	1	15	0	.203	.304	0	0	3B-20, 2B-3, DH-2, OF-2, SS-1
1988 CLE A	69	223	57	14	2	2	0.9	30	21	9	35	3	.256	.363	4	3	SS-54, 3B-8, 2B-7
9 yrs.	556	1579	413	64	22	20	1.3	189	146	65	262	28	.262	.368	44	10	SS-372, 2B-110, 3B-42, DH-29, OF-4, 1B-1

Mark Wasinger

WASINGER, MARK THOMAS
B. Aug. 4, 1961, Monterey, Calif.

BR TR 6' 165 lbs.

	G	AB	H	2B	3B	HR	HR %	R	RBI	BB	SO	SB	BA	SA	PH AB	PH H	G by POS
1986 SD N	3	8	0	0	0	0	0.0	0	1	0	2	0	.000	.000	0	0	3B-3, 2B-1
1987 SF N	44	80	22	3	0	1	1.3	16	3	8	14	2	.275	.350	11	1	3B-21, 2B-10, SS-2
1988	3	2	0	0	0	0	0.0	1	0	0	0	0	.000	.000	1	0	3B-1
3 yrs.	50	90	22	3	0	1	1.1	17	4	8	16	2	.244	.311	12	1	3B-25, 2B-11, SS-2

Mitch Webster

WEBSTER, MITCHELL DEAN
B. May 16, 1959, Larned, Kans.

BB TL 6'1½" 170 lbs.

	G	AB	H	2B	3B	HR	HR %	R	RBI	BB	SO	SB	BA	SA	PH AB	PH H	G by POS
1983 TOR A	11	11	2	0	0	0	0.0	2	0	1	1	0	.182	.182	1	0	OF-7, DH-2
1984	26	22	5	2	1	0	0.0	9	4	1	7	0	.227	.409	7	1	OF-10, DH-9, 1B-1
1985 2 teams			TOR	A	(4G –	.000)		MON	N	(74G –	.274)						
" total	78	213	58	8	2	11	5.2	32	30	20	33	15	.272	.484	9	1	OF-66, DH-2
1986 MON N	151	576	167	31	13	8	1.4	89	49	57	78	36	.290	.431	4	0	OF-146
1987	156	588	165	30	8	15	2.6	101	63	70	95	33	.281	.435	7	4	OF-153
1988 2 teams			MON	N	(81G –	.255)		CHI	N	(70G –	.265)						
" total	151	523	136	16	8	6	1.1	69	39	55	87	22	.260	.356	17	3	OF-136
6 yrs.	573	1933	533	87	32	40	2.1	302	185	204	301	106	.276	.416	45	10	OF-518, DH-13, 1B-1

	G	AB	H	2B	3B	HR	HR %	R	RBI	BB	SO	SB	BA	SA	Pinch Hit AB	H	G by POS

Walt Weiss

WEISS, WALTER WILLIAM
B. Nov. 28, 1963, Tuxedo, N. Y.   BB TR 6'   175 lbs.

	G	AB	H	2B	3B	HR	HR%	R	RBI	BB	SO	SB	BA	SA	AB	H	G by POS
1987 OAK A	16	26	12	4	0	0	0.0	3	1	2	2	1	.462	.615	1	0	SS-11
1988	147	452	113	17	3	3	0.7	44	39	35	56	4	.250	.321	1	0	SS-147
2 yrs.	163	478	125	21	3	3	0.6	47	40	37	58	5	.262	.337	2	0	SS-158

LEAGUE CHAMPIONSHIP SERIES

1988 OAK A	4	15	5	2	0	0	0.0	2	2	0	4	0	.333	.467	0	0	SS-4

WORLD SERIES

1988 OAK A	5	16	1	0	0	0	0.0	1	0	0	2	1	.063	.063	0	0	SS-5

Brad Wellman

WELLMAN, BRAD EUGENE
B. Aug. 17, 1959, Lodi, Calif.   BR TR 6'   165 lbs.

	G	AB	H	2B	3B	HR	HR%	R	RBI	BB	SO	SB	BA	SA	AB	H	G by POS
1982 SF N	6	4	1	0	0	0	0.0	1	0	0	1	0	.250	.250	2	0	2B-2
1983	82	182	39	3	0	1	0.5	15	16	22	39	5	.214	.247	4	0	2B-74, SS-2
1984	93	265	60	9	1	2	0.8	23	25	19	41	10	.226	.291	6	3	2B-54, SS-33, 3B-10
1985	71	174	41	11	1	0	0.0	16	16	4	33	5	.236	.310	6	1	2B-36, 3B-25, SS-3
1986	12	13	2	0	0	0	0.0	0	1	1	2	0	.154	.154	2	1	SS-8, 3B-1, 2B-1
1987 LA N	3	4	1	0	0	0	0.0	1	1	0	1	0	.250	.250	0	0	SS-1, 3B-1, 2B-1
1988 KC A	71	107	29	3	0	1	0.9	11	6	6	23	1	.271	.327	2	1	2B-46, SS-15, 3B-4
7 yrs.	338	749	173	26	2	4	0.5	67	65	52	140	21	.231	.287	22	6	2B-214, SS-62, 3B-41

Lou Whitaker

WHITAKER, LOUIS RODMAN (Sweet Lou)
B. May 12, 1957, Brooklyn, N. Y.   BL TR 5'11"   160 lbs.

	G	AB	H	2B	3B	HR	HR%	R	RBI	BB	SO	SB	BA	SA	AB	H	G by POS
1977 DET A	11	32	8	1	0	0	0.0	5	2	4	6	2	.250	.281	0	0	2B-9
1978	139	484	138	12	7	3	0.6	71	58	61	65	7	.285	.357	6	3	2B-136, DH-2
1979	127	423	121	14	8	3	0.7	75	42	78	66	20	.286	.378	5	0	2B-126
1980	145	477	111	19	1	1	0.2	68	45	73	79	8	.233	.283	8	2	2B-143
1981	109	335	88	14	4	5	1.5	48	36	40	42	5	.263	.373	2	1	2B-108
1982	152	560	160	22	8	15	2.7	76	65	48	58	11	.286	.434	4	1	2B-149, DH-1
1983	161	643	206	40	6	12	1.9	94	72	67	70	17	.320	.457	7	3	2B-160
1984	143	558	161	25	1	13	2.3	90	56	62	63	6	.289	.407	6	1	2B-142
1985	152	608	170	29	8	21	3.5	102	73	80	56	6	.280	.457	4	0	2B-150
1986	144	584	157	26	6	20	3.4	95	73	63	70	13	.269	.437	6	4	2B-141
1987	149	604	160	38	6	16	2.6	110	59	71	108	13	.265	.427	3	1	2B-148
1988	115	403	111	18	2	12	3.0	54	55	66	61	2	.275	.419	9	3	2B-110
12 yrs.	1547	5711	1591	258	57	121	2.1	888	636	713	744	110	.279	.407	60	19	2B-1522, DH-3

LEAGUE CHAMPIONSHIP SERIES

1984 DET A	3	14	2	0	0	0	0.0	3	0	0	3	0	.143	.143	0	0	2B-3
1987	5	17	3	0	0	1	5.9	4	1	7	3	1	.176	.353	0	0	2B-5
2 yrs.	8	31	5	0	0	1	3.2	7	1	7	6	1	.161	.258	0	0	2B-8

WORLD SERIES

1984 DET A	5	18	5	2	0	0	0.0	6	0	4	4	0	.278	.389	0	0	2B-5

Devon White

WHITE, DEVON MARKES
B. Dec. 29, 1962, Kingston, Jamaica   BB TR 6'1"   170 lbs.

	G	AB	H	2B	3B	HR	HR%	R	RBI	BB	SO	SB	BA	SA	AB	H	G by POS
1985 CAL A	21	7	1	0	0	0	0.0	7	0	1	3	3	.143	.143	0	0	OF-16
1986	28	51	12	1	1	1	2.0	8	3	6	8	6	.235	.353	0	0	OF-28
1987	159	639	168	33	5	24	3.8	103	87	39	135	32	.263	.443	0	0	OF-159
1988	122	455	118	22	2	11	2.4	76	51	23	84	17	.259	.389	5	2	OF-116
4 yrs.	330	1152	299	56	8	36	3.1	194	141	69	230	58	.260	.416	5	2	OF-319

LEAGUE CHAMPIONSHIP SERIES

1986 CAL A	3	2	1	0	0	0	0.0	2	0	0	1	0	.500	.500	0	0	OF-3

Frank White

WHITE, FRANK JR.
B. Sept. 4, 1950, Greenville, Miss.   BR TR 5'11"   165 lbs.

	G	AB	H	2B	3B	HR	HR%	R	RBI	BB	SO	SB	BA	SA	AB	H	G by POS
1973 KC A	51	139	31	6	1	0	0.0	20	5	8	23	3	.223	.281	1	0	SS-37, 2B-11
1974	99	204	45	6	3	1	0.5	19	18	5	33	3	.221	.294	3	0	2B-50, SS-29, 3B-16, DH-3
1975	111	304	76	10	2	7	2.3	43	36	20	39	11	.250	.365	0	0	2B-67, SS-42, 3B-4, DH-2
1976	152	446	102	17	6	2	0.4	39	46	19	42	20	.229	.307	0	0	2B-130, SS-37
1977	152	474	116	21	5	5	1.1	59	50	25	67	23	.245	.342	0	0	2B-152, SS-4
1978	143	461	127	24	6	7	1.5	66	50	26	59	13	.275	.399	3	0	2B-140
1979	127	467	124	26	4	10	2.1	73	48	25	54	28	.266	.403	1	0	2B-125
1980	154	560	148	23	4	7	1.3	70	60	19	69	19	.264	.357	3	0	2B-153
1981	94	364	91	17	1	9	2.5	35	38	19	50	4	.250	.376	1	1	2B-93
1982	145	524	156	45	6	11	2.1	71	56	16	65	10	.298	.469	1	0	2B-144
1983	146	549	143	35	6	11	2.0	52	77	20	51	13	.260	.406	3	2	2B-145
1984	129	479	130	22	5	17	3.5	58	56	27	72	5	.271	.445	1	0	2B-129
1985	149	563	140	25	1	22	3.9	62	69	28	86	10	.249	.414	0	0	2B-149
1986	151	566	154	37	3	22	3.9	76	84	43	88	4	.272	.465	6	1	2B-151, SS-1, 3B-1
1988	150	537	126	25	1	8	1.5	48	58	21	67	7	.235	.330	6	2	2B-148, DH-3
15 yrs.	1953	6637	1709	339	54	139	2.1	791	751	321	865	173	.257	.388	29	6	2B-1787, SS-150, 3B-21, DH-8

DIVISIONAL PLAYOFF SERIES

1981 KC A	3	11	2	0	0	0	0.0	1	0	1	1	0	.182	.182	0	0	2B-3

LEAGUE CHAMPIONSHIP SERIES

1976 KC A	4	8	1	0	0	0	0.0	2	0	0	1	0	.125	.125	0	0	2B-4
1977	5	18	5	1	0	0	0.0	1	2	0	4	1	.278	.333	0	0	2B-5
1978	4	13	3	0	0	0	0.0	1	2	0	0	0	.231	.231	0	0	2B-4
1980	3	11	6	1	0	1	9.1	3	3	0	0	1	.545	.909	0	0	2B-3
1984	3	12	1	0	0	0	0.0	1	0	0	3	0	.083	.083	0	0	2B-3
1985	7	25	5	0	0	0	0.0	1	3	1	2	0	.200	.200	0	0	2B-7
6 yrs.	26	87	21	2	0	1	1.1	9	10	1	10	2	.241	.299	0	0	2B-26

	G	AB	H	2B	3B	HR	HR %	R	RBI	BB	SO	SB	BA	SA	Pinch Hit AB	H	G by POS

Frank White continued

WORLD SERIES

	G	AB	H	2B	3B	HR	HR %	R	RBI	BB	SO	SB	BA	SA	PH AB	H	G by POS
1980 **KC A**	6	25	2	0	0	0	0.0	0	0	1	5	1	.080	.080	0	0	2B-6
1985	7	28	7	3	0	1	3.6	4	6	3	4	1	.250	.464	0	0	2B-7
2 yrs.	13	53	9	3	0	1	1.9	4	6	4	9	2	.170	.283	0	0	2B-13

Ernie Whitt
WHITT, LEO ERNEST
B. June 13, 1952, Detroit, Mich.

BL TR 6'2" 200 lbs.

	G	AB	H	2B	3B	HR	HR %	R	RBI	BB	SO	SB	BA	SA	PH AB	H	G by POS
1976 **BOS A**	8	18	4	2	0	1	5.6	4	3	2	2	0	.222	.500	1	0	C-8
1977 **TOR A**	23	41	7	3	0	0	0.0	4	6	2	12	0	.171	.244	9	1	C-14
1978	2	4	0	0	0	0	0.0	0	0	1	1	0	.000	.000	1	0	C-1
1980	106	295	70	12	2	6	2.0	23	34	22	30	1	.237	.353	1	0	C-105
1981	74	195	46	9	0	1	0.5	16	16	20	30	5	.236	.297	4	0	C-72
1982	105	284	74	14	2	11	3.9	28	42	26	34	3	.261	.440	21	7	C-98, DH-1
1983	123	344	88	15	2	17	4.9	53	56	50	55	1	.256	.459	17	5	C-119
1984	124	315	75	12	1	15	4.8	35	46	43	49	0	.238	.425	16	5	C-118
1985	139	412	101	21	2	19	4.6	55	64	47	59	3	.245	.444	16	2	C-134
1986	131	395	106	19	2	16	4.1	48	56	35	39	0	.268	.448	11	3	C-129
1987	135	446	120	24	1	19	4.3	57	75	44	50	0	.269	.455	12	1	C-131
1988	127	398	100	11	2	16	4.0	63	70	61	38	4	.251	.410	11	0	C-123
12 yrs.	1097	3147	791	142	14	121	3.8	386	468	353	399	17	.251	.421	120	24	C-1052, DH-1

LEAGUE CHAMPIONSHIP SERIES

	G	AB	H	2B	3B	HR	HR %	R	RBI	BB	SO	SB	BA	SA	PH AB	H	G by POS
1985 **TOR A**	7	21	4	1	0	0	0.0	1	2	2	4	0	.190	.238	0	0	C-7

Curtis Wilkerson
WILKERSON, CURTIS VERNON
B. Apr. 26, 1961, Petersburg, Va.

BB TR 5'8" 158 lbs.

	G	AB	H	2B	3B	HR	HR %	R	RBI	BB	SO	SB	BA	SA	PH AB	H	G by POS
1983 **TEX A**	16	35	6	0	1	0	0.0	7	1	2	5	3	.171	.229	1	0	SS-9, 3B-2, 2B-2
1984	153	484	120	12	0	1	0.0	47	26	22	72	12	.248	.279	0	0	SS-116, 2B-47
1985	129	360	88	11	6	0	0.0	35	22	22	63	14	.244	.308	2	1	SS-110, 2B-19, DH-2
1986	110	236	56	10	3	0	0.0	27	15	11	42	9	.237	.305	3	0	2B-60, SS-56, DH-2
1987	85	138	37	5	3	2	1.4	28	14	6	16	6	.268	.391	3	1	SS-33, 2B-28, 3B-18
1988	117	338	99	12	5	0	0.0	41	28	26	43	9	.293	.358	6	0	2B-87, SS-24, 3B-11
6 yrs.	610	1591	406	50	18	3	0.2	185	106	89	241	53	.255	.315	15	2	SS-348, 2B-243, 3B-31, DH-4

Eddie Williams
WILLIAMS, EDWARD LAQUAN
B. Nov. 1, 1964, Shreveport, La.

BR TR 6' 175 lbs.

	G	AB	H	2B	3B	HR	HR %	R	RBI	BB	SO	SB	BA	SA	PH AB	H	G by POS
1986 **CLE A**	5	7	1	0	0	0	0.0	2	1	0	3	0	.143	.143	2	0	OF-4
1987	22	64	11	4	0	1	1.6	9	4	9	19	0	.172	.281	0	0	3B-22
1988	10	21	4	0	0	0	0.0	3	1	0	3	0	.190	.190	0	0	3B-10
3 yrs.	37	92	16	4	0	1	1.1	14	6	9	25	0	.174	.250	2	0	3B-32, OF-4

Ken Williams
WILLIAMS, KENNETH ROYAL
B. Apr. 6, 1964, Berkeley, Calif.

BR TR 6'2" 187 lbs.

	G	AB	H	2B	3B	HR	HR %	R	RBI	BB	SO	SB	BA	SA	PH AB	H	G by POS
1986 **CHI A**	15	31	4	0	0	1	3.2	2	1	1	11	1	.129	.226	0	0	OF-10, DH-1
1987	116	391	110	18	2	11	2.8	48	50	10	83	21	.281	.422	1	0	OF-115
1988	73	220	35	4	2	8	3.6	18	28	10	64	6	.159	.305	2	1	OF-38, 3B-32, DH-3
3 yrs.	204	642	149	22	4	20	3.1	68	79	21	158	28	.232	.372	3	1	OF-163, 3B-32, DH-4

Matt Williams
WILLIAMS, MATTHEW DERRICK
B. Nov. 28, 1965, Bishop, Calif.

BR TR 6'2" 205 lbs.

	G	AB	H	2B	3B	HR	HR %	R	RBI	BB	SO	SB	BA	SA	PH AB	H	G by POS
1987 **SF N**	84	245	46	9	2	8	3.3	28	21	16	68	4	.188	.339	3	2	SS-70, 3B-17
1988	52	156	32	6	1	8	5.1	17	19	8	41	0	.205	.410	2	0	3B-43, SS-14
2 yrs.	136	401	78	15	3	16	4.0	45	40	24	109	4	.195	.367	5	2	SS-84, 3B-60

Reggie Williams
WILLIAMS, REGINALD DeWAYNE
B. Aug. 29, 1960, Memphis, Tenn.

BR TR 5'11" 185 lbs.

	G	AB	H	2B	3B	HR	HR %	R	RBI	BB	SO	SB	BA	SA	PH AB	H	G by POS
1985 **LA N**	22	9	3	0	0	0	0.0	4	0	0	4	1	.333	.333	3	1	OF-15
1986	128	303	84	14	2	4	1.3	35	32	23	57	9	.277	.376	11	1	OF-124
1987	39	36	4	0	0	0	0.0	6	4	5	9	1	.111	.111	9	0	OF-30
1988 **CLE A**	11	31	7	2	0	1	3.2	7	3	0	6	0	.226	.387	1	1	OF-11
4 yrs.	200	379	98	16	2	5	1.3	52	39	28	76	11	.259	.351	24	3	OF-180

Glenn Wilson
WILSON, GLENN DWIGHT
B. Dec. 22, 1958, Baytown, Tex.

BR TR 6'1" 190 lbs.

	G	AB	H	2B	3B	HR	HR %	R	RBI	BB	SO	SB	BA	SA	PH AB	H	G by POS
1982 **DET A**	84	322	94	15	1	12	3.7	39	34	15	51	2	.292	.457	2	0	OF-80, DH-4
1983	144	503	135	25	6	11	2.2	55	65	25	79	1	.268	.408	7	3	OF-143
1984 **PHI N**	132	341	82	21	3	6	1.8	28	31	17	56	7	.240	.372	19	2	OF-109, 3B-4
1985	161	608	167	39	5	14	2.3	73	102	35	117	7	.275	.424	5	2	OF-158
1986	155	584	158	30	4	15	2.6	70	84	42	91	5	.271	.413	3	0	OF-154
1987	154	569	150	21	2	14	2.5	55	54	38	82	3	.264	.381	2	1	OF-154, P-1
1988 **2 teams**		**SEA A** (78G – .250)				**PIT N** (37G – .270)											
" total	115	410	105	18	1	5	1.2	39	32	18	70	1	.256	.341	3	1	OF-110, DH-2
7 yrs.	945	3337	891	169	22	77	2.3	359	402	190	546	26	.267	.400	41	9	OF-908, DH-6, 3B-4, P-1

Mookie Wilson
WILSON, WILLIAM HAYWARD
B. Feb. 9, 1956, Bamberg, S. C.

BR TR 5'10" 170 lbs.

	G	AB	H	2B	3B	HR	HR %	R	RBI	BB	SO	SB	BA	SA	PH AB	H	G by POS
1980 **NY N**	27	105	26	5	3	0	0.0	16	4	12	19	7	.248	.352	0	0	OF-26
1981	92	328	89	8	8	3	0.9	49	14	20	59	24	.271	.372	10	1	OF-80
1982	159	639	178	25	9	5	0.8	90	55	32	102	58	.279	.369	7	2	OF-156
1983	152	638	176	25	6	7	1.1	91	51	18	103	54	.276	.367	7	0	OF-148
1984	154	587	162	28	10	10	1.7	88	54	26	90	46	.276	.409	8	5	OF-146
1985	93	337	93	16	8	6	1.8	56	26	18	52	24	.276	.424	8	1	OF-83
1986	123	381	110	17	5	9	2.4	61	45	32	72	25	.289	.430	20	7	OF-114
1987	124	385	115	19	7	9	2.3	58	34	35	85	21	.299	.455	32	10	OF-109

	G	AB	H	2B	3B	HR	HR %	R	RBI	BB	SO	SB	BA	SA	Pinch Hit AB	Pinch Hit H	G by POS

Mookie Wilson continued

	G	AB	H	2B	3B	HR	HR %	R	RBI	BB	SO	SB	BA	SA	PH AB	PH H	G by POS
1988	112	378	112	17	5	8	2.1	61	41	27	63	15	.296	.431	22	7	OF-104
9 yrs.	1036	3778	1061	160	61	57	1.5	570	324	230	645	274	.281	.401	114	33	OF-966

LEAGUE CHAMPIONSHIP SERIES

	G	AB	H	2B	3B	HR	HR %	R	RBI	BB	SO	SB	BA	SA	PH AB	PH H	G by POS
1986 NY N	6	26	3	0	0	0	0.0	2	1	1	7	1	.115	.115	0	0	OF-6
1988	4	13	2	0	0	0	0.0	2	1	2	2	0	.154	.154	0	0	OF-3
2 yrs.	10	39	5	0	0	0	0.0	4	2	3	9	1	.128	.128	1	0	OF-9

WORLD SERIES

	G	AB	H	2B	3B	HR	HR %	R	RBI	BB	SO	SB	BA	SA	PH AB	PH H	G by POS
1986 NY N	7	26	7	1	0	0	0.0	3	0	1	6	3	.269	.308	0	0	OF-7

Willie Wilson

WILSON, WILLIE JAMES
B. July 9, 1955, Montgomery, Ala.　　　　　BB TR 6'3"　190 lbs.

	G	AB	H	2B	3B	HR	HR %	R	RBI	BB	SO	SB	BA	SA	PH AB	PH H	G by POS
1976 KC A	12	6	1	0	0	0	0.0	0	0	0	2	2	.167	.167	0	0	OF-6
1977	13	34	11	2	0	0	0.0	10	1	1	8	6	.324	.382	0	0	OF-9, DH-2
1978	127	198	43	8	2	0	0.0	43	16	16	33	46	.217	.278	0	0	OF-112, DH-6
1979	154	588	185	18	13	6	1.0	113	49	28	92	83	.315	.420	0	0	OF-152, DH-2
1980	161	705¹	230	28	15	3	0.4	133	49	28	81	79	.326	.421	3	0	OF-159
1981	102	439	133	10	7	1	0.2	54	32	18	42	34	.303	.364	0	0	OF-101
1982	136	585	194	19	15	3	0.5	87	46	26	81	37	.332	.431	1	0	OF-135
1983	137	576	159	22	8	2	0.3	90	33	33	75	59	.276	.352	3	1	OF-136
1984	128	541	163	24	9	2	0.4	81	44	39	56	47	.301	.390	0	0	OF-128
1985	141	605	168	25	21	4	0.7	87	43	29	94	43	.278	.408	0	0	OF-140
1986	156	631	170	20	7	9	1.4	77	44	31	97	34	.269	.366	6	0	OF-155
1987	146	610	170	18	15	4	0.7	97	30	32	88	59	.279	.377	1	0	OF-143, DH-2
1988	147	591	155	17	11	1	0.2	81	37	22	106	35	.262	.333	4	1	OF-142
13 yrs.	1560	6109	1782	211	123	35	0.6	953	424	303	855	564	.292	.384	18	2	OF-1518, DH-12
												10th					

DIVISIONAL PLAYOFF SERIES

	G	AB	H	2B	3B	HR	HR %	R	RBI	BB	SO	SB	BA	SA	PH AB	PH H	G by POS
1981 KC A	3	13	4	0	0	0	0.0	0	1	0	0	0	.308	.308	0	0	OF-3

LEAGUE CHAMPIONSHIP SERIES

	G	AB	H	2B	3B	HR	HR %	R	RBI	BB	SO	SB	BA	SA	PH AB	PH H	G by POS
1978 KC A	3	4	1	0	0	0	0.0	0	0	0	2	0	.250	.250	0	0	OF-3
1980	3	13	4	2	1	0	0.0	2	4	1	2	0	.308	.615	0	0	OF-3
1984	3	13	2	0	0	0	0.0	0	0	1	2	0	.154	.154	0	0	OF-3
1985	7	29	9	0	0	1	3.4	5	2	1	5	1	.310	.414	0	0	OF-7
4 yrs.	16	59	16	2	1	1	1.7	7	6	3	11	1	.271	.390	0	0	OF-16

WORLD SERIES

	G	AB	H	2B	3B	HR	HR %	R	RBI	BB	SO	SB	BA	SA	PH AB	PH H	G by POS
1980 KC A	6	26	4	1	0	0	0.0	3	0	4	12	2	.154	.192	0	0	OF-6
1985	7	30	11	0	1	0	0.0	1	3	1	4	3	.367	.433	0	0	OF-7
2 yrs.	13	56	15	1	1	0	0.0	4	3	5	16	5	.268	.321	0	0	OF-13

Dave Winfield

WINFIELD, DAVID MARK (Winny)
B. Oct. 3, 1951, St. Paul, Minn.　　　　　BR TR 6'6"　220 lbs.

	G	AB	H	2B	3B	HR	HR %	R	RBI	BB	SO	SB	BA	SA	PH AB	PH H	G by POS
1973 SD N	56	141	39	4	1	3	2.1	9	12	12	19	0	.277	.383	17	8	OF-36, 1B-1
1974	145	498	132	18	4	20	4.0	57	75	40	96	9	.265	.438	15	4	OF-131
1975	143	509	136	20	2	15	2.9	74	76	69	82	23	.267	.403	2	0	OF-138
1976	137	492	139	26	4	13	2.6	81	69	65	78	26	.283	.431	2	1	OF-134
1977	157	615	169	29	7	25	4.1	104	92	58	75	16	.275	.467	2	1	OF-156
1978	158	587	181	30	5	24	4.1	88	97	55	81	21	.308	.499	5	1	OF-154, 1B-2
1979	159	597	184	27	10	34	5.7	97	118	85	71	15	.308	.558	2	0	OF-157
1980	162	558	154	25	6	20	3.6	89	87	79	83	23	.276	.450	9	3	OF-159
1981 NY A	105	388	114	25	1	13	3.4	52	68	43	41	11	.294	.464	4	3	OF-102, DH-1
1982	140	539	151	24	8	37	6.9	84	106	45	64	5	.280	.560	1	0	OF-135, DH-4
1983	152	598	169	26	8	32	5.4	99	116	58	77	15	.283	.513	3	2	OF-151
1984	141	567	193	34	4	19	3.4	106	100	53	71	6	.340	.515	0	0	OF-140
1985	155	633	174	34	6	26	4.1	105	114	52	96	19	.275	.471	1	1	OF-152, DH-2
1986	154	565	148	31	5	24	4.2	90	104	77	106	6	.262	.462	7	1	OF-145, DH-6, 3B-2
1987	156	575	158	22	1	27	4.7	83	97	76	96	5	.275	.457	4	2	OF-145, DH-8
1988	149	559	180	37	2	25	4.5	96	107	69	88	9	.322	.530	4	0	OF-141, DH-4
16 yrs.	2269	8421	2421	412	74	357	4.2	1314	1438	936	1224	209	.287	.481	78	27	OF-2176, DH-25, 1B-3, 3B-2

DIVISIONAL PLAYOFF SERIES

	G	AB	H	2B	3B	HR	HR %	R	RBI	BB	SO	SB	BA	SA	PH AB	PH H	G by POS
1981 NY A	5	20	7	3	0	0	0.0	2	0	1	5	0	.350	.500	0	0	OF-5

LEAGUE CHAMPIONSHIP SERIES

	G	AB	H	2B	3B	HR	HR %	R	RBI	BB	SO	SB	BA	SA	PH AB	PH H	G by POS
1981 NY A	3	13	2	1	0	0	0.0	2	2	2	2	1	.154	.231	0	0	OF-3

WORLD SERIES

	G	AB	H	2B	3B	HR	HR %	R	RBI	BB	SO	SB	BA	SA	PH AB	PH H	G by POS
1981 NY A	6	22	1	0	0	0	0.0	0	1	5	4	1	.045	.045	0	0	OF-6

Herm Winningham

WINNINGHAM, HERMAN SON
B. Dec. 1, 1961, Orangeburg, S. C.　　　　　BL TR 6'1"　170 lbs.

	G	AB	H	2B	3B	HR	HR %	R	RBI	BB	SO	SB	BA	SA	PH AB	PH H	G by POS
1984 NY N	14	27	11	1	1	0	0.0	5	5	1	7	2	.407	.519	4	1	OF-10
1985 MON N	125	312	74	6	5	3	1.0	30	21	28	72	20	.237	.317	13	6	OF-116
1986	90	185	40	6	3	4	2.2	23	11	18	51	12	.216	.346	23	3	OF-66, SS-1
1987	137	347	83	20	3	4	1.2	34	41	34	68	29	.239	.349	20	5	OF-131
1988 2 teams		MON N	(47G –	.233)					CIN N	(53G –	.230)						
" total	100	203	47	3	4	0	0.0	16	21	17	45	12	.232	.286	21	4	OF-72
5 yrs.	466	1074	255	36	16	11	1.0	108	99	98	243	75	.237	.331	81	19	OF-395, SS-1

Mike Woodard

WOODARD, MICHAEL CARY
B. Mar. 2, 1960, Melrose Park, Ill.　　　　　BL TR 5'9"　155 lbs.

	G	AB	H	2B	3B	HR	HR %	R	RBI	BB	SO	SB	BA	SA	PH AB	PH H	G by POS
1985 SF N	24	82	20	1	0	0	0.0	12	9	5	3	6	.244	.256	1	1	2B-23
1986	48	79	20	2	1	1	1.3	14	5	10	9	7	.253	.342	21	4	2B-23, SS-2, 3B-2
1987	10	19	4	1	0	0	0.0	0	1	0	1	0	.211	.263	2	0	2B-8
1988 CHI A	18	45	6	0	1	0	0.0	3	4	1	5	1	.133	.178	1	0	2B-14
4 yrs.	100	225	50	4	2	1	0.4	29	19	16	18	14	.222	.271	25	5	2B-68, SS-2, 3B-2

	G	AB	H	2B	3B	HR	HR %	R	RBI	BB	SO	SB	BA	SA	Pinch Hit AB	H	G by POS

Tracy Woodson

WOODSON, TRACY MICHAEL
B. Oct. 5, 1962, Richmond, Va.
BR TR 6'3" 215 lbs.

	G	AB	H	2B	3B	HR	HR %	R	RBI	BB	SO	SB	BA	SA	PH AB	H	G by POS
1987 LA N	53	136	31	8	1	1	0.7	14	11	9	21	1	.228	.324	4	1	3B-45, 1B-7
1988	65	173	43	4	1	3	1.7	15	15	7	32	1	.249	.335	9	3	3B-41, 1B-25
2 yrs.	118	309	74	12	2	4	1.3	29	26	16	53	2	.239	.330	13	4	3B-86, 1B-32

LEAGUE CHAMPIONSHIP SERIES

	G	AB	H	2B	3B	HR	HR %	R	RBI	BB	SO	SB	BA	SA	PH AB	H	G by POS
1988 LA N	3	4	1	0	0	0	0.0	0	0	0	1	0	.250	.250	2	1	1B-3

WORLD SERIES

	G	AB	H	2B	3B	HR	HR %	R	RBI	BB	SO	SB	BA	SA	PH AB	H	G by POS
1988 LA N	4	4	0	0	0	0	0.0	0	1	0	0	0	.000	.000	4	0	1B-3

Craig Worthington

WORTHINGTON, CRAIG RICHARD
B. Apr. 17, 1965, Los Angeles, Calif.
BR TR 6' 160 lbs.

	G	AB	H	2B	3B	HR	HR %	R	RBI	BB	SO	SB	BA	SA	PH AB	H	G by POS
1988 BAL A	26	81	15	2	0	2	2.5	5	4	9	24	1	.185	.284	0	0	3B-26

Rick Wrona

WRONA, RICHARD JAMES
B. Dec. 10, 1963, Tulsa, Okla.
BR TR 6'1" 185 lbs.

	G	AB	H	2B	3B	HR	HR %	R	RBI	BB	SO	SB	BA	SA	PH AB	H	G by POS
1988 CHI N	4	6	0	0	0	0	0.0	0	0	0	1	0	.000	.000	1	0	C-2

Butch Wynegar

WYNEGAR, HAROLD DELANO
B. Mar. 14, 1956, York, Pa.
BB TR 6'1" 190 lbs.

	G	AB	H	2B	3B	HR	HR %	R	RBI	BB	SO	SB	BA	SA	PH AB	H	G by POS
1976 MIN A	149	534	139	21	2	10	1.9	58	69	79	63	0	.260	.363	3	1	C-137, DH-15
1977	144	532	139	22	3	10	1.9	76	79	68	61	2	.261	.370	5	2	C-142, 3B-1
1978	135	454	104	22	1	4	0.9	36	45	47	42	1	.229	.308	8	1	C-131, 3B-1
1979	149	504	136	20	0	7	1.4	74	57	74	36	2	.270	.351	2	0	C-146, DH-2
1980	146	486	124	18	3	5	1.0	61	57	63	36	3	.255	.335	8	1	C-142, DH-1
1981	47	150	37	5	0	0	0.0	11	10	17	9	0	.247	.280	2	0	C-37, DH-9
1982 2 teams		MIN	A	(24G –	.209)		NY	A	(63G –	.293)							
" total	87	277	74	12	1	4	1.4	36	28	50	33	0	.267	.361	2	0	C-86
1983 NY A	94	301	89	18	2	6	2.0	40	42	52	29	1	.296	.429	4	0	C-93
1984	129	442	118	13	1	6	1.4	48	45	64	36	1	.267	.342	7	1	C-126
1985	102	309	69	15	0	5	1.6	27	32	64	43	0	.223	.320	8	3	C-96
1986	61	194	40	4	1	7	3.6	19	29	30	21	0	.206	.345	8	3	C-57
1987 CAL A	31	92	19	2	0	0	0.0	4	5	9	13	0	.207	.228	3	0	C-28, DH-1
1988	27	55	14	4	1	1	1.8	8	8	8	7	0	.255	.418	4	1	C-26
13 yrs.	1301	4330	1102	176	15	65	1.5	498	506	625	429	10	.255	.347	64	14	C-1247, DH-28, 3B-2

Marvell Wynne

WYNNE, MARVELL
B. Dec. 17, 1959, Chicago, Ill.
BL TL 5'11" 176 lbs.

	G	AB	H	2B	3B	HR	HR %	R	RBI	BB	SO	SB	BA	SA	PH AB	H	G by POS
1983 PIT N	103	366	89	16	2	7	1.9	66	26	38	52	12	.243	.355	1	0	OF-102
1984	154	653	174	24	11	0	0.0	77	39	42	81	24	.266	.337	0	0	OF-154
1985	103	337	69	6	3	2	0.6	21	18	18	48	10	.205	.258	3	0	OF-99
1986 SD N	137	288	76	19	2	7	2.4	34	37	15	45	11	.264	.417	12	3	OF-125
1987	98	188	47	8	2	2	1.1	17	24	20	37	11	.250	.346	30	6	OF-71
1988	128	333	88	13	4	11	3.3	37	42	31	62	3	.264	.426	23	2	OF-113
6 yrs.	723	2165	543	86	24	29	1.3	252	186	164	325	71	.251	.353	69	11	OF-664

Gerald Young

YOUNG, GERALD ANTHONY
B. Oct. 22, 1964, Tele, Honduras
BB TR 6'2" 185 lbs.

	G	AB	H	2B	3B	HR	HR %	R	RBI	BB	SO	SB	BA	SA	PH AB	H	G by POS
1987 HOU N	71	274	88	9	2	1	0.4	44	15	26	27	26	.321	.380	2	1	OF-67
1988	149	576	148	21	9	0	0.0	79	37	66	66	65	.257	.325	5	2	OF-145
2 yrs.	220	850	236	30	11	1	0.1	123	52	92	93	91	.278	.342	7	3	OF-212

Mike Young

YOUNG, MICHAEL DARREN
B. Mar. 20, 1960, Oakland, Calif.
BB TR 6'2" 195 lbs.

	G	AB	H	2B	3B	HR	HR %	R	RBI	BB	SO	SB	BA	SA	PH AB	H	G by POS
1982 BAL A	6	2	0	0	0	0	0.0	2	0	0	1	0	.000	.000	2	0	DH-2, OF-1
1983	25	36	6	2	1	0	0.0	5	2	2	8	1	.167	.278	5	0	OF-22, DH-3
1984	123	401	101	17	2	17	4.2	59	52	58	110	6	.252	.431	7	2	OF-115, DH-1
1985	139	450	123	22	1	28	6.2	72	81	48	104	1	.273	.513	18	6	OF-90, DH-37
1986	117	369	93	15	1	9	2.4	43	42	49	90	3	.252	.371	12	3	OF-75, DH-38
1987	110	363	87	10	1	16	4.4	46	39	46	91	10	.240	.405	10	4	OF-60, DH-47
1988 2 teams		PHI	N	(75G –	.226)		MIL	A	(8G –	.000)							
" total	83	160	33	14	0	1	0.6	15	14	28	48	0	.206	.313	40	7	OF-44, DH-5
7 yrs.	603	1781	443	80	6	71	4.0	242	230	231	452	21	.249	.420	94	22	OF-401, DH-133

Joel Youngblood

YOUNGBLOOD, JOEL RANDOLPH
B. Aug. 28, 1951, Houston, Tex.
BR TR 6' 180 lbs.

	G	AB	H	2B	3B	HR	HR %	R	RBI	BB	SO	SB	BA	SA	PH AB	H	G by POS
1976 CIN N	55	57	11	1	0	0	0.0	8	1	2	8	1	.193	.246	33	5	OF-9, 3B-6, 2B-1, C-1
1977 2 teams		STL	N	(25G –	.185)		NY	N	(70G –	.253)							
" total	95	209	51	13	1	0	0.0	17	12	16	45	1	.244	.316	22	5	OF-33, 2B-33, 3B-16
1978 NY N	113	266	67	12	8	7	2.6	40	30	16	39	4	.252	.436	23	7	OF-50, 2B-39, 3B-9, SS-1
1979	158	590	162	37	5	16	2.7	90	60	60	84	18	.275	.436	4	1	OF-147, 2B-13, 3B-12
1980	146	514	142	26	2	8	1.6	58	69	52	69	14	.276	.381	13	7	OF-121, 3B-21, 2B-6
1981	43	143	50	10	2	4	2.8	16	25	12	19	2	.350	.531	3	0	OF-41
1982 2 teams		NY	N	(80G –	.257)		MON	N	(40G –	.200)							
" total	120	292	70	14	0	3	1.0	37	29	17	58	2	.240	.318	15	2	OF-98, 2B-8, SS-1, 3B-1
1983 SF N	124	373	109	20	3	17	4.6	59	53	33	59	7	.292	.499	20	4	2B-64, 3B-28, OF-22
1984	134	469	119	17	1	10	2.1	50	51	48	86	5	.254	.358	6	1	3B-117, OF-11, 3B-5
1985	95	230	62	6	0	4	1.7	24	24	30	37	3	.270	.348	32	9	OF-56, 3B-1
1986	97	184	47	12	0	5	2.7	20	28	18	34	1	.255	.402	58	16	OF-45, 1B-7, 3B-5, 2B-4, SS-1
1987	69	91	23	9	0	3	3.3	9	11	5	13	1	.253	.385	44	13	OF-22, 3B-2
1988	83	123	31	4	0	0	0.0	12	16	10	17	1	.252	.285	49	15	OF-45
13 yrs.	1332	3541	944	175	23	77	2.2	440	409	319	568	60	.267	.394	322	85	OF-700, 3B-218, 2B-173, 1B-7, SS-3, C-1

	G	AB	H	2B	3B	HR	HR %	R	RBI	BB	SO	SB	BA	SA	Pinch Hit AB	H	G by POS

Robin Yount

YOUNT, ROBIN R.
Brother of Larry Yount.
B. Sept. 16, 1955, Danville, Ill.

BR TR 6' 165 lbs.

	G	AB	H	2B	3B	HR	HR %	R	RBI	BB	SO	SB	BA	SA	Pinch Hit AB	H	G by POS
1974 **MIL A**	107	344	86	14	5	3	0.9	48	26	12	46	7	.250	.346	0	0	SS-107
1975	147	558	149	28	2	8	1.4	67	52	33	69	12	.267	.367	2	0	SS-145
1976	161	638	161	19	3	2	0.3	59	54	38	69	16	.252	.301	0	0	SS-161, OF-1
1977	154	605	174	34	4	4	0.7	66	49	41	80	16	.288	.377	3	1	SS-153
1978	127	502	147	23	9	9	1.8	66	71	24	43	16	.293	.428	2	1	SS-125
1979	149	577	154	26	5	8	1.4	72	51	35	52	11	.267	.371	0	0	SS-149
1980	143	611	179	**49**	10	23	3.8	121	87	26	67	20	.293	.519	2	0	SS-133, DH-9
1981	96	377	103	15	5	10	2.7	50	49	22	37	4	.273	.419	1	1	SS-93, DH-3
1982	156	635	**210**	**46**	12	29	4.6	129	114	54	63	14	.331	**.578**	2	1	SS-154, DH-1
1983	149	578	178	42	**10**	17	2.9	102	80	72	58	12	.308	.503	2	2	SS-139, DH-8
1984	160	624	186	27	7	16	2.6	105	80	67	67	14	.298	.441	0	0	SS-120, DH-39
1985	122	466	129	26	3	15	3.2	76	68	49	56	10	.277	.442	0	0	OF-108, DH-12, 1B-3
1986	140	522	163	31	7	9	1.7	82	46	62	73	14	.312	.450	0	0	OF-131, DH-6, 1B-3
1987	158	635	198	25	9	21	3.3	99	103	76	94	19	.312	.479	0	0	OF-150, DH-8
1988	162	621	190	38	11	13	2.1	92	91	63	63	22	.306	.465	0	0	OF-158, DH-4
15 yrs.	2131	8293	2407	443	102	187	2.3	1234	1021	674	937	207	.290	.436	15	6	SS-1479, OF-548, DH-90, 1B-6

DIVISIONAL PLAYOFF SERIES

	G	AB	H	2B	3B	HR	HR %	R	RBI	BB	SO	SB	BA	SA	Pinch Hit AB	H	G by POS
1981 **MIL A**	5	19	6	0	1	0	0.0	4	1	2	2	1	.316	.421	0	0	SS-5

LEAGUE CHAMPIONSHIP SERIES

	G	AB	H	2B	3B	HR	HR %	R	RBI	BB	SO	SB	BA	SA	Pinch Hit AB	H	G by POS
1982 **MIL A**	5	16	4	0	0	0	0.0	1	0	5	0	0	.250	.250	0	0	SS-5

WORLD SERIES

	G	AB	H	2B	3B	HR	HR %	R	RBI	BB	SO	SB	BA	SA	Pinch Hit AB	H	G by POS
1982 **MIL A**	7	29	12	3	0	1	3.4	6	6	2	2	0	.414	.621	0	0	SS-7

Paul Zuvella

ZUVELLA, PAUL
B. Oct. 31, 1958, San Mateo, Calif.

BR TR 6' 173 lbs.

	G	AB	H	2B	3B	HR	HR %	R	RBI	BB	SO	SB	BA	SA	Pinch Hit AB	H	G by POS
1982 **ATL N**	2	1	0	0	0	0	0.0	0	0	0	0	0	.000	.000	0	0	SS-1
1983	3	5	0	0	0	0	0.0	0	0	2	1	0	.000	.000	1	0	SS-2
1984	11	25	5	1	0	0	0.0	2	1	2	3	0	.200	.240	0	0	SS-6, 2B-6
1985	81	190	48	8	1	0	0.0	16	4	16	14	2	.253	.305	5	1	2B-42, SS-33, 3B-5
1986 **NY A**	21	48	4	1	0	0	0.0	2	2	5	4	0	.083	.104	0	0	SS-21
1987	14	34	6	0	0	0	0.0	2	0	0	4	0	.176	.176	3	0	2B-7, SS-6, 3B-1
1988 **CLE A**	51	130	30	5	1	0	0.0	9	7	8	13	0	.231	.285	1	0	SS-49
7 yrs.	183	433	93	15	2	0	0.0	31	14	33	39	2	.215	.259	10	1	SS-118, 2B-55, 3B-6

Pitcher Register

The Pitcher Register is an alphabetical listing of every man who pitched in the major leagues in 1988. Also included are those players who played in 1988 and had pitched (however briefly) in previous seasons.

As in the Batter Register, bold-faced print indicates a league leader for the season. A superscript "1" means that the figure is the all-time single season record (since 1893, when the mound was fixed at a distance of 60 feet 6 inches), and figures underneath a player's career and World Series career totals provide his rank in the top ten all-time.

Partial innings pitched are indicated by adding ".1" or ".2" to the figure in the IP column; "55.2" would mean that he had pitched fifty-five and two-third innings. Meaningless averages are indicated with a dash; these would include the winning percentage of a pitcher with an 0-0 record, or the batting average of a pitcher with no at bats. Any time the infinity symbol "∞" is shown for a pitcher's earned run average, it means that he allowed at least one run in that season without retiring a batter.

An asterisk (*) shown in the lifetime batting totals means that that pitcher's complete batting record is included in the Player Register

	W	L	PCT	ERA	G	GS	CG	IP	H	BB	SO	ShO	Relief Pitching W	L	SV	BATTING AB	H	HR	BA

Don Aase

AASE, DONALD WILLIAM
B. Sept. 8, 1954, Orange, Calif.

BR TR 6'3" 190 lbs.

	W	L	PCT	ERA	G	GS	CG	IP	H	BB	SO	ShO	W	L	SV	AB	H	HR	BA
1977 **BOS A**	6	2	.750	3.12	13	13	4	92.1	85	19	49	2	0	0	0	0	0	0	–
1978 **CAL A**	11	8	.579	4.03	29	29	6	178.2	185	80	93	1	0	0	0	0	0	0	–
1979	9	10	.474	4.82	37	28	7	185	200	77	96	1	1	1	2	0	0	0	–
1980	8	13	.381	4.06	40	21	5	175	193	66	74	1	3	0	2	0	0	0	–
1981	4	4	.500	2.35	39	0	0	65	56	24	38	0	4	4	11	0	0	0	–
1982	3	3	.500	3.46	24	0	0	52	45	23	40	0	3	3	4	0	0	0	–
1984	4	1	.800	1.62	23	0	0	39	30	19	28	0	4	1	8	0	0	0	–
1985 **BAL A**	10	6	.625	3.78	54	0	0	88	83	35	67	0	10	6	14	0	0	0	–
1986	6	7	.462	2.98	66	0	0	81.2	71	28	67	0	6	7	34	0	0	0	–
1987	1	0	1.000	2.25	7	0	0	8	8	4	3	0	1	0	2	0	0	0	–
1988	0	0	–	4.05	35	0	0	46.2	40	37	28	0	0	0	0	0	0	0	–
11 yrs.	62	54	.534	3.75	367	91	22	1011.1	996	412	583	5	32	22	77	0	0	0	–

LEAGUE CHAMPIONSHIP SERIES

	W	L	PCT	ERA	G	GS	CG	IP	H	BB	SO	ShO	W	L	SV	AB	H	HR	BA
1979 **CAL A**	1	0	1.000	1.80	2	0	0	5	4	2	6	0	1	0	0	0	0	0	–

Jim Acker

ACKER, JAMES JUSTIN
B. Sept. 24, 1958, Freer, Tex.

BR TR 6'2" 210 lbs.

	W	L	PCT	ERA	G	GS	CG	IP	H	BB	SO	ShO	W	L	SV	AB	H	HR	BA
1983 **TOR A**	5	1	.833	4.33	38	5	0	97.2	103	38	44	0	2	1	1	0	0	0	–
1984	3	5	.375	4.38	32	3	0	72	79	25	33	0	3	4	1	0	0	0	–
1985	7	2	.778	3.23	61	0	0	86.1	86	43	42	0	7	2	10	0	0	0	–
1986 2 teams			**TOR**	A (23G 2–4)			**ATL**	N (21G 3–8)											
" total	5	12	.294	4.01	44	19	0	155	163	48	69	0	2	2	0	28	3	0	.107
1987 **ATL N**	4	9	.308	4.16	68	0	0	114.2	109	51	68	0	4	9	14	14	3	0	.214
1988	0	4	.000	4.71	21	1	0	42	45	14	25	0	0	3	0	5	2	0	.400
6 yrs.	24	33	.421	4.07	264	28	0	567.2	585	219	281	0	18	21	26	47	8	0	.170

LEAGUE CHAMPIONSHIP SERIES

	W	L	PCT	ERA	G	GS	CG	IP	H	BB	SO	ShO	W	L	SV	AB	H	HR	BA
1985 **TOR A**	0	0	–	0.00	2	0	0	6	2	0	5	0	0	0	0	0	0	0	–

Juan Agosto

AGOSTO, JUAN ROBERTO GONZALEZ
Born Juan Roberto Agosto y Gonzalez.
B. Feb. 23, 1958, Rio Pedras, Puerto Rico

BL TL 6' 175 lbs.

	W	L	PCT	ERA	G	GS	CG	IP	H	BB	SO	ShO	W	L	SV	AB	H	HR	BA
1981 **CHI A**	0	0	–	4.50	2	0	0	6	5	0	3	0	0	0	0	0	0	0	–
1982	0	0	–	18.00	1	0	0	2	7	0	1	0	0	0	0	0	0	0	–
1983	2	2	.500	4.10	39	0	0	41.2	41	11	29	0	2	2	7	0	0	0	–
1984	2	1	.667	3.09	49	0	0	55.1	54	34	26	0	2	1	7	0	0	0	–
1985	4	3	.571	3.58	54	0	0	60.1	45	23	39	0	4	3	1	0	0	0	–
1986 2 teams			**CHI**	A (9G 0–2)			**MIN**	A (17G 1–2)											
" total	1	4	.200	8.64	26	1	0	25	49	18	12	0	1	3	1	0	0	0	–
1987 **HOU N**	1	1	.500	2.63	27	0	0	27.1	26	10	6	0	1	1	2	1	0	0	.000
1988	10	2	.833	2.26	75	0	0	91.2	74	30	33	0	10	2	4	5	0	0	.000
8 yrs.	20	13	.606	3.61	273	1	0	309.1	301	126	149	0	20	12	22	6	0	0	.000

LEAGUE CHAMPIONSHIP SERIES

	W	L	PCT	ERA	G	GS	CG	IP	H	BB	SO	ShO	W	L	SV	AB	H	HR	BA
1983 **CHI A**	0	0	–	0.00	1	0	0	.1	0	0	0	0	0	0	0	0	0	0	–

Rick Aguilera

AGUILERA, RICHARD WARREN (Aggie)
B. Dec. 31, 1961, San Gabriel, Calif.

BR TR 6'5" 195 lbs.

	W	L	PCT	ERA	G	GS	CG	IP	H	BB	SO	ShO	W	L	SV	AB	H	HR	BA
1985 **NY N**	10	7	.588	3.24	21	19	2	122.1	118	37	74	0	1	0	0	36	10	0	.278
1986	10	7	.588	3.88	28	20	2	141.2	145	36	104	0	1	1	0	51	8	2	.157
1987	11	3	.786	3.60	18	17	1	115	124	33	77	0	0	0	0	40	9	1	.225
1988	0	4	.000	6.93	11	3	0	24.2	29	10	16	0	0	2	0	4	1	0	.250
4 yrs.	31	21	.596	3.79	78	59	5	403.2	416	116	271	0	2	3	0	131	28	3	.214

LEAGUE CHAMPIONSHIP SERIES

	W	L	PCT	ERA	G	GS	CG	IP	H	BB	SO	ShO	W	L	SV	AB	H	HR	BA
1986 **NY N**	0	0	–	0.00	2	0	0	5	2	2	2	0	0	0	0	0	0	0	–
1988	0	0	–	1.29	3	0	0	7	3	2	4	0	0	0	0	1	0	0	.000
2 yrs.	0	0	–	0.75	5	0	0	12	5	4	6	0	0	0	0	1	0	0	.000

WORLD SERIES

	W	L	PCT	ERA	G	GS	CG	IP	H	BB	SO	ShO	W	L	SV	AB	H	HR	BA
1986 **NY N**	1	0	1.000	12.00	2	0	0	3	8	1	4	0	1	0	0	0	0	0	–

Gibson Alba

ALBA, GIBSON ALBERTO
Born Gibson Alberto Alba y Rosando.
B. Jan. 18, 1960, Santiago, Dominican Republic

BL TL 6'2" 160 lbs.

	W	L	PCT	ERA	G	GS	CG	IP	H	BB	SO	ShO	W	L	SV	AB	H	HR	BA
1988 **STL N**	0	0	–	2.70	3	0	0	3.1	1	2	3	0	0	0	0	0	0	0	–

Doyle Alexander

ALEXANDER, DOYLE LAFAYETTE
B. Sept. 4, 1950, Cordova, Ala.

BR TR 6'3" 190 lbs.

	W	L	PCT	ERA	G	GS	CG	IP	H	BB	SO	ShO	W	L	SV	AB	H	HR	BA
1971 **LA N**	6	6	.500	3.82	17	12	4	92	105	18	30	0	1	0	0	33	9	0	.273
1972 **BAL A**	6	8	.429	2.45	35	9	2	106.1	78	30	49	2	4	5	2	25	2	0	.080
1973	12	8	.600	3.86	29	26	10	175	169	52	63	0	1	0	0	0	0	0	–
1974	6	9	.400	4.03	30	12	2	114	127	43	40	0	3	2	0	0	0	0	–
1975	8	8	.500	3.04	32	11	3	133.1	127	47	46	1	3	4	1	0	0	0	–
1976 2 teams			**BAL**	A (11G 3–4)			**NY**	A (19G 10–5)											
" total	13	9	.591	3.36	30	25	7	201	172	63	58	3	2	0	0	0	0	0	–
1977 **TEX A**	17	11	.607	3.65	34	34	12	237	221	82	82	1	0	0	0	0	0	0	–
1978	9	10	.474	3.86	31	28	7	191	198	71	81	1	0	0	0	0	0	0	–
1979	5	7	.417	4.46	23	18	0	113	114	69	50	0	0	0	0	0	0	0	–
1980 **ATL N**	14	11	.560	4.19	35	35	7	232	227	74	114	1	0	0	0	83	15	0	.181
1981 **SF N**	11	7	.611	2.90	24	24	1	152	156	44	77	1	0	0	0	51	9	0	.176
1982 **NY A**	1	7	.125	6.08	16	11	0	66.2	81	14	26	0	0	0	0	0	0	0	–
1983 2 teams			**NY**	A (8G 0–2)			**TOR**	A (17G 7–6)											
" total	7	8	.467	4.41	25	20	5	145	157	33	63	0	1	0	0	0	0	0	–
1984 **TOR A**	17	6	.739	3.13	36	35	11	261.2	238	59	139	2	0	0	0	0	0	0	–
1985	17	10	.630	3.45	36	36	6	260.2	268	67	142	1	0	0	0	0	0	0	–
1986 2 teams			**TOR**	A (17G 5–4)			**ATL**	N (17G 6–6)											
" total	11	10	.524	4.14	34	34	5	228.1	255	37	139	0	0	0	0	38	8	0	.211

	W	L	PCT	ERA	G	GS	CG	IP	H	BB	SO	ShO	Relief Pitching W	L	SV	BATTING AB	H	HR	BA

Doyle Alexander continued

	W	L	PCT	ERA	G	GS	CG	IP	H	BB	SO	ShO	W	L	SV	AB	H	HR	BA
1987 2 teams	ATL N (16G 5–10)				DET A (11G 9–0)														
" total	14	10	.583	3.01	27	27	6	206	178	53	108	3	0	0	0	35	1	0	.029
1988 DET A	14	11	.560	4.32	34	34	5	229	260	46	126	1	0	0	0	0	0	0	–
18 yrs.	188	156	.547	3.71	528	431	93	3144	3131	902	1433	17	15	11	3	265	44	0	.166

LEAGUE CHAMPIONSHIP SERIES

	W	L	PCT	ERA	G	GS	CG	IP	H	BB	SO	ShO	W	L	SV	AB	H	HR	BA
1973 BAL A	0	1	.000	4.91	1	1	0	3.2	5	0	1	0	0	0	0	0	0	0	–
1985 TOR A	0	1	.000	8.71	2	2	0	10.1	14	3	9	0	0	0	0	0	0	0	–
1987 DET A	0	2	.000	10.00	2	2	0	9	14	1	5	0	0	0	0	0	0	0	–
3 yrs.	0	4	.000	8.61	5	5	0	23	33	4	15	0	0	0	0	0	0	0	–

WORLD SERIES

	W	L	PCT	ERA	G	GS	CG	IP	H	BB	SO	ShO	W	L	SV	AB	H	HR	BA
1976 NY A	0	1	.000	7.50	1	1	0	6	9	2	1	0	0	0	0	0	0	0	–

Neil Allen

ALLEN, NEIL PATRICK   BR TR 6'3" 185 lbs.
B. Jan. 24, 1958, Kansas City, Kans.

	W	L	PCT	ERA	G	GS	CG	IP	H	BB	SO	ShO	W	L	SV	AB	H	HR	BA
1979 NY N	6	10	.375	3.55	50	5	0	99	100	47	65	0	6	6	8	14	0	0	.000
1980	7	10	.412	3.71	59	0	0	97	87	40	79	0	7	10	22	14	2	0	.143
1981	7	6	.538	2.96	43	0	0	67	64	26	50	0	7	6	18	5	1	0	.200
1982	3	7	.300	3.06	50	0	0	64.2	65	30	59	0	3	7	19	6	1	0	.167
1983 2 teams	NY N (21G 2–7)				STL N (25G 10–6)														
" total	12	13	.480	3.94	46	22	5	175.2	179	84	106	3	3	5	2	49	5	0	.102
1984 STL N	9	6	.600	3.55	57	1	0	119	105	49	66	0	9	5	3	25	6	0	.240
1985 2 teams	STL N (23G 1–4)				NY A (17G 1–0)														
" total	2	4	.333	4.17	40	1	0	58.1	58	30	26	0	2	3	3	2	0	0	.000
1986 CHI A	7	2	.778	3.82	22	17	2	113	101	38	57	2	0	0	0	0	0	0	–
1987 2 teams	CHI A (15G 0–7)				NY A (8G 0–1)														
" total	0	8	.000	5.93	23	11	0	74.1	97	36	42	0	0	0	0	0	0	0	–
1988 NY A	5	3	.625	3.84	41	2	0	117.1	121	37	61	1	5	1	0	0	0	0	–
10 yrs.	58	69	.457	3.85	431	59	7	985.1	977	417	611	6	42	43	75	115	15	0	.130

Jose Alvarez

ALVAREZ, JOSE LINO   BR TR 5'11" 175 lbs.
B. Apr. 12, 1956, Tampa, Fla.

	W	L	PCT	ERA	G	GS	CG	IP	H	BB	SO	ShO	W	L	SV	AB	H	HR	BA
1981 ATL N	0	0	–	0.00	1	0	0	2	0	0	2	0	0	0	0	0	0	0	–
1982	0	0	–	4.70	7	0	0	7.2	8	2	6	0	0	0	0	0	0	0	–
1988	5	6	.455	2.99	60	0	0	102.1	88	53	81	0	5	6	3	8	3	0	.375
3 yrs.	5	6	.455	3.05	68	0	0	112	96	55	89	0	5	6	3	8	3	0	.375

Larry Andersen

ANDERSEN, LARRY EUGENE   BR TR 6'3" 200 lbs.
B. May 6, 1953, Portland, Ore.

	W	L	PCT	ERA	G	GS	CG	IP	H	BB	SO	ShO	W	L	SV	AB	H	HR	BA
1975 CLE A	0	0	–	4.76	3	0	0	5.2	4	2	4	0	0	0	0	0	0	0	–
1977	0	1	.000	3.21	11	0	0	14	10	9	8	0	0	0	0	0	0	0	–
1979	0	0	–	7.41	8	0	0	17	25	4	7	0	0	0	0	0	0	0	–
1981 SEA A	3	3	.500	2.65	41	0	0	68	57	18	40	0	3	3	5	0	0	0	–
1982	0	0	–	5.99	40	1	0	79.2	100	23	32	0	0	0	1	0	0	0	–
1983 PHI N	1	0	1.000	2.39	17	0	0	26.1	19	9	14	0	1	0	0	2	0	0	.000
1984	3	7	.300	2.38	64	0	0	90.2	85	25	54	0	3	7	4	4	0	0	.000
1985	3	3	.500	4.32	57	0	0	73	78	26	50	0	3	3	3	4	0	0	.000
1986 2 teams	PHI N (10G 0–0)				HOU N (38G 2–1)														
" total	2	1	.667	3.03	48	0	0	77.1	83	26	42	0	2	1	1	6	0	0	.000
1987 HOU N	9	5	.643	3.45	67	0	0	101.2	95	41	94	0	9	5	5	6	1	0	.167
1988	2	4	.333	2.94	53	0	0	82.2	82	20	66	0	2	4	5 /	6	2	0	.333
11 yrs.	23	24	.489	3.58	409	1	0	636	638	203	411	0	23	23	24	28	3	0	.107

LEAGUE CHAMPIONSHIP SERIES

	W	L	PCT	ERA	G	GS	CG	IP	H	BB	SO	ShO	W	L	SV	AB	H	HR	BA
1986 HOU N	0	0	–	0.00	2	0	0	5	1	2	3	0	0	0	0	0	0	0	–

WORLD SERIES

	W	L	PCT	ERA	G	GS	CG	IP	H	BB	SO	ShO	W	L	SV	AB	H	HR	BA
1983 PHI N	0	0	–	2.25	2	0	0	4	4	0	1	0	0	0	0	0	0	0	–

Allan Anderson

ANDERSON, ALLAN LEE   BL TL 5'11" 169 lbs.
B. Jan. 7, 1964, Lancaster, Ohio

	W	L	PCT	ERA	G	GS	CG	IP	H	BB	SO	ShO	W	L	SV	AB	H	HR	BA
1986 MIN A	3	6	.333	5.55	21	10	1	84.1	106	30	51	0	1	1	1	0	0	0	–
1987	1	0	1.000	10.95	4	2	0	12.1	20	10	3	0	0	0	0	0	0	0	–
1988	16	9	.640	2.45	30	30	3	202.1	199	37	83	1	0	0	0	0	0	0	–
3 yrs.	20	15	.571	3.67	55	42	4	299	325	77	137	1	1	1	1	0	0	0	–

Rick Anderson

ANDERSON, RICHARD ARLEN   BR TR 6' 175 lbs.
B. Nov. 29, 1956, Everett, Wash.

	W	L	PCT	ERA	G	GS	CG	IP	H	BB	SO	ShO	W	L	SV	AB	H	HR	BA
1986 NY N	2	1	.667	2.72	15	5	0	49.2	45	11	21	0	0	0	1	11	1	0	.091
1987 KC A	0	2	.000	13.85	6	2	0	13	26	9	12	0	0	0	0	0	0	0	–
1988	2	1	.667	4.24	7	3	0	34	41	9	9	0	2	0	0	0	0	0	–
3 yrs.	4	4	.500	4.75	28	10	0	96.2	112	29	42	0	2	0	1	11	1	0	.091

Joaquin Andujar

ANDUJAR, JOAQUIN   BR TR 6' 170 lbs.
B. Dec. 21, 1952, San Pedro de Macoris, Dominican Republic

	W	L	PCT	ERA	G	GS	CG	IP	H	BB	SO	ShO	W	L	SV	AB	H	HR	BA
1976 HOU N	9	10	.474	3.61	28	25	9	172	163	75	59	4	0	0	0	57	8	0	.140
1977	11	8	.579	3.68	26	25	4	159	149	64	69	1	0	0	0	53	10	0	.189
1978	5	7	.417	3.41	35	13	2	111	88	58	55	0	2	3	1	23	3	0	.130
1979	12	12	.500	3.43	46	23	8	194	168	88	77	0	3	2	4	57	5	2	.088
1980	3	8	.273	3.91	35	14	0	122	132	43	75	0	0	2	2	29	5	1	.172
1981 2 teams	HOU N (9G 2–3)				STL N (11G 6–1)														
" total	8	4	.667	4.10	20	11	1	79	85	23	37	0	1	1	0	23	0	0	.000
1982 STL N	15	10	.600	2.47	38	37	9	265.2	237	50	137	5	0	0	0	95	15	0	.158
1983	6	16	.273	4.16	39	34	5	225	215	75	125	2	0	0	1	73	6	0	.082
1984	20	14	.588	3.34	36	36	12	261.1	218	70	147	4	0	0	0	84	11	2	.131
1985	21	12	.636	3.40	38	38	10	269.2	265	82	112	2	0	0	0	94	10	0	.106
1986 OAK A	12	7	.632	3.82	28	26	7	155.1	139	56	72	1	0	0	0	0	0	0	–
1987	3	5	.375	6.08	13	13	1	60.2	63	26	32	0	0	0	0	0	0	0	–

	W	L	PCT	ERA	G	GS	CG	IP	H	BB	SO	ShO	Relief Pitching W	L	SV	BATTING AB	H	HR	BA

Joaquin Andujar continued

	W	L	PCT	ERA	G	GS	CG	IP	H	BB	SO	ShO	W	L	SV	AB	H	HR	BA
1988 HOU N	2	5	.286	4.00	23	10	0	78.2	94	21	35	0	0	2	0	19	4	0	.211
13 yrs.	127	118	.518	3.58	405	305	68	2153.1	2016	731	1032	19	6	10	9	607	77	5	.127

LEAGUE CHAMPIONSHIP SERIES

	W	L	PCT	ERA	G	GS	CG	IP	H	BB	SO	ShO	W	L	SV	AB	H	HR	BA
1980 HOU N	0	0	—	0.00	1	0	0	1	0	1	0	0	0	0	1	0	0	0	—
1982 STL N	1	0	1.000	2.70	1	1	0	6.2	6	2	4	0	0	0	0	1	0	0	.000
1985	0	1	.000	6.97	2	2	0	10.1	14	4	9	0	0	0	0	4	1	0	.250
3 yrs.	1	1	.500	5.00	4	3	0	18	20	7	13	0	0	0	1	5	1	0	.200

WORLD SERIES

	W	L	PCT	ERA	G	GS	CG	IP	H	BB	SO	ShO	W	L	SV	AB	H	HR	BA
1982 STL N	2	0	1.000	1.35	2	2	0	13.1	10	1	4	0	0	0	0	0	0	0	—
1985	0	1	.000	9.00	2	1	0	4	10	4	3	0	0	0	0	1	0	0	.000
2 yrs.	2	1	.667	3.12	4	3	0	17.1	20	5	7	0	0	0	0	1	0	0	.000

Luis Aquino

AQUINO, LUIS ANTONI0
Born Luis Antonio Aquino y Colon.
B. May 19, 1964, Santurce, Puerto Rico

BR TR 6' 155 lbs.

	W	L	PCT	ERA	G	GS	CG	IP	H	BB	SO	ShO	W	L	SV	AB	H	HR	BA
1986 TOR A	1	1	.500	6.35	7	0	0	11.1	14	3	5	0	1	1	0	0	0	0	—
1988 KC A	1	0	1.000	2.79	7	5	1	29	33	17	11	1	0	0	0	0	0	0	—
2 yrs.	2	1	.667	3.79	14	5	1	40.1	47	20	16	1	1	1	0	0	0	0	—

Jack Armstrong

ARMSTRONG, JACK WILLIAM
B. Mar. 7, 1965, Englewood, N. J.

BR TR 6'5" 220 lbs.

	W	L	PCT	ERA	G	GS	CG	IP	H	BB	SO	ShO	W	L	SV	AB	H	HR	BA
1988 CIN N	4	7	.364	5.79	14	13	0	65.1	63	38	45	0	0	0	0	21	2	0	.095

Scott Arnold

ARNOLD, SCOTT GENTRY
B. Aug. 18, 1962, Lexington, Ky.

BR TR 6'2" 210 lbs.

	W	L	PCT	ERA	G	GS	CG	IP	H	BB	SO	ShO	W	L	SV	AB	H	HR	BA
1988 STL N	0	0	—	5.40	6	0	0	6.2	9	4	8	0	0	0	0	0	0	0	—

Paul Assenmacher

ASSENMACHER, PAUL ANDRE
B. Dec. 10, 1960, Detroit, Mich.

BL TL 6'3" 195 lbs.

	W	L	PCT	ERA	G	GS	CG	IP	H	BB	SO	ShO	W	L	SV	AB	H	HR	BA
1986 ATL N	7	3	.700	2.50	61	0	0	68.1	61	26	56	0	7	3	7	6	0	0	.000
1987	1	1	.500	5.10	52	0	0	54.2	58	24	39	0	1	1	2	4	0	0	.000
1988	8	7	.533	3.06	64	0	0	79.1	72	32	71	0	8	7	5	3	1	0	.333
3 yrs.	16	11	.593	3.43	177	0	0	202.1	191	82	166	0	16	11	14	13	1	0	.077

Keith Atherton

ATHERTON, KEITH ROWE
B. Feb. 19, 1959, Newport News, Va.

BR TR 6'5" 190 lbs.

	W	L	PCT	ERA	G	GS	CG	IP	H	BB	SO	ShO	W	L	SV	AB	H	HR	BA
1983 OAK A	2	5	.286	2.77	29	0	0	68.1	53	23	40	0	2	5	4	1	0	0	.000
1984	7	6	.538	4.33	57	1	0	104	110	39	58	0	7	6	2	0	0	0	—
1985	4	7	.364	4.30	56	0	0	104.2	89	42	77	0	4	7	3	0	0	0	—
1986 2 teams			OAK	A	(13G 1–2)		MIN	A	(47G 5–8)										
" total	6	10	.375	4.08	60	0	0	97	100	46	67	0	6	10	10	0	0	0	—
1987 MIN A	7	5	.583	4.54	59	0	0	79.1	81	30	51	0	7	5	2	0	0	0	—
1988	7	5	.583	3.41	49	0	0	74	65	22	43	0	7	5	3	0	0	0	—
6 yrs.	33	38	.465	3.98	310	1	0	527.1	498	202	336	0	33	38	24	1	0	0	.000

LEAGUE CHAMPIONSHIP SERIES

	W	L	PCT	ERA	G	GS	CG	IP	H	BB	SO	ShO	W	L	SV	AB	H	HR	BA
1987 MIN A	0	0	—	0.00	1	0	0	.1	1	0	0	0	0	0	0	0	0	0	—

WORLD SERIES

	W	L	PCT	ERA	G	GS	CG	IP	H	BB	SO	ShO	W	L	SV	AB	H	HR	BA
1987 MIN A	0	0	—	6.75	2	0	0	1.1	0	1	0	0	0	0	0	0	0	0	—

Don August

AUGUST, DONALD GLENN
B. July 3, 1963, Inglewood, Calif.

BR TR 6'3" 190 lbs.

	W	L	PCT	ERA	G	GS	CG	IP	H	BB	SO	ShO	W	L	SV	AB	H	HR	BA
1988 MIL A	13	7	.650	3.09	24	22	6	148.1	137	48	66	1	1	0	0	0	0	0	—

Scott Bailes

BAILES, SCOTT ALAN
B. Dec. 18, 1961, Chillicothe, Ohio

BL TL 6'2" 170 lbs.

	W	L	PCT	ERA	G	GS	CG	IP	H	BB	SO	ShO	W	L	SV	AB	H	HR	BA
1986 CLE A	10	10	.500	4.95	62	10	0	112.2	123	43	60	0	8	7	7	0	0	0	—
1987	7	8	.467	4.64	39	17	0	120.1	145	47	65	0	2	1	6	0	0	0	—
1988	9	14	.391	4.90	37	21	5	145	149	46	53	2	2	3	0	0	0	0	—
3 yrs.	26	32	.448	4.83	138	48	5	378	417	136	178	2	12	11	13	0	0	0	—

Doug Bair

BAIR, CHARLES DOUGLAS
B. Aug. 22, 1949, Defiance, Ohio

BR TR 6' 180 lbs.

	W	L	PCT	ERA	G	GS	CG	IP	H	BB	SO	ShO	W	L	SV	AB	H	HR	BA
1976 PIT N	0	0	—	5.68	4	0	0	6.1	4	5	4	0	0	0	0	0	0	0	—
1977 OAK A	4	6	.400	3.47	45	0	0	83	78	57	68	0	4	6	8	0	0	0	—
1978 CIN N	7	6	.538	1.98	70	0	0	100	87	38	91	0	7	6	28	14	2	0	.143
1979	11	7	.611	4.31	65	0	0	94	93	51	86	0	11	7	16	8	0	0	.000
1980	3	6	.333	4.24	61	0	0	85	91	39	62	0	3	6	6	2	0	0	.000
1981 2 teams			CIN	N	(24G 2–2)		STL	N	(11G 2–0)										
" total	4	2	.667	5.10	35	0	0	54.2	55	19	30	0	4	2	1	6	1	1	.167
1982 STL N	5	3	.625	2.55	63	0	0	91.2	69	36	68	0	5	3	8	13	1	0	.077
1983 2 teams			STL	N	(26G 1–1)		DET	A	(27G 7–3)										
" total	8	4	.667	3.59	53	1	0	85.1	75	32	60	0	7	4	5	2	0	0	.000
1984 DET A	5	3	.625	3.75	47	1	0	93.2	82	36	57	0	5	2	4	0	0	0	—
1985 2 teams			DET	A	(21G 2–0)		STL	N	(2G 0–0)										
" total	2	0	1.000	5.96	23	3	0	51.1	55	27	30	0	1	0	0	0	0	0	—
1986 OAK A	2	3	.400	3.00	31	0	0	45	37	18	40	0	2	3	4	0	0	0	—
1987 PHI N	2	0	1.000	5.96	11	0	0	13.2	17	5	10	0	2	0	0	1	0	0	.000
1988 TOR A	0	0	—	4.05	10	0	0	13.1	14	3	8	0	0	0	0	0	0	0	—
13 yrs.	53	40	.570	3.71	518	5	0	817	757	366	614	0	51	39	80	46	4	1	.087

LEAGUE CHAMPIONSHIP SERIES

	W	L	PCT	ERA	G	GS	CG	IP	H	BB	SO	ShO	W	L	SV	AB	H	HR	BA
1979 CIN N	0	1	.000	9.00	1	0	0	1	2	1	0	0	0	1	0	0	0	0	—
1982 STL N	0	0	—	0.00	1	0	0	1	2	3	0	0	0	0	0	0	0	0	—
2 yrs.	0	1	.000	4.50	2	0	0	2	4	4	0	0	0	1	0	0	0	0	—

	W	L	PCT	ERA	G	GS	CG	IP	H	BB	SO	ShO	Relief Pitching W	L	SV	BATTING AB	H	HR	BA

Doug Bair continued

WORLD SERIES

		W	L	PCT	ERA	G	GS	CG	IP	H	BB	SO	ShO	W	L	SV	AB	H	HR	BA
1982 STL N		0	1	.000	9.00	3	0	0	2	2	2	3	0	0	1	0	0	0	0	–
1984 DET A		0	0	–	0.00	1	0	0	.2	0	0	1	0	0	0	0	0	0	0	–
2 yrs.		0	1	.000	6.75	4	0	0	2.2	2	2	4	0	0	1	0	0	0	0	–

Jeff Ballard

BALLARD, JEFFREY SCOTT
B. Aug. 13, 1963, Billings, Mont.   BL TL 6'3"   210 lbs.

	W	L	PCT	ERA	G	GS	CG	IP	H	BB	SO	ShO	W	L	SV	AB	H	HR	BA
1987 BAL A	2	8	.200	6.59	14	14	0	69.2	100	35	27	0	0	0	0	0	0	0	–
1988	8	12	.400	4.40	25	25	6	153.1	167	42	41	1	0	0	0	0	0	0	–
2 yrs.	10	20	.333	5.09	39	39	6	223	267	77	68	1	0	0	0	0	0	0	–

Scott Bankhead

BANKHEAD, MICHAEL SCOTT
B. July 31, 1963, Raleigh, N. C.   BR TR 5'10"   175 lbs.

	W	L	PCT	ERA	G	GS	CG	IP	H	BB	SO	ShO	W	L	SV	AB	H	HR	BA
1986 KC A	8	9	.471	4.61	24	17	0	121	121	37	94	0	2	1	0	0	0	0	–
1987 SEA A	9	8	.529	5.42	27	25	2	149.1	168	37	95	0	0	0	0	0	0	0	–
1988	7	9	.438	3.07	21	21	2	135	115	38	102	1	0	0	0	0	0	0	–
3 yrs.	24	26	.480	4.40	72	63	4	405.1	404	112	291	1	2	1	0	0	0	0	–

Floyd Bannister

BANNISTER, FLOYD FRANKLIN
B. June 10, 1955, Pierre, S. D.   BL TL 6'1"   190 lbs.

	W	L	PCT	ERA	G	GS	CG	IP	H	BB	SO	ShO	W	L	SV	AB	H	HR	BA
1977 HOU N	8	9	.471	4.03	24	23	4	143	138	68	112	1	0	0	0	48	9	0	.188
1978	3	9	.250	4.83	28	16	2	110	120	63	94	2	0	0	0	31	5	0	.161
1979 SEA A	10	15	.400	4.05	30	30	6	182	185	68	115	2	0	0	0	0	0	0	–
1980	9	13	.409	3.47	32	32	8	218	200	66	155	0	0	0	0	0	0	0	–
1981	9	9	.500	4.46	21	20	5	121	128	39	85	2	0	0	0	0	0	0	–
1982	12	13	.480	3.43	35	35	5	247	225	77	**209**	3	0	0	0	0	0	0	–
1983 CHI A	16	10	.615	3.35	34	34	5	217.1	191	71	193	2	0	0	0	0	0	0	–
1984	14	11	.560	4.83	34	33	4	218	211	80	152	0	0	0	0	1	0	0	.000
1985	10	14	.417	4.87	34	34	4	210.2	211	100	198	1	0	0	0	0	0	0	–
1986	10	14	.417	3.54	28	27	6	165.1	162	48	92	1	1	0	0	0	0	0	–
1987	16	11	.593	3.58	34	34	11	228.2	216	49	124	2	0	0	0	0	0	0	–
1988 KC A	12	13	.480	4.33	31	31	2	189.1	182	68	113	0	0	0	0	0	0	0	–
12 yrs.	129	141	.478	4.01	365	349	62	2250.1	2169	797	1642	16	1	0	0	80	14	0	.175

LEAGUE CHAMPIONSHIP SERIES

	W	L	PCT	ERA	G	GS	CG	IP	H	BB	SO	ShO	W	L	SV	AB	H	HR	BA
1983 CHI A	0	1	.000	4.50	1	1	0	6	5	1	5	0	0	0	0	0	0	0	–

Salome Barojas

BAROJAS, SALOME ROMERO
Born Salome Barojas y Romero.
B. June 16, 1957, Cordoba, Mexico   BR TR 5'9"   160 lbs.

	W	L	PCT	ERA	G	GS	CG	IP	H	BB	SO	ShO	W	L	SV	AB	H	HR	BA
1982 CHI A	6	6	.500	3.54	61	0	0	106.2	96	46	56	0	6	6	21	0	0	0	–
1983	3	3	.500	2.47	52	0	0	87.1	70	32	38	0	3	3	12	0	0	0	–
1984 2 teams			CHI	A	(24G	3–2)		SEA	A	(19G	6–5)								
" total	9	7	.563	4.15	43	14	0	134.1	136	60	55	0	3	3	2	0	0	0	–
1985 SEA A	0	5	.000	5.98	17	4	0	52.2	65	33	27	0	0	1	0	0	0	0	–
1988 PHI N	0	0	–	8.31	6	0	0	8.2	7	8	1	0	0	0	0	0	0	0	–
5 yrs.	18	21	.462	3.95	179	18	0	389.2	374	179	177	0	12	13	35	0	0	0	–

LEAGUE CHAMPIONSHIP SERIES

	W	L	PCT	ERA	G	GS	CG	IP	H	BB	SO	ShO	W	L	SV	AB	H	HR	BA
1983 CHI A	0	0	–	18.00	2	0	0	1	4	0	0	0	0	0	0	0	0	0	–

Tim Barrett

BARRETT, TIMOTHY WAYNE
B. Jan. 24, 1961, Huntington, Ind.   BL TR 6'1"   185 lbs.

	W	L	PCT	ERA	G	GS	CG	IP	H	BB	SO	ShO	W	L	SV	AB	H	HR	BA
1988 MON N	0	0	–	5.79	4	0	0	9.1	10	2	5	0	0	0	1	2	0	0	.000

Jose Bautista

BAUTISTA, JOSE JOAQUIN
Born Jose Joaquin Bautista y Arias.
B. July 25, 1964, Bani, Dominican Republic   BR TR 6'1"   177 lbs.

	W	L	PCT	ERA	G	GS	CG	IP	H	BB	SO	ShO	W	L	SV	AB	H	HR	BA
1988 BAL A	6	15	.286	4.30	33	25	3	171.2	171	45	76	0	0	1	0	0	0	0	–

Steve Bedrosian

BEDROSIAN, STEPHEN WAYNE (Bedrock)
B. Dec. 6, 1957, Methuen, Mass.   BR TR 6'3"   200 lbs.

	W	L	PCT	ERA	G	GS	CG	IP	H	BB	SO	ShO	W	L	SV	AB	H	HR	BA
1981 ATL N	1	2	.333	4.50	15	1	0	24	15	15	9	0	1	1	0	2	0	0	.000
1982	8	6	.571	2.42	64	3	0	137.2	102	57	123	0	7	4	11	26	1	0	.038
1983	9	10	.474	3.60	70	1	0	120	100	51	114	0	9	10	19	19	2	0	.105
1984	9	6	.600	2.37	40	4	0	83.2	65	33	81	0	6	5	11	17	2	0	.118
1985	7	15	.318	3.83	37	37	0	206.2	198	111	134	0	0	0	0	64	5	0	.078
1986 PHI N	8	6	.571	3.39	68	0	0	90.1	79	34	82	0	8	6	29	5	1	0	.200
1987	5	3	.625	2.83	65	0	0	89	79	28	74	0	5	3	**40**	4	0	0	.000
1988	6	6	.500	3.75	57	0	0	74.1	75	27	61	0	6	6	28	2	0	0	.000
8 yrs.	53	54	.495	3.27	416	46	0	825.2	713	356	678	0	42	35	138	139	11	0	.079

LEAGUE CHAMPIONSHIP SERIES

	W	L	PCT	ERA	G	GS	CG	IP	H	BB	SO	ShO	W	L	SV	AB	H	HR	BA
1982 ATL N	0	0	–	18.00	2	0	0	1	3	1	2	0	0	0	0	0	0	0	–

Tim Belcher

BELCHER, TIMOTHY WAYNE
B. Oct. 19, 1961, Mount Gilead, Ohio   BR TR 6'3"   210 lbs.

	W	L	PCT	ERA	G	GS	CG	IP	H	BB	SO	ShO	W	L	SV	AB	H	HR	BA
1987 LA N	4	2	.667	2.38	6	5	0	34	30	7	23	0	1	0	0	10	2	0	.200
1988	12	6	.667	2.91	36	27	4	179.2	143	51	152	1	1	0	4	56	4	1	.071
2 yrs.	16	8	.667	2.82	42	32	4	213.2	173	58	175	1	2	0	4	66	6	1	.091

LEAGUE CHAMPIONSHIP SERIES

	W	L	PCT	ERA	G	GS	CG	IP	H	BB	SO	ShO	W	L	SV	AB	H	HR	BA
1988 LA N	2	0	1.000	4.11	2	2	0	15.1	12	4	16	0	0	0	0	8	1	0	.125

WORLD SERIES

	W	L	PCT	ERA	G	GS	CG	IP	H	BB	SO	ShO	W	L	SV	AB	H	HR	BA
1988 LA N	1	0	1.000	6.23	2	2	0	8.2	10	6	10	0	0	0	0	0	0	0	–

	W	L	PCT	ERA	G	GS	CG	IP	H	BB	SO	ShO	Relief Pitching W	L	SV	BATTING AB	H	HR	BA

Juan Berenguer

BERENGUER, JUAN BAUTISTA
B. Nov. 30, 1954, Aguadulce, Panama
BR TR 5'11" 186 lbs.

	W	L	PCT	ERA	G	GS	CG	IP	H	BB	SO	ShO	W	L	SV	AB	H	HR	BA
1978 NY N	0	2	.000	8.31	5	3	0	13	17	11	8	0	0	0	0	3	0	0	.000
1979	1	1	.500	2.90	5	5	0	31	28	12	25	0	0	0	0	7	1	0	.143
1980	0	1	.000	6.00	6	0	0	9	9	10	7	0	0	1	0	0	0	0	–
1981 2 teams				KC	A	(8G 0–4)		TOR	A	(12G 2–9)									
" total	2	13	.133	5.24	20	14	1	91	84	51	49	0	0	2	0	0	0	0	–
1982 DET A	0	0	–	6.75	2	1	0	6.2	5	9	8	0	0	0	0	0	0	0	–
1983	9	5	.643	3.14	37	19	2	157.2	110	71	129	1	2	0	1	0	0	0	–
1984	11	10	.524	3.48	31	27	2	168.1	146	79	118	1	0	0	0	0	0	0	–
1985	5	6	.455	5.59	31	13	0	95	96	48	82	0	1	1	0	0	0	0	–
1986 SF N	2	3	.400	2.70	46	4	0	73.1	64	44	72	0	2	2	4	7	1	0	.143
1987 MIN A	8	1	.889	3.94	47	6	0	112	100	47	110	0	6	1	4	0	0	0	–
1988	8	4	.667	3.96	57	1	0	100	74	61	99	0	8	4	2	0	0	0	–
11 yrs.	46	46	.500	3.99	287	93	5	857	733	443	707	2	19	11	11	17	2	0	.118

LEAGUE CHAMPIONSHIP SERIES
| 1987 MIN A | 0 | 0 | – | 1.50 | 4 | 0 | 0 | 6 | 1 | 3 | 6 | 0 | 0 | 0 | 1 | 0 | 0 | 0 | – |

WORLD SERIES
| 1987 MIN A | 0 | 1 | .000 | 10.38 | 3 | 0 | 0 | 4.1 | 10 | 0 | 1 | 0 | 0 | 1 | 0 | 0 | 0 | 0 | – |

Karl Best

BEST, KARL JON
B. Mar. 6, 1959, Aberdeen, Wash.
BR TR 6'4" 200 lbs.

	W	L	PCT	ERA	G	GS	CG	IP	H	BB	SO	ShO	W	L	SV	AB	H	HR	BA
1983 SEA A	0	1	.000	13.50	4	0	0	5.1	14	5	3	0	0	1	0	0	0	0	–
1984	1	1	.500	3.00	5	0	0	6	7	0	6	0	1	1	0	0	0	0	–
1985	2	1	.667	1.95	15	0	0	32.1	25	6	32	0	2	1	4	0	0	0	–
1986	2	3	.400	4.04	26	0	0	35.2	35	21	23	0	2	3	1	0	0	0	–
1988 MIN A	0	0	–	6.00	11	0	0	12	15	7	9	0	0	0	0	0	0	0	–
5 yrs.	5	6	.455	4.04	61	0	0	91.1	96	39	73	0	5	6	5	0	0	0	–

Mike Bielecki

BIELECKI, MICHAEL JOSEPH (Bie)
B. July 31, 1959, Baltimore, Md.
BR TR 6'3" 195 lbs.

	W	L	PCT	ERA	G	GS	CG	IP	H	BB	SO	ShO	W	L	SV	AB	H	HR	BA
1984 PIT N	0	0	–	0.00	4	0	0	4.1	4	0	1	0	0	0	0	0	0	0	–
1985	2	3	.400	4.53	12	7	0	45.2	45	31	22	0	0	0	0	10	0	0	.000
1986	6	11	.353	4.66	31	27	0	148.2	149	83	83	0	0	0	0	48	3	0	.063
1987	2	3	.400	4.73	8	8	2	45.2	43	12	25	0	0	0	0	16	1	0	.063
1988 CHI N	2	2	.500	3.35	19	5	0	48.1	55	16	33	0	1	0	0	10	1	0	.100
5 yrs.	12	19	.387	4.37	74	47	2	292.2	296	142	164	0	1	0	0	84	5	0	.060

Mike Birkbeck

BIRKBECK, MICHAEL LAWRENCE
B. Mar. 10, 1961, Orrville, Ohio
BR TR 6'1" 180 lbs.

	W	L	PCT	ERA	G	GS	CG	IP	H	BB	SO	ShO	W	L	SV	AB	H	HR	BA
1986 MIL A	1	1	.500	4.50	7	4	0	22	24	12	13	0	0	0	0	0	0	0	–
1987	1	4	.200	6.20	10	10	1	45	63	19	25	0	0	0	0	0	0	0	–
1988	10	8	.556	4.72	23	23	0	124	141	37	64	0	0	0	0	0	0	0	–
3 yrs.	12	13	.480	5.04	40	37	1	191	228	68	102	0	0	0	0	0	0	0	–

Tim Birtsas

BIRTSAS, TIMOTHY DEAN
B. Sept. 5, 1960, Pontiac, Mich.
BL TL 6'6" 235 lbs.

	W	L	PCT	ERA	G	GS	CG	IP	H	BB	SO	ShO	W	L	SV	AB	H	HR	BA
1985 OAK A	10	6	.625	4.01	29	25	2	141.1	124	91	94	0	0	0	0	0	0	0	–
1986	0	0	–	22.50	2	0	0	2	2	4	1	0	0	0	0	0	0	0	–
1988 CIN N	1	3	.250	4.20	36	4	0	64.1	61	24	38	0	1	0	0	10	0	0	.000
3 yrs.	11	9	.550	4.25	67	29	2	207.2	187	119	133	0	1	0	0	10	0	0	.000

Jeff Bittiger

BITTIGER, JEFFREY SCOTT
B. Apr. 13, 1962, Jersey City, N. J.
BR TR 5'10" 175 lbs.

	W	L	PCT	ERA	G	GS	CG	IP	H	BB	SO	ShO	W	L	SV	AB	H	HR	BA
1986 PHI N	1	1	.500	5.52	3	3	0	14.2	16	7	8	0	0	0	0	3	1	1	.333
1987 MIN A	1	0	1.000	5.40	3	1	0	8.1	11	0	5	0	0	0	0	0	0	0	–
1988 CHI A	2	4	.333	4.23	25	7	0	61.2	59	29	33	0	1	0	0	0	0	0	–
3 yrs.	4	5	.444	4.57	31	11	0	84.2	86	36	46	0	1	0	0	3	1	1	.333

Bud Black

BLACK, HARRY RALSTON
B. June 30, 1957, San Mateo, Calif.
BL TL 6'2" 180 lbs.

	W	L	PCT	ERA	G	GS	CG	IP	H	BB	SO	ShO	W	L	SV	AB	H	HR	BA
1981 SEA A	0	0	–	0.00	2	0	0	1	2	3	0	0	0	0	0	0	0	0	–
1982 KC A	4	6	.400	4.58	22	14	0	88.1	92	34	40	0	0	0	0	0	0	0	–
1983	10	7	.588	3.79	24	24	3	161.1	159	43	58	0	0	0	0	0	0	0	–
1984	17	12	.586	3.12	35	35	8	257	226	64	140	1	0	0	0	0	0	0	–
1985	10	15	.400	4.33	33	33	5	205.2	216	59	122	2	0	0	0	0	0	0	–
1986	5	10	.333	3.20	56	4	0	121	100	43	68	0	4	7	9	0	0	0	–
1987	8	6	.571	3.60	29	18	0	122.1	126	35	61	0	1	1	1	0	0	0	–
1988 2 teams				KC	A	(17G 2–1)		CLE	A	(16G 2–3)									
" total	4	4	.500	5.00	33	7	0	81	82	34	63	0	3	2	1	0	0	0	–
8 yrs.	58	60	.492	3.80	234	135	16	1037.2	1003	315	552	3	8	10	11	0	0	0	–

LEAGUE CHAMPIONSHIP SERIES
1984 KC A	0	1	.000	7.20	1	1	0	5	7	1	3	0	0	0	0	0	0	0	–
1985	0	0	–	1.69	3	1	0	10.2	11	4	8	0	0	0	0	0	0	0	–
2 yrs.	0	1	.000	3.45	4	2	0	15.2	18	5	11	0	0	0	0	0	0	0	–

WORLD SERIES
| 1985 KC A | 0 | 1 | .000 | 5.06 | 2 | 1 | 0 | 5.1 | 4 | 5 | 4 | 0 | 0 | 0 | 0 | 1 | 0 | 0 | .000 |

Kevin Blankenship

BLANKENSHIP, KEVIN DeWAYNE
B. Jan. 26, 1963, Anaheim, Calif.
BR TR 6' 180 lbs.

	W	L	PCT	ERA	G	GS	CG	IP	H	BB	SO	ShO	W	L	SV	AB	H	HR	BA
1988 2 teams				ATL	N	(2G 0–1)		CHI	N	(1G 1–0)									
" total	1	1	.500	4.60	3	3	0	15.2	14	8	9	0	0	0	0	6	0	0	.000

	W	L	PCT	ERA	G	GS	CG	IP	H	BB	SO	ShO	Relief Pitching W	L	SV	BATTING AB	H	HR	BA

Bert Blyleven

BLYLEVEN, RIK AALBERT
B. Apr. 6, 1951, Zeist, Netherlands   BR TR 6'3"   200 lbs.

	W	L	PCT	ERA	G	GS	CG	IP	H	BB	SO	ShO	W	L	SV	AB	H	HR	BA
1970 MIN A	10	9	.526	3.18	27	25	5	164	143	47	135	1	0	1	0	50	7	0	.140
1971	16	15	.516	2.82	38	38	17	278	267	59	224	5	0	0	0	91	12	0	.132
1972	17	17	.500	2.73	39	38	11	287	247	69	228	3	0	1	0	94	15	0	.160
1973	20	17	.541	2.52	40	40	25	325	296	67	258	9	0	0	0	0	0	0	–
1974	17	17	.500	2.66	37	37	19	281	244	77	249	3	0	0	0	0	0	0	–
1975	15	10	.600	3.00	35	35	20	275.2	219	84	233	3	0	0	0	0	0	0	–
1976 2 teams		MIN	A (12G 4–5)		TEX	A (24G 9–11)													
" total	13	16	.448	2.87	36	36	18	297.2	283	81	219	6	0	0	0	0	0	0	–
1977 TEX A	14	12	.538	2.72	30	30	15	235	181	69	182	5	0	0	0	0	0	0	–
1978 PIT N	14	10	.583	3.02	34	34	11	244	217	66	182	4	0	0	0	85	11	0	.129
1979	12	5	.706	3.61	37	37	4	237	238	92	172	0	0	0	0	70	9	0	.129
1980	8	13	.381	3.82	34	32	5	217	219	59	168	2	0	0	0	61	5	0	.082
1981 CLE A	11	7	.611	2.89	20	20	9	159	145	40	107	1	0	0	0	0	0	0	–
1982	2	2	.500	4.87	4	4	0	20.1	16	11	19	0	0	0	0	0	0	0	–
1983	7	10	.412	3.91	24	24	5	-156.1	160	44	123	0	0	0	0	0	0	0	–
1984	19	7	.731	2.87	33	32	12	245	204	74	170	4	0	0	0	0	0	0	–
1985 2 teams		CLE	A (23G 9–11)		MIN	A (14G 8–5)													
" total	17	16	.515	3.16	37	37	24	293.2	264	75	206	5	0	0	0	0	0	0	–
1986 MIN A	17	14	.548	4.01	36	36	16	271.2	262	58	215	3	0	0	0	0	0	0	–
1987	15	12	.556	4.01	37	37	8	267	249	101	196	1	0	0	0	0	0	0	–
1988	10	17	.370	5.43	33	33	7	207.1	240	51	145	0	0	0	0	0	0	0	–
19 yrs.	254	226	.529	3.25	611	605	231	4461.2	4094	1224	3431 7th	55	0	2	0	451	59	0	.131

LEAGUE CHAMPIONSHIP SERIES

	W	L	PCT	ERA	G	GS	CG	IP	H	BB	SO	ShO	W	L	SV	AB	H	HR	BA
1970 MIN A	0	0	–	0.00	1	0	0	2	2	0	2	0	0	0	0	0	0	0	–
1979 PIT N	1	0	1.000	1.00	1	1	1	9	8	0	9	0	0	0	0	3	1	0	.333
1987 MIN A	2	0	1.000	4.05	2	2	0	13.1	12	3	9	0	0	0	0	0	0	0	–
3 yrs.	3	0	1.000	2.59	4	3	1	24.1	22	3	20	0	0	0	0	3	1	0	.333

WORLD SERIES

	W	L	PCT	ERA	G	GS	CG	IP	H	BB	SO	ShO	W	L	SV	AB	H	HR	BA
1979 PIT N	1	0	1.000	1.80	2	1	0	10	8	3	4	0	0	0	0	3	0	0	.000
1987 MIN A	1	1	.500	2.77	2	2	0	13	13	2	12	0	0	0	0	1	0	0	.000
2 yrs.	2	1	.667	2.35	4	3	0	23	21	5	16	0	0	0	0	4	0	0	.000

Randy Bockus

BOCKUS, RANDY WALTER
B. Oct. 5, 1960, Canton, Ohio   BL TR 6'2"   190 lbs.

	W	L	PCT	ERA	G	GS	CG	IP	H	BB	SO	ShO	W	L	SV	AB	H	HR	BA
1986 SF N	0	0	–	2.57	5	0	0	7	7	6	4	0	0	0	0	1	0	0	.000
1987	1	0	1.000	3.63	12	0	0	17.1	17	4	9	0	1	0	0	1	0	0	.000
1988	1	1	.500	4.78	20	0	0	32	35	13	18	0	1	1	0	6	1	0	.167
3 yrs.	2	1	.667	4.15	37	0	0	56.1	59	23	31	0	2	1	0	8	1	0	.125

Mike Boddicker

BODDICKER, MICHAEL JAMES
B. Aug. 23, 1957, Cedar Rapids, Iowa   BR TR 5'11"   172 lbs.

	W	L	PCT	ERA	G	GS	CG	IP	H	BB	SO	ShO	W	L	SV	AB	H	HR	BA
1980 BAL A	0	1	.000	6.43	1	1	0	7	6	5	4	0	0	0	0	0	0	0	–
1981	0	0	–	4.50	2	0	0	6	6	2	2	0	0	0	0	0	0	0	–
1982	1	0	1.000	3.51	7	0	0	25.2	25	12	20	0	1	0	0	0	0	0	–
1983	16	8	.667	2.77	27	26	10	179	141	52	120	5	0	0	0	0	0	0	–
1984	20	11	.645	2.79	34	34	16	261.1	218	81	128	4	0	0	0	0	0	0	–
1985	12	17	.414	4.07	32	32	9	203.1	227	89	135	2	0	0	0	0	0	0	–
1986	14	12	.538	4.70	33	33	7	218.1	214	74	175	0	0	0	0	0	0	0	–
1987	10	12	.455	4.18	33	33	7	226	212	78	152	2	0	0	0	0	0	0	–
1988 2 teams		BAL	A (21G 6–12)		BOS	A (15G 7–3)													
" total	13	15	.464	3.39	36	35	5	236	234	77	156	1	0	0	0	0	0	0	–
9 yrs.	86	76	.531	3.66	205	194	54	1362.2	1283	470	892	14	1	0	0	0	0	0	–

LEAGUE CHAMPIONSHIP SERIES

	W	L	PCT	ERA	G	GS	CG	IP	H	BB	SO	ShO	W	L	SV	AB	H	HR	BA
1983 BAL A	1	0	1.000	0.00	1	1	1	9	5	3	14	1	0	0	0	0	0	0	–
1988 BOS A	0	1	.000	20.25	1	1	0	2.2	8	1	2	0	0	0	0	0	0	0	–
2 yrs.	1	1	.500	4.63	2	2	1	11.2	13	4	16	1	0	0	0	0	0	0	–

WORLD SERIES

	W	L	PCT	ERA	G	GS	CG	IP	H	BB	SO	ShO	W	L	SV	AB	H	HR	BA
1983 BAL A	1	0	1.000	0.00	1	1	1	9	3	0	6	0	0	0	0	3	0	0	.000

Joe Boever

BOEVER, JOSEPH MARTIN
B. Oct. 4, 1960, St. Louis, Mo.   BR TR 6'1"   200 lbs.

	W	L	PCT	ERA	G	GS	CG	IP	H	BB	SO	ShO	W	L	SV	AB	H	HR	BA
1985 STL N	0	0	–	4.41	13	0	0	16.1	17	4	20	0	0	0	0	0	0	0	–
1986	1	1	.500	1.66	11	0	0	21.2	19	11	8	0	0	1	0	2	1	0	.500
1987 ATL N	1	0	1.000	7.36	14	0	0	18.1	29	12	18	0	1	0	0	0	0	0	–
1988	0	2	.000	1.77	16	0	0	20.1	12	1	7	0	0	2	1	0	0	0	–
4 yrs.	1	3	.250	3.64	54	0	0	76.2	77	28	53	0	1	3	1	2	1	0	.500

Tom Bolton

BOLTON, THOMAS EDWARD
B. May 6, 1962, Nashville, Tenn.   BL TL 6'2"   172 lbs.

	W	L	PCT	ERA	G	GS	CG	IP	H	BB	SO	ShO	W	L	SV	AB	H	HR	BA
1987 BOS A	1	0	1.000	4.38	29	0	0	61.2	83	27	49	0	1	0	0	0	0	0	–
1988	1	3	.250	4.75	28	0	0	30.1	35	14	21	0	1	3	1	0	0	0	–
2 yrs.	2	3	.400	4.50	57	0	0	92	118	41	70	0	2	3	1	0	0	0	–

Greg Booker

BOOKER, GREGORY SCOTT
B. June 22, 1960, Lynchburg, Va.   BR TR 6'6"   230 lbs.

	W	L	PCT	ERA	G	GS	CG	IP	H	BB	SO	ShO	W	L	SV	AB	H	HR	BA
1983 SD N	0	1	.000	7.71	6	1	0	11.2	18	9	5	0	0	0	0	1	0	0	.000
1984	1	1	.500	3.30	32	1	0	57.1	67	27	28	0	1	1	0	7	2	0	.286
1985	0	1	.000	6.85	17	0	0	22.1	20	17	7	0	0	1	0	1	0	0	.000
1986	1	0	1.000	1.64	9	0	0	11	10	4	7	0	1	0	0	0	0	0	–
1987	1	1	.500	3.16	44	0	0	68.1	62	30	17	0	1	1	1	6	0	0	.000
1988	2	2	.500	3.39	34	2	0	63.2	68	19	43	0	1	2	0	8	2	0	.250
6 yrs.	5	6	.455	3.76	142	4	0	234.1	245	106	107	0	4	5	1	23	4	0	.174

	W	L	PCT	ERA	G	GS	CG	IP	H	BB	SO	ShO	Relief Pitching W	L	SV	BATTING AB	H	HR	BA

Greg Booker continued

LEAGUE CHAMPIONSHIP SERIES

	W	L	PCT	ERA	G	GS	CG	IP	H	BB	SO	ShO	W	L	SV	AB	H	HR	BA
1984 SD N	0	0	–	0.00	1	0	0	2	2	1	2	0	0	0	0	0	0	0	–

WORLD SERIES

1984 SD N	0	0	–	9.00	1	0	0	1	0	4	0	0	0	0	0	0	0	0	–

Rich Bordi

BORDI, RICHARD ALBERT
B. Apr. 18, 1959, San Francisco, Calif.
BR TR 6'7" 210 lbs.

	W	L	PCT	ERA	G	GS	CG	IP	H	BB	SO	ShO	W	L	SV	AB	H	HR	BA
1980 OAK A	0	0	–	4.50	1	0	0	2	4	0	0	0	0	0	0	0	0	0	–
1981	0	0	–	0.00	2	0	0	2	1	1	0	0	0	0	0	0	0	0	–
1982 SEA A	0	2	.000	8.31	7	2	0	13	18	1	10	0	0	0	0	0	0	0	–
1983 CHI N	0	2	.000	4.97	11	1	0	25.1	34	12	20	0	0	1	1	4	0	0	.000
1984	5	2	.714	3.46	31	7	0	83.1	78	20	41	0	1	1	4	19	1	0	.053
1985 NY A	6	8	.429	3.21	51	3	0	98	95	29	64	0	4	7	2	0	0	0	–
1986 BAL A	6	4	.600	4.46	52	1	0	107	105	41	83	0	6	3	3	0	0	0	–
1987 NY A	3	1	.750	7.64	16	1	0	33	42	12	23	0	3	0	0	0	0	0	–
1988 OAK A	0	1	.000	4.70	2	2	0	7.2	6	5	6	0	0	0	0	0	0	0	–
9 yrs.	20	20	.500	4.34	173	17	0	371.1	383	121	247	0	14	12	10	23	1	0	.043

Chris Bosio

BOSIO, CHRISTOPHER LOUIS
B. Apr. 3, 1963, Carmichael, Calif.
BR TR 6'3" 220 lbs.

	W	L	PCT	ERA	G	GS	CG	IP	H	BB	SO	ShO	W	L	SV	AB	H	HR	BA
1986 MIL A	0	4	.000	7.01	10	4	0	34.2	41	13	29	0	0	1	0	0	0	0	–
1987	11	8	.579	5.24	46	19	2	170	187	50	150	1	3	1	2	0	0	0	–
1988	7	15	.318	3.36	38	22	9	182	190	38	84	1	1	3	6	0	0	0	–
3 yrs.	18	27	.400	4.52	94	45	11	386.2	418	101	263	2	4	5	8	0	0	0	–

Oil Can Boyd

BOYD, DENNIS RAY
B. Oct. 6, 1959, Meridian, Miss.
BR TR 6'2" 160 lbs.

	W	L	PCT	ERA	G	GS	CG	IP	H	BB	SO	ShO	W	L	SV	AB	H	HR	BA
1982 BOS A	0	1	.000	5.40	3	1	0	8.1	11	2	2	0	0	0	0	0	0	0	–
1983	4	8	.333	3.28	15	13	5	98.2	103	23	43	0	0	0	0	0	0	0	–
1984	12	12	.500	4.37	29	26	10	197.2	207	53	134	3	0	1	0	0	0	0	–
1985	15	13	.536	3.70	35	35	13	272.1	273	67	154	3	0	0	0	0	0	0	–
1986	16	10	.615	3.78	30	30	10	214.1	222	45	129	0	0	0	0	0	0	0	–
1987	1	3	.250	5.89	7	7	0	36.2	47	9	12	0	0	0	0	0	0	0	–
1988	9	7	.563	5.34	23	23	1	129.2	147	41	71	0	0	0	0	0	0	0	–
7 yrs.	57	54	.514	4.14	142	135	39	957.2	1010	240	545	6	0	1	0	0	0	0	–

LEAGUE CHAMPIONSHIP SERIES

1986 BOS A	1	1	.500	4.61	2	2	0	13.2	17	3	8	0	0	0	0	0	0	0	–

WORLD SERIES

1986 BOS A	0	1	.000	7.71	1	1	0	7	9	1	3	0	0	0	0	0	0	0	–

Jeff Brantley

BRANTLEY, JEFFREY HOKE
B. Sept. 5, 1963, Florence, Ala.
BR TR 5'11" 180 lbs.

	W	L	PCT	ERA	G	GS	CG	IP	H	BB	SO	ShO	W	L	SV	AB	H	HR	BA
1988 SF N	0	1	.000	5.66	9	1	0	20.2	22	6	11	0	0	0	1	2	1	0	.500

William Brennan

BRENNAN, WILLIAM RAYMOND
B. Jan. 15, 1963, Tampa, Fla.
BR TR 6'3" 194 lbs.

	W	L	PCT	ERA	G	GS	CG	IP	H	BB	SO	ShO	W	L	SV	AB	H	HR	BA
1988 LA N	0	1	.000	6.75	4	2	0	9.1	13	6	7	0	0	0	0	2	0	0	.000

Keith Brown

BROWN, KEITH EDWARD
B. Feb. 14, 1964, Flagstaff, Ariz.
BR TR 6'4" 205 lbs.

	W	L	PCT	ERA	G	GS	CG	IP	H	BB	SO	ShO	W	L	SV	AB	H	HR	BA
1988 CIN N	2	1	.667	2.76	4	3	0	16.1	14	4	6	0	0	0	0	4	0	0	.000

Kevin Brown

BROWN, JAMES KEVIN
B. Mar. 14, 1965, Milledgeville, Ga.
BR TR 6'4" 195 lbs.

	W	L	PCT	ERA	G	GS	CG	IP	H	BB	SO	ShO	W	L	SV	AB	H	HR	BA
1986 TEX A	1	0	1.000	3.60	1	1	0	5	6	0	4	0	0	0	0	0	0	0	–
1988	1	1	.500	4.24	4	4	1	23.1	33	8	12	0	0	0	0	0	0	0	–
2 yrs.	2	1	.667	4.13	5	5	1	28.1	39	8	16	0	0	0	0	0	0	0	–

Tom Browning

BROWNING, THOMAS LEO
B. Apr. 28, 1960, Casper, Wyo.
BL TL 6'1" 180 lbs.

	W	L	PCT	ERA	G	GS	CG	IP	H	BB	SO	ShO	W	L	SV	AB	H	HR	BA
1984 CIN N	1	0	1.000	1.54	3	3	0	23.1	27	5	14	0	0	0	0	7	1	0	.143
1985	20	9	.690	3.55	38	38	6	261.1	242	73	155	4	0	0	0	88	17	0	.193
1986	14	13	.519	3.81	39	39	4	243.1	225	70	147	2	0	0	0	86	14	0	.163
1987	10	13	.435	5.02	32	31	2	183	201	61	117	0	0	0	0	52	8	0	.154
1988	18	5	.783	3.41	36	36	5	250.2	205	64	124	2	0	0	0	83	12	0	.145
5 yrs.	63	40	.612	3.81	148	147	17	961.2	900	273	557	8	0	0	0	316	52	0	.165

DeWayne Buice

BUICE, DeWAYNE ALLISON
B. Aug. 20, 1957, Lynwood, Calif.
BR TR 6' 170 lbs.

	W	L	PCT	ERA	G	GS	CG	IP	H	BB	SO	ShO	W	L	SV	AB	H	HR	BA
1987 CAL A	6	7	.462	3.39	57	0	0	114	87	40	109	0	6	7	17	0	0	0	–
1988	2	4	.333	5.88	32	0	0	41.1	45	19	38	0	2	4	3	0	0	0	–
2 yrs.	8	11	.421	4.06	89	0	0	155.1	132	59	147	0	8	11	20	0	0	0	–

Tim Burke

BURKE, TIMOTHY PHILIP
B. Feb. 19, 1959, Omaha, Neb.
BR TR 6'3" 205 lbs.

	W	L	PCT	ERA	G	GS	CG	IP	H	BB	SO	ShO	W	L	SV	AB	H	HR	BA
1985 MON N	9	4	.692	2.39	78	0	0	120.1	86	44	87	0	9	4	8	10	1	0	.100
1986	9	7	.563	2.93	68	2	0	101.1	103	46	82	0	8	7	4	7	0	0	.000
1987	7	0	1.000	1.19	55	0	0	91	64	17	58	0	7	0	18	10	0	0	.000
1988	3	5	.375	3.40	61	0	0	82	84	25	42	0	3	5	18	2	0	0	.000
4 yrs.	28	16	.636	2.46	262	2	0	394.2	337	132	269	0	27	16	48	29	1	0	.034

                                                 Pitcher Register

	W	L	PCT	ERA	G	GS	CG	IP	H	BB	SO	ShO	Relief Pitching W	L	SV	BATTING AB	H	HR	BA

Todd Burns

BURNS, TODD EDWARD
B. July 6, 1963, Maywood, Calif.   BR TR 6'2"   186 lbs.

	W	L	PCT	ERA	G	GS	CG	IP	H	BB	SO	ShO	W	L	SV	AB	H	HR	BA
1988 **OAK A**	8	2	.800	3.16	17	14	2	102.2	93	34	57	0	1	0	1	0	0	0	–
WORLD SERIES																			
1988 **OAK A**	0	0	–	0.00	1	0	0	.1	0	0	0	0	0	0	0	0	0	0	–

Sal Butera

BUTERA, SALVATORE PHILIP
B. Sept. 25, 1952, Richmond Hill, N. Y.   BR TR 6'   190 lbs.

	W	L	PCT	ERA	G	GS	CG	IP	H	BB	SO	ShO	W	L	SV	AB	H	HR	BA
1985 **MON N**	0	0	–	0.00	1	0	0	1	0	0	0	0	0	0	0	120	24	3	.200
1986 **CIN N**	0	0	–	0.00	1	0	0	1	0	1	1	0	0	0	0	113	27	2	.239
2 yrs.	0	0	–	0.00	2	0	0	2	0	1	1	0	0	0	0	*			

Greg Cadaret

CADARET, GREGORY JAMES
B. Feb. 27, 1962, Detroit, Mich.   BL TL 6'3"   200 lbs.

	W	L	PCT	ERA	G	GS	CG	IP	H	BB	SO	ShO	W	L	SV	AB	H	HR	BA
1987 **OAK A**	6	2	.750	4.54	29	0	0	39.2	37	24	30	0	6	2	0	0	0	0	–
1988	5	2	.714	2.89	58	0	0	71.2	60	36	64	0	5	2	3	0	0	0	–
2 yrs.	11	4	.733	3.48	87	0	0	111.1	97	60	94	0	11	4	3	0	0	0	–
LEAGUE CHAMPIONSHIP SERIES																			
1988 **OAK A**	0	0	–	27.00	1	0	0	.1	1	0	0	0	0	0	0	0	0	0	–
WORLD SERIES																			
1988 **OAK A**	0	0	–	0.00	3	0	0	2	2	0	3	0	0	0	0	0	0	0	–

Jeff Calhoun

. CALHOUN, JEFFREY WILTON
B. Apr. 11, 1958, LaGrange, Ga.   BL TL 6'2"   190 lbs.

	W	L	PCT	ERA	G	GS	CG	IP	H	BB	SO	ShO	W	L	SV	AB	H	HR	BA
1984 **HOU N**	0	1	.000	1.17	9	0	0	15.1	5	2	11	0	0	1	0	0	0	0	–
1985	2	5	.286	2.54	44	0	0	63.2	56	24	47	0	2	5	4	5	0	0	.000
1986	1	0	1.000	3.71	20	0	0	26.2	28	12	14	0	1	0	0	0	0	0	–
1987 **PHI N**	3	1	.750	1.48	42	0	0	42.2	25	26	31	0	3	1	1	1	0	0	.000
1988	0	0	–	15.43	3	0	0	2.1	6	1	1	0	0	0	0	0	0	0	–
5 yrs.	6	7	.462	2.51	118	0	0	150.2	120	65	104	0	6	7	5	6	0	0	.000
LEAGUE CHAMPIONSHIP SERIES																			
1986 **HOU N**	0	0	–	9.00	1	0	0	1	1	1	0	0	0	0	0	0	0	0	–

Ernie Camacho

CAMACHO, ERNEST CARLOS
B. Feb. 1, 1955, Salinas, Calif.   BR TR 6'1"   180 lbs.

	W	L	PCT	ERA	G	GS	CG	IP	H	BB	SO	ShO	W	L	SV	AB	H	HR	BA
1980 **OAK A**	0	0	–	6.75	5	0	0	12	20	5	9	0	0	0	0	0	0	0	–
1981 **PIT N**	0	1	.000	4.91	7	3	0	22	23	15	11	0	0	0	0	4	0	0	.000
1983 **CLE A**	0	1	.000	5.06	4	0	0	5.1	5	2	2	0	0	1	0	0	0	0	–
1984	5	9	.357	2.43	69	0	0	100	83	37	48	0	5	9	23	0	0	0	–
1985	0	1	.000	8.10	2	0	0	3.1	4	1	2	0	0	1	0	0	0	0	–
1986	2	4	.333	4.08	51	0	0	57.1	60	31	36	0	2	4	20	0	0	0	–
1987	0	1	.000	9.22	15	0	0	13.2	21	5	9	0	0	1	1	0	0	0	–
1988 **HOU N**	0	3	.000	7.64	13	0	0	17.2	25	12	13	0	0	3	1	1	0	0	.000
8 yrs.	7	20	.259	4.24	166	3	0	231.1	241	108	130	0	7	19	45	5	0	0	.000

Mike Campbell

CAMPBELL, MICHAEL THOMAS
B. Feb. 17, 1964, Seattle, Wash.   BR TR 6'3"   210 lbs.

	W	L	PCT	ERA	G	GS	CG	IP	H	BB	SO	ShO	W	L	SV	AB	H	HR	BA
1987 **SEA A**	1	4	.200	4.74	9	9	1	49.1	41	25	35	0	0	0	0	0	0	0	–
1988	6	10	.375	5.89	20	20	2	114.2	128	43	63	0	0	0	0	0	0	0	–
2 yrs.	7	14	.333	5.54	29	29	3	164	169	68	98	0	0	0	0	0	0	0	–

John Candelaria

CANDELARIA, JOHN ROBERT (The Candy Man)
B. Nov. 6, 1953, New York, N. Y.   BL TL 6'7"   205 lbs.

	W	L	PCT	ERA	G	GS	CG	IP	H	BB	SO	ShO	W	L	SV	AB	H	HR	BA
1975 **PIT N**	8	6	.571	2.75	18	18	4	121	95	36	95	1	0	0	0	43	6	0	.140
1976	16	7	.696	3.15	32	31	11	220	173	60	138	4	0	0	1	76	14	0	.184
1977	20	5	.800	2.34	33	33	6	231	197	50	133	1	0	0	0	80	18	0	.225
1978	12	11	.522	3.24	30	29	3	189	191	49	94	1	0	0	1	52	9	0	.173
1979	14	9	.609	3.22	33	30	8	207	201	41	101	0	0	1	0	68	9	0	.132
1980	11	14	.440	4.02	35	34	7	233	246	50	97	0	0	0	1	77	15	0	.195
1981	2	2	.500	3.51	6	6	0	41	42	11	14	0	0	0	0	13	3	0	.231
1982	12	7	.632	2.94	31	30	1	174.2	166	37	133	1	0	0	0	54	12	0	.222
1983	15	8	.652	3.23	33	32	2	197.2	191	45	157	0	0	0	0	65	9	0	.138
1984	12	11	.522	2.72	33	28	3	185.1	179	34	133	1	0	1	2	62	8	1	.129
1985 **2 teams**			**PIT**	**N (37G 2–4)**						**CAL**		**A (13G 7–3)**							
" total	9	7	.563	3.73	50	13	1	125.1	127	38	100	1	2	4	9	1	0	0	.000
1986 **CAL A**	10	2	.833	2.55	16	16	1	91.2	68	26	81	1	0	0	0	0	0	0	–
1987 **2 teams**			**CAL**	**A (20G 8–6)**						**NY**		**N (3G 2–0)**							
" total	10	6	.625	4.81	23	23	0	129	144	23	84	0	0	0	0	5	1	0	.200
1988 **NY A**	13	7	.650	3.38	25	24	6	157	150	23	121	2	0	0	0	0	0	0	–
14 yrs.	164	102	.617	3.23	398	347	53	2302.2	2170	523	1481	13	2	6	16	596	104	1	.174
LEAGUE CHAMPIONSHIP SERIES																			
1975 **PIT N**	0	0	–	3.52	1	1	0	7.2	3	2	14	0	0	0	0	3	0	0	.000
1979	0	0	–	2.57	1	1	0	7	5	1	4	0	0	0	0	3	0	0	.000
1986 **CAL A**	1	1	.500	0.84	2	2	0	10.2	11	6	7	0	0	0	0	0	0	0	–
3 yrs.	1	1	.500	2.13	4	4	0	25.1	19	9	25	0	0	0	0	6	0	0	.000
WORLD SERIES																			
1979 **PIT N**	1	1	.500	5.00	2	2	0	9	14	2	4	0	0	0	0	3	1	0	.333

Tom Candiotti

CANDIOTTI, THOMAS CAESAR
B. Aug. 31, 1957, Walnut Creek, Calif.   BR TR 6'3"   205 lbs.

	W	L	PCT	ERA	G	GS	CG	IP	H	BB	SO	ShO	W	L	SV	AB	H	HR	BA
1983 **MIL A**	4	4	.500	3.23	10	8	2	55.2	62	16	21	1	0	0	0	0	0	0	–
1984	2	2	.500	5.29	8	6	0	32.1	38	10	23	0	0	0	0	0	0	0	–
1986 **CLE A**	16	12	.571	3.57	36	34	17	252.1	234	106	167	3	0	0	0	0	0	0	–
1987	7	18	.280	4.78	32	32	7	201.2	193	93	111	2	0	0	0	0	0	0	–

	W	L	PCT	ERA	G	GS	CG	IP	H	BB	SO	ShO	Relief Pitching W	L	SV	BATTING AB	H	HR	BA

Tom Candiotti continued

	W	L	PCT	ERA	G	GS	CG	IP	H	BB	SO	ShO	W	L	SV	AB	H	HR	BA
1988	14	8	.636	3.28	31	31	11	216.2	225	53	137	1	0	0	0	0	0	0	–
5 yrs.	43	44	.494	3.86	117	111	37	758.2	752	278	459	7	0	0	0	0	0	0	–

John Cangelosi

CANGELOSI, JOHN ANTHONY
B. Mar. 10, 1963, Brooklyn, N. Y.

BB TL 5'8" 150 lbs.

		W	L	PCT	ERA	G	GS	CG	IP	H	BB	SO	ShO	W	L	SV	AB	H	HR	BA
1988 PIT	N	0	0	–	0.00	1	0	0	2	1	0	0	0	0	0	0	*		

Mike Capel

CAPEL, MICHAEL LEE
B. Oct. 13, 1961, Marshall, Tex.

BR TR 6'1" 175 lbs.

		W	L	PCT	ERA	G	GS	CG	IP	H	BB	SO	ShO	W	L	SV	AB	H	HR	BA
1988 CHI	N	2	1	.667	4.91	22	0	0	29.1	34	13	19	0	2	1	0	2	0	0	.000

Steve Carlton

CARLTON, STEPHEN NORMAN (Lefty)
B. Dec. 22, 1944, Miami, Fla.

BL TL 6'4" 210 lbs.

		W	L	PCT	ERA	G	GS	CG	IP	H	BB	SO	ShO	W	L	SV	AB	H	HR	BA
1965 STL	N	0	0	–	2.52	15	2	0	25	27	8	21	0	0	0	0	2	0	0	.000
1966		3	3	.500	3.12	9	9	2	52	56	18	25	1	0	0	0	15	4	0	.267
1967		14	9	.609	2.98	30	28	11	193	173	62	168	2	0	1	1	72	11	0	.153
1968		13	11	.542	2.99	34	33	10	232	214	61	162	5	0	1	0	73	12	2	.164
1969		17	11	.607	2.17	31	31	12	236	185	93	210	2	0	0	0	80	17	1	.213
1970		10	19	.345	3.72	34	33	13	254	239	109	193	2	0	0	0	80	16	0	.200
1971		20	9	.690	3.56	37	36	18	273	275	98	172	4	0	0	0	96	17	0	.177
1972 PHI	N	27	10	.730	1.97	41	41	30	346.1	257	87	310	8	0	0	0	117	23	1	.197
1973		13	20	.394	3.90	40	40	18	293.1	293	113	223	3	0	0	0	100	16	2	.160
1974		16	13	.552	3.22	39	39	17	291	249	136	240	1	0	0	0	102	25	0	.245
1975		15	14	.517	3.56	37	37	14	255	217	104	192	3	0	0	0	90	14	0	.156
1976		20	7	.741	3.13	35	35	13	252.2	224	72	195	2	0	0	0	92	20	0	.217
1977		23	10	.697	2.64	36	36	17	283	229	89	198	2	0	0	0	97	26	3	.268
1978		16	13	.552	2.84	34	34	12	247	228	63	161	3	0	0	0	86	25	0	.291
1979		18	11	.621	3.62	35	35	13	251	202	89	213	4	0	0	0	94	21	0	.223
1980		24	9	.727	2.34	38	38	13	304	243	90	286	3	0	0	0	101	19	0	.188
1981		13	4	.765	2.42	24	24	10	190	152	62	179	1	0	0	0	67	9	0	.134
1982		23	11	.676	3.10	38	38	19	295.2	253	86	286	6	0	0	0	101	22	2	.218
1983		15	16	.484	3.11	37	37	8	283.2	277	84	275	3	0	0	0	97	19	0	.196
1984		13	7	.650	3.58	33	33	1	229	214	79	163	0	0	0	0	84	16	1	.190
1985		1	8	.111	3.33	16	16	0	92	84	53	48	0	0	0	0	28	5	0	.179
1986 3 teams		PHI	N (16G 4–8)		SF	N (6G 1–3)		CHI	A (10G 4–3)											
" total		9	14	.391	5.10	32	32	0	176.1	196	86	120	0	0	0	0	45	9	1	.200
1987 2 teams		CLE	A (23G 5–9)		MIN	A (9G 1–5)														
" total		6	14	.300	5.74	32	21	3	152	165	86	91	0	2	2	1	0	0	0	–
1988 MIN	A	0	1	.000	16.76	4	1	0	9.2	20	5	5	0	0	0	0	0	0	0	–
24 yrs.		329	244	.574	3.22	741	709	254	5216.2	4672	1833	4136	55	2	4	2	1719	346	13	.201
			9th								8th			2nd	2nd					

DIVISIONAL PLAYOFF SERIES

		W	L	PCT	ERA	G	GS	CG	IP	H	BB	SO	ShO	W	L	SV	AB	H	HR	BA
1981 PHI	N	0	2	.000	3.86	2	2	0	14	14	8	13	0	0	0	0	4	1	0	.250

LEAGUE CHAMPIONSHIP SERIES

		W	L	PCT	ERA	G	GS	CG	IP	H	BB	SO	ShO	W	L	SV	AB	H	HR	BA
1976 PHI	N	0	1	.000	5.14	1	1	0	7	8	5	6	0	0	0	0	2	0	0	.000
1977		0	1	.000	6.94	2	2	0	11.2	13	8	6	0	0	0	0	4	2	0	.500
1978		1	0	1.000	4.00	1	1	1	9	8	2	8	0	0	0	0	4	2	1	.500
1980		1	0	1.000	2.19	2	2	0	12.1	11	8	6	0	0	0	0	4	0	0	.000
1983		2	0	1.000	0.66	2	2	0	13.2	13	5	13	0	0	0	0	5	1	0	.200
5 yrs.		4	2	.667	3.52	8	8	1	53.2	53	28	39	0	0	0	0	19	5	1	.263

WORLD SERIES

		W	L	PCT	ERA	G	GS	CG	IP	H	BB	SO	ShO	W	L	SV	AB	H	HR	BA
1967 STL	N	0	1	.000	0.00	1	1	0	6	3	2	5	0	0	0	0	1	0	0	.000
1968		0	0	–	6.75	2	0	0	4	7	1	3	0	0	0	0	0	0	0	–
1980 PHI	N	2	0	1.000	2.40	2	2	0	15	14	9	17	0	0	0	0	0	0	0	–
1983		0	1	.000	2.70	1	1	0	6.2	5	3	7	0	0	0	0	3	0	0	.000
4 yrs.		2	2	.500	2.56	6	4	0	31.2	29	15	32	0	0	0	0	4	0	0	.000

Don Carman

CARMAN, DONALD WAYNE
B. Aug. 14, 1959, Oklahoma City, Okla.

BL TL 6'3" 195 lbs.

		W	L	PCT	ERA	G	GS	CG	IP	H	BB	SO	ShO	W	L	SV	AB	H	HR	BA
1983 PHI	N	0	0	–	0.00	1	0	0	1	0	0	0	0	0	0	1	0	0	0	–
1984		0	1	.000	5.40	11	0	0	13.1	14	6	16	0	0	1	0	1	0	0	.000
1985		9	4	.692	2.08	71	0	0	86.1	52	38	87	0	9	4	7	3	0	0	.000
1986		10	5	.667	3.22	50	14	2	134.1	113	52	98	1	3	2	1	31	0	0	.000
1987		13	11	.542	4.22	35	35	3	211	194	69	125	2	0	0	0	61	5	0	.082
1988		10	14	.417	4.29	36	32	2	201.1	211	70	116	0	0	0	0	63	3	0	.048
6 yrs.		42	35	.545	3.77	204	81	7	647.1	584	235	442	3	12	7	9	159	8	0	.050

Cris Carpenter

CARPENTER, CRIS HOWELL
B. Apr. 5, 1965, St. Augustine, Fla.

BR TR 6'1" 185 lbs.

		W	L	PCT	ERA	G	GS	CG	IP	H	BB	SO	ShO	W	L	SV	AB	H	HR	BA
1988 STL	N	2	3	.400	4.72	8	8	1	47.2	56	9	24	0	0	0	0	14	2	0	.143

Chuck Cary

CARY, CHARLES DOUGLAS
B. Mar. 3, 1960, Whittier, Calif.

BL TL 6'4" 210 lbs.

		W	L	PCT	ERA	G	GS	CG	IP	H	BB	SO	ShO	W	L	SV	AB	H	HR	BA
1985 DET	A	0	1	.000	3.42	16	0	0	23.2	16	8	22	0	0	1	2	0	0	0	–
1986		1	2	.333	3.41	22	0	0	31.2	33	15	21	0	1	2	0	0	0	0	–
1987 ATL	N	1	1	.500	3.78	13	0	0	16.2	17	4	15	0	1	1	1	1	0	0	.000
1988		0	0	–	6.48	7	0	0	8.1	8	4	7	0	0	0	0	0	0	0	–
4 yrs.		2	4	.333	3.81	58	0	0	80.1	74	31	65	0	2	4	3	1	0	0	.000

	W	L	PCT	ERA	G	GS	CG	IP	H	BB	SO	ShO	Relief W	Relief L	SV	AB	H	HR	BA

Tony Castillo

CASTILLO, ANTONIO
B. Mar. 1, 1963, Quibor, Venezuela
BL TL 5'10" 177 lbs.

	W	L	PCT	ERA	G	GS	CG	IP	H	BB	SO	ShO	RW	RL	SV	AB	H	HR	BA
1988 TOR A	1	0	1.000	3.00	14	0	0	15	10	2	14	0	1	0	0	0	0	0	—

Jose Cecena

CECENA, JOSE ISABEL
Born Jose Isabel Cecena y Lugo.
B. Aug. 20, 1963, Ciudad Obregon, Mexico
BR TR 5'11" 180 lbs.

	W	L	PCT	ERA	G	GS	CG	IP	H	BB	SO	ShO	RW	RL	SV	AB	H	HR	BA
1988 TEX A	0	0	—	4.78	22	0	0	26.1	20	23	27	0	0	0	1	0	0	0	—

Rick Cerone

CERONE, RICHARD ALDO
B. May 19, 1954, Newark, N. J.
BR TR 5'11" 192 lbs.

	W	L	PCT	ERA	G	GS	CG	IP	H	BB	SO	ShO	RW	RL	SV	AB	H	HR	BA
1987 NY A	0	0	—	0.00	2	0	0	2	0	1	1	0	0	0	0	*			

John Cerutti

CERUTTI, JOHN JOSEPH
B. Apr. 28, 1960, Albany, N. Y.
BL TL 6'2" 190 lbs.

	W	L	PCT	ERA	G	GS	CG	IP	H	BB	SO	ShO	RW	RL	SV	AB	H	HR	BA
1985 TOR A	0	2	.000	5.40	4	1	0	6.2	10	4	5	0	0	1	0	0	0	0	—
1986	9	4	.692	4.15	34	20	2	145.1	150	47	89	1	2	0	1	0	0	0	—
1987	11	4	.733	4.40	44	21	2	151.1	144	59	92	0	2	0	0	0	0	0	—
1988	6	7	.462	3.13	46	12	0	123.2	120	42	65	0	1	3	1	0	0	0	—
4 yrs.	26	17	.605	3.96	128	54	4	427	424	152	251	1	5	4	2	0	0	0	—

Norm Charlton

CHARLTON, NORMAN WOOD
B. Jan. 6, 1963, Fort Polk, La.
BB TL 6'3" 195 lbs.

	W	L	PCT	ERA	G	GS	CG	IP	H	BB	SO	ShO	RW	RL	SV	AB	H	HR	BA
1988 CIN N	4	5	.444	3.96	10	10	0	61.1	60	20	39	0	0	0	0	15	0	0	.000

Rocky Childress

CHILDRESS, RODNEY OSBORNE
B. Feb. 18, 1962, Santa Rosa, Calif.
BR TR 6'2" 185 lbs.

	W	L	PCT	ERA	G	GS	CG	IP	H	BB	SO	ShO	RW	RL	SV	AB	H	HR	BA
1985 PHI N	0	1	.000	6.21	16	1	0	33.1	45	9	14	0	0	0	0	6	1	0	.167
1986	0	0	—	6.75	2	0	0	2.2	1	1	1	0	0	0	0	0	0	0	—
1987 HOU N	1	2	.333	2.98	32	0	0	48.1	46	18	26	0	1	2	0	2	0	0	.000
1988	1	0	1.000	6.17	11	0	0	23.1	26	9	24	0	1	0	0	4	1	0	.250
4 yrs.	2	3	.400	4.76	61	1	0	107.2	121	37	65	0	2	2	0	12	2	0	.167

Jim Clancy

CLANCY, JAMES
B. Dec. 18, 1955, Chicago, Ill.
BR TR 6'2" 185 lbs.

	W	L	PCT	ERA	G	GS	CG	IP	H	BB	SO	ShO	RW	RL	SV	AB	H	HR	BA
1977 TOR A	4	9	.308	5.03	13	13	4	77	80	47	44	1	0	0	0	0	0	0	—
1978	10	12	.455	4.09	31	30	7	193.2	199	91	106	0	0	0	0	0	0	0	—
1979	2	7	.222	5.48	12	11	2	64	65	31	33	0	0	0	0	0	0	0	—
1980	13	16	.448	3.30	34	34	15	251	217	128	152	2	0	0	0	0	0	0	—
1981	6	12	.333	4.90	22	22	2	125	126	64	56	0	0	0	0	0	0	0	—
1982	16	14	.533	3.71	40	40	11	266.2	251	77	139	3	0	0	0	0	0	0	—
1983	15	11	.577	3.91	34	34	11	223	238	61	99	1	0	0	0	0	0	0	—
1984	13	15	.464	5.12	36	36	5	219.2	249	88	118	0	0	0	0	0	0	0	—
1985	9	6	.600	3.78	23	23	1	128.2	117	37	66	0	0	0	0	0	0	0	—
1986	14	14	.500	3.94	34	34	6	219.1	202	63	126	3	0	0	0	0	0	0	—
1987	15	11	.577	3.54	37	37	5	241.1	234	80	180	1	0	0	0	0	0	0	—
1988	11	13	.458	4.49	36	31	4	196.1	207	47	118	0	0	0	1	0	0	0	—
12 yrs.	128	140	.478	4.10	352	345	73	2205.2	2185	814	1237	11	0	0	1	0	0	0	—

LEAGUE CHAMPIONSHIP SERIES

	W	L	PCT	ERA	G	GS	CG	IP	H	BB	SO	ShO	RW	RL	SV	AB	H	HR	BA
1985 TOR A	0	1	.000	9.00	1	0	0	1	2	1	0	0	0	1	0	0	0	0	—

Terry Clark

CLARK, TERRY LEE
B. Oct. 18, 1960, Los Angeles, Calif.
BR TR 6'2" 190 lbs.

	W	L	PCT	ERA	G	GS	CG	IP	H	BB	SO	ShO	RW	RL	SV	AB	H	HR	BA
1988 CAL A	6	6	.500	5.07	15	15	2	94	120	31	39	1	0	0	0	0	0	0	—

Danny Clay

CLAY, DANNY BRUCE
B. Oct. 24, 1961, Sun Valley, Calif.
BR TR 6'1" 190 lbs.

	W	L	PCT	ERA	G	GS	CG	IP	H	BB	SO	ShO	RW	RL	SV	AB	H	HR	BA
1988 PHI N	0	1	.000	6.00	17	0	0	24	27	21	12	0	0	1	0	2	0	0	.000

Mark Clear

CLEAR, MARK ALAN
B. May 27, 1956, Los Angeles, Calif.
BR TR 6'4" 200 lbs.

	W	L	PCT	ERA	G	GS	CG	IP	H	BB	SO	ShO	RW	RL	SV	AB	H	HR	BA
1979 CAL A	11	5	.688	3.63	52	0	0	109	87	68	98	0	11	5	14	0	0	0	—
1980	11	11	.500	3.31	58	0	0	106	82	65	105	0	11	11	9	0	0	0	—
1981 BOS A	8	3	.727	4.09	34	0	0	77	69	51	82	0	8	3	9	0	0	0	—
1982	14	9	.609	3.00	55	0	0	105	92	61	109	0	14	9	14	0	0	0	—
1983	4	5	.444	6.28	48	0	0	96	101	68	81	0	4	5	4	0	0	0	—
1984	8	3	.727	4.03	47	0	0	67	47	70	76	0	8	3	8	0	0	0	—
1985	1	3	.250	3.72	41	0	0	55.2	45	50	55	0	1	3	3	0	0	0	—
1986 MIL A	5	5	.500	2.20	59	0	0	73.2	53	36	85	0	5	5	16	0	0	0	—
1987	8	5	.615	4.48	58	1	0	78.1	70	55	81	0	8	4	6	0	0	0	—
1988	1	0	1.000	2.79	25	0	0	29	23	21	26	0	1	0	0	0	0	0	—
10 yrs.	71	49	.592	3.83	477	1	0	796.2	669	545	798	0	71	48	83	0	0	0	—

LEAGUE CHAMPIONSHIP SERIES

	W	L	PCT	ERA	G	GS	CG	IP	H	BB	SO	ShO	RW	RL	SV	AB	H	HR	BA
1979 CAL A	0	0	—	4.76	1	0	0	5.2	4	2	3	0	0	0	0	0	0	0	—

Roger Clemens

CLEMENS, WILLIAM ROGER (Rocket)
B. Aug. 4, 1962, Dayton, Ohio
BR TR 6'4" 205 lbs.

	W	L	PCT	ERA	G	GS	CG	IP	H	BB	SO	ShO	RW	RL	SV	AB	H	HR	BA
1984 BOS A	9	4	.692	4.32	21	20	5	133.1	146	29	126	1	0	0	0	0	0	0	—
1985	7	5	.583	3.29	15	15	3	98.1	83	37	74	1	0	0	0	0	0	0	—
1986	24	4	.857	2.48	33	33	10	254	179	67	238	1	0	0	0	0	0	0	—
1987	20	9	.690	2.97	36	36	18	281.2	248	83	256	7	0	0	0	0	0	0	—
1988	18	12	.600	2.93	35	35	14	264	217	62	291	8	0	0	0	0	0	0	—
5 yrs.	78	34	.696	3.05	140	139	50	1031.1	873	278	985	18	0	0	0	0	0	0	—

LEAGUE CHAMPIONSHIP SERIES

	W	L	PCT	ERA	G	GS	CG	IP	H	BB	SO	ShO	RW	RL	SV	AB	H	HR	BA
1986 BOS A	1	1	.500	4.37	3	3	0	22.2	22	7	17	0	0	0	0	0	0	0	—

	W	L	PCT	ERA	G	GS	CG	IP	H	BB	SO	ShO	Relief Pitching W	L	SV	BATTING AB	H	HR	BA

Roger Clemens continued

	W	L	PCT	ERA	G	GS	CG	IP	H	BB	SO	ShO	W	L	SV	AB	H	HR	BA
1988	0	0	–	3.86	1	1	0	7	6	0	8	0	0	0	0	0	0	0	–
2 yrs.	1	1	.500	4.25	4	4	0	29.2	28	7	25	0	0	0	0	0	0	0	–

WORLD SERIES

| 1986 **BOS A** | 0 | 0 | – | 3.18 | 2 | 2 | 0 | 11.1 | 9 | 6 | 11 | 0 | 0 | 0 | 0 | 4 | 0 | 0 | .000 |

Pat Clements

CLEMENTS, PATRICK BRIAN
B. Feb. 2, 1962, McCloud, Calif.

BR TL 6' 175 lbs.

	W	L	PCT	ERA	G	GS	CG	IP	H	BB	SO	ShO	W	L	SV	AB	H	HR	BA
1985 **2 teams**			CAL	A	(41G	5–0)		PIT	N	(27G	0–2)								
" total	5	2	.714	3.46	68	0	0	96.1	86	40	36	0	5	2	3	3	1	0	.333
1986 **PIT N**	0	4	.000	2.80	65	0	0	61	53	32	31	0	0	4	2	6	0	0	.000
1987 **NY A**	3	3	.500	4.95	55	0	0	80	91	30	36	0	3	3	7	0	0	0	–
1988	0	0	–	6.48	6	1	0	8.1	12	4	3	0	0	0	0	0	0	0	–
4 yrs.	8	9	.471	3.88	194	1	0	245.2	242	106	106	0	8	9	12	9	1	0	.111

Stu Cliburn

CLIBURN, STEWART WALKER
Brother of Stan Cliburn.
B. Dec. 19, 1956, Jackson, Miss.

BR TR 6' 195 lbs.

	W	L	PCT	ERA	G	GS	CG	IP	H	BB	SO	ShO	W	L	SV	AB	H	HR	BA
1984 **CAL A**	0	0	–	13.50	1	0	0	2	3	1	1	0	0	0	0	0	0	0	–
1985	9	3	.750	2.09	44	0	0	99	87	26	48	0	9	3	6	0	0	0	–
1988	4	2	.667	4.07	40	1	0	84	83	32	42	0	4	1	0	0	0	0	–
3 yrs.	13	5	.722	3.11	85	1	0	185	173	59	91	0	13	4	6	0	0	0	–

Chris Codiroli

CODIROLI, CHRISTOPHER ALLEN
B. Mar. 26, 1958, Oxnard, Calif.

BR TR 6'1" 160 lbs.

	W	L	PCT	ERA	G	GS	CG	IP	H	BB	SO	ShO	W	L	SV	AB	H	HR	BA
1982 **OAK A**	1	2	.333	4.32	3	3	0	16.2	16	4	5	0	0	0	0	0	0	0	–
1983	12	12	.500	4.46	37	31	7	205.2	208	72	85	2	1	1	1	0	0	0	–
1984	6	4	.600	5.84	28	14	1	89.1	111	34	44	0	0	0	1	0	0	0	–
1985	14	14	.500	4.46	37	37	4	226	228	78	111	0	0	0	0	0	0	0	–
1986	5	8	.385	4.03	16	16	1	91.2	91	38	43	0	0	0	0	0	0	0	–
1987	0	2	.000	8.74	3	3	0	11.1	12	8	4	0	0	0	0	0	0	0	–
1988 **CLE A**	0	4	.000	9.31	14	2	0	19.1	32	10	12	0	0	2	1	0	0	0	–
7 yrs.	38	46	.452	4.80	138	106	13	660	698	244	304	2	1	3	3	0	0	0	–

Kevin Coffman

COFFMAN, KEVIN REESE
B. Jan. 19, 1965, Austin, Tex.

BR TR 6'2" 175 lbs.

	W	L	PCT	ERA	G	GS	CG	IP	H	BB	SO	ShO	W	L	SV	AB	H	HR	BA
1987 **ATL N**	2	3	.400	4.62	5	5	0	25.1	31	22	14	0	0	0	0	10	1	0	.100
1988	2	6	.250	5.78	18	11	0	67	62	54	24	0	0	0	0	22	5	0	.227
2 yrs.	4	9	.308	5.46	23	16	0	92.1	93	76	38	0	0	0	0	32	6	0	.188

Keith Comstock

COMSTOCK, KEITH MARTIN
B. Dec. 23, 1955, San Francisco, Calif.

BL TL 6' 174 lbs.

	W	L	PCT	ERA	G	GS	CG	IP	H	BB	SO	ShO	W	L	SV	AB	H	HR	BA
1984 **MIN A**	0	0	–	8.53	4	0	0	6.1	6	4	2	0	0	0	0	0	0	0	–
1987 **2 teams**			SF	N	(15G	2–0)		SD	N	(26G	0–1)								
" total	2	1	.667	4.61	41	0	0	56.2	52	31	59	0	2	1	1	2	0	0	.000
1988 **SD N**	0	0	–	6.75	7	0	0	8	8	3	9	0	0	0	0	0	0	0	–
3 yrs.	2	1	.667	5.20	52	0	0	71	66	38	70	0	2	1	1	2	0	0	.000

Dave Concepcion

CONCEPCION, DAVID ISMAEL
Born David Ismael Concepcion Bonitez.
B. June 17, 1948, Aragua, Venezuela

BR TR 6'2" 155 lbs.

	W	L	PCT	ERA	G	GS	CG	IP	H	BB	SO	ShO	W	L	SV	AB	H	HR	BA
1988 **CIN N**	0	0	–	0.00	1	0	0	1.1	2	0	1	0	0	0	0	*			

David Cone

CONE, DAVID BRIAN
B. Jan. 2, 1963, Kansas City, Mo.

BL TR 6'1" 180 lbs.

	W	L	PCT	ERA	G	GS	CG	IP	H	BB	SO	ShO	W	L	SV	AB	H	HR	BA
1986 **KC A**	0	0	–	5.56	11	0	0	22.2	29	13	21	0	0	0	0	0	0	0	–
1987 **NY N**	5	6	.455	3.71	21	13	0	99.1	87	44	68	0	1	1	1	31	2	0	.065
1988	20	3	.870	2.22	35	28	8	231.1	178	80	213	4	2	0	0	80	12	0	.150
3 yrs.	25	9	.735	2.85	67	41	9	353.1	294	137	302	4	3	1	1	111	14	0	.126

LEAGUE CHAMPIONSHIP SERIES

| 1988 **NY N** | 1 | 1 | .500 | 4.50 | 3 | 2 | 1 | 12 | 10 | 5 | 9 | 0 | 0 | 0 | 0 | 4 | 0 | 0 | .000 |

Dennis Cook

COOK, DENNIS BRYAN
B. Oct. 4, 1962, LaMarque, Tex.

BL TL 6'3" 185 lbs.

	W	L	PCT	ERA	G	GS	CG	IP	H	BB	SO	ShO	W	L	SV	AB	H	HR	BA
1988 **SF N**	2	1	.667	2.86	4	4	1	22	9	11	13	1	0	0	0	4	0	0	.000

Mike Cook

COOK, MICHAEL HORACE
B. Aug. 14, 1963, Charleston, S. C.

BR TR 6'3" 200 lbs.

	W	L	PCT	ERA	G	GS	CG	IP	H	BB	SO	ShO	W	L	SV	AB	H	HR	BA
1986 **CAL A**	0	2	.000	9.00	5	1	0	9	13	7	6	0	0	1	0	0	0	0	–
1987	1	2	.333	5.50	16	1	0	34.1	34	18	27	0	1	1	0	0	0	0	–
1988	0	1	.000	4.91	3	0	0	3.2	4	1	2	0	0	0	0	0	0	0	–
3 yrs.	1	5	.167	6.13	24	2	0	47	51	26	35	0	1	3	0	0	0	0	–

Sherman Corbett

CORBETT, SHERMAN STANLEY
B. Nov. 3, 1962, New Braunfels, Tex.

BL TL 6'4" 205 lbs.

	W	L	PCT	ERA	G	GS	CG	IP	H	BB	SO	ShO	W	L	SV	AB	H	HR	BA
1988 **CAL A**	2	1	.667	4.14	34	0	0	45.2	47	23	28	1	2	1	1	0	0	0	–

Jim Corsi

CORSI, JAMES BERNARD
B. Sept. 9, 1961, Newton, Mass.

BR TR 6'1" 210 lbs.

	W	L	PCT	ERA	G	GS	CG	IP	H	BB	SO	ShO	W	L	SV	AB	H	HR	BA
1988 **OAK A**	0	1	.000	3.80	11	1	0	21.1	20	6	10	0	0	1	0	0	0	0	–

	W	L	PCT	ERA	G	GS	CG	IP	H	BB	SO	ShO	Relief Pitching W	L	SV	BATTING AB	H	HR	BA

John Costello

COSTELLO, JOHN REILLY
B. Dec. 24, 1960, New York, N. Y.   BR TR 6'1"   180 lbs.

	W	L	PCT	ERA	G	GS	CG	IP	H	BB	SO	ShO	W	L	SV	AB	H	HR	BA
1988 STL N	5	2	.714	1.81	36	0	0	49.2	44	25	38	0	5	2	1	5	0	0	.000

Danny Cox

COX, DANNY BRADFORD (Coxie)
B. Sept. 21, 1959, Northampton, England   BR TR 6'4"   220 lbs.

	W	L	PCT	ERA	G	GS	CG	IP	H	BB	SO	ShO	W	L	SV	AB	H	HR	BA
1983 STL N	3	6	.333	3.25	12	12	0	83	92	23	36	0	0	0	0	27	2	0	.074
1984	9	11	.450	4.03	29	27	1	156.1	171	54	70	1	1	0	0	53	7	0	.132
1985	18	9	.667	2.88	35	35	10	241	226	64	131	4	0	0	0	79	12	0	.152
1986	12	13	.480	2.90	32	32	8	220	189	60	108	0	0	0	0	65	5	0	.077
1987	11	9	.550	3.88	31	31	2	199.1	224	71	101	0	0	0	0	69	8	0	.116
1988	3	8	.273	3.98	13	13	0	86	89	25	47	0	0	0	0	23	1	0	.043
6 yrs.	56	56	.500	3.40	152	150	21	985.2	991	297	493	5	1	0	0	316	35	0	.111

LEAGUE CHAMPIONSHIP SERIES

	W	L	PCT	ERA	G	GS	CG	IP	H	BB	SO	ShO	W	L	SV	AB	H	HR	BA
1985 STL N	1	0	1.000	3.00	1	1	0	6	4	5	4	0	0	0	0	2	0	0	.000
1987	1	1	.500	2.12	2	2	2	17	17	3	11	1	0	0	0	6	2	0	.333
2 yrs.	2	1	.667	2.35	3	3	2	23	21	8	15	1	0	0	0	8	2	0	.250

WORLD SERIES

	W	L	PCT	ERA	G	GS	CG	IP	H	BB	SO	ShO	W	L	SV	AB	H	HR	BA
1985 STL N	0	0	–	1.29	2	2	0	14	14	4	13	0	0	0	0	4	0	0	.000
1987	1	2	.333	7.71	3	2	0	11.2	13	8	9	0	0	1	0	2	0	0	.000
2 yrs.	1	2	.333	4.21	5	4	0	25.2	27	12	22	0	0	1	0	6	0	0	.000

Tim Crews

CREWS, STANLEY TIMOTHY
B. Apr. 3, 1961, Tampa, Fla.   BR TR 6'   180 lbs.

	W	L	PCT	ERA	G	GS	CG	IP	H	BB	SO	ShO	W	L	SV	AB	H	HR	BA
1987 LA N	1	1	.500	2.48	20	0	0	29	30	8	20	0	1	1	3	2	0	0	.000
1988	4	0	1.000	3.14	42	0	0	71.2	77	16	45	0	4	0	0	5	1	0	.200
2 yrs.	5	1	.833	2.95	62	0	0	100.2	107	24	65	0	5	1	3	7	1	0	.143

Chuck Crim

CRIM, CHARLES ROBERT
B. July 23, 1961, Van Nuys, Calif.   BR TR 6'   175 lbs.

	W	L	PCT	ERA	G	GS	CG	IP	H	BB	SO	ShO	W	L	SV	AB	H	HR	BA
1987 MIL A	6	8	.429	3.67	53	5	0	130	133	39	56	0	5	4	12	0	0	0	–
1988	7	6	.538	2.91	70	0	0	105	95	28	58	0	7	6	9	0	0	0	–
2 yrs.	13	14	.481	3.33	123	5	0	235	228	67	114	0	12	10	21	0	0	0	–

Zach Crouch

CROUCH, ZACHARY QUINN
B. Oct. 26, 1965, Folsom, Calif.   BL TL 6'3"   190 lbs.

	W	L	PCT	ERA	G	GS	CG	IP	H	BB	SO	ShO	W	L	SV	AB	H	HR	BA
1988 BOS A	0	0	–	6.75	3	0	0	1.1	4	2	0	0	0	0	0	0	0	0	–

Steve Curry

CURRY, STEPHEN T.
B. Sept. 13, 1965, Winter Park, Fla.   BR TR 6'6"   217 lbs.

	W	L	PCT	ERA	G	GS	CG	IP	H	BB	SO	ShO	W	L	SV	AB	H	HR	BA
1988 BOS A	0	1	.000	8.18	3	3	0	11	15	14	4	0	0	0	0	0	0	0	–

Ron Darling

DARLING, RONALD MAURICE JR.
B. Aug. 19, 1960, Honolulu, Hawaii   BR TR 6'3"   205 lbs.

	W	L	PCT	ERA	G	GS	CG	IP	H	BB	SO	ShO	W	L	SV	AB	H	HR	BA
1983 NY N	1	3	.250	2.80	5	5	1	35.1	31	17	23	0	0	0	0	10	1	0	.100
1984	12	9	.571	3.81	33	33	2	205.2	179	104	136	2	0	0	0	67	10	0	.149
1985	16	6	.727	2.90	36	35	4	248	214	114	167	2	0	0	0	76	13	0	.171
1986	15	6	.714	2.81	34	34	4	237	203	81	184	2	0	0	0	81	8	0	.099
1987	12	8	.600	4.29	32	32	2	207.2	183	96	167	0	0	0	0	65	8	0	.123
1988	17	9	.654	3.25	34	34	7	240.2	218	60	161	4	0	0	0	82	18	0	.220
6 yrs.	73	41	.640	3.36	174	173	20	1174.1	1028	472	838	10	0	0	0	381	58	0	.152

LEAGUE CHAMPIONSHIP SERIES

	W	L	PCT	ERA	G	GS	CG	IP	H	BB	SO	ShO	W	L	SV	AB	H	HR	BA
1986 NY N	0	0	–	7.20	1	1	0	5	6	2	5	0	0	0	0	1	0	0	.000
1988	0	1	.000	7.71	2	2	0	7	11	4	7	0	0	0	0	3	0	0	.000
2 yrs.	0	1	.000	7.50	3	3	0	12	17	6	12	0	0	0	0	4	0	0	.000

WORLD SERIES

	W	L	PCT	ERA	G	GS	CG	IP	H	BB	SO	ShO	W	L	SV	AB	H	HR	BA
1986 NY N	1	1	.500	1.53	3	3	0	17.2	13	10	12	0	0	0	0	3	0	0	.000

Danny Darwin

DARWIN, DANNY WAYNE
B. Oct. 25, 1955, Bonham, Tex.   BR TR 6'3"   185 lbs.

	W	L	PCT	ERA	G	GS	CG	IP	H	BB	SO	ShO	W	L	SV	AB	H	HR	BA
1978 TEX A	1	0	1.000	4.15	3	1	0	8.2	11	1	8	0	1	0	0	0	0	0	–
1979	4	4	.500	4.04	20	6	1	78	50	30	58	0	1	3	0	0	0	0	–
1980	13	4	.765	2.62	53	2	0	110	98	50	104	0	12	3	8	0	0	0	–
1981	9	9	.500	3.64	22	22	6	146	115	57	98	2	0	0	0	0	0	0	–
1982	10	8	.556	3.44	56	1	0	89	95	37	61	0	10	7	7	0	0	0	–
1983	8	13	.381	3.49	28	26	9	183	175	62	92	2	0	0	0	0	0	0	–
1984	8	12	.400	3.94	35	32	5	223.2	249	54	123	1	0	0	0	0	0	0	–
1985 MIL A	8	18	.308	3.80	39	29	11	217.2	212	65	125	1	1	2	2	0	0	0	–
1986 2 teams			MIL	A (27G 6–8)		HOU		N (12G 5–2)											
" total	11	10	.524	3.17	39	22	6	184.2	170	44	120	1	3	1	0	16	1	0	.063
1987 HOU N	9	10	.474	3.59	33	30	3	195.2	184	69	134	1	0	0	0	66	12	0	.182
1988	8	13	.381	3.84	44	20	3	192	189	48	129	0	4	3	3	56	4	0	.071
11 yrs.	89	101	.468	3.59	372	191	44	1628.1	1548	517	1052	8	32	19	20	138	17	1	.123

Joel Davis

DAVIS, JOEL CLARK
B. Jan. 30, 1965, Jacksonville, Fla.   BL TR 6'5"   205 lbs.

	W	L	PCT	ERA	G	GS	CG	IP	H	BB	SO	ShO	W	L	SV	AB	H	HR	BA
1985 CHI A	3	3	.500	4.16	12	11	1	71.1	71	26	37	0	0	0	0	0	0	0	–
1986	4	5	.444	4.70	19	19	1	105.1	115	51	54	0	0	0	0	0	0	0	–
1987	1	5	.167	5.73	13	9	1	55	56	29	25	0	1	1	0	0	0	0	–
1988	0	1	.000	6.75	5	2	0	16	21	5	10	0	0	0	0	0	0	0	–
4 yrs.	8	14	.364	4.91	49	41	3	247.2	263	111	126	0	0	1	0	0	0	0	–

	W	L	PCT	ERA	G	GS	CG	IP	H	BB	SO	ShO	Relief Pitching W	L	SV	BATTING AB	H	HR	BA

John Davis

DAVIS, JOHN KIRK
B. Jan. 5, 1963, Chicago, Ill.
BR TR 6'7" 215 lbs.

		W	L	PCT	ERA	G	GS	CG	IP	H	BB	SO	ShO	W	L	SV	AB	H	HR	BA
1987	KC A	5	2	.714	2.27	27	0	0	43.2	29	26	24	0	5	2	2	0	0	0	–
1988	CHI A	2	5	.286	6.64	34	1	0	63.2	77	50	37	0	2	4	1	0	0	0	–
2 yrs.		7	7	.500	4.86	61	1	0	107.1	106	76	61	0	7	6	3	0	0	0	–

Mark Davis

DAVIS, MARK WILLIAM
B. Oct. 19, 1960, Livermore, Calif.
BL TL 6'3" 180 lbs.

		W	L	PCT	ERA	G	GS	CG	IP	H	BB	SO	ShO	W	L	SV	AB	H	HR	BA
1980	PHI N	0	0	–	2.57	2	1	0	7	4	5	5	0	0	0	0	2	1	0	.500
1981		1	4	.200	7.74	9	9	0	43	49	24	29	0	0	0	0	11	1	0	.091
1983	SF N	6	4	.600	3.49	20	20	2	111	93	50	83	2	0	0	0	30	4	0	.133
1984		5	17	.227	5.36	46	27	1	174.2	201	54	124	0	3	4	0	46	6	0	.130
1985		5	12	.294	3.54	77	1	0	114.1	89	41	131	0	5	11	7	12	3	0	.250
1986		5	7	.417	2.99	67	2	0	84.1	63	34	90	0	5	6	4	8	1	0	.125
1987 2 teams	SF N (20G 4–5)	SD N (43G 5–3)																		
" total		9	8	.529	3.99	63	11	1	133	123	59	98	0	5	3	2	30	7	0	.233
1988	SD N	5	10	.333	2.01	62	0	0	98.1	70	42	102	0	5	10	28	10	2	1	.200
8 yrs.		36	62	.367	4.00	346	71	4	765.2	692	309	662	2	23	34	41	149	25	1	.168

Ron Davis

DAVIS, RONALD GENE
B. Aug. 6, 1955, Houston, Tex.
BR TR 6'4" 205 lbs.

		W	L	PCT	ERA	G	GS	CG	IP	H	BB	SO	ShO	W	L	SV	AB	H	HR	BA
1978	NY A	0	0	–	11.57	4	0	0	2.1	3	3	0	0	0	0	0	0	0	0	–
1979		14	2	.875	2.86	44	0	0	85	84	28	43	0	14	2	9	1	0	0	.000
1980		9	3	.750	2.95	53	0	0	131	121	32	65	0	9	3	7	1	0	0	.000
1981		4	5	.444	2.71	43	0	0	73	47	25	83	0	4	5	6	0	0	0	–
1982	MIN A	3	9	.250	4.42	63	0	0	106	106	47	89	0	3	9	22	0	0	0	–
1983		5	8	.385	3.34	66	0	0	89	89	33	84	0	5	8	30	0	0	0	–
1984		7	11	.389	4.55	64	0	0	83	79	41	74	0	7	11	29	0	0	0	–
1985		2	6	.250	3.48	57	0	0	64.2	55	35	72	0	2	6	25	0	0	0	–
1986 2 teams	MIN A (36G 2–6)	CHI N (17G 0–2)																		
" total		2	8	.200	8.59	53	0	0	58.2	86	32	40	0	2	8	2	2	0	0	.000
1987 2 teams	CHI N (21G 0–0)	LA N (4G 0–0)																		
" total		0	0	–	5.94	25	0	0	36.1	50	18	32	0	0	0	0	0	0	0	–
1988	SF N	1	1	.500	4.67	9	0	0	17.1	15	6	15	0	1	1	0	2	0	0	.000
11 yrs.		47	53	.470	4.05	481	0	0	746.1	735	300	597	0	47	53	130	6	0	0	.000

DIVISIONAL PLAYOFF SERIES

		W	L	PCT	ERA	G	GS	CG	IP	H	BB	SO	ShO	W	L	SV	AB	H	HR	BA
1981	NY A	1	0	1.000	0.00	3	0	0	6	1	2	6	0	1	0	0	0	0	0	–

LEAGUE CHAMPIONSHIP SERIES

		W	L	PCT	ERA	G	GS	CG	IP	H	BB	SO	ShO	W	L	SV	AB	H	HR	BA
1980	NY A	0	0	–	2.25	1	0	0	4	1	3	3	0	0	0	0	0	0	0	–
1981		0	0	–	0.00	2	0	0	3.1	2	0	4	0	0	0	0	0	0	0	–
2 yrs.		0	0	–	1.23	3	0	0	7.1	3	3	7	0	0	0	0	0	0	0	–

WORLD SERIES

		W	L	PCT	ERA	G	GS	CG	IP	H	BB	SO	ShO	W	L	SV	AB	H	HR	BA
1981	NY A	0	0	–	23.14	4	0	0	2.1	4	5	4	0	0	0	0	0	0	0	–

Storm Davis

DAVIS, GEORGE EARL
B. Dec. 26, 1961, Dallas, Tex.
BR TR 6'4" 210 lbs.

		W	L	PCT	ERA	G	GS	CG	IP	H	BB	SO	ShO	W	L	SV	AB	H	HR	BA
1982	BAL A	8	4	.667	3.49	29	8	1	100.2	96	28	67	0	3	2	0	0	0	0	–
1983		13	7	.650	3.59	34	29	6	200.1	180	64	125	1	0	0	0	0	0	0	–
1984		14	9	.609	3.12	35	31	10	225	205	71	105	2	0	1	1	0	0	0	–
1985		10	8	.556	4.53	31	28	8	175	172	70	93	1	0	0	0	0	0	0	–
1986		9	12	.429	3.62	25	25	2	154	166	49	96	0	0	0	0	0	0	0	–
1987 2 teams	SD N (21G 2–7)	OAK A (5G 1–1)																		
" total		3	8	.273	5.23	26	15	0	93	98	47	65	0	0	1	0	16	1	0	.063
1988	OAK A	16	7	.696	3.70	33	33	1	201.2	211	91	127	0	0	0	0	0	0	0	–
7 yrs.		73	55	.570	3.79	213	169	28	1149.2	1128	420	678	4	3	4	1	16	1	0	.063

LEAGUE CHAMPIONSHIP SERIES

		W	L	PCT	ERA	G	GS	CG	IP	H	BB	SO	ShO	W	L	SV	AB	H	HR	BA
1983	BAL A	0	0	–	0.00	1	1	0	6	5	2	2	0	0	0	0	0	0	0	–
1988	OAK A	0	0	–	0.00	1	1	0	6.1	2	5	4	0	0	0	0	0	0	0	–
2 yrs.		0	0	–	0.00	2	2	0	12.1	7	7	6	0	0	0	0	0	0	0	–

WORLD SERIES

		W	L	PCT	ERA	G	GS	CG	IP	H	BB	SO	ShO	W	L	SV	AB	H	HR	BA
1983	BAL A	1	0	1.000	5.40	1	1	0	5	6	1	3	0	0	0	0	2	0	0	.000
1988	OAK A	0	2	.000	11.25	2	2	0	8	14	1	7	0	0	0	0	1	0	0	.000
2 yrs.		1	2	.333	9.00	3	3	0	13	20	2	10	0	0	0	0	3	0	0	.000

Bill Dawley

DAWLEY, WILLIAM CHESTER
B. Feb. 6, 1958, Norwich, Conn.
BR TR 6'5" 235 lbs.

		W	L	PCT	ERA	G	GS	CG	IP	H	BB	SO	ShO	W	L	SV	AB	H	HR	BA
1983	HOU N	6	6	.500	2.82	48	0	0	79.2	51	22	60	0	6	6	14	9	2	0	.222
1984		11	4	.733	1.93	60	0	0	98	82	35	47	0	11	4	5	9	3	0	.333
1985		5	3	.625	3.56	49	0	0	81	76	37	48	0	5	3	2	10	2	0	.200
1986	CHI A	0	7	.000	3.32	46	0	0	97.2	91	28	66	0	0	7	2	2	0	0	.000
1987	STL N	5	8	.385	4.47	60	0	0	96.2	93	38	65	0	5	8	2	12	2	0	.167
1988	PHI N	0	2	.000	13.50	8	0	0	8.2	16	4	3	0	0	2	0	0	0	0	–
6 yrs.		27	30	.474	3.41	271	0	0	461.2	409	164	289	0	27	30	25	42	9	0	.214

Ken Dayley

DAYLEY, KENNETH GRANT
B. Feb. 25, 1959, Jerome, Ida.
BL TL 6' 178 lbs.

		W	L	PCT	ERA	G	GS	CG	IP	H	BB	SO	ShO	W	L	SV	AB	H	HR	BA
1982	ATL N	5	6	.455	4.54	20	11	0	71.1	79	25	34	0	2	0	0	20	5	0	.250
1983		5	8	.385	4.30	24	16	0	104.2	100	39	70	0	1	2	0	32	7	0	.219
1984 2 teams	ATL N (4G 0–3)	STL N (3G 0–2)																		
" total		0	5	.000	7.99	7	6	0	23.2	44	11	10	0	0	0	0	4	2	0	.500
1985	STL N	4	4	.500	2.76	57	0	0	65.1	65	18	62	0	4	4	11	5	2	0	.400
1986		0	3	.000	3.26	31	0	0	38.2	42	11	33	0	0	3	5	5	1	0	.200
1987		9	5	.643	2.66	53	0	0	61	52	33	63	0	9	5	4	0	0	0	–
1988		2	7	.222	2.77	54	0	0	55.1	48	19	38	0	2	7	5	4	0	0	.000
7 yrs.		25	38	.397	3.77	246	33	0	420	430	156	310	0	18	21	25	70	17	0	.243

	W	L	PCT	ERA	G	GS	CG	IP	H	BB	SO	ShO	Relief Pitching W	L	SV	BATTING AB	H	HR	BA

Ken Dayley continued

LEAGUE CHAMPIONSHIP SERIES

	W	L	PCT	ERA	G	GS	CG	IP	H	BB	SO	ShO	W	L	SV	AB	H	HR	BA
1985 STL N	0	0	–	0.00	5	0	0	6	2	1	3	0	0	0	2	2	1	0	.500
1987	0	0	–	0.00	3	0	0	4	1	2	4	0	0	0	2	0	0	0	–
2 yrs.	0	0	–	0.00	8	0	0	10	3	3	7	0	0	0	4	2	1	0	.500

WORLD SERIES

	W	L	PCT	ERA	G	GS	CG	IP	H	BB	SO	ShO	W	L	SV	AB	H	HR	BA
1985 STL N	1	0	1.000	0.00	4	0	0	6	1	3	5	0	1	0	0	0	0	0	–
1987	0	0	–	1.93	4	0	0	4.2	2	0	3	0	0	0	1	1	0	0	.000
2 yrs.	1	0	1.000	0.84	8	0	0	10.2	3	3	8	0	1	0	1	1	0	0	.000

Jeff Dedmon

DEDMON, JEFFREY LINDEN
B. Mar. 4, 1960, Torrance, Calif.　　　BL TR 6'3"　185 lbs.

	W	L	PCT	ERA	G	GS	CG	IP	H	BB	SO	ShO	W	L	SV	AB	H	HR	BA
1983 ATL N	0	0	–	13.50	5	0	0	4	10	0	3	0	0	0	0	0	0	0	–
1984	4	3	.571	3.78	54	0	0	81	86	35	51	0	4	3	4	6	0	0	.000
1985	6	3	.667	4.08	60	0	0	86	84	49	41	0	6	3	0	9	1	0	.111
1986	6	6	.500	2.98	57	0	0	99.2	90	39	58	0	6	6	3	16	2	0	.125
1987	3	4	.429	3.91	53	3	0	89.2	82	42	40	0	3	3	4	16	4	0	.250
1988 CLE A	1	0	1.000	4.54	21	0	0	33.2	35	21	17	0	1	0	1	0	0	0	–
6 yrs.	20	16	.556	3.84	250	3	0	394	387	186	210	0	20	15	12	47	7	0	.149

Jose DeJesus

DeJESUS, JOSE LUIS
B. Jan. 6, 1965, Brooklyn, N. Y.　　　BR TR 6'5"　175 lbs.

	W	L	PCT	ERA	G	GS	CG	IP	H	BB	SO	ShO	W	L	SV	AB	H	HR	BA
1988 KC A	0	1	.000	27.00	2	0	0	2.2	6	5	2	0	0	0	0	0	0	0	–

Jose DeLeon

DeLEON, JOSE CHESTARO
Born Jose Deleon y Chestaro.
B. Dec. 20, 1960, La Vega, Dominican Republic　　　BR TR 6'3"　195 lbs.

	W	L	PCT	ERA	G	GS	CG	IP	H	BB	SO	ShO	W	L	SV	AB	H	HR	BA
1983 PIT N	7	3	.700	2.83	15	15	3	108	75	47	118	2	0	0	0	34	2	0	.059
1984	7	13	.350	3.74	30	28	5	192.1	147	92	153	1	1	0	0	59	5	0	.085
1985	2	19	.095	4.70	31	25	1	162.2	138	89	149	0	0	1	3	36	2	0	.056
1986 2 teams			PIT	N	(9G	1–3)		CHI	A	(13G	4–5)								
" total	5	8	.385	3.87	22	14	1	95.1	66	59	79	0	1	2	1	1	0	0	.000
1987 CHI A	11	12	.478	4.02	33	31	2	206	177	97	153	0	0	0	0	0	0	0	–
1988 STL N	13	10	.565	3.67	34	34	3	225.1	198	86	208	1	0	0	0	72	10	0	.139
6 yrs.	45	65	.409	3.86	165	147	15	989.2	801	470	860	4	2	3	4	202	19	0	.094

Jim Deshaies

DESHAIES, JAMES JOSEPH
B. June 23, 1960, Massena, N. Y.　　　BL TL 6'4"　222 lbs.

	W	L	PCT	ERA	G	GS	CG	IP	H	BB	SO	ShO	W	L	SV	AB	H	HR	BA
1984 NY A	0	1	.000	11.57	2	2	0	7	14	7	5	0	0	0	0	0	0	0	–
1985 HOU N	0	0	–	0.00	2	0	0	3	1	0	2	0	0	0	0	0	0	0	–
1986	12	5	.706	3.25	26	26	1	144	124	59	128	1	0	0	0	43	2	0	.047
1987	11	6	.647	4.62	26	25	1	152	149	57	104	0	0	0	0	53	5	0	.094
1988	11	14	.440	3.00	31	31	3	207	164	72	127	2	0	0	0	63	3	0	.048
5 yrs.	34	26	.567	3.65	87	84	5	513	452	195	366	3	0	0	0	159	10	0	.063

Rob Dibble

DIBBLE, ROBERT KEITH
B. Jan. 24, 1964, Bridgeport, Conn.　　　BL TR 6'4"　230 lbs.

	W	L	PCT	ERA	G	GS	CG	IP	H	BB	SO	ShO	W	L	SV	AB	H	HR	BA
1988 CIN N	1	1	.500	1.82	37	0	0	59.1	43	21	59	0	1	1	0	2	0	0	.000

Gordon Dillard

DILLARD, GORDON LEE
B. May 20, 1964, Salinas, Calif.　　　BL TL 6'1"　180 lbs.

	W	L	PCT	ERA	G	GS	CG	IP	H	BB	SO	ShO	W	L	SV	AB	H	HR	BA
1988 BAL A	0	0	–	6.00	2	1	0	3	3	4	2	0	0	0	0	0	0	0	–

Frank DiMichele

DiMICHELE, FRANK LAWRENCE
B. Feb. 16, 1965, Philadelphia, Pa.　　　BR TL 6'3"　205 lbs.

	W	L	PCT	ERA	G	GS	CG	IP	H	BB	SO	ShO	W	L	SV	AB	H	HR	BA
1988 CAL A	0	0	–	9.64	4	0	0	4.2	5	2	1	0	0	0	0	0	0	0	–

Frank DiPino

DiPINO, FRANK MICHAEL
B. Oct. 22, 1956, Syracuse, N. Y.　　　BL TL 5'10"　175 lbs.

	W	L	PCT	ERA	G	GS	CG	IP	H	BB	SO	ShO	W	L	SV	AB	H	HR	BA
1981 MIL A	0	0	–	0.00	2	0	0	2	0	3	3	0	0	0	0	0	0	0	–
1982 HOU N	2	2	.500	6.04	6	6	0	28.1	32	11	25	0	0	0	0	8	0	0	.000
1983	3	4	.429	2.65	53	0	0	71.1	52	20	67	0	3	4	20	6	1	0	.167
1984	4	9	.308	3.35	57	0	0	75.1	74	36	65	0	4	9	14	10	0	0	.000
1985	3	7	.300	4.03	54	0	0	76	69	43	49	0	3	7	6	12	2	0	.167
1986 2 teams			HOU	N	(31G	1–3)		CHI	N	(30G	2–4)								
" total	3	7	.300	4.37	61	0	0	80.1	74	30	70	0	3	7	3	6	1	0	.167
1987 CHI N	3	3	.500	3.15	69	0	0	80	75	34	61	0	3	3	4	2	1	0	.500
1988	2	3	.400	4.98	63	0	0	90.1	102	32	69	0	2	3	6	10	1	0	.100
8 yrs.	20	35	.364	3.91	365	6	0	503.2	478	209	409	0	18	33	53	54	6	0	.111

John Dopson

DOPSON, JOHN ROBERT JR.
B. July 14, 1963, Baltimore, Md.　　　BL TR 6'4"　205 lbs.

	W	L	PCT	ERA	G	GS	CG	IP	H	BB	SO	ShO	W	L	SV	AB	H	HR	BA
1985 MON N	0	2	.000	11.08	4	3	0	13	25	4	4	0	0	0	0	4	0	0	.000
1988	3	11	.214	3.04	26	26	1	168.2	150	58	101	0	0	0	0	51	3	0	.059
2 yrs.	3	13	.188	3.62	30	29	1	181.2	175	62	105	0	0	0	0	55	3	0	.055

Richard Dotson

DOTSON, RICHARD ELLIOTT
B. Jan. 10, 1959, Cincinnati, Ohio　　　BR TR 6'1"　190 lbs.

	W	L	PCT	ERA	G	GS	CG	IP	H	BB	SO	ShO	W	L	SV	AB	H	HR	BA
1979 CHI A	2	0	1.000	3.75	5	5	1	24	28	6	13	1	0	0	0	0	0	0	–
1980	12	10	.545	4.27	33	32	8	198	185	87	109	0	0	0	0	0	0	0	–
1981	9	8	.529	3.77	24	24	5	141	145	49	73	4	0	0	0	0	0	0	–
1982	11	15	.423	3.84	34	31	3	196.2	219	73	109	1	0	0	0	0	0	0	–
1983	22	7	.759	3.23	35	35	8	240	209	106	137	1	0	0	0	0	0	0	–
1984	14	15	.483	3.59	32	32	14	245.2	216	103	120	1	0	0	0	0	0	0	–
1985	3	4	.429	4.47	9	9	0	52.1	53	17	33	0	0	0	0	0	0	0	–
1986	10	17	.370	5.48	34	34	3	197	226	69	110	1	0	0	0	0	0	0	–

	W	L	PCT	ERA	G	GS	CG	IP	H	BB	SO	ShO	Relief Pitching W	L	SV	BATTING AB	H	HR	BA

Richard Dotson continued

	W	L	PCT	ERA	G	GS	CG	IP	H	BB	SO	ShO	W	L	SV	AB	H	HR	BA
1987	11	12	.478	4.17	31	31	7	211.1	201	86	114	2	0	0	0	0	0	0	—
1988 NY A	12	9	.571	5.00	32	29	4	171	178	72	77	0	0	0	0	0	0	0	—
10 yrs.	106	97	.522	4.13	269	262	53	1677	1660	668	895	11	0	0	0	0	0	0	—

LEAGUE CHAMPIONSHIP SERIES

	W	L	PCT	ERA	G	GS	CG	IP	H	BB	SO	ShO	W	L	SV	AB	H	HR	BA
1983 CHI A	0	1	.000	10.80	1	1	0	5	6	3	3	0	0	0	0	0	0	0	—

Kelly Downs

DOWNS, KELLY ROBERT
Brother of Dave Downs.
B. Oct. 25, 1960, Ogden, Utah

BR TR 6'4" 195 lbs.

	W	L	PCT	ERA	G	GS	CG	IP	H	BB	SO	ShO	W	L	SV	AB	H	HR	BA
1986 SF N	4	4	.500	2.75	14	14	1	88.1	78	30	64	0	0	0	0	29	5	0	.172
1987	12	9	.571	3.63	41	28	4	186	185	67	137	3	1	1	1	56	8	0	.143
1988	13	9	.591	3.32	27	26	6	168	140	47	118	3	0	0	0	54	9	0	.167
3 yrs.	29	22	.569	3.34	82	68	11	442.1	403	144	319	6	1	1	1	139	22	0	.158

LEAGUE CHAMPIONSHIP SERIES

	W	L	PCT	ERA	G	GS	CG	IP	H	BB	SO	ShO	W	L	SV	AB	H	HR	BA
1987 SF N	0	0	—	0.00	1	0	0	1.1	1	0	0	0	0	0	0	0	0	0	—

Doug Drabek

DRABEK, DOUGLAS DEAN
B. July 25, 1962, Victoria, Tex.

BR TR 6'1" 185 lbs.

	W	L	PCT	ERA	G	GS	CG	IP	H	BB	SO	ShO	W	L	SV	AB	H	HR	BA
1986 NY A	7	8	.467	4.10	27	21	0	131.2	126	50	76	0	0	0	0	0	0	0	—
1987 PIT N	11	12	.478	3.88	29	28	1	176.1	165	46	120	1	0	0	0	59	7	0	.119
1988	15	7	.682	3.08	33	32	3	219.1	194	50	127	1	0	0	0	76	13	0	.171
3 yrs.	33	27	.550	3.60	89	81	4	527.1	485	146	323	2	0	0	0	135	20	0	.148

Dave Dravecky

DRAVECKY, DAVID FRANCIS
B. Feb. 14, 1956, Youngstown, Ohio

BR TL 6'1" 195 lbs.

	W	L	PCT	ERA	G	GS	CG	IP	H	BB	SO	ShO	W	L	SV	AB	H	HR	BA
1982 SD N	5	3	.625	2.57	31	10	0	105	86	33	59	0	1	1	2	23	3	0	.130
1983	14	10	.583	3.58	28	28	9	183.2	181	44	74	1	0	0	0	61	6	0	.098
1984	9	8	.529	2.93	50	14	3	156.2	125	51	71	2	4	4	8	41	4	0	.098
1985	13	11	.542	2.93	34	31	7	214.2	200	57	105	2	0	1	0	69	8	0	.116
1986	9	11	.450	3.07	26	26	3	161.1	149	54	87	1	0	0	0	50	7	1	.140
1987 2 teams					SD	N	(30G 3–7)		SF	N	(18G 7–5)								
" total	10	12	.455	3.43	48	28	5	191.1	186	64	138	3	0	4	0	56	8	0	.143
1988 SF N	2	2	.500	3.16	7	7	1	37	33	8	19	0	0	0	0	10	1	0	.100
7 yrs.	62	57	.521	3.13	224	144	28	1049.2	960	311	553	9	5	10	10	310	37	1	.119

LEAGUE CHAMPIONSHIP SERIES

	W	L	PCT	ERA	G	GS	CG	IP	H	BB	SO	ShO	W	L	SV	AB	H	HR	BA
1984 SD N	0	0	—	0.00	3	0	0	6	2	0	5	0	0	0	0	0	0	0	—
1987 SF N	1	1	.500	0.60	2	2	1	15	7	4	14	1	0	0	0	6	1	0	.167
2 yrs.	1	1	.500	0.43	5	2	1	21	9	4	19	1	0	0	0	6	1	0	.167

WORLD SERIES

	W	L	PCT	ERA	G	GS	CG	IP	H	BB	SO	ShO	W	L	SV	AB	H	HR	BA
1984 SD N	0	0	—	0.00	2	0	0	4.2	3	1	5	0	0	0	0	0	0	0	—

Mike Dunne

DUNNE, MICHAEL DENNIS
B. Oct. 27, 1962, South Bend, Ind.

BR TR 6'4" 190 lbs.

	W	L	PCT	ERA	G	GS	CG	IP	H	BB	SO	ShO	W	L	SV	AB	H	HR	BA
1987 PIT N	13	6	.684	3.03	23	23	5	163.1	143	68	72	1	0	0	0	53	5	0	.094
1988	7	11	.389	3.92	30	28	1	170	163	88	70	0	0	0	0	46	5	0	.109
2 yrs.	20	17	.541	3.48	53	51	6	333.1	306	156	142	1	0	0	0	99	10	0	.101

Gary Eave

EAVE, GARY LOUIS
B. July 22, 1963, Monroe, La.

BR TR 6'4" 190 lbs.

	W	L	PCT	ERA	G	GS	CG	IP	H	BB	SO	ShO	W	L	SV	AB	H	HR	BA
1988 ATL N	0	0	—	9.00	5	0	0	5	7	3	0	0	0	0	0	0	0	0	—

Dennis Eckersley

ECKERSLEY, DENNIS LEE
B. Oct. 3, 1954, Oakland, Calif.

BR TR 6'2" 190 lbs.

	W	L	PCT	ERA	G	GS	CG	IP	H	BB	SO	ShO	W	L	SV	AB	H	HR	BA
1975 CLE A	13	7	.650	2.60	34	24	6	186.2	147	90	152	2	0	0	2	0	0	0	—
1976	13	12	.520	3.44	36	30	9	199	155	78	200	3	0	1	1	0	0	0	—
1977	14	13	.519	3.53	33	33	12	247	214	54	191	3	0	0	0	0	0	0	—
1978 BOS A	20	8	.714	2.99	35	35	16	268.1	258	71	162	3	0	0	0	0	0	0	—
1979	17	10	.630	2.99	33	33	17	247	234	59	150	2	0	0	0	0	0	0	—
1980	12	14	.462	4.27	30	30	8	198	188	44	121	0	0	0	0	0	0	0	—
1981	9	8	.529	4.27	23	23	8	154	160	35	79	2	0	0	0	0	0	0	—
1982	13	13	.500	3.73	33	33	11	224.1	228	43	127	3	0	0	0	0	0	0	—
1983	9	13	.409	5.61	28	28	2	176.1	223	39	77	0	0	0	0	0	0	0	—
1984 2 teams					BOS	A	(9G 4–4)		CHI	N	(24G 10–8)								
" total	14	12	.538	3.60	33	33	4	225	223	49	114	0	0	0	0	55	6	0	.109
1985 CHI N	11	7	.611	3.08	25	25	6	169.1	145	19	117	2	0	0	0	56	7	1	.125
1986	6	11	.353	4.57	33	32	1	201	226	43	137	0	0	0	0	69	11	2	.159
1987 OAK A	6	8	.429	3.03	54	2	0	115.2	99	17	113	0	6	6	16	0	0	0	—
1988	4	2	.667	2.35	60	0	0	72.2	52	11	70	0	4	2	45	0	0	0	—
14 yrs.	161	138	.538	3.61	490	361	100	2684.1	2552	652	1810	20	11	9	64	180	24	3	.133

LEAGUE CHAMPIONSHIP SERIES

	W	L	PCT	ERA	G	GS	CG	IP	H	BB	SO	ShO	W	L	SV	AB	H	HR	BA
1984 CHI N	0	1	.000	8.44	1	1	0	5.1	9	0	0	0	0	0	0	2	0	0	.000
1988 OAK A	0	0	—	0.00	4	0	0	6	1	2	5	0	0	0	4	0	0	0	—
2 yrs.	0	1	.000	3.97	5	1	0	11.1	10	2	5	0	0	0	4	2	0	0	.000

WORLD SERIES

	W	L	PCT	ERA	G	GS	CG	IP	H	BB	SO	ShO	W	L	SV	AB	H	HR	BA
1988 OAK A	0	1	.000	10.80	2	0	0	1.2	2	1	2	0	0	1	0	0	0	0	—

Juan Eichelberger

EICHELBERGER, JUAN TYRONE
B. Oct. 21, 1953, St. Louis, Mo.

BR TR 6'2" 195 lbs.

	W	L	PCT	ERA	G	GS	CG	IP	H	BB	SO	ShO	W	L	SV	AB	H	HR	BA
1978 SD N	0	0	—	12.00	3	0	0	3	4	2	2	0	0	0	0	0	0	0	—
1979	1	1	.500	3.43	3	3	1	21	15	11	12	0	0	0	0	5	2	0	.400
1980	4	2	.667	3.64	15	13	0	89	73	55	43	0	1	0	0	27	3	0	.111
1981	8	8	.500	3.51	25	24	3	141	136	74	81	1	0	0	0	46	4	0	.087
1982	7	14	.333	4.20	31	24	8	177.2	171	72	74	0	0	2	0	55	5	0	.091
1983 CLE A	4	11	.267	4.90	28	15	2	134	132	59	56	0	1	0	0	0	0	0	—

	W	L	PCT	ERA	G	GS	CG	IP	H	BB	SO	ShO	Relief Pitching W	L	SV	BATTING AB	H	HR	BA

Juan Eichelberger continued

	W	L	PCT	ERA	G	GS	CG	IP	H	BB	SO	ShO	W	L	SV	AB	H	HR	BA
1988 ATL N	2	0	1.000	3.86	20	0	0	37.1	44	10	13	0	2	0	0	3	0	0	.000
7 yrs.	26	36	.419	4.10	125	79	14	603	575	283	281	1	4	2	0	136	14	0	.103

Mark Eichhorn

EICHHORN, MARK ANTHONY
B. Nov. 21, 1960, San Jose, Calif.

BR TR 6'4"   200 lbs.

	W	L	PCT	ERA	G	GS	CG	IP	H	BB	SO	ShO	W	L	SV	AB	H	HR	BA
1982 TOR A	0	3	.000	5.45	7	7	0	38	40	14	16	0	0	0	0	0	0	0	–
1986	14	6	.700	1.72	69	0	0	157	105	45	166	0	14	6	10	0	0	0	–
1987	10	6	.625	3.17	89	0	0	127.2	110	52	96	0	10	6	4	0	0	0	–
1988	0	3	.000	4.19	37	0	0	66.2	79	27	28	0	0	3	1	0	0	0	–
4 yrs.	24	18	.571	2.98	202	7	0	389.1	334	138	306	0	24	15	15	0	0	0	–

Dave Eiland

EILAND, DAVID WILLIAM
B. July 5, 1966, Dade City, Fla.

BR TR 6'3"   210 lbs.

	W	L	PCT	ERA	G	GS	CG	IP	H	BB	SO	ShO	W	L	SV	AB	H	HR	BA
1988 NY A	0	0	–	6.39	3	3	0	12.2	15	4	7	0	0	0	0	0	0	0	–

Steve Ellsworth

ELLSWORTH, STEVEN CLARK
Son of Dick Ellsworth.
B. July 30, 1960, Chicago, Ill.

BR TR 6'8"   220 lbs.

	W	L	PCT	ERA	G	GS	CG	IP	H	BB	SO	ShO	W	L	SV	AB	H	HR	BA
1988 BOS A	1	6	.143	6.75	8	7	0	36	47	16	16	0	0	1	0	0	0	0	–

Steve Farr

FARR, STEVEN MICHAEL
B. Dec. 12, 1956, Cheverly, Md.

BR TR 5'10"   190 lbs.

	W	L	PCT	ERA	G	GS	CG	IP	H	BB	SO	ShO	W	L	SV	AB	H	HR	BA
1984 CLE A	3	11	.214	4.58	31	16	0	116	106	46	83	0	1	2	1	0	0	0	–
1985 KC A	2	1	.667	3.11	16	3	0	37.2	34	20	36	0	1	0	1	0	0	0	–
1986	8	4	.667	3.13	56	0	0	109.1	90	39	83	0	8	4	8	0	0	0	–
1987	4	3	.571	4.15	47	0	0	91	97	44	88	0	4	3	1	0	0	0	–
1988	5	4	.556	2.50	62	1	0	82.2	74	30	72	0	4	4	20	0	0	0	–
5 yrs.	22	23	.489	3.61	212	20	0	436.2	401	179	362	0	18	13	31	0	0	0	–

LEAGUE CHAMPIONSHIP SERIES

	W	L	PCT	ERA	G	GS	CG	IP	H	BB	SO	ShO	W	L	SV	AB	H	HR	BA
1985 KC A	1	0	1.000	1.42	2	0	0	6.1	4	1	3	0	1	0	0	0	0	0	–

John Farrell

FARRELL, JOHN EDWARD
B. Aug. 4, 1962, Monmouth Beach, N. J.

BR TR 6'4"   210 lbs.

	W	L	PCT	ERA	G	GS	CG	IP	H	BB	SO	ShO	W	L	SV	AB	H	HR	BA
1987 CLE A	5	1	.833	3.39	10	9	1	69	68	22	28	0	1	0	0	0	0	0	–
1988	14	10	.583	4.24	31	30	4	210.1	216	67	92	0	0	0	0	0	0	0	–
2 yrs.	19	11	.633	4.03	41	39	5	279.1	284	89	120	0	1	0	0	0	0	0	–

Sid Fernandez

FERNANDEZ, CHARLES SIDNEY (El Sid)
B. Oct. 12, 1962, Honolulu, Hawaii

BL TL 6'1"   220 lbs.

	W	L	PCT	ERA	G	GS	CG	IP	H	BB	SO	ShO	W	L	SV	AB	H	HR	BA
1983 LA N	0	1	.000	6.00	2	1	0	6	7	7	9	0	0	0	0	1	1	0	1.000
1984 NY N	6	6	.500	3.50	15	15	0	90	74	34	62	0	0	0	0	28	5	0	.179
1985	9	9	.500	2.80	26	26	3	170.1	108	80	180	0	0	0	0	52	11	0	.212
1986	16	6	.727	3.52	32	31	2	204.1	161	91	200	0	1	0	1	68	11	0	.162
1987	12	8	.600	3.81	28	27	3	156	130	67	134	1	0	0	0	43	7	0	.163
1988	12	10	.545	3.03	31	31	1	187	127	70	189	1	0	0	0	56	14	0	.250
6 yrs.	55	40	.579	3.33	134	131	9	813.2	607	349	774	3	0	0	1	248	49	0	.198

LEAGUE CHAMPIONSHIP SERIES

	W	L	PCT	ERA	G	GS	CG	IP	H	BB	SO	ShO	W	L	SV	AB	H	HR	BA
1986 NY N	0	1	.000	4.50	1	1	0	6	3	1	5	0	0	0	0	1	0	0	.000
1988	0	1	.000	13.50	1	1	0	4	7	1	5	0	0	0	0	1	0	0	.000
2 yrs.	0	2	.000	8.10	2	2	0	10	10	2	10	0	0	0	0	2	0	0	.000

WORLD SERIES

	W	L	PCT	ERA	G	GS	CG	IP	H	BB	SO	ShO	W	L	SV	AB	H	HR	BA
1986 NY N	0	0	–	1.35	3	0	0	6.2	6	1	10	0	0	0	0	0	0	0	–

Tom Filer

FILER, THOMAS CARSON
B. Dec. 1, 1956, Philadelphia, Pa.

BR TR 6'1"   195 lbs.

	W	L	PCT	ERA	G	GS	CG	IP	H	BB	SO	ShO	W	L	SV	AB	H	HR	BA
1982 CHI N	1	2	.333	5.53	8	8	0	40.2	50	18	15	0	0	0	0	12	1	0	.083
1985 TOR A	7	0	1.000	3.88	11	9	0	48.2	38	18	24	0	0	0	0	0	0	0	–
1988 MIL A	5	8	.385	4.43	19	16	2	101.2	108	33	39	1	0	1	0	0	0	0	–
3 yrs.	13	10	.565	4.52	38	33	2	191	196	69	78	1	0	1	0	12	1	0	.083

Chuck Finley

FINLEY, CHARLES EDWARD
B. Nov. 26, 1962, Monroe, La.

BL TL 6'6"   220 lbs.

	W	L	PCT	ERA	G	GS	CG	IP	H	BB	SO	ShO	W	L	SV	AB	H	HR	BA
1986 CAL A	3	1	.750	3.30	25	0	0	46.1	40	23	37	0	3	1	0	0	0	0	–
1987	2	7	.222	4.67	35	3	0	90.2	102	43	63	0	2	6	0	0	0	0	–
1988	9	15	.375	4.17	31	31	2	194.1	191	82	111	0	0	0	0	0	0	0	–
3 yrs.	14	23	.378	4.18	91	34	2	331.1	333	148	211	0	5	7	0	0	0	0	–

LEAGUE CHAMPIONSHIP SERIES

	W	L	PCT	ERA	G	GS	CG	IP	H	BB	SO	ShO	W	L	SV	AB	H	HR	BA
1986 CAL A	0	0	–	0.00	3	0	0	2	1	0	1	0	0	0	0	0	0	0	–

Brian Fisher

FISHER, BRIAN KEVIN
B. Mar. 18, 1962, Honolulu, Hawaii

BR TR 6'4"   210 lbs.

	W	L	PCT	ERA	G	GS	CG	IP	H	BB	SO	ShO	W	L	SV	AB	H	HR	BA
1985 NY A	4	4	.500	2.38	55	0	0	98.1	77	29	85	0	4	4	14	0	0	0	–
1986	9	5	.643	4.93	62	0	0	96.2	105	37	67	0	9	5	6	0	0	0	–
1987 PIT N	11	9	.550	4.52	37	26	6	185.1	185	72	117	3	0	0	0	58	11	2	.190
1988	8	10	.444	4.61	33	22	1	146.1	157	57	66	0	2	0	1	42	2	0	.048
4 yrs.	32	28	.533	4.22	187	48	7	526.2	524	195	335	4	15	9	21	100	13	2	.130

Mike Flanagan

FLANAGAN, MICHAEL KENDALL
B. Dec. 16, 1951, Manchester, N. H.

BL TL 6'   180 lbs.

	W	L	PCT	ERA	G	GS	CG	IP	H	BB	SO	ShO	W	L	SV	AB	H	HR	BA
1975 BAL A	0	1	.000	2.79	2	1	0	9.2	9	6	7	0	0	0	0	0	0	0	–
1976	3	5	.375	4.13	20	10	4	85	83	33	56	0	0	3	0	0	0	0	–
1977	15	10	.600	3.64	36	33	15	235	235	70	149	2	0	1	1	0	0	0	–
1978	19	15	.559	4.03	40	40	17	281.1	271	87	167	2	0	0	0	0	0	0	–
1979	23	9	.719	3.08	39	38	16	266	245	70	190	5	0	0	0	0	0	0	–

	W	L	PCT	ERA	G	GS	CG	IP	H	BB	SO	ShO	Relief Pitching W	L	SV	BATTING AB	H	HR	BA

Mike Flanagan continued

	W	L	PCT	ERA	G	GS	CG	IP	H	BB	SO	ShO	W	L	SV	AB	H	HR	BA
1980	16	13	.552	4.12	37	37	12	251	**278**	71	128	2	0	0	0	0	0	0	—
1981	9	6	.600	4.19	20	20	3	116	108	37	72	2	0	0	0	0	0	0	—
1982	15	11	.577	3.97	36	35	11	236	233	76	103	1	0	0	0	0	0	0	—
1983	12	4	.750	3.30	20	20	3	125.1	135	31	50	1	0	0	0	0	0	0	—
1984	13	13	.500	3.53	34	34	10	226.2	213	81	115	2	0	0	0	0	0	0	—
1985	4	5	.444	5.13	15	15	1	86	101	28	42	0	0	0	0	0	0	0	—
1986	7	11	.389	4.24	29	28	2	172	179	66	96	0	0	0	0	0	0	0	—
1987 2 teams		BAL	A (16G 3–6)		TOR	A	(7G 3–2)												
" total	6	8	.429	4.06	23	23	4	144	148	51	93	0	0	0	0	0	0	0	—
1988 TOR A	13	13	.500	4.18	34	34	2	211	220	80	99	1	0	0	0	0	0	0	—
14 yrs.	155	124	.556	3.88	385	368	100	2445	2458	787	1367	18	0	4	1	0	0	0	—

LEAGUE CHAMPIONSHIP SERIES

	W	L	PCT	ERA	G	GS	CG	IP	H	BB	SO	ShO	W	L	SV	AB	H	HR	BA
1979 BAL A	1	0	1.000	5.14	1	1	0	7	6	1	2	0	0	0	0	0	0	0	—
1983	1	0	1.000	1.80	1	1	0	5	5	0	1	0	0	0	0	0	0	0	—
2 yrs.	2	0	1.000	3.75	2	2	0	12	11	1	3	0	0	0	0	0	0	0	—

WORLD SERIES

	W	L	PCT	ERA	G	GS	CG	IP	H	BB	SO	ShO	W	L	SV	AB	H	HR	BA
1979 BAL A	1	1	.500	3.00	3	2	1	15	18	2	13	0	0	0	0	5	0	0	.000
1983	0	0	—	4.50	1	1	0	4	6	1	1	0	0	0	0	1	0	0	.000
2 yrs.	1	1	.500	3.32	4	3	1	19	24	3	14	0	0	0	0	6	0	0	.000

Bob Forsch

FORSCH, ROBERT HERBERT BR TR 6'4" 200 lbs.
Brother of Ken Forsch.
B. Jan. 13, 1950, Sacramento, Calif.

	W	L	PCT	ERA	G	GS	CG	IP	H	BB	SO	ShO	W	L	SV	AB	H	HR	BA
1974 STL N	7	4	.636	2.97	19	14	5	100	84	34	39	2	0	0	0	29	7	0	.241
1975	15	10	.600	2.86	34	34	7	230	213	70	108	4	0	0	0	78	24	1	.308
1976	8	10	.444	3.94	33	32	2	194	209	71	76	0	0	1	0	62	11	1	.177
1977	20	7	.741	3.48	35	35	8	217	210	69	95	2	0	0	0	72	12	0	.167
1978	11	17	.393	3.69	34	34	7	234	205	97	114	3	0	0	0	83	15	1	.181
1979	11	11	.500	3.82	33	32	7	219	215	52	92	1	0	0	0	73	8	0	.110
1980	11	10	.524	3.77	31	31	8	215	225	33	87	0	0	0	0	78	23	3	.295
1981	10	5	.667	3.19	20	20	1	124	106	29	41	0	0	0	0	41	5	0	.122
1982	15	9	.625	3.48	36	34	6	233	238	54	69	2	0	0	1	73	15	0	.205
1983	10	12	.455	4.28	34	30	6	187	190	54	56	2	1	0	0	54	13	1	.241
1984	2	5	.286	6.02	16	11	1	52.1	64	19	21	0	1	0	0	16	4	0	.250
1985	9	6	.600	3.90	34	19	3	136	132	47	48	1	1	0	2	45	11	1	.244
1986	14	10	.583	3.25	33	33	3	230	211	68	104	0	0	0	0	76	13	2	.171
1987	11	7	.611	4.32	33	30	2	179	189	45	89	1	0	0	0	57	17	2	.298
1988 2 teams		STL	N (30G 9–4)		HOU	N	(6G 1–4)												
" total	10	8	.556	4.29	36	18	1	136.1	153	44	54	1	4	2	0	32	8	0	.250
15 yrs.	164	131	.556	3.70	461	407	67	2686.2	2644	786	1093	19	7	3	3	869	186	12	.214

LEAGUE CHAMPIONSHIP SERIES

	W	L	PCT	ERA	G	GS	CG	IP	H	BB	SO	ShO	W	L	SV	AB	H	HR	BA
1982 STL N	1	0	1.000	0.00	1	1	1	9	3	0	6	1	0	0	0	3	2	0	.667
1985	0	0	—	5.40	1	1	0	3.1	3	2	0	0	0	0	0	0	0	0	—
1987	1	1	.500	12.00	3	0	0	3	4	1	3	0	1	1	0	0	0	0	—
3 yrs.	2	1	.667	3.52	5	2	1	15.1	10	3	9	1	1	1	0	3	2	0	.667

WORLD SERIES

	W	L	PCT	ERA	G	GS	CG	IP	H	BB	SO	ShO	W	L	SV	AB	H	HR	BA
1982 STL N	0	2	.000	4.97	2	2	0	12.2	18	3	4	0	0	0	0	0	0	0	—
1985	0	1	.000	12.00	2	1	0	3	6	1	3	0	0	0	0	0	0	0	—
1987	1	0	1.000	9.95	3	0	0	6.1	8	5	3	0	1	0	0	2	0	0	.000
3 yrs.	1	3	.250	7.36	7	3	0	22	32	9	10	0	1	0	0	2	0	0	.000

Tony Fossas

FOSSAS, EMILIO ANTONIO BL TL 6' 195 lbs.
B. Sept. 23, 1957, Havana, Cuba

	W	L	PCT	ERA	G	GS	CG	IP	H	BB	SO	ShO	W	L	SV	AB	H	HR	BA
1988 TEX A	0	0	—	4.76	5	0	0	5.2	11	2	0	0	0	0	0	0	0	0	—

John Franco

FRANCO, JOHN ANTHONY BL TL 5'10" 175 lbs.
B. Sept. 17, 1960, Brooklyn, N. Y.

	W	L	PCT	ERA	G	GS	CG	IP	H	BB	SO	ShO	W	L	SV	AB	H	HR	BA
1984 CIN N	6	2	.750	2.61	54	0	0	79.1	74	36	55	0	6	2	4	3	0	0	.000
1985	12	3	.800	2.18	67	0	0	99	83	40	61	0	12	3	12	6	2	0	.333
1986	6	6	.500	2.94	74	0	0	101	90	44	84	0	6	6	29	4	0	0	.000
1987	8	5	.615	2.52	68	0	0	82	76	27	61	0	8	5	32	2	0	0	.000
1988	6	6	.500	1.57	70	0	0	86	60	27	46	0	6	6	39	1	0	0	.000
5 yrs.	38	22	.633	2.37	333	0	0	447.1	383	174	307	0	38	22	116	16	2	0	.125

Willie Fraser

FRASER, WILLIAM PATRICK BR TR 6'3" 200 lbs.
B. May 26, 1964, New York, N. Y.

	W	L	PCT	ERA	G	GS	CG	IP	H	BB	SO	ShO	W	L	SV	AB	H	HR	BA
1986 CAL A	0	0	—	8.31	1	1	0	4.1	6	1	2	0	0	0	0	0	0	0	—
1987	10	10	.500	3.92	36	23	5	176.2	160	63	106	1	3	1	1	0	0	0	—
1988	12	13	.480	5.41	34	32	2	194.2	203	80	86	0	1	0	0	0	0	0	—
3 yrs.	22	23	.489	4.74	71	56	7	375.2	369	144	194	1	4	1	1	0	0	0	—

Marvin Freeman

FREEMAN, MARVIN (Starvin' Marvin) BR TR 6'7" 200 lbs.
B. Apr. 10, 1963, Chicago, Ill.

	W	L	PCT	ERA	G	GS	CG	IP	H	BB	SO	ShO	W	L	SV	AB	H	HR	BA
1986 PHI N	2	0	1.000	2.25	3	3	0	16	6	10	8	0	0	0	0	6	0	0	.000
1988	2	3	.400	6.10	11	11	0	51.2	55	43	37	0	0	0	0	14	3	0	.214
2 yrs.	4	3	.571	5.19	14	14	0	67.2	61	53	45	0	0	0	0	20	3	0	.150

Todd Frohwirth

FROHWIRTH, TODD GERARD BR TR 6'4" 190 lbs.
B. Sept. 28, 1962, Milwaukee, Wis.

	W	L	PCT	ERA	G	GS	CG	IP	H	BB	SO	ShO	W	L	SV	AB	H	HR	BA
1987 PHI N	1	0	1.000	0.00	10	0	0	11	12	2	9	0	1	0	0	1	0	0	.000
1988	1	2	.333	8.25	12	0	0	12	16	11	11	0	1	2	0	0	0	0	—
2 yrs.	2	2	.500	4.30	22	0	0	23	28	13	20	0	2	2	0	1	0	0	.000

	W	L	PCT	ERA	G	GS	CG	IP	H	BB	SO	ShO	Relief Pitching W	L	SV	BATTING AB	H	HR	BA

Jim Gantner

GANTNER, JAMES ELMER   BL TR 6'   180 lbs.
B. Jan. 5, 1953, Fond du Lac, Wis.

	W	L	PCT	ERA	G	GS	CG	IP	H	BB	SO	ShO	W	L	SV	AB	H	HR	BA
1979 MIL A	0	0	–	0.00	1	0	0	1	2	0	0	0	0	0	0	*			

Gene Garber

GARBER, HENRY EUGENE   BR TR 5'10"   175 lbs.
B. Nov. 13, 1947, Lancaster, Pa.

	W	L	PCT	ERA	G	GS	CG	IP	H	BB	SO	ShO	W	L	SV	AB	H	HR	BA
1969 PIT N	0	0	–	5.40	2	1	0	5	6	1	3	0	0	0	0	1	0	0	.000
1970	0	3	.000	5.32	14	0	0	22	22	10	7	0	0	3	0	3	2	0	.667
1972	0	0	–	7.50	4	0	0	6	7	3	3	0	0	0	0	1	0	0	.000
1973 KC A	9	9	.500	4.24	48	8	4	153	164	49	60	0	7	4	11	0	0	0	–
1974 2 teams			KC	A	(17G 1–2)		PHI	N	(34G 4–0)										
" total	5	2	.714	3.08	51	0	0	76	74	44	41	0	5	2	5	3	0	0	.000
1975 PHI N	10	12	.455	3.60	71	0	0	110	103	27	69	0	10	12	14	12	2	0	.167
1976	9	3	.750	2.82	59	0	0	92.2	78	30	92	0	9	3	11	7	2	0	.286
1977	8	6	.571	2.36	64	0	0	103	82	23	78	0	8	6	19	10	0	0	.000
1978 2 teams			PHI	N	(22G 2–1)		ATL	N	(43G 4–4)										
" total	6	5	.545	2.15	65	0	0	117	84	24	85	0	6	5	25	14	1	0	.071
1979 ATL N	6	16	.273	4.33	68	0	0	106	121	24	56	0	6	16¹	25	10	3	0	.300
1980	5	5	.500	3.84	68	0	0	82	95	24	51	0	5	5	7	2	1	0	.500
1981	4	6	.400	2.59	35	0	0	59	49	20	34	0	4	6	2	5	0	0	.000
1982	8	10	.444	2.34	69	0	0	119.1	100	32	68	0	8	10	30	15	2	0	.133
1983	4	5	.444	4.60	43	0	0	60.2	72	23	45	0	4	5	9	3	0	0	.000
1984	3	6	.333	3.06	62	0	0	106	103	24	55	0	3	6	11	14	2	0	.143
1985	6	6	.500	3.61	59	0	0	97.1	98	25	66	0	6	6	1	5	1	0	.200
1986	5	5	.500	2.54	61	0	0	78	76	20	56	0	5	5	24	6	1	0	.167
1987 2 teams			ATL	N	(49G 8–10)		KC	A	(13G 0–0)										
" total	8	10	.444	4.09	62	0	0	83.2	100	29	51	0	8	10	18	4	0	0	.000
1988 KC A	0	4	.000	3.58	26	0	0	32.2	29	13	20	0	0	4	6	0	0	0	–
19 yrs.	96	113	.459	3.34	931	9	4	1509.1	1463	445	940	0	94	108	218	115	17	0	.148
				5th									7th		8th				

LEAGUE CHAMPIONSHIP SERIES

	W	L	PCT	ERA	G	GS	CG	IP	H	BB	SO	ShO	W	L	SV	AB	H	HR	BA
1976 PHI N	0	1	.000	13.50	2	0	0	.2	2	1	0	0	0	1	0	0	0	0	–
1977	1	1	.500	3.38	3	0	0	5.1	4	0	3	0	1	1	0	0	0	0	–
1982 ATL N	0	1	.000	8.10	2	0	0	3.1	4	1	3	0	0	1	0	1	0	0	.000
3 yrs.	1	3	.250	5.79	7	0	0	9.1	10	2	6	0	1	3	0	1	0	0	.000

Miguel Garcia

GARCIA, MIGUEL ANGEL   BL TL 5'11"   173 lbs.
Born Miguel Angel Garcia y Sifontes.
B. Apr. 19, 1967, Caracas, Venezuela

	W	L	PCT	ERA	G	GS	CG	IP	H	BB	SO	ShO	W	L	SV	AB	H	HR	BA
1987 2 teams			CAL	A	(1G 0–0)		PIT	N	(1G 0–0)										
" total	0	0	–	11.57	2	0	0	2.1	3	3	0	0	0	0	0	0	0	0	–
1988 PIT N	0	0	–	4.50	1	0	0	2	3	2	2	0	0	0	0	0	0	0	–
2 yrs.	0	0	–	8.31	3	0	0	4.1	6	5	2	0	0	0	0	0	0	0	–

Wes Gardner

GARDNER, WESLEY BRIAN   BR TR 6'4"   195 lbs.
B. Apr. 29, 1961, Benton, Ark.

	W	L	PCT	ERA	G	GS	CG	IP	H	BB	SO	ShO	W	L	SV	AB	H	HR	BA
1984 NY N	1	1	.500	6.39	21	0	0	25.1	34	8	19	0	1	1	1	1	0	0	.000
1985	0	2	.000	5.25	9	0	0	12	18	8	11	0	0	2	0	0	0	0	–
1986 BOS A	0	0	–	9.00	1	0	0	1	1	0	1	0	0	0	0	0	0	0	–
1987	3	6	.333	5.42	49	1	0	89.2	98	42	70	0	3	6	10	0	0	0	–
1988	8	6	.571	3.50	36	18	1	149	119	64	106	0	1	1	2	0	0	0	–
5 yrs.	12	15	.444	4.48	116	19	1	277	270	122	207	0	5	10	13	1	0	0	.000

LEAGUE CHAMPIONSHIP SERIES

	W	L	PCT	ERA	G	GS	CG	IP	H	BB	SO	ShO	W	L	SV	AB	H	HR	BA
1988 BOS A	0	0	–	5.79	1	0	0	4.2	6	2	8	0	0	0	0	0	0	0	–

Scott Garrelts

GARRELTS, SCOTT WILLIAM   BR TR 6'4"   200 lbs.
B. Oct. 30, 1961, Champaign, Ill.

	W	L	PCT	ERA	G	GS	CG	IP	H	BB	SO	ShO	W	L	SV	AB	H	HR	BA
1982 SF N	0	0	–	13.50	1	0	0	2	3	2	4	0	0	0	0	0	0	0	–
1983	2	2	.500	2.52	5	5	1	35.2	33	19	16	1	0	0	0	9	2	0	.222
1984	2	3	.400	5.65	21	3	0	43	45	34	32	0	2	3	0	10	1	0	.100
1985	9	6	.600	2.30	74	0	0	105.2	76	58	106	0	9	6	13	9	2	0	.222
1986	13	9	.591	3.11	53	18	2	173.2	144	74	125	0	8	2	10	45	8	1	.178
1987	11	7	.611	3.22	64	0	0	106.1	70	55	127	0	11	7	12	10	2	0	.200
1988	5	9	.357	3.58	65	0	0	98	80	46	86	0	5	9	13	13	1	0	.077
7 yrs.	42	36	.538	3.25	283	26	3	564.1	451	288	496	1	35	27	48	96	16	1	.167

LEAGUE CHAMPIONSHIP SERIES

	W	L	PCT	ERA	G	GS	CG	IP	H	BB	SO	ShO	W	L	SV	AB	H	HR	BA
1987 SF N	0	0	–	6.75	2	0	0	2.2	2	4	4	0	0	0	0	0	0	0	–

Paul Gibson

GIBSON, PAUL MARSHALL   BR TL 6'   165 lbs.
B. Jan. 4, 1960, Southampton, N. Y.

	W	L	PCT	ERA	G	GS	CG	IP	H	BB	SO	ShO	W	L	SV	AB	H	HR	BA
1988 DET A	4	2	.667	2.93	40	1	0	92	83	34	50	0	3	2	0	0	0	0	–

Dan Gladden

GLADDEN, CLINTON DANIEL III   BR TR 5'11"   175 lbs.
B. July 7, 1957, San Jose, Calif.

	W	L	PCT	ERA	G	GS	CG	IP	H	BB	SO	ShO	W	L	SV	AB	H	HR	BA
1988 MIN A	0	0	–	0.00	1	0	0	1	0	0	0	0	0	0	0	*			

Tom Glavine

GLAVINE, THOMAS MICHAEL   BL TL 6'   175 lbs.
B. Mar. 25, 1966, Concord, Mass.

	W	L	PCT	ERA	G	GS	CG	IP	H	BB	SO	ShO	W	L	SV	AB	H	HR	BA
1987 ATL N	2	4	.333	5.54	9	9	0	50.1	55	33	20	0	0	0	0	16	2	0	.125
1988	7	17	.292	4.56	34	34	1	195.1	201	63	84	0	0	0	0	60	11	0	.183
2 yrs.	9	21	.300	4.76	43	43	1	245.2	256	96	104	0	0	0	0	76	13	0	.171

	W	L	PCT	ERA	G	GS	CG	IP	H	BB	SO	ShO	Relief Pitching W	L	SV	BATTING AB	H	HR	BA

Jerry Don Gleaton

GLEATON, JERRY DON
B. Sept. 14, 1957, Brownwood, Tex.   BL TL 6'3" 205 lbs.

	W	L	PCT	ERA	G	GS	CG	IP	H	BB	SO	ShO	W	L	SV	AB	H	HR	BA
1979 TEX A	0	1	.000	6.30	5	2	0	10	15	2	2	0	0	0	0	0	0	0	–
1980	0	0	–	2.57	5	0	0	7	5	4	2	0	0	0	0	0	0	0	–
1981 SEA A	4	7	.364	4.76	20	13	1	85	88	38	31	0	0	0	0	0	0	0	–
1982	0	0	–	13.50	3	0	0	4.2	7	2	1	0	0	0	0	0	0	0	–
1984 CHI A	1	2	.333	3.44	11	1	0	18.1	20	6	4	0	1	1	2	0	0	0	–
1985	1	0	1.000	5.76	31	0	0	29.2	37	13	22	0	1	0	1	0	0	0	–
1987 KC A	4	4	.500	4.26	48	0	0	50.2	38	28	44	0	4	4	5	0	0	0	–
1988	0	4	.000	3.55	42	0	0	38	33	17	29	0	0	4	3	0	0	0	–
8 yrs.	10	18	.357	4.66	165	16	1	243.1	243	110	135	0	6	9	11	0	0	0	–

German Gonzalez

GONZALEZ, GERMAN JOSE
Born German Jose Gonzalez y Caraballo.   BR TR 6' 170 lbs.
B. Mar. 7, 1962, Rio Caribe, Venezuela

	W	L	PCT	ERA	G	GS	CG	IP	H	BB	SO	ShO	W	L	SV	AB	H	HR	BA
1988 MIN A	0	0	–	3.38	16	0	0	21.1	20	8	19	0	0	0	1	0	0	0	–

Dwight Gooden

GOODEN, DWIGHT EUGENE (Doc, Dr. K)
B. Nov. 16, 1964, Tampa, Fla.   BR TR 6'2" 190 lbs.

	W	L	PCT	ERA	G	GS	CG	IP	H	BB	SO	ShO	W	L	SV	AB	H	HR	BA
1984 NY N	17	9	.654	2.60	31	31	7	218	161	73	**276**	3	0	0	0	70	14	0	.200
1985	24	4	.857	**1.53**	35	35	16	276.2	198	69	**268**	8	0	0	0	93	21	1	.226
1986	17	6	.739	2.84	33	33	12	250	197	80	200	2	0	0	0	81	7	0	.086
1987	15	7	.682	3.21	25	25	7	179.2	162	53	148	3	0	0	0	64	14	0	.219
1988	18	9	.667	3.19	34	34	10	248.1	242	57	175	3	0	0	0	90	16	1	.178
5 yrs.	91	35	.722	2.62	158	158	52	1172.2	960	332	1067	19	0	0	0	398	72	2	.181

LEAGUE CHAMPIONSHIP SERIES

	W	L	PCT	ERA	G	GS	CG	IP	H	BB	SO	ShO	W	L	SV	AB	H	HR	BA
1986 NY N	0	1	.000	1.06	2	2	0	17	16	5	9	0	0	0	0	5	0	0	.000
1988	0	0	–	2.95	3	2	0	18.1	10	8	20	0	0	0	0	5	1	0	.200
2 yrs.	0	1	.000	2.04	5	4	0	35.1	26	13	29	0	0	0	0	10	1	0	.100

WORLD SERIES

	W	L	PCT	ERA	G	GS	CG	IP	H	BB	SO	ShO	W	L	SV	AB	H	HR	BA
1986 NY N	0	2	.000	8.00	2	2	0	9	17	4	9	0	0	0	0	2	1	0	.500

Don Gordon

GORDON, DONALD THOMAS
B. Oct. 10, 1959, New York, N. Y.   BR TR 6'1" 175 lbs.

	W	L	PCT	ERA	G	GS	CG	IP	H	BB	SO	ShO	W	L	SV	AB	H	HR	BA
1986 TOR A	0	1	.000	7.06	14	0	0	21.2	28	8	13	0	0	1	1	0	0	0	–
1987 2 teams			TOR	A (5G 0–0)			CLE	A (21G 0–3)											
" total	0	3	.000	4.09	26	0	0	50.2	57	15	23	0	0	3	1	0	0	0	–
1988 CLE A	3	4	.429	4.40	38	0	0	59.1	65	19	20	0	3	4	1	0	0	0	–
3 yrs.	3	8	.273	4.72	78	0	0	131.2	150	42	56	0	3	8	3	0	0	0	–

Tom Gordon

GORDON, THOMAS (Flash)
B. Nov. 18, 1967, Sebring, Fla.   BR TR 5'9" 160 lbs.

	W	L	PCT	ERA	G	GS	CG	IP	H	BB	SO	ShO	W	L	SV	AB	H	HR	BA
1988 KC A	0	2	.000	5.17	5	2	0	15.2	16	7	18	0	0	0	0	0	0	0	–

Goose Gossage

GOSSAGE, RICHARD MICHAEL
B. July 5, 1951, Colorado Springs, Colo.   BR TR 6'3" 180 lbs.

	W	L	PCT	ERA	G	GS	CG	IP	H	BB	SO	ShO	W	L	SV	AB	H	HR	BA
1972 CHI A	7	1	.875	4.28	36	1	0	80	72	44	57	0	7	0	2	16	0	0	.000
1973	0	4	.000	7.43	20	4	1	49.2	57	37	33	0	0	0	0	0	0	0	–
1974	4	6	.400	4.15	39	3	0	89	92	47	64	0	4	5	1	0	0	0	–
1975	9	8	.529	1.84	62	0	0	141.2	99	70	130	0	9	8	26	0	0	0	–
1976	9	17	.346	3.94	31	29	15	224	214	90	135	0	0	1	1	0	0	0	–
1977 PIT N	11	9	.550	1.62	72	0	0	133	78	49	151	0	11	9	26	23	5	0	.217
1978 NY A	10	11	.476	2.01	63	0	0	134.1	87	59	122	0	10	11	27	0	0	0	–
1979	5	3	.625	2.64	36	0	0	58	48	19	41	0	5	3	18	0	0	0	–
1980	6	2	.750	2.27	64	0	0	99	74	37	103	0	6	2	33	0	0	0	–
1981	3	2	.600	0.77	32	0	0	47	22	14	48	0	3	2	20	0	0	0	–
1982	4	5	.444	2.23	56	0	0	93	63	28	102	0	4	5	30	0	0	0	–
1983	13	5	.722	2.27	57	0	0	87.1	82	25	90	0	13	5	22	0	0	0	–
1984 SD N	10	6	.625	2.90	62	0	0	102.1	75	36	84	0	10	6	25	22	4	0	.182
1985	5	3	.625	1.82	50	0	0	79	64	17	52	0	5	3	26	11	0	0	.000
1986	5	7	.417	4.45	45	0	0	64.2	69	20	63	0	5	7	21	7	0	0	.000
1987	5	4	.556	3.12	40	0	0	52	47	19	44	0	5	4	11	4	0	0	.000
1988 CHI N	4	4	.500	4.33	46	0	0	43.2	50	15	30	0	4	4	13	1	0	0	.000
17 yrs.	110	97	.531	2.92	811	37	16	1577.2	1293	626	1349	0	101 4th	75	302 2nd	84	9	0	.107

DIVISIONAL PLAYOFF SERIES

	W	L	PCT	ERA	G	GS	CG	IP	H	BB	SO	ShO	W	L	SV	AB	H	HR	BA
1981 NY A	0	0	–	0.00	3	0	0	6.2	3	2	8	0	0	0	3	0	0	0	–

LEAGUE CHAMPIONSHIP SERIES

	W	L	PCT	ERA	G	GS	CG	IP	H	BB	SO	ShO	W	L	SV	AB	H	HR	BA
1978 NY A	1	0	1.000	4.50	2	0	0	4	3	0	3	0	1	0	1	0	0	0	–
1980	0	1	.000	54.00	1	0	0	.1	3	0	0	0	0	1	0	0	0	0	–
1981	0	0	–	0.00	2	0	0	2.2	1	0	2	0	0	0	1	0	0	0	–
1984 SD N	0	0	–	4.50	3	0	0	4	5	1	5	0	0	0	1	0	0	0	–
4 yrs.	1	1	.500	4.91	8	0	0	11	12	1	10	0	1	1	3	0	0	0	–

WORLD SERIES

	W	L	PCT	ERA	G	GS	CG	IP	H	BB	SO	ShO	W	L	SV	AB	H	HR	BA
1978 NY A	1	0	1.000	0.00	6	0	0	6	1	1	4	0	1	0	0	0	0	0	–
1981	0	0	–	0.00	3	0	0	5	2	2	5	0	0	0	2	1	0	0	.000
1984 SD N	0	0	–	13.50	2	0	0	2.2	3	1	2	0	0	0	0	0	0	0	–
3 yrs.	1	0	1.000	2.63	8	0	0	13.2	6	4	11	0	1	0	2	1	0	0	.000

Jim Gott

GOTT, JAMES WILLIAM
B. Aug. 3, 1959, Hollywood, Calif.   BR TR 6'4" 200 lbs.

	W	L	PCT	ERA	G	GS	CG	IP	H	BB	SO	ShO	W	L	SV	AB	H	HR	BA
1982 TOR A	5	10	.333	4.43	30	23	1	136	134	66	82	1	0	0	0	0	0	0	–
1983	9	14	.391	4.74	34	30	6	176.2	195	68	121	1	0	1	0	0	0	0	–
1984	7	6	.538	4.02	35	12	1	109.2	93	49	73	1	2	1	2	0	0	0	–
1985 SF N	7	10	.412	3.88	26	26	2	148.1	144	51	78	0	0	0	0	51	10	3	.196

	W	L	PCT	ERA	G	GS	CG	IP	H	BB	SO	ShO	Relief Pitching W	L	SV	BATTING AB	H	HR	BA

Jim Gott continued

	W	L	PCT	ERA	G	GS	CG	IP	H	BB	SO	ShO	W	L	SV	AB	H	HR	BA
1986	0	0	–	7.62	9	2	0	13	16	13	9	0	0	0	1	3	0	0	.000
1987 2 teams			SF N (30G 1–0)			PIT N (25G 0–2)													
" total	1	2	.333	3.41	55	3	0	87	81	40	90	0	1	2	13	11	1	1	.091
1988 PIT N	6	6	.500	3.49	67	0	0	77.1	68	22	76	0	6	6	34	1	0	0	.000
7 yrs.	35	48	.422	4.18	256	96	10	748	731	309	529	3	9	10	50	66	11	4	.167

Mark Grant

GRANT, MARK ANDREW
B. Oct. 24, 1963, Aurora, Ill.
BR TR 6'2" 205 lbs.

	W	L	PCT	ERA	G	GS	CG	IP	H	BB	SO	ShO	W	L	SV	AB	H	HR	BA
1984 SF N	1	4	.200	6.37	11	10	0	53.2	56	19	32	0	0	0	1	17	0	0	.000
1986	0	1	.000	3.60	4	1	0	10	6	5	5	0	0	0	0	1	0	0	.000
1987 2 teams			SF N (16G 1–2)			SD N (17G 6–7)													
" total	7	9	.438	4.24	33	25	2	163.1	170	73	90	1	1	1	1	44	4	0	.091
1988 SD N	2	8	.200	3.69	33	11	0	97.2	97	36	61	0	1	3	0	16	0	0	.000
4 yrs.	10	22	.313	4.41	81	47	2	324.2	329	133	188	1	2	4	2	78	4	0	.051

Jeff Gray

GRAY, JEFFREY EDWARD
B. Apr. 10, 1963, Richmond, Va.
BR TR 6'1" 175 lbs.

	W	L	PCT	ERA	G	GS	CG	IP	H	BB	SO	ShO	W	L	SV	AB	H	HR	BA
1988 CIN N	0	0	–	3.86	5	0	0	9.1	12	4	5	0	0	0	0	1	0	0	.000

Greg Gross

GROSS, GREGORY EUGENE
B. Aug. 1, 1952, York, Pa.
BL TL 5'10" 160 lbs.

	W	L	PCT	ERA	G	GS	CG	IP	H	BB	SO	ShO	W	L	SV	AB	H	HR	BA
1986 PHI N	0	0	–	0.00	1	0	0	.2	1	1	2	0	0	0	0	*			

Kevin Gross

GROSS, KEVIN FRANK
B. June 8, 1961, Downey, Calif.
BR TR 6'5" 200 lbs.

	W	L	PCT	ERA	G	GS	CG	IP	H	BB	SO	ShO	W	L	SV	AB	H	HR	BA
1983 PHI N	4	6	.400	3.56	17	17	1	96	100	35	66	1	0	0	0	33	3	0	.091
1984	8	5	.615	4.12	44	14	1	129	140	44	84	0	4	0	1	30	2	0	.067
1985	15	13	.536	3.41	38	31	6	205.2	194	81	151	2	1	2	0	65	9	1	.138
1986	12	12	.500	4.02	37	36	7	241.2	240	94	154	2	0	0	0	80	15	1	.188
1987	9	16	.360	4.35	34	33	3	200.2	205	87	110	1	0	0	0	63	12	1	.190
1988	12	14	.462	3.69	33	33	5	231.2	209	89	162	1	0	0	0	75	13	0	.173
6 yrs.	60	66	.476	3.87	203	164	23	1104.2	1088	430	727	7	6	2	1	346	54	3	.156

Cecilio Guante

GUANTE, CECILIO MAGALLANE
Born Cecilio Guante y Magallane.
B. Feb. 1, 1960, Villa Mella, Dominican Republic
BR TR 6'3" 200 lbs.

	W	L	PCT	ERA	G	GS	CG	IP	H	BB	SO	ShO	W	L	SV	AB	H	HR	BA
1982 PIT N	0	0	–	3.33	10	0	0	27	28	5	26	0	0	0	0	5	0	0	.000
1983	2	6	.250	3.32	49	0	0	100.1	90	46	82	0	2	6	9	22	2	0	.091
1984	2	3	.400	2.61	27	0	0	41.1	32	16	30	0	2	3	2	4	0	0	.000
1985	4	6	.400	2.72	63	0	0	109	84	40	92	0	4	6	5	17	1	0	.059
1986	5	2	.714	3.35	52	0	0	78	65	29	63	0	5	2	4	1	0	0	.000
1987 NY A	3	2	.600	5.73	23	0	0	44	42	20	46	0	3	2	1	0	0	0	–
1988 2 teams			NY A (56G 5–6)			TEX A (7G 0–0)													
" total	5	6	.455	2.82	63	0	0	79.2	67	26	65	0	5	6	12	0	0	0	–
7 yrs.	21	25	.457	3.27	287	0	0	479.1	408	182	404	0	21	25	33	49	3	0	.061

Mark Gubicza

GUBICZA, MARK STEVEN
B. Aug. 14, 1962, Philadelphia, Pa.
BR TR 6'6" 215 lbs.

	W	L	PCT	ERA	G	GS	CG	IP	H	BB	SO	ShO	W	L	SV	AB	H	HR	BA
1984 KC A	10	14	.417	4.05	29	29	4	189	172	75	111	2	0	0	0	0	0	0	–
1985	14	10	.583	4.06	29	28	0	177.1	160	77	99	0	1	0	0	0	0	0	–
1986	12	6	.667	3.64	35	24	3	180.2	155	84	118	2	1	1	0	0	0	0	–
1987	13	18	.419	3.98	35	35	10	241.2	231	120	166	2	0	0	0	0	0	0	–
1988	20	8	.714	2.70	35	35	8	269.2	237	83	183	4	0	0	0	0	0	0	–
5 yrs.	69	56	.552	3.62	163	151	25	1058.1	955	439	677	10	2	1	0	0	0	0	–

LEAGUE CHAMPIONSHIP SERIES

	W	L	PCT	ERA	G	GS	CG	IP	H	BB	SO	ShO	W	L	SV	AB	H	HR	BA
1985 KC A	1	0	1.000	3.24	2	1	0	8.1	4	4	4	0	0	0	0	0	0	0	–

Lee Guetterman

GUETTERMAN, ARTHUR LEE
B. Nov. 22, 1958, Chattanooga, Tenn.
BL TL 6'8" 225 lbs.

	W	L	PCT	ERA	G	GS	CG	IP	H	BB	SO	ShO	W	L	SV	AB	H	HR	BA
1984 SEA A	0	0	–	4.15	3	0	0	4.1	9	2	2	0	0	0	0	0	0	0	–
1986	0	4	.000	7.34	41	4	1	76	108	30	38	0	0	2	0	0	0	0	–
1987	11	4	.733	3.81	25	17	2	113.1	117	35	42	1	1	0	0	0	0	0	–
1988 NY A	1	2	.333	4.65	20	2	0	40.2	49	14	15	0	1	0	0	0	0	0	–
4 yrs.	12	10	.545	5.11	89	23	3	234.1	283	81	97	1	2	2	0	0	0	0	–

Ron Guidry

GUIDRY, RONALD AMES (Louisiana Lightning, Gator)
B. Aug. 28, 1950, Lafayette, La.
BL TL 5'11" 161 lbs.

	W	L	PCT	ERA	G	GS	CG	IP	H	BB	SO	ShO	W	L	SV	AB	H	HR	BA
1975 NY A	0	1	.000	3.45	10	1	0	15.2	15	9	15	0	0	0	0	0	0	0	–
1976	0	0	–	5.63	7	0	0	16	20	4	12	0	0	0	0	0	0	0	–
1977	16	7	.696	2.82	31	25	9	211	174	65	176	5	1	0	1	0	0	0	–
1978	25	3	.893	1.74	35	35	16	273.2	187	72	248	9	0	0	0	0	0	0	–
1979	18	8	.692	2.78	33	30	15	236	203	71	201	2	1	0	2	0	0	0	–
1980	17	10	.630	3.56	37	29	5	220	215	80	166	3	1	1	1	0	0	0	–
1981	11	5	.688	2.76	23	21	0	127	100	26	104	0	0	0	0	0	0	0	–
1982	14	8	.636	3.81	34	33	6	222	216	69	162	1	0	0	0	0	0	0	–
1983	21	9	.700	3.42	31	31	21	250.1	232	60	156	3	0	0	0	0	0	0	–
1984	10	11	.476	4.51	29	28	5	195.2	223	44	127	1	0	0	0	0	0	0	–
1985	22	6	.786	3.27	34	33	11	259	243	42	143	2	0	0	0	0	0	0	–
1986	9	12	.429	3.98	30	30	5	192.1	202	38	140	0	0	0	0	0	0	0	–
1987	5	8	.385	3.67	22	17	2	117.2	111	38	96	0	0	1	0	0	0	0	–
1988	2	3	.400	4.18	12	10	0	56	57	15	32	0	0	0	0	0	0	0	–
14 yrs.	170	91	.651	3.29	368	323	95	2392.1	2198	633	1778	26	3	3	5	0	0	0	–

DIVISIONAL PLAYOFF SERIES

	W	L	PCT	ERA	G	GS	CG	IP	H	BB	SO	ShO	W	L	SV	AB	H	HR	BA
1981 NY A	0	0	–	5.40	2	2	0	8.1	11	3	8	0	0	0	0	0	0	0	–

	W	L	PCT	ERA	G	GS	CG	IP	H	BB	SO	ShO	Relief Pitching W	L	SV	BATTING AB	H	HR	BA

Ron Guidry continued

LEAGUE CHAMPIONSHIP SERIES

	W	L	PCT	ERA	G	GS	CG	IP	H	BB	SO	ShO	W	L	SV	AB	H	HR	BA
1977 NY A	1	0	1.000	3.97	2	2	1	11.1	9	3	8	0	0	0	0	0	0	0	–
1978	1	0	1.000	1.13	1	1	0	8	7	1	7	0	0	0	0	0	0	0	–
1980	0	1	.000	12.00	1	1	0	3	5	4	2	0	0	0	0	0	0	0	–
3 yrs.	2	1	.667	4.03	4	4	1	22.1	21	8	17	0	0	0	0	0	0	0	–

WORLD SERIES

	W	L	PCT	ERA	G	GS	CG	IP	H	BB	SO	ShO	W	L	SV	AB	H	HR	BA
1977 NY A	1	0	1.000	2.00	1	1	1	9	4	3	7	0	0	0	0	2	0	0	.000
1978	1	0	1.000	1.00	1	1	1	9	8	7	4	0	0	0	0	0	0	0	–
1981	1	1	.500	1.93	2	2	0	14	8	4	15	0	0	0	0	5	0	0	.000
3 yrs.	3	1	.750	1.69	4	4	2	32	20	14	26	0	0	0	0	7	0	0	.000

Jose Guzman

GUZMAN, JOSE ALBERTO
Born Jose Alberto Guzman y Mirabel.
B. Apr. 9, 1963, Santa Isabel, Puerto Rico

BR TR 6'2" 172 lbs.

	W	L	PCT	ERA	G	GS	CG	IP	H	BB	SO	ShO	W	L	SV	AB	H	HR	BA
1985 TEX A	3	2	.600	2.76	5	5	0	32.2	27	14	24	0	0	0	0	0	0	0	–
1986	9	15	.375	4.54	29	29	2	172.1	199	60	87	0	0	0	0	0	0	0	–
1987	14	14	.500	4.67	37	30	6	208.1	196	82	143	0	3	0	0	0	0	0	–
1988	11	13	.458	3.70	30	30	6	206.2	180	82	157	2	0	0	0	0	0	0	–
4 yrs.	37	44	.457	4.21	101	94	14	620	602	238	411	2	3	0	0	0	0	0	–

John Habyan

HABYAN, JOHN GABRIEL
B. Jan. 29, 1963, Bay Shore, N. Y.

BR TR 6'1" 195 lbs.

	W	L	PCT	ERA	G	GS	CG	IP	H	BB	SO	ShO	W	L	SV	AB	H	HR	BA
1985 BAL A	1	0	1.000	0.00	2	0	0	2.2	3	0	2	0	1	0	0	0	0	0	–
1986	1	3	.250	4.44	6	5	0	26.1	24	18	14	0	0	0	0	0	0	0	–
1987	6	7	.462	4.80	27	13	0	116.1	110	40	64	0	4	0	1	0	0	0	–
1988	1	0	1.000	4.30	7	0	0	14.2	22	4	4	0	1	0	0	0	0	0	–
4 yrs.	9	10	.474	4.61	42	18	0	160	159	62	84	0	6	0	1	0	0	0	–

Drew Hall

HALL, ANDREW CLARK
B. Mar. 27, 1963, Louisville, Ky.

BL TL 6'4" 220 lbs.

	W	L	PCT	ERA	G	GS	CG	IP	H	BB	SO	ShO	W	L	SV	AB	H	HR	BA
1986 CHI N	1	2	.333	4.56	5	4	1	23.2	24	10	21	0	0	0	1	7	1	0	.143
1987	1	1	.500	6.89	21	0	0	32.2	40	14	20	0	1	1	0	4	0	0	.000
1988	1	1	.500	7.66	19	0	0	22.1	26	9	22	0	1	1	1	1	0	0	.000
3 yrs.	3	4	.429	6.41	45	4	1	78.2	90	33	63	0	2	2	2	12	1	0	.083

Atlee Hammaker

HAMMAKER, CHARLTON ATLEE
B. Jan. 24, 1958, Carmel, Calif.

BB TL 6'3" 200 lbs.

	W	L	PCT	ERA	G	GS	CG	IP	H	BB	SO	ShO	W	L	SV	AB	H	HR	BA
1981 KC A	1	3	.250	5.54	10	6	0	39	44	12	11	0	0	0	0	0	0	0	–
1982 SF N	12	8	.600	4.11	29	27	4	175	189	28	102	1	0	0	0	59	4	0	.068
1983	10	9	.526	2.25	23	23	8	172.1	147	32	127	3	0	0	0	59	6	0	.102
1984	2	0	1.000	2.18	6	6	0	33	32	9	24	0	0	0	0	11	2	0	.182
1985	5	12	.294	3.74	29	29	1	170.2	161	47	100	1	0	0	0	47	4	0	.085
1987	10	10	.500	3.58	31	27	2	168.1	159	57	107	0	1	0	0	57	7	0	.123
1988	9	9	.500	3.73	43	17	3	144.2	136	41	65	1	4	2	5	33	4	0	.121
7 yrs.	49	51	.490	3.52	171	135	18	903	868	226	536	6	5	2	5	266	27	0	.102

LEAGUE CHAMPIONSHIP SERIES

	W	L	PCT	ERA	G	GS	CG	IP	H	BB	SO	ShO	W	L	SV	AB	H	HR	BA
1987 SF N	0	1	.000	7.88	2	2	0	8	12	0	7	0	0	0	0	3	0	0	.000

Erik Hanson

HANSON, ERIK BRIAN
B. May 18, 1965, Kinnelon, N. J.

BR TR 6'6" 205 lbs.

	W	L	PCT	ERA	G	GS	CG	IP	H	BB	SO	ShO	W	L	SV	AB	H	HR	BA
1988 SEA A	2	3	.400	3.24	6	6	0	41.2	35	12	36	0	0	0	0	0	0	0	–

Mike Harkey

HARKEY, MICHAEL ANTHONY
B. Oct. 25, 1966, San Diego, Calif.

BR TR 6'5" 220 lbs.

	W	L	PCT	ERA	G	GS	CG	IP	H	BB	SO	ShO	W	L	SV	AB	H	HR	BA
1988 CHI N	0	3	.000	2.60	5	5	0	34.2	33	15	18	0	0	0	0	11	1	0	.091

Pete Harnisch

HARNISCH, PETER THOMAS
B. Sept. 23, 1966, Commack, N. Y.

BB TR 6'1" 195 lbs.

	W	L	PCT	ERA	G	GS	CG	IP	H	BB	SO	ShO	W	L	SV	AB	H	HR	BA
1988 BAL A	0	2	.000	5.54	2	2	0	13	13	9	10	0	0	0	0	0	0	0	–

Greg Harris

HARRIS, GREG ALLEN
B. Nov. 2, 1955, Lynwood, Calif.

BB TR 6' 165 lbs.

	W	L	PCT	ERA	G	GS	CG	IP	H	BB	SO	ShO	W	L	SV	AB	H	HR	BA
1981 NY N	3	5	.375	4.43	16	14	0	69	65	28	54	0	0	0	1	22	4	0	.182
1982 CIN N	2	6	.250	4.83	34	10	1	91.1	96	37	67	0	0	1	1	18	3	0	.167
1983	0	0	–	27.00	1	0	0	1	2	3	1	0	0	0	0	1	0	0	.000
1984 2 teams						MON	N (15G 0–1)		SD		N (19G 2–1)								
" total	2	2	.500	2.48	34	1	0	54.1	38	25	45	0	1	2	3	9	3	0	.333
1985 TEX A	5	4	.556	2.47	58	0	0	113	74	43	111	0	5	4	11	0	0	0	–
1986	10	8	.556	2.83	73	0	0	111.1	103	42	95	0	10	8	20	0	0	0	–
1987	5	10	.333	4.86	42	19	0	140.2	157	56	106	0	1	4	0	0	0	0	–
1988 PHI N	4	6	.400	2.36	66	1	0	107	80	52	71	0	4	5	1	9	3	0	.333
8 yrs.	31	41	.431	3.55	324	45	1	687.2	615	286	550	0	21	24	37	59	13	0	.220

LEAGUE CHAMPIONSHIP SERIES

	W	L	PCT	ERA	G	GS	CG	IP	H	BB	SO	ShO	W	L	SV	AB	H	HR	BA
1984 SD N	0	0	–	31.50	1	0	0	2	9	3	2	0	0	0	0	0	0	0	–

WORLD SERIES

	W	L	PCT	ERA	G	GS	CG	IP	H	BB	SO	ShO	W	L	SV	AB	H	HR	BA
1984 SD N	0	0	–	0.00	1	0	0	5.1	3	3	5	0	0	0	0	0	0	0	–

Greg Harris

HARRIS, GREGORY WADE
B. Dec. 1, 1963, Greensboro, N. C.

BR TR 6'2" 190 lbs.

	W	L	PCT	ERA	G	GS	CG	IP	H	BB	SO	ShO	W	L	SV	AB	H	HR	BA
1988 SD N	2	0	1.000	1.50	3	1	1	18	13	3	15	0	1	0	0	7	0	0	.000

	W	L	PCT	ERA	G	GS	CG	IP	H	BB	SO	ShO	Relief Pitching W	L	SV	BATTING AB	H	HR	BA

Bryan Harvey

HARVEY, BRYAN STANLEY
B. June 2, 1963, Chattanooga, Tenn.   BR TR 6'3"   235 lbs.

	W	L	PCT	ERA	G	GS	CG	IP	H	BB	SO	ShO	W	L	SV	AB	H	HR	BA
1987 CAL A	0	0	–	0.00	3	0	0	5	6	2	3	0	0	0	0	0	0	0	–
1988	7	5	.583	2.13	50	0	0	76	59	20	67	0	7	5	17	0	0	0	–
2 yrs.	7	5	.583	2.00	53	0	0	81	65	22	70	0	7	5	17	0	0	0	–

Brad Havens

HAVENS, BRADLEY DAVID
B. Nov. 17, 1959, Highland Park, Mich.   BL TL 6'1"   180 lbs.

	W	L	PCT	ERA	G	GS	CG	IP	H	BB	SO	ShO	W	L	SV	AB	H	HR	BA
1981 MIN A	3	6	.333	3.58	14	12	1	78	76	24	43	1	0	0	0	0	0	0	–
1982	10	14	.417	4.31	33	32	4	208.2	201	80	129	1	0	1	0	0	0	0	–
1983	5	8	.385	8.18	16	14	1	80.1	110	38	40	0	0	1	0	0	0	0	–
1985 BAL A	0	1	.000	8.79	8	1	0	14.1	20	10	19	0	0	0	0	0	0	0	–
1986	3	3	.500	4.56	46	0	0	71	64	29	57	0	3	3	1	0	0	0	–
1987 LA N	0	0	–	4.33	31	1	0	35.1	30	23	23	0	0	0	1	2	0	0	.000
1988 2 teams		LA	N	(9G 0–0)	CLE	A	(28G 2–3)												
" total	2	3	.400	3.36	37	0	0	67	77	21	38	0	2	3	1	1	0	0	.000
7 yrs.	23	35	.397	4.80	185	60	6	554.2	578	225	349	2	5	8	3	3	0	0	.000

Andy Hawkins

HAWKINS, MELTON ANDREW
B. Jan. 21, 1960, Waco, Tex.   BR TR 6'3"   200 lbs.

	W	L	PCT	ERA	G	GS	CG	IP	H	BB	SO	ShO	W	L	SV	AB	H	HR	BA
1982 SD N	2	5	.286	4.10	15	10	1	63.2	66	27	25	0	0	0	0	15	0	0	.000
1983	5	7	.417	2.93	21	19	4	119.2	106	48	59	1	0	0	0	31	2	0	.065
1984	8	9	.471	4.68	36	22	2	146	143	72	77	1	2	1	0	41	8	0	.195
1985	18	8	.692	3.15	33	33	5	228.2	229	65	69	2	0	0	0	77	6	0	.078
1986	10	8	.556	4.30	37	35	3	209.1	218	75	117	1	1	0	0	67	10	0	.149
1987	3	10	.231	5.05	24	20	0	117.2	131	49	51	0	0	0	0	32	5	0	.156
1988	14	11	.560	3.35	33	33	4	217.2	196	76	91	2	0	0	0	62	7	0	.113
7 yrs.	60	58	.508	3.84	199	172	19	1102.2	1089	412	489	7	3	1	0	325	38	0	.117

LEAGUE CHAMPIONSHIP SERIES

	W	L	PCT	ERA	G	GS	CG	IP	H	BB	SO	ShO	W	L	SV	AB	H	HR	BA
1984 SD N	0	0	–	0.00	3	0	0	3.2	0	2	1	0	0	0	0	0	0	0	–

WORLD SERIES

	W	L	PCT	ERA	G	GS	CG	IP	H	BB	SO	ShO	W	L	SV	AB	H	HR	BA
1984 SD N	1	1	.500	0.75	3	0	0	12	4	6	4	0	1	1	0	0	0	0	–

Ray Hayward

HAYWARD, RAYMOND ALTON
B. Apr. 27, 1961, Enid, Okla.   BL TL 6'1"   190 lbs.

	W	L	PCT	ERA	G	GS	CG	IP	H	BB	SO	ShO	W	L	SV	AB	H	HR	BA
1986 SD N	0	2	.000	9.00	3	3	0	10	16	4	6	0	0	0	0	4	0	0	.000
1987	0	0	–	16.50	4	0	0	6	12	3	2	0	0	0	0	1	0	0	.000
1988 TEX A	4	6	.400	5.46	12	12	1	62.2	63	35	37	1	0	0	0	0	0	0	–
3 yrs.	4	8	.333	6.75	19	15	1	78.2	91	42	45	1	0	0	0	5	0	0	.000

Jeff Heathcock

HEATHCOCK, RONALD JEFFREY
B. Nov. 18, 1959, Covina, Calif.   BR TR 6'4"   195 lbs.

	W	L	PCT	ERA	G	GS	CG	IP	H	BB	SO	ShO	W	L	SV	AB	H	HR	BA
1983 HOU N	2	1	.667	3.21	6	3	0	28	19	4	12	0	1	0	1	6	0	0	.000
1985	3	1	.750	3.36	14	7	1	56.1	50	13	25	0	1	1	1	16	1	0	.063
1987	4	2	.667	3.16	19	2	0	42.2	44	9	15	0	3	1	1	10	0	0	.000
1988	0	5	.000	5.81	17	1	0	31	33	16	12	0	0	4	0	3	0	0	.000
4 yrs.	9	9	.500	3.76	56	13	1	158	146	42	64	0	5	6	3	35	1	0	.029

Neal Heaton

HEATON, NEAL
B. Mar. 3, 1960, Jamaica, N. Y.   BL TL 6'2"   195 lbs.

	W	L	PCT	ERA	G	GS	CG	IP	H	BB	SO	ShO	W	L	SV	AB	H	HR	BA
1982 CLE A	0	2	.000	5.23	8	4	0	31	32	16	14	0	0	0	0	0	0	0	–
1983	11	7	.611	4.16	39	16	4	149.1	157	44	75	3	4	2	7	0	0	0	–
1984	12	15	.444	5.21	38	34	4	198.2	231	75	75	1	0	1	0	0	0	0	–
1985	9	17	.346	4.90	36	33	5	207.2	244	80	82	1	0	1	0	0	0	0	–
1986 2 teams		CLE	A	(12G 3–6)	MIN	A	(21G 4–9)												
" total	7	15	.318	4.08	33	29	5	198.2	201	81	90	0	0	0	1	0	0	0	–
1987 MON N	13	10	.565	4.52	32	32	3	193.1	207	37	105	1	0	0	0	67	14	0	.209
1988	3	10	.231	4.99	32	11	0	97.1	98	43	43	0	1	4	2	21	3	0	.143
7 yrs.	55	76	.420	4.65	218	159	21	1076	1170	376	484	6	5	8	10	88	17	0	.193

Danny Heep

HEEP, DANIEL WILLIAM
B. July 3, 1957, San Antonio, Tex.   BL TL 5'11"   185 lbs.

	W	L	PCT	ERA	G	GS	CG	IP	H	BB	SO	ShO	W	L	SV	AB	H	HR	BA
1988 LA N	0	0	–	9.00	1	0	0	2	2	0	0	0	0	0	0	*			

Don Heinkel

HEINKEL, DONALD ELLIOTT
B. Oct. 20, 1959, Racine, Wis.   BL TR 6'   185 lbs.

	W	L	PCT	ERA	G	GS	CG	IP	H	BB	SO	ShO	W	L	SV	AB	H	HR	BA
1988 DET A	0	0	–	3.96	21	0	0	36.1	30	12	30	0	0	0	1	0	0	0	–

Tom Henke

HENKE, THOMAS ANTHONY (The Terminator)
B. Dec. 21, 1957, Kansas City, Mo.   BR TR 6'5"   215 lbs.

	W	L	PCT	ERA	G	GS	CG	IP	H	BB	SO	ShO	W	L	SV	AB	H	HR	BA
1982 TEX A	1	0	1.000	1.15	8	0	0	15.2	14	8	9	0	1	0	0	0	0	0	–
1983	1	0	1.000	3.38	8	0	0	16	16	4	17	0	1	0	1	0	0	0	–
1984	1	1	.500	6.35	25	0	0	28.1	36	20	25	0	1	1	2	0	0	0	–
1985 TOR A	3	3	.500	2.03	28	0	0	40	29	8	42	0	3	3	13	0	0	0	–
1986	9	5	.643	3.35	63	0	0	91.1	63	32	118	0	9	5	27	0	0	0	–
1987	0	6	.000	2.49	72	0	0	94	62	25	128	0	0	6	34	0	0	0	–
1988	4	4	.500	2.91	52	0	0	68	60	24	66	0	4	4	25	0	0	0	–
7 yrs.	19	19	.500	3.03	256	0	0	353.1	280	121	405	0	19	19	102	0	0	0	–

LEAGUE CHAMPIONSHIP SERIES

	W	L	PCT	ERA	G	GS	CG	IP	H	BB	SO	ShO	W	L	SV	AB	H	HR	BA
1985 TOR A	2	0	1.000	4.26	3	0	0	6.1	5	4	4	0	2	0	0	0	0	0	–

	W	L	PCT	ERA	G	GS	CG	IP	H	BB	SO	ShO	W	L	SV	AB	H	HR	BA

Mike Henneman

HENNEMAN, MICHAEL ALAN
B. Dec. 11, 1961, St. Charles, Mo.
BR TR 6'4" 205 lbs.

	W	L	PCT	ERA	G	GS	CG	IP	H	BB	SO	ShO	W	L	SV	AB	H	HR	BA
1987 DET A	11	3	.786	2.98	55	0	0	96.2	86	30	75	0	11	3	7	1	0	0	.000
1988	9	6	.600	1.87	65	0	0	91.1	72	24	58	0	9	6	22	0	0	0	–
2 yrs.	20	9	.690	2.44	120	0	0	188	158	54	133	0	20	9	29	1	0	0	.000
LEAGUE CHAMPIONSHIP SERIES																			
1987 DET A	1	0	1.000	10.80	3	0	0	5	6	6	3	0	1	0	0	0	0	0	–

Dwayne Henry

HENRY, DWAYNE ALLEN
B. Feb. 16, 1962, Elkton, Md.
BR TR 6'3" 210 lbs.

	W	L	PCT	ERA	G	GS	CG	IP	H	BB	SO	ShO	W	L	SV	AB	H	HR	BA
1984 TEX A	0	1	.000	8.31	3	0	0	4.1	5	7	2	0	0	1	0	0	0	0	–
1985	2	2	.500	2.57	16	0	0	21	16	7	20	0	2	2	3	0	0	0	–
1986	1	0	1.000	4.66	19	0	0	19.1	14	22	17	0	1	0	0	0	0	0	–
1987	0	0	–	9.00	5	0	0	10	12	9	7	0	0	0	0	0	0	0	–
1988	0	1	.000	8.71	11	0	0	10.1	15	9	10	0	0	1	1	0	0	0	–
5 yrs.	3	4	.429	5.54	54	0	0	65	62	54	56	0	3	4	4	0	0	0	–

Guillermo Hernandez

HERNANDEZ, GUILLERMO VILLANUEVA (Willie)
Born Guillermo Hernandez y Villanueva.
B. Nov. 14, 1954, Aguada, Puerto Rico
BL TL 6'3" 180 lbs.

	W	L	PCT	ERA	G	GS	CG	IP	H	BB	SO	ShO	W	L	SV	AB	H	HR	BA
1977 CHI N	8	7	.533	3.03	67	1	0	110	94	28	78	0	8	6	4	16	1	0	.063
1978	8	2	.800	3.75	54	0	0	60	57	35	38	0	8	2	3	1	0	0	.000
1979	4	4	.500	5.01	51	2	0	79	85	39	53	0	4	3	0	8	2	0	.250
1980	1	9	.100	4.42	53	7	0	108	115	45	75	0	1	3	0	19	4	0	.211
1981	0	0	–	3.86	12	0	0	14	14	8	13	0	0	0	2	0	0	0	–
1982	4	6	.400	3.00	75	0	0	75	74	24	54	0	4	6	10	3	0	0	.000
1983 2 teams			CHI N (11G 1–0)					PHI N (63G 8–4)											
" total	9	4	.692	3.28	74	1	0	115.1	109	32	93	0	9	4	8	15	6	0	.400
1984 DET A	9	3	.750	1.92	80	0	0	140.1	96	36	112	0	9	3	32	0	0	0	–
1985	8	10	.444	2.70	74	0	0	106.2	82	14	76	0	8	10	31	1	0	0	.000
1986	8	7	.533	3.55	64	0	0	88.2	87	21	77	0	8	7	24	0	0	0	–
1987	3	4	.429	3.67	45	0	0	49	53	20	30	0	3	4	8	0	0	0	–
1988	6	5	.545	3.06	63	0	0	67.2	50	31	59	0	6	5	10	0	0	0	–
12 yrs.	68	61	.527	3.30	712	11	0	1013.2	916	333	758	0	68	53	132	63	13	0	.206
LEAGUE CHAMPIONSHIP SERIES																			
1984 DET A	0	0	–	2.25	3	0	0	4	3	1	3	0	0	0	1	0	0	0	–
1987	0	0	–	0.00	1	0	0	.1	2	0	0	0	0	0	0	0	0	0	–
2 yrs.	0	0	–	2.08	4	0	0	4.1	5	1	3	0	0	0	1	0	0	0	–
WORLD SERIES																			
1983 PHI N	0	0	–	0.00	3	0	0	4	0	1	4	0	0	0	0	0	0	0	–
1984 DET A	0	0	–	1.69	3	0	0	5.1	4	0	0	0	0	0	2	0	0	0	–
2 yrs.	0	0	–	0.96	6	0	0	9.1	4	1	4	0	0	0	2	0	0	0	–

Orel Hershiser

HERSHISER, OREL LEONARD QUINTON (Bulldog)
B. Sept. 16, 1958, Buffalo, N. Y.
BR TR 6'3" 190 lbs.

	W	L	PCT	ERA	G	GS	CG	IP	H	BB	SO	ShO	W	L	SV	AB	H	HR	BA
1983 LA N	0	0	–	3.38	8	0	0	8	7	6	5	0	0	0	1	0	0	0	–
1984	11	8	.579	2.66	45	20	8	189.2	160	50	150	4	3	0	2	50	10	0	.200
1985	19	3	.864	2.03	36	34	9	239.2	179	68	157	5	1	0	0	76	15	0	.197
1986	14	14	.500	3.85	35	35	8	231.1	213	86	153	1	0	0	0	71	17	0	.239
1987	16	16	.500	3.06	37	35	10	264.2	247	74	190	1	0	1	1	90	19	0	.211
1988	23	8	.742	2.26	35	34	15	267	208	73	178	8	0	0	1	85	11	0	.129
6 yrs.	83	49	.629	2.77	196	158	50	1200.1	1014	357	833	19	4	1	5	372	72	0	.194
LEAGUE CHAMPIONSHIP SERIES																			
1985 LA N	1	0	1.000	3.52	2	2	1	15.1	17	6	5	0	0	0	0	7	2	0	.286
1988	1	0	1.000	1.09	4	3	1	24.2	18	7	15	1	0	0	1	9	0	0	.000
2 yrs.	2	0	1.000	2.03	6	5	2	40	35	13	20	1	0	0	1	16	2	0	.125
WORLD SERIES																			
1988 LA N	2	0	1.000	1.00	2	2	2	18	7	6	17	1	0	0	0	3	3	0	1.000

Joe Hesketh

HESKETH, JOSEPH THOMAS
B. Feb. 15, 1959, Lackawanna, N. Y.
BL TL 6'2" 165 lbs.

	W	L	PCT	ERA	G	GS	CG	IP	H	BB	SO	ShO	W	L	SV	AB	H	HR	BA
1984 MON N	2	2	.500	1.80	11	5	1	45	38	15	32	1	0	1	1	10	1	0	.100
1985	10	5	.667	2.49	25	25	2	155.1	125	45	113	1	0	0	0	44	4	0	.091
1986	6	5	.545	5.01	15	15	0	82.2	92	31	67	0	0	0	0	23	0	0	.000
1987	0	0	–	3.14	18	0	0	28.2	23	15	31	0	0	0	1	4	0	0	.000
1988	4	3	.571	2.85	60	0	0	72.2	63	35	64	0	4	3	9	2	0	0	.000
5 yrs.	22	15	.595	3.07	129	45	3	384.1	341	141	307	2	4	4	11	83	5	0	.060

Ted Higuera

HIGUERA, TEODORO VALENZUELA
Born Teodoro Valenzuela Higuera y Valenzuela.
B. Nov. 9, 1958, Los Mochis, Mexico
BB TL 5'10" 180 lbs.

	W	L	PCT	ERA	G	GS	CG	IP	H	BB	SO	ShO	W	L	SV	AB	H	HR	BA
1985 MIL A	15	8	.652	3.90	32	30	7	212.1	186	63	127	2	0	0	0	0	0	0	–
1986	20	11	.645	2.79	34	34	15	248.1	226	74	207	4	0	0	0	0	0	0	–
1987	18	10	.643	3.85	35	35	14	261.2	236	87	240	3	0	0	0	0	0	0	–
1988	16	9	.640	2.45	31	31	8	227.1	168	59	192	1	0	0	0	0	0	0	–
4 yrs.	69	38	.645	3.25	132	130	44	949.2	816	283	766	10	0	0	0	0	0	0	–

Ken Hill

HILL, KENNETH WADE
B. Dec. 14, 1965, Lynn, Mass.
BR TR 6'2" 175 lbs.

	W	L	PCT	ERA	G	GS	CG	IP	H	BB	SO	ShO	W	L	SV	AB	H	HR	BA
1988 STL N	0	1	.000	5.14	4	1	0	14	16	6	6	0	0	0	0	3	0	0	.000

Shawn Hillegas

HILLEGAS, SHAWN PATRICK
B. Aug. 21, 1964, Dos Palos, Calif.
BR TR 6'3" 205 lbs.

	W	L	PCT	ERA	G	GS	CG	IP	H	BB	SO	ShO	W	L	SV	AB	H	HR	BA
1987 LA N	4	3	.571	3.57	12	10	0	58	52	31	51	0	0	0	0	14	0	0	.000

	W	L	PCT	ERA	G	GS	CG	IP	H	BB	SO	ShO	Relief Pitching W	L	SV	BATTING AB	H	HR	BA

Shawn Hillegas continued

1988 2 teams	LA	N	(11G 3–4)		CHI	A	(6G 3–2)												
" total	6	6	.500	3.72	17	16	0	96.2	84	35	56	0	0	0	0	15	2	0	.133
2 yrs.	10	9	.526	3.67	29	26	0	154.2	136	66	107	0	0	0	0	29	2	0	.069

Guy Hoffman

HOFFMAN, GUY ALAN   BL   TL   5'9"   175 lbs.
B. July 9, 1956, Ottawa, Ill.

	W	L	PCT	ERA	G	GS	CG	IP	H	BB	SO	ShO	W	L	SV	AB	H	HR	BA
1979 CHI A	0	5	.000	5.40	24	0	0	30	30	23	18	0	0	5	2	0	0	0	–
1980	1	0	1.000	2.61	23	1	0	38	38	17	24	0	1	0	1	0	0	0	–
1983	1	0	1.000	7.50	11	0	0	6	14	2	2	0	1	0	0	0	0	0	–
1986 CHI N	6	2	.750	3.86	32	8	1	84	92	29	47	0	4	0	0	15	1	0	.067
1987 CIN N	9	10	.474	4.37	36	22	0	158.2	160	49	87	0	3	0	0	45	5	0	.111
1988 TEX A	0	0	–	5.24	11	0	0	22.1	22	8	9	0	0	0	0	0	0	0	–
6 yrs.	17	17	.500	4.25	137	31	1	339	356	128	187	0	9	5	3	60	6	0	.100

Brian Holman

HOLMAN, BRIAN SCOTT   BR   TR   6'4"   185 lbs.
B. Jan. 25, 1965, Denver, Colo.

	W	L	PCT	ERA	G	GS	CG	IP	H	BB	SO	ShO	W	L	SV	AB	H	HR	BA
1988 MON N	4	8	.333	3.23	18	16	1	100.1	101	34	58	1	0	0	0	28	3	0	.107

Brian Holton

HOLTON, BRIAN JOHN   BR   TR   6'3"   190 lbs.
B. Nov. 29, 1959, McKeesport, Pa.

	W	L	PCT	ERA	G	GS	CG	IP	H	BB	SO	ShO	W	L	SV	AB	H	HR	BA
1985 LA N	1	1	.500	9.00	3	0	0	4	9	1	1	0	1	1	0	0	0	0	–
1986	2	3	.400	4.44	12	3	0	24.1	28	6	24	0	2	1	0	5	0	0	.000
1987	3	2	.600	3.89	53	1	0	83.1	87	32	58	0	3	2	2	5	1	0	.200
1988	7	3	.700	1.70	45	0	0	84.2	69	26	49	0	7	3	1	10	0	0	.000
4 yrs.	13	9	.591	3.12	113	4	0	196.1	193	65	132	0	13	7	3	20	1	0	.050

LEAGUE CHAMPIONSHIP SERIES

	W	L	PCT	ERA	G	GS	CG	IP	H	BB	SO	ShO	W	L	SV	AB	H	HR	BA
1988 LA N	0	0	–	2.25	3	0	0	4	2	1	2	0	0	0	1	1	1	0	1.000

WORLD SERIES

	W	L	PCT	ERA	G	GS	CG	IP	H	BB	SO	ShO	W	L	SV	AB	H	HR	BA
1988 LA N	0	0	–	0.00	1	0	0	2	0	1	0	0	0	0	0	0	0	0	–

Rick Honeycutt

HONEYCUTT, FREDERICK WAYNE   BL   TL   6'1"   185 lbs.
B. June 29, 1952, Chattanooga, Tenn.

	W	L	PCT	ERA	G	GS	CG	IP	H	BB	SO	ShO	W	L	SV	AB	H	HR	BA
1977 SEA A	0	1	.000	4.34	10	3	0	29	26	11	17	0	0	0	0	0	0	0	–
1978	5	11	.313	4.89	26	24	4	134.1	150	49	50	1	0	0	0	0	0	0	–
1979	11	12	.478	4.04	33	28	8	194	201	67	83	1	1	3	0	0	0	0	–
1980	10	17	.370	3.95	30	30	9	203	221	60	79	1	0	0	0	0	0	0	–
1981 TEX A	11	6	.647	3.30	20	20	8	128	120	17	40	2	0	0	0	0	0	0	–
1982	5	17	.227	5.27	30	26	4	164	201	54	64	1	0	0	0	0	0	0	–
1983 2 teams	TEX	A	(25G 14–8)		LA	N	(9G 2–3)												
" total	16	11	.593	3.03	34	32	6	213.2	214	50	74	2	0	0	0	12	1	0	.083
1984 LA N	10	9	.526	2.84	29	28	6	183.2	180	51	75	2	0	0	0	56	8	0	.143
1985	8	12	.400	3.42	31	25	1	142	141	49	67	0	0	1	1	38	5	0	.132
1986	11	9	.550	3.32	32	28	0	171	164	45	100	0	1	0	0	43	3	0	.070
1987 2 teams	LA	N	(27G 2–12)		OAK	A	(7G 1–4)												
" total	3	16	.158	4.72	34	24	1	139.1	158	54	102	1	0	1	0	30	7	0	.233
1988 OAK A	3	2	.600	3.50	55	0	0	79.2	74	25	47	0	3	2	7	0	0	0	–
12 yrs.	93	123	.431	3.82	364	268	47	1781.2	1850	532	798	11	5	7	8	179	24	0	.134

LEAGUE CHAMPIONSHIP SERIES

	W	L	PCT	ERA	G	GS	CG	IP	H	BB	SO	ShO	W	L	SV	AB	H	HR	BA
1983 LA N	0	0	–	21.60	2	0	0	1.2	4	0	2	0	0	0	0	0	0	0	–
1985	0	0	–	13.50	2	0	0	1.1	4	2	1	0	0	0	0	0	0	0	–
1988 OAK A	1	0	1.000	0.00	3	0	0	2	0	2	0	0	1	0	0	0	0	0	–
3 yrs.	1	0	1.000	10.80	7	0	0	5	8	4	3	0	1	0	0	0	0	0	–

WORLD SERIES

	W	L	PCT	ERA	G	GS	CG	IP	H	BB	SO	ShO	W	L	SV	AB	H	HR	BA
1988 OAK A	1	0	1.000	0.00	3	0	0	3.1	0	0	5	0	1	0	0	0	0	0	–

Ricky Horton

HORTON, RICKY NEAL   BL   TL   6'2"   197 lbs.
B. July 30, 1959, Poughkeepsie, N. Y.

	W	L	PCT	ERA	G	GS	CG	IP	H	BB	SO	ShO	W	L	SV	AB	H	HR	BA
1984 STL N	9	4	.692	3.44	37	18	1	125.2	140	39	76	1	1	0	1	31	2	0	.065
1985	3	2	.600	2.91	49	3	0	89.2	84	34	59	0	2	2	1	16	1	0	.063
1986	4	3	.571	2.24	42	9	1	100.1	77	26	49	0	1	0	3	18	1	0	.056
1987	8	3	.727	3.82	67	6	0	125	127	42	55	0	6	2	7	29	5	0	.172
1988 2 teams	CHI	A	(52G 6–10)		LA	N	(12G 1–1)												
" total	7	11	.389	4.87	64	9	1	118.1	131	38	36	0	4	5	2	0	0	0	–
5 yrs.	31	23	.574	3.53	259	45	3	559	559	179	275	1	14	9	14	94	9	0	.096

LEAGUE CHAMPIONSHIP SERIES

	W	L	PCT	ERA	G	GS	CG	IP	H	BB	SO	ShO	W	L	SV	AB	H	HR	BA
1985 STL N	0	0	–	9.00	3	0	0	3	4	2	1	0	0	0	0	0	0	0	–
1987	0	0	–	0.00	1	0	0	3	2	0	2	0	0	0	0	0	0	0	–
1988 LA N	0	0	–	0.00	4	0	0	4.1	4	2	3	0	0	0	0	0	0	0	–
3 yrs.	0	0	–	2.61	8	0	0	10.1	10	4	6	0	0	0	0	0	0	0	–

WORLD SERIES

	W	L	PCT	ERA	G	GS	CG	IP	H	BB	SO	ShO	W	L	SV	AB	H	HR	BA
1985 STL N	0	0	–	6.75	3	0	0	4	4	5	5	0	0	0	0	1	0	0	.000
1987	0	0	–	6.00	2	0	0	3	5	0	1	0	0	0	0	0	0	0	–
2 yrs.	0	0	–	6.43	5	0	0	7	9	5	6	0	0	0	0	1	0	0	.000

Charlie Hough

HOUGH, CHARLES OLIVER   BR   TR   6'2"   190 lbs.
B. Jan. 5, 1948, Honolulu, Hawaii

	W	L	PCT	ERA	G	GS	CG	IP	H	BB	SO	ShO	W	L	SV	AB	H	HR	BA
1970 LA N	0	0	–	5.29	8	0	0	17	18	11	8	0	0	0	2	3	1	0	.333
1971	0	0	–	4.50	4	0	0	4	3	3	4	0	0	0	0	0	0	0	–
1972	0	0	–	3.38	2	0	0	2.2	2	2	4	0	0	0	0	0	0	0	–
1973	4	2	.667	2.76	37	0	0	71.2	52	45	70	0	4	2	5	14	3	0	.214
1974	9	4	.692	3.75	49	0	0	96	65	40	63	0	9	4	1	12	0	0	.000
1975	3	7	.300	2.95	38	0	0	61	43	34	34	0	3	7	4	6	2	0	.333
1976	12	8	.600	2.21	77	0	0	142.2	102	77	81	0	12	8	18	21	6	0	.286
1977	6	12	.333	3.33	70	1	0	127	98	70	105	0	5	12	22	22	4	1	.182

	W	L	PCT	ERA	G	GS	CG	IP	H	BB	SO	ShO	Relief Pitching W	L	SV	BATTING AB	H	HR	BA

Charlie Hough continued

	W	L	PCT	ERA	G	GS	CG	IP	H	BB	SO	ShO	W	L	SV	AB	H	HR	BA
1978	5	5	.500	3.29	55	0	0	93	69	48	66	0	5	5	7	12	4	0	.333
1979	7	5	.583	4.77	42	14	0	151	152	66	76	0	1	2	0	38	6	0	.158
1980 2 teams			LA	N	(19G 1–3)		TEX	A	(16G 2–2)										
" total	3	5	.375	4.55	35	3	2	93	91	58	72	1	2	3	1	2	1	0	.500
1981 TEX A	4	1	.800	2.96	21	5	2	82	61	31	69	0	0	0	1	0	0	0	—
1982	16	13	.552	3.95	34	34	12	228	217	72	128	2	0	0	0	0	0	0	—
1983	15	13	.536	3.18	34	33	11	252	219	95	152	3	1	0	0	0	0	0	—
1984	16	14	.533	3.76	36	**36**	17	266	**260**	94	165	1	0	0	0	0	0	0	—
1985	14	16	.467	3.31	34	34	14	250.1	198	83	141	1	0	0	0	0	0	0	—
1986	17	10	.630	3.79	33	33	7	230.1	188	89	146	2	0	0	0	0	0	0	—
1987	18	13	.581	3.79	40	**40**	13	**285.1**	238	124	223	0	0	0	0	0	0	0	—
1988	15	16	.484	3.32	34	34	10	252	202	**126**	174	0	0	0	0	0	0	0	—
19 yrs.	164	144	.532	3.55	683	267	88	2705	2278	1168	1781	10	42	43	61	130	27	1	.208

LEAGUE CHAMPIONSHIP SERIES

	W	L	PCT	ERA	G	GS	CG	IP	H	BB	SO	ShO	W	L	SV	AB	H	HR	BA
1974 LA N	0	0	—	7.71	1	0	0	2.1	4	0	2	0	0	0	0	0	0	0	—
1977	0	0	—	4.50	1	0	0	2	2	0	3	0	0	0	0	0	0	0	—
1978	0	0	—	4.50	1	0	0	2	1	0	1	0	0	0	0	0	0	0	—
3 yrs.	0	0	—	5.68	3	0	0	6.1	7	0	6	0	0	0	0	0	0	0	—

WORLD SERIES

	W	L	PCT	ERA	G	GS	CG	IP	H	BB	SO	ShO	W	L	SV	AB	H	HR	BA
1974 LA N	0	0	—	0.00	1	0	0	2	0	1	4	0	0	0	0	0	0	0	—
1977	0	0	—	1.80	2	0	0	5	3	0	5	0	0	0	0	0	0	0	—
1978	0	0	—	8.44	2	0	0	5.1	10	2	5	0	0	0	0	0	0	0	—
3 yrs.	0	0	—	4.38	5	0	0	12.1	13	3	14	0	0	0	0	0	0	0	—

Jay Howell

HOWELL, JAY CANFIELD
B. Nov. 26, 1955, Miami, Fla.   BR TR 6'3"   200 lbs.

	W	L	PCT	ERA	G	GS	CG	IP	H	BB	SO	ShO	W	L	SV	AB	H	HR	BA
1980 CIN N	0	0	—	15.00	5	0	0	3	8	0	1	0	0	0	0	0	0	0	—
1981 CHI N	2	0	1.000	4.91	10	2	0	22	23	10	10	0	0	0	0	2	0	0	.000
1982 NY A	2	3	.400	7.71	6	6	0	28	42	13	21	0	0	0	0	0	0	0	—
1983	1	5	.167	5.38	19	12	2	82	89	35	61	0	0	0	0	0	0	0	—
1984	9	4	.692	2.69	61	1	0	103.2	86	34	109	0	8	4	7	0	0	0	—
1985 OAK A	9	8	.529	2.85	63	0	0	98	98	31	68	0	9	8	29	0	0	0	—
1986	3	6	.333	3.38	38	0	0	53.1	53	23	42	0	3	6	16	0	0	0	—
1987	3	4	.429	5.89	36	0	0	44.1	48	21	35	0	3	4	16	0	0	0	—
1988 LA N	5	3	.625	2.08	50	0	0	65	44	21	70	0	5	3	21	2	0	0	.000
9 yrs.	34	33	.507	3.89	288	21	2	499.1	491	188	417	0	28	25	89	4	0	0	.000

LEAGUE CHAMPIONSHIP SERIES

	W	L	PCT	ERA	G	GS	CG	IP	H	BB	SO	ShO	W	L	SV	AB	H	HR	BA
1988 LA N	0	1	.000	27.00	2	0	0	.2	1	2	1	0	0	1	0	0	0	0	—

WORLD SERIES

	W	L	PCT	ERA	G	GS	CG	IP	H	BB	SO	ShO	W	L	SV	AB	H	HR	BA
1988 LA N	0	1	.000	3.38	2	0	0	2.2	3	1	2	0	0	1	1	0	0	0	—

Ken Howell

HOWELL, KENNETH
B. Nov. 28, 1960, Detroit, Mich.   BR TR 6'3"   195 lbs.

	W	L	PCT	ERA	G	GS	CG	IP	H	BB	SO	ShO	W	L	SV	AB	H	HR	BA
1984 LA N	5	5	.500	3.33	32	1	0	51.1	51	9	54	0	5	5	6	5	0	0	.000
1985	4	7	.364	3.77	56	0	0	86	66	35	85	0	4	7	12	4	0	0	.000
1986	6	12	.333	3.87	62	0	0	97.2	86	63	104	0	6	12	12	5	0	0	.000
1987	3	4	.429	4.91	40	2	0	55	54	29	60	0	2	3	1	4	1	0	.250
1988	0	1	.000	6.39	4	1	0	12.2	16	4	12	0	0	0	0	1	0	0	.000
5 yrs.	18	29	.383	4.04	194	4	0	302.2	273	140	315	0	17	27	31	19	1	0	.053

LEAGUE CHAMPIONSHIP SERIES

	W	L	PCT	ERA	G	GS	CG	IP	H	BB	SO	ShO	W	L	SV	AB	H	HR	BA
1985 LA N	0	0	—	0.00	1	0	0	2	0	0	2	0	0	0	0	0	0	0	—

Charles Hudson

HUDSON, CHARLES LYNN
B. Mar. 16, 1959, Ennis, Tex.   BB TR 6'3"   185 lbs.

	W	L	PCT	ERA	G	GS	CG	IP	H	BB	SO	ShO	W	L	SV	AB	H	HR	BA
1983 PHI N	8	8	.500	3.35	26	26	3	169.1	158	53	101	0	0	0	0	54	5	0	.093
1984	9	11	.450	4.04	30	30	1	173.2	181	52	94	1	0	0	0	56	5	0	.089
1985	8	13	.381	3.78	38	26	3	193	188	74	122	0	0	2	0	57	8	0	.140
1986	7	10	.412	4.94	33	23	0	144	165	58	82	0	1	0	0	43	2	0	.047
1987 NY A	11	7	.611	3.61	35	16	6	154.2	137	57	100	2	5	2	0	0	0	0	—
1988	6	6	.500	4.49	28	12	1	106.1	93	36	58	0	2	2	2	0	0	0	—
6 yrs.	49	55	.471	3.98	190	133	14	941	922	330	557	3	8	6	2	210	20	0	.095

LEAGUE CHAMPIONSHIP SERIES

	W	L	PCT	ERA	G	GS	CG	IP	H	BB	SO	ShO	W	L	SV	AB	H	HR	BA
1983 PHI N	1	0	1.000	2.00	1	1	1	9	4	2	9	0	0	0	0	4	0	0	.000

WORLD SERIES

	W	L	PCT	ERA	G	GS	CG	IP	H	BB	SO	ShO	W	L	SV	AB	H	HR	BA
1983 PHI N	0	2	.000	8.64	2	2	0	8.1	9	1	6	0	0	0	0	2	0	0	.000

Mark Huismann

HUISMANN, MARK LAWRENCE
B. May 11, 1958, Lincoln, Neb.   BR TR 6'3"   195 lbs.

	W	L	PCT	ERA	G	GS	CG	IP	H	BB	SO	ShO	W	L	SV	AB	H	HR	BA
1983 KC A	2	1	.667	5.58	13	0	0	30.2	29	17	20	0	2	1	0	0	0	0	—
1984	3	3	.500	4.08	38	0	0	75	83	21	54	0	3	3	3	0	0	0	—
1985	1	0	1.000	1.93	9	0	0	18.2	14	3	9	0	1	0	0	0	0	0	—
1986 2 teams			KC	A	(10G 0–1)		SEA	A	(36G 3–3)										
" total	3	4	.429	3.79	46	1	0	97.1	98	25	72	0	3	3	5	0	0	0	—
1987 2 teams			SEA	A	(6G 0–0)		CLE	A	(20G 2–3)										
" total	2	3	.400	5.04	26	0	0	50	48	12	38	0	2	3	2	0	0	0	—
1988 DET A	1	0	1.000	5.06	5	0	0	5.1	6	2	6	0	1	0	0	0	0	0	—
6 yrs.	12	11	.522	4.19	137	1	0	277	278	80	199	0	12	10	10	0	0	0	—

LEAGUE CHAMPIONSHIP SERIES

	W	L	PCT	ERA	G	GS	CG	IP	H	BB	SO	ShO	W	L	SV	AB	H	HR	BA
1984 KC A	0	0	—	10.13	1	0	0	2.2	6	1	2	0	0	0	0	0	0	0	—

	W	L	PCT	ERA	G	GS	CG	IP	H	BB	SO	ShO	W	L	SV	AB	H	HR	BA
													Relief Pitching			**BATTING**			

Bruce Hurst

HURST, BRUCE VEE
B. Mar. 24, 1958, St. George, Utah

BL TL 6'4"   200 lbs.

	W	L	PCT	ERA	G	GS	CG	IP	H	BB	SO	ShO	W	L	SV	AB	H	HR	BA
1980 BOS A	2	2	.500	9.00	12	7	0	31	39	16	16	0	0	0	0	0	0	0	–
1981	2	0	1.000	4.30	5	5	0	23	23	12	11	0	0	0	0	0	0	0	–
1982	3	7	.300	5.77	28	19	0	117	161	40	53	0	0	1	0	0	0	0	–
1983	12	12	.500	4.09	33	32	6	211.1	241	62	115	2	0	0	0	0	0	0	–
1984	12	12	.500	3.92	33	33	9	218	232	88	136	2	0	0	0	0	0	0	–
1985	11	13	.458	4.51	35	31	6	229.1	243	70	189	1	0	2	0	0	0	0	–
1986	13	8	.619	2.99	25	25	11	174.1	169	50	167	4	0	0	0	0	0	0	–
1987	15	13	.536	4.41	33	33	15	238.2	239	76	190	3	0	0	0	0	0	0	–
1988	18	6	.750	3.66	33	32	7	216.2	222	65	166	1	0	0	0	0	0	0	–
9 yrs.	88	73	.547	4.23	237	217	54	1459.1	1569	479	1043	13	0	3	0	0	0	0	–

LEAGUE CHAMPIONSHIP SERIES

	W	L	PCT	ERA	G	GS	CG	IP	H	BB	SO	ShO	W	L	SV	AB	H	HR	BA
1986 BOS A	1	0	1.000	2.40	2	2	1	15	18	1	8	0	0	0	0	0	0	0	–
1988	0	2	.000	2.77	2	2	1	13	10	5	12	0	0	0	0	0	0	0	–
2 yrs.	1	2	.333	2.57	4	4	2	28	28	6	20	0	0	0	0	0	0	0	–

WORLD SERIES

	W	L	PCT	ERA	G	GS	CG	IP	H	BB	SO	ShO	W	L	SV	AB	H	HR	BA
1986 BOS A	2	0	1.000	1.96	3	3	1	23	18	6	17	0	0	0	0	3	0	0	.000

Jeff Innis

INNIS, JEFFREY DAVID
B. July 5, 1962, Decatur, Ill.

BR TR 6'1"   170 lbs.

	W	L	PCT	ERA	G	GS	CG	IP	H	BB	SO	ShO	W	L	SV	AB	H	HR	BA
1987 NY N	0	1	.000	3.16	17	1	0	25.2	29	4	28	0	0	1	0	3	0	0	.000
1988	1	1	.500	1.89	12	0	0	19	19	2	14	0	1	1	0	0	0	0	–
2 yrs.	1	2	.333	2.62	29	1	0	44.2	48	6	42	0	1	2	0	3	0	0	.000

Danny Jackson

JACKSON, DANNY LYNN
B. Jan. 5, 1962, San Antonio, Tex.

BR TL 6'   190 lbs.

	W	L	PCT	ERA	G	GS	CG	IP	H	BB	SO	ShO	W	L	SV	AB	H	HR	BA
1983 KC A	1	1	.500	5.21	4	3	0	19	26	6	9	0	1	0	0	0	0	0	–
1984	2	6	.250	4.26	15	11	1	76	84	35	40	0	1	0	0	0	0	0	–
1985	14	12	.538	3.42	32	32	4	208	209	76	114	3	0	0	0	0	0	0	–
1986	11	12	.478	3.20	32	27	4	185.2	177	79	115	1	0	0	1	0	0	0	–
1987	9	18	.333	4.02	36	34	11	224	219	109	152	2	0	0	0	0	0	0	–
1988 CIN N	23	8	.742	2.73	35	35	15	260.2	206	71	161	6	0	0	0	90	13	0	.144
6 yrs.	60	57	.513	3.43	154	142	35	973.1	921	376	591	12	2	0	1	90	13	0	.144

LEAGUE CHAMPIONSHIP SERIES

	W	L	PCT	ERA	G	GS	CG	IP	H	BB	SO	ShO	W	L	SV	AB	H	HR	BA
1985 KC A	1	0	1.000	0.00	2	1	1	10	10	1	7	1	0	0	0	0	0	0	–

WORLD SERIES

	W	L	PCT	ERA	G	GS	CG	IP	H	BB	SO	ShO	W	L	SV	AB	H	HR	BA
1985 KC A	1	1	.500	1.69	2	2	1	16	9	5	12	0	0	0	0	6	0	0	.000

Mike Jackson

JACKSON, MICHAEL RAY
B. Dec. 22, 1964, Houston, Tex.

BR TR 6'1"   185 lbs.

	W	L	PCT	ERA	G	GS	CG	IP	H	BB	SO	ShO	W	L	SV	AB	H	HR	BA
1986 PHI N	0	0	–	3.38	9	0	0	13.1	12	4	3	0	0	0	0	0	0	0	–
1987	3	10	.231	4.20	55	7	0	109.1	88	56	93	0	2	6	1	17	2	0	.118
1988 SEA A	6	5	.545	2.63	62	0	0	99.1	74	43	76	0	6	5	4	0	0	0	–
3 yrs.	9	15	.375	3.45	126	7	0	222	174	103	172	0	8	11	5	17	2	0	.118

Mike Jeffcoat

JEFFCOAT, JAMES MICHAEL
B. Aug. 3, 1959, Pine Bluff, Ark.

BL TL 6'2"   185 lbs.

	W	L	PCT	ERA	G	GS	CG	IP	H	BB	SO	ShO	W	L	SV	AB	H	HR	BA
1983 CLE A	1	3	.250	3.31	11	2	0	32.2	32	13	9	0	1	1	0	0	0	0	–
1984	5	2	.714	2.99	63	1	0	75.1	82	24	41	0	4	2	1	0	0	0	–
1985 2 teams			CLE	A	(9G	0-0)		SF	N	(19G	0-2)								
" total	0	2	.000	4.55	28	1	0	31.2	35	12	14	0	0	2	0	1	0	0	.000
1987 TEX A	0	1	.000	12.86	2	2	0	7	11	4	1	0	0	0	0	0	0	0	–
1988	0	2	.000	11.70	5	2	0	10	19	5	5	0	0	0	0	0	0	0	–
5 yrs.	6	10	.375	4.37	109	8	0	156.2	179	58	70	0	5	5	1	1	0	0	.000

German Jimenez

JIMENEZ, GERMAN
Born German Jimenez y Camarena.
B. Dec. 5, 1962, Santiago, Mexico

BL TL 5'10"   200 lbs.

	W	L	PCT	ERA	G	GS	CG	IP	H	BB	SO	ShO	W	L	SV	AB	H	HR	BA
1988 ATL N	1	6	.143	5.01	15	9	0	55.2	65	12	26	0	0	1	0	17	1	0	.059

Tommy John

JOHN, THOMAS EDWARD (T. J.)
B. May 22, 1943, Terre Haute, Ind.

BR TL 6'3"   180 lbs.

	W	L	PCT	ERA	G	GS	CG	IP	H	BB	SO	ShO	W	L	SV	AB	H	HR	BA
1963 CLE A	0	2	.000	2.21	6	3	0	20.1	23	6	9	0	0	0	0	6	0	0	.000
1964	2	9	.182	3.91	25	14	2	94.1	97	35	65	1	0	0	0	24	5	0	.208
1965 CHI A	14	7	.667	3.09	39	27	6	183.2	162	58	126	1	1	1	3	59	10	1	.169
1966	14	11	.560	2.62	34	33	10	223	195	57	138	5	0	0	0	69	10	2	.145
1967	10	13	.435	2.47	31	29	9	178.1	143	47	110	6	0	1	0	51	8	0	.157
1968	10	5	.667	1.98	25	25	5	177.1	135	49	117	1	0	0	0	62	12	1	.194
1969	9	11	.450	3.25	33	33	6	232.1	230	90	128	2	0	0	0	79	9	0	.114
1970	12	17	.414	3.28	37	37	10	269	253	101	138	3	0	0	0	84	17	0	.202
1971	13	16	.448	3.62	38	35	10	229	244	58	131	3	0	0	0	69	10	0	.145
1972 LA N	11	5	.688	2.89	29	29	4	186.2	172	40	117	1	0	0	0	63	10	0	.159
1973	16	7	.696	3.10	36	31	4	218	202	50	116	2	0	0	0	74	15	0	.203
1974	13	3	.813	2.59	22	22	5	153	133	42	78	3	0	0	0	51	6	0	.118
1976	10	10	.500	3.09	31	31	6	207	207	61	91	2	0	0	0	64	7	0	.109
1977	20	7	.741	2.78	31	31	11	220	225	50	123	3	0	0	0	79	14	1	.177
1978	17	10	.630	3.30	33	30	7	213	230	53	124	0	1	0	1	66	8	0	.121
1979 NY A	21	9	.700	2.97	37	36	17	276	268	65	111	3	1	0	0	0	0	0	–
1980	22	9	.710	3.43	36	36	16	265	270	56	78	6	0	0	0	0	0	0	–
1981	9	8	.529	2.64	20	20	7	140	135	39	50	0	0	0	0	0	0	0	–
1982 2 teams			NY	A	(30G	10-10)		CAL	A	(7G	4-2)								
" total	14	12	.538	3.69	37	33	10	221.2	239	39	68	2	0	0	0	0	0	0	–
1983 CAL A	11	13	.458	4.33	34	34	9	234.2	287	49	65	0	0	0	0	0	0	0	–
1984	7	13	.350	4.52	32	29	4	181.1	223	56	47	1	0	0	0	0	0	0	–

	W	L	PCT	ERA	G	GS	CG	IP	H	BB	SO	ShO	Relief Pitching W	L	SV	BATTING AB	H	HR	BA

Tommy John continued

	W	L	PCT	ERA	G	GS	CG	IP	H	BB	SO	ShO	W	L	SV	AB	H	HR	BA
1985 **2 teams** CAL A (12G 2–4)					OAK	A	(11G 2–6)												
" total	4	10	.286	5.53	23	17	0	86.1	117	28	25	0	1	1	0	0	0	0	–
1986 NY A	5	3	.625	2.93	13	10	1	70.2	73	15	28	0	0	0	0	0	0	0	–
1987	13	6	.684	4.03	33	33	3	187.2	212	47	63	1	0	0	0	0	0	0	–
1988	9	8	.529	4.49	35	32	0	176.1	221	46	81	0	0	0	0	0	0	0	–
25 yrs.	286	224	.561	3.31	750	690	162	4644.2	4696	1237	2227	46	4	3	4	900	141	5	.157

DIVISIONAL PLAYOFF SERIES

	W	L	PCT	ERA	G	GS	CG	IP	H	BB	SO	ShO	W	L	SV	AB	H	HR	BA
1981 NY A	0	1	.000	6.43	1	1	0	7	8	2	0	0	0	0	0	0	0	0	–

LEAGUE CHAMPIONSHIP SERIES

	W	L	PCT	ERA	G	GS	CG	IP	H	BB	SO	ShO	W	L	SV	AB	H	HR	BA
1977 LA N	1	0	1.000	0.66	2	2	1	13.2	11	5	11	0	0	0	0	5	1	0	.200
1978	1	0	1.000	0.00	1	1	1	9	4	2	4	1	0	0	0	3	0	0	.000
1980 NY A	0	0	–	2.70	1	1	0	6.2	8	1	3	0	0	0	0	0	0	0	–
1981	1	0	1.000	1.50	1	1	0	6	6	1	3	0	0	0	0	0	0	0	–
1982 CAL A	1	1	.500	5.11	2	2	1	12.1	11	6	6	0	0	0	0	0	0	0	–
5 yrs.	4	1	.800	2.08	7	7	3	47.2	40	15	27	1	0	0	0	8	1	0	.125

WORLD SERIES

	W	L	PCT	ERA	G	GS	CG	IP	H	BB	SO	ShO	W	L	SV	AB	H	HR	BA
1977 LA N	0	1	.000	6.00	1	1	0	6	9	3	7	0	0	0	0	2	0	0	.000
1978	1	0	1.000	3.07	2	2	0	14.2	14	4	6	0	0	0	0	0	0	0	–
1981 NY A	1	0	1.000	0.69	3	2	0	13	11	0	8	0	0	0	0	2	0	0	.000
3 yrs.	2	1	.667	2.67	6	5	0	33.2	34	7	21	0	0	0	0	4	0	0	.000

Randy Johnson

JOHNSON, RANDALL DAVID
B. Sept. 10, 1963, Walnut Creek, Calif.   BL TR 6'10" 225 lbs.

	W	L	PCT	ERA	G	GS	CG	IP	H	BB	SO	ShO	W	L	SV	AB	H	HR	BA
1988 MON N	3	0	1.000	2.42	4	4	1	26	23	7	25	0	0	0	0	9	1	0	.111

Barry Jones

JONES, BARRY LOUIS
B. Feb. 15, 1963, Centerville, Ind.   BR TR 6'2" 215 lbs.

	W	L	PCT	ERA	G	GS	CG	IP	H	BB	SO	ShO	W	L	SV	AB	H	HR	BA
1986 PIT N	3	4	.429	2.89	26	0	0	37.1	29	21	29	0	3	4	3	5	1	0	.200
1987	2	4	.333	5.61	32	0	0	43.1	55	23	28	0	2	4	1	3	0	0	.000
1988 **2 teams** PIT N (42G 1–1)					CHI	A	(17G 2–2)												
" total	3	3	.500	2.84	59	0	0	82.1	72	38	48	0	3	3	3	5	0	0	.000
3 yrs.	8	11	.421	3.59	117	0	0	163	156	82	105	0	8	11	7	13	1	0	.077

Doug Jones

JONES, DOUGLAS REID
B. June 24, 1957, Covina, Calif.   BR TR 6'2" 170 lbs.

	W	L	PCT	ERA	G	GS	CG	IP	H	BB	SO	ShO	W	L	SV	AB	H	HR	BA
1982 MIL A	0	0	–	10.13	4	0	0	2.2	5	1	1	0	0	0	0	0	0	0	–
1986 CLE A	1	0	1.000	2.50	11	0	0	18	18	6	12	0	1	0	1	0	0	0	–
1987	6	5	.545	3.15	49	0	0	91.1	101	24	87	0	6	5	8	0	0	0	–
1988	3	4	.429	2.27	51	0	0	83.1	69	16	72	0	3	4	37	0	0	0	–
4 yrs.	10	9	.526	2.81	115	0	0	195.1	193	47	172	0	10	9	46	0	0	0	–

Jimmy Jones

JONES, JAMES CONDIA
B. Apr. 20, 1964, Dallas, Tex.   BR TR 6'2" 175 lbs.

	W	L	PCT	ERA	G	GS	CG	IP	H	BB	SO	ShO	W	L	SV	AB	H	HR	BA
1986 SD N	2	0	1.000	2.50	3	3	1	18	10	3	15	1	0	0	0	6	1	0	.167
1987	9	7	.563	4.14	30	22	2	145.2	154	54	51	1	2	0	0	49	8	1	.163
1988	9	14	.391	4.12	29	29	3	179	192	44	82	0	0	0	0	55	9	1	.164
3 yrs.	20	21	.488	4.04	62	54	6	342.2	356	101	148	2	2	0	0	110	18	2	.164

Odell Jones

JONES, ODELL
B. Jan. 13, 1953, Tulare, Calif.   BR TR 6'3" 175 lbs.

	W	L	PCT	ERA	G	GS	CG	IP	H	BB	SO	ShO	W	L	SV	AB	H	HR	BA
1975 PIT N	0	0	–	0.00	2	0	0	3	1	1	2	0	0	0	0	0	0	0	–
1977	3	7	.300	5.08	34	15	1	108	118	31	66	0	1	1	0	28	4	0	.143
1978	2	0	1.000	2.00	3	1	0	9	7	4	10	0	1	0	0	1	0	0	.000
1979 SEA A	3	11	.214	6.05	25	19	3	119	151	58	72	0	0	2	0	0	0	0	–
1981 PIT N	4	5	.444	3.33	13	8	0	54	51	23	30	0	1	1	0	10	2	0	.200
1983 TEX A	3	6	.333	3.09	42	0	0	67	56	22	50	0	3	6	10	0	0	0	–
1984	2	4	.333	3.64	33	0	0	59.1	62	23	28	0	2	4	2	0	0	0	–
1986 BAL A	2	2	.500	3.83	21	0	0	49.1	58	23	32	0	2	2	0	0	0	0	–
1988 MIL A	5	0	1.000	4.35	28	2	0	80.2	75	29	48	0	4	0	1	0	0	0	–
9 yrs.	24	35	.407	4.42	201	45	4	549.1	579	213	338	0	14	16	13	39	6	0	.154

Jeff Kaiser

KAISER, JEFFREY PATRICK
B. July 24, 1960, Wyandotte, Mich.   BR TL 6'3" 195 lbs.

	W	L	PCT	ERA	G	GS	CG	IP	H	BB	SO	ShO	W	L	SV	AB	H	HR	BA
1985 OAK A	0	0	–	14.58	15	0	0	16.2	25	20	10	0	0	0	0	0	0	0	–
1987 CLE A	0	0	–	16.20	2	0	0	3.1	4	3	2	0	0	0	0	0	0	0	–
1988	0	0	–	13.10	3	0	0	2.2	1	1	0	0	0	0	0	0	0	0	–
3 yrs.	0	0	–	13.10	20	0	0	22.2	31	24	12	0	0	0	0	0	0	0	–

Jimmy Key

KEY, JAMES EDWARD
B. Apr. 22, 1961, Huntsville, Ala.   BR TL 6'1" 180 lbs.

	W	L	PCT	ERA	G	GS	CG	IP	H	BB	SO	ShO	W	L	SV	AB	H	HR	BA
1984 TOR A	4	5	.444	4.65	63	0	0	62	70	32	44	0	4	5	10	0	0	0	–
1985	14	6	.700	3.00	35	32	3	212.2	188	50	85	0	1	0	0	0	0	0	–
1986	14	11	.560	3.57	36	35	4	232	222	74	141	2	0	0	0	0	0	0	–
1987	17	8	.680	2.76	36	36	8	261	210	66	161	1	0	0	0	0	0	0	–
1988	12	5	.706	3.29	21	21	2	131.1	127	30	65	2	0	0	0	0	0	0	–
5 yrs.	61	35	.635	3.23	191	124	17	899	817	252	496	5	5	5	10	0	0	0	–

LEAGUE CHAMPIONSHIP SERIES

	W	L	PCT	ERA	G	GS	CG	IP	H	BB	SO	ShO	W	L	SV	AB	H	HR	BA
1985 TOR A	0	1	.000	5.19	2	2	0	8.2	15	2	5	0	0	0	0	0	0	0	–

Paul Kilgus

KILGUS, PAUL NELSON
B. Feb. 2, 1962, Bowling Green, Ky.   BL TL 6'1" 175 lbs.

	W	L	PCT	ERA	G	GS	CG	IP	H	BB	SO	ShO	W	L	SV	AB	H	HR	BA
1987 TEX A	2	7	.222	4.13	25	12	0	89.1	95	31	42	0	0	2	0	0	0	0	–
1988	12	15	.444	4.16	32	32	5	203.1	190	71	88	3	0	0	0	0	0	0	–
2 yrs.	14	22	.389	4.15	57	44	5	292.2	285	102	130	3	0	2	0	0	0	0	–

	W	L	PCT	ERA	G	GS	CG	IP	H	BB	SO	ShO	Relief Pitching W	L	SV	BATTING AB	H	HR	BA

Eric King

KING, ERIC STEVEN
B. Apr. 10, 1964, Oxnard, Calif.
BR TR 6'2" 180 lbs.

	W	L	PCT	ERA	G	GS	CG	IP	H	BB	SO	ShO	W	L	SV	AB	H	HR	BA
1986 DET A	11	4	.733	3.51	33	16	3	138.1	108	63	79	1	3	0	3	0	0	0	–
1987	6	9	.400	4.89	55	4	0	116	111	60	89	0	6	7	9	0	0	0	–
1988	4	1	.800	3.41	23	5	0	68.2	60	34	45	0	1	0	3	0	0	0	–
3 yrs.	21	14	.600	3.98	111	25	3	323	279	157	213	1	10	7	15	0	0	0	–

LEAGUE CHAMPIONSHIP SERIES

	W	L	PCT	ERA	G	GS	CG	IP	H	BB	SO	ShO	W	L	SV	AB	H	HR	BA
1987 DET A	0	0	–	1.69	2	0	0	5.1	3	2	4	0	0	0	0	0	0	0	–

Bob Kipper

KIPPER, ROBERT WAYNE
B. July 8, 1964, Aurora, Ill.
BR TL 6'2" 190 lbs.

	W	L	PCT	ERA	G	GS	CG	IP	H	BB	SO	ShO	W	L	SV	AB	H	HR	BA
1985 2 teams			CAL	A (2G 0–1)			PIT	N (5G 1–2)											
" total	1	3	.250	7.07	7	5	0	28	28	10	13	0	0	0	0	8	2	0	.250
1986 PIT N	6	8	.429	4.03	20	19	0	114	123	34	81	0	0	0	0	33	1	0	.030
1987	5	9	.357	5.94	24	20	1	110.2	117	52	83	1	0	0	0	33	8	0	.242
1988	2	6	.250	3.74	50	0	0	65	54	26	39	0	2	6	0	4	0	0	.000
4 yrs.	14	26	.350	4.90	101	44	1	317.2	322	122	216	1	2	6	0	78	11	0	.141

Bob Knepper

KNEPPER, ROBERT WESLEY
B. May 25, 1954, Akron, Ohio
BL TL 6'3" 195 lbs.

	W	L	PCT	ERA	G	GS	CG	IP	H	BB	SO	ShO	W	L	SV	AB	H	HR	BA
1976 SF N	1	2	.333	3.24	4	4	0	25	26	7	11	0	0	0	0	9	1	0	.111
1977	11	9	.550	3.36	27	27	6	166	151	72	100	2	0	0	0	55	10	0	.182
1978	17	11	.607	2.63	36	35	16	260	218	85	147	6	0	0	0	79	5	0	.063
1979	9	12	.429	4.65	34	34	6	207	241	77	123	2	0	0	0	66	12	1	.182
1980	9	16	.360	4.10	35	33	8	215	242	61	103	1	0	0	0	66	10	0	.152
1981 HOU N	9	5	.643	2.18	22	22	6	157	128	38	75	5	0	0	0	47	7	1	.149
1982	5	15	.250	4.45	33	29	4	180	193	60	108	0	0	0	1	52	3	0	.058
1983	6	13	.316	3.19	35	29	4	203	202	71	125	3	1	1	0	66	12	1	.182
1984	15	10	.600	3.20	35	34	11	233.2	223	55	140	3	0	0	0	76	13	1	.171
1985	15	13	.536	3.55	37	37	4	241	253	54	131	0	0	0	0	78	11	1	.141
1986	17	12	.586	3.14	40	38	8	258	232	62	143	5	1	0	0	91	9	0	.099
1987	8	17	.320	5.27	33	31	1	177.2	226	54	76	0	0	0	0	51	5	0	.098
1988	14	5	.737	3.14	27	27	3	175	156	67	103	2	0	0	0	48	6	0	.125
13 yrs.	136	140	.493	3.54	398	380	77	2498.1	2491	763	1385	29	2	1	1	784	104	5	.133

DIVISIONAL PLAYOFF SERIES

	W	L	PCT	ERA	G	GS	CG	IP	H	BB	SO	ShO	W	L	SV	AB	H	HR	BA
1981 HOU N	0	1	.000	5.40	1	1	0	5	6	2	4	0	0	0	0	1	0	0	.000

LEAGUE CHAMPIONSHIP SERIES

	W	L	PCT	ERA	G	GS	CG	IP	H	BB	SO	ShO	W	L	SV	AB	H	HR	BA
1986 HOU N	0	0	–	3.52	2	2	0	15.1	13	1	9	0	0	0	0	5	0	0	.000

Mark Knudson

KNUDSON, MARK RICHARD
B. Oct. 28, 1960, Denver, Colo.
BR TR 6'5" 215 lbs.

	W	L	PCT	ERA	G	GS	CG	IP	H	BB	SO	ShO	W	L	SV	AB	H	HR	BA
1985 HOU N	0	2	.000	9.00	2	2	0	11	21	3	4	0	0	0	0	2	0	0	.000
1986 2 teams			HOU	N (9G 1–5)			MIL	A (4G 0–1)											
" total	1	6	.143	5.22	13	8	0	60.1	70	20	29	0	0	0	0	10	0	0	.000
1987 MIL A	4	4	.500	5.37	15	8	1	62	88	14	26	0	2	1	0	0	0	0	–
1988	0	0	–	1.13	5	0	0	16	17	2	7	0	0	0	0	0	0	0	–
4 yrs.	5	12	.294	5.12	35	18	1	149.1	196	39	66	0	2	1	0	12	0	0	.000

Randy Kramer

KRAMER, RANDALL JOHN
B. Sept. 20, 1960, Palo Alto, Calif.
BR TR 6'2" 170 lbs.

	W	L	PCT	ERA	G	GS	CG	IP	H	BB	SO	ShO	W	L	SV	AB	H	HR	BA
1988 PIT N	1	2	.333	5.40	5	1	0	12	12	1	7	0	1	1	0	2	0	0	.000

Ray Krawczyk

KRAWCZYK, RAYMOND ALLEN
B. Oct. 9, 1959, Sewickley, Pa.
BR TR 6'2" 190 lbs.

	W	L	PCT	ERA	G	GS	CG	IP	H	BB	SO	ShO	W	L	SV	AB	H	HR	BA
1984 PIT N	0	0	–	3.38	4	0	0	5.1	7	4	3	0	0	0	0	0	0	0	–
1985	0	2	.000	14.04	8	0	0	8.1	20	6	9	0	0	2	0	0	0	0	–
1986	0	1	.000	7.30	12	0	0	12.1	17	10	7	0	0	1	0	0	0	0	–
1988 CAL A	0	1	.000	4.81	14	1	0	24.1	29	8	17	0	0	0	1	0	0	0	–
4 yrs.	0	4	.000	6.79	38	1	0	50.1	73	28	36	0	0	3	1	0	0	0	–

Bill Krueger

KRUEGER, WILLIAM CULP
B. Apr. 24, 1958, Waukegan, Ill.
BL TL 6'5" 205 lbs.

	W	L	PCT	ERA	G	GS	CG	IP	H	BB	SO	ShO	W	L	SV	AB	H	HR	BA
1983 OAK A	7	6	.538	3.61	17	16	2	109.2	104	53	58	0	1	0	0	0	0	0	–
1984	10	10	.500	4.75	26	24	1	142	156	85	61	0	0	0	0	0	0	0	–
1985	9	10	.474	4.52	32	23	2	151.1	165	69	56	0	1	0	0	0	0	0	–
1986	1	2	.333	6.03	11	3	0	34.1	40	13	10	0	0	1	1	0	0	0	–
1987 2 teams			OAK	A (9G 0–3)			LA	N (2G 0–0)											
" total	0	3	.000	6.75	11	0	0	8	12	9	4	0	0	3	0	0	0	0	–
1988 LA N	0	0	–	11.57	1	1	0	2.1	4	2	1	0	0	0	0	0	0	0	–
6 yrs.	27	31	.466	4.56	98	67	5	447.2	481	231	190	0	2	4	1	0	0	0	–

Mike Krukow

KRUKOW, MICHAEL EDWARD
B. Jan. 21, 1952, Long Beach, Calif.
BR TR 6'5" 205 lbs.

	W	L	PCT	ERA	G	GS	CG	IP	H	BB	SO	ShO	W	L	SV	AB	H	HR	BA
1976 CHI N	0	0	–	9.00	2	0	0	4	6	2	1	0	0	0	0	1	0	0	.000
1977	8	14	.364	4.40	34	33	1	172	195	61	106	1	0	0	0	55	11	0	.200
1978	9	3	.750	3.91	27	20	3	138	125	53	81	1	0	0	0	45	11	0	.244
1979	9	9	.500	4.20	28	28	0	165	172	81	119	0	0	0	0	51	16	1	.314
1980	10	15	.400	4.39	34	34	3	205	200	80	130	0	0	0	0	65	16	1	.246
1981	9	9	.500	3.69	25	25	2	144	146	55	101	1	0	0	0	50	9	0	.180
1982 PHI N	13	11	.542	3.12	33	33	7	208	211	82	138	2	0	0	0	72	13	0	.181
1983 SF N	11	11	.500	3.95	31	31	2	184.1	189	76	136	1	0	0	0	63	16	1	.254
1984	11	12	.478	4.56	35	33	3	199.1	234	78	141	1	0	0	1	72	10	0	.139
1985	8	11	.421	3.38	28	28	6	194.2	176	49	150	1	0	0	0	55	12	1	.218
1986	20	9	.690	3.05	34	34	10	245	204	55	178	2	0	0	0	82	12	0	.146
1987	5	6	.455	4.80	30	28	3	163	182	46	104	0	0	0	0	54	9	0	.167

	W	L	PCT	ERA	G	GS	CG	IP	H	BB	SO	ShO	Relief Pitching W	L	SV	BATTING AB	H	HR	BA

Mike Krukow continued

	W	L	PCT	ERA	G	GS	CG	IP	H	BB	SO	ShO	W	L	SV	AB	H	HR	BA
1988	7	4	.636	3.54	20	20	1	124.2	111	31	75	0	0	0	0	41	3	1	.073
13 yrs.	120	114	.513	3.90	361	347	41	2147	2151	749	1460	10	0	0	1	706	138	5	.195

LEAGUE CHAMPIONSHIP SERIES

	W	L	PCT	ERA	G	GS	CG	IP	H	BB	SO	ShO	W	L	SV	AB	H	HR	BA
1987 SF N	1	0	1.000	2.00	1	1	1	9	9	1	3	0	0	0	0	2	0	0	.000

Jeff Kunkel

KUNKEL, JEFFREY WILLIAM
Son of Bill Kunkel.
B. Mar. 25, 1962, West Palm Beach, Fla.

BR TR 6'2" 175 lbs.

	W	L	PCT	ERA	G	GS	CG	IP	H	BB	SO	ShO	W	L	SV	AB	H	HR	BA
1988 TEX A	0	0	–	0.00	1	0	0	1	0	0	1	0	0	0	0	*			

Mike LaCoss

LaCOSS, MICHAEL JAMES
B. May 30, 1956, Glendale, Calif.

BR TR 6'5" 185 lbs.

	W	L	PCT	ERA	G	GS	CG	IP	H	BB	SO	ShO	W	L	SV	AB	H	HR	BA
1978 CIN N	4	8	.333	4.50	16	15	2	96	104	46	31	1	0	0	0	30	2	0	.067
1979	14	8	.636	3.50	35	32	6	206	202	79	73	1	0	0	0	70	9	0	.129
1980	10	12	.455	4.63	34	29	4	169	207	68	59	2	2	0	0	55	5	0	.091
1981	4	7	.364	6.12	20	13	1	78	102	30	22	1	2	0	1	19	0	0	.000
1982 HOU N	6	6	.500	2.90	41	8	0	115	107	54	51	0	3	3	0	24	6	0	.250
1983	5	7	.417	4.43	38	17	2	138	142	56	53	0	0	1	1	35	3	0	.086
1984	7	5	.583	4.02	39	18	2	132	132	55	86	1	1	0	3	31	4	0	.129
1985 KC A	1	1	.500	5.09	21	0	0	40.2	49	29	26	0	1	1	1	0	0	0	–
1986 SF N	10	13	.435	3.57	37	31	4	204.1	179	70	86	1	0	0	0	61	14	2	.230
1987	13	10	.565	3.68	39	26	2	171	184	63	79	1	1	0	0	50	3	0	.060
1988	7	7	.500	3.62	19	19	1	114.1	99	47	70	1	0	0	0	33	8	0	.242
11 yrs.	81	84	.491	4.01	339	208	24	1464.1	1507	597	636	9	10	5	6	408	54	2	.132

LEAGUE CHAMPIONSHIP SERIES

	W	L	PCT	ERA	G	GS	CG	IP	H	BB	SO	ShO	W	L	SV	AB	H	HR	BA
1979 CIN N	0	1	.000	10.80	1	1	0	1.2	1	4	0	0	0	0	0	0	0	0	–
1987 SF N	0	0	–	0.00	2	0	0	3.1	1	3	2	0	0	0	0	0	0	0	–
2 yrs.	0	1	.000	3.60	3	1	0	5	2	7	2	0	0	0	0	0	0	0	–

Dennis Lamp

LAMP, DENNIS PATRICK
B. Sept. 23, 1952, Los Angeles, Calif.

BR TR 6'4" 200 lbs.

	W	L	PCT	ERA	G	GS	CG	IP	H	BB	SO	ShO	W	L	SV	AB	H	HR	BA
1977 CHI N	0	2	.000	6.30	11	3	0	30	43	8	12	0	0	0	0	8	3	0	.375
1978	7	15	.318	3.29	37	36	6	224	221	56	73	3	0	0	0	73	15	0	.205
1979	11	10	.524	3.51	38	32	6	200	223	46	86	1	0	0	0	58	9	0	.155
1980	10	14	.417	5.19	41	37	2	203	259	82	83	1	1	2	0	61	6	0	.098
1981 CHI A	7	6	.538	2.41	27	10	3	127	103	43	71	0	3	1	0	0	0	0	–
1982	11	8	.579	3.99	44	27	3	189.2	206	59	78	2	1	1	5	0	0	0	–
1983	7	7	.500	3.71	49	5	1	116.1	123	29	44	0	4	5	15	0	0	0	–
1984 TOR A	8	8	.500	4.55	56	4	0	85	97	38	45	0	5	7	9	0	0	0	–
1985	11	0	1.000	3.32	53	1	0	105.2	96	27	68	0	11	0	2	0	0	0	–
1986	2	6	.250	5.05	40	2	0	73	93	23	30	0	2	4	2	0	0	0	–
1987 OAK A	1	3	.250	5.08	36	5	0	56.2	76	22	36	0	0	0	0	0	0	0	–
1988 BOS A	7	6	.538	3.48	46	0	0	82.2	92	19	49	0	7	6	0	0	0	0	–
12 yrs.	82	85	.491	3.92	478	162	21	1493	1632	452	675	7	34	26	33	200	33	0	.165

LEAGUE CHAMPIONSHIP SERIES

	W	L	PCT	ERA	G	GS	CG	IP	H	BB	SO	ShO	W	L	SV	AB	H	HR	BA
1983 CHI A	0	0	–	0.00	3	0	0	2	0	2	1	0	0	0	0	0	0	0	–
1985 TOR A	0	0	–	0.00	3	0	0	9.1	2	1	10	0	0	0	0	0	0	0	–
2 yrs.	0	0	–	0.00	6	0	0	11.1	2	3	11	0	0	0	0	0	0	0	–

Les Lancaster

LANCASTER, LESTER WAYNE
B. Apr. 21, 1962, Dallas, Tex.

BR TR 6'2" 200 lbs.

	W	L	PCT	ERA	G	GS	CG	IP	H	BB	SO	ShO	W	L	SV	AB	H	HR	BA
1987 CHI N	8	3	.727	4.90	27	18	0	132.1	138	51	78	0	1	0	0	49	4	0	.082
1988	4	6	.400	3.78	44	3	1	85.2	89	34	36	0	3	6	5	20	1	0	.050
2 yrs.	12	9	.571	4.46	71	21	1	218	227	85	114	0	4	6	5	69	5	0	.072

Bill Landrum

LANDRUM, THOMAS WILLIAM
Son of Joe Landrum.
B. Aug. 17, 1957, Columbia, S. C.

BR TR 6'2" 185 lbs.

	W	L	PCT	ERA	G	GS	CG	IP	H	BB	SO	ShO	W	L	SV	AB	H	HR	BA
1986 CIN N	0	0	–	6.75	10	0	0	13.1	23	4	14	0	0	0	0	2	0	0	.000
1987	3	2	.600	4.71	44	2	0	65	68	34	42	0	3	1	2	5	1	0	.200
1988 CHI N	1	0	1.000	5.84	7	0	0	12.1	19	3	6	0	1	0	0	2	0	0	.000
3 yrs.	4	2	.667	5.16	61	2	0	90.2	110	41	62	0	4	1	2	9	1	0	.111

Mark Langston

LANGSTON, MARK EDWARD
B. Aug. 20, 1960, San Diego, Calif.

BR TL 6'2" 175 lbs.

	W	L	PCT	ERA	G	GS	CG	IP	H	BB	SO	ShO	W	L	SV	AB	H	HR	BA
1984 SEA A	17	10	.630	3.40	35	33	5	225	188	118	204	2	1	0	0	0	0	0	–
1985	7	14	.333	5.47	24	24	2	126.2	122	91	72	0	0	0	0	0	0	0	–
1986	12	14	.462	4.85	37	36	9	239.1	234	123	245	0	0	0	0	0	0	0	–
1987	19	13	.594	3.84	35	35	14	272	242	114	262	3	0	0	0	0	0	0	–
1988	15	11	.577	3.34	35	35	9	261.1	222	110	235	3	0	0	0	0	0	0	–
5 yrs.	70	62	.530	4.03	166	163	39	1124.1	1008	556	1018	8	1	0	0	0	0	0	–

Dave LaPoint

LaPOINT, DAVID JEFFREY
B. July 29, 1959, Glens Falls, N. Y.

BL TL 6'3" 205 lbs.

	W	L	PCT	ERA	G	GS	CG	IP	H	BB	SO	ShO	W	L	SV	AB	H	HR	BA
1980 MIL A	1	0	1.000	6.00	5	3	0	15	17	13	5	0	1	0	1	0	0	0	–
1981 STL N	1	0	1.000	4.09	3	2	0	11	12	2	4	0	0	0	0	5	0	0	.000
1982	9	3	.750	3.42	42	21	0	152.2	170	52	81	0	1	0	0	38	2	0	.053
1983	12	9	.571	3.95	37	29	1	191.1	191	84	113	0	2	1	0	59	9	0	.153
1984	12	10	.545	3.96	33	33	2	193	205	77	130	1	0	0	0	59	4	0	.068
1985 SF N	7	17	.292	3.57	31	31	2	206.2	215	74	122	1	0	0	0	60	10	0	.167
1986 2 teams			DET	A (16G 3–6)		SD		N (24G 1–4)											
" total	4	10	.286	5.02	40	12	0	129	152	56	77	0	0	3	0	8	0	0	.000

	W	L	PCT	ERA	G	GS	CG	IP	H	BB	SO	ShO	Relief Pitching W	L	SV	BATTING AB	H	HR	BA

Dave LaPoint continued

1987 2 teams	STL	N	(6G 1–1)		CHI	A	(14G 6–3)												
" total	7	4	.636	3.56	20	14	2	98.2	95	36	51	1	1	1	0	4	0	0	.000
1988 2 teams	CHI	A	(25G 10–11)		PIT	N	(8G 4–2)												
" total	14	13	.519	3.25	33	33	2	213.1	205	57	98	1	0	0	0	16	1	0	.063
9 yrs.	67	66	.504	3.81	244	178	9	1210.2	1262	451	681	4	5	5	1	249	26	0	.104

WORLD SERIES

	W	L	PCT	ERA	G	GS	CG	IP	H	BB	SO	ShO	W	L	SV	AB	H	HR	BA
1982 STL N	0	0	–	3.24	2	1	0	8.1	10	2	3	0	0	0	0	0	0	0	–

Bill Laskey

LASKEY, WILLIAM ALAN   BR TR 6'5"   190 lbs.
B. Dec. 20, 1957, Toledo, Ohio

	W	L	PCT	ERA	G	GS	CG	IP	H	BB	SO	ShO	W	L	SV	AB	H	HR	BA
1982 SF N	13	12	.520	3.14	32	31	7	189.1	186	43	88	1	0	0	0	62	8	0	.129
1983	13	10	.565	4.19	25	25	1	148.1	151	45	81	0	0	0	0	47	5	0	.106
1984	9	14	.391	4.33	35	34	2	207.2	222	50	71	0	1	0	0	63	4	0	.063
1985 2 teams			SF	N	(19G 5–11)		MON	N	(11G 0–5)										
" total	5	16	.238	4.91	30	26	0	148.1	165	53	60	0	0	0	0	37	5	0	.135
1986 SF N	1	1	.500	4.28	20	0	0	27.1	28	13	8	0	1	1	1	1	0	0	.000
1988 CLE A	1	0	1.000	5.18	17	0	0	24.1	32	6	17	0	1	0	1	0	0	0	–
6 yrs.	42	53	.442	4.14	159	116	10	745.1	784	210	325	1	3	1	2	210	22	0	.105

Vance Law

LAW, VANCE AARON   BR TR 6'2"   185 lbs.
Son of Vern Law.
B. Oct. 1, 1956, Boise, Ida.

	W	L	PCT	ERA	G	GS	CG	IP	H	BB	SO	ShO	W	L	SV	AB	H	HR	BA
1986 MON N	0	0	–	2.25	3	0	0	4	3	2	0	0	0	0	0	360	81	5	.225
1987	0	0	–	5.40	3	0	0	3.1	5	0	2	0	0	0	0	436	119	12	.273
2 yrs.	0	0	–	3.68	6	0	0	7.1	8	2	2	0	0	0	0	*			

Jack Lazorko

LAZORKO, JACK THOMAS   BR TR 5'11"   198 lbs.
B. Mar. 30, 1956, Hoboken, N. J.

	W	L	PCT	ERA	G	GS	CG	IP	H	BB	SO	ShO	W	L	SV	AB	H	HR	BA
1984 MIL A	0	1	.000	4.31	15	1	0	39.2	37	22	24	0	0	1	1	0	0	0	–
1985 SEA A	0	0	–	3.54	15	0	0	20.1	23	8	7	0	0	0	1	0	0	0	–
1986 DET A	0	0	–	4.05	3	0	0	6.2	8	4	3	0	0	0	0	0	0	0	–
1987 CAL A	5	6	.455	4.59	26	11	2	117.2	108	44	55	0	2	1	0	0	0	0	–
1988	0	1	.000	3.35	10	3	0	37.2	37	16	19	0	0	0	0	0	0	0	–
5 yrs.	5	8	.385	4.22	69	15	2	222	213	94	108	0	2	2	2	0	0	0	–

Charlie Lea

LEA, CHARLES WILLIAM   BR TR 6'4"   194 lbs.
B. Dec. 25, 1956, Orleans, France

	W	L	PCT	ERA	G	GS	CG	IP	H	BB	SO	ShO	W	L	SV	AB	H	HR	BA
1980 MON N	7	5	.583	3.72	21	19	0	104	103	55	56	0	0	0	0	37	3	0	.081
1981	5	4	.556	4.64	16	11	2	64	63	26	31	2	0	0	0	15	2	0	.133
1982	12	10	.545	3.24	27	27	4	177.2	145	56	115	2	0	0	0	65	8	0	.123
1983	16	11	.593	3.12	33	33	8	222	195	84	137	4	0	0	0	70	8	0	.114
1984	15	10	.600	2.89	30	30	8	224.1	198	68	123	0	0	0	0	72	8	0	.111
1987	0	1	.000	36.00	1	1	0	1	4	2	1	0	0	0	0	0	0	0	–
1988 MIN A	7	7	.500	4.85	24	23	0	130	156	50	72	0	0	0	0	0	0	0	–
7 yrs.	62	48	.564	3.54	152	144	22	923	864	341	535	8	0	0	0	259	29	0	.112

Rick Leach

LEACH, RICHARD MAX   BL TL 6'1"   180 lbs.
B. May 4, 1957, Ann Arbor, Mich.

	W	L	PCT	ERA	G	GS	CG	IP	H	BB	SO	ShO	W	L	SV	AB	H	HR	BA
1984 TOR A	0	0	–	27.00	1	0	0	1	2	2	0	0	0	0	0	*			

Terry Leach

LEACH, TERRY HESTER   BR TR 6'   215 lbs.
B. Mar. 13, 1954, Selma, Ala.

	W	L	PCT	ERA	G	GS	CG	IP	H	BB	SO	ShO	W	L	SV	AB	H	HR	BA
1981 NY N	1	1	.500	2.57	21	1	0	35	26	12	16	0	1	0	0	1	0	0	.000
1982	2	1	.667	2.91	21	1	1	45.1	46	18	30	1	1	1	3	8	1	0	.125
1985	3	4	.429	2.91	22	4	1	55.2	48	14	30	1	0	3	1	12	2	0	.167
1986	0	0	–	2.70	6	0	0	6.2	6	3	4	0	0	0	0	0	0	0	–
1987	11	1	.917	3.22	44	12	1	131.1	132	29	61	1	4	0	0	33	2	0	.061
1988	7	2	.778	2.54	52	0	0	92	95	24	51	0	7	2	3	14	2	0	.143
6 yrs.	24	9	.727	3.05	166	18	3	366	353	100	192	3	13	4	7	68	7	0	.103

LEAGUE CHAMPIONSHIP SERIES

	W	L	PCT	ERA	G	GS	CG	IP	H	BB	SO	ShO	W	L	SV	AB	H	HR	BA
1988 NY N	0	0	–	0.00	3	0	0	5	4	1	4	0	0	0	0	0	0	0	–

Tim Leary

LEARY, TIMOTHY JAMES   BR TR 6'3"   205 lbs.
B. Mar. 21, 1958, Santa Monica, Calif.

	W	L	PCT	ERA	G	GS	CG	IP	H	BB	SO	ShO	W	L	SV	AB	H	HR	BA
1981 NY N	0	0	–	0.00	1	1	0	5	1	3	3	0	0	0	0	1	0	0	.000
1983	1	1	.500	3.38	2	2	1	10.2	15	4	9	0	0	0	0	3	1	0	.333
1984	3	3	.500	4.02	20	7	0	53.2	61	18	29	0	3	0	0	10	3	1	.300
1985 MIL A	1	4	.200	4.05	5	5	0	33.1	40	8	29	0	0	0	0	0	0	0	–
1986	12	12	.500	4.21	33	30	3	188.1	216	53	110	2	0	0	0	0	0	0	–
1987 LA N	3	11	.214	4.76	39	12	0	107.2	121	36	61	0	1	4	1	23	7	0	.304
1988	17	11	.607	2.91	35	34	9	228.2	201	56	180	6	0	0	0	67	18	0	.269
7 yrs.	37	42	.468	3.78	135	91	13	624.1	654	176	421	8	4	4	1	104	29	1	.279

LEAGUE CHAMPIONSHIP SERIES

	W	L	PCT	ERA	G	GS	CG	IP	H	BB	SO	ShO	W	L	SV	AB	H	HR	BA
1988 LA N	0	1	.000	6.23	2	1	0	4.1	8	3	3	0	0	0	0	1	0	0	.000

WORLD SERIES

	W	L	PCT	ERA	G	GS	CG	IP	H	BB	SO	ShO	W	L	SV	AB	H	HR	BA
1988 LA N	0	0	–	1.35	2	0	0	6.2	6	2	4	0	0	0	0	0	0	0	–

Mark Lee

LEE, MARK OWEN   BL TL 6'3"   198 lbs.
B. July 20, 1964, Williston, N. D.

	W	L	PCT	ERA	G	GS	CG	IP	H	BB	SO	ShO	W	L	SV	AB	H	HR	BA
1988 KC A	0	0	–	3.60	4	0	0	5	6	1	0	0	0	0	0	0	0	0	–

	W	L	PCT	ERA	G	GS	CG	IP	H	BB	SO	ShO	W	L	SV	AB	H	HR	BA

Relief Pitching columns: W L SV. *BATTING* columns: AB H HR BA.

Craig Lefferts

LEFFERTS, CRAIG LINDSAY
B. Sept. 29, 1957, Munich, West Germany
BL TL 6'1" 180 lbs.

	W	L	PCT	ERA	G	GS	CG	IP	H	BB	SO	ShO	W	L	SV	AB	H	HR	BA
1983 CHI N	3	4	.429	3.13	56	5	0	89	80	29	60	0	2	3	1	18	2	0	.111
1984 SD N	3	4	.429	2.13	62	0	0	105.2	88	24	56	0	3	4	10	17	5	0	.294
1985	7	6	.538	3.35	60	0	0	83.1	75	30	48	0	7	6	2	4	1	0	.250
1986	9	8	.529	3.09	83	0	0	107.2	98	44	72	0	9	8	4	8	1	1	.125
1987 2 teams	SD	N	(33G 2–2)				SF	N	(44G 3–3)										
" total	5	5	.500	3.83	77	0	0	98.2	92	33	57	0	5	5	6	7	2	0	.286
1988 SF N	3	8	.273	2.92	64	0	0	92.1	74	23	58	0	3	8	11	9	0	0	.000
6 yrs.	30	35	.462	3.06	402	5	0	576.2	507	183	351	0	29	34	34	63	11	1	.175

LEAGUE CHAMPIONSHIP SERIES

	W	L	PCT	ERA	G	GS	CG	IP	H	BB	SO	ShO	W	L	SV	AB	H	HR	BA
1984 SD N	2	0	1.000	0.00	3	0	0	4	1	1	1	0	2	0	0	0	0	0	–
1987 SF N	0	0	–	0.00	3	0	0	2	3	1	0	0	0	0	0	0	0	0	–
2 yrs.	2	0	1.000	0.00	6	0	0	6	4	2	1	0	2	0	0	0	0	0	–

WORLD SERIES

	W	L	PCT	ERA	G	GS	CG	IP	H	BB	SO	ShO	W	L	SV	AB	H	HR	BA
1984 SD N	0	0	–	0.00	3	0	0	6	2	1	7	0	0	0	1	0	0	0	–

Charlie Leibrandt

LEIBRANDT, CHARLES LOUIS, JR.
B. Oct. 4, 1956, Chicago, Ill.
BR TL 6'3" 195 lbs.

	W	L	PCT	ERA	G	GS	CG	IP	H	BB	SO	ShO	W	L	SV	AB	H	HR	BA
1979 CIN N	0	0	–	0.00	3	0	0	4	2	2	1	0	0	0	0	0	0	0	–
1980	10	9	.526	4.24	36	27	5	174	200	54	62	2	0	0	0	56	11	0	.196
1981	1	1	.500	3.60	7	4	1	30	28	15	9	1	0	0	0	8	0	0	.000
1982	5	7	.417	5.10	36	11	0	107.2	130	48	34	0	2	1	2	25	2	0	.080
1984 KC A	11	7	.611	3.63	23	23	0	143.2	158	38	53	0	0	0	0	0	0	0	–
1985	17	9	.654	2.69	33	33	8	237.2	223	68	108	3	0	0	0	0	0	0	–
1986	14	11	.560	4.09	35	34	8	231.1	238	63	108	1	0	0	0	0	0	0	–
1987	16	11	.593	3.41	35	35	8	240.1	235	74	151	3	0	0	0	0	0	0	–
1988	13	12	.520	3.19	35	35	7	243	244	62	125	2	0	0	0	0	0	0	–
9 yrs.	87	67	.565	3.61	243	202	37	1411.2	1458	424	651	12	2	1	2	89	13	0	.146

LEAGUE CHAMPIONSHIP SERIES

	W	L	PCT	ERA	G	GS	CG	IP	H	BB	SO	ShO	W	L	SV	AB	H	HR	BA
1979 CIN N	0	0	–	0.00	1	0	0	.1	0	0	0	0	0	0	0	0	0	0	–
1984 KC A	0	1	.000	1.13	1	1	1	8	3	4	6	0	0	0	0	0	0	0	–
1985	1	2	.333	5.28	3	2	0	15.1	17	4	6	0	1	0	0	0	0	0	–
3 yrs.	1	3	.250	3.80	5	3	1	23.2	20	8	12	0	1	0	0	0	0	0	–

WORLD SERIES

	W	L	PCT	ERA	G	GS	CG	IP	H	BB	SO	ShO	W	L	SV	AB	H	HR	BA
1985 KC A	0	1	.000	2.76	2	2	0	16.1	10	4	10	0	0	0	0	4	0	0	.000

Dave Leiper

LEIPER, DAVID PAUL
B. June 18, 1962, Whittier, Calif.
BL TL 6'1" 160 lbs.

	W	L	PCT	ERA	G	GS	CG	IP	H	BB	SO	ShO	W	L	SV	AB	H	HR	BA
1984 OAK A	1	0	1.000	9.00	8	0	0	7	12	5	3	0	1	0	0	0	0	0	–
1986	2	2	.500	4.83	33	0	0	31.2	28	18	15	0	2	2	1	0	0	0	–
1987 2 teams	OAK	A	(45G 2–1)				SD	N	(12G 1–0)										
" total	3	1	.750	3.95	57	0	0	68.1	65	23	43	0	3	1	2	0	0	0	–
1988 SD N	3	0	1.000	2.17	35	0	0	54	45	14	33	0	3	0	1	2	1	0	.500
4 yrs.	9	3	.750	3.75	133	0	0	161	150	60	94	0	9	3	4	2	1	0	.500

Al Leiter

LEITER, ALOIS TERRY
B. Oct. 23, 1965, Toms River, N. J.
BL TL 6'2" 200 lbs.

	W	L	PCT	ERA	G	GS	CG	IP	H	BB	SO	ShO	W	L	SV	AB	H	HR	BA
1987 NY A	2	2	.500	6.35	4	4	0	22.2	24	15	28	0	0	0	0	0	0	0	–
1988	4	4	.500	3.92	14	14	0	57.1	49	33	60	0	0	0	0	0	0	0	–
2 yrs.	6	6	.500	4.61	18	18	0	80	73	48	88	0	0	0	0	0	0	0	–

Bill Long

LONG, WILLIAM DOUGLAS
B. Feb. 29, 1960, Cincinnati, Ohio
BR TR 6' 185 lbs.

	W	L	PCT	ERA	G	GS	CG	IP	H	BB	SO	ShO	W	L	SV	AB	H	HR	BA
1985 CHI A	0	1	.000	10.29	4	3	0	14	25	5	13	0	0	0	0	0	0	0	–
1987	8	8	.500	4.37	29	23	5	169	179	28	72	2	1	1	1	0	0	0	–
1988	8	11	.421	4.03	47	18	3	174	187	43	77	0	2	2	2	0	0	0	–
3 yrs.	16	20	.444	4.44	80	44	8	357	391	76	162	2	3	3	3	0	0	0	–

Vance Lovelace

LOVELACE, VANCE ODELL
B. Aug. 9, 1963, Tampa, Fla.
BL TL 6'5" 205 lbs.

	W	L	PCT	ERA	G	GS	CG	IP	H	BB	SO	ShO	W	L	SV	AB	H	HR	BA
1988 CAL A	0	0	–	13.50	3	0	0	1.1	2	3	0	0	0	0	0	0	0	0	–

Urbano Lugo

LUGO, URBANO RAFAEL
Born Rafael Urbano Lugo y Colina.
B. Aug. 12, 1962, Punto Fijo, Venezuela
BR TR 6' 185 lbs.

	W	L	PCT	ERA	G	GS	CG	IP	H	BB	SO	ShO	W	L	SV	AB	H	HR	BA
1985 CAL A	3	4	.429	3.69	20	10	1	83	86	29	42	0	0	0	0	0	0	0	–
1986	1	1	.500	3.80	6	3	0	21.1	21	6	9	0	0	0	0	0	0	0	–
1987	0	2	.000	9.32	7	5	0	28	42	18	24	0	0	0	0	0	0	0	–
1988	0	0	–	9.00	1	0	0	2	2	1	1	0	0	0	0	0	0	0	–
4 yrs.	4	7	.364	4.96	34	18	1	134.1	151	54	76	0	0	0	0	0	0	0	–

Morris Madden

MADDEN, MORRIS DeWAYNE
B. Aug. 31, 1960, Laurens, S. C.
BL TL 6' 155 lbs.

	W	L	PCT	ERA	G	GS	CG	IP	H	BB	SO	ShO	W	L	SV	AB	H	HR	BA
1987 DET A	0	0	–	16.20	2	0	0	1.2	4	3	0	0	0	0	0	0	0	0	–
1988 PIT N	0	0	–	0.00	5	0	0	5.2	5	7	3	0	0	0	0	0	0	0	–
2 yrs.	0	0	–	3.68	7	0	0	7.1	9	10	3	0	0	0	0	0	0	0	–

Greg Maddux

MADDUX, GREGORY ALAN
Brother of Mike Maddux.
B. Apr. 14, 1966, San Angelo, Tex.
BR TR 6' 170 lbs.

	W	L	PCT	ERA	G	GS	CG	IP	H	BB	SO	ShO	W	L	SV	AB	H	HR	BA
1986 CHI N	2	4	.333	5.52	6	5	1	31	44	11	20	0	0	1	0	12	4	0	.333
1987	6	14	.300	5.61	30	27	1	155.2	181	74	101	1	0	0	0	42	5	0	.119
1988	18	8	.692	3.18	34	34	9	249	230	81	140	3	0	0	0	96	19	0	.198
3 yrs.	26	26	.500	4.21	70	66	11	435.2	455	166	261	4	0	1	0	150	28	0	.187

	W	L	PCT	ERA	G	GS	CG	IP	H	BB	SO	ShO	Relief Pitching W	L	SV	BATTING AB	H	HR	BA

Mike Maddux

MADDUX, MICHAEL AUSLEY
Brother of Greg Maddux.
B. Aug. 27, 1961, Dayton, Ohio

BL TR 6'2" 180 lbs.

	W	L	PCT	ERA	G	GS	CG	IP	H	BB	SO	ShO	W	L	SV	AB	H	HR	BA
1986 PHI N	3	7	.300	5.42	16	16	0	78	88	34	44	0	0	0	0	22	1	0	.045
1987	2	0	1.000	2.65	7	2	0	17	17	5	15	0	1	0	0	3	0	0	.000
1988	4	3	.571	3.76	25	11	0	88.2	91	34	59	0	2	0	0	23	3	0	.130
3 yrs.	9	10	.474	4.36	48	29	0	183.2	196	73	118	0	3	0	0	48	4	0	.083

Alex Madrid

MADRID, ALEXANDER
B. Apr. 18, 1963, Springerville, Ariz.

BR TR 6'3" 200 lbs.

	W	L	PCT	ERA	G	GS	CG	IP	H	BB	SO	ShO	W	L	SV	AB	H	HR	BA
1987 MIL A	0	0	–	15.19	3	0	0	5.1	11	1	1	0	0	0	0	3	0	0	–
1988 PHI N	1	1	.500	2.76	5	2	1	16.1	15	6	2	0	0	0	0	3	0	0	.000
2 yrs.	1	1	.500	5.82	8	2	1	21.2	26	7	3	0	0	0	0	3	0	0	.000

Joe Magrane

MAGRANE, JOSEPH DAVID
B. July 2, 1964, Des Moines, Iowa

BR TL 6'6" 225 lbs.

	W	L	PCT	ERA	G	GS	CG	IP	H	BB	SO	ShO	W	L	SV	AB	H	HR	BA
1987 STL N	9	7	.563	3.54	27	26	4	170.1	157	60	101	2	0	0	0	52	7	1	.135
1988	5	9	.357	2.18	24	24	4	165.1	133	51	100	3	0	0	0	48	8	1	.167
2 yrs.	14	16	.467	2.87	51	50	8	335.2	290	111	201	5	0	0	0	100	15	2	.150

LEAGUE CHAMPIONSHIP SERIES
| 1987 STL N | 0 | 0 | – | 9.00 | 1 | 1 | 0 | 4 | 4 | 2 | 3 | 0 | 0 | 0 | 0 | 1 | 0 | 0 | .000 |

WORLD SERIES
| 1987 STL N | 0 | 1 | .000 | 8.59 | 2 | 2 | 0 | 7.1 | 9 | 5 | 5 | 0 | 0 | 0 | 0 | 0 | 0 | 0 | – |

Rick Mahler

MAHLER, RICHARD KEITH
Brother of Mickey Mahler.
B. Aug. 5, 1953, Austin, Tex.

BR TR 6'1" 195 lbs.

	W	L	PCT	ERA	G	GS	CG	IP	H	BB	SO	ShO	W	L	SV	AB	H	HR	BA
1979 ATL N	0	0	–	6.14	15	0	0	22	28	11	12	0	0	0	0	2	1	0	.500
1980	0	0	–	2.25	2	0	0	4	2	0	1	0	0	0	0	0	0	0	–
1981	8	6	.571	2.81	34	14	1	112	109	43	54	0	2	0	2	27	4	0	.148
1982	9	10	.474	4.21	39	33	5	205.1	213	62	105	2	0	0	0	58	11	1	.190
1983	0	0	–	5.02	10	0	0	14.1	16	9	7	0	0	0	0	2	0	0	.000
1984	13	10	.565	3.12	38	29	9	222	209	62	106	1	0	0	0	71	21	0	.296
1985	17	15	.531	3.48	39	39	6	266.2	272	79	107	1	0	0	0	90	14	0	.156
1986	14	18	.438	4.88	39	39	7	237.2	283	95	137	1	0	0	0	83	16	0	.193
1987	8	13	.381	4.98	39	28	3	197	212	85	95	1	2	1	0	65	11	0	.169
1988	9	16	.360	3.69	39	34	5	249	279	42	131	0	2	0	0	72	9	0	.125
10 yrs.	78	88	.470	3.97	294	216	36	1530	1623	488	755	6	6	1	2	470	87	1	.185

LEAGUE CHAMPIONSHIP SERIES
| 1982 ATL N | 0 | 0 | – | 0.00 | 1 | 0 | 0 | 1.2 | 3 | 2 | 0 | 0 | 0 | 0 | 0 | 0 | 0 | 0 | – |

Ravelo Manzanillo

MANZANILLO, RAVELO
Born Ravelo Manzanillo y Adams.
B. Oct. 17, 1963, San Pedro deMacoris, Dominican Republic

BL TL 6' 200 lbs.

	W	L	PCT	ERA	G	GS	CG	IP	H	BB	SO	ShO	W	L	SV	AB	H	HR	BA
1988 CHI A	0	1	.000	5.79	2	2	0	9.1	7	12	10	0	0	0	0	0	0	0	–

Dennis Martinez

MARTINEZ, JOSE DENNIS
Born Jose Dennis Martinez y Emilia.
B. May 14, 1955, Granada, Nicaragua

BR TR 6'1" 175 lbs.

	W	L	PCT	ERA	G	GS	CG	IP	H	BB	SO	ShO	W	L	SV	AB	H	HR	BA
1976 BAL A	1	2	.333	2.57	4	2	1	28	23	8	18	0	0	0	0	0	0	0	–
1977	14	7	.667	4.10	42	13	5	167	157	64	107	0	8	4	4	0	0	0	–
1978	16	11	.593	3.52	40	38	15	276.1	257	93	142	2	0	0	0	0	0	0	–
1979	15	16	.484	3.67	40	39	18	292	279	78	132	3	0	0	0	0	0	0	–
1980	6	4	.600	3.96	25	12	2	100	103	44	42	0	0	1	1	0	0	0	–
1981	14	5	.737	3.32	25	24	9	179	173	62	88	2	0	0	0	0	0	0	–
1982	16	12	.571	4.21	40	39	10	252	262	87	111	2	0	0	0	0	0	0	–
1983	7	16	.304	5.53	32	25	4	153	209	45	71	0	1	0	0	0	0	0	–
1984	6	9	.400	5.02	34	20	2	141.2	145	37	77	0	1	2	0	0	0	0	–
1985	13	11	.542	5.15	33	31	3	180	203	63	68	1	1	0	0	0	0	0	–
1986 2 teams	BAL A	(4G 0–0)		MON	N	(19G 3–6)													
" total	3	6	.333	4.73	23	15	1	104.2	114	30	65	1	0	0	0	30	3	0	.100
1987 MON N	11	4	.733	3.30	22	22	2	144.2	133	40	84	1	0	0	0	46	3	0	.065
1988	15	13	.536	2.72	34	34	9	235.1	215	55	120	2	0	0	0	78	15	0	.192
13 yrs.	137	116	.542	3.97	394	314	81	2253.2	2273	706	1125	14	11	7	5	154	21	0	.136

LEAGUE CHAMPIONSHIP SERIES
| 1979 BAL A | 0 | 0 | – | 3.24 | 1 | 1 | 0 | 8.1 | 8 | 0 | 4 | 0 | 0 | 0 | 0 | 0 | 0 | 0 | – |

WORLD SERIES
| 1979 BAL A | 0 | 0 | – | 18.00 | 2 | 1 | 0 | 2 | 6 | 0 | 0 | 0 | 0 | 0 | 0 | 0 | 0 | 0 | – |

Ramon Martinez

MARTINEZ, RAMON JAIME
B. Mar. 22, 1968, Santo Domingo, Dominican Republic

BR TR 6'4" 165 lbs.

	W	L	PCT	ERA	G	GS	CG	IP	H	BB	SO	ShO	W	L	SV	AB	H	HR	BA
1988 LA N	1	3	.250	3.79	9	6	0	35.2	27	22	23	0	0	0	0	7	0	0	.000

Tippy Martinez

MARTINEZ, FELIX ANTHONY
B. May 31, 1950, LaJunta, Colo.

BL TL 5'10" 180 lbs.

	W	L	PCT	ERA	G	GS	CG	IP	H	BB	SO	ShO	W	L	SV	AB	H	HR	BA
1974 NY A	0	0	–	4.15	10	0	0	13	14	9	10	0	0	0	0	0	0	0	–
1975	1	2	.333	2.68	23	2	0	37	27	32	20	0	1	1	8	0	0	0	–
1976 2 teams	NY	A	(11G 2–0)		BAL	A	(28G 3–1)												
" total	5	1	.833	2.33	39	0	0	69.2	50	42	45	0	5	1	10	0	0	0	–
1977 BAL A	5	1	.833	2.70	41	0	0	50	47	27	29	0	5	1	9	0	0	0	–
1978	3	3	.500	4.83	42	0	0	69	77	40	57	0	3	3	5	0	0	0	–
1979	10	3	.769	2.88	39	0	0	78	59	31	61	0	10	3	3	0	0	0	–
1980	4	4	.500	3.00	53	0	0	81	69	34	68	0	4	4	10	0	0	0	–
1981	3	3	.500	2.90	37	0	0	59	48	32	50	0	3	3	11	0	0	0	–
1982	8	8	.500	3.41	76	0	0	95	81	37	78	0	8	8	16	0	0	0	–

	W	L	PCT	ERA	G	GS	CG	IP	H	BB	SO	ShO	Relief Pitching W	L	SV	BATTING AB	H	HR	BA

Tippy Martinez continued

	W	L	PCT	ERA	G	GS	CG	IP	H	BB	SO	ShO	W	L	SV	AB	H	HR	BA
1983	9	3	.750	2.35	65	0	0	103.1	76	37	81	0	9	3	21	0	0	0	–
1984	4	9	.308	3.91	55	0	0	89.2	88	51	71	0	4	9	17	0	0	0	–
1985	3	3	.500	5.40	49	0	0	70	70	37	47	0	3	3	4	0	0	0	–
1986	0	2	.000	5.63	14	0	0	16	18	12	11	0	0	2	1	0	0	0	–
1988 **MIN A**	0	0	–	18.00	3	0	0	4	8	4	3	0	0	0	0	0	0	0	–
14 yrs.	55	42	.567	3.45	546	2	0	834.2	732	425	631	0	55	41	115	0	0	0	–

LEAGUE CHAMPIONSHIP SERIES

	W	L	PCT	ERA	G	GS	CG	IP	H	BB	SO	ShO	W	L	SV	AB	H	HR	BA
1983 **BAL A**	1	0	1.000	0.00	2	0	0	6	5	3	5	0	1	0	0	0	0	0	–

WORLD SERIES

	W	L	PCT	ERA	G	GS	CG	IP	H	BB	SO	ShO	W	L	SV	AB	H	HR	BA
1979 **BAL A**	0	0	–	6.75	3	0	0	1.1	3	0	1	0	0	0	0	0	0	0	–
1983	0	0	–	3.00	3	0	0	3	3	0	0	0	0	0	2	0	0	0	–
2 yrs.	0	0	–	4.15	6	0	0	4.1	6	0	1	0	0	0	2	0	0	0	–

Mike Mason

MASON, MICHAEL PAUL
B. Nov. 21, 1958, Fairbault, Minn.   BL TL 6'2"   205 lbs.

	W	L	PCT	ERA	G	GS	CG	IP	H	BB	SO	ShO	W	L	SV	AB	H	HR	BA
1982 **TEX A**	1	2	.333	5.09	4	4	0	23	21	9	8	0	0	0	0	0	0	0	–
1983	0	2	.000	5.91	5	0	0	10.2	10	6	9	0	0	2	0	0	0	0	–
1984	9	13	.409	3.61	36	24	4	184.1	159	51	113	0	3	0	0	0	0	0	–
1985	8	15	.348	4.83	38	30	1	179	212	73	92	1	0	0	0	0	0	0	–
1986	7	3	.700	4.33	27	22	2	135	135	56	85	1	0	0	0	0	0	0	–
1987 2 teams				TEX	A	(8G 0–2)		CHI	N	(17G 4–1)									
" total	4	3	.571	5.64	25	10	0	67	80	45	49	0	2	0	0	9	2	0	.222
1988 **MIN A**	0	1	.000	10.80	5	0	0	6.2	8	9	7	0	0	1	0	0	0	0	–
7 yrs.	29	39	.426	4.53	140	90	7	605.2	625	249	363	2	5	3	0	9	2	0	.222

Greg Mathews

MATHEWS, GREGORY INMAN
B. May 17, 1962, Harbor City, Calif.   BB TL 6'2"   180 lbs.

	W	L	PCT	ERA	G	GS	CG	IP	H	BB	SO	ShO	W	L	SV	AB	H	HR	BA
1986 **STL N**	11	8	.579	3.65	23	22	1	145.1	139	44	67	0	0	0	0	43	2	0	.047
1987	11	11	.500	3.73	32	32	2	197.2	184	71	108	1	0	0	0	68	13	0	.191
1988	4	6	.400	4.24	13	13	1	68	61	33	31	0	0	0	0	23	4	0	.174
3 yrs.	26	25	.510	3.79	68	67	4	411	384	148	206	1	0	0	0	134	19	0	.142

LEAGUE CHAMPIONSHIP SERIES

	W	L	PCT	ERA	G	GS	CG	IP	H	BB	SO	ShO	W	L	SV	AB	H	HR	BA
1987 **STL N**	1	0	1.000	3.48	2	2	0	10.1	6	3	10	0	0	0	0	2	2	0	1.000

WORLD SERIES

	W	L	PCT	ERA	G	GS	CG	IP	H	BB	SO	ShO	W	L	SV	AB	H	HR	BA
1987 **STL N**	0	0	–	2.45	1	1	0	3.2	2	2	3	0	0	0	0	1	0	0	.000

Scott May

MAY, SCOTT FRANCIS
B. Nov. 11, 1961, West Bend, Wis.   BR TR 6'1"   185 lbs.

	W	L	PCT	ERA	G	GS	CG	IP	H	BB	SO	ShO	W	L	SV	AB	H	HR	BA
1988 **TEX A**	0	0	–	8.59	3	1	0	7.1	8	4	4	0	0	0	0	0	0	0	–

Tom McCarthy

McCARTHY, THOMAS MICHAEL
B. June 18, 1961, Lundstahl, West Germany   BR TR 6'   180 lbs.

	W	L	PCT	ERA	G	GS	CG	IP	H	BB	SO	ShO	W	L	SV	AB	H	HR	BA
1985 **BOS A**	0	0	–	10.80	3	0	0	5	7	4	2	0	0	0	0	0	0	0	–
1988 **CHI A**	2	0	1.000	1.38	6	0	0	13	9	2	5	0	2	0	1	0	0	0	–
2 yrs.	2	0	1.000	4.00	9	0	0	18	16	6	7	0	2	0	1	0	0	0	–

Kirk McCaskill

McCASKILL, KIRK EDWARD
B. Apr. 9, 1961, Kapuskasing, Ont., Canada   BR TR 6'1"   195 lbs.

	W	L	PCT	ERA	G	GS	CG	IP	H	BB	SO	ShO	W	L	SV	AB	H	HR	BA
1985 **CAL A**	12	12	.500	4.70	30	29	6	189.2	189	64	102	1	0	0	0	0	0	0	–
1986	17	10	.630	3.36	34	33	10	246.1	207	92	202	2	0	0	0	0	0	0	–
1987	4	6	.400	5.67	14	13	1	74.2	84	34	56	0	0	0	0	0	0	0	–
1988	8	6	.571	4.31	23	23	4	146.1	155	61	98	2	0	0	0	0	0	0	–
4 yrs.	41	34	.547	4.22	101	98	21	657	635	251	458	6	0	0	0	0	0	0	–

LEAGUE CHAMPIONSHIP SERIES

	W	L	PCT	ERA	G	GS	CG	IP	H	BB	SO	ShO	W	L	SV	AB	H	HR	BA
1986 **CAL A**	0	2	.000	7.71	2	2	0	9.1	16	5	7	0	0	0	0	0	0	0	–

Bob McClure

McCLURE, ROBERT CRAIG
B. Apr. 29, 1952, Oakland, Calif.   BB TL 5'11"   170 lbs.

	W	L	PCT	ERA	G	GS	CG	IP	H	BB	SO	ShO	W	L	SV	AB	H	HR	BA
1975 **KC A**	1	0	1.000	0.00	12	0	0	15.1	4	14	15	0	1	0	1	0	0	0	–
1976	0	0	–	9.00	8	0	0	4	3	8	3	0	0	0	0	0	0	0	–
1977 **MIL A**	2	1	.667	2.54	68	0	0	71	64	34	57	0	2	1	6	0	0	0	–
1978	2	6	.250	3.74	44	0	0	65	53	30	47	0	2	6	9	0	0	0	–
1979	5	2	.714	3.88	36	0	0	51	53	24	37	0	5	2	5	0	0	0	–
1980	5	8	.385	3.07	52	5	2	91	83	37	47	1	1	7	10	0	0	0	–
1981	0	0	–	3.38	4	0	0	8	7	4	6	0	0	0	0	0	0	0	–
1982	12	7	.632	4.22	34	26	5	172.2	160	74	99	0	2	0	0	0	0	0	–
1983	9	9	.500	4.50	24	23	4	142	152	68	68	0	0	0	0	0	0	0	–
1984	4	8	.333	4.38	39	18	1	139.2	154	52	68	0	0	2	1	0	0	0	–
1985	4	1	.800	4.31	38	1	0	85.2	91	30	57	0	4	1	3	0	0	0	–
1986 2 teams					**MIL A**	(13G 2–1)		**MON N**	(52G 2–5)										
" total	4	6	.400	3.19	65	0	0	79	71	33	53	0	4	6	6	4	1	0	.250
1987 **MON N**	6	1	.857	3.44	52	0	0	52.1	47	20	33	0	6	1	5	2	0	0	.000
1988 2 teams					**MON N**	(19G 1–3)		**NY N**	(14G 1–0)										
" total	2	3	.400	5.40	33	0	0	30	35	8	19	0	2	3	3	2	0	0	.000
14 yrs.	56	52	.519	3.88	509	73	12	1006.2	977	436	609	1	29	29	49	8	1	0	.125

DIVISIONAL PLAYOFF SERIES

	W	L	PCT	ERA	G	GS	CG	IP	H	BB	SO	ShO	W	L	SV	AB	H	HR	BA
1981 **MIL A**	0	0	–	0.00	3	0	0	3.1	4	0	2	0	0	0	0	0	0	0	–

LEAGUE CHAMPIONSHIP SERIES

	W	L	PCT	ERA	G	GS	CG	IP	H	BB	SO	ShO	W	L	SV	AB	H	HR	BA
1982 **MIL A**	1	0	1.000	0.00	1	0	0	1.2	2	0	0	0	1	0	0	0	0	0	–

WORLD SERIES

	W	L	PCT	ERA	G	GS	CG	IP	H	BB	SO	ShO	W	L	SV	AB	H	HR	BA
1982 **MIL A**	0	2	.000	4.15	5	0	0	4.1	5	3	5	0	0	2	2	0	0	0	–

2nd

	W	L	PCT	ERA	G	GS	CG	IP	H	BB	SO	ShO	Relief Pitching W	L	SV	BATTING AB	H	HR	BA

Lance McCullers
McCULLERS, LANCE GRAYE
B. Mar. 8, 1964, Tampa, Fla.
BB TR 6'1" 185 lbs.

	W	L	PCT	ERA	G	GS	CG	IP	H	BB	SO	ShO	W	L	SV	AB	H	HR	BA
1985 SD N	0	2	.000	2.31	21	0	0	35	23	16	27	0	0	2	5	4	0	0	.000
1986	10	10	.500	2.78	70	7	0	136	103	58	92	0	9	6	5	22	2	0	.091
1987	8	10	.444	3.72	78	0	0	123.1	115	59	126	0	8	10	16	14	1	0	.071
1988	3	6	.333	2.49	60	0	0	97.2	70	55	81	0	3	6	10	8	2	0	.250
4 yrs.	21	28	.429	2.96	229	7	0	392	311	188	326	0	20	24	36	48	5	0	.104

Jack McDowell
McDOWELL, JACK BURNS
B. Jan. 16, 1966, Van Nuys, Calif.
BR TR 6'5" 180 lbs.

	W	L	PCT	ERA	G	GS	CG	IP	H	BB	SO	ShO	W	L	SV	AB	H	HR	BA
1987 CHI A	3	0	1.000	1.93	4	4	0	28	16	6	15	0	0	0	0	0	0	0	–
1988	5	10	.333	3.97	26	26	1	158.2	147	68	84	0	0	0	0	0	0	0	–
2 yrs.	8	10	.444	3.66	30	30	1	186.2	163	74	99	0	0	0	0	0	0	0	–

Roger McDowell
McDOWELL, ROGER ALAN
B. Dec. 21, 1960, Cincinnati, Ohio
BR TR 6'1" 175 lbs.

	W	L	PCT	ERA	G	GS	CG	IP	H	BB	SO	ShO	W	L	SV	AB	H	HR	BA
1985 NY N	6	5	.545	2.83	62	2	0	127.1	108	37	70	0	6	4	17	19	3	0	.158
1986	14	9	.609	3.02	75	0	0	128	107	42	65	0	14	9	22	18	5	0	.278
1987	7	5	.583	4.16	56	0	0	88.2	95	28	32	0	7	5	25	13	3	0	.231
1988	5	5	.500	2.63	62	0	0	89	80	31	46	0	5	5	16	9	3	0	.333
4 yrs.	32	24	.571	3.12	255	2	0	433	390	138	213	0	32	23	80	59	14	0	.237

LEAGUE CHAMPIONSHIP SERIES

	W	L	PCT	ERA	G	GS	CG	IP	H	BB	SO	ShO	W	L	SV	AB	H	HR	BA
1986 NY N	0	0	–	0.00	2	0	0	7	1	0	3	0	0	0	0	1	0	0	.000
1988	0	1	.000	4.50	4	0	0	6	6	2	5	0	0	1	0	0	0	0	–
2 yrs.	0	1	.000	2.08	6	0	0	13	7	2	8	0	0	1	0	1	0	0	.000

WORLD SERIES

	W	L	PCT	ERA	G	GS	CG	IP	H	BB	SO	ShO	W	L	SV	AB	H	HR	BA
1986 NY N	1	0	1.000	4.91	5	0	0	7.1	10	6	2	0	1	0	0	0	0	0	–

Andy McGaffigan
McGAFFIGAN, ANDREW JOSEPH
B. Oct. 25, 1956, West Palm Beach, Fla.
BR TR 6'3" 185 lbs.

	W	L	PCT	ERA	G	GS	CG	IP	H	BB	SO	ShO	W	L	SV	AB	H	HR	BA
1981 NY A	0	0	–	2.57	2	0	0	7	5	3	2	0	0	0	0	0	0	0	–
1982 SF N	1	0	1.000	0.00	4	0	0	8	5	1	4	0	1	0	0	1	0	0	.000
1983	3	9	.250	4.29	43	16	0	134.1	131	39	93	0	1	0	2	30	2	0	.067
1984 2 teams	MON	N (21G 3–4)		CIN	N	(9G 0–2)													
" total	3	6	.333	3.52	30	6	0	69	60	23	57	0	1	3	1	10	0	0	.000
1985 CIN N	3	3	.500	3.72	15	15	2	94.1	88	30	83	0	0	0	0	29	1	0	.034
1986 MON N	10	5	.667	2.65	48	14	1	142.2	114	55	104	1	5	1	2	33	2	0	.061
1987	5	2	.714	2.39	69	0	0	120.1	105	42	100	0	5	2	12	17	0	0	.000
1988	6	0	1.000	2.76	63	0	0	91.1	81	37	71	0	6	0	4	5	0	0	.000
8 yrs.	31	25	.554	3.16	274	51	3	667	589	230	514	1	19	6	21	125	5	0	.040

Scott McGregor
McGREGOR, SCOTT HOUSTON
B. Jan. 18, 1954, Inglewood, Calif.
BB TL 6'1" 190 lbs.

	W	L	PCT	ERA	G	GS	CG	IP	H	BB	SO	ShO	W	L	SV	AB	H	HR	BA
1976 BAL A	0	1	.000	3.60	3	2	0	15	17	5	6	0	0	0	0	0	0	0	–
1977	3	5	.375	4.42	29	5	1	114	119	30	55	0	1	4	4	0	0	0	–
1978	15	13	.536	3.32	35	32	13	233	217	47	94	4	1	0	1	0	0	0	–
1979	13	6	.684	3.34	27	23	7	175	165	23	81	2	0	0	0	0	0	0	–
1980	20	8	.714	3.32	36	36	12	252	254	58	119	4	0	0	0	0	0	0	–
1981	13	5	.722	3.26	24	22	8	160	167	40	82	3	0	0	0	0	0	0	–
1982	14	12	.538	4.61	37	37	7	226.1	238	52	84	1	0	0	0	0	0	0	–
1983	18	7	.720	3.18	36	36	10	260	271	45	86	2	0	0	0	0	0	0	–
1984	15	12	.556	3.94	30	30	10	196.1	216	54	67	3	0	0	0	0	0	0	–
1985	14	14	.500	4.81	35	34	8	204	226	65	86	1	0	0	0	0	0	0	–
1986	11	15	.423	4.52	34	33	4	203	216	57	95	2	0	0	0	0	0	0	–
1987	2	7	.222	6.64	26	15	1	85.1	112	35	39	1	0	0	0	0	0	0	–
1988	0	3	.000	8.83	4	4	0	17.1	27	7	10	0	0	0	0	0	0	0	–
13 yrs.	138	108	.561	3.99	356	309	83	2141.1	2245	518	904	23	2	4	5	0	0	0	–

LEAGUE CHAMPIONSHIP SERIES

	W	L	PCT	ERA	G	GS	CG	IP	H	BB	SO	ShO	W	L	SV	AB	H	HR	BA
1979 BAL A	1	0	1.000	0.00	1	1	1	9	6	1	4	1	0	0	0	0	0	0	–
1983	0	1	.000	1.35	1	1	0	6.2	6	3	2	0	0	0	0	0	0	0	–
2 yrs.	1	1	.500	0.57	2	2	1	15.2	12	4	6	1	0	0	0	0	0	0	–

WORLD SERIES

	W	L	PCT	ERA	G	GS	CG	IP	H	BB	SO	ShO	W	L	SV	AB	H	HR	BA
1979 BAL A	1	1	.500	3.18	2	2	1	17	16	2	8	0	0	0	0	4	0	0	.000
1983	1	1	.500	1.06	2	2	1	17	9	2	12	1	0	0	0	5	0	0	.000
2 yrs.	2	2	.500	2.12	4	4	2	34	25	4	20	1	0	0	0	9	0	0	.000

Craig McMurtry
McMURTRY, JOE CRAIG
B. Nov. 5, 1959, Temple, Tex.
BR TR 6'5" 195 lbs.

	W	L	PCT	ERA	G	GS	CG	IP	H	BB	SO	ShO	W	L	SV	AB	H	HR	BA
1983 ATL N	15	9	.625	3.08	36	35	6	224.2	204	88	105	3	0	0	0	70	6	0	.086
1984	9	17	.346	4.32	37	30	0	183.1	184	102	99	0	0	2	0	52	6	0	.115
1985	0	3	.000	6.60	17	6	0	45	56	27	28	0	0	0	1	14	1	0	.071
1986	1	6	.143	4.74	37	5	0	79.2	82	43	50	0	1	3	0	16	2	0	.125
1988 TEX A	3	3	.500	2.25	32	0	0	60	37	24	35	0	3	3	3	0	0	0	–
5 yrs.	28	38	.424	3.87	159	76	6	592.2	563	284	317	3	4	8	4	152	15	0	.099

Larry McWilliams
McWILLIAMS, LARRY DEAN
B. Feb. 10, 1954, Wichita, Kans.
BL TL 6'5" 180 lbs.

	W	L	PCT	ERA	G	GS	CG	IP	H	BB	SO	ShO	W	L	SV	AB	H	HR	BA
1978 ATL N	9	3	.750	2.82	15	15	3	99	84	35	42	1	0	0	0	32	2	0	.063
1979	3	2	.600	5.59	13	13	1	66	69	22	32	0	0	0	0	24	5	0	.208
1980	9	14	.391	4.94	30	30	4	164	188	39	77	1	0	0	0	51	8	0	.157
1981	2	1	.667	3.08	9	5	2	38	31	8	23	1	0	0	0	10	1	0	.100
1982 2 teams	ATL	N (27G 2–3)		PIT	N	(19G 6–5)													
" total	8	8	.500	3.84	46	20	2	159.1	158	44	118	2	2	2	1	38	7	0	.184
1983 PIT N	15	8	.652	3.25	35	35	8	238	205	87	199	4	0	0	0	79	9	0	.114
1984	12	11	.522	2.93	34	32	7	227.1	226	78	149	2	0	0	1	74	9	0	.122
1985	7	9	.438	4.70	30	19	2	126.1	139	62	52	0	1	1	0	40	5	0	.125
1986	3	11	.214	5.15	49	15	0	122.1	129	49	80	0	2	3	0	29	4	0	.138

	W	L	PCT	ERA	G	GS	CG	IP	H	BB	SO	ShO	Relief Pitching W	L	SV	BATTING AB	H	HR	BA

Larry McWilliams continued

1987 ATL N	0	1	.000	5.75	9	2	0	20.1	25	7	13	0	0	0	0	5	1	0	.200
1988 STL N	6	9	.400	3.90	42	17	2	136	130	45	70	1	1	3	1	37	6	0	.162
11 yrs.	74	77	.490	3.94	309	203	31	1396.2	1384	476	855	12	6	9	3	419	57	0	.136

Dave Meads

MEADS, DAVID DONALD
B. Jan. 7, 1964, Montclair, N. J.   BL TL 6'½"   175 lbs.

1987 HOU N	5	3	.625	5.55	45	0	0	48.2	60	16	32	0	5	3	0	3	1	0	.333
1988	3	1	.750	3.18	22	2	0	39.2	37	14	27	0	2	0	0	4	1	0	.250
2 yrs.	8	4	.667	4.48	67	2	0	88.1	97	30	59	0	7	3	0	7	2	0	.286

Scott Medvin

MEDVIN, SCOTT HOWARD
B. Sept. 16, 1961, North Olmsted, Ohio   BR TR 6'   190 lbs.

1988 PIT N	3	0	1.000	4.88	17	0	0	27.2	23	9	16	0	3	0	0	3	0	0	.000

Brian Meyer

MEYER, BRIAN SCOTT
B. Jan. 29, 1963, Camden, N. J.   BR TR 6'   190 lbs.

1988 HOU N	0	0	–	1.46	8	0	0	12.1	9	4	10	0	0	0	0	0	0	0	–

Bob Milacki

MILACKI, ROBERT
B. July 28, 1964, Trenton, N. J.   BR TR 6'4"   220 lbs.

1988 BAL A	2	0	1.000	0.72	3	3	1	25	9	9	18	1	0	0	0	0	0	0	–

Greg Minton

MINTON, GREGORY BRIAN
B. July 29, 1951, Lubbock, Tex.   BB TR 6'2"   180 lbs.

1975 SF N	1	1	.500	6.88	4	2	0	17	19	11	6	0	0	0	0	6	0	0	.000
1976	0	3	.000	4.91	10	2	0	25.2	32	12	7	0	0	2	0	5	1	0	.200
1977	1	1	.500	4.50	2	2	0	14	14	4	5	0	0	0	0	3	1	0	.333
1978	0	1	.000	7.88	11	0	0	16	22	8	6	0	0	1	0	1	0	0	.000
1979	4	3	.571	1.80	46	0	0	80	59	27	33	0	4	3	4	4	0	0	.000
1980	4	6	.400	2.47	68	0	0	91	81	34	42	0	4	6	19	8	1	0	.125
1981	4	5	.444	2.89	55	0	0	84	84	36	29	0	4	5	21	12	0	0	.000
1982	10	4	.714	1.83	78	0	0	123	108	42	58	0	10	4	30	17	3	0	.176
1983	7	11	.389	3.54	73	0	0	106.2	117	47	38	0	7	11	22	11	6	1	.545
1984	4	9	.308	3.76	74	1	0	124.1	130	57	48	0	3	9	19	21	1	0	.048
1985	5	4	.556	3.54	68	0	0	96.2	98	54	37	0	5	4	4	8	0	0	.000
1986	4	4	.500	3.93	48	0	0	68.2	63	34	34	0	4	4	5	5	2	0	.400
1987 2 teams					SF	N	(15G 1–0)		CAL	A	(41G 5–4)								
" total	6	4	.600	3.17	56	0	0	99.1	101	39	44	0	6	4	11	2	0	0	.000
1988 CAL A	4	5	.444	2.85	44	0	0	79	67	34	46	0	4	5	7	0	0	0	–
14 yrs.	54	61	.470	3.19	637	7	0	1025.1	995	439	433	0	51	58	142	103	15	1	.146

Paul Mirabella

MIRABELLA, PAUL THOMAS
B. Mar. 20, 1954, Belleville, N. J.   BL TL 6'1"   190 lbs.

1978 TEX A	3	2	.600	5.79	10	4	0	28	30	17	23	0	1	1	1	0	0	0	–
1979 NY A	0	4	.000	9.00	10	1	0	14	16	10	4	0	0	3	0	0	0	0	–
1980 TOR A	5	12	.294	4.33	33	22	3	131	151	66	53	1	0	0	0	0	0	0	–
1981	0	0	–	7.20	8	1	0	15	20	7	9	0	0	0	0	0	0	0	–
1982 TEX A	1	1	.500	4.80	40	0	0	50.2	46	22	29	0	1	1	3	0	0	0	–
1983 BAL A	0	0	–	5.59	3	2	0	9.2	9	7	4	0	0	0	0	0	0	0	–
1984 SEA A	2	5	.286	4.37	52	1	0	68	74	32	41	0	2	4	3	0	0	0	–
1985	0	0	–	1.32	10	0	0	13.2	9	4	8	0	0	0	0	0	0	0	–
1986	0	0	–	8.53	8	0	0	6.1	13	3	6	0	0	0	0	0	0	0	–
1987 MIL A	2	1	.667	4.91	29	0	0	29.1	30	16	14	0	2	1	2	0	0	0	–
1988	2	2	.500	1.65	38	0	0	60	44	21	33	0	2	2	4	0	0	0	–
11 yrs.	15	27	.357	4.40	241	31	3	425.2	442	205	224	1	8	12	13	0	0	0	–

John Mitchell

MITCHELL, JOHN KYLE
Brother of Charlie Mitchell.
B. Aug. 11, 1965, Dickson, Tenn.   BR TR 6'2"   165 lbs.

1986 NY N	0	1	.000	3.60	4	1	0	10	10	4	2	0	0	0	0	2	0	0	.000
1987	3	6	.333	4.11	20	19	1	111.2	124	36	57	0	0	0	0	35	4	0	.114
1988	0	0	–	0.00	1	0	0	1	2	1	1	0	0	0	0	1	0	0	.000
3 yrs.	3	7	.300	4.04	25	20	1	122.2	136	41	60	0	0	0	0	38	4	0	.105

Dale Mohorcic

MOHORCIC, DALE ROBERT
B. Jan. 25, 1956, Cleveland, Ohio   BR TR 6'3"   220 lbs.

1986 TEX A	2	4	.333	2.51	58	0	0	79	86	15	29	0	2	4	7	0	0	0	–
1987	7	6	.538	2.99	74	0	0	99.1	88	19	48	0	7	6	16	0	0	0	–
1988 2 teams			TEX	A	(43G 2–6)	NY	A	(13G 2–2)											
" total	4	8	.333	4.22	56	0	0	74.2	83	29	44	0	4	8	6	0	0	0	–
3 yrs.	13	18	.419	3.20	188	0	0	253	257	63	121	0	13	18	29	0	0	0	–

Rich Monteleone

MONTELEONE, RICHARD
B. Mar. 22, 1963, Tampa, Fla.   BR TR 6'2"   205 lbs.

1987 SEA A	0	0	–	6.43	3	0	0	7	10	4	2	0	0	0	0	0	0	0	–
1988 CAL A	0	0	–	0.00	3	0	0	4.1	4	1	3	0	0	0	0	0	0	0	–
2 yrs.	0	0	–	3.97	6	0	0	11.1	14	5	5	0	0	0	0	0	0	0	–

Jeff Montgomery

MONTGOMERY, JEFFREY THOMAS
B. Jan. 7, 1962, Wellston, Ohio   BR TR 5'11"   170 lbs.

1987 CIN N	2	2	.500	6.52	14	1	0	19.1	25	9	13	0	2	1	0	2	0	0	.000
1988 KC A	7	2	.778	3.45	45	0	0	62.2	54	30	47	0	7	2	1	0	0	0	–
2 yrs.	9	4	.692	4.17	59	1	0	82	79	39	60	0	9	3	1	2	0	0	.000

	W	L	PCT	ERA	G	GS	CG	IP	H	BB	SO	ShO	Relief Pitching W	L	SV	BATTING AB	H	HR	BA

Brad Moore

MOORE, BRADLEY ALAN
B. June 21, 1964, Loveland, Colo. BR TR 6'1" 185 lbs.

	W	L	PCT	ERA	G	GS	CG	IP	H	BB	SO	ShO	RW	RL	SV	AB	H	HR	BA
1988 PHI N	0	0	—	0.00	5	0	0	5.2	4	4	2	0	0	0	0	0	0	0	—

Donnie Moore

MOORE, DONNIE RAY
B. Feb. 13, 1954, Lubbock, Tex. BL TR 6' 175 lbs.

	W	L	PCT	ERA	G	GS	CG	IP	H	BB	SO	ShO	RW	RL	SV	AB	H	HR	BA
1975 CHI N	0	0	—	4.00	4	1	0	9	12	4	8	0	0	0	0	3	0	0	.000
1977	4	2	.667	4.04	27	1	0	49	51	18	34	0	3	2	0	10	3	0	.300
1978	9	7	.563	4.11	71	1	0	103	117	31	50	0	9	7	4	15	4	0	.267
1979	1	4	.200	5.18	39	1	0	73	95	25	43	0	1	3	1	13	2	0	.154
1980 STL N	1	1	.500	6.14	11	0	0	22	25	5	10	0	1	1	0	4	3	0	.750
1981 MIL A	0	0	—	6.75	3	0	0	4	4	4	2	0	0	0	0	0	0	0	—
1982 ATL N	3	1	.750	4.23	16	0	0	27.2	32	7	17	0	3	1	1	1	0	0	.000
1983	2	3	.400	3.67	43	0	0	68.2	72	10	41	0	2	3	6	8	4	0	.500
1984	4	5	.444	2.94	47	0	0	64.1	63	18	47	0	4	5	16	3	0	0	.000
1985 CAL A	8	8	.500	1.92	65	0	0	103	91	21	72	0	8	8	31	0	0	0	—
1986	4	5	.444	2.97	49	0	0	72.2	60	22	53	0	4	5	21	0	0	0	—
1987	2	2	.500	2.70	14	0	0	26.2	28	13	17	0	2	2	5	0	0	0	—
1988	5	2	.714	4.91	27	0	0	33	48	8	22	0	5	2	4	0	0	0	—
13 yrs.	43	40	.518	3.66	416	4	0	656	698	186	416	0	42	39	89	57	16	0	.281

LEAGUE CHAMPIONSHIP SERIES

	W	L	PCT	ERA	G	GS	CG	IP	H	BB	SO	ShO	RW	RL	SV	AB	H	HR	BA
1982 ATL N	0	0	—	0.00	2	0	0	2.2	2	0	1	0	0	0	0	0	0	0	—
1986 CAL A	0	1	.000	7.20	3	0	0	5	8	2	0	0	0	1	1	0	0	0	—
2 yrs.	0	1	.000	4.70	5	0	0	7.2	10	2	1	0	0	1	1	0	0	0	—

Mike Moore

MOORE, MICHAEL WAYNE
B. Nov. 26, 1959, Carnegie, Okla. BR TR 6'4" 205 lbs.

	W	L	PCT	ERA	G	GS	CG	IP	H	BB	SO	ShO	RW	RL	SV	AB	H	HR	BA
1982 SEA A	7	14	.333	5.36	28	27	1	144.1	159	79	73	1	0	0	0	0	0	0	—
1983	6	8	.429	4.71	22	21	3	128	130	60	108	2	0	0	0	0	0	0	—
1984	7	17	.292	4.97	34	33	6	212	236	85	158	0	0	0	0	0	0	0	—
1985	17	10	.630	3.46	35	34	14	247	230	70	155	2	0	0	0	0	0	0	—
1986	11	13	.458	4.30	38	37	11	266	279	94	146	1	0	0	1	0	0	0	—
1987	9	19	.321	4.71	33	33	12	231	268	84	115	0	0	0	0	1	0	0	.000
1988	9	15	.375	3.78	37	32	9	228.2	196	63	182	3	1	0	1	0	0	0	—
7 yrs.	66	96	.407	4.38	227	217	56	1457	1498	535	937	9	1	0	2	1	0	0	.000

Mike Morgan

MORGAN, MICHAEL THOMAS
B. Oct. 8, 1959, Tulare, Calif. BR TR 6'3" 195 lbs.

	W	L	PCT	ERA	G	GS	CG	IP	H	BB	SO	ShO	RW	RL	SV	AB	H	HR	BA
1978 OAK A	0	3	.000	7.30	3	3	1	12.1	19	8	0	0	0	0	0	0	0	0	—
1979	2	10	.167	5.96	13	13	2	77	102	50	17	0	0	0	0	0	0	0	—
1982 NY A	7	11	.389	4.37	30	23	2	150.1	167	67	71	0	2	1	0	0	0	0	—
1983 TOR A	0	3	.000	5.16	16	4	0	45.1	48	21	22	0	0	1	0	0	0	0	—
1985 SEA A	1	1	.500	12.00	2	2	0	6	11	5	2	0	0	0	0	0	0	0	—
1986	11	17	.393	4.53	37	33	9	216.1	243	86	116	1	0	0	1	0	0	0	—
1987	12	17	.414	4.65	34	31	8	207	245	53	85	2	0	0	0	0	0	0	—
1988 BAL A	1	6	.143	5.43	22	10	2	71.1	70	23	29	0	1	0	1	0	0	0	—
8 yrs.	34	68	.333	4.89	157	119	24	785.2	905	313	342	3	3	2	2	0	0	0	—

Jack Morris

MORRIS, JOHN SCOTT
B. May 16, 1955, St. Paul, Minn. BR TR 6'3" 195 lbs.

	W	L	PCT	ERA	G	GS	CG	IP	H	BB	SO	ShO	RW	RL	SV	AB	H	HR	BA
1977 DET A	1	1	.500	3.72	7	6	1	46	38	23	28	0	0	0	0	0	0	0	—
1978	3	5	.375	4.33	28	7	0	106	107	49	48	0	3	3	0	0	0	0	—
1979	17	7	.708	3.27	27	27	9	198	179	59	113	1	0	0	0	0	0	0	—
1980	16	15	.516	4.18	36	36	11	250	252	87	112	2	0	0	0	0	0	0	—
1981	14	7	.667	3.05	25	25	15	198	153	78	97	1	0	0	0	0	0	0	—
1982	17	16	.515	4.06	37	37	17	266.1	247	96	135	3	0	0	0	0	0	0	—
1983	20	13	.606	3.34	37	37	20	293.2	257	83	232	1	0	0	0	0	0	0	—
1984	19	11	.633	3.65	35	35	9	241.1	224	87	149	1	0	0	0	0	0	0	—
1985	16	11	.593	3.33	35	35	13	257	212	110	191	4	0	0	0	0	0	0	—
1986	21	8	.724	3.27	35	35	15	267	229	82	223	6	0	0	0	0	0	0	—
1987	18	11	.621	3.38	34	34	13	266	227	93	208	0	0	0	0	1	0	0	.000
1988	15	13	.536	3.94	34	34	10	235	225	83	168	2	0	0	0	0	0	0	—
12 yrs.	177	118	.600	3.59	370	348	133	2624.1	2350	930	1704	21	3	3	0	1	0	0	.000

LEAGUE CHAMPIONSHIP SERIES

	W	L	PCT	ERA	G	GS	CG	IP	H	BB	SO	ShO	RW	RL	SV	AB	H	HR	BA
1984 DET A	1	0	1.000	1.29	1	1	0	7	5	1	4	0	0	0	0	0	0	0	—
1987	0	1	.000	6.75	1	1	1	8	6	3	7	0	0	0	0	0	0	0	—
2 yrs.	1	1	.500	4.20	2	2	1	15	11	4	11	0	0	0	0	0	0	0	—

WORLD SERIES

	W	L	PCT	ERA	G	GS	CG	IP	H	BB	SO	ShO	RW	RL	SV	AB	H	HR	BA
1984 DET A	2	0	1.000	2.00	2	2	2	18	13	3	13	0	0	0	0	0	0	0	—

Jim Morrison

MORRISON, JAMES FORREST
B. Sept. 23, 1952, Pensacola, Fla. BR TR 5'11" 175 lbs.

	W	L	PCT	ERA	G	GS	CG	IP	H	BB	SO	ShO	RW	RL	SV	AB	H	HR	BA
1988 DET A	0	0	—	0.00	3	0	0	3.2	3	2	1	0	0	0	0	*			

Jamie Moyer

MOYER, JAMIE
B. Nov. 11, 1962, Sellersville, Pa. BL TL 6' 170 lbs.

	W	L	PCT	ERA	G	GS	CG	IP	H	BB	SO	ShO	RW	RL	SV	AB	H	HR	BA
1986 CHI N	7	4	.636	5.05	16	16	1	87.1	107	42	45	1	0	0	0	22	2	0	.091
1987	12	15	.444	5.10	35	33	1	201	210	97	147	0	1	0	0	61	14	0	.230
1988	9	15	.375	3.48	34	30	3	202	212	55	121	1	1	0	0	60	5	0	.083
3 yrs.	28	34	.452	4.42	85	79	5	490.1	529	194	313	2	2	0	0	143	21	0	.147

	W	L	PCT	ERA	G	GS	CG	IP	H	BB	SO	ShO	Relief Pitching			BATTING			BA
													W	L	SV	AB	H	HR	

Terry Mulholland

MULHOLLAND, TERENCE JOHN
B. Mar. 9, 1963, Uniontown, Pa.   BR TL 6'3"   200 lbs.

	W	L	PCT	ERA	G	GS	CG	IP	H	BB	SO	ShO	W	L	SV	AB	H	HR	BA
1986 SF N	1	7	.125	4.94	15	10	0	54.2	51	35	27	0	0	0	0	19	1	0	.053
1988	2	1	.667	3.72	9	6	2	46	50	7	18	1	0	0	0	14	0	0	.000
2 yrs.	3	8	.273	4.38	24	16	2	100.2	101	42	45	1	0	0	0	33	1	0	.030

Rob Murphy

MURPHY, ROBERT ALBERT JR.
B. May 26, 1960, Miami, Fla.   BL TL 6'2"   200 lbs.

	W	L	PCT	ERA	G	GS	CG	IP	H	BB	SO	ShO	W	L	SV	AB	H	HR	BA
1985 CIN N	0	0	–	6.00	2	0	0	3	2	2	1	0	0	0	0	0	0	0	–
1986	6	0	1.000	0.72	34	0	0	50.1	26	21	36	0	6	0	1	3	0	0	.000
1987	8	5	.615	3.04	87	0	0	100.2	91	32	99	0	8	5	3	5	1	0	.200
1988	0	6	.000	3.08	76	0	0	84.2	69	38	74	0	0	6	3	0	0	0	–
4 yrs.	14	11	.560	2.60	199	0	0	238.2	188	93	210	0	14	11	7	8	1	0	.125

Jeff Musselman

MUSSELMAN, JEFFREY JOSEPH
B. June 21, 1963, Doylestown, Pa.   BL TL 6'   180 lbs.

	W	L	PCT	ERA	G	GS	CG	IP	H	BB	SO	ShO	W	L	SV	AB	H	HR	BA
1986 TOR A	0	0	–	10.13	6	0	0	5.1	8	5	4	0	0	0	0	0	0	0	–
1987	12	5	.706	4.15	68	1	0	89	75	54	54	0	12	5	3	0	0	0	–
1988	8	5	.615	3.18	15	15	0	85	80	30	39	0	0	0	0	0	0	0	–
3 yrs.	20	10	.667	3.86	89	16	0	179.1	163	89	97	0	12	5	3	0	0	0	–

Randy Myers

MYERS, RANDALL KIRK
B. Sept. 19, 1962, Vancouver, Wash.   BL TL 6'1"   190 lbs.

	W	L	PCT	ERA	G	GS	CG	IP	H	BB	SO	ShO	W	L	SV	AB	H	HR	BA
1985 NY N	0	0	–	0.00	1	0	0	2	0	1	2	0	0	0	0	0	0	0	–
1986	0	0	–	4.22	10	0	0	10.2	11	9	13	0	0	0	0	0	0	0	–
1987	3	6	.333	3.96	54	0	0	75	61	30	92	0	3	6	6	7	2	0	.286
1988	7	3	.700	1.72	55	0	0	68	45	17	69	0	7	3	26	4	1	0	.250
4 yrs.	10	9	.526	2.95	120	0	0	155.2	117	57	176	0	10	9	32	11	3	0	.273

LEAGUE CHAMPIONSHIP SERIES

	W	L	PCT	ERA	G	GS	CG	IP	H	BB	SO	ShO	W	L	SV	AB	H	HR	BA
1988 NY N	2	0	1.000	0.00	3	0	0	4.2	1	2	0	0	2	0	0	0	0	0	–

Gene Nelson

NELSON, WAYLAND EUGENE
B. Dec. 3, 1960, Tampa, Fla.   BR TR 6'   172 lbs.

	W	L	PCT	ERA	G	GS	CG	IP	H	BB	SO	ShO	W	L	SV	AB	H	HR	BA
1981 NY A	3	1	.750	4.85	8	7	0	39	40	23	16	0	0	0	0	0	0	0	–
1982 SEA A	6	9	.400	4.62	22	19	2	122.2	133	60	71	1	0	1	0	0	0	0	–
1983	0	3	.000	7.88	10	5	1	32	38	21	11	0	0	0	0	0	0	0	–
1984 CHI A	3	5	.375	4.46	20	9	2	74.2	72	17	36	0	2	0	1	0	0	0	–
1985	10	10	.500	4.26	46	18	1	145.2	144	67	101	0	4	3	2	1	0	0	.000
1986	6	6	.500	3.85	54	1	0	114.2	118	41	70	0	6	5	6	0	0	0	–
1987 OAK A	6	5	.545	3.93	54	6	0	123.2	120	35	94	0	5	2	3	0	0	0	–
1988	9	6	.600	3.06	54	1	0	111.2	93	38	67	0	9	5	3	0	0	0	–
8 yrs.	43	45	.489	4.23	268	66	6	764	758	302	466	1	26	16	15	1	0	0	.000

LEAGUE CHAMPIONSHIP SERIES

	W	L	PCT	ERA	G	GS	CG	IP	H	BB	SO	ShO	W	L	SV	AB	H	HR	BA
1988 OAK A	2	0	1.000	0.00	2	0	0	4.2	5	1	0	0	2	0	0	0	0	0	–

WORLD SERIES

	W	L	PCT	ERA	G	GS	CG	IP	H	BB	SO	ShO	W	L	SV	AB	H	HR	BA
1988 OAK A	0	0	–	1.42	3	0	0	6.1	4	3	3	0	0	0	0	0	0	0	–

Rod Nichols

NICHOLS, RODNEY LEA
B. Dec. 29, 1964, Burlington, Iowa   BR TR 6'2"   190 lbs.

	W	L	PCT	ERA	G	GS	CG	IP	H	BB	SO	ShO	W	L	SV	AB	H	HR	BA
1988 CLE A	1	7	.125	5.06	11	10	3	69.1	73	23	31	0	0	1	0	0	0	0	–

Tom Niedenfuer

NIEDENFUER, THOMAS EDWARD
B. Aug. 13, 1959, St. Louis Park, Minn.   BR TR 6'5"   225 lbs.

	W	L	PCT	ERA	G	GS	CG	IP	H	BB	SO	ShO	W	L	SV	AB	H	HR	BA
1981 LA N	3	1	.750	3.81	17	0	0	26	25	6	12	0	3	1	2	0	0	0	–
1982	3	4	.429	2.71	55	0	0	69.2	71	25	60	0	3	4	9	3	0	0	.000
1983	8	3	.727	1.90	66	0	0	94.2	55	29	66	0	8	3	11	4	0	0	.000
1984	2	5	.286	2.47	33	0	0	47.1	39	23	45	0	2	5	11	3	0	0	.000
1985	7	9	.438	2.71	64	0	0	106.1	86	24	102	0	7	9	19	9	1	0	.111
1986	6	6	.500	3.71	60	0	0	80	86	29	55	0	6	6	11	4	2	0	.500
1987 2 teams	LA	N	(15G 1–0)	BAL	A	(45G 3–5)													
" total	4	5	.444	4.46	60	0	0	68.2	68	31	47	0	4	5	14	0	0	0	–
1988 BAL A	3	4	.429	3.51	52	0	0	59	59	19	40	0	3	4	18	0	0	0	–
8 yrs.	36	37	.493	3.05	407	0	0	551.2	489	186	427	0	36	37	95	23	3	0	.130

DIVISIONAL PLAYOFF SERIES

	W	L	PCT	ERA	G	GS	CG	IP	H	BB	SO	ShO	W	L	SV	AB	H	HR	BA
1981 LA N	0	0	–	0.00	1	0	0	.1	1	1	1	0	0	0	0	0	0	0	–

LEAGUE CHAMPIONSHIP SERIES

	W	L	PCT	ERA	G	GS	CG	IP	H	BB	SO	ShO	W	L	SV	AB	H	HR	BA
1981 LA N	0	0	–	0.00	1	0	0	.1	2	0	0	0	0	0	0	0	0	0	–
1983	0	0	–	0.00	2	0	0	2	0	1	3	0	0	0	1	0	0	0	–
1985	0	2	.000	6.35	3	0	0	5.2	5	2	5	0	0	2	1	1	0	0	.000
3 yrs.	0	2	.000	4.50	6	0	0	8	7	3	8	0	0	2	2	1	0	0	.000

WORLD SERIES

	W	L	PCT	ERA	G	GS	CG	IP	H	BB	SO	ShO	W	L	SV	AB	H	HR	BA
1981 LA N	0	0	–	0.00	2	0	0	5	3	1	0	0	0	0	0	0	0	0	–

Joe Niekro

NIEKRO, JOSEPH FRANKLIN
Brother of Phil Niekro.
B. Nov. 7, 1944, Martins Ferry, Ohio   BR TR 6'1"   185 lbs.

	W	L	PCT	ERA	G	GS	CG	IP	H	BB	SO	ShO	W	L	SV	AB	H	HR	BA
1967 CHI N	10	7	.588	3.34	36	22	7	169.2	171	32	77	2	1	1	0	46	9	0	.196
1968	14	10	.583	4.31	34	29	2	177.1	204	59	65	1	1	0	2	60	6	0	.100
1969 2 teams	CHI	N	(4G 0–1)	SD	N	(37G 8–17)													
" total	8	18	.308	3.70	41	34	8	221.1	237	51	62	3	0	0	0	56	7	0	.125
1970 DET A	12	13	.480	4.06	38	34	6	213	221	72	101	2	1	0	0	66	13	0	.197
1971	6	7	.462	4.50	31	15	0	122	136	49	43	0	2	0	1	30	4	0	.133
1972	3	2	.600	3.83	18	7	1	47	62	8	24	0	1	1	1	12	3	0	.250
1973 ATL N	2	4	.333	4.13	20	0	0	24	23	11	12	0	2	4	3	3	1	0	.333
1974	3	2	.600	3.56	27	2	0	43	36	18	31	0	3	2	0	5	0	0	.000

	W	L	PCT	ERA	G	GS	CG	IP	H	BB	SO	ShO	Relief Pitching W	L	SV	BATTING AB	H	HR	BA

Joe Niekro continued

	W	L	PCT	ERA	G	GS	CG	IP	H	BB	SO	ShO	W	L	SV	AB	H	HR	BA
1975 HOU N	6	4	.600	3.07	40	4	1	88	79	39	54	1	3	4	4	14	3	0	.214
1976	4	8	.333	3.36	36	13	0	118	107	56	77	0	0	2	0	27	5	1	.185
1977	13	8	.619	3.03	44	14	9	181	155	64	101	2	4	4	5	50	7	0	.140
1978	14	14	.500	3.86	35	29	10	203	190	73	97	1	1	0	0	65	9	0	.138
1979	21	11	.656	3.00	38	38	11	264	221	107	119	5	0	0	0	83	10	0	.120
1980	20	12	.625	3.55	37	36	11	256	268	79	127	2	1	0	0	80	22	0	.275
1981	9	9	.500	2.82	24	24	5	166	150	47	77	2	0	0	0	51	9	0	.176
1982	17	12	.586	2.47	35	35	16	270	224	64	130	5	0	0	0	89	8	0	.090
1983	15	14	.517	3.48	38	38	9	263.2	238	101	152	1	0	0	0	85	8	0	.094
1984	16	12	.571	3.04	38	38	6	248.1	223	89	127	1	0	0	0	83	11	0	.133
1985 2 teams			HOU	N	(32G	9–12)		NY	A	(3G	2–1)								
" total	11	13	.458	3.83	35	35	4	225.1	211	107	121	1	0	0	0	68	17	0	.250
1986 NY A	9	10	.474	4.87	25	25	0	125.2	139	63	59	0	0	0	0	0	0	0	–
1987 2 teams			NY	A	(8G	3–4)		MIN	A	(19G	4–9)								
" total	7	13	.350	5.33	27	26	1	147	155	64	84	0	0	0	0	0	0	0	–
1988 MIN A	1	1	.500	10.03	5	2	0	11.2	16	9	7	0	1	0	0	0	0	0	–
22 yrs.	221	204	.520	3.59	702	500	107	3585	3466	1262	1747	29	20	18	16	973	152	1	.156

DIVISIONAL PLAYOFF SERIES
| 1981 HOU N | 0 | 0 | – | 0.00 | 1 | 1 | 0 | 8 | 7 | 3 | 4 | 0 | 0 | 0 | 0 | 2 | 0 | 0 | .000 |

LEAGUE CHAMPIONSHIP SERIES
| 1980 HOU N | 0 | 0 | – | 0.00 | 1 | 1 | 0 | 10 | 6 | 1 | 2 | 0 | 0 | 0 | 0 | 3 | 0 | 0 | .000 |

WORLD SERIES
| 1987 MIN A | 0 | 0 | – | 0.00 | 1 | 0 | 0 | 2 | 1 | 1 | 1 | 0 | 0 | 0 | 0 | 0 | 0 | 0 | – |

Scott Nielsen

NIELSEN, JEFFREY SCOTT
B. Dec. 18, 1958, Salt Lake City, Utah
BR TR 6'1"   190 lbs.

	W	L	PCT	ERA	G	GS	CG	IP	H	BB	SO	ShO	W	L	SV	AB	H	HR	BA
1986 NY A	4	4	.500	4.02	10	9	2	56	66	12	20	2	0	0	0	0	0	0	–
1987 CHI A	3	5	.375	6.24	19	7	1	66.1	83	25	23	1	1	0	2	0	0	0	–
1988 NY A	1	2	.333	6.86	7	2	0	19.2	27	13	4	0	1	0	0	0	0	0	–
3 yrs.	8	11	.421	5.45	36	18	3	142	176	50	47	3	2	0	2	0	0	0	–

Juan Nieves

NIEVES, JUAN MANUEL
Born Juan Manuel Nieves y Cruz.
B. Jan. 5, 1965, Santurce, Puerto Rico
BL TL 6'3"   175 lbs.

	W	L	PCT	ERA	G	GS	CG	IP	H	BB	SO	ShO	W	L	SV	AB	H	HR	BA
1986 MIL A	11	12	.478	4.92	35	33	4	184.2	224	77	116	3	1	0	0	0	0	0	–
1987	14	8	.636	4.88	34	33	3	195.2	199	100	163	1	0	0	0	0	0	0	–
1988	7	5	.583	4.08	25	15	1	110.1	84	50	73	1	1	0	1	0	0	0	–
3 yrs.	32	25	.561	4.71	94	81	8	490.2	507	227	352	5	2	0	1	0	0	0	–

Al Nipper

NIPPER, ALBERT SAMUEL
B. Apr. 2, 1959, San Diego, Calif.
BR TR 6'   188 lbs.

	W	L	PCT	ERA	G	GS	CG	IP	H	BB	SO	ShO	W	L	SV	AB	H	HR	BA
1983 BOS A	1	1	.500	2.25	3	2	1	16	17	7	5	0	0	0	0	0	0	0	–
1984	11	6	.647	3.89	29	24	6	182.2	183	52	84	0	0	0	0	0	0	0	–
1985	9	12	.429	4.06	25	25	5	162	157	82	85	0	0	0	0	0	0	0	–
1986	10	12	.455	5.38	26	26	3	159	186	47	79	0	0	0	0	0	0	0	–
1987	11	12	.478	5.43	30	30	6	174	196	62	89	0	0	0	0	0	0	0	–
1988 CHI N	2	4	.333	3.04	22	12	0	80	72	34	27	0	0	1	1	23	2	0	.087
6 yrs.	44	47	.484	4.46	135	119	21	773.2	811	284	369	0	0	1	1	23	2	0	.087

WORLD SERIES
| 1986 BOS A | 0 | 1 | .000 | 7.11 | 2 | 1 | 0 | 6.1 | 10 | 2 | 2 | 0 | 0 | 0 | 0 | 0 | 0 | 0 | – |

Dickie Noles

NOLES, DICKIE RAY
B. Nov. 19, 1956, Charlotte, N. C.
BR TR 6'2"   160 lbs.

	W	L	PCT	ERA	G	GS	CG	IP	H	BB	SO	ShO	W	L	SV	AB	H	HR	BA
1979 PHI N	3	4	.429	3.80	14	14	0	90	80	38	42	0	0	0	0	30	3	0	.100
1980	1	4	.200	3.89	48	3	0	81	80	42	57	0	0	4	6	13	4	0	.308
1981	2	2	.500	4.19	13	8	0	58	57	23	34	0	0	0	0	19	2	0	.105
1982 CHI N	10	13	.435	4.42	31	30	2	171	180	61	85	2	0	0	0	56	6	0	.107
1983	5	10	.333	4.72	24	18	1	116.1	133	37	59	1	0	1	0	38	9	0	.237
1984 2 teams			CHI	N	(21G	2–2)		TEX	A	(18G	2–3)								
" total	4	5	.444	5.15	39	7	0	108.1	120	46	53	0	4	3	0	10	0	0	.000
1985 TEX A	4	8	.333	5.06	28	13	0	110.1	129	33	59	0	1	1	1	0	0	0	–
1986 CLE A	3	2	.600	5.10	32	0	0	54.2	56	30	32	0	3	2	0	0	0	0	–
1987 2 teams			CHI	N	(41G	4–2)		DET	A	(4G	0–0)								
" total	4	2	.667	3.53	45	1	0	66.1	61	28	33	0	4	1	4	11	0	0	.000
1988 BAL A	0	2	.000	24.30	2	2	0	3.1	11	0	1	0	0	0	0	0	0	0	–
10 yrs.	36	52	.409	4.56	276	96	3	859.1	907	338	455	3	12	12	11	177	24	0	.136

DIVISIONAL PLAYOFF SERIES
| 1981 PHI N | 0 | 0 | – | 4.50 | 1 | 1 | 0 | 4 | 4 | 2 | 5 | 0 | 0 | 0 | 0 | 0 | 0 | 0 | – |

LEAGUE CHAMPIONSHIP SERIES
| 1980 PHI N | 0 | 0 | – | 0.00 | 2 | 0 | 0 | 2.2 | 1 | 3 | 0 | 0 | 0 | 0 | 0 | 0 | 0 | 0 | – |

WORLD SERIES
| 1980 PHI N | 0 | 0 | – | 1.93 | 1 | 0 | 0 | 4.2 | 5 | 2 | 6 | 0 | 0 | 0 | 0 | 0 | 0 | 0 | – |

Eric Nolte

NOLTE, ERIC CARL
B. Apr. 28, 1964, Canoga Park, Calif.
BL TL 6'3"   205 lbs.

	W	L	PCT	ERA	G	GS	CG	IP	H	BB	SO	ShO	W	L	SV	AB	H	HR	BA
1987 SD N	2	6	.250	3.21	12	12	1	67.1	57	36	44	0	0	0	0	21	2	0	.095
1988	0	0	–	6.00	2	0	0	3	3	2	1	0	0	0	0	0	0	0	–
2 yrs.	2	6	.250	3.33	14	12	1	70.1	60	38	45	0	0	0	0	21	2	0	.095

	W	L	PCT	ERA	G	GS	CG	IP	H	BB	SO	ShO	Relief Pitching W	L	SV	BATTING AB	H	HR	BA

Edwin Nunez

NUNEZ, EDWIN MARTINEZ
Born Edwin Nunez y Martinez.
B. May 27, 1963, Humacao, Puerto Rico

BR TR 6'5" 207 lbs.

	W	L	PCT	ERA	G	GS	CG	IP	H	BB	SO	ShO	W	L	SV	AB	H	HR	BA
1982 SEA A	1	2	.333	4.58	8	5	0	35.1	36	16	27	0	0	0	0	0	0	0	–
1983	0	4	.000	4.38	14	5	0	37	40	22	35	0	0	0	0	0	0	0	–
1984	2	2	.500	3.18	37	0	0	68	55	21	57	0	2	2	7	0	0	0	–
1985	7	3	.700	3.09	70	0	0	90.1	79	34	58	0	7	3	16	0	0	0	–
1986	1	2	.333	5.82	14	1	0	21.2	25	5	17	0	0	2	0	0	0	0	–
1987	3	4	.429	3.80	48	0	0	47.1	45	18	34	0	3	4	12	0	0	0	–
1988 2 teams		SEA	A (14G 1–4)		NY	N	(10G 1–0)												
" total	2	4	.333	6.85	24	3	0	43.1	66	17	27	0	2	1	0	0	0	0	–
7 yrs.	16	21	.432	4.15	215	14	0	343	346	133	255	0	14	12	35	0	0	0	–

Jose Nunez

NUNEZ, JOSE
Born Jose Nunez y Jiminez.
B. Jan. 13, 1964, Jarabacoa, Dominican Republic

BR TR 6'3" 175 lbs.

	W	L	PCT	ERA	G	GS	CG	IP	H	BB	SO	ShO	W	L	SV	AB	H	HR	BA
1987 TOR A	5	2	.714	5.01	37	9	0	97	91	58	99	0	3	1	0	0	0	0	–
1988	0	1	.000	3.07	13	2	0	29.1	28	17	18	0	0	1	0	0	0	0	–
2 yrs.	5	3	.625	4.56	50	11	0	126.1	119	75	117	0	3	2	0	0	0	0	–

Bob Ojeda

OJEDA, ROBERT MICHAEL (Bobby O.)
B. Dec. 17, 1957, Los Angeles, Calif.

BL TL 6'1" 185 lbs.

	W	L	PCT	ERA	G	GS	CG	IP	H	BB	SO	ShO	W	L	SV	AB	H	HR	BA
1980 BOS A	1	1	.500	6.92	7	7	0	26	39	14	12	0	0	0	0	0	0	0	–
1981	6	2	.750	3.14	10	10	2	66	50	25	28	0	0	0	0	0	0	0	–
1982	4	6	.400	5.63	22	14	0	78.1	95	29	52	0	1	0	0	0	0	0	–
1983	12	7	.632	4.04	29	28	5	173.2	173	73	94	0	0	0	0	0	0	0	–
1984	12	12	.500	3.99	33	32	8	216.2	211	96	137	5	0	0	0	0	0	0	–
1985	9	11	.450	4.00	39	22	5	157.2	166	48	102	0	2	1	1	0	0	0	–
1986 NY N	18	5	.783	2.57	32	30	7	217.1	185	52	148	2	1	0	0	71	8	0	.113
1987	3	5	.375	3.88	10	7	0	46.1	45	10	21	0	0	1	0	14	1	0	.071
1988	10	13	.435	2.88	29	29	5	190.1	158	33	133	5	0	0	0	61	10	0	.164
9 yrs.	75	62	.547	3.68	211	179	32	1172.1	1122	380	727	12	4	2	1	146	19	0	.130

LEAGUE CHAMPIONSHIP SERIES

	W	L	PCT	ERA	G	GS	CG	IP	H	BB	SO	ShO	W	L	SV	AB	H	HR	BA
1986 NY N	1	0	1.000	2.57	2	2	1	14	15	4	6	0	0	0	0	5	0	0	.000

WORLD SERIES

	W	L	PCT	ERA	G	GS	CG	IP	H	BB	SO	ShO	W	L	SV	AB	H	HR	BA
1986 NY N	1	0	1.000	2.08	2	2	0	13	13	5	9	0	0	0	0	2	0	0	.000

Gregg Olson

OLSON, GREGGORY WILLIAM
B. Oct. 11, 1966, Scribner, Neb.

BR TR 6'4" 210 lbs.

	W	L	PCT	ERA	G	GS	CG	IP	H	BB	SO	ShO	W	L	SV	AB	H	HR	BA
1988 BAL A	1	1	.500	3.27	10	0	0	11	10	10	9	0	1	1	0	0	0	0	–

Ed Olwine

OLWINE, EDWARD R.
B. May 28, 1958, Greenville, Ohio

BR TL 6'2" 165 lbs.

	W	L	PCT	ERA	G	GS	CG	IP	H	BB	SO	ShO	W	L	SV	AB	H	HR	BA
1986 ATL N	0	0	–	3.40	37	0	0	47.2	35	17	37	0	0	0	0	3	1	0	.333
1987	0	1	.000	5.01	27	0	0	23.1	25	8	12	0	0	1	1	0	0	0	–
1988	0	0		6.75	16	0	0	18.2	22	4	5	0	0	0	1	0	0	0	–
3 yrs.	0	1	.000	4.52	80	0	0	89.2	82	29	54	0	0	1	3	3	1	0	.333

Randy O'Neal

O'NEAL, RANDALL JEFFREY
B. Aug. 30, 1960, Ashland, Ky.

BR TR 6'2" 195 lbs.

	W	L	PCT	ERA	G	GS	CG	IP	H	BB	SO	ShO	W	L	SV	AB	H	HR	BA
1984 DET A	2	1	.667	3.38	4	3	0	18.2	16	6	12	0	0	0	0	0	0	0	–
1985	5	5	.500	3.24	28	12	1	94.1	82	36	52	0	0	0	1	0	0	0	–
1986	3	7	.300	4.33	37	11	1	122.2	121	44	68	0	0	3	2	0	0	0	–
1987 2 teams		ATL	N (16G 4–2)		STL	N	(1G 0–0)												
" total	4	2	.667	5.32	17	11	0	66	81	26	37	0	0	0	0	20	3	0	.150
1988 STL N	2	3	.400	4.58	10	8	0	53	57	10	20	0	0	1	0	19	0	0	.000
5 yrs.	16	18	.471	4.21	96	45	2	354.2	357	122	189	0	0	4	3	39	3	0	.077

Paul O'Neill

O'NEILL, PAUL ANDREW
B. Feb. 25, 1963, Columbus, Ohio

BL TL 6'4" 200 lbs.

	W	L	PCT	ERA	G	GS	CG	IP	H	BB	SO	ShO	W	L	SV	AB	H	HR	BA
1987 CIN N	0	0	–	13.50	1	0	0	2	2	4	2	0	0	0	0	*			

Steve Ontiveros

ONTIVEROS, STEVEN
B. Mar. 5, 1961, Tularosa, N. M.

BR TR 6' 180 lbs.

	W	L	PCT	ERA	G	GS	CG	IP	H	BB	SO	ShO	W	L	SV	AB	H	HR	BA
1985 OAK A	1	3	.250	1.93	39	0	0	74.2	45	19	36	0	1	3	8	0	0	0	–
1986	2	2	.500	4.71	46	0	0	72.2	72	25	54	0	2	2	10	0	0	0	–
1987	10	8	.556	4.00	35	22	2	150.2	141	50	97	1	1	2	1	0	0	0	–
1988	3	4	.429	4.61	10	10	0	54.2	57	21	30	0	0	0	0	0	0	0	–
4 yrs.	16	17	.485	3.80	130	32	2	352.2	315	115	217	1	4	7	19	0	0	0	–

Jose Oquendo

OQUENDO, JOSE MANUEL CONTRERAS
Born Jose Manuel Oquendo y Contreras.
B. July 4, 1963, Rio Peidras, Puerto Rico

BB TR 5'10" 160 lbs.

	W	L	PCT	ERA	G	GS	CG	IP	H	BB	SO	ShO	W	L	SV	AB	H	HR	BA
1987 STL N	0	0	–	27.00	1	0	0	1	4	1	0	0	0	0	0	248	71	1	.286
1988	0	1	.000	4.50	1	0	0	4	4	6	1	0	0	1	0	451	125	7	.277
2 yrs.	0	1	.000	9.00	2	0	0	5	8	7	1	0	0	1	0	*			

Jesse Orosco

OROSCO, JESSE
B. Apr. 21, 1957, Santa Barbara, Calif.

BR TL 6'2" 174 lbs.

	W	L	PCT	ERA	G	GS	CG	IP	H	BB	SO	ShO	W	L	SV	AB	H	HR	BA
1979 NY N	1	2	.333	4.89	18	2	0	35	33	22	22	0	1	2	0	6	0	0	.000
1981	0	1	.000	1.59	8	0	0	17	13	6	18	0	0	1	1	2	0	0	.000
1982	4	10	.286	2.72	54	2	0	109.1	92	40	89	0	4	8	4	14	2	0	.143
1983	13	7	.650	1.47	62	0	0	110	76	38	84	0	13	7	17	12	4	0	.333
1984	10	6	.625	2.59	60	0	0	87	58	34	85	0	10	6	31	4	1	0	.250
1985	8	6	.571	2.73	54	0	0	79	66	34	68	0	8	6	17	7	3	0	.429
1986	8	6	.571	2.33	58	0	0	81	64	35	62	0	8	6	21	3	0	0	.000

	W	L	PCT	ERA	G	GS	CG	IP	H	BB	SO	ShO	Relief Pitching W	L	SV	BATTING AB	H	HR	BA

Jesse Orosco continued

	W	L	PCT	ERA	G	GS	CG	IP	H	BB	SO	ShO	W	L	SV	AB	H	HR	BA
1987	3	9	.250	4.44	58	0	0	77	78	31	78	0	3	9	16	8	0	0	.000
1988 LA N	3	2	.600	2.72	55	0	0	53	41	30	43	0	3	2	9	2	0	0	.000
9 yrs.	50	49	.505	2.73	427	4	0	648.1	521	270	549	0	50	47	116	58	10	0	.172

LEAGUE CHAMPIONSHIP SERIES

	W	L	PCT	ERA	G	GS	CG	IP	H	BB	SO	ShO	W	L	SV	AB	H	HR	BA
1986 NY N	3	0	1.000	3.38	4	0	0	8	5	2	10	0	3	0	0	0	0	0	–
1988 LA N	0	0	–	7.71	4	0	0	2.1	4	3	0	0	0	0	0	0	0	0	–
2 yrs.	3	0	1.000	4.35	8	0	0	10.1	9	5	10	0	3	0	0	0	0	0	–

WORLD SERIES

	W	L	PCT	ERA	G	GS	CG	IP	H	BB	SO	ShO	W	L	SV	AB	H	HR	BA
1986 NY N	0	0	–	0.00	4	0	0	5.2	2	0	6	0	0	0	2	1	1	0	1.000

Dave Otto

OTTO, DAVID ALAN   BL TL 6'7" 210 lbs.
B. Nov. 12, 1964, Chicago, Ill.

	W	L	PCT	ERA	G	GS	CG	IP	H	BB	SO	ShO	W	L	SV	AB	H	HR	BA
1987 OAK A	0	0	–	9.00	3	0	0	6	7	1	3	0	0	0	0	0	0	0	–
1988	0	0	–	1.80	3	2	0	10	9	6	7	0	0	0	0	0	0	0	–
2 yrs.	0	0	–	4.50	6	2	0	16	16	7	10	0	0	0	0	0	0	0	–

Pat Pacillo

PACILLO, PATRICK MICHAEL   BR TR 6'2" 205 lbs.
B. July 23, 1963, Jersey City, N. J.

	W	L	PCT	ERA	G	GS	CG	IP	H	BB	SO	ShO	W	L	SV	AB	H	HR	BA
1987 CIN N	3	3	.500	6.13	12	7	0	39.2	41	19	23	0	1	0	0	11	1	0	.091
1988	1	0	1.000	5.06	6	0	0	10.2	14	4	11	0	1	0	0	1	0	0	.000
2 yrs.	4	3	.571	5.90	18	7	0	50.1	55	23	34	0	2	0	0	12	1	0	.083

Vicente Palacios

PALACIOS, VICENTE   BR TR 6'3" 165 lbs.
Born Vicente Palacios y Hernandez.
B. July 19, 1963, Veracruz, Mexico

	W	L	PCT	ERA	G	GS	CG	IP	H	BB	SO	ShO	W	L	SV	AB	H	HR	BA
1987 PIT N	2	1	.667	4.30	6	4	0	29.1	27	9	13	0	0	0	0	9	1	0	.111
1988	1	2	.333	6.66	7	3	0	24.1	28	15	15	0	0	1	0	8	0	0	.000
2 yrs.	3	3	.500	5.37	13	7	0	53.2	55	24	28	0	0	1	0	17	1	0	.059

Donn Pall

PALL, DONN STEVEN   BR TR 6'1" 180 lbs.
B. Jan. 11, 1962, Chicago, Ill.

	W	L	PCT	ERA	G	GS	CG	IP	H	BB	SO	ShO	W	L	SV	AB	H	HR	BA
1988 CHI A	0	2	.000	3.45	17	0	0	28.2	39	8	16	0	0	2	0	0	0	0	–

David Palmer

PALMER, DAVID WILLIAM   BR TR 6'1" 195 lbs.
B. Aug. 19, 1957, Glens Falls, N. Y.

	W	L	PCT	ERA	G	GS	CG	IP	H	BB	SO	ShO	W	L	SV	AB	H	HR	BA
1978 MON N	0	1	.000	2.70	5	1	0	10	9	2	7	0	0	0	0	1	0	0	.000
1979	10	2	.833	2.63	36	11	2	123	110	30	72	1	1	0	2	31	1	0	.032
1980	8	6	.571	2.98	24	19	3	130	124	30	73	1	0	0	0	45	9	0	.200
1982	6	4	.600	3.18	13	13	1	73.2	60	36	46	0	0	0	0	24	1	0	.042
1984	7	3	.700	3.84	20	19	1	105.1	101	44	66	1	0	1	0	33	5	1	.152
1985	7	10	.412	3.71	24	24	0	135.2	128	67	106	0	0	0	0	36	4	0	.111
1986 ATL N	11	10	.524	3.65	35	35	2	209.2	181	102	170	0	0	0	0	66	12	1	.182
1987	8	11	.421	4.90	28	28	0	152.1	169	64	111	0	0	0	0	48	6	1	.125
1988 PHI N	7	9	.438	4.47	22	22	1	129	129	48	85	1	0	0	0	39	10	2	.256
9 yrs.	64	56	.533	3.71	207	171	10	1068.2	1011	423	736	4	1	1	2	323	48	5	.149

Jeff Parrett

PARRETT, JEFFREY DALE   BR TR 6'4" 185 lbs.
B. Aug. 26, 1961, Indianapolis, Ind.

	W	L	PCT	ERA	G	GS	CG	IP	H	BB	SO	ShO	W	L	SV	AB	H	HR	BA
1986 MON N	0	1	.000	4.87	12	0	0	20.1	19	13	21	0	0	1	0	2	1	0	.500
1987	7	6	.538	4.21	45	0	0	62	53	30	56	0	7	6	6	5	0	0	.000
1988	12	4	.750	2.65	61	0	0	91.2	66	45	62	0	12	4	6	0	0	0	–
3 yrs.	19	11	.633	3.47	118	0	0	174	138	88	139	0	19	11	12	7	1	0	.143

Ken Patterson

PATTERSON, KENNETH BRIAN   BL TL 6'4" 210 lbs.
B. July 8, 1964, Costa Mesa, Calif.

	W	L	PCT	ERA	G	GS	CG	IP	H	BB	SO	ShO	W	L	SV	AB	H	HR	BA
1988 CHI A	0	2	.000	4.79	9	2	0	20.2	25	7	8	0	0	1	1	0	0	0	–

John Pawlowski

PAWLOWSKI, JOHN   BR TR 6'2" 175 lbs.
B. Sept. 6, 1963, Johnson City, N. Y.

	W	L	PCT	ERA	G	GS	CG	IP	H	BB	SO	ShO	W	L	SV	AB	H	HR	BA
1987 CHI A	0	0	–	4.91	2	0	0	3.2	7	3	2	0	0	0	0	0	0	0	–
1988	1	0	1.000	8.36	6	0	0	14	20	3	10	0	1	0	0	0	0	0	–
2 yrs.	1	0	1.000	7.64	8	0	0	17.2	27	6	12	0	1	0	0	0	0	0	–

Alejandro Pena

PENA, ALEJANDRO   BR TR 6'3" 200 lbs.
Born Alejandro Pena y Vasquez.
B. June 25, 1959, Cambiaso Puerto Plata, Dominican Republic

	W	L	PCT	ERA	G	GS	CG	IP	H	BB	SO	ShO	W	L	SV	AB	H	HR	BA
1981 LA N	1	1	.500	2.88	14	0	0	25	18	11	14	0	1	1	2	6	0	0	.000
1982	0	2	.000	4.79	29	0	0	35.2	37	21	20	0	0	2	0	0	0	0	–
1983	12	9	.571	2.75	34	26	4	177	152	51	120	3	2	1	1	60	6	1	.100
1984	12	6	.667	2.48	28	28	8	199.1	186	46	135	4	0	0	0	66	8	0	.121
1985	0	1	.000	8.31	2	1	0	4.1	7	3	2	0	0	1	0	1	0	0	.000
1986	1	2	.333	4.89	24	10	0	70	74	30	46	0	0	1	1	17	3	0	.176
1987	2	7	.222	3.50	37	7	0	87.1	82	37	76	0	2	2	11	13	1	0	.077
1988	6	7	.462	1.91	60	0	0	94.1	75	27	83	0	6	7	12	6	0	0	.000
8 yrs.	34	35	.493	3.01	228	72	12	693	631	226	496	7	11	15	27	169	18	1	.107

LEAGUE CHAMPIONSHIP SERIES

	W	L	PCT	ERA	G	GS	CG	IP	H	BB	SO	ShO	W	L	SV	AB	H	HR	BA
1981 LA N	0	0	–	0.00	2	0	0	2.1	1	0	0	0	0	0	0	0	0	0	–
1983	0	0	–	6.75	1	0	0	2.2	4	1	3	0	0	0	0	1	1	0	1.000
1988	1	1	.500	4.15	3	0	0	4.1	1	5	1	0	1	1	1	0	0	0	–
3 yrs.	1	1	.500	3.86	6	0	0	9.1	6	6	4	0	1	1	1	1	1	0	1.000

WORLD SERIES

	W	L	PCT	ERA	G	GS	CG	IP	H	BB	SO	ShO	W	L	SV	AB	H	HR	BA
1988 LA N	1	0	1.000	0.00	2	0	0	5	2	1	7	0	1	0	0	0	0	0	–

	W	L	PCT	ERA	G	GS	CG	IP	H	BB	SO	ShO	Relief Pitching W	L	SV	BATTING AB	H	HR	BA

Hipolito Pena

PENA, HIPOLITO
Born Hipolito Pena y Concepcion.
B. Jan. 30, 1964, Fantino, Dominican Republic

BL TL 6'3"   168 lbs.

	W	L	PCT	ERA	G	GS	CG	IP	H	BB	SO	ShO	W	L	SV	AB	H	HR	BA
1986 PIT N	0	3	.000	8.64	10	1	0	8.1	7	3	6	0	0	2	1	0	0	0	–
1987	0	3	.000	4.56	16	1	0	25.2	16	26	16	0	0	2	1	6	1	0	.167
1988 NY A	1	1	.500	3.14	16	0	0	14.1	10	9	10	0	1	1	0	0	0	0	–
3 yrs.	1	7	.125	4.84	42	2	0	48.1	33	38	32	0	1	5	2	6	1	0	.167

Oswaldo Peraza

PERAZA, OSWALD JOSE
B. Oct. 19, 1962, Puerto Cabello, Venezuela

BR TR 6'4"   172 lbs.

	W	L	PCT	ERA	G	GS	CG	IP	H	BB	SO	ShO	W	L	SV	AB	H	HR	BA
1988 BAL A	5	7	.417	5.55	19	15	1	86	98	37	61	0	0	0	0	0	0	0	–

Melido Perez

PEREZ, MELIDO TURPEN GROSS
Born Melido Turpen Gross y Perez.   Brother of Pascual Perez.
B. Feb. 15, 1966, San Cristobal, Dominican Republic

BR TR 6'4"   180 lbs.

	W	L	PCT	ERA	G	GS	CG	IP	H	BB	SO	ShO	W	L	SV	AB	H	HR	BA
1987 KC A	1	1	.500	7.84	3	3	0	10.1	18	5	5	0	0	0	0	0	0	0	–
1988 CHI A	12	10	.545	3.79	32	32	3	197	186	72	138	1	0	0	0	0	0	0	–
2 yrs.	13	11	.542	3.99	35	35	3	207.1	204	77	143	1	0	0	0	0	0	0	–

Pascual Perez

PEREZ, PASCUAL GROSS
Born Pascual Gross y Perez.   Brother of Melido Perez.
B. May 17, 1957, San Cristobal, Dominican Republic

BR TR 6'2"   162 lbs.

	W	L	PCT	ERA	G	GS	CG	IP	H	BB	SO	ShO	W	L	SV	AB	H	HR	BA
1980 PIT N	0	1	.000	3.75	2	2	0	12	15	2	7	0	0	0	0	4	1	0	.250
1981	2	7	.222	3.98	17	13	2	86	92	34	46	0	0	1	0	22	3	0	.136
1982 ATL N	4	4	.500	3.06	16	11	0	79.1	85	17	29	0	2	0	0	18	3	0	.167
1983	15	8	.652	3.43	33	33	7	215.1	213	51	144	1	0	0	0	75	12	0	.160
1984	14	8	.636	3.74	30	30	4	211.2	208	51	145	1	0	0	0	66	5	0	.076
1985	1	13	.071	6.14	22	22	0	95.1	115	57	57	0	0	0	0	25	3	0	.120
1987 MON N	7	0	1.000	2.30	10	10	2	70.1	52	16	58	0	0	0	0	24	1	0	.042
1988	12	8	.600	2.44	27	27	4	188	133	44	131	2	0	0	0	54	2	0	.037
8 yrs.	55	49	.529	3.51	157	148	19	958	913	272	617	4	2	1	0	288	30	0	.104

LEAGUE CHAMPIONSHIP SERIES

	W	L	PCT	ERA	G	GS	CG	IP	H	BB	SO	ShO	W	L	SV	AB	H	HR	BA
1982 ATL N	0	1	.000	5.19	2	1	0	8.2	10	2	4	0	0	0	0	3	0	0	.000

Jon Perlman

PERLMAN, JONATHAN SAMUEL
B. Dec. 13, 1956, Dallas, Tex.

BL TR 6'3"   185 lbs.

	W	L	PCT	ERA	G	GS	CG	IP	H	BB	SO	ShO	W	L	SV	AB	H	HR	BA
1985 CHI N	1	0	1.000	11.42	6	0	0	8.2	10	8	4	0	1	0	0	1	0	0	.000
1987 SF N	0	0	–	3.97	10	0	0	11.1	11	4	3	0	0	0	0	0	0	0	–
1988 CLE A	0	2	.000	5.49	10	0	0	19.2	25	11	10	0	0	2	0	0	0	0	–
3 yrs.	1	2	.333	6.35	26	0	0	39.2	46	23	17	0	1	2	0	1	0	0	.000

Pat Perry

PERRY, WILLIAM PATRICK (Atlas)
B. Feb. 4, 1959, Taylorville, Ill.

BL TL 6'1"   190 lbs.

	W	L	PCT	ERA	G	GS	CG	IP	H	BB	SO	ShO	W	L	SV	AB	H	HR	BA
1985 STL N	1	0	1.000	0.00	6	0	0	12.1	3	3	6	0	1	0	0	2	1	0	.500
1986	2	3	.400	3.80	46	0	0	68.2	59	34	29	0	2	3	2	8	0	0	.000
1987 2 teams				STL	N	(45G 4–2)		CIN	N	(12G 1–0)									
" total	5	2	.714	3.56	57	0	0	81	60	25	39	0	5	2	2	7	1	0	.143
1988 2 teams				CIN	N	(12G 2–2)		CHI	N	(35G 2–2)									
" total	4	4	.500	4.14	47	0	0	58.2	61	16	35	0	4	4	1	3	1	1	.333
4 yrs.	12	9	.571	3.59	156	0	0	220.2	183	78	109	0	12	9	5	20	3	1	.150

Steve Peters

PETERS, STEVEN BRADLEY
B. Nov. 14, 1962, Oklahoma City, Okla.

BL TL 5'10"   170 lbs.

	W	L	PCT	ERA	G	GS	CG	IP	H	BB	SO	ShO	W	L	SV	AB	H	HR	BA
1987 STL N	0	0	–	1.80	12	0	0	15	17	6	11	0	0	0	1	2	0	0	.000
1988	3	3	.500	6.40	44	0	0	45	57	22	30	0	3	3	0	3	0	0	.000
2 yrs.	3	3	.500	5.25	56	0	0	60	74	28	41	0	3	3	1	5	0	0	.000

Adam Peterson

PETERSON, ADAM CHARLES
B. Dec. 11, 1965, Long Beach, Calif.

BR TR 6'3"   190 lbs.

	W	L	PCT	ERA	G	GS	CG	IP	H	BB	SO	ShO	W	L	SV	AB	H	HR	BA
1987 CHI A	0	0	–	13.50	1	1	0	4	8	3	1	0	0	0	0	0	0	0	–
1988	0	1	.000	13.50	2	2	0	6	6	6	5	0	0	0	0	0	0	0	–
2 yrs.	0	1	.000	13.50	3	3	0	10	14	9	6	0	0	0	0	0	0	0	–

Dan Petry

PETRY, DANIEL JOSEPH
B. Nov. 13, 1958, Palo Alto, Calif.

BR TR 6'4"   185 lbs.

	W	L	PCT	ERA	G	GS	CG	IP	H	BB	SO	ShO	W	L	SV	AB	H	HR	BA
1979 DET A	6	5	.545	3.95	15	15	2	98	90	33	43	0	0	0	0	0	0	0	–
1980	10	9	.526	3.93	27	25	4	165	156	83	88	3	1	0	0	0	0	0	–
1981	10	9	.526	3.00	23	22	7	141	115	57	79	2	0	0	0	0	0	0	–
1982	15	9	.625	3.22	35	35	8	246	220	100	132	1	0	0	0	0	0	0	–
1983	19	11	.633	3.92	38	38	9	266.1	256	99	122	2	0	0	0	0	0	0	–
1984	18	8	.692	3.24	35	35	7	233.1	231	66	144	2	0	0	0	0	0	0	–
1985	15	13	.536	3.36	34	34	8	238.2	190	81	109	0	0	0	0	0	0	0	–
1986	5	10	.333	4.66	20	20	2	116	122	53	56	0	0	0	0	0	0	0	–
1987	9	7	.563	5.61	30	21	0	134.2	148	76	93	0	2	0	0	0	0	0	–
1988 CAL A	3	9	.250	4.38	22	22	4	139.2	139	59	64	1	0	0	0	0	0	0	–
10 yrs.	110	90	.550	3.80	279	267	51	1778.2	1667	707	930	11	3	0	0	0	0	0	–

LEAGUE CHAMPIONSHIP SERIES

	W	L	PCT	ERA	G	GS	CG	IP	H	BB	SO	ShO	W	L	SV	AB	H	HR	BA
1984 DET A	0	0	–	2.57	1	1	0	7	4	1	4	0	0	0	0	0	0	0	–
1987	0	0	–	0.00	1	0	0	3.1	1	0	1	0	0	0	0	0	0	0	–
2 yrs.	0	0	–	1.74	2	1	0	10.1	5	1	5	0	0	0	0	0	0	0	–

WORLD SERIES

	W	L	PCT	ERA	G	GS	CG	IP	H	BB	SO	ShO	W	L	SV	AB	H	HR	BA
1984 DET A	0	1	.000	9.00	2	2	0	8	14	5	4	0	0	0	0	0	0	0	–

	W	L	PCT	ERA	G	GS	CG	IP	H	BB	SO	ShO	Relief Pitching W	L	SV	BATTING AB	H	HR	BA

Jeff Pico

PICO, JEFFREY MARK
B. Feb. 12, 1966, Antioch, Calif.   BR TR 6'1"   180 lbs.

	W	L	PCT	ERA	G	GS	CG	IP	H	BB	SO	ShO	RW	RL	SV	AB	H	HR	BA
1988 CHI N	6	7	.462	4.15	29	13	3	112.2	108	37	57	2	2	1	1	34	5	0	.147

Dan Plesac

PLESAC, DANIEL THOMAS
B. Feb. 4, 1962, Gary, Ind.   BL TL 6'5"   205 lbs.

	W	L	PCT	ERA	G	GS	CG	IP	H	BB	SO	ShO	RW	RL	SV	AB	H	HR	BA
1986 MIL A	10	7	.588	2.97	51	0	0	91	81	29	75	0	10	7	14	0	0	0	—
1987	5	6	.455	2.61	57	0	0	79.1	63	23	89	0	5	6	23	0	0	0	—
1988	1	2	.333	2.41	50	0	0	52.1	46	12	52	0	1	2	30	0	0	0	—
3 yrs.	16	15	.516	2.71	158	0	0	222.2	190	64	216	0	16	15	67	0	0	0	—

Eric Plunk

PLUNK, ERIC VAUGHN
B. Sept. 3, 1963, Wilmington, Calif.   BR TR 6'5"   210 lbs.

	W	L	PCT	ERA	G	GS	CG	IP	H	BB	SO	ShO	RW	RL	SV	AB	H	HR	BA
1986 OAK A	4	7	.364	5.31	26	15	0	120.1	91	102	98	0	0	1	0	0	0	0	—
1987	4	6	.400	4.74	32	11	0	95	91	62	90	0	3	2	2	0	0	0	—
1988	7	2	.778	3.00	49	0	0	78	62	39	79	0	7	2	5	0	0	0	—
3 yrs.	15	15	.500	4.51	107	26	0	293.1	244	203	267	0	10	5	7	0	0	0	—

LEAGUE CHAMPIONSHIP SERIES

	W	L	PCT	ERA	G	GS	CG	IP	H	BB	SO	ShO	RW	RL	SV	AB	H	HR	BA
1988 OAK A	0	0	—	0.00	1	0	0	.1	1	0	1	0	0	0	0	0	0	0	—

WORLD SERIES

	W	L	PCT	ERA	G	GS	CG	IP	H	BB	SO	ShO	RW	RL	SV	AB	H	HR	BA
1988 OAK A	0	0	—	0.00	2	0	0	1.2	0	0	3	0	0	0	0	0	0	0	—

Mark Portugal

PORTUGAL, MARK STEVEN
B. Oct. 30, 1962, Los Angeles, Calif.   BR TR 6'   170 lbs.

	W	L	PCT	ERA	G	GS	CG	IP	H	BB	SO	ShO	RW	RL	SV	AB	H	HR	BA
1985 MIN A	1	3	.250	5.55	6	4	0	24.1	24	14	12	0	0	0	0	0	0	0	—
1986	6	10	.375	4.31	27	15	3	112.2	112	50	67	0	2	4	1	0	0	0	—
1987	1	3	.250	7.77	13	7	0	44	58	24	28	0	0	1	0	0	0	0	—
1988	3	3	.500	4.53	26	0	0	57.2	60	17	31	0	3	3	3	0	0	0	—
4 yrs.	11	19	.367	5.13	72	26	3	238.2	254	105	138	0	5	8	4	0	0	0	—

Dennis Powell

POWELL, DENNIS CLAY
B. Aug. 13, 1963, Moultrie, Ga.   BR TL 6'3"   175 lbs.

	W	L	PCT	ERA	G	GS	CG	IP	H	BB	SO	ShO	RW	RL	SV	AB	H	HR	BA
1985 LA N	1	1	.500	5.22	16	2	0	29.1	30	13	19	0	1	0	1	3	0	0	.000
1986	2	7	.222	4.27	27	6	0	65.1	65	25	31	0	1	2	0	14	3	0	.214
1987 SEA A	1	3	.250	3.15	16	3	0	34.1	32	15	17	0	1	2	0	0	0	0	—
1988	1	3	.250	8.68	12	2	0	18.2	29	11	15	0	1	2	0	0	0	0	—
4 yrs.	5	14	.263	4.75	71	13	0	147.2	156	64	82	0	4	6	1	17	3	0	.176

Ted Power

POWER, TED HENRY
B. Jan. 31, 1955, Guthrie, Okla.   BR TR 6'4"   220 lbs.

	W	L	PCT	ERA	G	GS	CG	IP	H	BB	SO	ShO	RW	RL	SV	AB	H	HR	BA
1981 LA N	1	3	.250	3.21	5	2	0	14	16	7	7	0	1	1	0	3	0	0	.000
1982	1	1	.500	6.68	12	4	0	33.2	38	23	15	0	0	0	0	6	0	0	.000
1983 CIN N	5	6	.455	4.54	49	6	1	111	120	49	57	0	4	3	2	16	0	0	.000
1984	9	7	.563	2.82	78	0	0	108.2	93	46	81	0	9	7	11	5	0	0	.000
1985	8	6	.571	2.70	64	0	0	80	65	45	42	0	8	6	27	0	0	0	—
1986	10	6	.625	3.70	56	10	0	129	115	52	95	0	4	5	1	24	3	0	.125
1987	10	13	.435	4.50	34	34	2	204	213	71	133	1	0	0	0	59	7	1	.119
1988 2 teams	KC	A	(22G 5–6)	DET	A	(4G 1–1)													
" total	6	7	.462	5.91	26	14	2	99	121	38	57	0	3	2	0	0	0	0	—
8 yrs.	50	49	.505	4.20	324	70	5	779.1	781	331	487	3	29	24	41	113	10	1	.088

Joe Price

PRICE, JOSEPH WALTER
B. Nov. 29, 1956, Inglewood, Calif.   BR TL 6'4"   220 lbs.

	W	L	PCT	ERA	G	GS	CG	IP	H	BB	SO	ShO	RW	RL	SV	AB	H	HR	BA
1980 CIN N	7	3	.700	3.57	24	13	2	111	95	37	44	0	2	0	0	39	5	0	.128
1981	6	1	.857	2.50	41	0	0	54	42	18	41	0	6	1	4	3	0	0	.000
1982	3	4	.429	2.85	59	1	0	72.2	73	32	71	0	3	3	3	3	1	0	.333
1983	10	6	.625	2.88	21	21	5	144	118	46	83	0	0	0	0	41	4	0	.098
1984	7	13	.350	4.19	30	30	3	171.2	176	61	129	1	0	0	0	48	7	0	.146
1985	2	2	.500	3.90	26	8	0	64.2	59	23	52	0	0	0	1	14	0	0	.000
1986	1	2	.333	5.40	25	2	0	41.2	49	22	30	0	1	1	0	7	1	0	.143
1987 SF N	2	2	.500	2.57	20	0	0	35	19	13	42	0	2	2	1	6	1	0	.167
1988	1	6	.143	3.94	38	3	0	61.2	59	27	49	0	1	6	4	8	0	0	.000
9 yrs.	39	39	.500	3.55	284	78	10	756.1	690	279	541	1	15	13	13	169	19	0	.112

LEAGUE CHAMPIONSHIP SERIES

	W	L	PCT	ERA	G	GS	CG	IP	H	BB	SO	ShO	RW	RL	SV	AB	H	HR	BA
1987 SF N	1	0	1.000	0.00	2	0	0	5.2	3	1	7	0	1	0	0	1	0	0	.000

Charlie Puleo

PULEO, CHARLES MICHAEL
B. Feb. 7, 1955, Glen Ridge, N. J.   BR TR 6'2"   190 lbs.

	W	L	PCT	ERA	G	GS	CG	IP	H	BB	SO	ShO	RW	RL	SV	AB	H	HR	BA
1981 NY N	0	0	—	0.00	4	1	0	13	8	8	8	0	0	0	0	2	0	0	.000
1982	9	9	.500	4.47	36	24	1	171	179	90	98	1	2	1	1	48	6	0	.125
1983 CIN N	6	12	.333	4.89	27	24	0	143.2	145	91	71	0	0	0	0	50	5	0	.100
1984	1	2	.333	5.73	5	4	0	22	27	15	6	0	0	0	0	5	1	0	.200
1986 ATL N	1	2	.333	2.96	5	3	1	24.1	13	12	18	0	0	1	0	6	2	0	.333
1987	6	8	.429	4.23	35	16	1	123.1	122	40	99	0	2	0	0	28	5	1	.179
1988	5	5	.500	3.47	53	3	0	106.1	101	47	70	0	5	3	1	13	3	0	.231
7 yrs.	28	38	.424	4.23	165	75	3	603.2	595	303	370	1	9	5	2	152	22	1	.145

Dan Quisenberry

QUISENBERRY, DANIEL RAYMOND (Quiz)
B. Feb. 7, 1953, Santa Monica, Calif.   BR TR 6'2"   170 lbs.

	W	L	PCT	ERA	G	GS	CG	IP	H	BB	SO	ShO	RW	RL	SV	AB	H	HR	BA
1979 KC A	3	2	.600	3.15	32	0	0	40	42	7	13	0	3	2	5	0	0	0	—
1980	12	7	.632	3.09	75	0	0	128	129	27	37	0	12	7	33	0	0	0	—
1981	1	4	.200	1.74	40	0	0	62	59	15	20	0	1	4	18	0	0	0	—
1982	9	7	.563	2.57	72	0	0	136.2	126	12	46	0	9	7	35	0	0	0	—
1983	5	3	.625	1.94	69	0	0	139	118	11	48	0	5	3	45	0	0	0	—
1984	6	3	.667	2.64	72	0	0	129.1	121	12	41	0	6	3	44	0	0	0	—

	W	L	PCT	ERA	G	GS	CG	IP	H	BB	SO	ShO	Relief Pitching			BATTING			BA
													W	L	SV	AB	H	HR	

Dan Quisenberry continued

	W	L	PCT	ERA	G	GS	CG	IP	H	BB	SO	ShO	W	L	SV	AB	H	HR	BA
1985	8	9	.471	2.37	84	0	0	129	142	16	54	0	8	9	37	0	0	0	—
1986	3	7	.300	2.77	62	0	0	81.1	92	24	36	0	3	7	12	0	0	0	—
1987	4	1	.800	2.76	47	0	0	49	58	10	17	0	4	1	8	0	0	0	—
1988 2 teams	KC	A	(20G 0-1)		STL	N	(33G 2-0)												
" total	2	1	.667	5.12	53	0	0	63.1	86	11	28	0	2	1	1	1	0	0	.000
10 yrs.	53	44	.546	2.70	606	0	0	957.2	973	145	340	0	53	44	238	1	0	0	.000
															4th				

DIVISIONAL PLAYOFF SERIES

	W	L	PCT	ERA	G	GS	CG	IP	H	BB	SO	ShO	W	L	SV	AB	H	HR	BA
1981 KC A	0	0	—	0.00	1	0	0	1	1	0	0	0	0	0	0	0	0	0	

LEAGUE CHAMPIONSHIP SERIES

	W	L	PCT	ERA	G	GS	CG	IP	H	BB	SO	ShO	W	L	SV	AB	H	HR	BA
1980 KC A	1	0	1.000	0.00	2	0	0	4.2	4	2	1	0	1	0	1	0	0	0	—
1984	0	1	.000	3.00	1	0	0	3	2	1	1	0	0	1	0	0	0	0	—
1985	0	1	.000	3.86	4	0	0	4.2	7	0	3	0	0	1	1	0	0	0	—
3 yrs.	1	2	.333	2.19	7	0	0	12.1	13	3	5	0	1	2	2	0	0	0	

WORLD SERIES

	W	L	PCT	ERA	G	GS	CG	IP	H	BB	SO	ShO	W	L	SV	AB	H	HR	BA
1980 KC A	1	2	.333	5.23	6	0	0	10.1	10	3	0	0	1	2	1	0	0	0	—
1985	1	0	1.000	2.08	4	0	0	4.1	5	3	3	0	1	0	0	0	0	0	—
2 yrs.	2	2	.500	4.30	10	0	0	14.2	15	6	3	0	2	2	1	0	0	0	
													2nd	2nd					

Dennis Rasmussen

RASMUSSEN, DENNIS LEE   BL TL 6'7"   230 lbs.
B. Apr. 18, 1959, Los Angeles, Calif.

	W	L	PCT	ERA	G	GS	CG	IP	H	BB	SO	ShO	W	L	SV	AB	H	HR	BA
1983 SD N	0	0	—	1.98	4	1	0	13.2	10	8	13	0	0	0	0	3	0	0	.000
1984 NY A	9	6	.600	4.57	24	24	1	147.2	127	60	110	0	0	0	0	0	0	0	—
1985	3	5	.375	3.98	22	16	2	101.2	97	42	63	0	0	0	0	0	0	0	—
1986	18	6	.750	3.88	31	31	3	202	160	74	131	1	0	0	0	0	0	0	—
1987 2 teams	NY	A	(26G 9-7)		CIN	N	(7G 4-1)												
" total	13	8	.619	4.56	33	32	2	191.1	184	67	128	0	0	0	0	15	1	0	.067
1988 2 teams	CIN	N	(11G 2-6)		SD	N	(20G 14-4)												
" total	16	10	.615	3.43	31	31	7	204.2	199	58	112	1	0	0	0	70	14	0	.200
6 yrs.	59	35	.628	4.02	145	135	15	861	777	309	557	2	0	0	0	88	15	0	.170

Shane Rawley

RAWLEY, SHANE WILLIAM   BR TL 6'   170 lbs.
B. July 27, 1955, Racine, Wis.

	W	L	PCT	ERA	G	GS	CG	IP	H	BB	SO	ShO	W	L	SV	AB	H	HR	BA
1978 SEA A	4	9	.308	4.12	52	2	0	111.1	114	51	66	0	4	7	4	0	0	0	—
1979	5	9	.357	3.86	48	3	0	84	88	40	48	0	5	9	11	0	0	0	—
1980	7	7	.500	3.32	59	0	0	114	103	63	68	0	7	7	13	0	0	0	—
1981	4	6	.400	3.97	46	0	0	68	64	38	35	0	4	6	8	0	0	0	—
1982 NY A	11	10	.524	4.06	47	17	3	164	165	54	111	0	4	5	3	0	0	0	—
1983	14	14	.500	3.78	34	33	13	238.1	246	79	124	2	0	0	1	0	0	0	—
1984 2 teams	NY	A	(11G 2-3)		PHI	N	(18G 10-6)												
" total	12	9	.571	4.44	29	28	3	162.1	163	54	82	0	0	0	0	43	5	0	.116
1985 PHI N	13	8	.619	3.31	36	31	6	198.2	188	81	106	2	1	0	0	58	8	0	.138
1986	11	7	.611	3.54	23	23	7	157.2	166	50	73	1	0	0	0	52	9	0	.173
1987	17	11	.607	4.39	36	36	4	229.2	250	86	123	1	0	0	0	79	12	0	.152
1988	8	16	.333	4.18	32	32	4	198	220	78	87	1	0	0	0	57	6	0	.105
11 yrs.	106	106	.500	3.92	442	205	40	1726	1767	674	923	7	25	34	40	289	40	0	.138

Jeff Reardon

REARDON, JEFFREY JAMES   BR TR 6'   190 lbs.
B. Oct. 1, 1955, Pittsfield, Mass.

	W	L	PCT	ERA	G	GS	CG	IP	H	BB	SO	ShO	W	L	SV	AB	H	HR	BA
1979 NY N	1	2	.333	1.71	18	0	0	21	12	9	10	0	1	2	2	0	0	0	—
1980	8	7	.533	2.62	61	0	0	110	96	47	101	0	8	7	6	8	0	0	.000
1981 2 teams	NY	N	(18G 1-0)		MON	N	(25G 2-0)												
" total	3	0	1.000	2.18	43	0	0	70.1	48	21	49	0	3	0	8	5	0	0	.000
1982 MON N	7	4	.636	2.06	75	0	0	109	87	36	86	0	7	4	26	10	1	0	.100
1983	7	9	.438	3.03	66	0	0	92	87	44	78	0	7	9	21	8	1	0	.125
1984	7	7	.500	2.90	68	0	0	87	70	37	79	0	7	7	23	9	0	0	.000
1985	2	8	.200	3.18	63	0	0	87.2	68	26	67	0	2	8	41	7	2	0	.286
1986	7	9	.438	3.94	62	0	0	89	83	26	67	0	7	9	35	8	1	0	.125
1987 MIN A	8	8	.500	4.48	63	0	0	80.1	70	28	83	0	8	8	31	0	0	0	—
1988	2	4	.333	2.47	63	0	0	73	68	15	56	0	2	4	42	0	0	0	—
10 yrs.	52	58	.473	2.93	582	0	0	819.1	689	289	676	0	52	58	235	55	5	0	.091
															6th				

DIVISIONAL PLAYOFF SERIES

	W	L	PCT	ERA	G	GS	CG	IP	H	BB	SO	ShO	W	L	SV	AB	H	HR	BA
1981 MON N	0	1	.000	2.08	3	0	0	4.1	1	1	2	0	0	1	2	1	0	0	.000

LEAGUE CHAMPIONSHIP SERIES

	W	L	PCT	ERA	G	GS	CG	IP	H	BB	SO	ShO	W	L	SV	AB	H	HR	BA
1981 MON N	0	0	—	27.00	1	0	0	1	3	0	0	0	0	0	0	0	0	0	—
1987 MIN A	1	1	.500	5.06	4	0	0	5.1	7	3	5	0	1	1	2	0	0	0	—
2 yrs.	1	1	.500	8.53	5	0	0	6.1	10	3	5	0	1	1	2	0	0	0	

WORLD SERIES

	W	L	PCT	ERA	G	GS	CG	IP	H	BB	SO	ShO	W	L	SV	AB	H	HR	BA
1987 MIN A	0	0	—	0.00	4	0	0	4.2	5	0	3	0	0	0	1	0	0	0	—

Jerry Reed

REED, JERRY MAXWELL   BR TR 6'1"   190 lbs.
B. Oct. 8, 1955, Bryson City, N. C.

	W	L	PCT	ERA	G	GS	CG	IP	H	BB	SO	ShO	W	L	SV	AB	H	HR	BA
1981 PHI N	0	1	.000	7.20	4	0	0	5	7	6	5	0	0	1	0	0	0	0	—
1982 2 teams	PHI	N	(7G 1-0)		CLE	A	(6G 1-1)												
" total	2	1	.667	4.07	13	1	0	24.1	26	6	11	0	2	0	0	0	0	0	—
1983 CLE A	0	0	—	7.17	7	0	0	21.1	26	9	11	0	0	0	0	0	0	0	—
1985	3	5	.375	4.11	33	5	0	72.1	67	19	37	0	3	2	8	0	0	0	—
1986 SEA A	4	0	1.000	3.12	11	4	0	34.2	38	13	16	0	1	0	0	0	0	0	—
1987	1	2	.333	3.42	39	1	0	81.2	79	24	51	0	1	2	7	0	0	0	—
1988	1	1	.500	3.96	46	0	0	86.1	82	33	48	0	1	1	1	0	0	0	—
7 yrs.	11	10	.524	4.03	153	11	0	325.2	325	110	179	0	8	6	16	0	0	0	—

	W	L	PCT	ERA	G	GS	CG	IP	H	BB	SO	ShO	Relief Pitching W	L	SV	BATTING AB	H	HR	BA

Rick Reed — REED, RICHARD ALLEN   B. Aug. 16, 1964, Huntington, W. Va.   BR TR 6'   195 lbs.

	W	L	PCT	ERA	G	GS	CG	IP	H	BB	SO	ShO	W	L	SV	AB	H	HR	BA
1988 PIT N	1	0	1.000	3.00	2	2	0	12	10	2	6	0	0	0	0	4	0	0	.000

Rick Reuschel — REUSCHEL, RICKEY EUGENE (Big Daddy)   Brother of Paul Reuschel.   B. May 16, 1949, Quincy, Ill.   BR TR 6'3"   215 lbs.

	W	L	PCT	ERA	G	GS	CG	IP	H	BB	SO	ShO	W	L	SV	AB	H	HR	BA
1972 CHI N	10	8	.556	2.93	21	18	5	129	127	29	87	4	1	0	0	44	6	0	.136
1973	14	15	.483	3.00	36	36	7	237	244	62	168	3	0	0	0	73	9	0	.123
1974	13	12	.520	4.29	41	38	8	241	262	83	160	2	1	0	0	86	19	0	.221
1975	11	17	.393	3.73	38	37	6	234	244	67	155	0	0	0	1	77	16	1	.208
1976	14	12	.538	3.46	38	37	9	260	260	64	146	2	0	0	1	83	19	0	.229
1977	20	10	.667	2.79	39	37	8	252	233	74	166	4	1	0	1	87	18	1	.207
1978	14	15	.483	3.41	35	35	9	243	235	54	115	1	0	0	0	73	10	0	.137
1979	18	12	.600	3.62	36	36	5	239	251	75	125	1	0	0	0	79	13	0	.165
1980	11	13	.458	3.40	38	**38**	6	257	**281**	76	140	0	0	0	0	82	13	0	.159
1981 2 teams			CHI	N	(13G	4–7)	NY	A	(12G	4–4)									
" total	8	11	.421	3.10	25	24	4	157	162	33	75	0	0	0	0	25	2	0	.080
1983 CHI N	1	1	.500	3.92	4	4	0	20.2	18	10	9	0	0	0	0	7	1	0	.143
1984	5	5	.500	5.17	19	14	1	92.1	123	23	43	0	1	0	0	29	7	0	.241
1985 PIT N	14	8	.636	2.27	31	26	9	194	153	52	138	1	2	0	1	59	10	1	.169
1986	9	16	.360	3.96	35	34	4	215.2	232	57	125	2	0	0	0	70	11	0	.157
1987 2 teams			PIT	N	(25G	8–6)	SF	N	(9G	5–3)									
" total	13	9	.591	3.09	34	33	12	227	207	42	107	4	0	1	0	79	11	1	.139
1988 SF N	19	11	.633	3.12	36	**36**	7	245	242	42	92	2	0	0	0	73	8	0	.110
16 yrs.	194	175	.526	3.38	506	483	100	3243.2	3274	843	1851	26	6	1	4	1026	173	4	.169

DIVISIONAL PLAYOFF SERIES
| 1981 NY A | 0 | 1 | .000 | 3.00 | 1 | 1 | 0 | 6 | 4 | 1 | 3 | 0 | 0 | 0 | 0 | 0 | 0 | 0 | – |

LEAGUE CHAMPIONSHIP SERIES
| 1987 SF N | 0 | 1 | .000 | 6.30 | 2 | 2 | 0 | 10 | 15 | 2 | 2 | 0 | 0 | 0 | 0 | 2 | 0 | 0 | .000 |

WORLD SERIES
| 1981 NY A | 0 | 0 | – | 4.91 | 2 | 1 | 0 | 3.2 | 7 | 3 | 2 | 0 | 0 | 0 | 0 | 2 | 0 | 0 | .000 |

Jerry Reuss — REUSS, JERRY (Rolls)   B. June 19, 1949, St. Louis, Mo.   BL TL 6'5"   200 lbs.

	W	L	PCT	ERA	G	GS	CG	IP	H	BB	SO	ShO	W	L	SV	AB	H	HR	BA
1969 STL N	1	0	1.000	0.00	1	1	0	7	2	3	3	0	0	0	0	3	1	0	.333
1970	7	8	.467	4.11	20	20	5	127	132	49	74	2	0	0	0	40	2	0	.050
1971	14	14	.500	4.78	36	35	7	211	228	109	131	2	0	0	0	65	8	0	.123
1972 HOU N	9	13	.409	4.17	33	30	4	192	177	83	174	1	0	0	1	66	7	0	.106
1973	16	13	.552	3.74	41	40	12	279.1	271	117	177	3	1	0	0	95	13	0	.137
1974 PIT N	16	11	.593	3.50	35	35	14	260	259	101	105	1	0	0	0	86	13	0	.151
1975	18	11	.621	2.54	32	32	15	237	224	78	131	6	0	0	0	71	14	0	.197
1976	14	9	.609	3.53	31	29	11	209.1	209	51	108	3	0	0	2	66	16	0	.242
1977	10	13	.435	4.11	33	33	8	208	225	71	116	2	0	0	0	70	12	0	.171
1978	3	2	.600	4.88	23	12	3	83	97	23	42	0	0	0	0	27	5	0	.185
1979 LA N	7	14	.333	3.54	39	21	4	160	178	60	83	1	2	4	3	42	7	0	.167
1980	18	6	.750	2.52	37	29	10	229	193	40	111	6	3	0	3	68	6	1	.088
1981	10	4	.714	2.29	22	22	8	153	138	27	51	2	0	0	0	51	10	0	.196
1982	18	11	.621	3.11	39	37	8	254.2	232	50	138	4	1	0	0	77	17	0	.221
1983	12	11	.522	2.94	32	31	7	223.1	233	50	143	0	0	0	0	71	20	0	.282
1984	5	7	.417	3.82	30	15	2	99	102	31	44	0	0	2	1	24	4	0	.167
1985	14	10	.583	2.92	34	33	5	212.2	210	58	84	3	0	0	0	74	10	0	.135
1986	2	6	.250	5.84	19	13	0	74	96	17	29	0	0	0	1	20	5	0	.250
1987 3 teams			LA	N	(1G	0–0)	CIN	N	(7G	0–5)	CAL	A	(17G	4–5)					
" total	4	10	.286	5.97	25	23	1	119	166	29	49	1	0	0	0	8	1	0	.125
1988 CHI A	13	9	.591	3.44	32	29	2	183	183	43	73	0	0	0	0	0	0	0	–
20 yrs.	211	182	.537	3.58	594	520	126	3521.1	3555	1090	1866	37	7	6	11	1024	171	1	.167

DIVISIONAL PLAYOFF SERIES
| 1981 LA N | 1 | 0 | 1.000 | 0.00 | 2 | 2 | 1 | 18 | 10 | 5 | 7 | 1 | 0 | 0 | 0 | 8 | 0 | 0 | .000 |

LEAGUE CHAMPIONSHIP SERIES
1974 PIT N	0	2	.000	3.72	2	2	0	9.2	7	8	3	0	0	0	0	2	0	0	.000
1975	0	1	.000	13.50	1	1	0	2.2	4	4	1	0	0	0	0	1	0	0	.000
1981 LA N	0	1	.000	5.14	1	1	0	7	7	1	2	0	0	0	0	2	0	0	.000
1983	0	2	.000	4.50	2	2	0	12	14	3	4	0	0	0	0	3	0	0	.000
1985	0	1	.000	10.80	1	1	0	1.2	5	1	0	0	0	0	0	0	0	0	–
5 yrs.	0	7	.000	5.45	7	7	0	33	37	17	10	0	0	0	0	8	0	0	.000

WORLD SERIES
| 1981 LA N | 1 | 1 | .500 | 3.86 | 2 | 2 | 1 | 11.2 | 10 | 3 | 8 | 0 | 0 | 0 | 0 | 3 | 0 | 0 | .000 |

Craig Reynolds — REYNOLDS, GORDON CRAIG   B. Dec. 27, 1952, Houston, Tex.   BL TR 6'1"   175 lbs.

	W	L	PCT	ERA	G	GS	CG	IP	H	BB	SO	ShO	W	L	SV	AB	H	HR	BA
1986 HOU N	0	0	–	27.00	1	0	0	1	3	2	1	0	0	0	0	*			

Rick Rhoden — RHODEN, RICHARD ALAN   B. May 16, 1953, Boynton Beach, Fla.   BR TR 6'3"   195 lbs.

	W	L	PCT	ERA	G	GS	CG	IP	H	BB	SO	ShO	W	L	SV	AB	H	HR	BA
1974 LA N	1	0	1.000	2.00	4	0	0	9	5	4	7	0	1	0	0	2	1	0	.500
1975	3	3	.500	3.09	26	11	1	99	94	32	40	0	0	1	0	28	2	0	.071
1976	12	3	.800	2.98	27	26	10	181	165	53	77	3	0	0	0	65	20	1	.308
1977	16	10	.615	3.75	31	31	4	216	223	63	122	1	0	0	0	78	18	3	.231
1978	10	8	.556	3.65	30	23	6	165	160	51	79	3	0	0	0	52	7	0	.135
1979 PIT N	0	1	.000	7.20	1	1	0	5	5	2	2	0	0	0	0	1	1	0	1.000
1980	7	5	.583	3.83	20	19	2	127	133	40	70	0	0	0	0	40	15	1	.375
1981	9	4	.692	3.90	21	21	4	136	147	53	76	2	0	0	0	48	9	0	.188
1982	11	14	.440	4.14	35	35	6	230.1	239	70	128	1	0	0	0	83	22	3	.265
1983	13	13	.500	3.09	36	35	7	244.1	256	68	153	2	0	0	1	86	13	0	.151

	W	L	PCT	ERA	G	GS	CG	IP	H	BB	SO	ShO	Relief Pitching W	L	SV	BATTING AB	H	HR	BA

Rick Rhoden continued

	W	L	PCT	ERA	G	GS	CG	IP	H	BB	SO	ShO	W	L	SV	AB	H	HR	BA
1984	14	9	.609	2.72	33	33	6	238.1	216	62	136	3	0	0	0	84	28	0	.333
1985	10	15	.400	4.47	35	35	2	213.1	254	69	128	0	0	0	0	74	14	0	.189
1986	15	12	.556	2.84	34	34	12	253.2	211	76	159	1	0	0	0	90	25	1	.278
1987 NY A	16	10	.615	3.86	30	29	4	181.2	184	61	107	0	0	0	0	0	0	0	—
1988	12	12	.500	4.29	30	30	5	197	206	56	94	1	0	0	0	1	0	0	.000
15 yrs.	149	119	.556	3.57	393	363	69	2496.2	2498	760	1378	17	1	3	1	732	175	9	.239

LEAGUE CHAMPIONSHIP SERIES

	W	L	PCT	ERA	G	GS	CG	IP	H	BB	SO	ShO	W	L	SV	AB	H	HR	BA
1977 LA N	0	0	—	0.00	1	0	0	4.1	2	2	0	0	0	0	0	1	0	0	.000
1978	0	0	—	2.25	1	0	0	4	2	1	3	0	0	0	0	1	0	0	.000
2 yrs.	0	0	—	1.08	2	0	0	8.1	4	3	3	0	0	0	0	2	0	0	.000

WORLD SERIES

	W	L	PCT	ERA	G	GS	CG	IP	H	BB	SO	ShO	W	L	SV	AB	H	HR	BA
1977 LA N	0	1	.000	2.57	2	0	0	7	4	1	5	0	0	1	0	2	1	0	.500

Dave Righetti

RIGHETTI, DAVID ALLAN (Rags)
B. Nov. 28, 1958, San Jose, Calif.

BL TL 6'2" 170 lbs.

	W	L	PCT	ERA	G	GS	CG	IP	H	BB	SO	ShO	W	L	SV	AB	H	HR	BA
1979 NY A	0	1	.000	3.71	3	3	0	17	10	10	13	0	0	0	0	0	0	0	—
1981	8	4	.667	2.06	15	15	2	105	75	38	89	0	0	0	0	0	0	0	—
1982	11	10	.524	3.79	33	27	4	183	155	**108**	163	0	0	0	1	0	0	0	—
1983	14	8	.636	3.44	31	31	7	217	194	67	169	2	0	0	0	0	0	0	—
1984	5	6	.455	2.34	64	0	0	96.1	79	37	90	0	5	6	31	0	0	0	—
1985	12	7	.632	2.78	74	0	0	107	96	45	92	0	12	7	29	0	0	0	—
1986	8	8	.500	2.45	74	0	0	106.2	88	35	83	0	8	8	46[1]	0	0	0	—
1987	8	6	.571	3.51	60	0	0	95	95	44	77	0	8	6	31	0	0	0	—
1988	5	4	.556	3.52	60	0	0	87	86	37	70	0	5	4	25	0	0	0	—
9 yrs.	71	54	.568	3.10	414	76	13	1014	878	421	846	2	38	31	163	0	0	0	—

DIVISIONAL PLAYOFF SERIES

	W	L	PCT	ERA	G	GS	CG	IP	H	BB	SO	ShO	W	L	SV	AB	H	HR	BA
1981 NY A	2	0	1.000	1.00	2	1	0	9	8	3	13	0	1	0	0	0	0	0	—

LEAGUE CHAMPIONSHIP SERIES

	W	L	PCT	ERA	G	GS	CG	IP	H	BB	SO	ShO	W	L	SV	AB	H	HR	BA
1981 NY A	1	0	1.000	0.00	1	1	0	6	4	2	4	0	0	0	0	0	0	0	—

WORLD SERIES

	W	L	PCT	ERA	G	GS	CG	IP	H	BB	SO	ShO	W	L	SV	AB	H	HR	BA
1981 NY A	0	0	—	13.50	1	1	0	2	5	2	1	0	0	0	0	1	0	0	.000

Jose Rijo

RIJO, JOSE ANTONIO ABREU
Born Jose Antonio Rijo y Abreu.
B. May 13, 1965, San Cristobal, Dominican Republic

BR TR 6'1" 160 lbs.

	W	L	PCT	ERA	G	GS	CG	IP	H	BB	SO	ShO	W	L	SV	AB	H	HR	BA
1984 NY A	2	8	.200	4.76	24	5	0	62.1	74	33	47	0	2	4	2	0	0	0	—
1985 OAK A	6	4	.600	3.53	12	9	0	63.2	57	28	65	0	2	1	0	0	0	0	—
1986	9	11	.450	4.65	39	26	4	193.2	172	108	176	0	0	4	1	0	0	0	—
1987	2	7	.222	5.90	21	14	1	82.1	106	41	67	0	0	0	0	0	0	0	—
1988 CIN N	13	8	.619	2.39	49	19	0	162	120	63	160	0	6	1	0	37	2	1	.054
5 yrs.	32	38	.457	4.07	145	73	5	564	529	273	515	0	10	10	3	37	2	1	.054

Wally Ritchie

RITCHIE, WALLACE REID
B. July 12, 1965, Glendale, Calif.

BL TL 6'2" 180 lbs.

	W	L	PCT	ERA	G	GS	CG	IP	H	BB	SO	ShO	W	L	SV	AB	H	HR	BA
1987 PHI N	3	2	.600	3.75	49	0	0	62.1	60	29	45	0	3	2	3	4	1	0	.250
1988	0	0	—	3.12	19	0	0	26	19	17	8	0	0	0	0	0	0	0	—
2 yrs.	3	2	.600	3.57	68	0	0	88.1	79	46	53	0	3	2	3	4	1	0	.250

Don Robinson

ROBINSON, DON ALLEN
B. June 8, 1957, Ashland, Ky.

BR TR 6'4" 225 lbs.

	W	L	PCT	ERA	G	GS	CG	IP	H	BB	SO	ShO	W	L	SV	AB	H	HR	BA
1978 PIT N	14	6	.700	3.47	35	32	9	228	203	57	135	1	0	0	1	85	20	0	.235
1979	8	8	.500	3.86	29	25	4	161	171	52	96	0	0	1	0	49	10	0	.204
1980	7	10	.412	3.99	29	24	3	160	157	45	103	2	0	0	1	57	19	1	.333
1981	0	3	.000	5.92	16	2	0	38	47	23	17	0	0	2	2	12	3	0	.250
1982	15	13	.536	4.28	38	30	6	227	213	103	165	0	2	0	0	85	24	2	.282
1983	2	2	.500	4.46	9	6	0	36.1	43	21	28	0	1	0	0	13	2	1	.154
1984	5	6	.455	3.02	51	1	0	122	99	49	110	0	5	5	10	31	9	1	.290
1985	5	11	.313	3.87	44	6	0	95.1	95	42	65	0	4	7	3	21	5	1	.238
1986	3	4	.429	3.38	50	0	0	69.1	61	27	53	0	3	4	14	6	4	0	.667
1987 2 teams			PIT	N	(42G	6–6)		SF	N	(25G	5–1)								
" total	11	7	.611	3.42	67	0	0	108	105	40	79	0	11	7	19	18	4	1	.222
1988 SF N	10	5	.667	2.45	51	19	3	176.2	152	49	122	2	2	1	6	52	9	1	.173
11 yrs.	80	75	.516	3.65	419	145	25	1421.2	1346	508	973	5	28	27	56	429	109	8	.254

LEAGUE CHAMPIONSHIP SERIES

	W	L	PCT	ERA	G	GS	CG	IP	H	BB	SO	ShO	W	L	SV	AB	H	HR	BA
1979 PIT N	1	0	1.000	0.00	2	0	0	2	0	1	3	0	1	0	1	0	0	0	—
1987 SF N	0	1	.000	9.00	3	0	0	3	3	0	3	0	0	1	0	0	0	0	—
2 yrs.	1	1	.500	5.40	5	0	0	5	3	1	6	0	1	1	1	0	0	0	—

WORLD SERIES

	W	L	PCT	ERA	G	GS	CG	IP	H	BB	SO	ShO	W	L	SV	AB	H	HR	BA
1979 PIT N	1	0	1.000	5.40	4	0	0	5	4	6	3	0	1	0	0	0	0	0	—

Jeff Robinson

ROBINSON, JEFFREY DANIEL
B. Dec. 13, 1960, Santa Ana, Calif.

BR TR 6'4" 195 lbs.

	W	L	PCT	ERA	G	GS	CG	IP	H	BB	SO	ShO	W	L	SV	AB	H	HR	BA
1984 SF N	7	15	.318	4.56	34	33	1	171.2	195	52	102	0	0	0	0	61	7	0	.115
1985	0	0	—	5.11	8	0	0	12.1	16	10	8	0	0	0	0	0	0	0	—
1986	6	3	.667	3.36	64	1	0	104.1	92	32	90	0	6	3	8	15	1	0	.067
1987 2 teams			SF	N	(63G	6–8)		PIT	N	(18G	2–1)								
" total	8	9	.471	2.85	81	0	0	123.1	89	54	101	0	8	9	14	22	3	1	.136
1988 PIT N	11	5	.688	3.03	75	0	0	124.2	113	39	87	0	11	5	9	16	3	0	.188
5 yrs.	32	32	.500	3.59	262	34	1	536.1	505	187	388	1	25	17	31	114	14	1	.123

	W	L	PCT	ERA	G	GS	CG	IP	H	BB	SO	ShO	Relief Pitching W	L	SV	BATTING AB	H	HR	BA

Jeff Robinson

ROBINSON, JEFFREY MARK
B. Dec. 14, 1961, Ventura, Calif.
BR TR 6'6"   210 lbs.

	W	L	PCT	ERA	G	GS	CG	IP	H	BB	SO	ShO	W	L	SV	AB	H	HR	BA
1987 DET A	9	6	.600	5.37	29	21	2	127.1	132	54	98	1	1	1	0	0	0	0	–
1988	13	6	.684	2.98	24	23	6	172	121	72	114	2	0	0	0	0	0	0	–
2 yrs.	22	12	.647	4.00	53	44	8	299.1	253	126	212	3	1	1	0	0	0	0	–

LEAGUE CHAMPIONSHIP SERIES

	W	L	PCT	ERA	G	GS	CG	IP	H	BB	SO	ShO	W	L	SV	AB	H	HR	BA
1987 DET A	0	0	–	0.00	1	0	0	.1	1	0	0	0	0	0	0	0	0	0	–

Ron Robinson

ROBINSON, RONALD DEAN
B. Mar. 24, 1962, Exeter, Calif.
BR TR 6'4"   200 lbs.

	W	L	PCT	ERA	G	GS	CG	IP	H	BB	SO	ShO	W	L	SV	AB	H	HR	BA
1984 CIN N	1	2	.333	2.72	12	5	1	39.2	35	13	24	0	0	0	0	8	0	0	.000
1985	7	7	.500	3.99	33	12	0	108.1	107	32	76	0	3	1	1	22	2	0	.091
1986	10	3	.769	3.24	70	0	0	116.2	110	43	117	0	10	3	14	14	1	0	.071
1987	7	5	.583	3.68	48	18	0	154	148	43	99	0	1	2	4	36	7	0	.194
1988	3	7	.300	4.12	17	16	0	78.2	88	26	38	0	0	0	0	25	5	0	.200
5 yrs.	28	24	.538	3.64	180	51	1	497.1	488	157	354	0	14	6	19	105	15	0	.143

Mike Rochford

ROCHFORD, MICHAEL JOSEPH
B. Mar. 14, 1963, Methuen, Mass.
BL TL 6'4"   205 lbs.

	W	L	PCT	ERA	G	GS	CG	IP	H	BB	SO	ShO	W	L	SV	AB	H	HR	BA
1988 BOS A	0	0	–	0.00	2	0	0	2.1	4	1	1	0	0	0	0	0	0	0	–

Rick Rodriguez

RODRIGUEZ, RICARDO
B. Sept. 21, 1960, Oakland, Calif.
BR TR 6'3"   190 lbs.

	W	L	PCT	ERA	G	GS	CG	IP	H	BB	SO	ShO	W	L	SV	AB	H	HR	BA
1986 OAK A	1	2	.333	6.61	3	3	0	16.1	17	7	2	0	0	0	0	0	0	0	–
1987	1	0	1.000	2.96	15	0	0	24.1	32	15	9	0	1	0	0	0	0	0	–
1988 CLE A	1	2	.333	7.09	10	5	0	33	43	17	9	0	0	0	0	0	0	0	–
3 yrs.	3	4	.429	5.62	28	8	0	73.2	92	39	20	0	1	0	0	0	0	0	–

Steve Rosenberg

ROSENBERG, STEVEN ALLEN
B. Oct. 31, 1964, Brooklyn, N. Y.
BL TL 6'   180 lbs.

	W	L	PCT	ERA	G	GS	CG	IP	H	BB	SO	ShO	W	L	SV	AB	H	HR	BA
1988 CHI A	0	1	.000	4.30	33	0	0	46	53	19	28	0	0	1	1	0	0	0	–

Mark Ross

ROSS, MARK JOSEPH
B. Aug. 8, 1954, Galveston, Tex.
BR TR 6'   195 lbs.

	W	L	PCT	ERA	G	GS	CG	IP	H	BB	SO	ShO	W	L	SV	AB	H	HR	BA
1982 HOU N	0	0	–	1.50	4	0	0	6	3	0	4	0	0	0	0	0	0	0	–
1984	1	0	1.000	0.00	2	0	0	2.1	1	0	1	0	1	0	0	0	0	0	–
1985	0	2	.000	4.85	8	0	0	13	12	2	3	0	0	2	1	1	0	0	.000
1987 PIT N	0	0	–	9.00	1	0	0	1	1	0	0	0	0	0	0	0	0	0	–
1988 TOR A	0	0	–	4.91	3	0	0	7.1	5	4	4	0	0	0	0	0	0	0	–
5 yrs.	1	2	.333	3.94	18	0	0	29.2	22	6	12	0	1	2	1	1	0	0	.000

Dave Rucker

RUCKER, DAVID MICHAEL
B. Sept. 1, 1957, San Bernardino, Calif.
BL TL 6'1"   185 lbs.

	W	L	PCT	ERA	G	GS	CG	IP	H	BB	SO	ShO	W	L	SV	AB	H	HR	BA
1981 DET A	0	0	–	6.75	2	0	0	4	3	1	2	0	0	0	0	0	0	0	–
1982	5	6	.455	3.38	27	4	1	64	62	23	31	0	4	4	0	0	0	0	–
1983 2 teams		DET	A (4G 1–2)		STL	N	(34G 5–3)												
" total	6	5	.545	5.28	38	3	0	46	54	26	28	0	5	4	0	4	0	0	.000
1984 STL N	2	3	.400	2.10	50	0	0	73	62	34	38	0	2	3	0	7	1	0	.143
1985 PHI N	3	2	.600	4.31	39	0	0	79.1	83	40	41	0	2	1	1	12	4	0	.333
1986	2	2	.000	5.76	19	0	0	25	34	14	14	0	0	2	0	1	0	0	.000
1988 PIT N	0	2	.000	4.76	31	0	0	28.1	39	9	16	0	0	2	0	2	0	0	.000
7 yrs.	16	20	.444	3.94	206	10	1	319.2	337	147	170	0	13	16	1	26	5	0	.192

Bruce Ruffin

RUFFIN, BRUCE WAYNE
B. Oct. 4, 1963, Lubbock, Tex.
BR TL 6'2"   205 lbs.

	W	L	PCT	ERA	G	GS	CG	IP	H	BB	SO	ShO	W	L	SV	AB	H	HR	BA
1986 PHI N	9	4	.692	2.46	21	21	6	146.1	138	44	70	0	0	0	0	55	4	0	.073
1987	11	14	.440	4.35	35	35	3	204.2	236	73	93	1	0	0	0	73	4	0	.055
1988	6	10	.375	4.43	55	15	3	144.1	151	80	82	0	2	4	3	33	4	0	.121
3 yrs.	26	28	.481	3.82	111	71	12	495.1	525	197	245	1	2	4	3	161	12	0	.075

Jeff Russell

RUSSELL, JEFFREY LEE
B. Sept. 2, 1961, Cincinnati, Ohio
BR TR 6'4"   200 lbs.

	W	L	PCT	ERA	G	GS	CG	IP	H	BB	SO	ShO	W	L	SV	AB	H	HR	BA
1983 CIN N	4	5	.444	3.03	10	10	2	68.1	58	22	40	0	0	0	0	21	3	1	.143
1984	6	18	.250	4.26	33	30	4	181.2	186	65	101	2	0	0	0	57	8	0	.140
1985 TEX A	3	6	.333	7.55	13	13	0	62	85	27	44	0	0	0	0	0	0	0	–
1986	5	2	.714	3.40	37	0	0	82	74	31	54	0	5	2	2	0	0	0	–
1987	5	4	.556	4.44	52	2	0	97.1	109	52	56	0	5	3	3	0	0	0	–
1988	10	9	.526	3.82	34	24	5	188.2	183	66	88	0	1	0	0	1	0	0	.000
6 yrs.	33	44	.429	4.24	179	79	11	680	695	263	383	2	11	5	5	79	11	1	.139

Nolan Ryan

RYAN, LYNN NOLAN (The Express)
B. Jan. 31, 1947, Refugio, Tex.
BR TR 6'2"   170 lbs.

	W	L	PCT	ERA	G	GS	CG	IP	H	BB	SO	ShO	W	L	SV	AB	H	HR	BA
1966 NY N	0	1	.000	15.00	2	1	0	3	5	3	6	0	0	0	0	0	0	0	–
1968	6	9	.400	3.09	21	18	3	134	93	75	133	0	0	0	0	44	5	0	.114
1969	6	3	.667	3.53	25	10	2	89.1	60	53	92	0	3	0	1	29	3	0	.103
1970	7	11	.389	3.41	27	19	5	132	86	97	125	2	0	0	1	45	8	0	.178
1971	10	14	.417	3.97	30	26	3	152	125	116	137	0	1	0	0	47	6	0	.128
1972 CAL A	19	16	.543	2.28	39	39	20	284	166	157	329	9	0	0	0	96	13	0	.135
1973	21	16	.568	2.87	41	39	26	326	238	162	383[1]	4	0	0	1	0	0	0	–
1974	22	16	.579	2.89	42	41	26	333	221	202	367	3	1	0	0	0	0	0	–
1975	14	12	.538	3.45	28	28	10	198	152	132	186	5	0	0	0	0	0	0	–
1976	17	18	.486	3.36	39	39	21	284	193	183	327	7	0	0	0	0	0	0	–
1977	19	16	.543	2.77	37	37	22	299	198	204	341	4	0	0	0	0	0	0	–
1978	10	13	.435	3.71	31	31	14	235	183	148	260	3	0	0	0	0	0	0	–
1979	16	14	.533	3.59	34	34	17	223	169	114	223	5	0	0	0	0	0	0	–
1980 HOU N	11	10	.524	3.35	35	35	4	234	205	98	200	2	0	0	0	70	6	1	.086
1981	11	5	.688	1.69	21	21	5	149	99	68	140	3	0	0	0	51	11	0	.216

	W	L	PCT	ERA	G	GS	CG	IP	H	BB	SO	ShO	Relief Pitching W	L	SV	BATTING AB	H	HR	BA

Nolan Ryan continued

	W	L	PCT	ERA	G	GS	CG	IP	H	BB	SO	ShO	W	L	SV	AB	H	HR	BA
1982	16	12	.571	3.16	35	35	10	250.1	196	109	245	3	0	0	0	83	10	0	.120
1983	14	9	.609	2.98	29	29	5	196.1	134	101	183	2	0	0	0	69	5	0	.072
1984	12	11	.522	3.04	30	30	5	183.2	143	69	197	2	0	0	0	61	6	0	.098
1985	10	12	.455	3.80	35	35	4	232	205	95	209	0	0	0	0	63	7	0	.111
1986	12	8	.600	3.34	30	30	1	178	119	82	194	0	0	0	0	59	6	0	.102
1987	8	16	.333	**2.76**	34	34	0	211.2	154	87	**270**	0	0	0	0	65	4	1	.062
1988	12	11	.522	3.52	33	33	4	220	186	87	**228**	1	0	0	0	70	4	0	.057
22 yrs.	273	253	.519	3.15	678	644	207	4547.1	3330	2442	4775	55	5	0	3	852	94	2	.110
			8th							1st	1st								

DIVISIONAL PLAYOFF SERIES

	W	L	PCT	ERA	G	GS	CG	IP	H	BB	SO	ShO	W	L	SV	AB	H	HR	BA
1981 HOU N	1	1	.500	1.80	2	2	1	15	6	3	14	0	0	0	0	4	1	0	.250

LEAGUE CHAMPIONSHIP SERIES

	W	L	PCT	ERA	G	GS	CG	IP	H	BB	SO	ShO	W	L	SV	AB	H	HR	BA
1969 NY N	1	0	1.000	2.57	1	0	0	7	3	2	7	0	1	0	0	4	2	0	.500
1979 CAL A	0	0	—	1.29	1	1	0	7	4	3	8	0	0	0	0	0	0	0	—
1980 HOU N	0	0	—	5.40	2	2	0	13.1	16	3	14	0	0	0	0	4	0	0	.000
1986	0	1	.000	3.86	2	2	0	14	9	1	17	0	0	0	0	4	0	0	.000
4 yrs.	1	1	.500	3.70	6	5	0	41.1	32	9	46	0	1	0	0	12	2	0	.167

WORLD SERIES

	W	L	PCT	ERA	G	GS	CG	IP	H	BB	SO	ShO	W	L	SV	AB	H	HR	BA
1969 NY N	0	0	—	0.00	1	0	0	2.1	1	2	3	0	0	0	1	0	0	0	—

Bret Saberhagen

SABERHAGEN, BRET WILLIAM
B. Apr. 11, 1964, Chicago Heights, Ill.

BR TR 6'1" 160 lbs.

	W	L	PCT	ERA	G	GS	CG	IP	H	BB	SO	ShO	W	L	SV	AB	H	HR	BA
1984 KC A	10	11	.476	3.48	38	18	2	157.2	138	36	73	1	4	1	1	0	0	0	—
1985	20	6	.769	2.87	32	32	10	235.1	211	38	158	1	0	0	0	0	0	0	—
1986	7	12	.368	4.15	30	25	4	156	165	29	112	2	1	0	0	0	0	0	—
1987	18	10	.643	3.36	33	33	15	257	246	53	163	4	0	0	0	0	0	0	—
1988	14	16	.467	3.80	35	35	9	260.2	**271**	59	171	0	0	0	0	0	0	0	—
5 yrs.	69	55	.556	3.49	168	143	40	1066.2	1031	215	677	8	5	1	1	0	0	0	—

LEAGUE CHAMPIONSHIP SERIES

	W	L	PCT	ERA	G	GS	CG	IP	H	BB	SO	ShO	W	L	SV	AB	H	HR	BA
1984 KC A	0	0	—	2.25	1	1	0	8	6	1	5	0	0	0	0	0	0	0	—
1985	0	0	—	6.14	2	2	0	7.1	12	2	6	0	0	0	0	0	0	0	—
2 yrs.	0	0	—	4.11	3	3	0	15.1	18	3	11	0	0	0	0	0	0	0	—

WORLD SERIES

	W	L	PCT	ERA	G	GS	CG	IP	H	BB	SO	ShO	W	L	SV	AB	H	HR	BA
1985 KC A	2	0	1.000	0.50	2	2	2	18	11	1	10	1	0	0	0	7	0	0	.000

Randy St. Claire

ST. CLAIRE, RANDY ANTHONY
Son of Ebba St. Claire.
B. Aug. 23, 1960, Glens Falls, N. Y.

BR TR 6'3" 180 lbs.

	W	L	PCT	ERA	G	GS	CG	IP	H	BB	SO	ShO	W	L	SV	AB	H	HR	BA
1984 MON N	0	0	—	4.50	4	0	0	8	11	2	4	0	0	0	0	0	0	0	—
1985	5	3	.625	3.93	42	0	0	68.2	69	26	25	0	5	3	0	5	1	0	.200
1986	2	0	1.000	2.37	11	0	0	19	13	6	21	0	2	0	1	1	0	0	.000
1987	3	3	.500	4.03	44	0	0	67	64	20	43	0	3	3	7	6	2	0	.333
1988 2 teams			MON	N (6G 0–0)			CIN	N (10G 1–0)											
" total	1	0	1.000	3.86	16	0	0	21	24	10	14	0	1	0	0	1	0	0	.000
5 yrs.	11	6	.647	3.82	117	0	0	183.2	181	64	107	0	11	6	8	13	3	0	.231

Luis Salazar

SALAZAR, LLUIS ERNESTO GARCIA
Born Luis Ernesto Salazar y Garacia.
B. May 19, 1956, Barcelona, Venezuela

BR TR 6' 185 lbs.

	W	L	PCT	ERA	G	GS	CG	IP	H	BB	SO	ShO	W	L	SV	AB	H	HR	BA
1987 SD N	0	0	—	4.50	2	0	0	2	2	1	0	0	0	0	0	*			

Roger Samuels

SAMUELS, ROGER HOWARD
B. Jan. 5, 1961, San Jose, Calif.

BL TL 6'5" 210 lbs.

	W	L	PCT	ERA	G	GS	CG	IP	H	BB	SO	ShO	W	L	SV	AB	H	HR	BA
1988 SF N	1	2	.333	3.47	15	0	0	23.1	17	7	22	0	1	2	0	3	0	0	.000

Israel Sanchez

SANCHEZ, ISRAEL
Born Israel Sanchez y Matos.
B. Aug. 20, 1963, Falcon Lasvias, Cuba

BL TL 5'9" 170 lbs.

	W	L	PCT	ERA	G	GS	CG	IP	H	BB	SO	ShO	W	L	SV	AB	H	HR	BA
1988 KC A	3	2	.600	4.54	19	1	0	35.2	36	18	14	0	3	2	1	0	0	0	—

Scott Sanderson

SANDERSON, SCOTT DOUGLAS
B. July 22, 1956, Dearborn, Mich.

BR TR 6'5" 195 lbs.

	W	L	PCT	ERA	G	GS	CG	IP	H	BB	SO	ShO	W	L	SV	AB	H	HR	BA
1978 MON N	4	2	.667	2.51	10	9	1	61	52	21	50	1	0	0	0	19	2	0	.105
1979	9	8	.529	3.43	34	24	5	168	148	54	138	3	1	1	1	50	8	0	.160
1980	16	11	.593	3.11	33	33	7	211	206	56	125	3	0	0	0	64	5	0	.078
1981	9	7	.563	2.96	22	22	4	137	122	31	77	1	0	0	0	35	4	0	.114
1982	12	12	.500	3.46	32	32	7	224	212	58	158	0	0	0	0	57	8	1	.140
1983	6	7	.462	4.65	18	16	0	81.1	98	20	55	0	0	0	1	28	4	0	.143
1984 CHI N	8	5	.615	3.14	24	24	3	140.2	140	24	76	0	0	0	0	42	5	0	.119
1985	5	6	.455	3.12	19	19	2	121	100	27	80	0	0	0	0	31	2	0	.065
1986	9	11	.450	4.19	37	28	1	169.2	165	37	124	1	2	0	1	51	3	0	.059
1987	8	9	.471	4.29	32	22	0	144.2	156	50	106	0	1	2	2	40	3	1	.075
1988	1	2	.333	5.28	11	9	0	15.1	13	3	6	0	1	0	0	0	0	0	—
11 yrs.	87	80	.521	3.51	272	229	30	1473.2	1412	381	995	9	5	5	5	417	44	2	.106

DIVISIONAL PLAYOFF SERIES

	W	L	PCT	ERA	G	GS	CG	IP	H	BB	SO	ShO	W	L	SV	AB	H	HR	BA
1981 MON N	0	0	—	6.75	1	1	0	2.2	4	1	2	0	0	0	0	1	0	0	.000

LEAGUE CHAMPIONSHIP SERIES

	W	L	PCT	ERA	G	GS	CG	IP	H	BB	SO	ShO	W	L	SV	AB	H	HR	BA
1984 CHI N	0	0	—	5.79	1	1	0	4.2	6	1	2	0	0	0	0	2	0	0	.000

	W	L	PCT	ERA	G	GS	CG	IP	H	BB	SO	ShO	Relief Pitching W	L	SV	BATTING AB	H	HR	BA

Rich Sauveur
SAUVEUR, RICHARD DANIEL
B. Nov. 23, 1963, Arlington, Va.　　　　BL TL 6'4"　163 lbs.

	W	L	PCT	ERA	G	GS	CG	IP	H	BB	SO	ShO	W	L	SV	AB	H	HR	BA
1986 PIT N	0	0	–	6.00	3	3	0	12	17	6	6	0	0	0	0	3	1	0	.333
1988 MON N	0	0	–	6.00	4	0	0	3	3	2	3	0	0	0	0	0	0	0	–
2 yrs.	0	0	–	6.00	7	3	0	15	20	8	9	0	0	0	0	3	1	0	.333

Dan Schatzeder
SCHATZEDER, DANIEL ERNEST
B. Dec. 1, 1954, Elmhurst, Ill.　　　　BL TL 6'　185 lbs.

	W	L	PCT	ERA	G	GS	CG	IP	H	BB	SO	ShO	W	L	SV	AB	H	HR	BA
1977 MON N	2	1	.667	2.45	6	3	1	22	16	13	14	1	0	0	0	6	2	0	.333
1978	7	7	.500	3.06	29	18	2	144	108	68	69	0	2	0	0	45	10	1	.222
1979	10	5	.667	2.83	32	21	3	162	136	59	106	0	1	1	1	51	11	1	.216
1980 DET A	11	13	.458	4.01	32	26	9	193	178	58	94	2	2	0	0	0	0	0	–
1981	6	8	.429	6.08	17	14	1	71	74	29	20	0	0	0	0	0	0	0	–
1982 2 teams					SF N (13G 1–4)			MON N (26G 0–2)											
" total	1	6	.143	5.32	39	4	0	69.1	84	24	33	0	1	3	0	13	3	0	.231
1983 MON N	5	2	.714	3.21	58	2	0	87	88	25	48	0	4	1	2	10	2	0	.200
1984	7	7	.500	2.71	36	14	1	136	112	36	89	1	1	1	1	35	11	0	.314
1985	3	5	.375	3.80	24	15	1	104.1	101	31	64	0	0	0	0	31	6	2	.194
1986 2 teams					MON N (30G 3–2)			PHI N (25G 3–3)											
" total	6	5	.545	3.26	55	1	0	88.1	81	35	47	0	6	5	2	26	10	1	.385
1987 2 teams					PHI N (26G 3–1)			MIN A (30G 3–1)											
" total	6	2	.750	5.31	56	1	0	81.1	104	32	58	0	6	2	0	12	2	0	.167
1988 2 teams					CLE A (15G 0–1)			MIN A (10G 0–1)											
" total	0	3	.000	6.49	25	0	0	26.1	34	7	17	0	0	3	3	0	0	0	–
12 yrs.	64	64	.500	3.77	409	119	18	1184.2	1116	417	659	4	23	16	9	229	57	5	.249

LEAGUE CHAMPIONSHIP SERIES

	W	L	PCT	ERA	G	GS	CG	IP	H	BB	SO	ShO	W	L	SV	AB	H	HR	BA
1987 MIN A	0	0	–	0.00	2	0	0	4.1	2	0	5	0	0	0	0	0	0	0	–

WORLD SERIES

	W	L	PCT	ERA	G	GS	CG	IP	H	BB	SO	ShO	W	L	SV	AB	H	HR	BA
1987 MIN A	1	0	1.000	6.23	3	0	0	4.1	4	3	3	0	1	0	0	0	0	0	–

Bill Scherrer
SCHERRER, WILLIAM JOSEPH
B. Jan. 20, 1958, Tonawanda, N. Y.　　　　BL TL 6'4"　180 lbs.

	W	L	PCT	ERA	G	GS	CG	IP	H	BB	SO	ShO	W	L	SV	AB	H	HR	BA
1982 CIN N	0	1	.000	2.60	5	2	0	17.1	17	0	7	0	0	0	0	2	1	0	.500
1983	2	3	.400	2.74	73	0	0	92	73	33	57	0	2	3	10	11	1	0	.091
1984 2 teams					CIN N (36G 1–1)			DET A (18G 1–0)											
" total	2	1	.667	4.16	54	0	0	71.1	78	23	51	0	2	1	1	3	0	0	.000
1985 DET A	3	2	.600	4.36	48	0	0	66	62	41	46	0	3	2	0	0	0	0	–
1986	0	1	.000	7.29	13	0	0	21	19	22	16	0	0	1	0	0	0	0	–
1987 CIN N	1	1	.500	4.36	23	0	0	33	43	16	24	0	1	1	0	1	0	0	.000
1988 2 teams					BAL A (4G 0–1)			PHI N (8G 0–0)											
" total	0	1	.000	8.44	12	0	0	10.2	15	5	6	0	0	1	0	0	0	0	–
7 yrs.	8	10	.444	4.08	228	2	0	311.1	307	140	207	0	8	9	11	17	2	0	.118

WORLD SERIES

	W	L	PCT	ERA	G	GS	CG	IP	H	BB	SO	ShO	W	L	SV	AB	H	HR	BA
1984 DET A	0	0	–	3.00	3	0	0	3	5	0	0	0	0	0	0	0	0	0	–

Curt Schilling
SCHILLING, CURIS MONTAGUE
B. Nov. 14, 1966, Anchorage, Alaska　　　　BR TR 6'5"　205 lbs.

	W	L	PCT	ERA	G	GS	CG	IP	H	BB	SO	ShO	W	L	SV	AB	H	HR	BA
1988 BAL A	0	3	.000	9.82	4	4	0	14.2	22	10	4	0	0	0	0	0	0	0	–

Calvin Schiraldi
SCHIRALDI, CALVIN DREW
B. June 16, 1962, Houston, Tex.　　　　BR TR 6'5"　215 lbs.

	W	L	PCT	ERA	G	GS	CG	IP	H	BB	SO	ShO	W	L	SV	AB	H	HR	BA
1984 NY N	0	2	.000	5.71	5	3	0	17.1	20	10	16	0	0	0	0	3	0	0	.000
1985	1	2	.667	8.89	10	4	0	26.1	43	11	21	0	0	0	0	8	1	0	.125
1986 BOS A	4	2	.667	1.41	25	0	0	51	36	15	55	0	4	2	9	0	0	0	–
1987	8	5	.615	4.41	62	1	0	83.2	75	40	93	0	8	5	6	0	0	0	–
1988 CHI N	9	13	.409	4.38	29	27	2	166.1	166	63	140	1	0	0	1	60	6	0	.100
5 yrs.	23	23	.500	4.36	131	35	2	344.2	340	139	325	1	12	7	16	71	7	0	.099

LEAGUE CHAMPIONSHIP SERIES

	W	L	PCT	ERA	G	GS	CG	IP	H	BB	SO	ShO	W	L	SV	AB	H	HR	BA
1986 BOS A	0	1	.000	1.50	4	0	0	6	5	3	9	0	0	1	1	0	0	0	–

WORLD SERIES

	W	L	PCT	ERA	G	GS	CG	IP	H	BB	SO	ShO	W	L	SV	AB	H	HR	BA
1986 BOS A	0	2	.000	13.50	3	0	0	4	7	3	2	0	0	2 (2nd)	1	1	0	0	.000

Dave Schmidt
SCHMIDT, DAVID JOSEPH
B. Apr. 22, 1957, Niles, Mich.　　　　BR TR 6'1"　185 lbs.

	W	L	PCT	ERA	G	GS	CG	IP	H	BB	SO	ShO	W	L	SV	AB	H	HR	BA
1981 TEX A	0	1	.000	3.09	14	1	0	32	31	11	13	0	0	0	1	0	0	0	–
1982	4	6	.400	3.20	33	8	0	109.2	118	25	69	0	3	1	6	0	0	0	–
1983	3	3	.500	3.88	31	0	0	46.1	42	14	29	0	3	3	2	0	0	0	–
1984	6	6	.500	2.56	43	0	0	70.1	69	20	46	0	6	6	12	0	0	0	–
1985	7	6	.538	3.15	51	4	1	85.2	81	22	46	1	5	4	5	0	0	0	–
1986 CHI A	3	6	.333	3.31	49	1	0	92.1	94	27	67	0	3	5	8	0	0	0	–
1987 BAL A	10	5	.667	3.77	35	14	2	124	128	26	70	2	6	1	1	0	0	0	–
1988	8	5	.615	3.40	41	9	0	129.2	129	38	67	0	3	3	2	0	0	0	–
8 yrs.	41	38	.519	3.33	297	37	3	690	692	183	407	3	29	23	37	0	0	0	–

Mike Schooler
SCHOOLER, MICHAEL RALPH
B. Aug. 10, 1962, Anaheim, Calif.　　　　BR TR 6'3"　220 lbs.

	W	L	PCT	ERA	G	GS	CG	IP	H	BB	SO	ShO	W	L	SV	AB	H	HR	BA
1988 SEA A	5	8	.385	3.54	40	0	0	48.1	45	24	54	0	5	8	15	0	0	0	–

Mike Scott
SCOTT, MICHAEL WARREN
B. Apr. 26, 1955, Santa Monica, Calif.　　　　BR TR 6'2"　210 lbs.

	W	L	PCT	ERA	G	GS	CG	IP	H	BB	SO	ShO	W	L	SV	AB	H	HR	BA
1979 NY N	1	3	.250	5.37	18	9	0	52	59	20	21	0	0	0	0	12	0	0	.000
1980	1	1	.500	4.34	6	6	1	29	40	8	13	1	0	0	0	9	1	0	.111
1981	5	10	.333	3.90	23	23	1	136	130	34	54	0	0	0	0	41	3	0	.073
1982	7	13	.350	5.14	37	22	1	147	185	60	63	0	1	3	3	48	7	0	.146
1983 HOU N	10	6	.625	3.72	24	24	2	145	143	46	73	2	0	0	0	48	8	0	.167

	W	L	PCT	ERA	G	GS	CG	IP	H	BB	SO	ShO	W	L	SV	AB	H	HR	BA
													Relief Pitching			BATTING			

Mike Scott continued

	W	L	PCT	ERA	G	GS	CG	IP	H	BB	SO	ShO	W	L	SV	AB	H	HR	BA
1984	5	11	.313	4.68	31	29	0	154	179	43	83	0	0	0	0	47	6	0	.128
1985	18	8	.692	3.29	36	35	4	221.2	194	80	137	2	0	0	0	72	11	1	.153
1986	18	10	.643	**2.22**	37	37	7	**275.1**	182	72	**306**	5	0	0	0	95	12	0	.126
1987	16	13	.552	3.23	36	**36**	8	247.2	199	79	233	3	0	0	0	80	10	0	.125
1988	14	8	.636	2.92	32	32	8	218.2	162	53	190	5	0	0	0	71	6	0	.085
10 yrs.	95	83	.534	3.53	280	253	32	1626.1	1473	495	1173	18	1	3	3	523	64	1	.122

LEAGUE CHAMPIONSHIP SERIES

	W	L	PCT	ERA	G	GS	CG	IP	H	BB	SO	ShO	W	L	SV	AB	H	HR	BA
1986 HOU N	2	0	1.000	0.50	2	2	2	18	8	1	19	1	0	0	0	6	0	0	.000

Rod Scurry

SCURRY, RODNEY GRANT BL TL 6'2" 180 lbs.
B. Mar. 17, 1956, Sacramento, Calif.

	W	L	PCT	ERA	G	GS	CG	IP	H	BB	SO	ShO	W	L	SV	AB	H	HR	BA
1980 PIT N	0	2	.000	2.13	20	0	0	38	23	17	28	0	0	2	0	4	1	0	.250
1981	4	5	.444	3.77	27	7	0	74	74	40	65	0	1	2	7	19	3	0	.158
1982	4	5	.444	1.74	76	0	0	103.2	79	64	94	0	4	5	14	21	5	0	.238
1983	4	9	.308	5.56	61	0	0	68	63	53	67	0	4	9	7	5	0	0	.000
1984	5	6	.455	2.53	43	0	0	46.1	28	22	48	0	5	6	4	2	0	0	.000
1985 2 teams			PIT N	(30G 0–1)			NY	A	(5G 1–0)										
" total	1	1	.500	3.13	35	0	0	60.1	47	38	60	0	1	1	3	4	0	0	.000
1986 NY A	1	2	.333	3.66	31	0	0	39.1	38	22	36	0	1	2	2	0	0	0	–
1988 SEA A	0	2	.000	4.02	39	0	0	31.1	32	18	33	0	0	2	2	0	0	0	–
8 yrs.	19	32	.373	3.24	332	7	0	461	384	274	431	0	16	29	39	55	9	0	.164

Steve Searcy

SEARCY, WILLIAM STEVEN BL TL 6'1" 185 lbs.
B. June 4, 1964, Knoxville, Tenn.

	W	L	PCT	ERA	G	GS	CG	IP	H	BB	SO	ShO	W	L	SV	AB	H	HR	BA
1988 DET A	0	2	.000	5.63	2	2	0	8	8	4	5	0	0	0	0	0	0	0	–

Bob Sebra

SEBRA, ROBERT BUSH BR TR 6'2" 200 lbs.
B. Dec. 11, 1961, Ridgewood, N. J.

	W	L	PCT	ERA	G	GS	CG	IP	H	BB	SO	ShO	W	L	SV	AB	H	HR	BA
1985 TEX A	0	2	.000	7.52	7	4	0	20.1	26	14	13	0	0	0	0	0	0	0	–
1986 MON N	5	5	.500	3.55	17	13	3	91.1	82	25	66	1	1	1	0	29	6	0	.207
1987	6	15	.286	4.42	36	27	4	177.1	184	67	156	1	0	0	0	51	8	0	.157
1988 PHI N	1	2	.333	7.94	3	3	0	11.1	15	10	7	0	0	0	0	5	0	0	.000
4 yrs.	12	24	.333	4.50	63	47	7	300.1	307	116	242	2	1	1	0	85	14	0	.165

Jose Segura

SEGURA, JOSE ALTAGRACIA BR TR 5'11" 180 lbs.
Born Jose Altagracia Segura y Mota.
B. Jan. 26, 1963, Fundacion, Dominican Republic

	W	L	PCT	ERA	G	GS	CG	IP	H	BB	SO	ShO	W	L	SV	AB	H	HR	BA
1988 CHI A	0	0	–	13.50	4	0	0	8.2	19	8	2	0	0	0	0	0	0	0	–

Jeff Sellers

SELLERS, JEFFREY DOYLE BR TR 6'1" 195 lbs.
B. May 11, 1964, Compton, Calif.

	W	L	PCT	ERA	G	GS	CG	IP	H	BB	SO	ShO	W	L	SV	AB	H	HR	BA
1985 BOS A	2	0	1.000	3.63	4	4	1	22.1	24	7	6	0	0	0	0	0	0	0	–
1986	3	7	.300	4.94	14	13	1	82	90	40	51	0	0	0	0	0	0	0	–
1987	7	8	.467	5.28	25	22	4	139.2	161	61	99	2	0	0	0	0	0	0	–
1988	1	7	.125	4.83	18	12	1	85.2	89	56	70	0	1	0	0	0	0	0	–
4 yrs.	13	22	.371	4.97	61	51	7	329.2	364	164	226	2	1	0	0	0	0	0	–

Scott Service

SERVICE, DAVID SCOTT BR TR 6'6" 225 lbs.
B. Feb. 26, 1967, Cincinnati, Ohio

	W	L	PCT	ERA	G	GS	CG	IP	H	BB	SO	ShO	W	L	SV	AB	H	HR	BA
1988 PHI N	0	0	–	1.69	5	0	0	5.1	7	1	6	0	0	0	0	0	0	0	–

Jeff Shaver

SHAVER, JEFFREY THOMAS BR TR 6'3" 185 lbs.
B. July 30, 1963, Beaver Falls, Pa.

	W	L	PCT	ERA	G	GS	CG	IP	H	BB	SO	ShO	W	L	SV	AB	H	HR	BA
1988 OAK A	0	0	–	0.00	1	0	0	1	0	0	0	0	0	0	0	0	0	0	–

Steve Shields

SHIELDS, STEPHEN MACK BR TR 6'5" 220 lbs.
B. Nov. 30, 1958, Gadsden, Ala.

	W	L	PCT	ERA	G	GS	CG	IP	H	BB	SO	ShO	W	L	SV	AB	H	HR	BA
1985 ATL N	1	2	.333	5.16	23	6	0	68	86	32	29	0	0	0	0	18	2	0	.111
1986 2 teams			ATL	N (6G 0–0)			KC	A	(3G 0–0)										
" total	0	0	–	5.06	9	0	0	21.1	16	11	8	0	0	0	0	1	0	0	.000
1987 SEA A	2	0	1.000	6.60	20	0	0	30	43	12	22	0	2	0	3	0	0	0	–
1988 NY A	5	5	.500	4.37	39	0	0	82.1	96	30	55	0	5	5	0	0	0	0	–
4 yrs.	8	7	.533	5.04	91	6	0	201.2	241	85	114	0	7	5	3	19	2	0	.105

Eric Show

SHOW, ERIC VAUGHN BR TR 6'1" 185 lbs.
B. May 19, 1956, Riverside, Calif.

	W	L	PCT	ERA	G	GS	CG	IP	H	BB	SO	ShO	W	L	SV	AB	H	HR	BA
1981 SD N	1	3	.250	3.13	15	0	0	23	17	9	22	0	1	3	3	0	0	0	–
1982	10	6	.625	2.64	47	14	2	150	117	48	88	2	6	3	3	41	6	0	.146
1983	15	12	.556	4.17	35	33	4	200.2	201	74	120	2	0	0	0	64	11	0	.172
1984	15	9	.625	3.40	32	32	3	206.2	175	88	104	1	0	0	0	69	17	3	.246
1985	12	11	.522	3.09	35	35	5	233	212	87	141	2	0	0	0	79	10	1	.127
1986	9	5	.643	2.97	24	22	2	136.1	109	69	94	0	1	0	0	43	7	0	.163
1987	8	16	.333	3.84	34	34	5	206.1	188	85	117	3	0	0	0	70	5	0	.071
1988	16	11	.593	3.26	32	32	13	234.2	201	53	144	1	0	0	0	81	12	0	.148
8 yrs.	86	73	.541	3.37	254	202	34	1390.2	1220	513	830	11	8	6	6	447	68	4	.152

LEAGUE CHAMPIONSHIP SERIES

	W	L	PCT	ERA	G	GS	CG	IP	H	BB	SO	ShO	W	L	SV	AB	H	HR	BA
1984 SD N	0	1	.000	13.50	2	2	0	5.1	8	4	2	0	0	0	0	1	0	0	.000

WORLD SERIES

	W	L	PCT	ERA	G	GS	CG	IP	H	BB	SO	ShO	W	L	SV	AB	H	HR	BA
1984 SD N	0	1	.000	10.13	1	1	0	2.2	4	1	2	0	0	0	0	0	0	0	–

	W	L	PCT	ERA	G	GS	CG	IP	H	BB	SO	ShO	Relief Pitching W	L	SV	BATTING AB	H	HR	BA

Candy Sierra

SIERRA, ULISES
Born Ulises Sierra y Pizarro.
B. Mar. 27, 1967, Rio Piedras, Puerto Rico　　　　　BR　TR　6'2"　　190 lbs.

	W	L	PCT	ERA	G	GS	CG	IP	H	BB	SO	ShO	W	L	SV	AB	H	HR	BA
1988 2 teams			SD	N (15G 0–1)				CIN	N (1G 0–0)										
" total	0	1	.000	5.53	16	0	0	27.2	41	12	24	0	0	1	0	4	0	0	.000

Doug Sisk

SISK, DOUGLAS RANDALL
B. Sept. 26, 1957, Renton, Wash.　　　　　　　　　　BR　TR　6'2"　　210 lbs.

	W	L	PCT	ERA	G	GS	CG	IP	H	BB	SO	ShO	W	L	SV	AB	H	HR	BA
1982 NY N	0	1	.000	1.04	8	0	0	8.2	5	4	4	0	0	1	1	0	0	0	–
1983	5	4	.556	2.24	67	0	0	104.1	88	59	33	0	5	4	11	6	3	0	.500
1984	1	3	.250	2.09	50	0	0	77.2	57	54	32	0	1	3	15	11	1	0	.091
1985	4	5	.444	5.30	42	0	0	73	86	40	26	0	4	5	2	12	0	0	.000
1986	4	2	.667	3.06	41	0	0	70.2	77	31	31	0	4	2	1	4	0	0	.000
1987	3	1	.750	3.46	55	0	0	78	83	22	37	0	3	1	3	5	0	0	.000
1988 BAL A	3	3	.500	3.72	52	0	0	94.1	109	45	26	0	3	3	0	0	0	0	–
7 yrs.	20	19	.513	3.22	315	0	0	506.2	505	255	189	0	20	19	33	38	4	0	.105

LEAGUE CHAMPIONSHIP SERIES

	W	L	PCT	ERA	G	GS	CG	IP	H	BB	SO	ShO	W	L	SV	AB	H	HR	BA
1986 NY N	0	0	–	0.00	1	0	0	1	1	1	0	0	0	0	0	0	0	0	–

WORLD SERIES

	W	L	PCT	ERA	G	GS	CG	IP	H	BB	SO	ShO	W	L	SV	AB	H	HR	BA
1986 NY N	0	0	–	0.00	1	0	0	.2	0	1	1	0	0	0	0	0	0	0	–

John Smiley

SMILEY, JOHN PATRICK
B. Mar. 17, 1965, Phoenixville, Pa.　　　　　　　　　BL　TL　6'4"　　180 lbs.

	W	L	PCT	ERA	G	GS	CG	IP	H	BB	SO	ShO	W	L	SV	AB	H	HR	BA
1986 PIT N	1	0	1.000	3.86	12	0	0	11.2	4	4	9	0	1	0	0	0	0	0	–
1987	5	5	.500	5.76	63	0	0	75	69	50	58	0	5	5	4	7	1	0	.143
1988	13	11	.542	3.25	34	32	5	205	185	46	129	1	0	0	0	63	5	0	.079
3 yrs.	19	16	.543	3.92	109	32	5	291.2	258	100	196	1	6	5	4	70	6	0	.086

Bryn Smith

SMITH, BRYN NELSON
B. Aug. 11, 1955, Marietta, Ga.　　　　　　　　　　BR　TR　6'2"　　200 lbs.

	W	L	PCT	ERA	G	GS	CG	IP	H	BB	SO	ShO	W	L	SV	AB	H	HR	BA
1981 MON N	1	0	1.000	2.77	7	0	0	13	14	3	9	0	1	0	0	1	0	0	.000
1982	2	4	.333	4.20	47	1	0	79.1	81	23	50	0	2	3	3	8	0	0	.000
1983	6	11	.353	2.49	49	12	5	155.1	142	43	101	3	1	4	3	30	5	0	.167
1984	12	13	.480	3.32	28	28	4	179	178	51	101	2	0	0	0	53	7	0	.132
1985	18	5	.783	2.91	32	32	4	222.1	193	41	127	2	0	0	0	72	14	1	.194
1986	10	8	.556	3.94	30	30	1	187.1	182	63	105	0	0	0	0	58	8	1	.138
1987	10	9	.526	4.37	26	26	2	150.1	164	31	94	0	0	0	0	44	6	0	.136
1988	12	10	.545	3.00	32	32	1	198	179	32	122	0	0	0	0	55	6	0	.109
8 yrs.	71	60	.542	3.37	251	161	17	1184.2	1133	287	709	7	4	7	6	321	46	2	.143

Dave Smith

SMITH, DAVID STANLEY
B. Jan. 21, 1955, Richmond, Calif.　　　　　　　　　BR　TR　6'1"　　195 lbs.

	W	L	PCT	ERA	G	GS	CG	IP	H	BB	SO	ShO	W	L	SV	AB	H	HR	BA
1980 HOU N	7	5	.583	1.92	57	0	0	103	90	32	85	0	7	5	10	12	0	0	.000
1981	5	3	.625	2.76	42	0	0	75	54	23	52	0	5	3	8	8	2	0	.250
1982	5	4	.556	3.84	49	1	0	63.1	69	31	28	0	5	4	11	2	0	0	.000
1983	3	1	.750	3.10	42	0	0	72.2	72	36	41	0	3	1	6	5	0	0	.000
1984	5	4	.556	2.21	53	0	0	77.1	60	20	45	0	5	4	5	4	0	0	.000
1985	9	5	.643	2.27	64	0	0	79.1	69	17	40	0	9	5	27	3	0	0	.000
1986	4	7	.364	2.73	54	0	0	56	39	22	46	0	4	7	33	2	0	0	.000
1987	2	3	.400	1.65	50	0	0	60	39	21	73	0	2	3	24	2	1	0	.500
1988	4	5	.444	2.67	51	0	0	57.1	60	19	38	0	4	5	27	2	0	0	.000
9 yrs.	44	37	.543	2.53	462	1	0	644	552	221	448	0	44	37	151	40	3	0	.075

DIVISIONAL PLAYOFF SERIES

	W	L	PCT	ERA	G	GS	CG	IP	H	BB	SO	ShO	W	L	SV	AB	H	HR	BA
1981 HOU N	0	0	–	3.86	2	0	0	2.1	2	0	4	0	0	0	0	0	0	0	–

LEAGUE CHAMPIONSHIP SERIES

	W	L	PCT	ERA	G	GS	CG	IP	H	BB	SO	ShO	W	L	SV	AB	H	HR	BA
1980 HOU N	1	0	1.000	3.86	3	0	0	2.1	4	2	4	0	1	0	0	0	0	0	–
1986	0	1	.000	9.00	2	0	0	2	2	3	2	0	0	1	0	0	0	0	–
2 yrs.	1	1	.500	6.23	5	0	0	4.1	6	5	6	0	1	1	0	0	0	0	–

Lee Smith

SMITH, LEE ARTHUR JR.
B. Dec. 4, 1957, Jamestown, La.　　　　　　　　　　BR　TR　6'5"　　220 lbs.

	W	L	PCT	ERA	G	GS	CG	IP	H	BB	SO	ShO	W	L	SV	AB	H	HR	BA
1980 CHI N	2	0	1.000	2.86	18	0	0	22	21	14	17	0	2	0	0	0	0	0	–
1981	3	6	.333	3.49	40	1	0	67	57	31	50	0	3	5	1	9	0	0	.000
1982	2	5	.286	2.69	72	5	0	117	105	37	99	0	2	1	17	16	1	1	.063
1983	4	10	.286	1.65	66	0	0	103.1	70	41	91	0	4	10	29	9	1	0	.111
1984	9	7	.563	3.65	69	0	0	101	98	35	86	0	9	7	33	13	1	0	.077
1985	7	4	.636	3.04	65	0	0	97.2	87	32	112	0	7	4	33	6	0	0	.000
1986	9	9	.500	3.09	66	0	0	90.1	69	42	93	0	9	9	31	5	0	0	.000
1987	4	10	.286	3.12	62	0	0	83.2	84	32	96	0	4	10	36	2	0	0	.000
1988 BOS A	4	5	.444	2.80	64	0	0	83.2	72	37	96	0	4	5	29	0	0	0	–
9 yrs.	44	56	.440	2.90	522	6	0	765.2	663	301	740	0	44	51	209 9th	60	3	1	.050

LEAGUE CHAMPIONSHIP SERIES

	W	L	PCT	ERA	G	GS	CG	IP	H	BB	SO	ShO	W	L	SV	AB	H	HR	BA
1984 CHI N	0	1	.000	9.00	2	0	0	2	3	0	3	0	0	1	1	0	0	0	–
1988 BOS A	0	1	.000	8.10	2	0	0	3.1	6	1	4	0	0	1	0	0	0	0	–
2 yrs.	0	2	.000	8.44	4	0	0	5.1	9	1	7	0	0	2	1	0	0	0	–

Mike Smith

SMITH, MICHAEL ANTHONY
B. Feb. 23, 1961, Hinds, Miss.　　　　　　　　　　BB　TR　6'1"　　195 lbs.

	W	L	PCT	ERA	G	GS	CG	IP	H	BB	SO	ShO	W	L	SV	AB	H	HR	BA
1984 CIN N	1	0	1.000	5.23	8	0	0	10.1	12	5	7	0	1	0	0	0	0	0	–
1985	0	0	–	5.40	2	0	0	3.1	2	1	2	0	0	0	0	0	0	0	–
1986	0	0	–	13.50	2	1	0	3.1	7	1	1	0	0	0	0	0	0	0	–
1988 MON N	0	0	–	3.12	5	0	0	8.2	6	5	4	0	0	0	1	2	0	0	.000
4 yrs.	1	0	1.000	5.61	17	1	0	25.2	27	12	14	0	1	0	1	2	0	0	.000

	W	L	PCT	ERA	G	GS	CG	IP	H	BB	SO	ShO	Relief Pitching W	L	SV	BATTING AB	H	HR	BA

Pete Smith

SMITH, PETER JOHN — B. Feb. 27, 1966, Abington, Mass. — BR TR 6'2" 185 lbs.

	W	L	PCT	ERA	G	GS	CG	IP	H	BB	SO	ShO	W	L	SV	AB	H	HR	BA
1987 ATL N	1	2	.333	4.83	6	6	0	31.2	39	14	11	0	0	0	0	11	1	0	.091
1988	7	15	.318	3.69	32	32	5	195.1	183	88	124	3	0	0	0	53	6	0	.113
2 yrs.	8	17	.320	3.85	38	38	5	227	222	102	135	3	0	0	0	64	7	0	.109

Roy Smith

SMITH, LEROY PURDY III — B. Sept. 6, 1961, Mt. Vernon, N. Y. — BR TR 6'3" 205 lbs.

	W	L	PCT	ERA	G	GS	CG	IP	H	BB	SO	ShO	W	L	SV	AB	H	HR	BA
1984 CLE A	5	5	.500	4.59	22	14	0	86.1	91	40	55	0	0	0	0	0	0	0	–
1985	1	4	.200	5.34	12	11	1	62.1	84	17	28	0	0	0	0	0	0	0	–
1986 MIN A	0	2	.000	6.97	5	0	0	10.1	13	5	8	0	0	2	0	0	0	0	–
1987	1	0	1.000	4.96	7	1	0	16.1	20	6	8	0	0	0	0	0	0	0	–
1988	3	0	1.000	2.68	9	4	0	37	29	12	17	0	1	0	0	0	0	0	–
5 yrs.	10	11	.476	4.62	55	30	1	212.1	237	80	116	0	1	2	0	0	0	0	–

Zane Smith

SMITH, ZANE WILLIAM — B. Dec. 28, 1960, Madison, Wis. — BL TL 6'2" 195 lbs.

	W	L	PCT	ERA	G	GS	CG	IP	H	BB	SO	ShO	W	L	SV	AB	H	HR	BA
1984 ATL N	1	0	1.000	2.25	3	3	0	20	16	13	16	0	0	0	0	9	5	0	.556
1985	9	10	.474	3.80	42	18	2	147	135	80	85	2	3	4	0	37	6	0	.162
1986	8	16	.333	4.05	38	32	3	204.2	209	105	139	1	1	0	1	59	5	0	.085
1987	15	10	.600	4.09	36	36	9	242	245	91	130	3	0	0	0	76	10	0	.132
1988	5	10	.333	4.30	23	22	3	140.1	159	44	59	0	0	0	0	42	7	0	.167
5 yrs.	38	46	.452	4.01	142	111	17	754	764	333	429	6	4	4	1	223	33	0	.148

Mike Smithson

SMITHSON, BILLY MIKE — B. Jan. 21, 1955, Centerville, Tenn. — BL TR 6'8" 200 lbs.

	W	L	PCT	ERA	G	GS	CG	IP	H	BB	SO	ShO	W	L	SV	AB	H	HR	BA
1982 TEX A	3	4	.429	5.01	8	8	3	46.2	51	13	24	0	0	0	0	0	0	0	–
1983	10	14	.417	3.91	33	33	10	223.1	233	71	135	0	0	0	0	0	0	0	–
1984 MIN A	15	13	.536	3.68	36	36	10	252	246	54	144	1	0	0	0	0	0	0	–
1985	15	14	.517	4.34	37	37	8	257	264	78	127	3	0	0	0	0	0	0	–
1986	13	14	.481	4.77	34	33	8	198	234	57	114	1	0	1	0	0	0	0	–
1987	4	7	.364	5.94	21	20	0	109	126	38	53	0	0	0	0	0	0	0	–
1988 BOS A	9	6	.600	5.97	31	18	1	126.2	149	37	73	0	1	1	0	0	0	0	–
7 yrs.	69	72	.489	4.53	200	185	40	1212.2	1303	348	670	5	1	2	0	0	0	0	–

LEAGUE CHAMPIONSHIP SERIES

	W	L	PCT	ERA	G	GS	CG	IP	H	BB	SO	ShO	W	L	SV	AB	H	HR	BA
1988 BOS A	0	0	–	0.00	1	0	0	2.1	3	0	1	0	0	0	0	0	0	0	–

John Smoltz

SMOLTZ, JOHN ANDREW — B. May 15, 1967, Detroit, Mich. — BR TR 6'3" 180 lbs.

	W	L	PCT	ERA	G	GS	CG	IP	H	BB	SO	ShO	W	L	SV	AB	H	HR	BA
1988 ATL N	2	7	.222	5.48	12	12	0	64	74	33	37	0	0	0	0	17	2	0	.118

Julio Solano

SOLANO, JULIO CESAR MERCADO — Born Julio Cesar Mercado Solano. B. Jan. 8, 1960, Aqua Blanca, Dominican Republic — BR TR 6'1" 157 lbs.

	W	L	PCT	ERA	G	GS	CG	IP	H	BB	SO	ShO	W	L	SV	AB	H	HR	BA
1983 HOU N	0	2	.000	6.00	4	0	0	6	5	4	3	0	0	2	0	0	0	0	–
1984	1	3	.250	1.95	31	0	0	50.2	31	18	33	0	1	3	0	3	1	0	.333
1985	2	2	.500	3.48	20	0	0	33.2	34	13	17	0	2	2	0	2	0	0	.000
1986	3	1	.750	7.59	16	1	0	32	39	22	21	0	3	0	0	6	0	0	.000
1987	0	0	–	7.65	11	0	0	20	25	9	12	0	0	0	0	2	0	0	.000
1988 SEA A	0	0	–	4.09	17	0	0	22	22	12	10	0	0	0	3	0	0	0	–
6 yrs.	6	8	.429	4.49	99	1	0	164.1	156	78	96	0	6	7	3	13	1	0	.077

Lary Sorensen

SORENSEN, LARY ALAN — B. Oct. 4, 1955, Detroit, Mich. — BR TR 6'2" 200 lbs.

	W	L	PCT	ERA	G	GS	CG	IP	H	BB	SO	ShO	W	L	SV	AB	H	HR	BA
1977 MIL A	7	10	.412	4.37	23	20	9	142	147	36	57	0	0	1	0	0	0	0	–
1978	18	12	.600	3.21	37	36	17	280.2	277	50	78	3	0	0	1	0	0	0	–
1979	15	14	.517	3.98	34	34	16	235	250	42	63	2	0	0	0	0	0	0	–
1980	12	10	.545	3.67	35	29	8	196	242	45	54	2	0	1	1	0	0	0	–
1981 STL N	7	7	.500	3.28	23	23	3	140	149	26	52	1	0	0	0	46	3	0	.065
1982 CLE A	10	15	.400	5.61	32	30	6	189.1	251	55	62	1	0	0	0	0	0	0	–
1983	12	11	.522	4.24	36	34	8	222.2	238	65	76	1	0	0	0	0	0	0	–
1984 OAK A	6	13	.316	4.91	46	21	2	183.1	240	44	63	0	1	2	1	0	0	0	–
1985 CHI N	3	7	.300	4.26	45	3	0	82.1	86	24	34	0	3	5	0	6	0	0	.000
1987 MON N	3	4	.429	4.72	23	5	0	47.2	56	12	21	0	1	1	1	8	0	0	.000
1988 SF N	0	0	–	4.86	12	0	0	16.2	24	3	9	0	0	0	2	1	0	0	.000
11 yrs.	93	103	.474	4.15	346	235	69	1735.2	1960	402	569	10	5	10	6	61	3	0	.049

Mario Soto

SOTO, MARIO MELVIN — B. July 12, 1956, Bani, Dominican Republic — BR TR 6' 174 lbs.

	W	L	PCT	ERA	G	GS	CG	IP	H	BB	SO	ShO	W	L	SV	AB	H	HR	BA
1977 CIN N	2	6	.250	5.31	12	10	2	61	60	26	44	1	0	0	0	13	1	0	.077
1978	1	0	1.000	2.50	5	1	0	18	13	13	13	0	1	0	0	2	0	0	.000
1979	3	2	.600	5.35	25	0	0	37	33	30	32	0	3	2	0	7	4	0	.571
1980	10	8	.556	3.08	53	12	3	190	126	84	182	1	3	8	4	46	2	0	.043
1981	12	9	.571	3.29	25	25	10	175	142	61	151	3	0	0	0	59	4	0	.068
1982	14	13	.519	2.79	35	34	13	257.2	202	71	274	2	1	0	0	84	14	0	.167
1983	17	13	.567	2.70	34	34	18	273.2	207	95	242	3	0	0	0	88	11	0	.125
1984	18	7	.720	3.53	33	33	13	237.1	181	87	185	0	0	0	0	87	18	1	.207
1985	12	15	.444	3.58	36	36	9	256.2	196	104	214	1	0	0	0	83	11	0	.133
1986	5	10	.333	4.71	19	19	1	105	113	46	67	1	0	0	0	27	3	0	.111
1987	3	2	.600	5.12	6	6	0	31.2	34	12	11	0	0	0	0	12	1	0	.083
1988	3	3	.300	4.66	14	14	3	87	88	28	34	1	0	0	0	22	1	0	.045
12 yrs.	100	92	.521	3.47	297	224	72	1730	1395	657	1449	13	8	10	4	530	70	1	.132

LEAGUE CHAMPIONSHIP SERIES

	W	L	PCT	ERA	G	GS	CG	IP	H	BB	SO	ShO	W	L	SV	AB	H	HR	BA
1979 CIN N	0	0	–	0.00	1	0	0	2	0	0	1	0	0	0	0	0	0	0	–

	W	L	PCT	ERA	G	GS	CG	IP	H	BB	SO	ShO	Relief Pitching W	L	SV	BATTING AB	H	HR	BA

Bob Stanley

STANLEY, ROBERT WILLIAM (Bigfoot)   BR TR 6'4"   210 lbs.
B. Nov. 10, 1954, Portland, Me.

	W	L	PCT	ERA	G	GS	CG	IP	H	BB	SO	ShO	W	L	SV	AB	H	HR	BA
1977 **BOS A**	8	7	.533	3.99	41	13	3	151	176	43	44	1	3	0	3	0	0	0	–
1978	15	2	.882	2.60	52	3	0	141.2	142	34	38	0	12	2	10	0	0	0	–
1979	16	12	.571	3.98	40	30	9	217	250	44	56	4	3	1	1	0	0	0	–
1980	10	8	.556	3.39	52	17	5	175	186	52	71	1	4	2	14	0	0	0	–
1981	10	8	.556	3.82	35	1	0	99	110	38	28	0	10	7	0	0	0	0	–
1982	12	7	.632	3.10	48	0	0	168.1	161	50	83	0	12	7	14	0	0	0	–
1983	8	10	.444	2.85	64	0	0	145.1	145	38	65	0	8	10	33	0	0	0	–
1984	9	10	.474	3.54	57	0	0	106.2	113	23	52	0	9	10	22	0	0	0	–
1985	6	6	.500	2.87	48	0	0	87.2	76	30	46	0	6	6	10	0	0	0	–
1986	6	6	.500	4.37	66	1	0	82.1	109	22	54	0	6	5	16	0	0	0	–
1987	4	15	.211	5.01	34	20	4	152.2	198	42	67	1	0	3	0	0	0	0	–
1988	6	4	.600	3.19	57	0	0	101.2	90	29	57	0	6	4	5	0	0	0	–
12 yrs.	110	95	.537	3.58	594	85	21	1628.1	1756	445	661	7	79	57	128	0	0	0	–

LEAGUE CHAMPIONSHIP SERIES

1986 **BOS A**	0	0	–	4.76	3	0	0	5.2	7	3	1	0	0	0	0	0	0	0	–
1988	0	0	–	9.00	2	0	0	1	2	1	0	0	0	0	0	0	0	0	–
2 yrs.	0	0	–	5.40	5	0	0	6.2	9	4	1	0	0	0	0	0	0	0	–

WORLD SERIES

1986 **BOS A**	0	0	–	0.00	5	0	0	6.1	5	1	4	0	0	0	1	1	0	0	.000

Dave Stapleton

STAPLETON, DAVID EARL   BL TL 6'1"   185 lbs.
B. Oct. 16, 1961, Miami, Ariz.

1987 **MIL A**	2	0	1.000	1.84	4	0	0	14.2	13	3	14	0	2	0	0	0	0	0	–
1988	0	0	–	5.93	6	0	0	13.2	20	9	6	0	0	0	0	0	0	0	–
2 yrs.	2	0	1.000	3.81	10	0	0	28.1	33	12	20	0	2	0	0	0	0	0	–

Dave Stewart

STEWART, DAVID KEITH   BR TR 6'2"   200 lbs.
B. Feb. 19, 1957, Oakland, Calif.

1978 **LA N**	0	0	–	0.00	1	0	0	2	1	0	1	0	0	0	0	0	0	0	–
1981	4	3	.571	2.51	32	0	0	43	40	14	29	0	4	3	6	5	2	0	.400
1982	9	8	.529	3.81	45	14	0	146.1	137	49	80	0	6	3	1	39	7	0	.179
1983 **2 teams**					**LA**	N	(46G 5–2)		**TEX**	A	(8G 5–2)								
" total	10	4	.714	2.60	54	9	2	135	117	50	78	0	5	2	8	7	1	0	.143
1984 **TEX A**	7	14	.333	4.73	32	27	3	192.1	193	87	119	0	0	1	0	0	0	0	–
1985 **2 teams**					**TEX**	A	(42G 0–6)		**PHI**	N	(4G 0–0)								
" total	0	6	.000	5.46	46	5	0	85.2	91	41	66	0	0	4	4	0	0	0	–
1986 **2 teams**					**PHI**	N	(8G 0–0)		**OAK**	A	(29G 9–5)								
" total	9	5	.643	3.95	37	17	4	161.2	152	69	111	1	0	0	0	0	0	0	–
1987 **OAK A**	20	13	.606	3.68	37	37	8	261.1	224	105	205	1	0	0	0	0	0	0	–
1988	21	12	.636	3.23	37	37	14	275.2	240	110	192	2	0	0	0	0	0	0	–
9 yrs.	80	65	.552	3.75	321	146	31	1303	1195	525	881	4	15	13	19	51	10	0	.196

DIVISIONAL PLAYOFF SERIES

1981 **LA N**	0	2	.000	40.50	2	0	0	.2	4	0	1	0	0	2	0	0	0	0	–

LEAGUE CHAMPIONSHIP SERIES

1988 **OAK A**	1	0	1.000	1.35	2	2	0	13.1	9	6	11	0	0	0	0	0	0	0	–

WORLD SERIES

1981 **LA N**	0	0	–	0.00	2	0	0	1.2	1	2	1	0	0	0	0	0	0	0	–
1988 **OAK A**	0	1	.000	3.14	2	2	0	14.1	12	5	5	0	0	0	0	3	0	0	.000
2 yrs.	0	1	.000	2.81	4	2	0	16	13	7	6	0	0	0	0	3	0	0	.000

Dave Stieb

STIEB, DAVID ANDREW   BR TR 6'   185 lbs.
B. July 22, 1957, Santa Ana, Calif.

1979 **TOR A**	8	8	.500	4.33	18	18	7	129	139	48	52	1	0	0	0	0	0	0	–
1980	12	15	.444	3.70	34	32	14	243	232	83	108	4	0	0	0	1	0	0	.000
1981	11	10	.524	3.18	25	25	11	184	148	61	89	2	0	0	0	0	0	0	–
1982	17	14	.548	3.25	38	38	19	288.1	271	75	141	5	0	0	0	0	0	0	–
1983	17	12	.586	3.04	36	36	14	278	223	93	187	4	0	0	0	0	0	0	–
1984	16	8	.667	2.83	35	35	11	267	215	88	198	2	0	0	0	0	0	0	–
1985	14	13	.519	2.48	36	36	8	265	206	96	167	2	0	0	0	0	0	0	–
1986	7	12	.368	4.74	37	34	1	205	239	87	127	1	0	0	1	0	0	0	–
1987	13	9	.591	4.09	33	31	3	185	164	87	115	1	0	0	0	0	0	0	–
1988	16	8	.667	3.04	32	31	8	207.1	157	79	147	4	0	0	0	0	0	0	–
10 yrs.	131	109	.546	3.37	324	316	96	2251.2	1994	797	1331	26	0	0	1	1	0	0	.000

LEAGUE CHAMPIONSHIP SERIES

1985 **TOR A**	1	1	.500	3.10	3	3	0	20.1	11	10	18	0	0	0	0	0	0	0	–

Tim Stoddard

STODDARD, TIMOTHY PAUL   BR TR 6'7"   230 lbs.
B. Jan. 24, 1953, East Chicago, Ind.

1975 **CHI A**	0	0	–	9.00	1	0	0	1	2	0	0	0	0	0	0	0	0	0	–
1978 **BAL A**	0	1	.000	6.00	8	0	0	18	22	8	14	0	0	1	0	0	0	0	–
1979	3	1	.750	1.71	29	0	0	58	44	19	47	0	3	1	3	0	0	0	–
1980	5	3	.625	2.51	64	0	0	86	72	38	64	0	5	3	26	0	0	0	–
1981	4	2	.667	3.89	31	0	0	37	38	18	32	0	4	2	7	0	0	0	–
1982	3	4	.429	4.02	50	0	0	56	53	29	42	0	3	4	12	0	0	0	–
1983	4	3	.571	6.09	47	0	0	57.2	65	29	50	0	4	3	9	0	0	0	–
1984 **CHI N**	10	6	.625	3.82	58	0	0	92	77	57	87	0	10	6	7	11	1	0	.091
1985 **SD N**	1	6	.143	4.65	44	0	0	60	63	37	42	0	1	6	1	5	0	0	.000
1986 **2 teams**					**SD**	N	(30G 1–3)		**NY**	A	(24G 4–1)								
" total	5	4	.556	3.80	54	0	0	94.2	74	57	81	0	5	4	0	4	1	1	.250
1987 **NY A**	4	3	.571	3.50	57	0	0	92.2	83	30	78	0	4	3	8	0	0	0	–
1988	2	2	.500	6.38	28	0	0	55	62	27	33	0	2	2	3	0	0	0	–
12 yrs.	41	35	.539	3.98	471	0	0	708	655	349	570	0	41	35	76	20	2	1	.100

	W	L	PCT	ERA	G	GS	CG	IP	H	BB	SO	ShO	Relief Pitching W	L	SV	BATTING AB	H	HR	BA

Tim Stoddard <small>continued</small>

LEAGUE CHAMPIONSHIP SERIES

	W	L	PCT	ERA	G	GS	CG	IP	H	BB	SO	ShO	W	L	SV	AB	H	HR	BA
1984 **CHI N**	0	0	–	4.50	2	0	0	2	1	2	2	0	0	0	0	0	0	0	–

WORLD SERIES

	W	L	PCT	ERA	G	GS	CG	IP	H	BB	SO	ShO	W	L	SV	AB	H	HR	BA
1979 **BAL A**	1	0	1.000	5.40	4	0	0	5	6	1	3	0	1	0	0	1	1	0	1.000

Todd Stottlemyre

STOTTLEMYRE, TODD VERNON
Son of Mel Stottlemyre.
B. May 20, 1965, Sunnyside, Wash.

BL TR 6'3" 190 lbs.

	W	L	PCT	ERA	G	GS	CG	IP	H	BB	SO	ShO	W	L	SV	AB	H	HR	BA
1988 **TOR A**	4	8	.333	5.69	28	16	0	98	109	46	67	0	2	1	0	0	0	0	–

Les Straker

STRAKER, LESTER PAUL
Born Lester Paul Straker y Bolnalda.
B. Oct. 10, 1959, Ciudad Bolivar, Venezuela

BR TR 6'1" 193 lbs.

	W	L	PCT	ERA	G	GS	CG	IP	H	BB	SO	ShO	W	L	SV	AB	H	HR	BA
1987 **MIN A**	8	10	.444	4.37	31	26	1	154.1	150	59	76	0	0	1	0	0	0	0	–
1988	2	5	.286	3.92	16	14	1	82.2	86	25	23	1	0	0	1	0	0	0	–
2 yrs.	10	15	.400	4.22	47	40	2	237	236	84	99	1	0	1	1	0	0	0	–

LEAGUE CHAMPIONSHIP SERIES

	W	L	PCT	ERA	G	GS	CG	IP	H	BB	SO	ShO	W	L	SV	AB	H	HR	BA
1987 **MIN A**	0	0	–	16.88	1	1	0	2.2	3	4	1	0	0	0	0	0	0	0	–

WORLD SERIES

	W	L	PCT	ERA	G	GS	CG	IP	H	BB	SO	ShO	W	L	SV	AB	H	HR	BA
1987 **MIN A**	0	0	–	4.00	2	2	0	9	9	3	6	0	0	0	0	2	0	0	.000

Rick Sutcliffe

SUTCLIFFE, RICHARD LEE
B. June 21, 1956, Independence, Mo.

BL TR 6'7" 215 lbs.

	W	L	PCT	ERA	G	GS	CG	IP	H	BB	SO	ShO	W	L	SV	AB	H	HR	BA
1976 **LA N**	0	0	–	0.00	1	1	0	5	2	1	3	0	0	0	0	1	0	0	.000
1978	0	0	–	0.00	2	0	0	2	2	1	0	0	0	0	0	0	0	0	–
1979	17	10	.630	3.46	39	30	5	242	217	97	117	1	1	2	0	85	21	1	.247
1980	3	9	.250	5.56	42	10	1	110	122	55	59	1	2	5	5	27	4	0	.148
1981	2	2	.500	4.02	14	6	0	47	41	20	16	0	0	0	0	11	2	0	.182
1982 **CLE A**	14	8	.636	**2.96**	34	27	6	216	174	98	142	1	2	1	1	0	0	0	–
1983	17	11	.607	4.29	36	35	10	243.1	251	102	160	2	1	0	0	0	0	0	–
1984 **2 teams**		CLE	A (15G 4–5)		CHI	N (20G 16–1)													
" total	20	6	.769	3.64	35	35	9	244.2	234	85	213	3	0	0	0	56	14	0	.250
1985 **CHI N**	8	8	.500	3.18	20	20	6	130	119	44	102	3	0	0	0	43	10	1	.233
1986	5	14	.263	4.64	28	27	4	176.2	166	96	122	1	0	0	0	53	11	1	.208
1987	**18**	10	.643	3.68	34	34	6	237.1	223	106	174	1	0	0	0	81	12	0	.148
1988	13	14	.481	3.86	32	32	12	226	232	70	144	2	0	0	0	75	12	1	.160
12 yrs.	117	92	.560	3.83	317	257	59	1880	1783	775	1252	15	6	8	6	432	86	4	.199

LEAGUE CHAMPIONSHIP SERIES

	W	L	PCT	ERA	G	GS	CG	IP	H	BB	SO	ShO	W	L	SV	AB	H	HR	BA
1984 **CHI N**	1	1	.500	3.38	2	2	0	13.1	9	8	10	0	0	0	0	6	3	1	.500

Bruce Sutter

SUTTER, HOWARD BRUCE
B. Jan. 8, 1953, Lancaster, Pa.

BR TR 6'2" 190 lbs.

	W	L	PCT	ERA	G	GS	CG	IP	H	BB	SO	ShO	W	L	SV	AB	H	HR	BA
1976 **CHI N**	6	3	.667	2.71	52	0	0	83	63	26	73	0	6	3	10	8	0	0	.000
1977	7	3	.700	1.35	62	0	0	107	69	23	129	0	7	3	31	20	3	0	.150
1978	8	10	.444	3.18	64	0	0	99	82	34	106	0	8	10	27	13	1	0	.077
1979	6	6	.500	2.23	62	0	0	101	67	32	110	0	6	6	**37**	12	3	0	.250
1980	5	8	.385	2.65	60	0	0	102	90	34	76	0	5	8	**28**	9	1	0	.111
1981 **STL N**	3	5	.375	2.63	48	0	0	82	64	24	57	0	3	5	**25**	9	0	0	.000
1982	9	8	.529	2.90	70	0	0	102.1	88	34	61	0	9	8	**36**	8	1	0	.125
1983	9	10	.474	4.23	60	0	0	89.1	90	30	64	0	9	10	21	7	0	0	.000
1984	5	7	.417	1.54	71	0	0	122.2	109	23	77	0	5	7	**45**	10	0	0	.000
1985 **ATL N**	7	7	.500	4.48	58	0	0	88.1	91	29	52	0	7	7	23	4	0	0	.000
1986	2	0	1.000	4.34	16	0	0	18.2	17	9	16	0	2	0	3	1	0	0	.000
1988	1	4	.200	4.76	38	0	0	45.1	49	11	40	0	1	4	14	1	0	0	.000
12 yrs.	68	71	.489	2.84	661	0	0	1040.2	879	309	861	0	68	71	300 3rd	102	9	0	.088

LEAGUE CHAMPIONSHIP SERIES

	W	L	PCT	ERA	G	GS	CG	IP	H	BB	SO	ShO	W	L	SV	AB	H	HR	BA
1982 **STL N**	1	0	1.000	0.00	2	0	0	4.1	0	0	1	0	1	0	1	1	0	0	.000

WORLD SERIES

	W	L	PCT	ERA	G	GS	CG	IP	H	BB	SO	ShO	W	L	SV	AB	H	HR	BA
1982 **STL N**	1	0	1.000	4.70	4	0	0	7.2	6	3	6	0	1	0	2	0	0	0	–

Don Sutton

SUTTON, DONALD HOWARD
B. Apr. 2, 1945, Clio, Ala.

BR TR 6'1" 185 lbs.

	W	L	PCT	ERA	G	GS	CG	IP	H	BB	SO	ShO	W	L	SV	AB	H	HR	BA
1966 **LA N**	12	12	.500	2.99	37	35	6	225.2	192	52	209	2	0	1	0	82	15	0	.183
1967	11	15	.423	3.95	37	34	11	232.2	223	57	169	3	0	1	1	75	10	0	.133
1968	11	15	.423	2.60	35	27	7	207.2	179	59	162	2	1	1	1	62	11	0	.177
1969	17	18	.486	3.47	41	41	11	293	269	91	217	4	0	0	0	98	15	0	.153
1970	15	13	.536	4.08	38	38	10	260	251	78	201	4	0	0	0	84	13	0	.155
1971	17	12	.586	2.55	38	37	12	265	231	55	194	4	0	0	1	88	19	0	.216
1972	19	9	.679	2.08	33	33	18	272.2	186	63	207	9	0	0	0	91	13	0	.143
1973	18	10	.643	2.42	33	33	14	256.1	196	56	200	3	0	0	0	84	10	0	.119
1974	19	9	.679	3.23	40	**40**	10	276	241	80	179	5	0	0	0	98	18	0	.184
1975	16	13	.552	2.87	35	35	11	254	202	62	175	4	0	0	0	80	11	0	.138
1976	21	10	.677	3.06	35	34	15	267.2	231	82	161	4	1	0	0	84	7	0	.083
1977	14	8	.636	3.19	33	33	9	240	207	69	150	3	0	0	0	73	11	0	.151
1978	15	11	.577	3.55	34	34	12	238	228	54	154	2	0	0	0	72	6	0	.083
1979	12	15	.444	3.82	33	32	6	226	201	61	146	1	0	0	1	77	11	0	.143
1980	13	5	.722	**2.21**	32	31	4	212	163	47	128	2	0	0	1	64	5	0	.078
1981 **HOU N**	11	9	.550	2.60	23	23	6	159	132	29	104	3	0	0	0	51	7	0	.137
1982 **2 teams**		HOU	N (27G 13–8)		MIL	A (7G 4–1)													
" total	17	9	.654	3.06	34	34	6	249.2	224	64	175	1	0	0	0	68	11	0	.162
1983 **MIL A**	8	13	.381	4.08	31	31	4	220.1	209	54	134	0	0	0	0	0	0	0	–

	W	L	PCT	ERA	G	GS	CG	IP	H	BB	SO	ShO	Relief Pitching W	L	SV	BATTING AB	H	HR	BA

Don Sutton continued

	W	L	PCT	ERA	G	GS	CG	IP	H	BB	SO	ShO	W	L	SV	AB	H	HR	BA
1984	14	12	.538	3.77	33	33	1	212.2	224	51	143	0	0	0	0	0	0	0	–
1985 2 teams		OAK	A	(29G 13–8)		CAL	A	(5G 2–2)											
" total	15	10	.600	3.86	34	34	1	226	221	59	107	1	0	0	0	0	0	0	–
1986 CAL A	15	11	.577	3.74	34	34	3	207	192	49	116	1	0	0	0	0	0	0	–
1987	11	11	.500	4.70	35	34	1	191.2	199	41	99	0	1	0	0	0	0	0	–
1988 LA N	3	6	.333	3.92	16	16	0	87.1	91	30	44	0	0	0	0	23	2	0	.087
23 yrs.	324	256	.559	3.26	774	756	178	5280.1	4692	1343	3574	58	3	3	5	1354	195	0	.144
			6th					6th			4th	8th							

LEAGUE CHAMPIONSHIP SERIES

	W	L	PCT	ERA	G	GS	CG	IP	H	BB	SO	ShO	W	L	SV	AB	H	HR	BA
1974 LA N	2	0	1.000	0.53	2	2	1	17	7	2	13	1	0	0	0	7	2	0	.286
1977	1	0	1.000	1.00	1	1	1	9	9	0	4	0	0	0	0	3	0	0	.000
1978	0	1	.000	6.35	1	1	0	5.2	7	2	0	0	0	0	0	2	0	0	.000
1982 MIL A	1	0	1.000	3.52	1	1	0	7.2	8	2	9	0	0	0	0	0	0	0	–
1986 CAL A	0	0	–	1.86	2	1	0	9.2	6	1	4	0	0	0	0	0	0	0	–
5 yrs.	4	1	.800	2.02	7	6	2	49	37	7	30	1	0	0	0	12	2	0	.167

WORLD SERIES

	W	L	PCT	ERA	G	GS	CG	IP	H	BB	SO	ShO	W	L	SV	AB	H	HR	BA
1974 LA N	1	0	1.000	2.77	2	2	0	13	9	3	12	0	0	0	0	3	0	0	.000
1977	1	0	1.000	3.94	2	2	1	16	17	1	6	0	0	0	0	6	0	0	.000
1978	0	2	.000	7.50	2	2	0	12	17	4	8	0	0	0	0	0	0	0	–
1982 MIL A	0	1	.000	7.84	2	2	0	10.1	12	1	5	0	0	0	0	0	0	0	–
4 yrs.	2	3	.400	5.26	8	8	1	51.1	55	9	31	0	0	0	0	9	0	0	.000
						10th			9th										

Bill Swift

SWIFT, WILLIAM CHARLES
B. Oct. 27, 1961, Portland, Me.

BR TR 6'   170 lbs.

	W	L	PCT	ERA	G	GS	CG	IP	H	BB	SO	ShO	W	L	SV	AB	H	HR	BA
1985 SEA A	6	10	.375	4.77	23	21	0	120.2	131	48	55	0	1	0	0	0	0	0	–
1986	2	9	.182	5.46	29	17	1	115.1	148	55	55	0	0	0	0	0	0	0	–
1988	8	12	.400	4.59	38	24	6	174.2	199	65	47	1	3	1	0	0	0	0	–
3 yrs.	16	31	.340	4.89	90	62	7	410.2	478	168	157	1	4	1	0	0	0	0	–

Greg Swindell

SWINDELL, FORREST GREGORY
B. Jan. 2, 1965, Houston, Tex.

BR TL 6'2"   225 lbs.

	W	L	PCT	ERA	G	GS	CG	IP	H	BB	SO	ShO	W	L	SV	AB	H	HR	BA
1986 CLE A	5	2	.714	4.23	9	9	1	61.2	57	15	46	0	0	0	0	0	0	0	–
1987	3	8	.273	5.10	16	15	4	102.1	112	37	97	1	0	0	0	0	0	0	–
1988	18	14	.563	3.20	33	33	12	242	234	45	180	4	0	0	0	0	0	0	–
3 yrs.	26	24	.520	3.83	58	57	17	406	403	97	323	5	0	0	0	0	0	0	–

Frank Tanana

TANANA, FRANK DARYL
B. July 3, 1953, Detroit, Mich.

BL TL 6'2"   180 lbs.

	W	L	PCT	ERA	G	GS	CG	IP	H	BB	SO	ShO	W	L	SV	AB	H	HR	BA
1973 CAL A	2	2	.500	3.08	4	4	2	26.1	20	8	22	1	0	0	0	0	0	0	–
1974	14	19	.424	3.11	39	35	12	269	262	77	180	4	2	0	0	0	0	0	–
1975	16	9	.640	2.62	34	33	16	257.1	211	73	269	5	0	0	0	0	0	0	–
1976	19	10	.655	2.44	34	34	23	288	212	73	261	2	0	0	0	0	0	0	–
1977	15	9	.625	2.54	31	31	20	241.1	201	61	205	7	0	0	0	0	0	0	–
1978	18	12	.600	3.65	33	33	10	239	239	60	137	4	0	0	0	0	0	0	–
1979	7	5	.583	3.90	18	17	2	90	93	25	46	1	0	0	0	0	0	0	–
1980	11	12	.478	4.15	32	31	7	204	223	45	113	0	0	0	0	0	0	0	–
1981 BOS A	4	10	.286	4.02	24	23	5	141	142	43	78	2	0	0	0	0	0	0	–
1982 TEX A	7	18	.280	4.21	30	30	7	194.1	199	55	87	0	0	0	0	0	0	0	–
1983	7	9	.438	3.16	29	22	3	159.1	144	49	108	0	1	0	0	0	0	0	–
1984	15	15	.500	3.25	35	35	9	246.1	234	81	141	1	0	0	0	0	0	0	–
1985 2 teams		TEX	A	(13G 2–7)		DET	A	(20G 10–7)											
" total	12	14	.462	4.27	33	33	4	215	220	57	159	0	0	0	0	0	0	0	–
1986 DET A	12	9	.571	4.16	32	31	3	188.1	196	65	119	1	0	0	0	0	0	0	–
1987	15	10	.600	3.91	34	34	5	218.2	216	56	146	3	0	0	0	0	0	0	–
1988	14	11	.560	4.21	32	32	2	203	213	64	127	0	0	0	0	0	0	0	–
16 yrs.	188	174	.519	3.48	474	458	130	3181	3025	892	2198	31	3	0	0	0	0	0	–

LEAGUE CHAMPIONSHIP SERIES

	W	L	PCT	ERA	G	GS	CG	IP	H	BB	SO	ShO	W	L	SV	AB	H	HR	BA
1979 CAL A	0	0	–	3.60	1	1	0	5	6	2	3	0	0	0	0	0	0	0	–
1987 DET A	0	1	.000	5.06	1	1	0	5.1	6	4	1	0	0	0	0	0	0	0	–
2 yrs.	0	1	.000	4.35	2	2	0	10.1	12	6	4	0	0	0	0	0	0	0	–

Terry Taylor

TAYLOR, TERRY DERRELL
B. July 28, 1964, Crestview, Fla.

BR TR 6'1"   180 lbs.

	W	L	PCT	ERA	G	GS	CG	IP	H	BB	SO	ShO	W	L	SV	AB	H	HR	BA
1988 SEA A	0	1	.000	6.26	5	5	0	23	26	11	9	0	0	0	0	0	0	0	–

Kent Tekulve

TEKULVE, KENTON CHARLES
B. Mar. 5, 1947, Cincinnati, Ohio

BR TR 6'4"   180 lbs.

	W	L	PCT	ERA	G	GS	CG	IP	H	BB	SO	ShO	W	L	SV	AB	H	HR	BA
1974 PIT N	1	1	.500	6.00	8	0	0	9	12	5	6	0	1	1	0	0	0	0	–
1975	1	2	.333	2.25	34	0	0	56	43	23	28	0	1	2	5	11	1	0	.091
1976	5	3	.625	2.45	64	0	0	102.2	91	25	68	0	5	3	9	9	0	0	.000
1977	10	1	.909	3.06	72	0	0	103	89	33	59	0	10	1	7	12	3	0	.250
1978	8	7	.533	2.33	91	0	0	135	115	55	77	0	8	7	31	21	2	0	.095
1979	10	8	.556	2.75	94	0	0	134	109	49	75	0	10	8	31	15	2	0	.133
1980	8	12	.400	3.39	78	0	0	93	96	40	47	0	8	12	21	9	0	0	.000
1981	5	5	.500	2.49	45	0	0	65	61	17	34	0	5	5	3	2	0	0	.000
1982	12	8	.600	2.87	85	0	0	128.2	113	46	66	0	12	8	20	14	1	0	.071
1983	7	5	.583	1.64	76	0	0	99	78	36	52	0	7	5	18	8	0	0	.000
1984	3	9	.250	2.66	72	0	0	88	86	33	36	0	3	9	13	7	0	0	.000
1985 2 teams		PIT	N	(3G 0–0)		PHI	N	(58G 4–10)											
" total	4	10	.286	3.57	61	0	0	75.2	74	30	40	0	4	10	14	3	0	0	.000
1986 PHI N	11	5	.688	2.54	73	0	0	110	99	25	57	0	11	5	4	5	0	0	.000
1987	6	4	.600	3.09	90	0	0	105	96	29	60	0	6	4	3	1	0	0	.000
1988	3	7	.300	3.60	70	0	0	80	87	22	43	0	3	7	4	2	0	0	.000
15 yrs.	94	87	.519	2.77	1013	0	0	1384	1249	468	748	0	94	87	183	119	9	0	.076
					2nd								7th						

	W	L	PCT	ERA	G	GS	CG	IP	H	BB	SO	ShO	Relief Pitching W	L	SV	BATTING AB	H	HR	BA

Kent Tekulve continued

LEAGUE CHAMPIONSHIP SERIES

	W	L	PCT	ERA	G	GS	CG	IP	H	BB	SO	ShO	W	L	SV	AB	H	HR	BA
1975 PIT N	0	0	–	6.75	2	0	0	1.1	3	1	2	0	0	0	0	0	0	0	–
1979	0	0	–	3.00	2	0	0	3	2	2	2	0	0	0	0	1	0	0	.000
2 yrs.	0	0	–	4.15	4	0	0	4.1	5	3	4	0	0	0	0	1	0	0	.000

WORLD SERIES

	W	L	PCT	ERA	G	GS	CG	IP	H	BB	SO	ShO	W	L	SV	AB	H	HR	BA
1979 PIT N	0	1	.000	2.89	5	0	0	9.1	4	3	10	0	0	1	3 4th	2	0	0	.000

Walt Terrell

TERRELL, CHARLES WALTER
B. May 11, 1958, Jeffersonville, Ind.   BL TR 6'2"   205 lbs.

	W	L	PCT	ERA	G	GS	CG	IP	H	BB	SO	ShO	W	L	SV	AB	H	HR	BA
1982 NY N	0	3	.000	3.43	3	3	0	21	22	14	8	0	0	0	0	5	2	0	.400
1983	8	8	.500	3.57	21	20	4	133.2	123	55	59	2	0	0	0	44	8	3	.182
1984	11	12	.478	3.52	33	33	3	215	232	80	114	1	0	0	0	75	6	0	.080
1985 DET A	15	10	.600	3.85	34	34	5	229	221	95	130	3	0	0	0	0	0	0	–
1986	15	12	.556	4.56	34	33	9	217.1	199	98	93	2	0	0	0	0	0	0	–
1987	17	10	.630	4.05	35	35	10	244.2	254	94	143	1	0	0	0	0	0	0	–
1988	7	16	.304	3.97	29	29	11	206.1	199	78	84	1	0	0	0	0	0	0	–
7 yrs.	73	71	.507	3.94	189	187	42	1267	1250	514	631	10	0	0	0	124	16	3	.129

LEAGUE CHAMPIONSHIP SERIES

	W	L	PCT	ERA	G	GS	CG	IP	H	BB	SO	ShO	W	L	SV	AB	H	HR	BA
1987 DET A	0	0	–	9.00	1	1	0	6	7	4	4	0	0	0	0	0	0	0	–

Scott Terry

TERRY, SCOTT RAY
B. Nov. 21, 1959, Hobbs, N. M.   BR TR 5'11"   185 lbs.

	W	L	PCT	ERA	G	GS	CG	IP	H	BB	SO	ShO	W	L	SV	AB	H	HR	BA
1986 CIN N	1	2	.333	6.14	28	3	0	55.2	66	32	32	0	1	1	0	4	1	0	.250
1987 STL N	0	0	–	0.00	0	0	0	0	0	0	0	0	0	0	0	0	0	0	–
1988	9	6	.600	2.92	51	11	1	129.1	119	34	65	0	2	3	3	28	7	0	.250
3 yrs.	10	8	.556	3.89	79	14	1	185	185	66	97	0	3	4	3	32	8	0	.250

Bob Tewksbury

TEWKSBURY, ROBERT ALAN
B. Nov. 30, 1960, Concord, N. H.   BR TR 6'4"   200 lbs.

	W	L	PCT	ERA	G	GS	CG	IP	H	BB	SO	ShO	W	L	SV	AB	H	HR	BA
1986 NY A	9	5	.643	3.31	23	20	2	130.1	144	31	49	0	0	0	0	0	0	0	–
1987 2 teams					NY	A (8G 1–4)		CHI	N	(7G 0–4)									
" total	1	8	.111	6.66	15	9	0	51.1	79	20	22	0	0	1	0	5	0	0	.000
1988 CHI N	0	0	–	8.10	1	1	0	3.1	6	2	1	0	0	0	0	2	0	0	.000
3 yrs.	10	13	.435	4.33	39	30	2	185	229	53	72	0	0	1	0	7	0	0	.000

Bobby Thigpen

THIGPEN, ROBERT THOMAS
B. July 17, 1963, Tallahassee, Fla.   BR TR 6'3"   195 lbs.

	W	L	PCT	ERA	G	GS	CG	IP	H	BB	SO	ShO	W	L	SV	AB	H	HR	BA
1986 CHI A	2	0	1.000	1.77	20	0	0	35.2	26	12	20	0	2	0	7	0	0	0	–
1987	7	5	.583	2.73	51	0	0	89	86	24	52	0	7	5	16	0	0	0	–
1988	5	8	.385	3.30	68	0	0	90	96	33	62	0	5	8	34	0	0	0	–
3 yrs.	14	13	.519	2.81	139	0	0	214.2	208	69	134	0	14	13	57	0	0	0	–

Mark Thurmond

THURMOND, MARK ANTHONY
B. Sept. 12, 1956, Houston, Tex.   BL TL 6'   190 lbs.

	W	L	PCT	ERA	G	GS	CG	IP	H	BB	SO	ShO	W	L	SV	AB	H	HR	BA
1983 SD N	7	3	.700	2.65	21	18	2	115.1	104	33	49	0	0	0	0	37	2	0	.054
1984	14	8	.636	2.97	32	29	1	178.2	174	55	57	1	0	1	0	58	11	0	.190
1985	7	11	.389	3.97	36	23	1	138.1	154	44	57	1	1	1	2	34	3	0	.088
1986 2 teams					SD	N (17G 3–7)		DET	A	(25G 4–1)									
" total	7	8	.467	4.56	42	19	2	122.1	140	44	49	1	2	0	3	24	6	0	.250
1987 DET A	1	0	1.000	4.23	48	0	0	61.2	83	24	21	0	0	1	5	0	0	0	–
1988 BAL A	1	8	.111	4.58	43	6	0	74.2	80	27	29	0	1	2	3	0	0	0	–
6 yrs.	36	39	.480	3.69	222	95	6	691	735	227	262	3	4	5	13	153	22	0	.144

LEAGUE CHAMPIONSHIP SERIES

	W	L	PCT	ERA	G	GS	CG	IP	H	BB	SO	ShO	W	L	SV	AB	H	HR	BA
1984 SD N	0	1	.000	9.82	1	1	0	3.2	7	2	1	0	0	0	0	1	1	0	1.000
1987 DET A	0	0	–	0.00	1	0	0	.1	0	0	0	0	0	0	0	0	0	0	–
2 yrs.	0	1	.000	9.00	2	1	0	4	7	2	1	0	0	0	0	1	1	0	1.000

WORLD SERIES

	W	L	PCT	ERA	G	GS	CG	IP	H	BB	SO	ShO	W	L	SV	AB	H	HR	BA
1984 SD N	0	1	.000	10.13	2	2	0	5.1	12	3	2	0	0	0	0	0	0	0	–

Jay Tibbs

TIBBS, JAY LINDSEY
B. Jan. 4, 1962, Birmingham, Ala.   BR TR 6'3"   185 lbs.

	W	L	PCT	ERA	G	GS	CG	IP	H	BB	SO	ShO	W	L	SV	AB	H	HR	BA
1984 CIN N	6	2	.750	2.86	14	14	3	100.2	87	33	40	1	0	0	0	36	5	0	.139
1985	10	16	.385	3.92	35	34	5	218	216	83	98	2	0	1	0	65	6	0	.092
1986 MON N	7	9	.438	3.97	35	31	3	190.1	181	70	117	2	0	0	0	54	7	0	.130
1987	4	5	.444	4.99	19	12	0	83	95	34	54	0	0	0	0	25	3	0	.120
1988 BAL A	4	15	.211	5.39	30	24	1	158.2	184	63	82	0	0	1	0	0	0	0	–
5 yrs.	31	47	.397	4.22	133	115	12	750.2	763	283	391	5	0	2	0	180	21	0	.117

Fred Toliver

TOLIVER, FREDDIE LEE
B. Feb. 3, 1961, Natchez, Miss.   BR TR 6'1"   170 lbs.

	W	L	PCT	ERA	G	GS	CG	IP	H	BB	SO	ShO	W	L	SV	AB	H	HR	BA
1984 CIN N	0	0	–	0.90	3	1	0	10	7	7	4	0	0	0	0	1	0	0	.000
1985 PHI N	0	4	.000	4.68	11	3	0	25	27	17	23	0	0	1	1	4	2	0	.500
1986	0	2	.000	3.51	5	5	0	25.2	28	11	20	0	0	0	0	6	0	0	.000
1987	1	1	.500	5.64	10	4	0	30.1	34	17	25	0	0	0	0	5	0	0	.000
1988 MIN A	7	6	.538	4.24	21	19	0	114.2	116	52	69	0	0	0	0	0	0	0	–
5 yrs.	8	13	.381	4.24	50	32	0	205.2	212	104	141	0	0	1	1	16	2	0	.125

John Trautwein

TRAUTWEIN, JOHN HOWARD
B. Aug. 7, 1962, Lafayette Hills, Pa.   BR TR 6'3"   195 lbs.

	W	L	PCT	ERA	G	GS	CG	IP	H	BB	SO	ShO	W	L	SV	AB	H	HR	BA
1988 BOS A	0	1	.000	9.00	9	0	0	16	26	9	8	0	0	1	0	0	0	0	–

	W	L	PCT	ERA	G	GS	CG	IP	H	BB	SO	ShO	Relief Pitching W	L	SV	BATTING AB	H	HR	BA

Steve Trout

TROUT, STEVEN RUSSELL (Rainbow)
Son of Dizzy Trout.
B. July 30, 1957, Detroit, Mich.
BL TL 6'4" 195 lbs.

	W	L	PCT	ERA	G	GS	CG	IP	H	BB	SO	ShO	W	L	SV	AB	H	HR	BA
1978 CHI A	3	0	1.000	4.03	4	3	1	22.1	19	11	11	0	0	0	0	0	0	0	–
1979	11	8	.579	3.89	34	18	6	155	165	59	76	2	1	2	4	0	0	0	–
1980	9	16	.360	3.69	32	30	7	200	229	49	89	2	0	0	0	0	0	0	–
1981	8	7	.533	3.46	20	18	3	125	122	38	54	0	1	0	0	0	0	0	–
1982	6	9	.400	4.26	25	19	2	120.1	130	50	62	0	0	0	0	0	0	0	–
1983 CHI N	10	14	.417	4.65	34	32	1	180	217	59	80	0	1	0	0	62	12	0	.194
1984	13	7	.650	3.41	32	31	6	190	205	59	81	2	0	1	0	61	8	0	.131
1985	9	7	.563	3.39	24	24	3	140.2	142	63	44	1	0	0	0	46	5	0	.109
1986	5	7	.417	4.75	37	25	0	161	184	78	69	0	1	0	0	43	9	0	.209
1987 2 teams			CHI	N (11G 6–3)		NY	A (14G 0–4)												
" total	6	7	.462	4.38	25	20	3	121.1	123	64	59	2	0	0	0	26	4	0	.154
1988 SEA A	4	7	.364	7.83	15	13	0	56.1	86	31	14	0	0	0	0	0	0	0	–
11 yrs.	84	89	.486	4.13	282	233	32	1472	1622	561	639	9	4	3	4	238	38	0	.160

LEAGUE CHAMPIONSHIP SERIES

	W	L	PCT	ERA	G	GS	CG	IP	H	BB	SO	ShO	W	L	SV	AB	H	HR	BA
1984 CHI N	1	0	1.000	2.00	2	1	0	9	5	3	3	0	0	0	0	2	1	0	.500

Mike Trujillo

TRUJILLO, MICHAEL ANDREW
B. Jan. 12, 1960, Denver, Colo.
BR TR 6'1" 180 lbs.

	W	L	PCT	ERA	G	GS	CG	IP	H	BB	SO	ShO	W	L	SV	AB	H	HR	BA
1985 BOS A	4	4	.500	4.82	27	7	1	84	112	23	19	0	2	1	1	0	0	0	–
1986 2 teams			BOS	A (3G 0–0)		SEA	A (11G 3–2)												
" total	3	2	.600	3.26	14	4	1	47	39	21	23	1	1	1	1	0	0	0	–
1987 SEA A	4	4	.500	6.17	28	7	0	65.2	70	26	36	0	2	1	1	0	0	0	–
1988 DET A	0	0	–	5.11	6	0	0	12.1	11	5	5	0	0	0	0	0	0	0	–
4 yrs.	11	10	.524	4.91	75	18	2	209	232	75	83	1	5	3	3	0	0	0	–

John Tudor

TUDOR, JOHN THOMAS
B. Feb. 2, 1954, Schenectady, N. Y.
BL TL 6' 185 lbs.

	W	L	PCT	ERA	G	GS	CG	IP	H	BB	SO	ShO	W	L	SV	AB	H	HR	BA
1979 BOS A	2	1	.333	6.43	6	6	1	28	39	9	11	0	0	0	0	0	0	0	–
1980	8	5	.615	3.03	16	13	5	92	81	31	45	0	0	1	0	0	0	0	–
1981	4	3	.571	4.56	18	11	2	79	74	28	44	0	1	1	1	0	0	0	–
1982	13	10	.565	3.63	32	30	6	195.2	215	59	146	1	0	0	0	0	0	0	–
1983	13	12	.520	4.09	34	34	7	242	236	81	136	2	0	0	0	0	0	0	–
1984 PIT N	12	11	.522	3.27	32	32	6	212	200	56	117	1	0	0	0	76	16	0	.211
1985 STL N	21	8	.724	1.93	36	36	14	275	209	49	169	10	0	0	0	94	13	0	.138
1986	13	7	.650	2.92	30	30	3	219	197	53	107	0	0	0	0	72	11	0	.153
1987	10	2	.833	3.84	16	16	0	96	100	32	54	0	0	0	0	35	7	0	.200
1988 2 teams			STL	N (21G 6–5)		LA	N (9G 4–3)												
" total	10	8	.556	2.32	30	30	5	197.2	189	41	87	1	0	0	0	59	5	0	.085
10 yrs.	105	68	.607	3.18	250	238	49	1636.1	1540	439	916	15	1	2	1	336	52	0	.155

LEAGUE CHAMPIONSHIP SERIES

	W	L	PCT	ERA	G	GS	CG	IP	H	BB	SO	ShO	W	L	SV	AB	H	HR	BA
1985 STL N	1	1	.500	2.84	2	2	0	12.2	10	3	8	0	0	0	0	4	0	0	.000
1987	1	1	.500	1.76	2	2	0	15.1	16	5	12	0	0	0	0	4	0	0	.000
1988 LA N	0	0	–	7.20	1	1	0	5	8	1	1	0	0	0	0	2	0	0	.000
3 yrs.	2	2	.500	3.00	5	5	0	33	34	9	21	0	0	0	0	10	0	0	.000

WORLD SERIES

	W	L	PCT	ERA	G	GS	CG	IP	H	BB	SO	ShO	W	L	SV	AB	H	HR	BA
1985 STL N	2	1	.667	3.00	3	3	1	18	15	7	14	1	0	0	0	5	0	0	.000
1987	1	1	.500	5.73	2	2	0	11	15	3	8	0	0	0	0	2	0	0	.000
1988 LA N	0	0	–	0.00	1	1	0	1.1	0	0	1	0	0	0	0	0	0	0	–
3 yrs.	3	2	.600	3.86	6	6	1	30.1	30	10	23	1	0	0	0	7	0	0	.000

Fernando Valenzuela

VALENZUELA, FERNAND ANGUAMEA
Born Fernando Valenzuela y Anguamea.
B. Nov. 1, 1960, Navajoa, Mexico
BL TL 5'11" 180 lbs.

	W	L	PCT	ERA	G	GS	CG	IP	H	BB	SO	ShO	W	L	SV	AB	H	HR	BA
1980 LA N	2	0	1.000	0.00	10	0	0	18	8	5	16	0	2	0	1	1	0	0	.000
1981	13	7	.650	2.48	25	25	11	192	140	61	180	8	0	0	0	64	16	0	.250
1982	19	13	.594	2.87	37	37	18	285	247	83	199	4	0	0	0	95	16	1	.168
1983	15	10	.600	3.75	35	35	9	257	245	99	189	4	0	0	0	91	17	1	.187
1984	12	17	.414	3.03	34	34	12	261	218	106	240	2	0	0	0	79	15	3	.190
1985	17	10	.630	2.45	35	35	14	272.1	211	101	208	5	0	0	0	97	21	1	.216
1986	21	11	.656	3.14	34	34	20	269.1	226	85	242	3	0	0	0	109	24	0	.220
1987	14	14	.500	3.98	34	34	12	251	254	124	190	1	0	0	0	92	13	1	.141
1988	5	8	.385	4.24	23	22	3	142.1	142	76	64	0	0	0	1	44	8	0	.182
9 yrs.	118	90	.567	3.16	267	256	99	1948	1691	740	1528	27	2	0	2	672	130	7	.193

DIVISIONAL PLAYOFF SERIES

	W	L	PCT	ERA	G	GS	CG	IP	H	BB	SO	ShO	W	L	SV	AB	H	HR	BA
1981 LA N	1	0	1.000	1.06	2	2	1	17	10	3	10	0	0	0	0	4	0	0	.000

LEAGUE CHAMPIONSHIP SERIES

	W	L	PCT	ERA	G	GS	CG	IP	H	BB	SO	ShO	W	L	SV	AB	H	HR	BA
1981 LA N	1	1	.500	2.45	2	2	0	14.2	10	5	10	0	0	0	0	5	0	0	.000
1983	1	0	1.000	1.13	1	1	0	8	7	4	5	0	0	0	0	3	0	0	.000
1985	1	0	1.000	1.88	2	2	0	14.1	11	10	13	0	0	0	0	5	1	0	.200
3 yrs.	3	1	.750	1.95	5	5	0	37	28	19	28	0	0	0	0	13	1	0	.077

WORLD SERIES

	W	L	PCT	ERA	G	GS	CG	IP	H	BB	SO	ShO	W	L	SV	AB	H	HR	BA
1981 LA N	1	0	1.000	4.00	1	1	1	9	9	7	6	0	0	0	0	3	0	0	.000

Ed Vande Berg

VANDE BERG, EDWARD JOHN
B. Oct. 26, 1958, Redlands, Calif.
BR TL 6'2" 175 lbs.

	W	L	PCT	ERA	G	GS	CG	IP	H	BB	SO	ShO	W	L	SV	AB	H	HR	BA
1982 SEA A	9	4	.692	2.37	78	0	0	76	54	32	60	0	9	4	5	0	0	0	–
1983	2	4	.333	3.36	68	0	0	64.1	59	22	49	0	2	4	5	0	0	0	–
1984	8	12	.400	4.76	50	17	2	130.1	165	50	71	0	3	1	7	0	0	0	–
1985	1	2	.667	3.72	76	0	0	67.2	71	31	34	0	2	1	3	0	0	0	–
1986 LA N	1	5	.167	3.41	60	0	0	71.1	83	33	42	0	1	5	0	1	0	0	.000
1987 CLE A	1	0	1.000	5.10	55	0	0	72.1	96	21	40	0	1	0	0	0	0	0	–
1988 TEX A	2	1	.500	4.14	26	0	0	37	44	11	18	0	2	2	2	0	0	0	–
7 yrs.	25	28	.472	3.92	413	17	2	519	572	200	314	0	20	17	22	1	0	0	.000

	W	L	PCT	ERA	G	GS	CG	IP	H	BB	SO	ShO	W	L	SV	AB	H	HR	BA
													Relief Pitching			**BATTING**			

DeWayne Vaughn

VAUGHN, DeWAYNE MATHEW
B. July 22, 1959, Oklahoma City, Okla.
BR TR 6'1" 175 lbs.

	W	L	PCT	ERA	G	GS	CG	IP	H	BB	SO	ShO	W	L	SV	AB	H	HR	BA
1988 TEX A	0	0	—	7.63	8	0	0	15.1	24	4	8	0	0	0	0	0	0	0	—

Frank Viola

VIOLA, FRANK JOHN JR. (Sweet Music)
B. Apr. 19, 1960, Hempstead, N. Y.
BL TL 6'4" 195 lbs.

	W	L	PCT	ERA	G	GS	CG	IP	H	BB	SO	ShO	W	L	SV	AB	H	HR	BA
1982 MIN A	4	10	.286	5.21	22	22	3	126	152	38	84	1	0	0	0	0	0	0	—
1983	7	15	.318	5.49	35	34	4	210	242	92	127	0	0	0	0	0	0	0	—
1984	18	12	.600	3.21	35	35	10	257.2	225	73	149	4	0	0	0	0	0	0	—
1985	18	14	.563	4.09	36	36	9	250.2	262	68	135	0	0	0	0	0	0	0	—
1986	16	13	.552	4.51	37	37	7	245.2	257	83	191	1	0	0	0	0	0	0	—
1987	17	10	.630	2.90	36	36	7	251.2	230	66	197	1	0	0	0	0	0	0	—
1988	24	7	**.774**	2.64	35	35	7	255.1	236	54	193	2	0	0	0	0	0	0	—
7 yrs.	104	81	.562	3.87	236	235	47	1597	1604	474	1076	9	0	0	0	0	0	0	—
LEAGUE CHAMPIONSHIP SERIES																			
1987 MIN A	1	0	1.000	5.25	2	2	0	12	14	5	9	0	0	0	0	0	0	0	—
WORLD SERIES																			
1987 MIN A	2	1	.667	3.72	3	3	0	19.1	17	3	16	0	0	0	0	1	0	0	.000

Bob Walk

WALK, ROBERT VERNON
B. Nov. 26, 1956, Van Nuys, Calif.
BR TR 6'3" 185 lbs.

	W	L	PCT	ERA	G	GS	CG	IP	H	BB	SO	ShO	W	L	SV	AB	H	HR	BA
1980 PHI N	11	7	.611	4.56	27	27	2	152	163	71	94	0	0	0	0	50	7	0	.140
1981 ATL N	1	4	.200	4.60	12	8	0	43	41	23	16	0	0	0	0	7	1	0	.143
1982	11	9	.550	4.87	32	27	3	164.1	179	59	84	1	0	0	0	51	10	0	.196
1983	0	0	—	7.36	1	1	0	3.2	7	2	4	0	0	0	0	1	0	0	.000
1984 PIT N	1	1	.500	2.61	2	2	0	10.1	8	4	10	0	0	0	0	3	0	0	.000
1985	2	3	.400	3.68	9	9	1	58.2	60	18	40	1	0	0	0	17	0	0	.000
1986	7	8	.467	3.75	44	15	1	141.2	129	64	78	1	2	3	2	39	6	0	.154
1987	8	2	.800	3.31	39	12	1	117	107	51	78	1	2	1	0	26	6	0	.231
1988	12	10	.545	2.71	32	32	1	212.2	183	65	81	1	0	0	0	69	6	0	.087
9 yrs.	53	44	.546	3.83	198	133	9	903.1	877	357	485	5	4	4	2	263	36	0	.137
LEAGUE CHAMPIONSHIP SERIES																			
1982 ATL N	0	0	—	9.00	1	0	0	1	2	1	1	0	0	0	0	0	0	0	—
WORLD SERIES																			
1980 PHI N	1	0	1.000	7.71	1	1	0	7	8	3	3	0	0	0	0	0	0	0	—

Mike Walker

WALKER, MICHAEL CHARLES
B. Oct. 4, 1966, Chicago, Ill.
BR TR 6'1" 175 lbs.

	W	L	PCT	ERA	G	GS	CG	IP	H	BB	SO	ShO	W	L	SV	AB	H	HR	BA
1988 CLE A	0	1	.000	7.27	3	1	0	8.2	8	10	7	0	0	0	0	0	0	0	—

Gene Walter

WALTER, GENE WINSTON
B. Nov. 22, 1960, Chicago, Ill.
BL TL 6'4" 200 lbs.

	W	L	PCT	ERA	G	GS	CG	IP	H	BB	SO	ShO	W	L	SV	AB	H	HR	BA
1985 SD N	0	2	.000	2.05	15	0	0	22	12	8	18	0	0	2	3	1	0	0	.000
1986	2	2	.500	3.86	57	0	0	98	89	49	84	0	2	2	1	10	2	0	.200
1987 NY N	1	2	.333	3.20	21	0	0	19.2	18	13	11	0	1	2	0	1	0	0	.000
1988 2 teams		NY	N (19G 0–1)			SEA	A (16G 1–0)												
" total	1	1	.500	4.60	35	0	0	43	42	26	27	0	1	1	0	0	0	0	—
4 yrs.	4	7	.364	3.74	128	0	0	182.2	161	96	140	0	4	7	4	12	2	0	.167

Duane Ward

WARD, ROY DUANE
B. May 28, 1964, Park View, N. M.
BR TR 6'4" 185 lbs.

	W	L	PCT	ERA	G	GS	CG	IP	H	BB	SO	ShO	W	L	SV	AB	H	HR	BA
1986 2 teams		ATL	N (10G 0–1)			TOR	A (2G 0–0)												
" total	0	2	.000	8.00	12	1	0	18	25	12	9	0	0	1	0	1	0	0	.000
1987 TOR A	1	0	1.000	6.94	12	1	0	11.2	14	12	10	0	1	0	0	0	0	0	—
1988	9	3	.750	3.30	64	0	0	111.2	101	60	91	0	9	3	15	0	0	0	—
3 yrs.	10	5	.667	4.20	88	2	0	141.1	140	84	110	0	10	4	15	1	0	0	.000

Bill Wegman

WEGMAN, WILLIAM EDWARD
B. Dec. 19, 1962, Cincinnati, Ohio
BR TR 6'5" 200 lbs.

	W	L	PCT	ERA	G	GS	CG	IP	H	BB	SO	ShO	W	L	SV	AB	H	HR	BA
1985 MIL A	2	0	1.000	3.57	3	3	0	17.2	17	3	6	0	0	0	0	0	0	0	—
1986	5	12	.294	5.13	35	32	2	198.1	217	43	82	0	0	0	0	0	0	0	—
1987	12	11	.522	4.24	34	33	7	225	229	53	102	0	0	1	0	0	0	0	—
1988	13	13	.500	4.12	32	31	4	199	207	50	84	1	0	0	0	0	0	0	—
4 yrs.	32	36	.471	4.46	104	99	13	640	670	149	274	1	0	1	0	0	0	0	—

Bob Welch

WELCH, ROBERT LYNN
B. Nov. 3, 1956, Detroit, Mich.
BR TR 6'3" 190 lbs.

	W	L	PCT	ERA	G	GS	CG	IP	H	BB	SO	ShO	W	L	SV	AB	H	HR	BA
1978 LA N	7	4	.636	2.03	23	13	4	111	92	26	66	3	1	0	3	29	5	0	.172
1979	5	6	.455	4.00	25	12	1	81	82	32	64	0	3	1	5	19	3	0	.158
1980	14	9	.609	3.28	32	32	3	214	190	79	141	2	0	0	0	70	17	0	.243
1981	9	5	.643	3.45	23	23	2	141	141	41	88	1	0	0	0	45	10	0	.222
1982	16	11	.593	3.36	36	36	9	235.2	199	81	176	3	0	0	0	85	12	0	.141
1983	15	12	.556	2.65	31	31	4	204	164	72	156	3	0	0	0	73	7	1	.096
1984	13	13	.500	3.78	31	29	3	178.2	191	58	126	1	0	0	0	51	4	0	.078
1985	14	4	.778	2.31	23	23	8	167.1	141	35	96	3	0	0	0	50	9	0	.180
1986	7	13	.350	3.28	33	33	7	235.2	227	55	183	3	0	0	0	76	8	1	.105
1987	15	9	.625	3.22	35	35	6	251.2	204	86	196	4	0	0	0	83	13	0	.157
1988 OAK A	17	9	.654	3.64	36	36	4	244.2	237	81	158	2	0	0	0	0	0	0	—
11 yrs.	132	95	.581	3.20	328	303	51	2064.2	1868	646	1450	25	4	1	8	581	88	2	.151
DIVISIONAL PLAYOFF SERIES																			
1981 LA N	0	0	—	0.00	1	0	0	1	0	1	1	0	0	0	0	0	0	0	—
LEAGUE CHAMPIONSHIP SERIES																			
1978 LA N	1	0	1.000	2.08	1	0	0	4.1	2	0	5	0	1	0	0	2	0	0	.000
1981	0	0	—	5.40	3	0	0	1.2	2	0	2	0	0	0	1	0	0	0	—
1983	0	1	.000	6.75	1	1	0	1.1	2	0	0	0	0	0	0	0	0	0	—

	W	L	PCT	ERA	G	GS	CG	IP	H	BB	SO	ShO	Relief Pitching W	L	SV	BATTING AB	H	HR	BA

Bob Welch continued

	W	L	PCT	ERA	G	GS	CG	IP	H	BB	SO	ShO	W	L	SV	AB	H	HR	BA
1985	0	1	.000	6.75	1	1	0	2.2	5	6	2	0	0	0	0	1	0	0	.000
1988 OAK A	0	0	–	27.00	1	1	0	1.2	6	2	0	0	0	0	0	0	0	0	–
5 yrs.	1	2	.333	7.71	7	3	0	11.2	15	10	9	0	1	0	1	3	0	0	.000

WORLD SERIES

	W	L	PCT	ERA	G	GS	CG	IP	H	BB	SO	ShO	W	L	SV	AB	H	HR	BA
1978 LA N	0	1	.000	6.23	3	0	0	4.1	4	2	6	0	0	1	1	0	0	0	–
1981	0	0	–	∞	1	1	0		3	1	0	0	0	0	0	0	0	0	–
1988 OAK A	0	0	–	1.80	1	1	0	5	6	3	8	0	0	0	0	0	0	0	–
3 yrs.	0	1	.000	5.79	5	2	0	9.1	13	6	14	0	0	1	1	/	0	0	–

David Wells

WELLS, DAVID LEE
B. May 20, 1963, Torrance, Calif.

BL TL 6'3"   187 lbs.

	W	L	PCT	ERA	G	GS	CG	IP	H	BB	SO	ShO	W	L	SV	AB	H	HR	BA
1987 TOR A	4	3	.571	3.99	18	2	0	29.1	37	12	32	0	4	1	1	0	0	0	–
1988	3	5	.375	4.62	41	0	0	64.1	65	31	56	0	3	5	4	0	0	0	–
2 yrs.	7	8	.467	4.42	59	2	0	93.2	102	43	88	0	7	6	5	0	0	0	–

Dave West

WEST, DAVID LEE
B. Sept. 1, 1964, Memphis, Tenn.

BL TL 6'6"   205 lbs.

	W	L	PCT	ERA	G	GS	CG	IP	H	BB	SO	ShO	W	L	SV	AB	H	HR	BA
1988 NY N	1	0	1.000	3.00	2	1	0	6	6	3	3	0	0	0	0	2	2	0	1.000

Ed Whitson

WHITSON, EDDIE LEE
B. May 19, 1955, Johnson City, Tenn.

BR TR 6'3"   195 lbs.

	W	L	PCT	ERA	G	GS	CG	IP	H	BB	SO	ShO	W	L	SV	AB	H	HR	BA
1977 PIT N	1	0	1.000	3.38	5	2	0	16	11	9	10	0	1	0	0	4	0	0	.000
1978	5	6	.455	3.28	43	0	0	74	66	37	64	0	5	6	4	11	2	0	.182
1979 2 teams			PIT N	(19G 2–3)		SF N	(18G 5–8)												
" total	7	11	.389	4.10	37	24	2	158	151	75	93	0	0	3	1	45	5	0	.111
1980 SF N	11	13	.458	3.10	34	34	6	212	222	56	90	2	0	0	0	66	6	0	.091
1981	6	9	.400	4.02	22	22	2	123	130	47	65	1	0	0	0	33	3	0	.091
1982 CLE A	4	2	.667	3.26	40	9	1	107.2	91	58	61	1	2	1	2	0	0	0	–
1983 SD N	5	7	.417	4.30	31	21	2	144.1	143	50	81	0	0	0	1	44	8	0	.182
1984	14	8	.636	3.24	31	31	1	189	181	42	103	0	0	0	0	61	3	0	.049
1985 NY A	10	8	.556	4.88	30	30	2	158.2	201	43	89	2	0	0	0	0	0	0	–
1986 2 teams			NY A	(14G 5–2)		SD N	(17G 1–7)												
" total	6	9	.400	6.23	31	16	0	112.2	139	60	73	0	4	0	0	18	3	0	.167
1987 SD N	10	13	.435	4.73	36	34	3	205.2	197	64	135	1	0	0	0	65	8	0	.123
1988	13	11	.542	3.77	34	33	3	205.1	202	45	118	1	1	0	0	66	11	0	.167
12 yrs.	92	97	.487	4.05	374	256	22	1706.1	1734	586	982	8	13	10	8	413	49	0	.119

LEAGUE CHAMPIONSHIP SERIES

	W	L	PCT	ERA	G	GS	CG	IP	H	BB	SO	ShO	W	L	SV	AB	H	HR	BA
1984 SD N	1	0	1.000	1.13	1	1	0	8	5	2	6	0	0	0	0	3	0	0	.000

WORLD SERIES

	W	L	PCT	ERA	G	GS	CG	IP	H	BB	SO	ShO	W	L	SV	AB	H	HR	BA
1984 SD N	0	0	–	40.50	1	1	0	.2	5	0	0	0	0	0	0	0	0	0	–

Bill Wilkinson

WILKINSON, WILLIAM CARL
B. Aug. 10, 1964, Greybull, Wyo.

BR TL 5'10"   160 lbs.

	W	L	PCT	ERA	G	GS	CG	IP	H	BB	SO	ShO	W	L	SV	AB	H	HR	BA
1985 SEA A	0	2	.000	13.50	2	2	0	6	8	6	5	0	0	0	0	0	0	0	–
1987	3	4	.429	3.66	56	0	0	76.1	61	21	73	0	3	4	10	0	0	0	–
1988	2	2	.500	3.48	30	0	0	31	28	15	25	0	2	2	2	0	0	0	–
3 yrs.	5	8	.385	4.13	88	2	0	113.1	97	42	103	0	5	6	12	0	0	0	–

Frank Williams

WILLIAMS, FRANK LEE
B. Feb. 13, 1958, Seattle, Wash.

BR TR 6'1"   180 lbs.

	W	L	PCT	ERA	G	GS	CG	IP	H	BB	SO	ShO	W	L	SV	AB	H	HR	BA
1984 SF N	9	4	.692	3.55	61	1	1	106.1	88	51	91	1	8	4	3	18	4	0	.222
1985	2	4	.333	4.19	49	0	0	73	65	35	54	0	2	4	0	3	0	0	.000
1986	3	1	.750	1.20	36	0	0	52.1	35	21	33	0	3	1	1	2	1	0	.500
1987 CIN N	4	0	1.000	2.30	85	0	0	105.2	101	39	60	0	4	0	2	5	0	0	.000
1988	3	2	.600	2.59	60	0	0	62.2	59	35	43	0	3	2	1	1	0	0	.000
5 yrs.	21	11	.656	2.88	291	1	1	400	348	181	281	1	20	11	7	29	5	0	.172

Mitch Williams

WILLIAMS, MITCHELL STEVEN
B. Nov. 17, 1964, Santa Ana, Calif.

BL TL 6'3"   180 lbs.

	W	L	PCT	ERA	G	GS	CG	IP	H	BB	SO	ShO	W	L	SV	AB	H	HR	BA
1986 TEX A	8	6	.571	3.58	80	0	0	98	69	79	90	0	8	6	8	0	0	0	–
1987	8	6	.571	3.23	85	1	0	108.2	63	94	129	0	8	5	6	0	0	0	–
1988	2	7	.222	4.63	67	0	0	68	48	47	61	0	2	7	18	0	0	0	–
3 yrs.	18	19	.486	3.70	232	1	0	274.2	180	220	280	0	18	18	32	0	0	0	–

Mark Williamson

WILLIAMSON, MARK ALAN
B. July 21, 1959, Corpus Christi, Tex.

BR TR 6'   155 lbs.

	W	L	PCT	ERA	G	GS	CG	IP	H	BB	SO	ShO	W	L	SV	AB	H	HR	BA
1987 BAL A	8	9	.471	4.03	61	2	0	125	122	41	73	0	8	8	3	0	0	0	–
1988	5	8	.385	4.90	37	10	2	117.2	125	40	69	0	4	2	2	0	0	0	–
2 yrs.	13	17	.433	4.45	98	12	2	242.2	247	81	142	0	12	10	5	0	0	0	–

Carl Willis

WILLIS, CARL BLAKE
B. Dec. 28, 1960, Danville, Va.

BL TR 6'4"   210 lbs.

	W	L	PCT	ERA	G	GS	CG	IP	H	BB	SO	ShO	W	L	SV	AB	H	HR	BA
1984 2 teams			DET A	(10G 0–2)		CIN N	(7G 0–1)												
" total	0	3	.000	5.96	17	2	0	25.2	33	7	7	0	0	2	1	0	0	0	–
1985 CIN N	1	0	1.000	9.22	11	0	0	13.2	21	5	6	0	1	0	1	1	0	0	.000
1986	1	3	.250	4.47	29	0	0	52.1	54	32	24	0	1	3	0	3	1	0	.333
1988 CHI A	0	0	–	8.25	6	0	0	12	17	7	6	0	0	0	0	0	0	0	–
4 yrs.	2	6	.250	5.90	63	2	0	103.2	125	51	43	0	2	5	2	4	1	0	.250

Frank Wills

WILLS, FRANK LEE JR.
B. Oct. 26, 1958, New Orleans, La.

BR TR 6'2"   200 lbs.

	W	L	PCT	ERA	G	GS	CG	IP	H	BB	SO	ShO	W	L	SV	AB	H	HR	BA
1983 KC A	2	1	.667	4.15	6	4	0	34.2	35	15	23	0	0	0	0	0	0	0	–
1984	2	3	.400	5.11	10	5	0	37	39	13	21	0	1	0	0	0	0	0	–
1985 SEA A	5	11	.313	6.00	24	18	1	123	122	68	67	0	0	0	1	0	0	0	–

	W	L	PCT	ERA	G	GS	CG	IP	H	BB	SO	ShO	Relief Pitching W	L	SV	BATTING AB	H	HR	BA

Frank Wills continued

	W	L	PCT	ERA	G	GS	CG	IP	H	BB	SO	ShO	W	L	SV	AB	H	HR	BA
1986 CLE A	4	4	.500	4.91	26	0	0	40.1	43	16	32	0	4	4	4	0	0	0	–
1987	0	1	.000	5.06	6	0	0	5.1	3	7	4	0	0	1	1	0	0	0	–
1988 TOR A	0	0	–	5.23	10	0	0	20.2	22	6	19	0	0	0	0	0	0	0	–
6 yrs.	13	20	.394	5.38	82	27	1	261	264	125	166	0	5	5	6	0	0	0	

Glenn Wilson

WILSON, GLENN DWIGHT B. Dec. 22, 1958, Baytown, Tex.   BR TR 6'1"   190 lbs.

	W	L	PCT	ERA	G	GS	CG	IP	H	BB	SO	ShO	W	L	SV	AB	H	HR	BA
1987 PHI N	0	0	–	0.00	1	0	0	1	0	0	1	0	0	0	0	*			

Steve Wilson

WILSON, STEPHEN DOUGLAS B. Dec. 13, 1964, Victoria, B. C., Canada   BL TL 6'4"   195 lbs.

	W	L	PCT	ERA	G	GS	CG	IP	H	BB	SO	ShO	W	L	SV	AB	H	HR	BA
1988 TEX A	0	0	–	5.87	3	0	0	7.2	7	4	1	0	0	0	0	0	0	0	–

Trevor Wilson

WILSON, TREVOR KIRK B. June 7, 1966, Torrance, Calif.   BL TL 6'   175 lbs.

	W	L	PCT	ERA	G	GS	CG	IP	H	BB	SO	ShO	W	L	SV	AB	H	HR	BA
1988 SF N	0	2	.000	4.09	4	4	0	22	25	8	15	0	0	0	0	7	2	0	.286

Jim Winn

WINN, JAMES FRANCIS B. Sept. 23, 1959, Stockton, Calif.   BR TR 6'3"   190 lbs.

	W	L	PCT	ERA	G	GS	CG	IP	H	BB	SO	ShO	W	L	SV	AB	H	HR	BA
1983 PIT N	0	0	–	7.36	7	0	0	11	12	6	3	0	0	0	0	0	0	0	–
1984	1	0	1.000	3.86	9	0	0	18.2	19	9	11	0	1	0	1	1	0	0	.000
1985	3	6	.333	5.23	30	7	0	75.2	77	31	22	0	1	4	0	18	2	0	.111
1986	3	5	.375	3.58	50	3	0	88	85	38	70	0	3	3	3	16	1	0	.063
1987 CHI A	4	6	.400	4.79	56	0	0	94	95	62	44	0	4	6	6	0	0	0	–
1988 MIN A	1	0	1.000	6.00	9	0	0	21	33	10	9	0	1	0	0	0	0	0	–
6 yrs.	12	17	.414	4.67	161	10	0	308.1	321	156	159	0	10	13	10	35	3	0	.086

Bobby Witt

WITT, ROBERT ANDREW B. May 11, 1964, Arlington, Mass.   BR TR 6'2"   190 lbs.

	W	L	PCT	ERA	G	GS	CG	IP	H	BB	SO	ShO	W	L	SV	AB	H	HR	BA
1986 TEX A	11	9	.550	5.48	31	31	0	157.2	130	143	174	0	0	0	0	0	0	0	–
1987	8	10	.444	4.91	26	25	1	143	114	140	160	0	0	0	0	1	0	0	.000
1988	8	10	.444	3.92	22	22	13	174.1	134	101	148	2	0	0	0	0	0	0	–
3 yrs.	27	29	.482	4.74	79	78	14	475	378	384	482	2	0	0	0	1	0	0	.000

Mike Witt

WITT, MICHAEL ATWATER B. July 20, 1960, Fullerton, Calif.   BR TR 6'7"   185 lbs.

	W	L	PCT	ERA	G	GS	CG	IP	H	BB	SO	ShO	W	L	SV	AB	H	HR	BA
1981 CAL A	8	9	.471	3.28	22	21	7	129	123	47	75	1	0	1	0	0	0	0	–
1982	8	6	.571	3.51	33	26	5	179.2	177	47	85	1	0	1	0	0	0	0	–
1983	7	14	.333	4.91	43	19	2	154	173	75	77	0	3	3	5	0	0	0	–
1984	15	11	.577	3.47	34	34	9	246.2	227	84	196	2	0	0	0	0	0	0	–
1985	15	9	.625	3.56	35	35	6	250	228	98	180	1	0	0	0	0	0	0	–
1986	18	10	.643	2.84	34	34	14	269	218	73	208	3	0	0	0	0	0	0	–
1987	16	14	.533	4.01	36	36	10	247	252	84	192	0	0	0	0	0	0	0	–
1988	13	16	.448	4.15	34	34	12	249.2	263	87	133	2	0	0	0	0	0	0	–
8 yrs.	100	89	.529	3.68	271	239	65	1725	1661	595	1146	10	3	5	5	0	0	0	–

LEAGUE CHAMPIONSHIP SERIES

	W	L	PCT	ERA	G	GS	CG	IP	H	BB	SO	ShO	W	L	SV	AB	H	HR	BA
1982 CAL A	0	0	–	6.00	1	0	0	3	2	2	3	0	0	0	0	0	0	0	–
1986	1	0	1.000	2.55	2	2	1	17.2	13	2	8	0	0	0	0	0	0	0	–
2 yrs.	1	0	1.000	3.05	3	2	1	20.2	15	4	11	0	0	0	0	0	0	0	–

Rob Woodward

WOODWARD, ROBERT JOHN B. Sept. 28, 1962, Hanover, N. H.   BR TR 6'3"   185 lbs.

	W	L	PCT	ERA	G	GS	CG	IP	H	BB	SO	ShO	W	L	SV	AB	H	HR	BA
1985 BOS A	1	0	1.000	1.69	5	2	0	26.2	17	9	16	0	0	0	0	0	0	0	–
1986	2	3	.400	5.30	9	6	0	35.2	46	11	14	0	1	0	0	0	0	0	–
1987	1	1	.500	7.05	9	6	0	37	53	15	15	0	0	0	0	0	0	0	–
1988	0	0	–	13.50	1	0	0	.2	2	1	0	0	0	0	0	0	0	0	–
4 yrs.	4	4	.500	5.04	24	14	0	100	118	36	45	0	1	0	0	0	0	0	–

Todd Worrell

WORRELL, TODD ROLAND B. Sept. 28, 1959, Arcadia, Calif.   BR TR 6'5"   215 lbs.

	W	L	PCT	ERA	G	GS	CG	IP	H	BB	SO	ShO	W	L	SV	AB	H	HR	BA
1985 STL N	3	0	1.000	2.91	17	0	0	21.2	17	7	17	0	3	0	5	1	0	0	.000
1986	9	10	.474	2.08	74	0	0	103.2	86	41	73	0	9	10	36	7	1	0	.143
1987	8	6	.571	2.66	75	0	0	94.2	86	34	92	0	8	6	33	10	1	0	.100
1988	5	9	.357	3.00	68	0	0	90	69	34	78	0	5	9	32	6	0	0	.000
4 yrs.	25	25	.500	2.58	234	0	0	310	258	116	260	0	25	25	106	24	2	0	.083

LEAGUE CHAMPIONSHIP SERIES

	W	L	PCT	ERA	G	GS	CG	IP	H	BB	SO	ShO	W	L	SV	AB	H	HR	BA
1985 STL N	1	0	1.000	1.42	4	0	0	6.1	4	2	3	0	1	0	0	0	0	0	–
1987	0	0	–	2.08	3	0	0	4.1	4	1	6	0	0	0	1	1	0	0	.000
2 yrs.	1	0	1.000	1.69	7	0	0	10.2	8	3	9	0	1	0	1	1	0	0	.000

WORLD SERIES

	W	L	PCT	ERA	G	GS	CG	IP	H	BB	SO	ShO	W	L	SV	AB	H	HR	BA
1985 STL N	0	1	.000	3.86	3	0	0	4.2	4	2	6	0	0	1	1	1	0	0	.000
1987	0	0	–	1.29	4	0	0	7	6	4	3	0	0	0	2	0	0	0	–
2 yrs.	0	1	.000	2.31	7	0	0	11.2	10	6	9	0	0	1	3 (4th)	1	0	0	.000

Rich Yett

YETT, RICHARD MARTIN B. Oct. 6, 1962, Pomona, Calif.   BR TR 6'2"   187 lbs.

	W	L	PCT	ERA	G	GS	CG	IP	H	BB	SO	ShO	W	L	SV	AB	H	HR	BA
1985 MIN A	0	0	–	27.00	1	1	0	.1	1	2	0	0	0	0	0	0	0	0	–
1986 CLE A	5	3	.625	5.15	39	3	1	78.2	84	37	50	1	4	2	1	0	0	0	–
1987	3	9	.250	5.25	37	11	0	97.2	96	49	59	0	1	5	1	0	0	0	–
1988	9	6	.600	4.62	23	22	0	134.1	146	55	71	0	0	0	0	0	0	0	–
4 yrs.	17	18	.486	4.98	100	37	3	311	327	143	180	1	5	7	2	0	0	0	–

	W	L	PCT	ERA	G	GS	CG	IP	H	BB	SO	ShO	Relief Pitching W	L	SV	BATTING AB	H	HR	BA

Floyd Youmans

YOUMANS, FLOYD EVERETT
B. May 11, 1964, Tampa, Fla.

BR TR 6'2"   180 lbs.

Year	Team	W	L	PCT	ERA	G	GS	CG	IP	H	BB	SO	ShO	W	L	SV	AB	H	HR	BA
1985	MON N	4	3	.571	2.45	14	12	0	77	57	49	54	0	1	0	0	19	1	0	.053
1986		13	12	.520	3.53	33	32	6	219	145	118	202	2	0	1	0	75	12	1	.160
1987		9	8	.529	4.64	23	23	3	116.1	112	47	94	3	0	0	0	40	6	1	.150
1988		3	6	.333	3.21	14	13	1	84	64	41	54	1	0	0	0	26	4	0	.154
4 yrs.		29	29	.500	3.57	84	80	10	496.1	378	255	404	6	1	1	0	160	23	2	.144

Curt Young

YOUNG, CURTIS ALLEN
B. Apr. 16, 1960, Saginaw, Mich.

BR TL 6'   175 lbs.

Year	Team	W	L	PCT	ERA	G	GS	CG	IP	H	BB	SO	ShO	W	L	SV	AB	H	HR	BA
1983	OAK A	0	1	.000	16.00	8	2	0	9	17	5	5	0	0	0	0	0	0	0	–
1984		9	4	.692	4.06	20	17	2	108.2	118	31	41	1	0	0	0	0	0	0	–
1985		0	4	.000	7.24	19	7	0	46	57	22	19	0	0	0	0	0	0	0	–
1986		13	9	.591	3.45	29	27	5	198	176	57	116	2	1	0	0	0	0	0	–
1987		13	7	.650	4.08	31	31	6	203	194	44	124	0	0	0	0	1	0	0	.000
1988		11	8	.579	4.14	26	26	1	156.1	162	50	69	0	0	0	0	0	0	0	–
6 yrs.		46	33	.582	4.27	133	110	14	721	724	209	374	3	1	0	0	1	0	0	.000

LEAGUE CHAMPIONSHIP SERIES

Year	Team	W	L	PCT	ERA	G	GS	CG	IP	H	BB	SO	ShO	W	L	SV	AB	H	HR	BA
1988	OAK A	0	0	–	0.00	1	0	0	1.1	1	0	2	0	0	0	0	0	0	0	–

WORLD SERIES

Year	Team	W	L	PCT	ERA	G	GS	CG	IP	H	BB	SO	ShO	W	L	SV	AB	H	HR	BA
1988	OAK A	0	0	–	0.00	1	0	0	1	1	0	0	0	0	0	0	0	0	0	–

Manager Register

The Manager Register is an alphabetical listing of every man who managed in the major leagues in 1988. Most of the information is self-explanatory; note that tie games are included in the games column, but not reflected in wins or losses.

The figures in the Standing column show where the team stood at the end of the season and when there was a managerial change. There are four possible cases:

Only Manager for the Team That Year. Indicated by a single bold faced figure that appears in the extreme left-hand column and shows the final standing of the team.

Manager Started Season, but Did Not Finish. Indicated by two figures; the first is bold faced and shows the standing of the team when this manager left; the second shows the final standing of the team. (See Tony LaRussa, Chicago, 1988).

Manager Finished Season, but Did Not Start. Indicated by two figures; the first shows the standing of the team when this manager started; the second is bold faced and shows the final standing of the team. (See Tony LaRussa, Oakland, 1988).

Manager Did Not Start or Finish Season. Indicated by three figures: the first shows the standing of the team when this manager started; the second is bold faced and shows the standing of the team when this manager; the third shows the final standing of the team. (See Jeff Newman.)

The managers' records for the 1981 split season are given separately for each half. "(1st)" or "(2nd)" will appear to the right of the standings to indicate which half.

	G	W	L	PCT	Standing				G	W	L	PCT	Standing

Sparky Anderson
ANDERSON, GEORGE LEE
B. Feb. 22, 1934, Bridgewater, S. D.

		G	W	L	PCT	Standing	
1970	CIN N	162	102	60	.630	1	
1971		162	79	83	.488	4	
1972		154	95	59	.617	1	
1973		162	99	63	.611	1	
1974		162	98	64	.605	2	
1975		162	108	54	.667	1	
1976		162	102	60	.630	1	
1977		162	88	74	.543	2	
1978		161	92	69	.571	2	
1979	DET A	105	56	49	.533	5	5
1980		163	84	78	.519	4	
1981		57	31	26	.544	4	(1st)
1981		52	29	23	.558	2	(2nd)
1982		162	83	79	.512	4	
1983		162	92	70	.568	2	
1984		162	104	58	.642	1	
1985		161	84	77	.522	3	
1986		162	87	75	.537	3	
1987		162	98	64	.605	1	
1988		162	88	74	.543	2	
19 yrs.		2959	1699	1259	.574	10th	

LEAGUE CHAMPIONSHIP SERIES

		G	W	L	PCT	
1970	CIN N	3	3	0	1.000	
1972		5	3	2	.600	
1973		5	2	3	.400	
1975		3	3	0	1.000	
1976		3	3	0	1.000	
1984	DET A	3	3	0	1.000	
1987		5	1	4	.200	
7 yrs.		27	18	9	.667	
		3rd	1st	5th	2nd	

WORLD SERIES

		G	W	L	PCT	
1970	CIN N	5	1	4	.200	
1972		7	3	4	.429	
1975		7	4	3	.571	
1976		4	4	0	1.000	
1984	DET A	5	4	1	.800	
5 yrs.		28	16	12	.571	
		7th	7th	10th	3rd	

Larry Bowa
BOWA, LAWRENCE ROBERT
B. Dec. 6, 1945, Sacramento, Calif.

		G	W	L	PCT	Standing	
1987	SD N	162	65	97	.401	6	
1988		46	16	30	.348	5	3
2 yrs.		208	81	127	.389		

Roger Craig
CRAIG, ROGER LEE
B. Feb. 17, 1930, Durham, N. C.

		G	W	L	PCT	Standing	
1978	SD N	162	84	78	.519	4	
1979		161	68	93	.422	5	
1985	SF N	18	6	12	.333	6	6
1986		162	83	79	.512	3	
1987		162	90	72	.556	1	
1988		162	83	79	.512	4	
6 yrs.		827	414	413	.501		

LEAGUE CHAMPIONSHIP SERIES

		G	W	L	PCT
1987	SF N	7	3	4	.429

Doc Edwards
EDWARDS, HOWARD RODNEY
B. Dec. 10, 1936, Red Jacket, W. Va.

		G	W	L	PCT	Standing	
1987	CLE A	75	30	45	.400	7	7
1988		162	78	84	.481	6	
2 yrs.		237	108	129	.456		

Lee Elia
ELIA, LEE CONSTANTINE
B. July 16, 1937, Philadelphia, Pa.

		G	W	L	PCT	Standing	
1982	CHI N	162	73	89	.451	5	
1983		123	54	69	.439	5	5
1987	PHI N	101	51	50	.505	5	4
1988		153	60	92	.395	6	6
4 yrs.		539	238	300	.442		

Jim Fregosi
FREGOSI, JAMES LOUIS
B. Apr. 4, 1942, San Francisco, Calif.

		G	W	L	PCT	Standing		
1978	CAL A	117	62	55	.530	3	2	
1979		162	88	74	.543	1		
1980		160	65	95	.406	6		
1981		47	22	25	.468	4	4	(1st)
1986	CHI A	96	45	51	.469	5	5	
1987		162	77	85	.475	5		
1988		161	71	90	.441	5		
7 yrs.		905	430	475	.475			

LEAGUE CHAMPIONSHIP SERIES

		G	W	L	PCT
1979	CAL A	4	1	3	.250

Tommy Helms
HELMS, TOMMY VAN
B. May 5, 1941, Charlotte, N. C.

		G	W	L	PCT	Standing		
1988	CIN N	27	12	15	.444	4	4	2

Whitey Herzog
HERZOG, DORREL NORMAN ELVERT (The White Rat)
B. Nov. 9, 1931, New Athens, Ill.

		G	W	L	PCT	Standing		
1973	TEX A	138	47	91	.341	6	6	
1975	KC A	66	41	25	.621	2	2	
1976		162	90	72	.556	1		
1977		162	102	60	.630	1		
1978		162	92	70	.568	1		
1979		162	85	77	.525	2		
1980	STL N	73	38	35	.521	6	5	4
1981		51	30	20	.600	2		(1st)
1981		52	29	23	.558	2		(2nd)
1982		162	92	70	.568	1		
1983		162	79	83	.488	4		
1984		162	84	78	.519	3		
1985		162	101	61	.623	1		
1986		161	79	82	.491	3		
1987		162	95	67	.586	1		
1988		162	76	86	.469	5		
15 yrs.		2161	1160	1000	.537			

LEAGUE CHAMPIONSHIP SERIES

		G	W	L	PCT
1976	KC A	5	2	3	.400
1977		5	2	3	.400
1978		4	1	3	.250
1982	STL N	3	3	0	1.000
1985		6	4	2	.667
1987		7	4	3	.571
6 yrs.		30	16	14	.533
		1st	2nd	1st	4th

WORLD SERIES

		G	W	L	PCT
1982	STL N	7	4	3	.571
1985		7	3	4	.429
1987		7	3	4	.429
3 yrs.		21	10	11	.476

Davey Johnson
JOHNSON, DAVID ALLEN
B. Jan. 30, 1943, Orlando, Fla.

		G	W	L	PCT	Standing	
1984	NY N	162	90	72	.556	2	
1985		162	98	64	.605	2	
1986		162	108	54	.667	1	
1987		162	92	70	.568	2	
1988		160	100	60	.625	1	
5 yrs.		808	488	320	.604		

	G	W	L	PCT	Standing				G	W	L	PCT	Standing

Davey Johnson continued

LEAGUE CHAMPIONSHIP SERIES

	G	W	L	PCT
1986 NY N	6	4	2	.667
1988	7	3	4	.429
2 yrs.	13	7	6	.538
	8th	7th		3rd

WORLD SERIES

	G	W	L	PCT
1986 NY N	7	4	3	.571

Tom Kelly

KELLY, JAY THOMAS
B. Aug. 15, 1950, Graceville, Minn.

	G	W	L	PCT	Standing	
1986 MIN A	23	12	11	.522	7	6
1987	162	85	77	.525	1	
1988	162	91	71	.562	2	
3 yrs.	347	188	159	.542		

LEAGUE CHAMPIONSHIP SERIES

	G	W	L	PCT
1987 MIN A	5	4	1	.800

WORLD SERIES

	G	W	L	PCT
1987 MIN A	7	4	3	.571

Hal Lanier

LANIER, HAROLD CLIFTON
Son of Max Lanier.
B. July 4, 1942, Denton, N. C.

	G	W	L	PCT	Standing
1986 HOU N	162	96	66	.593	1
1987	162	76	86	.469	3
1988	162	82	80	.506	5
3 yrs.	486	254	232	.523	

LEAGUE CHAMPIONSHIP SERIES

	G	W	L	PCT
1986 HOU N	6	2	4	.333

Tony LaRussa

LaRUSSA, ANTHONY
B. Oct. 4, 1944, Tampa, Fla.

	G	W	L	PCT	Standing		
1979 CHI A	54	27	27	.500	5	5	
1980	162	70	90	.438	5		
1981	53	31	22	.585	3		(1st)
1981	53	23	30	.434	6		(2nd)
1982	162	87	75	.537	3		
1983	162	99	63	.611	1		
1984	162	74	88	.457	5		
1985	163	85	77	.525	3		
1986	64	26	38	.406	6	5	
1986 OAK A	79	45	34	.570	7	3	
1987	162	81	81	.500	3		
1988	162	104	58	.642	1		
10 yrs.	1438	752	683	.524			

LEAGUE CHAMPIONSHIP SERIES

	G	W	L	PCT
1983 CHI A	4	1	3	.250
1988 OAK A	4	4	0	1.000
2 yrs.	8	5	3	.625

WORLD SERIES

	G	W	L	PCT
1988 OAK A	5	1	4	.200

Tommy Lasorda

LASORDA, THOMAS CHARLES
B. Sept. 22, 1927, Norristown, Pa.

	G	W	L	PCT	Standing		
1976 LA N	4	2	2	.500	2	2	
1977	162	98	64	.605	1		
1978	162	95	67	.586	1		
1979	162	79	83	.488	3		
1980	163	92	71	.564	2		
1981	57	36	21	.632	1		(1st)
1981	53	27	26	.509	4		(2nd)
1982	162	88	74	.543	2		
1983	162	91	71	.562	1		
1984	162	79	83	.488	4		
1985	162	95	67	.586	1		
1986	162	73	89	.451	5		
1987	162	73	89	.451	4		
1988	162	94	67	.584	1		
13 yrs.	1897	1022	874	.539			

Tommy Lasorda continued

DIVISIONAL PLAYOFF SERIES

	G	W	L	PCT
1981 LA N	5	3	2	.600

LEAGUE CHAMPIONSHIP SERIES

	G	W	L	PCT
1977 LA N	4	3	1	.750
1978	4	3	1	.750
1981	5	3	2	.600
1983	4	1	3	.250
1985	6	2	4	.333
1988	7	4	3	.571
6 yrs.	30	16	14	.533
	1st	2nd	1st	4th

WORLD SERIES

	G	W	L	PCT
1977 LA N	6	2	4	.333
1978	6	2	4	.333
1981	6	4	2	.667
1988	5	4	1	.800
4 yrs.	23	12	11	.522
	10th	8th		8th

Jim Leyland

LEYLAND, JAMES RICHARD
B. Dec. 15, 1944, Toledo, Ohio

	G	W	L	PCT	Standing
1986 PIT N	162	64	98	.395	6
1987	162	80	82	.494	4
1988	160	85	75	.531	2
3 yrs.	484	229	255	.473	

Billy Martin

MARTIN, ALFRED MANUEL
Born Alfred Manuel Pesano.
B. May 16, 1928, Berkeley, Calif.

	G	W	L	PCT	Standing		
1969 MIN A	162	97	65	.599	1		
1971 DET A	162	91	71	.562	2		
1972	156	86	70	.551	1		
1973	143	76	67	.531	3	3	
1974 TEX A	160	84	76	.525	2		
1975	95	44	51	.463	4	3	
1975 NY A	56	30	26	.536	3	3	
1976	159	97	62	.610	1		
1977	162	100	62	.617	1		
1978	94	52	42	.553	3	1	
1979	96	55	41	.573	4	4	
1980 OAK A	162	83	79	.512	2		
1981	60	37	23	.617	1		(1st)
1981	49	27	22	.551	2		(2nd)
1982	162	68	94	.420	5		
1983 NY A	162	91	71	.562	3		
1985	145	91	54	.628	7	2	
1988	68	40	28	.588	2	5	
16 yrs.	2253	1249	1004	.554			

DIVISIONAL PLAYOFF SERIES

	G	W	L	PCT
1981 OAK A	3	3	0	1.000

LEAGUE CHAMPIONSHIP SERIES

	G	W	L	PCT
1969 MIN A	3	0	3	.000
1972 DET A	5	2	3	.400
1976 NY A	5	3	2	.600
1977	5	3	2	.600
1981 OAK A	3	0	3	.000
5 yrs.	21	8	13	.381
	5th	6th	3rd	10th

WORLD SERIES

	G	W	L	PCT
1976 NY A	4	0	4	.000
1977	6	4	2	.667
2 yrs.	10	4	6	.400

Jack McKeon

McKEON, JOHN ALOYSIUS
B. Nov. 23, 1930, South Amboy, N. J.

	G	W	L	PCT	Standing	
1973 KC A	162	88	74	.543	2	
1974	162	77	85	.475	5	
1975	96	50	46	.521	2	2
1977 OAK A	53	26	27	.491	7	7
1978	123	45	78	.366	6	6
1988 SD N	115	67	48	.583	5	3
6 yrs.	711	353	358	.496		

	G	W	L	PCT	Standing				G	W	L	PCT	Standing	

John McNamara

McNAMARA, JOHN FRANCIS
B. June 4, 1932, Sacramento, Calif.

	G	W	L	PCT	Standing	
1969 OAK A	13	8	5	.615	2	2
1970	162	89	73	.549	2	
1974 SD N	162	60	102	.370	6	
1975	162	71	91	.438	4	
1976	162	73	89	.451	5	
1977	48	20	28	.417	5	5
1979 CIN N	161	90	71	.559	1	
1980	163	89	73	.549	3	
1981	56	35	21	.625	2	(1st)
1981	52	31	21	.596	2	(2nd)
1982	92	34	58	.370	6	6
1983 CAL A	162	70	92	.432	5	
1984	162	81	81	.500	2	
1985 BOS A	163	81	81	.500	5	
1986	161	95	66	.590	1	
1987	162	78	84	.481	5	
1988	85	43	42	.506	4	1
16 yrs.	2128	1048	1078	.493		

LEAGUE CHAMPIONSHIP SERIES

	G	W	L	PCT		
1979 CIN N	3	0	3	.000		
1986 BOS A	7	4	3	.571		
2 yrs.	10	4	6	.400		
		9th	8th			

WORLD SERIES

	G	W	L	PCT		
1986 BOS A	7	3	4	.429		

Joe Morgan

MORGAN, JOSEPH MICHAEL
B. Nov. 19, 1930, Walpole, Mass.

	G	W	L	PCT	Standing	
1988 BOS A	77	46	31	.597	4	1

LEAGUE CHAMPIONSHIP SERIES

	G	W	L	PCT		
1988 BOS A	4	0	4	.000		

Russ Nixon

NIXON, RUSSELL EUGENE
B. Feb. 19, 1935, Cleveland, Ohio

	G	W	L	PCT	Standing	
1982 CIN N	70	27	43	.386	6	6
1983	162	74	88	.457	6	
1988 ATL N	121	42	79	.347	6	6
3 yrs.	353	143	210	.405		

Lou Piniella

PINIELLA, LOUIS VICTOR (Sweet Lou)
B. Aug. 28, 1943, Tampa, Fla.

	G	W	L	PCT	Standing	
1986 NY A	162	90	72	.556	2	
1987	162	89	73	.549	4	
1988	93	45	48	.484	2	5
3 yrs.	417	224	193	.537		

Cal Ripken

RIPKEN, CALVIN EDWARD SR.
Father of Cal Ripken.
Father of Billy Ripken.
B. Dec. 17, 1935, Aberdeen, Md.

	G	W	L	PCT	Standing		
1985 BAL A	1	1	0	1.000	4	4	4
1987	162	67	95	.414	6		
1988	6	0	6	.000	6	7	
3 yrs.	169	68	101	.402			

Frank Robinson

ROBINSON, FRANK
B. Aug. 31, 1935, Beaumont, Tex.
Hall of Fame 1982.

	G	W	L	PCT	Standing	
1975 CLE A	159	79	80	.497	4	
1976	159	81	78	.509	4	
1977	57	26	31	.456	6	5
1981 SF N	59	27	32	.458	5	(1st)
1981	52	29	23	.558	3	(2nd)
1982	162	87	75	.537	3	

Frank Robinson continued

	G	W	L	PCT	Standing	
1983	162	79	83	.488	5	
1984	106	42	64	.396	6	6
1988 BAL A	155	54	101	.348	6	7
8 yrs.	1071	504	567	.471		

Buck Rodgers

RODGERS, ROBERT LEROY
B. Aug. 16, 1938, Delaware, Ohio

	G	W	L	PCT	Standing	
1980 MIL A	47	26	21	.553	2	3
1980	23	13	10	.565	4	3
1981	56	31	25	.554	3	(1st)
1981	53	31	22	.585	1	(2nd)
1982	47	23	24	.489	5	1
1985 MON N	161	84	77	.522	3	
1986	161	78	83	.484	4	
1987	162	91	71	.562	3	
1988	163	81	81	.500	3	
7 yrs.	873	458	414	.525		

DIVISIONAL PLAYOFF SERIES

	G	W	L	PCT		
1981 MIL A	5	2	3	.400		

Cookie Rojas

ROJAS, OCTAVIO VICTOR RIVAS
Born Octavio Victor Rojas y Rivas.
B. Mar. 6, 1939, Havana, Cuba

	G	W	L	PCT	Standing	
1988 CAL A	154	75	79	.487	4	4

Pete Rose

ROSE, PETER EDWARD (Charlie Hustle)
B. Apr. 14, 1941, Cincinnati, Ohio

	G	W	L	PCT	Standing	
1984 CIN N	42	19	23	.452	5	5
1985	162	89	72	.553	2	
1986	162	86	76	.531	2	
1987	162	84	78	.519	2	
1988	23	11	12	.478	4	2
1988	111	64	47	.577	4	2
5 yrs.	662	353	308	.534		

Jimmy Snyder

SNYDER, JAMES ROBERT
B. Aug. 13, 1932, Dearborn, Mich.

	G	W	L	PCT	Standing	
1988 SEA A	104	44	60	.423	6	7

Larry Stubing

STUBING, LAWRENCE GEORGE (Moose)
B. Mar. 31, 1938, Bronx, N. Y.

	G	W	L	PCT	Standing	
1988 CAL A	8	0	8	.000	4	4

Chuck Tanner

TANNER, CHARLES WILLIAM
Father of Bruce Tanner.
B. July 4, 1929, New Castle, Pa.

	G	W	L	PCT	Standing	
1970 CHI A	16	3	13	.188	6	6
1971	162	79	83	.488	3	
1972	154	87	67	.565	2	
1973	162	77	85	.475	5	
1974	160	80	80	.500	4	
1975	161	75	86	.466	5	
1976 OAK A	161	87	74	.540	2	
1977 PIT N	162	96	66	.593	2	
1978	161	88	73	.547	2	
1979	162	98	64	.605	1	
1980	162	83	79	.512	3	
1981	49	25	23	.521	4	(1st)
1981	54	21	33	.389	6	(2nd)
1982	162	84	78	.519	4	
1983	162	84	78	.519	2	
1984	162	75	87	.463	6	
1985	161	57	104	.354	6	

	G	W	L	PCT	Standing				G	W	L	PCT	Standing

Chuck Tanner continued

	G	W	L	PCT		
1986 ATL N	161	72	89	.447	6	
1987	161	69	92	.429	5	
1988	39	12	27	.308	6	6
19 yrs.	2734	1352	1381	.495		

LEAGUE CHAMPIONSHIP SERIES

	G	W	L	PCT
1979 PIT N	3	3	0	1.000

WORLD SERIES

	G	W	L	PCT
1979 PIT N	7	4	3	.571

Tom Trebelhorn

TREBELHORN, THOMAS LYNN
B. Jan. 27, 1948, Portland, Ore.

	G	W	L	PCT		
1986 MIL A	9	6	3	.667	6	6
1987	162	91	71	.562	3	
1988	162	87	75	.537	3	
3 yrs.	333	184	149	.553		

Bobby Valentine

VALENTINE, ROBERT JOHN
B. May 13, 1950, Stamford, Conn.

	G	W	L	PCT		
1985 TEX A	129	53	76	.411	7	7
1986	162	87	75	.537	2	
1987	162	75	87	.463	6	
1988	161	70	91	.435	6	
4 yrs.	614	285	329	.464		

John Vukovich

VUKOVICH, JOHN CHRISTOPHER
B. July 31, 1947, Sacramento, Calif.

	G	W	L	PCT			
1986 CHI N	2	1	1	.500	5	5	5
1988 PHI N	9	5	4	.556	6	6	
2 yrs.	11	6	5	.545			

John Wathan

WATHAN, JOHN DAVID (Duke)
B. Oct. 4, 1949, Cedar Rapids, Iowa

	G	W	L	PCT		
1987 KC A	36	21	15	.583	4	2
1988	161	84	77	.522	3	
2 yrs.	197	105	92	.533		

Dick Williams

WILLIAMS, RICHARD HIRSCHFELD
B. May 7, 1928, St. Louis, Mo.

	G	W	L	PCT			
1967 BOS A	162	92	70	.568	1		
1968	162	86	76	.531	4		
1969	153	82	71	.536	3	3	
1971 OAK A	161	101	60	.627	1		
1972	155	93	62	.600	1		
1973	162	94	68	.580	1		
1974 CAL A	84	36	48	.429	6	6	
1975	161	72	89	.447	6		
1976	96	39	57	.406	4	4	
1977 MON N	162	75	87	.463	5		
1978	162	76	86	.469	4		
1979	160	95	65	.594	2		
1980	162	90	72	.556	2		
1981	55	30	25	.545	3		(1st)
1981	26	14	12	.538	2	1	(2nd)
1982 SD N	162	81	81	.500	4		
1983	162	81	81	.500	4		
1984	162	92	70	.568	1		
1985	162	83	79	.512	3		
1986 SEA A	133	58	75	.436	6	7	
1987	162	78	84	.481	4		
1988	57	24	33	.421	6	7	
21 yrs.	3023	1572	1451	.520			

LEAGUE CHAMPIONSHIP SERIES

	G	W	L	PCT
1971 OAK A	3	0	3	.000
1972	5	3	2	.600
1973	5	3	2	.600

Dick Williams continued

	G	W	L	PCT
1984 SD N	5	3	2	.600
4 yrs.	18	9	9	.500
	6th	5th	5th	6th

WORLD SERIES

	G	W	L	PCT
1967 BOS A	7	3	4	.429
1972 OAK A	7	4	3	.571
1973	7	4	3	.571
1984 SD N	5	1	4	.200
4 yrs.	26	12	14	.462
	8th	8th	6th	

Jimy Williams

WILLIAMS, JAMES FRANCIS
B. Oct. 4, 1943, Santa Maria, Calif.

	G	W	L	PCT	
1986 TOR A	163	86	76	.531	4
1987	162	96	66	.593	2
1988	162	87	75	.537	3
3 yrs.	487	269	217	.553	

Don Zimmer

ZIMMER, DONALD WILLIAM
B. Jan. 17, 1931, Cincinnati, Ohio

	G	W	L	PCT			
1972 SD N	142	54	88	.380	4	6	
1973	162	60	102	.370	6		
1976 BOS A	76	42	34	.553	3	3	
1977	161	97	64	.602	2		
1978	163	99	64	.607	2		
1979	160	91	69	.569	3		
1980	156	82	74	.526	4	4	
1981 TEX A	55	33	22	.600	2		(1st)
1981	50	24	26	.480	3		(2nd)
1982	96	38	58	.396	6	6	
1988 CHI N	163	77	85	.475	4		
10 yrs.	1384	697	686	.504			

World Series and League Championship Series

This section provides details of the National and American League Championship Series and World Series of 1988. Provided are facts about the individual games, including line scores and highlights.

Pitchers are listed in order of appearance. In parentheses following each pitcher's name is the number of innings he worked. "Doe (2.1)" would indicate that Doe worked two and on-third innings; "(2.0)" would mean that he had faced at least one batter in his third inning of work, but did not retire anyone. The winning and losing pitchers are listed in bold faced print; a pitcher who is credited with a save has a bold "SV" after his innings pitched.

Home runs are listed in the order they were hit.

LINE SCORES & PITCHERS (inn. pit.) | **HOME RUNS (men on)** | **HIGHLIGHTS**

Los Angeles (West) defeats New York (East) 4 games to 3

GAME 1 - OCTOBER 4

NY E 000 000 003   3 8 1
LA W 100 000 100   2 4 0
Gooden (7), **Myers** (2)
Hershiser (8.1), **Howell** (0.2)

Mets rallied for three ninth inning runs to overcome a 2-0 deficit. Strawberry doubled home the first run against Hershiser, and Carter's 2-out double off Howell plated the tying and winning runs.

GAME 2 - OCTOBER 5

NY E 000 200 001   3 6 0
LA W 140 010 00x   6 7 0
Cone (2), Aguilera (3), Leach (2),
  McDowell (1)
Belcher (8.1), Orosco (0), Pena (0.2) **SV**

Hernandez (1 on)

Los Angeles jumped to an early 5-0 lead behind the rookie Belcher, who struck out 10. Hernandez homered and drove in all three New York runs.

GAME 3 - OCTOBER 8

LA W 021 000 010   4 7 2
NY E 001 002 05x   8 9 2
Hershiser (7), Howell (0), **Pena** (0.2)
  Orosco (0), Horton (0.1)
Darling (6), McDowell (1.2), **Myers** (0.1),
  Cone (1)

New York sent 10 men to the plate during a 5-run eighth inning rally in which Dodger reliever Howell was ejected and subsequently suspended for having pine tar in his glove.

GAME 4 - OCTOBER 9

LA W 200 000 002 001   5 7 1
NY E 000 301 000 000   4 10 2
Tudor (5), Holton (1), Horton (2),
  Pena (3), Leary (0.1), Orosco (0.1),
  Hershiser (0.1) **SV**
Gooden (8.1), Myers (2.1), **McDowell**

Scioscia (1 on), Gibson
Strawberry (1 on),
McReynolds

Scioscia belted a 2-run homer in the ninth inning off Gooden to tie the game, then Gibson connected off McDowell in the 12th as Los Angeles evened the series 2-2.

GAME 5 - OCTOBER 10

LA W 000 330 001   7 12 0
NY E 000 030 010   4 9 1
Belcher (7), Horton (0.1), Holton (1.2) **SV**
Fernandez (4), Leach (1), Aguilera (2),
  McDowell (2)

Gibson (2 on)
Dykstra (2 on)

Dodgers scored three times in both the fourth and fifth innings and held off Mets to take series lead for the first time. Big blow was Gibson's three-run homer which gave Los Angeles a 6-0 lead.

GAME 6 - OCTOBER 11

NY E 101 021 000   5 11 0
LA W 000 010 000   1 5 2
Cone (9)
Leary (4), Holton (1.1), Horton (1.2),
  Orosco (2)

McReynolds (1 on)

Cone went the distance on a five-hitter, while McReynolds went 4-for-4 with a home run and 3 RBI as Mets forced a seventh game.

GAME 7 - OCTOBER 12

NY E 000 000 000   0 5 2
LA W 150 000 00x   6 10 0
Darling (1), Gooden (3), Leach (2),
  Aguilera (2)
Hershiser (9)

Los Angeles completed upset of Mets, who had beaten them 10 times in 11 meetings during the regular season. Series MVP Hershiser pitched a 5-hit shutout to wrap up Dodgers' first flag in seven years.

Team Totals

		W	AB	H	2B	3B	HR	R	RBI	BA	BB	SO	ERA
LA	W	4	243	52	7	1	3	31	30	.214	25	54	3.32
NY	E	3	240	58	12	1	5	27	27	.242	28	42	3.94

Individual Batting

LOS ANGELES (WEST)

	AB	H	2B	3B	HR	R	RBI	BA
M. Marshall, of	30	7	1	1	0	3	5	.233
S. Sax, 2b	30	8	0	0	0	7	3	.267
K. Gibson, of	26	4	0	0	2	2	6	.154
A. Griffin, ss	25	4	1	0	0	1	3	.160
J. Shelby, of	24	4	0	0	0	3	3	.167
J. Hamilton, 3b	23	5	0	0	0	2	1	.217
M. Scioscia, c	22	8	1	0	1	3	2	.364
M. Hatcher, 1b, of	21	5	2	0	0	4	3	.238
O. Hershiser, p	9	0	0	0	0	1	1	.000
F. Stubbs, of	8	2	0	0	0	0	0	.250
T. Belcher, p	8	1	0	0	0	1	0	.125
R. Dempsey, c	5	2	2	0	0	1	2	.400
T. Woodson, 1b	4	1	0	0	0	0	0	.250
J. Tudor, p	2	0	0	0	0	0	0	.000
M. Davis	2	0	0	0	0	0	0	.000
T. Leary, p	1	0	0	0	0	0	0	.000
D. Heep	1	0	0	0	0	0	0	.000
Sharperson, 3b, ss	1	0	0	0	0	0	1	.000
B. Holton, p	1	1	0	0	0	1	0	1.000
J. Gonzalez, of	0	0	0	0	0	2	0	—

Errors: M. Hatcher (2), J. Hamilton (2)
Stolen bases: S. Sax (5), J. Shelby (2), K. Gibson (2)

NEW YORK (EAST)

	AB	H	2B	3B	HR	R	RBI	BA
Strawberry, of	30	9	2	0	1	5	6	.300
McReynolds, of	28	7	2	0	2	4	4	.250
G. Jefferies, 3b	27	9	2	0	0	2	1	.333
G. Carter, c	27	6	1	1	0	0	4	.222
K. Hernandez, 1b	26	7	0	0	1	2	5	.269
W. Backman, 2b	22	6	1	0	0	2	2	.273
H. Johnson, 3b, ss	18	1	0	0	0	3	0	.056
L. Dykstra, of	14	6	3	0	1	6	3	.429
M. Wilson, of	13	2	0	0	0	2	1	.154
K. Elster, ss	8	2	1	0	0	1	0	.250
M. Sasser, c	5	1	0	0	0	0	0	.200
D. Gooden, p	5	1	0	0	0	0	0	.200
D. Cone, p	4	0	0	0	0	0	0	.000
D. Magadan	3	0	0	0	0	0	0	.000
R. Darling, p	3	0	0	0	0	0	0	.000
T. Teufel, 2b	3	0	0	0	0	0	0	.000
L. Mazzilli	2	1	0	0	0	0	0	.500
S. Fernandez, p	1	0	0	0	0	0	0	.000
R. Aguilera, p	1	0	0	0	0	0	0	.000

Errors: K. Elster (2), W. Backman (2), H. Johnson,
R. McDowell, K. Hernandez, G. Jefferies
Stolen bases: McReynolds (2), K. Hernandez, L. Mazzilli,
W. Backman, H. Johnson

Individual Pitching

LOS ANGELES (WEST)

	W	L	ERA	IP	H	BB	SO	SV
O. Hershiser	1	0	1.09	24.2	18	7	15	1
T. Belcher	2	0	4.11	15.1	12	4	16	0
J. Tudor	0	0	7.20	5	8	1	1	0
T. Leary	0	1	6.23	4.1	8	3	3	0
A. Pena	1	1	4.15	4.1	1	5	1	1
R. Horton	0	0	0.00	4.1	4	2	3	0
B. Holton	0	0	2.25	4	2	1	2	1
J. Orosco	0	0	7.71	2.1	4	3	0	0
J. Howell	0	1	27.00	0.2	1	2	1	0

NEW YORK (EAST)

	W	L	ERA	IP	H	BB	SO	SV
D. Gooden	0	0	2.95	18.1	10	8	20	0
D. Cone	1	1	4.50	12	10	5	9	0
R. Darling	0	1	7.71	7	11	4	7	0
R. Aguilera	0	0	1.29	7	3	2	4	0
R. McDowell	0	1	4.50	6	6	2	5	0
T. Leach	0	0	0.00	5	4	1	4	0
S. Fernandez	0	1	13.50	4	7	1	5	0
R. Myers	2	0	0.00	4.2	1	2	0	0

LINE SCORES & PITCHERS (inn. pit.)	HOME RUNS (men on)	HIGHLIGHTS

Oakland (West) defeats Boston (East) 4 games to 0

GAME 1 - OCTOBER 5

OAK W 000 100 010   2 6 0
BOS E 000 000 100   1 6 0
Stewart (6.1), **Honeycutt** (0.2),
 Eckersley (2) **SV**
Hurst (9)

Canseco

Henderson's eighth-inning single gave Oakland the series opener. A's scored on Canseco's fourth-inning homer, before Boston drew even on sacrifice fly by Boggs in seventh. Hurst pitched a complete game in losing effort for Red Sox.

GAME 2 - OCTOBER 6

OAK W 000 000 301   4 6 1
BOS E 000 002 100   3 4 1
Davis (6.1), Caderet (0.1),
 Nelson (1.1), Eckersley (1) **SV**
Clemens (7), Stanley (0.1), **Smith** (1.2)

Canseco (1 on)
Gedman

Oakland posted their second consecutive late-inning victory as Weiss singled home winning run in ninth inning. Boston scored twice in sixth to lead 2-0, but Oakland responded an inning later with Canseco's two-run homer and McGwire's RBI single off Clemens. Boston tied it in bottom of the seventh on Gedman's homer.

GAME 3 - OCTOBER 8

BOS E 320 000 100   6 12 0
OAK W 042 010 12x   10 15 1
Boddicker (2.2), Gardner (4.2),
 Stanley (0.2)
Welch (1.2), **Nelson** (3.1), Young (1.1),
 Plunk (0.1), Honeycutt (0.1),
 Eckersley (2) **SV**

Greenwell
McGwire,
Lansford (1 on),
Hassey (1 on),
Henderson (1 on)

Oakland slammed four homers to charge back from early 5-0 deficit. McGwire's solo shot got Athletics on the board, then Lansford's 2-run homer brought them within a run in the second. Hassey gave them the lead for good an inning later with his two-run homer. Henderson added another two-run blast in the eighth to close out the scoring.

GAME 4 - OCTOBER 9

BOS E 000 001 000   1 4 0
OAK W 101 000 02x   4 10 0
Hurst (4), Smithson (2.1), Smith (1.2)
Stewart (7), Honeycutt (1),
 Eckersley (1) **SV**

Canseco

In winning their first pennant since 1974, Oakland became the first team to sweep a best-of-seven League Championship Series. Eckersley saved all 4 games to set a playoff record and win the series MVP award. Canseco hit his third homer of the series to open the scoring.

Team Totals

		W	AB	H	2B	3B	HR	R	RBI	BA	BB	SO	ERA
OAK	W	4	137	41	8	0	7	20	20	.299	10	35	2.00
BOS	E	0	126	26	4	0	2	11	10	.206	18	23	5.29

Individual Batting

OAKLAND (WEST)

	AB	H	2B	3B	HR	R	RBI	BA
C. Lansford, 3b	17	5	1	0	1	4	2	.294
D. Henderson, of	16	6	1	0	1	2	4	.375
J. Canseco, of	16	5	1	0	3	4	4	.313
M. McGwire, 1b	15	5	0	0	1	4	3	.333
W. Weiss, ss	15	5	2	0	0	2	2	.333
D. Parker, of, dh	12	3	1	0	0	1	0	.250
M. Gallego, 2b	12	1	0	0	0	1	0	.083
R. Hassey, c	8	4	1	0	1	2	3	.500
T. Phillips, 2b, of	7	2	1	0	0	0	0	.286
D. Baylor, of	6	0	0	0	0	0	1	.000
L. Polonia, of	5	2	0	0	0	0	0	.400
S. Javier, of	4	2	0	0	0	0	1	.500
T. Steinbach, c	4	1	0	0	0	0	0	.250

Errors: D. Henderson (2), D. Parker
Stolen bases: J. Canseco

BOSTON (EAST)

	AB	H	2B	3B	HR	R	RBI	BA
E. Burks, of	17	4	1	0	0	2	1	.235
M. Barrett, 2b	15	1	0	0	0	2	0	.067
R. Gedman, c	14	5	0	0	1	1	1	.357
M. Greenwell, of	14	3	1	0	1	2	3	.214
W. Boggs, 3b	13	5	0	0	0	2	3	.385
J. Rice, dh	13	2	0	0	0	0	1	.154
D. Evans, of	12	2	1	0	0	1	1	.167
T. Benzinger, 1b	11	1	0	0	0	0	0	.091
J. Reed, ss	11	3	1	0	0	0	0	.273
L. Parrish, 1b, dh	6	0	0	0	0	0	0	.000
E. Romero	0	0	0	0	0	0	0	–
K. Romine	0	0	0	0	0	1	0	–
S. Owen	0	0	0	0	0	0	0	–

Errors: R. Clemens

Individual Pitching

OAKLAND (WEST)

	W	L	ERA	IP	H	BB	SO	SV
D. Stewart	1	0	1.35	13.1	9	6	11	0
D. Eckersley	0	0	0.00	6	1	2	5	4
S. Davis	0	0	0.00	6.1	2	5	4	0
G. Nelson	2	0	0.00	4.2	5	1	0	0
R. Honeycutt	1	0	0.00	2	0	2	0	0
B. Welch	0	0	27.00	1.2	6	2	0	0
C. Young	0	0	0.00	1.1	1	0	2	0
E. Plunk	0	0	0.00	0.1	1	0	1	0
G. Cadaret	0	0	27.00	0.1	1	0	0	0

BOSTON (EAST)

	W	L	ERA	IP	H	BB	SO	SV
B. Hurst	0	2	2.77	13	10	5	12	0
R. Clemens	0	0	3.86	7	6	0	8	0
W. Gardner	0	0	5.79	4.2	6	2	8	0
L. Smith	0	1	8.10	3.1	6	1	4	0
M. Smithson	0	0	0.00	2.1	3	0	1	0
M. Boddicker	0	1	20.25	2.2	8	1	2	0
B. Stanley	0	0	9.00	1	2	1	0	0

LINE SCORES & PITCHERS (inn. pit.)	HOME RUNS (men on)	HIGHLIGHTS

Los Angeles (N.L.) defeats Oakland (A.L.) 4 games to 1

GAME 1 - OCTOBER 15

```
OAK  A  040 000 000    4  7  0
LA   N  200 001 002    5  7  0
```
Stewart (8), **Eckersley** (0.2)
Belcher (2), Leary (3), Holton (2),
Pena (2)

Canseco (3 on)
Hatcher (1 on),
Gibson (1 on)

Two-out, two-run pinch homer by Gibson in ninth off relief ace Eckersley gave Dodgers a dramatic series opening victory. Grand slam by Canseco gave Oakland the lead until Gibson's blast. It was to be injured Gibson's only appearance in the series.

GAME 2 - OCTOBER 16

```
OAK  A  000 000 000    0  3  0
LA   N  005 100 00x    6  10 1
```
Davis (3.1), Nelson (1.2), Young (1),
Plunk (1), Honeycutt (1)
Hershiser (9)

Marshall (2 on)

Hershiser limited Oakland to three hits while collecting three himself, as Los Angeles took a 2-0 series lead. Dodgers tallied five times in the third inning, capped by Marshall's 3-run homer. Parker had all three Oakland hits off Hershiser.

GAME 3 - OCTOBER 18

```
LA   N  000 010 000    1  8  1
OAK  A  001 000 001    2  5  0
```
Tudor (1.1), Leary (3.2), Pena (3),
Howell (0.1)
Welch (5), Cadaret (0.1), Nelson (1.2),
Honeycutt (2)

McGwire

Ninth-inning homer by McGwire powered Athletics to their only victory of the series. Los Angeles left 10 runners on base and failed to capitalize on a bases loaded, nobody out opportunity in the sixth inning.

GAME 4 - OCTOBER 19

```
LA   N  201 000 100    4  8  1
OAK  A  100 001 100    3  9  2
```
Belcher (6.2), Howell (2.1) **SV**
Stewart (6.1), Cadaret (1.2),
Eckersley (1)

Los Angeles took advantage of sloppy fielding by Oakland to take a 3-1 lead in the series. Errors by infielders Hubbard and Weiss, along with Steinbach's passed ball led to Dodgers' first three runs. Strong relief work by Howell saved win for Belcher.

GAME 5 - OCTOBER 20

```
LA   N  200 201 000    5  8  0

OAK  A  001 000 010    2  4  0
```
Hershiser (9)
Davis (4.2), Cadaret (0), Nelson (3)
Honeycutt (0.1), Plunk (0.2), Burns (0.1)

Hatcher (1 on),
Davis (1 on)

Injury-riddled Dodgers climaxed a miraculous postseason by defeating Athletics 4 games to 1 to win their second World Championship of the 1980's. Series MVP Hershiser wrapped up the title with a 4-hitter, receiving support from Hatcher and Davis, who each smacked a two-run homer.

Team Totals

		W	AB	H	2B	3B	HR	R	RBI	BA	BB	SO	ERA
LA	N	4	167	41	8	1	5	19	19	.246	13	36	2.05
OAK	A	1	158	28	3	0	2	11	11	.177	17	41	3.89

Individual Batting

LOS ANGELES (N.L.)

	AB	H	2B	3B	HR	R	RBI	BA
S. Sax, 2b	20	6	0	0	0	3	0	.300
M. Hatcher, of	19	7	1	0	2	5	5	.368
J. Hamilton, 3b	19	2	0	0	0	1	0	.105
J. Shelby, of	18	4	1	0	0	0	1	.222
F. Stubbs, 1b	17	5	2	0	0	3	2	.294
A. Griffin, ss	16	3	0	0	0	2	0	.188
M. Scioscia, c	14	3	0	0	0	0	1	.214
M. Marshall, of	13	3	0	1	1	2	3	.231
D. Heep, dh	8	2	1	0	0	0	0	.250
M. Davis, of, dh	7	1	0	0	1	3	2	.143
R. Dempsey, c	5	1	1	0	0	0	1	.200
T. Woodson, 1b	4	0	0	0	0	0	0	.000
O. Hershiser, p	3	3	2	0	0	1	1	1.000
J. Gonzalez, dh	2	0	0	0	0	0	0	.000
D. Anderson, dh	1	0	0	0	0	0	0	.000
K. Gibson	1	1	0	0	1	1	2	1.000

Errors: A. Griffin, M. Scioscia, J. Hamilton
Stolen bases: M. Davis (2), S. Sax, J. Shelby

OAKLAND (A.L.)

	AB	H	2B	3B	HR	R	RBI	BA
D. Henderson, of	20	6	2	0	0	1	1	.300
J. Canseco, of	19	1	0	0	1	1	5	.053
C. Lansford, 3b	18	3	0	0	0	2	1	.167
M. McGwire, 1b	17	1	0	0	1	1	1	.059
W. Weiss, ss	16	1	0	0	0	1	0	.063
D. Parker, of, dh	15	3	0	0	0	0	0	.200
G. Hubbard, 2b	12	3	0	0	0	2	0	.250
T. Steinbach, c, dh	11	4	1	0	0	0	0	.364
L. Polonia, of	9	1	0	0	0	1	0	.111
R. Hassey, c	8	2	0	0	0	0	1	.250
T. Phillips, 2b, of	4	1	0	0	0	1	0	.250
S. Javier, of	4	2	0	0	0	0	2	.500
D. Stewart, p	3	0	0	0	0	1	0	.000
D. Baylor	1	0	0	0	0	0	0	.000
S. Davis, p	1	0	0	0	0	0	0	.000
M. Gallego, 2b	0	0	0	0	0	0	0	—

Errors: G. Hubbard, W. Weiss
Stolen bases: G. Hubbard, J. Canseco, W. Weiss

Individual Pitching

LOS ANGELES (N.L.)

	W	L	ERA	IP	H	BB	SO	SV
O. Hershiser	2	0	1.00	18	7	6	17	0
T. Belcher	1	0	6.23	8.2	10	6	10	0
T. Leary	0	0	1.35	6.2	6	2	4	0
A. Pena	1	0	0.00	5	2	1	7	0
J. Howell	0	1	3.38	2.2	3	1	2	1
B. Holton	0	0	0.00	2	0	1	0	0
J. Tudor	0	0	0.00	1.1	0	0	1	0

OAKLAND (A.L.)

	W	L	ERA	IP	H	BB	SO	SV
D. Stewart	0	1	3.14	14.1	12	5	5	0
S. Davis	0	2	11.25	8	14	1	7	0
G. Nelson	0	0	1.42	6.1	4	3	3	0
B. Welch	0	0	1.80	5	6	3	8	0
R. Honeycutt	1	0	0.00	3.1	0	0	5	0
G. Cadaret	0	0	0.00	2	2	0	3	0
C. Young	0	0	0.00	1	1	0	0	0
E. Plunk	0	0	0.00	1.2	0	0	3	0
D. Eckersley	0	1	10.80	1.2	2	1	2	0
T. Burns	0	0	0.00	0.1	0	0	0	0